THE ROUTLEDGE HANDBOOK OF PHILOSOPHY OF SKILL AND EXPERTISE

Philosophical questions surrounding skill and expertise can be traced back as far as Ancient Greece, China, and India. In the twentieth century, skilled action was an important factor in the work of phenomenologists such as Heidegger and Merleau-Ponty and analytic philosophers including Gilbert Ryle. However, as a subject in its own right it has, until now, remained largely in the background.

The Routledge Handbook of Philosophy of Skill and Expertise is an outstanding reference source and the first major collection of its kind, reflecting the explosion of interest in the topic in recent years. Comprising thirty-nine chapters written by leading international contributors, the *Handbook* is organized into six clear parts:

- Skill in the history of philosophy (East and West)
- Skill in epistemology
- Skill, intelligence, and agency
- Skill in perception, imagination, and emotion
- Skill, language, and social cognition
- Skill and expertise in normative philosophy

Essential reading for students and researchers in philosophy of mind and psychology, epistemology, and ethics, *The Routledge Handbook of Philosophy of Skill and Expertise* is also suitable for those in related disciplines such as social psychology and cognitive science. It is also relevant to those who are interested in conceptual issues underlying skill and expertise in fields such as sport, the performing arts, and medicine.

Ellen Fridland is a philosopher of mind and cognitive science at King's College London, UK.

Carlotta Pavese is an Associate Professor of Philosophy at Cornell University, USA.

ROUTLEDGE HANDBOOKS IN PHILOSOPHY

Routledge Handbooks in Philosophy are state-of-the-art surveys of emerging, newly refreshed, and important fields in philosophy, providing accessible yet thorough assessments of key problems, themes, thinkers, and recent developments in research.

All chapters for each volume are specially commissioned, and written by leading scholars in the field. Carefully edited and organized, *Routledge Handbooks in Philosophy* provide indispensable reference tools for students and researchers seeking a comprehensive overview of new and exciting topics in philosophy. They are also valuable teaching resources as accompaniments to textbooks, anthologies, and research-orientated publications.

Also available:

The Routledge Handbook of Metaphysical Grounding
Edited by Michael J. Raven

The Routledge Handbook of Philosophy of Colour
Edited by Derek H. Brown and Fiona Macpherson

The Routledge Handbook of Collective Responsibility
Edited by Saba Bazargan-Forward and Deborah Tollefsen

The Routledge Handbook of Phenomenology of Emotion
Edited by Thomas Szanto and Hilge Landweer

The Routledge Handbook of Hellenistic Philosophy
Edited by Kelly Arenson

The Routledge Handbook of Trust and Philosophy
Edited by Judith Simon

The Routledge Handbook of Philosophy of Humility
Edited by Mark Alfano, Michael P. Lynch and Alessandra Tanesini

The Routledge Handbook of Metametaphysics
Edited by Ricki Bliss and JTM Miller

The Routledge Handbook of Philosophy of Skill and Expertise
Edited by Ellen Fridland and Carlotta Pavese

The Routledge Handbook of Phenomenology and Phenomenological Philosophy
Edited by Daniele De Santis, Burt Hopkins and Claudio Majolino

For more information about this series, please visit:
www.routledge.com/Routledge-Handbooks-in-Philosophy/book-series/RHP

THE ROUTLEDGE HANDBOOK OF PHILOSOPHY OF SKILL AND EXPERTISE

Edited by Ellen Fridland and Carlotta Pavese

LONDON AND NEW YORK

First published 2021
by Routledge
2 Park Square, Milton Park, Abingdon, Oxon OX14 4RN

and by Routledge
52 Vanderbilt Avenue, New York, NY 10017

Routledge is an imprint of the Taylor & Francis Group, an informa business

British Library Cataloguing-in-Publication Data
A catalogue record for this book is available from the British Library

Library of Congress Cataloging-in-Publication Data
Names: Fridland, Ellen, editor. | Pavese, Carlotta, editor.
Title: The Routledge handbook of philosophy of skill and expertise /
edited by Ellen Fridland and Carlotta Pavese.
Description: Abingdon, Oxon; New York, NY: Routledge, 2021. |
Series: Routledge handbooks in philosophy |
Includes bibliographical references and index.
Identifiers: LCCN 2020012636 (print) | LCCN 2020012637 (ebook) |
ISBN 9781138744776 (hbk) | ISBN 9781315180809 (ebk)
Subjects: LCSH: Philosophy. | Knowledge, Theory of. | Ability. | Expertise.
Classification: LCC BD161 .R694 2020 (print) |
LCC BD161 (ebook) | DDC 128/.3–dc23
LC record available at https://lccn.loc.gov/2020012636
LC ebook record available at https://lccn.loc.gov/2020012637

ISBN: 978-1-138-74477-6 (hbk)
ISBN: 978-1-315-18080-9 (ebk)

Typeset in Bembo
by Newgen Publishing UK

MIX
Paper from
responsible sources
FSC   FSC® C013985
www.fsc.org

Printed in the United Kingdom
by Henry Ling Limited

CONTENTS

Contents

Contents

CONTRIBUTORS

Tom Angier is a Senior Lecturer in Philosophy at the University of Cape Town, South Africa. He works on Aristotelian and Neo-Aristotelian ethical and political theory. He is editor of *The Cambridge Companion to Natural Law Ethics* (2019) and author of *Natural Law Theory* (2020) in Cambridge's "Elements in Ethics" series.

Valentina Bambini is an Associate Professor of Linguistics at the University School for Advanced Studies IUSS Pavia, Italy. Her interests focus on the cognitive and neural underpinnings of linguistic and pragmatic abilities, both in healthy individuals and in pathological conditions. She is co-founder of the research network XPRAG.it.

Bana Bashour is an Associate Professor of Philosophy at the American University of Beirut. Her research interests are mainly in moral psychology, a sub-field that is at the intersection of philosophy of mind, metaphysics, and ethics. She earned her PhD from CUNY's Graduate Center in 2007.

Kath Bicknell is a Postdoctoral Researcher in Cognitive Science at Macquarie University, Sydney. Her research draws on case studies from cycling and circus to investigate and describe the relations between thinking and doing in live performance. She is internationally recognized for her sports journalism.

Paul Bloomfield is Professor of Philosophy at the University of Connecticut, specializing in moral philosophy and metaphysics. His publications include: *Moral Reality* (2001), *The Virtues of Happiness* (2014) and, as editor, *Morality and Self-Interest* (2008).

Michael Brownstein is Associate Professor of Philosophy at John Jay College and the Graduate Center, CUNY. He lives in Brooklyn, New York.

Stephen A. Butterfill is a Professor in the Department of Philosophy, University of Warwick, UK.

Laura Frances Callahan is an Assistant Professor of Philosophy at the University of Notre Dame. Her research focuses on questions at the intersection of ethics and epistemology, including responsibility for beliefs and desiderata for moral and religious beliefs.

Yuri Cath is a Senior Lecturer in Philosophy at La Trobe University, in Melbourne Australia. His main research is in epistemology, and his publications include "Intellectualism and Testimony" (2017), "Knowing What It Is Like and Testimony" (2018), and "The Ability Hypothesis and the New Knowledge-How" (2009).

Emily S. Cross currently holds positions as a Professor of Human Neuroscience within the Department of Cognitive Science at Macquarie University, in Sydney, Australia, and as a Professor of Social Robotics within the Institute of Neuroscience and Psychology at the University of Glasgow, Scotland. Through her research, she brings brain imaging techniques, robots, and action training paradigms to explore experience-dependent plasticity in the human brain and behavior.

Filippo Domaneschi is an Assistant Professor in Language Sciences at the University of Genoa, Italy. His research interests concern experimental and theoretical semantics and pragmatics and experimental philosophy. He is co-founder of the research network XPRAG.it.

Julia Driver is a Professor of Philosophy at The University of Texas at Austin. She received her PhD in Philosophy from Johns Hopkins University. She works in normative ethics, metaethics, moral psychology, and the history of sentimentalism, especially with respect to the work of David Hume. She is the author of three books: *Uneasy Virtue* (2001), *Ethics: The Fundamentals* (2006), and *Consequentialism* (2011). Her articles have appeared in journals such as the *Journal of Philosophy*, *Noûs*, *Philosophy & Phenomenological Research*, *Hypatia*, *Philosophy*, *Philosophical Studies*, and *The Australasian Journal of Philosophy*.

Gen Eickers is a postdoc at the University of Education Ludwigsburg, Germany. After finishing their PhD in philosophy at the Berlin School of Mind and Brain, Humboldt-Universität zu Berlin, and Freie Universität Berlin, they continue to work at the intersections of philosophy of mind, social psychology, and social epistemology, specifically addressing questions around social interaction, emotion, and social norms.

Keota Fields is an Associate Professor of Philosophy at the University of Massachusetts, Dartmouth. He works in contemporary metaphysics and epistemology, particularly perception, as well as early modern philosophy.

Ellen Fridland is a philosopher of mind and cognitive science at King's College London. She has held visiting appointments at Tufts University's Center for Cognitive Studies and Harvard University. Her work focuses on skill and how to understand the intelligence of embodied, skilled action.

Shaun Gallagher is the Lillian and Morrie Moss Professor of Excellence in Philosophy at the University of Memphis, and Professorial Fellow at the Faculty of Law, Humanities and the Arts, University of Wollongong (Australia). He held the Humboldt Foundation Anneliese Maier Research Fellowship (2012–18). Publications include *Action and Interaction* (2020); *Enactivist Interventions: Rethinking the Mind* (2017); *The Neurophenomenology of Awe and Wonder* (2015);

Phenomenology (2012); *The Phenomenological Mind* (with Dan Zahavi, 2012); *How the Body Shapes the Mind* (2005). He is also Editor-in-Chief of the journal *Phenomenology and the Cognitive Sciences*.

Jay L. Garfield is Doris Silbert Professor in the Humanities, Chair of the Philosophy department, and director of the Logic program and Buddhist Studies program at Smith College. He is also Visiting Professor of Buddhist Philosophy at Harvard Divinity School.

Kristina Gehrman is an Assistant Professor of Philosophy at the University of Tennessee, Knoxville. Her research and teaching interests lie in contemporary Aristotelian ethics and value theory, action theory, and environmental ethics.

Alexander A. Guerrero is an Associate Professor of Philosophy at Rutgers University—New Brunswick. He works on a number of topics in political philosophy, legal philosophy, and moral philosophy, and is the author of the forthcoming book, *Lottocracy: A New Kind of Democracy*.

Stephen Hetherington is a Professor of Philosophy at the University of New South Wales, Sydney, and Editor-in-Chief of the *Australasian Journal of Philosophy*. His books include *How to Know* (2011), *Knowledge and the Gettier Problem* (2016/2018), and *What Is Epistemology?* (2019).

Jesús Ilundáin-Agurruza is a Professor of Philosophy at Linfield University, in Oregon. His areas of expertise include phenomenology, philosophy of mind, comparative philosophy, and the philosophy of sport. His research program centers on expertise, particularly in sports, martial and performing arts.

Thomas K. Johansen is a Professor of Philosophy at the University of Oslo. His publications include *The Powers of Aristotle's Soul* (2012), *Plato's Natural Philosophy* (2004), *Aristotle on the Sense-Organs* (1997), and, as editor, *Productive Knowledge in Ancient Philosophy* (2020).

Amy Kind is Russell K. Pitzer Professor of Philosophy at Claremont McKenna College. In addition to authoring the introductory textbook *Persons and Personal Identity* (2015), she has edited *Philosophy of Mind in the Twentieth and Twenty-First Centuries* (2018), *The Routledge Handbook of Philosophy of Imagination* (2016), and *Knowledge Through Imagination* (with Peter Kung, 2016).

Günther Knoblich is a Professor of Cognitive Science and Co-Director of the Social Mind Center at Central European University. He studies how humans perceive, act, think, and learn, alone and together.

John W. Krakauer is currently the John C. Malone Professor, Professor of Neurology, Neuroscience, and Physical Medicine and Rehabilitation, and Director of the Brain, Learning, Animation, and Movement Lab (www.BLAM-lab.org) at The Johns Hopkins University School of Medicine. His areas of research interest are: (1) Experimental and computational studies of motor control and motor learning in humans; (2) Tracking long-term motor skill learning and its relation to higher cognitive processes such as decision-making; (3) Prediction of motor recovery after stroke; (4) Mechanisms of spontaneous motor recovery after stroke in humans and in mouse models; (5) New neuro-rehabilitation approaches for patients in the first three months after stroke.

Michael Kremer is the Mary R. Morton Professor of Philosophy and in the College at the University of Chicago, USA. His main interests are in the history of analytic philosophy. His current research focuses on the philosophy of Gilbert Ryle.

Matthew MacKenzie is a Professor of Philosophy and Department Chair at Colorado State University, USA. He works at the intersection of Indian philosophy and philosophy of mind and has published widely in those areas.

Diego Marconi (PhD, Pittsburgh 1980) was a Professor of Philosophy of Language in the University of Torino until 2017; he had taught Logic, Philosophy of Science and Philosophy of Language at other universities, both in Italy and in other European countries. His main work is on Wittgenstein's philosophy, Hegel's dialectic, paraconsistent logic, and several topics in the philosophy of language, particularly lexical meaning, and he is the author of *Lexical Competence* (1997). Recently, he has been working at the interface of philosophy of language and neuro-psychology, publishing papers in *Cortex* (2013) and *Neuropsychologia* (2019). He is a member of the Accademia delle Scienze of Torino and the Academia Europaea.

Melissa Merritt is an Associate Professor at the University of New South Wales in Sydney, Australia. She currently holds a Future Fellowship from the Australian Research Council, and is working on a long-term research project on the significance of Stoic philosophy in Kant's ethics.

Barbara Gail Montero is a Professor of Philosophy at the CUNY. Her research has been recognized by the National Endowment for the Humanities, the American Council of Learned Societies, and the Mellon Foundation. She is the author of *Thought in Action: Expertise and the Conscious Mind* (2016).

Richard Moore wrote his chapter in this volume while a Wissenschaftlicher Mitarbeiter at the Berlin School of Mind and Brain, Humboldt-Universität zu Berlin, and during an RSSS Visiting Fellowship in the Department of Philosophy at the Australian National University. He is now a UKRI Future Leaders Fellow in the Department of Philosophy at the University of Warwick. His research addresses the cultural and cognitive foundations of human development in ontogeny and phylogeny.

Myrto Mylopoulos is an Assistant Professor of Philosophy and Cognitive Science at Carleton University. She works on issues in the philosophy of mind, philosophy of action, and philosophy of cognitive science with a special focus on agency, control, and consciousness.

Bence Nanay is a BOF Research Professor of Philosophy at the Centre for Philosophical Psychology at the University of Antwerp. He has published more than 100 peer-reviewed articles on philosophy of mind and cognitive science and three monographs with Oxford University Press, with three more under contract. His work is supported by a large number of high-profile grants, including a two million euro grant from the ERC.

Carlotta Pavese is an Associate Professor of Philosophy at Cornell University. She has broad interests and writes on topics in philosophy of mind, language, epistemology, action theory, and philosophical logic. Her articles have appeared in *Philosophers' imprint*, *Philosophical Review*, *Synthese*, *Analysis*, *Philosophical Psychology*, *Philosophy and Phenomenological Research*, and

Philosophical Issues. She is currently working on a book project on the nature of skills and the practical mind.

Graham Priest is a Distinguished Professor of Philosophy at the Graduate Center of the CUNY, and Boyce Gibson Professor Emeritus at the University of Melbourne. Further details about him can be found at grahampriest.net.

Jesse Prinz is a Distinguished Professor of Philosophy and Director of Interdisciplinary Science Studies at the Graduate Center of the CUNY. His books include *Furnishing the Mind* (2002), *Gut Reactions* (2004), *Beyond Human Nature* (2012), and *The Conscious Brain* (2012).

Duncan Pritchard is the Chancellor's Professor of Philosophy at the University of California, Irvine. Professor Pritchard's research is mainly in the area of epistemology, and he has published broadly in this field. His monographs include *Epistemic Luck* (2005), *The Nature and Value of Knowledge* (with Alan Millar and Adrian Haddock, 2010), *Epistemological Disjunctivism* (2012), and *Epistemic Angst: Radical Skepticism and the Groundlessness of Our Believing* (2015).

Hagop Sarkissian is an Associate Professor of Philosophy at the CUNY, Baruch College, and the CUNY Graduate Center. His research spans topics in moral psychology, metaethics, and the history of Chinese philosophy.

John Schwenkler is an Associate Professor of Philosophy at Florida State University. He is the author of *Anscombe's* Intention: *A Guide* (2019) and co-editor, with Enoch Lambert, of *Becoming Someone New: Essays on Transformative Experience, Choice, and Change* (2020).

Natalie Sebanz is a Professor of Cognitive Science at Central European University and Co-Director of its Social Mind Center. She investigates how people take others' perspectives, how they act together, and how they learn from each other.

Joshua Shepherd is an Assistant Professor at Carleton University, a CIFAR Azrieli Global Scholar, and a Senior Fellow with the LOGOS research group at the University of Barcelona, where he leads the project Rethinking Conscious Agency, funded by the European Research Council, grant 757698.

Susanna Siegel is the Edgar Pierce Professor of Philosophy at Harvard University, USA and author of *The Rationality of Perception* (2017), *The Contents of Visual Experience* (2010), and numerous articles about perception and the relationship between individual minds and culture.

Corrado Sinigaglia is a Professor of Philosophy of Science in the Department of Philosophy, and Director of the Cognition in Action Lab (http://cialab.unimi.it/) at Università degli Studi di Milano, Italy. His main research interest is to explore the role of motor processes and representations in perception, cognition, and everyday social interaction. Publications include (with G. Rizzolatti) *Mirrors in the Brain: How our Minds Share Actions and Emotions* (2008).

Will Small is an Assistant Professor of Philosophy at the University of Illinois at Chicago. He works in the philosophy of action, and on related topics in ethics, epistemology, and the philosophy of mind. He has a special interest in the topic of practical knowledge, and in the works of Elizabeth Anscombe and Gilbert Ryle.

Ernest Sosa is the Board of Governors Professor of Philosophy at Rutgers University. These days he works mainly in epistemology, but with overlaps.

Matt Stichter is an Associate Professor of Philosophy in the School of Politics, Philosophy, & Public Affairs at Washington State University. He pursues research at the intersection of moral psychology, virtue ethics, and the philosophy of expertise.

Dustin Stokes is an Associate Professor in the Department of Philosophy at the University of Utah. He works primarily in philosophy of mind and cognitive science, in particular on perceptual experience and its relation to cognition, imagination and imagery, and creative thought and action.

James Strachan is a postdoctoral researcher in the Social Mind and Body lab in the Department of Cognitive Science at Central European University. His research interests relate to how people coordinate, communicate, and learn from each other in social interactions.

John Sutton is a Professor of Cognitive Science at Macquarie University, Sydney, where he was previously Head of the Department of Philosophy. His research addresses personal and social memory, distributed cognition, embodied skills, and cognitive history.

Antonella Tramacere is a postdoctoral researcher in the Department of Linguistic and Cultural Evolution at the Max Planck Institute for the Science of Human History in Jena. Her philosophical research concerns the neurobiology and functional role of action–perception coupling for understanding the development of the human mind.

Wayne Wu is an Associate Professor in the Neuroscience Institute at Carnegie Mellon University. He is the author of *Attention* (2014).

ACKNOWLEDGMENTS

We would like to thank Routledge for their assistance and encouragement with this project and all the authors for their contributions. Many authors have helped us review at least one of the chapters of this Handbook and we would like to thank them for their helpful comments. Additionally, we would like to thank the following scholars for providing advice and comments on some of the chapters: Taylor Carman (Barnard College), Mohan Matthen (University of Toronto), Francesca Bosco (University of Turin), Walter Sinnott-Armstrong (Duke University), Gopal Sreenivasan (Duke University), David Wong (Duke University), Anton Ford (University of Chicago). We are thankful to Shao-Pu Kang (Cornell University) and Amy Ramirez (Cornell University) for being extremely efficient copy-editors. Thanks are due to Cornell University for providing research funds that made the completion of this project possible and also to the Templeton World Charity Foundation.

INTRODUCTION TO *THE ROUTLEDGE HANDBOOK OF PHILOSOPHY OF SKILL AND EXPERTISE*

Ellen Fridland and Carlotta Pavese[1]

The diverse and breathtaking intelligence of the human animal is often embodied in skills. People, throughout their lifetimes, acquire and refine a vast number of skills. And there seems to be no upper limit to the creativity and beauty expressed by them. Think, for instance, of Olympic gymnastics: the amount of strength, flexibility, and control required to perform even a simple beam routine amazes, startles, and delights. In addition to the sheer beauty of skill, performances at the pinnacle of expertise often display a kind of brilliance or genius. We observe an intelligence that saturates the body. The unity of physicality and intellect, mind and body, meshed and melded.

Apart from sports, people develop a host of other skills, including musical and artistic skills, linguistic and social skills, scientific and medical skills, military and political skills, engineering skills, computer skills, business skills, etc. What's more, skill acquisition and refinement occur throughout the human lifespan. Children work on skills from infancy and throughout development and adults will often continue to refine skills through old age. The variety, ubiquity, and centrality of skills in the lives of humans is quite simply remarkable.

Although notions of skill and expertise have always figured prominently in a variety of philosophical discussions, the last couple of decades have seen an explosion of direct interest in skill and practical expertise. Crucially, debates about know-how and virtue epistemology have fueled interest in the notion of skill and practical knowledge in areas such as epistemology, ethics, and action theory. Also, philosophers of cognitive science, as well as neuroscientists and psychologists, have become increasingly interested in issues concerning the nature of embodied expertise, motor skill, motor representation, and bodily control. As a result, across a variety of subfields from ancient and eastern philosophy, philosophy of mind, cognitive science, philosophy of perception, epistemology, action theory, ethics, political and social philosophy, and aesthetics, the debate concerning skill and practical intelligence is growing and thriving.

It is the aim of this Handbook to collect and systematize the most relevant positions in these burgeoning areas of philosophy and cognitive science. Contained within are thirty-nine chapters written by leaders in their fields, addressing the role of skill in the history of philosophy both East and West, epistemology, political philosophy, ethics, and various areas of the cognitive sciences, including perception, imagination, emotion, motor control, language, and social cognition. The chapters offer both accessible overviews of the most relevant, current debates in their respective areas and, in many cases, also develop novel, substantive positions.

It should be noted that questions of skill and expertise are important not only for our particular, theoretical understanding of these specific notions but, more broadly, for our understanding of intelligence, cognition, and practical knowledge, full stop. That is, in thinking seriously about skill and expertise, we develop a fuller, richer picture of the nature of human cognition: moral, social, political, and embodied. This understanding, rooted in both theoretical and empirical views, provides us with the opportunity to properly and substantively conceptualize the nature of practical intelligence. This, in turn, allows and sometimes forces us to reformulate our current understanding of more familiar notions, such as knowledge, action, intention, virtue, perception, imagination, emotion, and even mental representation and intelligence. In all, then, questions concerning skill are significant in and of themselves, but also highly relevant for our overall understanding of the human mind.

Below, we introduce and contextualize the parts and chapters covered by this Handbook.

I.1 Skill in the history of philosophy (East & West)

I.1.1 Skill in the history of Eastern philosophy

Skill and expertise have played a prominent role in several traditions of Eastern thought, especially as those notions are connected to living the good, virtuous, or ethical life. For instance, skillful means or *upaya* in Indian Buddhism, examples of expert swimmers or butchers in Daoism, and karate and calligraphy in the Chan/Zen tradition are all taken either directly or indirectly to concern the cultivation of appropriate awareness, attention, and perception, which is thought essential for living the good life. Across traditions, spontaneity, naturalness, effortlessness, and absorption are central to the notion of skill, though exactly how these features ought to be understood is still a matter of some debate. The authors who have written about skill in the history of Eastern philosophy in this Handbook have provided us both with badly needed context and accessible but substantive overviews of the particular ways in which skill is relevant to various discussions in Indian, Chinese, and Japanese philosophy. Moreover, each chapter offers its own way of making sense of the balance and/or tension between spontaneity and wisdom.

In their chapter, "Skill and Virtuosity in Buddhist and Daoist Philosophy," Jay L. Garfield and Graham Priest examine the various roles that skill plays in the Indian school of Mahayana Buddhism, in Daoism, and in Chan/Zen thought. In Indian Buddhism, the notion of *upaya* or skillful means is important for understanding not only skilled pedagogy, that is, teaching in a way that is appropriate to the understanding of the student, but also for grasping fundamental truths concerning the nonduality of practice and awakened consciousness. In this way, the ultimate state of personal wisdom is a state of skillful engagement with the world. This skillful engagement is necessarily a moral engagement, though it is not simply the possession of virtue but, rather, the embodied moral skill of the virtuoso—effortless, natural, spontaneous, and responsive to context.

In Daoism as well as in Chan/Zen Buddhism, the emphasis on skill is also connected, fundamentally, to concerns about living a good and ethical life. The characteristics of spontaneous, natural, absorbed, attentive, engaged, and mindful action that are found in skill are exactly those features that are required for living in an ethical and natural way. Garfield and Priest go on to present a substantive proposal for how to understand the spontaneity of skill—they claim that acting without reflective thinking does not imply that skilled action is thoughtless. Moreover, the skilled person knows both when and how to deliberate. Thus, thought and skill are not necessarily at odds, though skill is necessarily immediate and spontaneous. In fact, they claim that in eastern traditions, "practical knowledge embodied in skill is our principal cognitive achievement."

Further examining the role of skill in Daoism but also in other schools within the Chinese tradition, Hagop Sarkissian provides an overview of skill and expertise in Chinese philosophy from the 6th–3rd centuries BCE. His chapter, "Skill and Expertise in Three Schools of Classical Chinese Thought," focuses on two prominent types of expertise that are often encountered in ancient Chinese thought: The first is expertise at a particular craft, occupation, or *dao*, as is most famously presented in the Daoist anthology *Zhuangzi*. The second is ethical expertise in the Ruist (Confucian) and Mohist schools.

Sarkissian provides several accessible examples of skilled agents as they are described in key Chinese texts. This gives the nonspecialist reader an opportunity to grasp the range of cases where an appeal to the spontaneity, absorption, and effortlessness of skill becomes relevant to understanding the truly good and ethical life. Interestingly, Sarkissian also connects the intuitiveness and spontaneity of skilled action to Antonio Damasio's (1999) somatic marker hypothesis, offering a way for us to understand how decision-making can become fine-tuned through practice and arise immediately with the appropriate emotional valence.

Next, Matthew MacKenzie's chapter, "Volition, Action, and Skill in Indian Buddhist Philosophy," examines the specific tensions in Buddhist philosophy between acting skillfully, with intention, volition, causal efficacy, and the production of karma and also without a self (*anatman*). In the course of deflating this tension, MacKenzie provides a primer in Buddhist psychology, ethics, and soteriology. First, MacKenzie argues that intentional action is central to the Buddhist conception of the human condition and the attendant prescriptions for how to liberate oneself from those conditions. However, the doctrine of no-self, which reduces the self to a collection of physical and psychological events is also incompatible with a full-blooded notion of agent-causation. In this way, the Buddhist is both robustly committed to intentional and skillful actions while also holding that the only causes of action are a complex of psycho-physical events (i.e., not a self). As such, agents should not be identified with selves but, rather, with the complex psycho-physical system in which phenomena arise and lead to other phenomena.

MacKenzie goes on to explain that this complex system or continuum of psycho-physical events (the practical agent) is required to develop both wisdom and skillful means (*upaya*) in order to produce liberated action. However, there is a further paradox in that such action, in its maximal skillfulness, should be without intention, volition, and effort. Rather, such action is spontaneous, wise, compassionate but without even the practical illusion of a self. MacKenzie ends by providing two ways of understanding the transition from unawakened to awakened agency: one constructivist, which he connects to Hubert Dreyfus' conception of expertise and the other innateist.

I.1.2 Skill in history of Western philosophy

The topic of skill and expertise (*technē*) in Plato and Aristotle has received attention both in relation to the notion of virtue and in the interpretation of Plato's and Aristotle's theories of knowledge. Although both Plato and Aristotle took *technē* to be a kind of knowledge, there is significant controversy about their conceptions regarding the nature of this kind of knowledge and its relation to experience (*empeiria*) on one hand, and scientific knowledge (*epistēmē*) on the other (Johansen 2017; Lorenz and Morison 2019; Coope forthcoming). The work of Julias Annas (1995, 2001, 2011) has renewed interest on the relation between skill and virtue (or *phronēsis*) in the *Nicomachean Ethics* and also to Aristotle's action theory. Two chapters in our Handbook discuss Plato and Aristotle's views precisely on the relation between *technē* and *phronēsis*.

In "*Technē* in the Platonic Dialogues," Tom Angier introduces us to the complexities of Plato's views on *technē*. Angier argues that Plato's conception of skill and expertise goes against modern expectations in at least two ways. First, the Greek concept of *technē* has a wider extension than the English "skill" or "expertise." In the dialogues, Socrates uses it not only to refer to crafts that yield a physical product but it is also used for activities whose outcome is either internal to the activity such as lyre-playing, or even purely theoretical, such as mathematics. The second respect under which Plato's conception of skill goes against modern expectations, according to Angier, is that while ethics and skill or expertise are not always conjoined in modern philosophy, Plato's interest in *technē* is primarily *ethical*. In a striking analogy with what we have seen above as a unifying theme in the Buddhist, Daoist, Chan/Zen, Ruist, and Mohist traditions, a central question throughout the Platonic corpus is: can virtue be construed as a kind of skill or expertise?

Angier makes a systematic case that Plato saw in *technē* a model of precision that approximates a science (*epistēmē*). As Angier points out, there are several benefits of thinking of virtue in this fashion. First, a science of virtue would *professionalize* the ethical life and so secure it firmer grounds. To be *technikos* is contrasted with having a mere *empeiria* or "knack" and so if virtue were a matter of having a *technē*, it would be taken out of the hands of those with a mere knack (or *empeiros*). For Plato, like later for Aristotle, *technē* involves a *logos*, or a rational account of one's expertise. Possessing a rational grasp of what one is doing would be highly beneficial to the virtuous person, for it would give them mastery and control of their practice. Moreover, *technē* embodies knowledge and, because of this, it is transmissible through teaching. Angier points out that for Plato the transmissibility of *technē*, primarily illustrated by theoretical *technai* such as mathematics, is the paradigm source and locus of *agreement*. The upshot is, perhaps surprisingly, both political and social: if virtue were subject to the rigors of a *technē*, we would be spared much social disagreement and conflict.

In Chapter 5, "*Technē* in Aristotle's Taxonomy of Knowledge," Thomas Johansen moves from Plato to Aristotle and highlights the differences in their conceptions of the relation between *technē* and *phronēsis*. The chapter starts by revisiting Aristotle's notion that rational capacities are to do with truths and are accompanied by a true account (*logos*). Among rational capacities, Aristotle distinguished between *theoretical knowledge*, *productive knowledge*, and *practical knowledge*. While theoretical knowledge is concerned with necessary and eternal truths, productive and practical knowledge are concerned with contingent truths that can be under our influence and that can be changed. So while theoretical knowledge is a *demonstrative* state of reason concerned with eternal truths accompanied by a true account, and practical knowledge is a *practical* state of reason accompanied by a true account, productive knowledge is a *productive* state of reason accompanied by a true account.

So, while for Aristotle both *technē* and *phronēsis* are rational capacities involving an account, *technē* involves a distinctive sort of intelligence. *Technē* and *phronēsis* differ in at least two respects. While *phronēsis* is of an end without qualification (*telos haplôs*), *technē* is of "an end in relation to something and of something" (*telos pros ti and tinos*); second, *technē* is of production and *phronēsis* is of action. Johansen guides us through several possible interpretations of these putative differences between *technē* and *phronēsis* and highlights several difficulties. As Johansen points out, the crucial point of contention of Aristotle's response to Plato might also have been the most philosophically problematic for Aristotle.

Despite Aristotle's attack, the Platonic idea that virtue can be conceived of as a certain sort of skill reemerges in modern thought in an exchange deftly reconstructed by Melissa Meritt in "Mendelssohn and Kant on Virtue as a Skill." As Meritt teaches us, Moses Mendelssohn played a pivotal role in rehabilitating the "skill model" of virtue for the German rationalist tradition. According to Mendelssohn, the execution of skill characteristically displays a certain automatism and unreflectiveness. Mendelssohn took this feature of skill, together with the skill model of virtue, to provide the resources for overcoming an objection against agent-based ethics, namely, that a virtuous person would seem to act for the sake of realizing his own perfection in everything that he does, thereby taking a morally inappropriate interest in his own character. By contrast, Kant rejects the automatism featured in Mendelssohn's account, on grounds that it would make virtue mindless and unreflective. As Merritt points out, that does not mean that Kant was thereby led to reject the skill model of virtue. Rather, Kant argued that reflection is central to the manifestation of certain kinds of skills too and, because of that, he was able to cling to a version of the *virtue as skill* model.

The next chapter of this historical section moves to the contemporary philosophy of skill. In "Gilbert Ryle on Skill as Knowledge-how," Michael Kremer deepens our understanding of Ryle's theory of skill. For Ryle, skill is a form of knowledge, or knowledge-how, that is constitutively acquired through practical and experimental learning and that depends on a critical capacity for self-regulation and continued improvement. Kremer makes the case that, while Ryle's notion of knowledge-how is sharply distinguished from knowledge-that, for him, knowledge-how is also substantively related to knowledge-that. Kremer reconstructs two of the classic Rylean arguments against the intellectualist legend—the regress argument and the argument from learning and gradability—and puts Ryle in a dialogue with recent debates concerning intellectualism and anti-intellectualism about know-how. Kremer argues that Ryle considered the intellectual and perceptual skills needed to produce knowledge-that to be kinds of know-how and that those intellectual skills, on his account, were the barriers to the regress which he thought afflicted intellectualism. Although knowledge-that depends on skills, Ryle also thought that skilled behavior depends in some ways on knowledge-that, especially since critical reflection on one's successes and failures requires an awareness of what one is doing and what its results are. Kremer's discussion of Ryle's conception of skill ends by looking at some of Ryle's less well-known writings (e.g., Ryle 1967, 1970, 1972) in order to reconstruct how Ryle's reflection on philosophical skill relates to his experience as a teacher and to his theoretical approach to the teaching of philosophy.

In the next chapter, Will Small discusses "Anscombe on Action and Practical Knowledge." While for Ryle know-how is a *standing general knowledge* that is put into practice on different occasions of action, Anscombe's notion of practical knowledge is that of a distinctive kind of agential knowledge that an agent has of her particular intentional actions while she performs them. Anscombe held that if someone is X-ing *intentionally*, she knows without observation not only that she is X-ing; she knows without observation *why* she is X-ing. Small explains that Anscombe arrives at this well-known "non-observational claim" through a negative specification of the "rough outline" of the "area of intentional actions." For Anscombe, the class of things that can be known without observation is a very heterogeneous class; hence, to know that intentional actions fall in that class is not to know much at all about what it is to be an intentional action, for it is not to know anything about *why* intentional actions fall in that class. The remainder of *Intention* (Anscombe 1957) develops a positive account of intentional action and agential knowledge. On this account, agential knowledge is knowledge "in intention"—hence not just knowledge of intention but knowledge in intention *of* what is going to happen. This knowledge is practical not just because its object is practical. It is practical in *form*, for it relates to its object in a different way from that in which theoretical knowledge relates to its—in the case of practical knowledge, the knowledge itself is the *cause* of what it understands. In this sense, agential knowledge is non-observational *because* it is practical: what is going on is a case of intentional action, there to be observed, only because it is already known agentially.

Does agential knowledge, as Anscombe understands it, depend on skill/know-how? Small provides evidence that, for Anscombe, one can intentionally do *A* only provided that one knows how to *A*, otherwise it would surely be some accident if her activity culminated in her having successfully done *A*. So Anscombe did endorse an entailment—that from intentionally *A* to knowing how to *A*—that is widely endorsed in the current debate on knowing-how by both intellectualists and anti-intellectualists (Ryle 1949; Stanley and Williamson 2001; Setiya 2012; Pavese 2018). According to Small, however, Anscombe's conception of know-how, though fully compatible with certain versions of intellectualism, fits most naturally with a "bifurcationist" conception of know-how, according to which there is propositional know-how but also non-propositional "basic know-how."

While Anscombe insists that exercises of know-how are intentional, this is denied by Dreyfus (2001); and while Anscombe argued that an agent exercising know-how knows that she is doing what she is doing and why, Dreyfus (2007) explicitly rejected this model of intentional action. These and other complexities of Dreyfus' view on agency are discussed by Kristina Gehrman and John Schwenkler in their chapter, "Hubert Dreyfus on Practical and Embodied Intelligence." Gehrman and Schwenkler locate Dreyfus' account of "skilled coping" as part of a bigger picture that aimed to demonstrate the primacy of practical intelligence over all other forms of intelligence. It is in response to a standard picture of intentional action defended by his U.C. Berkeley colleague John Searle that Dreyfus came to elaborate his alternative to what he considered a standard and prevailing Platonic picture of human beings as essentially rational, individual agents. Like many contemporary action theories, Searle thought that an action is intentional only if the agent is in a mental state that represents the goal of her action; he also thought that this mental state is the cause of the bodily movement whereby the agent acts as she intends to and, in acting intentionally, an agent enjoys an *experience* that represents her action as the cause of her bodily movement. Dreyfus attacked all of these claims, arguing that they are not supported by the phenomenology of purposive activity. If we returned to the phenomenon with open minds, Dreyfus thought that what we would find would be that human beings can relate to the world in an organized purposive manner without their actions being accompanied by a representational state representing the goal of the action. Paradigmatic examples of these representation-less and yet purposive activities were, for Dreyfus, skillful activities like playing tennis or habitual activity like rolling over in bed or making gestures while speaking. In this sort of skillful coping, Dreyfus thought we find humans fundamentally embedded, absorbed, and embodied. Gehrman and Schwenkler document how these commitments to a non-mentalistic form of intentionality are present throughout Dreyfus' philosophical writings, from his critique of Artificial Intelligence research in the 1970s and 1980s to his rejection of John McDowell's conceptualism in his 2005 APA Presidential Address. Because Dreyfus was, in the end, most interested in presenting an *at least equally plausible* phenomenological account of skillful coping that could represent a viable alternative to the standard Platonic picture, Gehrman and Schwenkler guide us through Dreyfus' radical proposal for a contentless and non-mentalistic form of intentionality and practical intelligence, through to its deepest motivations.

I.2 Skill in epistemology

Knowledge and skill are intimately connected. Scientists cannot collect new knowledge without developing their skills for devising experiments. And skilled artists, scientists, and mathematicians must know a lot about their area of expertise in order to perform skillfully and to routinely manifest that knowledge through their skillful performances.

Despite this obvious interrelationship, knowledge and skill have received different treatment in analytic epistemology. Although philosophers in this tradition have long been in the business of understanding and defining knowledge, the topic of skill has been marginalized. It is only quite recently that skills have made a powerful entrance in two epistemological debates: the debate on virtue epistemology and the debate on the nature of know-how. Part II encompasses four different chapters that take positions on these two central epistemological debates.

According to virtue epistemology, skill and know-how come before knowledge: knowledge is to be understood as a kind of skillful performance (Zagzebski 1996; Sosa 2007, 2015; Pritchard 2012; Turri 2018). This approach to epistemology is represented by two chapters of this handbook. In "Knowledge, Skill, and Virtue Epistemology," Duncan Pritchard provides an overview of different ways of understanding the virtue epistemological thesis that knowledge is to be conceived of in terms of the relationship between cognitive success and cognitive agency. Virtue epistemology is motivated by one key platitude: the *ability intuition*—according to which guesswork, for example, cannot amount to knowledge, for in it the subject displays no cognitive agency. According to *robust virtue epistemology*, there is nothing more to knowledge than virtuously formed true belief. Robust virtue epistemology is motivated by the idea that knowledge is a distinctive kind of cognitive achievement. Although theoretically attractive, Pritchard points out that it faces several objections, in that it cannot always account for another prominent intuition, the *anti-luck intuition* – the intuition that lucky belief cannot amount to knowledge. In this chapter, Pritchard argues that a form of modest virtue epistemology—anti-luck virtue epistemology—that combines the ability intuition with the anti-luck intuition, fares better. On these sorts of virtue epistemologies, knowledge is to be understood as *safe (non-lucky) cognitive success* which is attributable to one's manifestation of the relevant cognitive skills. According to Pritchard, anti-luck virtue epistemology thus has the resources to account for how knowledge demands both the avoidance of high levels of epistemic luck (and thus epistemic risk) and the manifestation of significant levels of relevant cognitive skill.

The second chapter on virtue epistemology is "Skill and Knowledge" by Ernest Sosa and Laura Frances Callahan. Following Sosa's (2007, 2015) prominent work in virtue epistemology, Sosa and Callahan take knowledge to be a form of action, which one might attempt and fail. Attempts can be either accurate, as when the aim of the attempt is attained, adroit, as when the attempt manifests a competence, or apt, where accuracy of the attempt manifests the competence. A competence is defined as a *disposition to succeed* and is understood as having a tripartite structure, for whether one is competent to perform on a certain occasion depends not only on one's pertinent skills (Skill) but also on the shape one is in (Shape) and on the favorability of one's relevant situation (Situation). Here, the authors present a detailed, and in some respects novel, robust virtue epistemological account. On this view, skills are *not* the same as competences. While competences have a triple structure, only the innermost competence counts as a skill: for one might have a skill without being in good shape or while being in a bad situation. Because of this, Sosa and Callahan observe that only full competence, rather than mere skill, is the most important kind of power for epistemology, for the highest epistemic success (knowledge) manifests full competence: one knows if and only if one has a *true* belief in virtue of one's having exercised skill in an appropriate shape and situation. This account differs from

Pritchard's anti-luck virtue epistemology where both a virtue condition and an anti-luck condition play a role in defining knowledge. It also differs from modal virtue epistemologies (e.g., Beddor and Pavese 2018) that understand skillfulness in modal terms as counterfactual success. In fact, on Sosa and Callahan's proposal, the modal profile of a performance is irrelevant to its counting as apt.

A novel aspect of the virtue epistemological account defended by Sosa and Callahan in this chapter is that they appeal to knowledge in an understanding of justification: epistemic performances that manifest skill without aptness are *mere* justified beliefs, which fall short of knowledge. The resulting virtue epistemology gives knowledge a central explanatory role to play vis-à-vis other concepts central to epistemology, such as that of justification. In this sense, Sosa and Callahan's counts as a "knowledge-friendly" virtue epistemology.

In addition to their role in virtue epistemology, skills and know-how have been central to epistemological discussions concerning the nature of know-how and skill. As we have seen, Ryle (1949) defended a form of anti-intellectualism about skill: skill is a kind of know-how and know-how is irreducible to propositional knowledge. Despite Ryle's attack on the intellectualist legend, the last twenty years have seen a resurgence of intellectualism (Stanley and Williamson 2001; Stanley 2011a; Pavese 2013), in a variety of forms. Stanley and Williamson (2001) responded to Ryle by arguing that know-how and skill come apart and that knowledge-how consists in a distinctive kind of propositional knowledge about how to perform actions — a state of knowing an answer to the question how one could perform the action under a distinctively *practical mode of presentation*. Moreover, they argued that one of Ryle's main motivations — he regress argument—fails.

This form of intellectualism was primarily motivated by linguistic considerations about how to ascribe know-how in English and kin languages. It focused on know-how and it conceded to Ryle that skills are a different matter from know-how. It even denied that know-how entails practical ability. A rich literature ensued, featuring responses and attacks to this version of intellectualism, some questioning the original linguistic argument (e.g., Schiffer 2002; Rumfitt 2003; Brogaard 2009; Bengson and Moffett 2011; Wiggins 2012; Hornsby 2016); others reformulating the Rylean regress argument (Fridland 2013; Weatherson 2017); others still questioning the epistemic parallel between know-how and knowledge-that (Poston 2009; Cath 2011, 2015; Setiya 2012; Carter and Pritchard 2015; Carter and Navarro 2018), the intelligibility of practical modes of presentation (Schiffer 2002; Noë 2005; Glick 2015), the compatibility of intellectualism with fundamental posits in cognitive science (e.g., Devitt 2011) and Stanley's (2011b) and Stanley and Krakauer's (2013) characterization of automatic processes (Fridland 2014, 2017a, 2017b). These attacks have, in turn, generated more intellectualist responses, aiming at defending the linguistic argument for intellectualism (Stanley 2011a, 2011b), the intelligibility of practical modes of presentation (Pavese 2015, 2019), at providing extra-linguistic motivations for the view (Pavese 2013), at defending the epistemic parallel between know-how and knowledge-that (Marley-Payne 2016; Pavese 2018), at debunking the cognitive science argument (Stanley and Krakauer 2013; Pavese 2019), the gradability argument (Pavese 2017), or the most recent versions of the regress argument (Cath 2013; Beddor and Pavese 2020).

The debate on know-how is ongoing. But the recent years have seen an important shift in attention. While earlier intellectualists agreed with Ryle that skill and know-how come apart, now intellectualists have extended their focus from know-how to skill. There is, however, wide disagreement on how intellectualism about skills ought to be understood. Stanley and Krakauer (2013) argue that skill consists in part in knowledge about how to perform an action but is not exhausted by it. In addition to knowledge, "motor acuity" is needed, as a sort of motor ability that can be tuned through practice and exercise. In contrast with this "hybrid view" of skill,

Stanley and Williamson (2017) argue that skills are not themselves knowledge states but rather dispositions to know. Starting from considerations stemming from the role of knowledge in action theory, Pavese (2013) and Beddor and Pavese (2020) argue instead for a radical form of intellectualism, according to which both skill and know-how are knowledge states, for only knowledge states appropriately characterized can explain the distinctive intentionality and control of skillful performance.

Though different in several respects, these forms of intellectualism all agree in taking skill and know-how to be understood in terms of a fundamental epistemic state of knowledge. By contrast, in the chapter "Know-how and Skill: The Puzzles of Priority and Equivalence," Yuri Cath defends a still different form of intellectualism—a "practical attitude intellectualism" as he calls it. Cath agrees with radical forms of intellectualism that skill and know-how are one and the same. However, Cath's intellectualism differs from radical intellectualism on two scores. First, Cath's intellectualism is *revisionary*, for according to Cath know-how and skill are not knowledge states but rather belief states of a kind. In particular, Cath appeals to his earlier work (Cath 2011, 2015) to argue that know-how can be Gettiered, while knowledge-that cannot. Because he thinks that know-how and knowledge-that differ in their epistemic and modal profile, Cath argues that know-how and skill cannot be knowledge states but must, rather, be belief states. Second, while intellectualists typically appeal to distinctively practical modes of presentation when characterizing the sort of knowledge states know-how and skill consist in, Cath develops a form of intellectualism that does not appeal to practical modes of presentation. For one to know how to perform a certain task one need not entertain a proposition under a practical mode of presentation; rather, it is enough that one entertains the propositional attitude practically.

While radical intellectualism understands skills in terms of knowledge, in the last chapter of Part II, "Knowledge as Skill," Stephen Hetherington reverses the order of explanation by defending *practicalism*—the view that knowledge is a kind of skill or know-how and defends it from several objections. While knowledge of a fact or truth has long been conceived of as a belief with epistemically propitious features, Hetherington argues that this picture fails to explain the distinctive role of knowledge vis-à-vis action. According to Hetherington, a paramount question for a theory of knowledge that is often neglected by epistemologists is: how can knowledge so conceived ever motivate and guide action? This chapter introduces a novel answer to this question—*practicalism*—whereby any instance of knowledge is a skillful power to act, or a form of knowledge-how. Hetherington argues that this pragmatist conception of knowledge can tell a powerful story about what links knowledge and action: many actions are expressions or manifestations of knowledge, which is itself the power to act in such ways.

While skills figure prominently in virtue epistemology, in the debate between intellectualists and anti-intellectualists, and in discussions about the relation between knowledge and action, the interest in skill in epistemology goes beyond these debates and expands to social epistemology. The notions of skill and expertise are central to today's discussions about what counts as a political expert (e.g., Goldman 2001; Buchanan 2004, 2009; Guerrero 2016) as well as in the debate about virtue ethics and moral expertise (Driver 2013, 2015). The importance of skill and know-how for moral and social/political epistemology will reappear in the final part of this Handbook.

I.3 Skill, intelligence, and agency

The notions of skill and know-how figure prominently in the philosophy of action. As we have seen, for Anscombe (1957), intentional action is understood in terms of agential knowledge and, moreover, it requires know-how. By contrast, Dreyfus (2000, 2001, 2005, 2007) thought that skillful action is the locus of embodied, embedded agency and used such action as an example motivating a non-representational theory of intentional action. Because of the centrality of skills in an account of intentional and intelligent action, Part III of this Handbook is devoted to chapters that discuss skills in relation to theories of agency.

In the first chapter of this section, "Consciousness and Skill," Barbara Gail Montero launches a sustained attack on the broadly Dreyfusian account of skillful coping as mindless. Developing several lines of arguments from Montero (2016), the author targets the "the *just-do-it principle*," that permeates much of the Dreyfusian discussion of skillful and mindless coping. According to the *just-do-it principle*, experts perform best when their conscious minds are disengaged from their actions, when they are performing "automatically." Montero critically assesses several arguments for the *just-do-it* principle. One particular argument starts from the phenomenon of choking under pressure, where an individual performs significantly worse than would be expected in a high-pressure situation. This phenomenon has been taken to be evidence that skillful action proceeds without conscious attention, because choking episodes are thought to arise from the fact that anxiety leads one to focus and direct one's mind on the performance, which would otherwise proceed smoothly if mindless. The "explicit monitoring hypothesis" has it that in normal circumstances conscious monitoring interferes with high level of performance. Montero reviews the extant empirical literature and shows not only that the methodology underlying the experiments for the explicit monitoring hypothesis is controversial, relying on artificial experimental settings, but also that there are other possible explanations for the choking effects, which emphasize that changing the locus of the focus, more than the focus itself might be detrimental to the performance in choking under pressure. By carefully highlighting the shortcomings of this and other arguments for the *just-do-it* principle, Montero argues that online conscious thought about what one is doing is compatible with expertise and surveys some empirical evidence that in fact skillful performance might require the full consciousness of the expert.

Montero's critique of the *just-do-it* principle confronts Dreyfus and its other proponent in their own terms—i.e., by taking seriously phenomenological evidence and first personal reports and by looking at skillful performance from the perspective of the embodied experiences of the real experts. This "ecological" approach to the study of skillful performance is theorized and defended in the following chapter, "Embodied Experience in the Cognitive Ecologies of Skilled Performance," by John Sutton and Kath Bicknell. They argue that a properly ecological methodology requires looking at the real performances of experts in the environment where they are intelligently attuned, rather than in artificial and regimented experimental settings. It requires expanding standard sources for skill theory, to look not only at specialist work in sport psychology, music cognition or other rich bodies of applied research but also at practitioners' own fallible but unique self-understandings. In order to anticipate concerns about the reliability of self-reports, Sutton and Bicknell survey related methods from cognitive psychology, sport science, and cognitive ethnography, and home in on apprenticeship methods and work by researcher-practitioners. They illustrate the methodology by looking at an extended case study of cyclist Chloe Hosking's account of the closing stages of her winning ride in the 2016 La Course by Le Tour de France. Sutton and Bicknell argue that by triangulating Hosking's narrative against other evidence, one can learn about the multiplicity of diverse cues to which this athlete was responding in on-the-fly decision-making.

The link between skill and agency, and the relation between automaticity on one hand, and control and attention on the other, is further investigated by Wayne Wu in "Automaticity, Control and Attention in Skill." Skill emerges from a shifting balance between automaticity and control over time. But how can a skillful performance be both automatic and controlled? As Wu teaches us, a rich psychological literature has assumed an overly simple connection between automaticity and control, assuming that performance can be under one's control if and only if it is not automatic. This connection, so understood, stands in the way of a full understanding of skillful performance as both automatic and controlled. Wu argues that in order to understand this feature of skillful performance, we ought to think of the structure of intentional agency as the locus where automaticity and control merge. While it is true that the same process cannot be wholly automatic and at the same time wholly controlled, certain features of the process might be automatic while other features of the same process can be under one's control. In particular, Wu proposes we individuate the properties of an intentional action that are under agentive control as those that are the result of the agent's executive intention to perform the action in this or that way. On the other hand, the properties of a process that are not under agential control are those that are not the result of the agent's executive intention. Wu argues that this way of retaining a strong division between automaticity and control also allows one to accommodate the observed gradualism in automaticity and control manifested in skill learning, for the set of properties that are automatic or controlled changes over time and so does the tuning of the specific action properties. Finally, Wu shows us how to apply this theoretical framework to a case study—the research on overt attention in batting sports.

The role of intentions and intentionality in skillful performance has long motivated intellectualist theories about know-how (Pavese 2013, 2018, 2020; Stanley and Krakauer 2013). If manifestations of knowing-how are intentional, because intentional action seems to require knowing what to do to initiate the action, intellectualists have argued that propositional knowledge about how to perform an action is central to skillful action. On this basis, Stanley and Krakauer (2013) argued that motor skill depends on knowledge of facts, forwarding a challenge to the standard interpretation of amnesiac cases, such as patient HM, that have led to the familiar dichotomy between procedural and declarative knowledge in psychology. In "Automatizing Knowledge: Confusion Over What Cognitive Neuroscience Tells Us About Intellectualism," John W. Krakauer recapitulates his argument to the effect that neuroscientific evidence suggesting that procedural knowledge and declarative knowledge dissociate has been misinterpreted as evidence for an anti-intellectualist position. The right understanding of HM and other amnesiac cases, Krakauer argues, supports a version of intellectualism about know-how. Krakauer goes on to respond to some critiques of this earlier position. As Krakauer himself acknowledges, something was missing from Stanley and Krakauer's (2013) version of intellectualism about know-how and skill—i.e., the role of a distinctively motor and procedural representation in the explanation of know-how and skill (see also Pavese, Chapter 18 in this volume). Krakauer proposes that we integrate that account of skillful action by appealing to what he calls "control policies" (cf. Shmuelof et al. 2012; Haith and Krakauer 2013, 2018). As he understands them, control policies are "rules that automatize and are cached with practice" and which are no longer propositional once cached. For example, the policy for mirror drawing is to go left rather than right after making a leftward error; with practice this policy gets cached, which is why it does not have to be explicitly remembered by HM.

The role of procedural and practical representation in intellectualist theories about know-how and skills is discussed in the next chapter, "Practical Representation." Carlotta Pavese elucidates the notion of a practical mode of presentation, first introduced by intellectualist theories of know-how, by comparing it to more familiar kinds of modes of presentation—perceptual and conceptual modes of presentation. By looking at psychological theories of motor control, Pavese forwards an account of the sort of motor and procedural representations that are posited by those theories and, against a widespread skepticism about the representational status of motor representation, provides a novel argument for thinking that motor representations are *bona fide* representations, in that they are assessable for accuracy and inaccuracy as they succeed or fail to accurately represent the intended target of the motor task. In the second half of the chapter, Pavese explores the theoretical need for practical concepts—or practical ways of thinking—that often make appearances in the intellectualist theories of know-how (Stanley and Williamson 2001; Pavese 2015), in order to account for a distinctively *productive* kind of reasoning—the capacity for which seems to be lost in motor deficits such as ideo-motor apraxia (Pacherie 2006; Pavese forthcoming). As she argues, far from being an unwelcome commitment of intellectualist theories of know-how, practical representation (both conceptual practical representation and non-conceptual practical representation) ought to play a central role in any theory of skill, whether or not intellectualist, that takes into serious account psychological and neuroscientific evidence.

In the next chapter, "The Nature of Skill: Functions and Control Structures," Ellen Fridland introduces a *functional* view of skill, where skills are to be understood as functions from intentions to actions that are implemented by a variety of control structures, which have been learned through practice. Fridland argues that this way of conceiving of skill incorporates the strengths and avoids the weaknesses of extant versions of intellectualism and anti-intellectualism about know-how. For Fridland, control structures are responsible for the flexible modification, adaptation, and adjustment of goal-directed action. Further, on her account, control structures are hierarchically organized on at least three levels: *strategic*, which includes practical planning and knowledge in action; *attention*, which selects perceptual information in an intention-sensitive way and integrates that information with online motor representations; and, *motor*, which involves motor representations that have been diachronically shaped through deliberate practice and which are, themselves, means-ends coherent with goal contents. In this way, Fridland maintains that motor representations are intelligent in several ways: in their capacity to adjust and adapt online to an unfolding action environment, in virtue of their learning history, and also because of their connection to states or structures of strategic control.

Further fleshing out how we ought to understand the intelligence of motor control, Myrto Mylopoulos, in "The Intelligence of Motor Control," argues that motor representations are intelligent not merely derivatively, as a result of their connection to intentions, but in their own right. To establish this position, Mylopoulos begins by introducing *the puzzle of skilled action*—a version of which we have seen appear in Wu's chapter: How can skilled action display robust intelligence despite being largely governed by motor control processes that are often characterized as brute, reflex-like, automatic, and paradigmatically unintelligent? For Mylopoulos, intelligence is cashed out in terms of flexibility and, thus, her challenge is to show that motor representations of the kind involved in skilled action are flexible in the relevant ways. To establish this, Mylopoulos argues for a hybrid view of skilled action, which acknowledges the role of intentions and propositional knowledge but also holds that motor representations are themselves intelligent in virtue of their temporal and functional organization. According to Mylopoulos, motor learning is a process that involves both refining the structure of a motor program but also fine-tuning the parameterization of that program. Accordingly, Mylopoulos locates the difference between the expert and novice in the complexity of their respective motor representations (see Pavese, Chapter 18 in this volume). As such, Mylopoulos's solution to *the puzzle of skilled action* involves elucidating the complex structure of motor representations in order to show that construing them as unintelligent is mistaken.

The final chapter of this part, "The Targets of Skill, and Their Importance," discusses a crucial methodological question that arises when studying skilled performance: What is this something that one is skilled *at*? Joshua Shepherd points out that skill essentially involves an agent's being excellent in *some* way: the skilled agent is skilled at *something*. This is the question of the "target of skills." According to Shepherd, one ought to be pluralist about the target of skills: agents display skill at actions, at games, and at a wide range of practices and activities. And this sort of pluralism about the target correspondingly motivates a sort of pluralism about skills, for it suggests that skills display variable structure, depending upon the target.

I.4 Skill in perception, imagination, and emotion

The next section of the Handbook is devoted to chapters that explore the connections between skill and perception, imagination and emotion. When it comes to phenomena like perception, especially visual perception, the connection to bodily skill has been forwarded as central in debates concerning embodied and enactive perception. For instance, as Siegel discusses below, Merleau-Ponty (2013/1945) made the connection to bodily action central to his theory of visual perception. Also, famously, J. J. Gibson (2014/1979) argued that perception involved perception not only of colors or static properties but direct sensitivity to affordances or possibilities for action. Importantly, affordances are relational properties, which depend on the kinds of actions or skills that an agent could perform in the perceived environment. More recently, Kevin O'Regan and Alva Noë (O'Regan and Noë 2001; Noë 2004) have argued that perceptual experience is constituted in part by an agent's know-how. More specifically, they argue that what one sees depends on one's embodied knowledge of sensorimotor contingencies or, put another way, perception depends on sensorimotor skills. In contrast, connections between skill and imagination and skill and emotion, though implicit in some discussions, are still nascent but rich areas of philosophical inquiry.

Taking up the connection between action and perception, we begin with a chapter by Emily S. Cross. Cross provides us with a terrific overview of how the development and possession of embodied expertise affects action observation in her chapter, "Embodying Expertise as a Performer and Perceiver: Insights from the Arts and Robotics." Cross begins with a brief overview of the history of thought—philosophical, psychological, and neuroscientific—as it pertains to the connections, or lack thereof, between perception and action. She goes on to review key empirical studies in the domain of the performing arts, which demonstrate a robust relationship between the possession of embodied expertise, both longstanding and *de novo*, and the perception of action in that domain. That is, empirical research seems to indicate that the better one is at performing an action, the more one simulates that action when observing it. Cross goes on to review studies relating embodied expertise to aesthetic and affective experience and also to possible applications of this knowledge to social robotics, where understanding how humans relate to the actions of others may be crucial for developing well-calibrated, artificial, social agents. Part of the utility of Cross's chapter is its evenhandedness in both presenting research that robustly supports a simulation theory of action and perception and also highlighting various studies that complicate a straightforward or linear relationship between greater amounts of embodied expertise and greater engagement of sensorimotor cortices, greater aesthetic enjoyment, and even greater interpersonal rapport.

Working in a similar domain, Corrado Sinigaglia and Stephen A. Butterfill build out a theoretical framework for understanding the evidence that Cross introduces above by offering a substantive explanation of the connection between skill and observational knowledge. In "Motor Representation and Knowledge of Skilled Action," Sinigaglia and Butterfill begin by reviewing empirical evidence of increased skill or expertise leading to increased knowledge or accuracy in predicting the outcomes of observed actions within the domain of expertise.

Sinigaglia and Butterfill go on to ask why developing motor skill should provide agents with the ability to acquire observational knowledge concerning that skill. They answer that it is because both performing motor skill and observing skill involve a common element: namely, a motor representation. That is, they claim that the same motor representation is involved in both guiding action and observing someone perform that same action.

Next, Sinigaglia and Butterfill go on to consider an objection concerning the proposal that motor representations play this dual role. The objection runs that representations can only have one direction of fit, but the role suggested above to motor representations has two. Sinigaglia and Butterfill respond to this potential objection by claiming that motor representations can have both a control and epistemic function relative to a system. As such, relative to one system, the motor representation can have a control function but, relative to another system, that same representation can take on an epistemic function. Sinigaglia and Butterfill end by considering a further potential issue with their view: the problem of how the content of motor representations can interface directly with that of personal-level epistemic states. They offer four proposals for how one might solve the interface problem that comes up at this juncture and go on to suggest empirical avenues to pursue in order to make progress on determining which of those solutions is true.

Moving from the connection between embodied expertises and action observation to questions about how skill might influence or constitute the processes of visual perception, we turn to Susanna Siegel's chapter, "Skill and Expertise in Perception." In order to understand how skill or expertise might be related to perception, Siegel proposes we work with a broad notion of skill, where exercises of skill are not necessarily instances of intentional action, and she further focuses on conscious perceptual experience. Siegel discusses three main ways in which perceptual experiences might be thought to manifest a subject's skills in this broader sense. According to the first, perceptual experience consists in, or necessarily engages motor skills. This idea traces back to the philosophy of Merleau-Ponty (2013/1945), according to whom in paradigmatic cases of perception, the flow of information is inseparable from the way a perceiver moves through a perceptual scene. Siegel reviews how this model of perceptual experience as necessarily engaging motor skills has inspired contemporary thinkers such as Noë (2004) and Kelly (2005) to generalize it to cases of apparently static perception. According to one such proposal, static perception also engages the body, for it involves the bodily activity of finding optimal viewpoints. Siegel then turns to the second way in which perception might be thought to manifest skills—i.e., by involving recognitional capacities. Siegel points out that one way to articulate this idea is to embrace Lewis's (1990) ability hypothesis: knowing what something looks like amounts to possessing certain sorts of practical abilities or know-how.

Finally, the third way in which perceptual experiences involve skills is by patterns of attention being affected by the skill and expertise that we have. As Siegel notes, distributions of attention might depend on scientific expertise: for example, faced with the same sequence of X-ray images, a radiologist and a novice will parse each image differently. Perceptual learning might also depend on improved acuity in categorization. For example, gaining practice and expertise in music can improve the ability to find the beat in a piece of music and keep track of it. Finally, cultural embeddings can shape our perceptual experience and attention. Here, Siegel reviews some important work providing experimental evidence that cultural stereotype can direct attention toward stereotype-congruent information, and away from stereotype-incongruent information (Eberhardt et al. 2004) and that the extent of gaze-following behavior can be sometimes sensitive to race and social power (Adams and Kveraga 2015).

Extending considerations of perceptual learning to perceptual expertise, Dustin Stokes and Bence Nanay's chapter, "Perceptual Skills," starts out by offering a way of distinguishing between properly perceptual and post-perceptual or cognitive skills. Stokes and Nanay go on to argue that cases of perceptual expertise, such as those found in expert birdwatchers or fingerprint examiners, involve properly perceptual skills. That is, these cases of expert perception involve skills of the perceptual system. Stokes and Nanay go on to consider the case of picture perception and likewise conclude that such perception involves perceptual skill. Importantly, what this shows is that possession of different visual skills will result in differences in the phenomenology of viewing the same picture. They end their chapter by isolating what they call "mechanisms" of perceptual skill: perceptual attention and mental imagery. In both cases, what's most central to skill is that the development of both perceptual attention and mental imagery are sensitive to top-down information and are thus robustly connected to the semantic and epistemic states of agents. Because of this, at least some perceptual skills, Stokes and Nanay argue, are properly attributable to the agent. Stokes and Nanay conclude by highlighting the fact that far from being some peripheral or niche area of theoretical work, perceptual skill is central to our full understanding of perception in general.

The last chapter in this part to address skills of perception or, more particularly, skills of the visual system, is Keota Fields' ambitious chapter, "Skill, Visual Prejudice, and Know-How." Fields contends that the visual system learns to see in roughly the same way as a person learns to swim. More specifically, the suggestion Fields endorses is to treat visual perception, generally, as skilled Bayesian inference. Treating vision as a skill, Fields maintains, does justice to the central commitments of a constructivist model of visual perception and, further, explains in a fairly straightforward manner the mechanisms of cognitive penetration.

Using this approach to visual perception, Fields goes on to argue that at least some cases of visual prejudice offer a counterexample to the often assumed identity between skill and know-how. This is because visual prejudice, as Fields argues, is an instance of skilled visual perception but does not manifest knowledge of facts. Using the example of implicit-bias infused visual perception, Fields argues that such an episode is an instance of skilled seeing because the episode is characterized by features that are diagnostic of skill: automaticity, diachronic refinement (i.e., improvement through training), intelligent task sensitivity, selective attention, and control. Moreover, Fields argues that a proper construal of control, for which Fields reaches for Wayne Wu's account (see Wu, Chapter 16 in this volume), shows that episodes of visual prejudice are in fact intentional. However, since cases of visual prejudice do not manifest knowledge of facts, these skilled seeings cannot be instances of know-how. In this way, Fields argues that skills and knowledge-how cannot be identical.

Moving from perception to imagination, Amy Kind in "The Skill of Imagination," lays out the case for thinking of imagination as a type of skill. Kind begins by extracting from the literature three central features of skill: Skill (1) can be done more or less well; (2) is under one's intentional control; and (3) can be improved via practice/training. These conditions serve as a general framework for categorization rather than as necessary and sufficient conditions of skill. Kind goes on to argue that at least certain types of imagination, namely sensory and experiential imagining, meet these conditions. Thus, she concludes, sensory and experiential imagining should be classified as skills. Kind ends by considering various objections to classifying imagination as a skill: what she calls the Socratic objection (i.e., where are the skilled imaginers?), the nativist objection (i.e., imagination cannot be improved via training), and the no feedback objection (i.e., what kind of feedback could possibly be used to improve imagination?). By reviewing several lovely cases of imagination's role in invention, art, and empirical study, Kind responds to objections and ends by noting the importance of thinking of imagination as a skill. She claims that not only can this conception of imagination help rein in philosophers who draw metaphysical conclusions from their stunted abilities at imagination but it can perhaps also entice us to train skills of imagination through childhood education and beyond.

In the final chapter of Part IV, "Emotion Recognition as a Social Skill," Gen Eickers and Jesse Prinz argue that emotional recognition, which is often thought of as static, passive, and innate is actually best construed as a type of skill. Eickers and Prinz not only maintain that emotional recognition is a skill, but suggest that emotions themselves may actually be skills as well. Like Kind and Fields above, Eickers and Prinz begin by extracting from the literature several central characteristics of skill. For them, the most notable features of skills are their improvability, practicality, and flexibility. Eickers and Prinz then go on to show that emotional recognition is characterized by these properties and, further, that these properties of emotional recognition are often overlooked in one way or another by extant theories of social cognition: Evolved Expression Recognition, Theory Theory, Simulation Theory, and Direct Perception. Eickers and Prinz end by forwarding a positive conception of emotional recognition in terms of the skilled recognition of emotional scripts. On this way of understanding emotions, they are sequences of subevents "that include: causes, beliefs, feelings, physiological changes, desires, overt actions, and vocal and facial expressions." They are called scripts because they are in some ways like a playwright's scripts but, unlike a playwright's script, they are flexible and embody norms that are both statistical and philosophical. This view entails that recognizing emotions requires fluency with these emotional scripts, which are variable, contextual, intelligent, embodied, and practical.

I.5 Skill, language, and social cognition

Human skills can manifest socially: in joint and coordinated action generally and in linguistic and communicative skill specifically. Part V includes chapters that look at skills in language and social cognition.

The section starts with the chapter "Skill and Expertise in Joint Action" by James Strachan, Günther Knoblich, and Natalie Sebanz, which focuses on the question: What are the mechanisms that allow people to perform skilled joint actions playing in a band, in a sports team, or in a collective dance? Investigating the mechanisms whereby people come to be able to perform joint actions skilfully raises the question of how *coordination* can be achieved in the course of cooperative and competitive interaction. In addressing this question, this chapter draws on studies from a wide range of skilled joint actions, including music, sports, and dance, as well as on more basic coordination tasks designed to investigate fundamental mechanisms of coordination. The chapter describes empirical evidence for three main coordination mechanisms: *strategic action modulations, joint action planning and monitoring*, and *action prediction*. Evidence for strategic action modulations comes from studies in joint improvisation, where it was found that people tend to make themselves more predictable by systematically modulating the velocity profile of their movements in order to achieve synchrony with their partner, by increasing the amount of ancillary movements, which can also play the collaborative function to adapt to adverse conditions, and by controlling, and in some cases resisting, *entrainment*, the process whereby two or more individuals producing regular patterns of behavior fall into the same rhythm. The chapter details the importance of expert action perception for prediction (see Sinigaglia and Butterfill, Chapter 23 in this volume)—i.e., for coming to be able to read and anticipate the actions of others; the most recent studies on action perception showing the connection between motor expertise and the sophistication of one's ability to perceive features of motor actions; and the mechanics of how people represent others' affordances and limitations as well as the extent to which representation of the others' action is helpful or detrimental to joint action. As a joint action requires the input of more than one individual to achieve a joint goal, it is not sufficient to represent what another could do. It is also necessary to monitor what that person *does*, particularly with regard to any errors made, so that one can adjust one's own behavior or prepare for any costs incurred. After introducing the most recent research on collaborative action, the chapter ends by discussing joint action in *competitive* interactions. The authors show that perhaps surprisingly, competition involves some of the same coordination mechanisms described for cooperative joint action, such as strategic modulations of action, action prediction, monitoring, and co-representation.

Joint action also raises questions for phenomenological concepts of expert performance on which an expert operates completely on the pre-reflective level of experience. As we have seen by looking at Dreyfus' conception of skillful action, on some phenomenological conceptions of expert performance, the expert operates completely on the pre-reflective (i.e., tacit, non-observational, non-objectifying) level of experience (Dreyfus 1997, 2002, 2005). In "Self- and Other-Awareness in Joint Expert Performance," Shaun Gallagher and Jesús Ilundáin-Agurruza critically assess this view by looking at the role of self-awareness and the awareness of others during joint actions. They start by introducing a theoretical debate about the nature and the extent of individual self-awareness during experts' performance and by reviewing the evidence motivating Shusterman's (2008) and Montero's (2016) "trained awareness model," according to which expert performance requires a particular type of trained awareness. Then Gallagher and Ilundáin-Agurruza move to examining questions about the role of self-awareness of others in team and collaborative performances. Just like in the case of individual performance, the phenomenological tradition features accounts suggesting that reflection also interrupts team or cooperative performance, and that working together best remains pre-reflective (e.g., Schutz 1976). In order to assess this position, Gallagher and Ilundáin-Agurruza review a detailed study of expert musical performance by Høffding (2015). In his study of the Danish String Quartet, Høffding conducted phenomenological interviews and focused on the precise experiences the musicians had while playing their best. It turns out that each member of the quartet had different experiences while playing but all of them reported they could be thinking of or experiencing different things. As they point out, these studies might show that Dreyfus was wrong to think that any kind of reflective thinking necessarily interrupts performance. On the other hand, some of these studies also suggest that *explicit* consciousness of the other players, or an explicit attending to one's actions might not always be needed to make the performance work. At least in some cases, in line with Dreyfus' analysis and against the trained awareness model, the real work seems to be done in a manner that involves skillful automaticity or a minimally pre-reflective level. They conclude that the contrasting positions represented by Dreyfus and Shusterman might both be off the mark, and they advocate an alternative *pluralist* model that helps refine the analysis of self- and other-awareness in expert performance.

Among our distinctively and perhaps uniquely human skills are the uses of a range of sophisticated motor tools and cognitive and communicative tools. Are these human-specific skills biologically inherited, or are they learned? These questions are investigated by Antonella Tramacere and Richard Moore in "The Evolution of Skilled Imitative learning: A Social Attention Hypothesis." Tramacere and Moore discuss the hypothesis that these uniquely human skills arise on the back of our possession of a more fundamental skill: *imitation*. Imitation is a form of action copying in which an agent is concerned to replicate the precise strategy of an observed demonstration. Tramacere and Moore review the ongoing debate about the origins of human imitation. According to one influential view, defended by Michael Arbib (2005, 2012, 2017) among others, the Mirror Neuron System in humans is a candidate for being the neural substrate of action copying behavior. As such there is an important innate component to imitation that is the result of biological evolution. Against this view, a group of psychologists led by Celia Heyes (2018) have argued that imitation is a product of cultural and not biological evolution. As an alternative to both nativism and non-nativism about imitation, Tramacere and Moore propose a third account of the origins of imitation, that borrows elements from both the nativist and non-nativist hypotheses while offering a parsimonious explanation of the cognitive and neurobiological differences between humans and other species.

As Tramacere and Moore make clear, imitation is central not only to the mastery of manual tools but also to the development of another distinctively human skill: *language*. This brings us to the other main topic of this section: linguistic competence and its nature, which is discussed in two chapters of this Handbook. In "Semantic Competence," Diego Marconi outlines a history of the debates concerning the ability to understand sentences of a natural language, ranging from Chomsky's (1965, 1985) discussion of linguistic competence and his critique of philosophical semantics to the recent debate about simulation theories. For Chomsky, linguistic competence was a sort of knowledge underlying our syntactic competence that could not be simply identified with a practical ability but that was not straightforwardly to be identified to propositional knowledge either—in the standard epistemological sense of knowledge available at the personal level and that requires justification. Marconi reviews Chomsky's criticism of philosophical semantics, as well as the main philosophically originated semantic theories (Montague's and Davidson's). Both Davidson (1967) and Montague (see Thomason 1974) agreed in identifying the aim of semantics with providing a theory of how the meanings of sentences depended on the meaning of the composing words and neither intended their theories as models of human semantic competence. Neither projects, nor their more recent cognitive developments, involved attention to psychological or neurophysiological plausibility of the semantic categories and processes that they posited. Marconi explains that this sort of criticism, raised prominently by Partee (1981) and others, gave rise to diverging responses. Some, like Jackendoff (1992) and Johnson-Laird (1983) opted for a form of *internalism* about the meaning of words according to which words got their meanings not by being suitably related to the environment but by being connected with internal representations and processes. By contrast, non-cognitive externalists such as Putnam (1975) thought that the meaning of natural kind words was fixed by objective causal connections with objects and properties in the world. Finally, cognitive externalists such as Marconi (1997) maintained that lexical competence was partly based on perceptual and motor connections with the world out there. According to this view, knowing the meaning of words such as "pear" and "bed" involves the ability to perceptually recognize pears and beds as well as the ability to appropriately respond to commands involving such things. This sort of position was motivated by debates within and about Artificial Intelligence which emphasized the role of perception and motor action in the exercise of semantic competence as well as by neuroscientific results that appeared to prove involvement of motor and perceptual brain areas in comprehension and, more generally, in language processing. Such research generated a partly new paradigm, which made language understanding *consist in* such perceptual and motor activations—i.e., the prominent simulationist paradigm (Barsalou 1999; Gallese and Lakoff 2005, among others). Marconi ends the chapter by discussing this radical position and highlights some of its difficulties.

In "Pragmatic Competence," Filippo Domaneschi and Valentina Bambini give an overview of the field of pragmatics, which studies language in contexts. They start from reviewing Grice's (1957, 1975) understanding of meaning in terms of a speaker's intentions and his distinction between what a speaker says by using a sentence and what the speaker intends to communicate. According to a Gricean analysis of the notion of meaning in terms of speakers' intentions, what a speaker *means* to communicate does not need to coincide with what she explicitly says. The Gricean analysis has led contemporary linguists and philosophers to a mainstream view of pragmatics as the study of the speaker's meaning and of the inferential processes of reconstruction of communicative intentions. Domaneschi and Bambini carefully investigate the reason why only in the 1980s did pragmatics become the subject of cognitive studies. Until then, it was conceived as having to do with the linguistic performance, rather than linguistic competence, and as such it was excluded from linguistic investigations having to do with the level of competence, pertaining to syntax. Fodor's (1983) modular theory of mind refused to view pragmatic processing as governed by a specific and independently analyzable module in the way classic Chomskyan competence (Chomsky 1957, 1980) was. And the Gricean roots of pragmatic studies contributed to pragmatic processing being viewed in strict relation with the ability of attributing mental states to others and hence largely tied with general and not module-specific mind reading abilities—i.e., with the theory of mind (ToM). Cognitive pragmatics arose as a revision of the Fodorian notion of module in order to account for pragmatic processing within the modular framework. Domaneschi and Bambini survey the most recent research in Experimental Pragmatics—where pragmatic phenomena are investigated via behavioral and neurolinguistic methods—that offer solid evidence in support of the thesis that pragmatic competence is not limited to the ability to understand speaker's intentions and, hence, pragmatic competence cannot be reduced to a ToM ability. They review experimental work on the cognitive mechanisms governing processing of presupposition, conversational mechanisms such as turn-taking, understanding of metaphors, suggesting instead that pragmatic competence has specific characterization in terms of developmental trajectories, patterns of decay, and neural substrates—a characterization that is distinct and independent of a characterization in terms of mind reading abilities.

I.6 Skill and expertise in normative philosophy

In the final part of the Handbook, six chapters address questions of skill and expertise in normative philosophy. As will be familiar to the reader, virtue ethicists have often appealed to skill in order to articulate the nature of moral cognition and judgment. That is, morality, for the virtue ethicist, amounts to a kind of expertise. However, there remain crucial questions about whether moral judgment and behavior is best construed as a kind of skill (Annas 1995, 2001; Stichter 2018) and whether wisdom can be construed as a sort of moral expertise (Driver 2013, 2015), about what kind of thing such a skill could be, whether morality might require skill even if morality itself is not a skill, and, importantly, how the practical demands of morality may require the development of moral perception or other perceptual and emotional skills. Questions of education, persuasion, and implicit bias and stereotype threat also arise in connection to these considerations, since it remains an open question whether and how we might be able to actually change not only our beliefs and attitudes but also our automatic, immediate, reactions, responses, perceptions, or associations through training, argument, or the development of virtue (Gendler 2011; Saul 2013).

The first chapter in Part VI is Julia Driver's, "Moral Expertise," where the author provides a superb overview of the major debates in the literature concerning moral expertise. She begins by comparing moral expertise to more familiar types of expertise, like those in the domains of science or mathematics. An important distinction between kinds of expertise that Driver highlights concerns the fact that moral expertise is normative and not merely descriptive. It is not only about how the world is but about how it *ought* to be. And also, perhaps importantly, about how *one ought to be/act oneself.*

Driver goes on to discuss in some detail the distinction between moral knowledge and moral understanding, and to consider which may be required for moral expertise. Driver herself thinks there are various ways to gain moral expertise, some of which do not require a full, systematic or articulable understanding of morality. In fact, moral expertise, in some cases, may simply amount to having an ability to make reliable judgments about moral matters. Driver ends by examining the role of empirical facts and moral action in moral expertise. In contrast to others in this section (e.g., Stichter and Bashour), Driver maintains that the way in which moral expertise is acquired is merely a contingent fact about what moral expertise is. As such, she holds that analysis of the normal development of moral expertise, even if in actual fact for humans it requires practice, does not tell us anything substantive about the nature of that expertise.

Moving from moral expertise to political expertise, Alexander A. Guerrero provides a contextualist, functionalist account of the normative political expert and expert political actor in "A Theory of Political Expertise." First, Guerrero distinguishes between, on the one hand, what he calls the *expert political analyst* (someone who has extensive knowledge about political topics) and the *exceptionally effective political actor* (someone who is able to navigate political institutions effectively, regardless of moral outcome) and, on the other, the *normative political expert* (someone who knows what ought to be done) and *expert political actor* (someone who is particularly skillful in doing what ought to be done). It is the latter type of expertise that concerns Guerrero and that he considers to be the proper domain of political experts.

It is important to note that since Guerrero's account of political expertise is functionalist and contextualist, it requires asking both about the purposes or ends of the political agent but also recognizing that those ends or purposes are not universal but relative to context and role. Doing justice to the embedded and contextual nature of political expertise, Guerrero explores what it means to be a normative political expert and expert political actor specifically as an elected political representative. Guerrero argues that the proper end or purpose of the elected political representative is to achieve the legitimating purposes of political institutions. These purposes include: preventing domination and harm; minority rights and justice; working together under conditions of disagreement and distrust; information management and use; respecting and promoting equality; respecting and promoting autonomy; and promoting welfare. He goes on to explain that achieving these legitimating purposes requires more than moral expertise but also a variety of epistemic virtues, including epistemic humility and open-mindedness. It will also involve disagreement navigation, which requires knowing which paths are feasible and available under conditions of disagreement and also the skills of compromise, conflict resolution, mediation, and the need to override dissenting opinion. For political expertise of the kind characteristic of the elected political representative, one should also exhibit the moral virtues of ethical leadership in addition to being a relatively expert moral analyst, so as to be able to make appropriate moral judgments in situations of complexity. Together, these conditions combine to form a theoretical or philosophical proposal for what expertise for the elected political representative consists in. Guerrero insists, however, that such a framework is not the end of the project but should be tested through modeling and empirical study.

Expanding what it means to possess the virtue of justice from the political, social or moral domain to the individual, Paul Bloomfield develops a historically grounded account of justice as a personal, moral and intellectual virtue in "Skills of Justice." The skills of justice apply broadly, Bloomfield argues, because they concern, very generally, making appropriate, measured judgments or just assessments. This way of thinking of justice, locates justice not only in the moral domain but also squarely in the epistemological domain, as a good moral, political or social judgment requires not only moral fairness but also epistemic accuracy. Moreover, the skills of justice apply not only interpersonally but intrapersonally, since making morally fair and epistemically accurate judgments concerns not only how we judge others but also how we judge ourselves. Strikingly, Bloomfield sees the skills of justice as applying even beyond the moral domain, since even in making e.g., scientific judgments, one has to judge judiciously, putting like with like and doing justice to relevant differences. In this way, the virtue of justice, as Bloomfield conceives of it, is an individual, intellectual virtue that applies across the board.

Moving from moral judgment to its connection with moral or virtuous behavior, Bana Bashour, in her chapter, "Why Moral Philosophers Are Not the Most Virtuous People," provides us with an account of moral behavior that is grounded in skill. Bashour begins by providing examples that highlight the double-dissociation between moral judgment and virtuous behavior: on the one hand, an example of a philosopher who reliably makes strong moral arguments but often acts selfishly and, on the other, Huck Finn who makes the wrong moral judgment but still acts virtuously.

Bashour argues that moral judgment and moral action come apart because moral or virtuous behavior is a kind of skill and moral judgment is either not a skill at all or relies on a distinct set of skills. Bashour goes on to review the main intellectualist and anti-intellectualist positions concerning skill in general, as well as virtue as skill, in particular and argues that both positions have shortcomings. Bashour recommends pursuing instead the blended account that Ellen Fridland develops (see Chapter 19 in this volume) where skill involves three levels of control. Bashour ends with two striking and timely examples of virtuous behavior where she describes how control at different levels is relevant for moral action. Importantly, Bashour emphasizes that even in cases of virtuous action, motor control is substantively implicated in moral behavior.

From an analysis of virtuous, skilled action to an account of how virtue might be acquired and improved, Matt Stichter, in his chapter, "Virtue as Skill, Self-Regulation and Social Psychology," develops a skill-based account of moral virtue in order to respond to situationist critiques of virtue ethics. Notably, the skill as virtue account that Stichter develops is heavily informed by empirical studies in psychology and he combines the lessons of those studies in order to recommend a way forward for moral education.

Stichter begins by claiming that skill is essentially a sophisticated form of self-regulation. As such, understanding skill requires understanding the literature on self-regulation. Critically, we should begin by differentiating between goal setting and goal striving. That is, differentiating between the process of setting an intention, even a complex one with subgoals, and the process of striving to attain that intention via planning and action. On Stichter's view, goal striving has often been overlooked by the literature on virtue, which emphasizes making the right judgment or setting the right intention but not developing the proper skills for achieving the ends to which one has already committed.

In contrast, a view informed by empirical psychology allows us to home in on effective strategies for reaching goals, such as, for example, implementation intentions. Such *if-then* intentions allow agents to deliberately set situation-specific strategies that can be used automatically in specified circumstances. Moreover, deliberate practice of specific strategies can provide further refinement of the means or skills necessary to reach one's already set goals. This is especially important, Stichter argues, because much of the actual literature in social psychology (e.g., the bystander effect) shows deficits in moral behavior can be attributed not to a lack of good intentions but to a lack in competencies and the related beliefs concerning one's self-efficacy. As such, Stichter argues that moral education should be concerned not only with setting the right intentions or making the correct judgment concerning morality but with developing the often complex skills required for attaining our moral goals. It is through such skill-based education that stable virtue can be developed and that situation-specific forces may be overcome.

Pursuing a similar approach to Stichter, Michael Brownstein, in "De-biasing, Skill, and Intergroup Virtue," consults the literature in empirical psychology in order to develop an account of the skills involved in de-biasing others, that is, in diminishing the prejudices, stereotypes, and biases that others possess. Brownstein begins by noting that changing people's opinions, attitudes, and beliefs is at the heart of a healthy democracy but goes on to review some depressing results concerning the actual success of changing others' minds. Brownstein then goes on to highlight which skills, strategies, knowledge, and abilities are likely involved in successful de-biasing. Importantly, Brownstein thinks of the power to de-bias as a skill because it is something one can learn and improve over time with practice. So, what does the skill of de-biasing require? Unfortunately for the philosopher, Brownstein is pretty pessimistic about the power of argument or "going factual" to change people's attitudes. Instead, Brownstein suggests that changing the perception of norms is at the heart of de-biasing because people are not only motivated to conform with norms but they are also concerned about the rewards and punishments associated with them. In order to change the perception of norms, Brownstein suggests that de-biasers do not directly try to change the attitudes that others have toward norms but, rather, the perception of what other people believe and feel. Skill in de-biasing then, may involve becoming a social referent, that is, a person with particular influence over other people's perception of norms due to one's e.g., status or prestige. Social referents can model virtuous norms, such as tolerance, compassion, open-mindedness, etc. and in so doing change what others think is acceptable, thereby also changing others' motivation to conform with these new virtuous norms.

Note

1 The order of the authors is alphabetical.

References

Adams, R., and Kveraga, K. (2015) "Social Vision: Functional Forecasting and the Integration of Compound Social Cues," *Review of Philosophy and Psychology* 6: 591–610.

Annas, J. (1995) "Virtue as a Skill," *International Journal of Philosophical Studies* 3: 227–43.

——— (2001) "Moral Knowledge as Practical Knowledge," in E. F. Paul, F. D. Miller, and J. Paul (eds.) *Moral Knowledge*, 236–56, Cambridge: Cambridge University Press.

——— (2011) "Practical Expertise," in J. Bengson and M. Moffett (eds.) *Knowing How: Essays on Knowledge, Mind, and Action*, 101–12, Oxford: Oxford University Press.

Anscombe, G. E. M. (1957) *Intention*. Basil Blackwell: England.

Arbib, M. A. (2005) "From Monkey-Like Action Recognition to Human Language: An Evolutionary Framework for Neurolinguistics," *Behavioral and Brain Sciences* 28: 105–24.

——— (2012) "Tool Use and Constructions," *Behavioral and Brain Sciences* 35: 218–19.

——— (2017) "Toward the Language-Ready Brain: Biological Evolution and Primate Comparisons," *Psychonomic Bulletin & Review* 24: 142–50.

Barsalou, L. (1999) "Perceptual Symbol Systems," *Behavioral and Brain Sciences* 22: 577–660.

Beddor, B., and Pavese, C. (2018) "Modal Virtue Epistemology," *Philosophy and Phenomenological Research*, doi: 10.1111/phpr.12562.

——— (2020) "Skill as Knowledge," manuscript.

Bengson, J., and Moffett, M. (2011) "Nonpropositional Intellectualism," in J. Bengson and M. Moffett (eds.) *Knowing How: Essays on Knowledge, Mind, and Action*, 161–95, Oxford: Oxford University Press.

Brogaard, B. (2009) "What Mary Did Yesterday: Reflections on Knowledge-Wh," *Philosophy and Phenomenological Research* 78: 439–67.

Buchanan, A. (2004) "Political Liberalism and Social Epistemology," *Philosophy & Public Affairs* 32: 95–130.

——— (2009) "Social Moral Epistemology and Public Policy," *Journal of Applied Philosophy* 19: 126–52.

Carter, A., and Navarro, J. (2018) "The Defeasibility of Knowledge-How," *Philosophy and Phenomenological Research* 95: 662–85.

Carter, A., and Pritchard, D. (2015) "Knowledge-How and Epistemic Luck," *Noûs* 49: 440–53.

Cath, Y. (2011) "Knowing How Without Knowing That," in J. Bengson and M. Moffett (eds.) *Knowing How: Essays on Knowledge, Mind and Action*, 136–60, Oxford: Oxford University Press.

—— (2013) "Regarding a Regress," *Pacific Philosophical Quarterly* 94: 358–88.

—— (2015) "Revisionary Intellectualism and Gettier," *Philosophical Studies* 172: 7–27.

Chomsky, N. (1957) *Syntactic Structures*, The Hague: Mouton.

—— (1965) *Aspects of the Theory of Syntax*, Cambridge, MA: MIT Press.

—— (1980) *Rules and Representations*, New York: Columbia University Press.

—— (1985) *Knowledge of Language*, New York: Praeger.

Coope, U. (forthcoming) "Aristotle on Productive Understanding and Completeness," in T. K. Johansen (ed.) *Technê in Ancient Philosophy*, Cambridge: Cambridge University Press.

Damasio, A. R. (1999) *The Feeling of What Happens: Body and Emotion in the Making of Consciousness*, New York: Houghton Mifflin Harcourt.

Davidson, D. (1967) "Truth and Meaning," *Synthese* 17: 304–23.

Devitt, M. (2011) "Methodology and the Nature of Knowing How," *The Journal of Philosophy* 108: 205–18.

Dreyfus, H. L. (1997) "Intuitive, Deliberative, and Calculative Models of Expert Performance," in C. Zsambok and G. Klein (eds.) *Naturalistic Decision Making*, 17–28, Mahwah, NJ: Lawrence Erlbaum.

—— (2000) "A Merleau-Pontian Critique of Husserl's and Searle's Representationalist Accounts of Action," *Proceedings of the Aristotelian Society* 100: 287–302.

—— (2001) "The Primacy of Phenomenology over Logical Analysis," *Philosophical Topics* 27: 3–24.

—— (2002) "Intelligence Without Representation: Merleau-Ponty's Critique of Mental Representation," *Phenomenology and the Cognitive Sciences* 1: 367–83.

—— (2005) "Overcoming the Myth of the Mental: How Philosophers Can Profit from the Phenomenology of Everyday Expertise," *Proceedings and Addresses of the American Philosophical Association* 79: 47–65.

—— (2007) "Response to McDowell," *Inquiry* 50: 371–7.

Driver, J. (2013) "Moral Expertise: Judgment, Practice, and Analysis," *Social Philosophy and Policy* 30: 280–96.

—— (2015) "Virtue and Moral Deference," *Etica & Politica* 17: 27–40.

Eberhardt, J. L., Goff, P. A., Purdie, V. J., and Davies, P. G. (2004) "Seeing Black: Race, Crime, and Visual Processing," *Journal of Personality and Social Psychology* 87: 876–93.

Fodor, J. A. (1983) *The Modularity of Mind: An Essay on Faculty Psychology*, Cambridge, MA: MIT Press.

Fridland, E. (2013) "Problems with Intellectualism," *Philosophical Studies* 165: 879–91.

—— (2014) "They've Lost Control: Reflections on Skill," *Synthese* 91: 2729–50.

—— (2017a) "Skill and Motor Control: Intelligence All the Way Down," *Philosophical Studies* 174: 1539–60.

—— (2017b) "Automatically Minded," *Synthese* 194: 4337–63.

Gallese, V., and Lakoff, G. (2005) "The Brain's Concepts: The Role of the Sensory-Motor System in Conceptual Knowledge," *Cognitive Neuropsychology* 21: 455–479.

Gendler, T. S. (2011) "On the Epistemic Costs of Implicit Bias," *Philosophical Studies* 156: 33–63.

Gibson, J. J. (2014/1979) *The Ecological Approach to Visual Perception: Classic Edition*, New York: Psychology Press.

Goldman, A. (2001) "Experts: Which Ones Should You Trust?" *Philosophy and Phenomenological Research* 63: 85–109.

Grice, H. P. (1957) "Meaning," *The Philosophical Review* 66: 377–88.

—— (1975) "Logic and Conversation," in P. Cole and J. Morgan (eds.) *Syntax and Semantics, Vol. 3, Speech Acts*, New York: Academic Press.

Guerrero, A. (2016) "Living with Ignorance in a World of Experts," in R. Peels (ed.) *Perspectives on Ignorance from Moral and Social Philosophy*, New York: Routledge.

Haith, A. M., and Krakauer, J. W. (2013) "Model-Based and Model-Free Mechanisms of Human Motor Learning," *Advances in Experimental Medicine and Biology*, 782: 1–21. doi:10.1007/978-1-4614-5465-6_1.

—— (2018) "The Multiple Effects of Practice: Skill, Habit and Reduced Cognitive Load," *Current Opinion in Behavioral Sciences* 20: 196–201.

Heyes, C. (2018) *Cognitive Gadgets: The Cultural Evolution of Thinking*, Cambridge, MA: Harvard University Press.

Høffding, S. (2015) *A Phenomenology of Expert Musicianship* (PhD thesis), Department of Philosophy, University of Copenhagen, Copenhagen.

Hornsby, J. (2016) "Intending, Knowing How, Infinitives," *Canadian Journal of Philosophy* 46: 1–17.

Jackendoff, R. (1992) *Languages of the Mind*, Cambridge, MA: MIT Press.

Johansen, T. K. (2017) "Aristotle on the Logos of the Craftsman," *Phronesis* 62: 97–135.

Johnson-Laird, P. (1983) *Mental Models*, Cambridge: Cambridge University Press.

Kelly, S. D. (2005) "Seeing Things in Merleau-Ponty," in T. Carman and M. Hansen (eds.) *The Cambridge Companion to Merleau-Ponty*, 74–110, Cambridge: Cambridge University Press

Lewis, D. (1990) "What Experience Teaches," in W. Lycan (ed.) *Mind and Cognition*, 499–519, New York: Blackwell.

Lorenz, H., and Morison, B. (2019) "Aristotle's Empiricist Theory of Doxastic Knowledge," *Phronesis* 64: 431–64.

Marconi, D. (1997) *Lexical Competence*, Cambridge, MA: MIT Press.

Marley-Payne, J. (2016) *Action-First Attitudes* (PhD thesis), Massachusetts Institute of Technology.

Merleau-Ponty, M. (2013/1945) *Phenomenology of Perception*, New York: Routledge.

Montero, B. (2016) *Thought in Action: Expertise and the Conscious Mind*, New York: Oxford University Press.

Noë, A. (2004) *Action in Perception*, Cambridge, MA: MIT Press.

—— (2005) "Anti-Intellectualism," *Analysis* 65: 278–90.

O'Regan, J. K., and Noë, A. (2001) "A Sensorimotor Account of Vision and Visual Consciousness," *Behavioral and Brain Sciences* 24: 939–73.

Pacherie, E. (2006) "Towards a Dynamic Theory of Intentions," in S. Pockett, W. Banks, and S. Gallagher (eds.) *Does Consciousness Cause Behavior? An Investigation of the Nature of Volition*, 145–67, Cambridge, MA: MIT Press.

Partee, B. (1981) "Montague Grammar, Mental Representations and Reality," in S. Kanger and S. Öhman (eds.) *Philosophy and Grammar*, 59–78, Dordrecht: Reidel.

Pavese, C. (2013) *The Unity and Scope of Knowledge* (PhD thesis), Rutgers University.

—— (2015) "Practical Senses," *Philosophers' Imprint* 15: 1–25.

—— (2017) "Know-How and Gradability," *Philosophical Review* 126: 345–83.

—— (2018) "Know How, Action, and Luck," *Synthese*, https://doi.org/10.1007/s11229-018-1823-7.

—— (2019) "The Psychological Reality of Practical Representation," *Philosophical Psychology* 32: 784–821.

—— (forthcoming 2020) "Knowledge, Action, and Defeasibility," in J. Brown and M. Simion (eds.) *Reasons, Justification, and Defeaters*, Oxford: Oxford University Press.

—— (forthcoming) "An Empirical Case for Practical Concepts," *Synthese*.

Poston, T. (2009) "Know How to Be Gettiered?" *Philosophy and Phenomenological Research* 79: 743–7.

Pritchard, D. (2012) "Anti-Luck Virtue Epistemology," *The Journal of Philosophy* 109: 247–79.

Putnam, H. (1975) "The Meaning of 'Meaning'," in K. Gunderson (ed.) *Language, Mind, and Knowledge*, 131–93, Minneapolis, MN: University of Minnesota Press.

Ryle, G. (1949) *The Concept of Mind*, London: Hutchinson & Co.

—— (1967) "Teaching and Training," reprinted in G. Ryle, *Collected Essays 1929–1968: Collected Papers Volume 2*, 80–9, Abingdon: Routledge.

—— (1970) "Bertrand Russell 1872–1970," *Proceedings of the Aristotelian Society* 71: 77–84.

—— (1972) "Thinking and Self-Teaching," reprinted in G. Ryle, *On Thinking*, 18–23, Totowa, NJ: Rowman and Littlefield.

Schiffer, S. (2002) "Amazing Knowledge," *The Journal of Philosophy* 99: 200–2.

Schutz, A. (1976) *Collected Papers* Vol. II, Dordrecht: Springer.

Setiya, K. (2012) "Know How," *Proceedings of the Aristotelian Society* 112: 285–307.

Shmuelof, L., Krakauer, J. W., and Mazzoni, P. (2012) "How Is a Motor Skill Learned? Change and Invariance at the Levels of Task Success and Trajectory Control," *Journal of Neurophysiology* 108: 578–94.

Shusterman, R. (2008) *Body Consciousness: A Philosophy of Mindfulness and Somaesthetics*, Cambridge: Cambridge University Press.

Sosa, E. (2007) *A Virtue Epistemology*, Oxford: Oxford University Press.

—— (2015) *Judgment and Agency*, Oxford: Oxford University Press.

Stanley, J. (2011a) *Know How*, Oxford: Oxford University Press.

—— (2011b) "Knowing (How)," *Noûs*, 45: 207–38.

Stanley, J., and Williamson, T. (2001) "Knowing How," *Journal of Philosophy* 98: 411–44.

—— (2017) "Skill," *Noûs* 51: 713–26.

Stanley, J., and Krakauer, J. W. (2013) "Motor Skill Depends on Knowledge of Facts," *Frontiers in Human Neuroscience* 7: 1–11.

Stichter, M. (2018) *The Skillfulness of Virtue: Improving Our Moral and Epistemic Lives*, Cambridge: Cambridge University Press.

Thomason, R. H. (1974) *"Introduction" to Formal Philosophy: Selected Papers of Richard Montague*, 1–69, New Haven, CT and London: Yale University Press.

Turri, J. (2018) "Virtue Epistemology and Abilism on Knowledge," in H. Battaly (ed.) *The Routledge Handbook of Virtue Epistemology*, 309–16, New York: Routledge.

Weatherson, B. (2017) "Intellectual Skill and the Rylean Regress," *The Philosophical Quarterly* 67: 370–86.

Wiggins, D. (2012) "Practical Knowledge: Knowing How to and Knowing That," *Mind* 121: 97–130.

Zagzebski, L. (1996) *Virtues of the Mind*, Cambridge: Cambridge University Press.

PART I

Skill in the history of philosophy (East and West)

1

SKILL AND VIRTUOSITY IN BUDDHIST AND DAOIST PHILOSOPHY

Jay L. Garfield and Graham Priest

1.1 *Upāy* in the *Lotus Sūtra*

The idea of *upāya*, usually translated as *skillful means*,[1] plays a large role in Mahāyāna Buddhist ethics and epistemology, where it used to motivate hermeneutic practice, to sort out ethical conundrums, and to defend a particular approach to moral psychology and phenomenology. It comes to provide an overarching conception of what it is to live well, to live a *virtuoso* life of skilled perceptual and ethical engagement, and so can be seen as providing one vision of the nature of awakening, particularly in the context of a nondual understanding of samsara and nirvana—an understanding according to which there is no ontological difference between them.

Despite the centrality of this idea in Mahāyāna thought, it plays virtually no discernible role in pre-Mahāyāna Buddhist literature, except perhaps by implication. *Upāya* is mentioned briefly in a long list of qualities to be cultivated in the *Suttanipāta* and gets one brief mention in the *Therigāta*. Beyond that, only the frequent mention of the metaphor of the raft to describe the need to discard the Buddha's teachings once one has achieved awakening, just as one discards a raft after using it to cross a river, can be taken as indicating the role of *upāya* in early Buddhist teachings.

The *Lotus Sūtra*, an early Mahāyāna text (possibly 1st or 2nd century BCE), is probably the earliest text that specifically thematizes *upāya* and takes it to be an essential ethical and pedagogical skill. The sutra deploys the example of a man whose children are in a burning house but who are oblivious to their danger and reluctant to leave. He lures them from the house by offering them various toys, none of which he actually can deliver to them. The sutra compares the probity of his using a falsehood to save the children's lives to a bodhisattva's use of Buddhist teachings that are not literally true to educate beginning disciples in Buddhist philosophy.

The Buddhist canon contains many sets of doctrines that are mutually inconsistent, and which are canonically arranged in a hierarchy from the most elementary to the most advanced, with only the most advanced regarded as literally true, or definitive in meaning (*nithārtha*), while the others are regarded as only provisional (*neyārtha*), to be abandoned when one is sufficiently advanced to understand a higher-level teaching (much as one might be taught Newtonian physics as true, as a prolegomenon to relativistic physics). The bodhisattva's ability to select the right teaching for the right disciple, as opposed to trying to teach the definitive doctrine to everyone, is valorized in this sutra as *upāya*, skill in teaching.

But we might equally note that the fact that the behavior of the father is praised despite the fact that it violates the precept against lying indicates a more literal understanding of *upāya* at work, that in the ethical domain. Ethical conduct itself is regarded as requiring skill and judgment, and cannot involve merely following rules or conforming to precepts. The *Lotus* thus valorizes *upāya* in at least two domains, that of teaching doctrine, and that of ethical conduct.

So much for background. We will begin what we have to say about *upāya* with a discussion of the ways in which skill is treated in the Indian Madhyamaka and Yogācāra Buddhist traditions. We will then consider the way skill is treated in the Chinese Daoist tradition. This sets the stage for an examination of how these conceptions of skill inform the martial arts traditions of East Asia which emerge from this philosophical matrix. Finally, we turn to a treatment of the larger picture of skill as underlying an ethical life, as understood from these Asian perspectives.

1.2 *Upāya* in teaching: the *Vimalakīrtinirdeśa-sūtra* and *Saṃdhinirmocana-sūtra*

Upāya is a central theme of two Mahāyāna sutras.[2] The *Vimalakīrtinirdeśa* (*The Teaching of Vimalakīrti*, henceforth *VKN* (Thurman 1976)) takes it as its principal topic; in the *Saṃdhinirmocana* (*The Discourse Untangling the Thought*, henceforth *SNS* (Powers 1995)) it is introduced only as a hermeneutical device to explain the relationship between the three cycles of Buddhist teachings distinguished in that text. Although it is a later text, it will be convenient to begin with the *SNS*. The *SNS* addresses a hermeneutical question posed by the fact that Buddhist sutra literature is apparently an inconsistent corpus, with the Buddha asserting some things in one sutra that he denies in others. The *SNS* resolves this conundrum by sorting this literature into three collections, referred to as the three turnings of the wheel of dharma, and by arguing that these are progressively more sophisticated articulations of Buddhist doctrine. The sutra does not, however, argue that the Buddha's own thought evolved, since that would be to deny his omniscience; instead, it argues that the Buddha, being a highly skilled teacher, produced three sets of teachings, each ideally suited to a different audience. Skill here is explicitly pedagogical skill, and it consists in being able to adjust one's speech and approach to one's audience.

The *VKN*, on the other hand, develops an expansive theory of *upāya* and its role in all of life. Indeed, the two central themes of the sutra are *upāya* and nonduality, and, by linking them, the sutra makes a case for the nonduality of *upāya* and awakening, a case that sets the stage for much of the Chan/Zen tradition's discourse about the nonduality of practice and awakening, the fact that genuine practice is already a manifestation of awakening, and that awakening can only be manifested in practice. Vimalakīrti himself, the hero of the sutra, is a layperson valorized for his mastery of *upāya*. He is a businessman, but earns money as a lesson to others, and for their benefit; he hangs out in bars and brothels, but does so to benefit others, etc. His life is described as one in which every action he performs and every word he speaks is a manifestation of perfect *upāya*, and this constitutes a complete union of ordinary life and awakened consciousness. Awakening, then, according to the *VKN* consists in a kind of spontaneous, skillful engagement in, rather than a withdrawal from, the world.

A striking illustration of this idea is the most famous moment in the sutra—Vimalakīrti's "lion's roar of silence" at the culmination of the ninth chapter. The scene for the sutra is Vimalakīrti's house, now occupied by large assemblies of monks who follow the Śrāvakayāna, or *disciples' vehicle* (the first turning sutras, if we follow the classification introduced in the *SNS*) and a large assembly of bodhisattvas (followers of the second). The *VKN* itself is a second turning (Mahāyāna, or *Great Vehicle*—a term comprising the second and third turnings) text, and is part of a body of literature that disparages the disciples' vehicle as *Hināyāya* (an inferior vehicle) and a great deal of the sutra involves scenes that are meant to show the superiority of the bodhisattvas of the Mahāyāna over the monks of the Śrāvakayāna. These are often followed by demonstrations that Vimalakīrti, the embodiment of *upāya*, surpasses all of the bodhisattvas, enshrining the idea that skill—understood as the union of wisdom and practice—is the highest form of awakened knowledge.

Before we get to the dénouement of this chapter, let us consider a bit more context. In the seventh chapter of the sutra, an amusing episode is reported in which, in the midst of a complex philosophical debate, a goddess pops out of a closet in Vimalakīrti's house. This poses a problem for the Śrāvakayāna monks, who are not supposed to be in houses with women present. Śāriputra, renowned as the wisest of the śrāvakas, enters into a discussion of this issue with the goddess which leads, after some amusing incidents involving flowers and miraculous gender reassignment surgery (all manifestations of the goddess' *upāya*) to Śāriputra being asked a difficult question about how long he has been awakened.

The question is skillful because it gives poor Śāriputra no way to answer. If he speaks, he will be using language to characterize the inexpressible, and will be distinguishing awakened from non-awakened consciousness, in the context of a sutra whose very point is the nonduality of the ordinary and the awakened states; if he is silent, he does not answer a straightforward question.[3] Śāriputra walks into the trap, taking the horn of silence. When the goddess chides him for not answering, he replies that since awakening is inexpressible, there is nothing he can say. She then ridicules his lack of *upāya*, noting that the Buddha himself said plenty of stuff. Silence, when you are asked a direct question, she suggests, is not skillful.

The ninth chapter opens with Vimalakīrti asking an assembly of bodhisattvas how one enters "the dharma door of nonduality," that is, how one achieves a nondual understanding of reality, an understanding in which the distinction between subject and object is not thematized, and in which distinctions between apparently contrary phenomena (good and bad; conventional and ultimate; freedom and bondage; etc.) are not seen as reflecting reality, but rather our conceptual superimpositions on reality. After a long sequence of perfectly good replies by the assembled adepts, Vimalakīrti turns to Mañjuśrī, the celestial bodhisattva who embodies wisdom and asks him to comment. Mañjuśrī replies that while all of the answers were fine, they are all deficient, because each of them is expressed in language, a medium that itself embodies and reinscribes duality. This, in itself, is an indictment of the bodhisattvas for a failure of *upāya*. The problem, Mañjuśrī indicates, is not with *what* the bodhisattvas said, but in *how* they said it. Their method undercuts their message. The only way to really communicate nonduality, he says, is to remain silent. So far, so good.

Mañjuśrī then turns to Vimalakīrti and asks him for a comment. Vimalakīrti remains silent, a silence received with enormous admiration by all present. Mañjuśrī, chiding the other bodhisattvas for undermining their own explanations through the unskillful use of language, we now see, despite having himself spoken the truth about their failure to live up to the truths they articulated, was just as lacking in skill as were they, using language to say that only silence is appropriate as a way to communicate nonduality. Only Vimalakīrti, who remains silent, demonstrates real *upāya* here. Even though what he says, and what Mañjuśrī says are exactly the same, his silent affirmation is skillful; Mañjuśrī's explicit statement of exactly the same thing is not.

But wait! Wasn't Śāriputra's silence just the same? A refusal to say anything when language could only undermine what one wants to say? Why was the first silence unskillful and the second skillful? The juxtaposition of these two silences is the heart of the sutra. Śāriputra's silence has no context; it is unskillful because *he* is unskillful, and has been maneuvered into a spot where there is no right thing to say or to do. Vimalakīrti's silence is skillful precisely because Mañjuśrī provided the context for him. His silence could be articulate because its content was already available. The silences are the same; their circumstances differ and so their meanings do as well; similarly, the meanings of Mañjuśrī's speech and Vimalakīrti's silence are the same; but in the context, only one can be skillful (and, like Śāriputra, Mañjuśrī had no good options: speaking opened him up to Vimalakīrti's critique just as silence opened Śāriputra to that of the goddess). Everything is in the timing, the circumstance, the context. To pay attention to figure is to fail to be skillful; to pay attention to ground, though, risks making it figure.

This is meant to indicate what a virtuoso life is like. A virtuoso life is one lived effortlessly and spontaneously constantly responsive to context, and a life in which one places oneself in the right contexts. The spontaneity of Vimalakīrti's silence contrasts with Śāriputra's studied consternation; his skill in following Mañjuśrī shows that getting to the right context is half the game. The nonduality between what he expresses so articulately and Mañjuśrī does so clumsily demonstrates that real wisdom is in skill, not in declarative knowledge.

1.3 Ethical skill, perception and perfection on the bodhisattva path

The centrality of skill in a virtuoso life is adumbrated further in an explicitly ethical context in Śāntideva's (8th century CE) *Bodhichāryāvatāra* (*How to Lead an Awakened Life* (1995)). In this text Śāntideva characterizes ethical development as the acquisition of a suite of complex perceptual and affective skills which together transform one's experience of oneself and others. Those skills include the ability to give effectively; to concentrate and to avoid distraction; the ability to be patient; the ability to see oneself as intimately bound to others; and the ability to free oneself from egocentric attachment. One can become an effective moral agent, Śāntideva argues, if, and only if, one acquires this suite of skills. Much of his text is devoted to making that argument in detail. Here we only sketch the broad picture.

One of the skills Śāntideva argues we should cultivate is generosity. He emphasizes that to give generously is to give without attachment to what is given, to the beneficiary of the gift, to oneself, or to the act of giving. A truly generous act is a spontaneous act. He points out that this is hard, and, like any skill, requires cultivation and training. The goal is to be able to offer one's own life when appropriate. But, he suggests, this is not for beginners. They should begin with cheap vegetables and work their way up. This way of characterizing generosity and its cultivation makes clear the model of skill development in Śāntideva's account of moral cultivation. By suggesting that moral progress begins with easy actions and progresses to the more challenging, he allies moral maturation with the development of skill.

The ability to concentrate—to focus on a situation and on one's own motivations—Śāntideva argues, is also essential for moral development. Otherwise, one forgets one's own values and goals, loses discipline, and behaves in ways that are destructive, rather than constructive, creating, rather than reducing, suffering and dysfunction. For that reason, he devotes a great deal of attention to the cultivation of attention, focusing on the skill of fixing the mind on an appropriate object (*smṛti*), the skill of maintaining that fixation (*samprajaña*), and the skill of making automatic and integrating into one's way of taking up with the world the skills one develops through meditation.

Patience is an important skill to cultivate in moral development, and Śāntideva emphasizes not only its moral importance but the fact that the cultivation of patience is a matter of practice and skill development. It requires coming to see others and ourselves differently; acquiring the habit of reflecting before responding, instead of reacting; and, importantly, developing the right kinds of reflective skills to deploy in those moments. In the end, we replace the disposition to anger with the disposition to care when we or others act in harmful ways.

One of the distinctive aspects of Śāntideva's analysis of moral development and moral perfection is his insistence on the development of new perceptual skills. Moral immaturity on his view is grounded in seeing ourselves and others as isolated individuals in competition with one another, a perceptual set that leads to fear, self-grasping, clinging to friends and aversion to those we see as adversaries, issuing in selfishness, partiality and hostility. But by cultivating, through reflection and meditation, the skill of seeing ourselves as inextricably bound to others, and our interests and values as inextricably bound to theirs, we come to respond to others with generosity, patience, thoughtfulness and care. The entire set of behavioral skills we want to cultivate, on this model, rests on a foundation of perceptual skills. These skills are revealed in the immediate categorization of others in terms appropriate to virtue, not to vice, just as a skilled botanist or an art historian's perceptual skills are revealed in her seeing plants *as* members of a particular species, or a painting *as* an early Monet (see, in this volume, Siegel, Chapter 24 and Stokes and Nanay, Chapter 25).

On this model of ethical perfection, we come to be effective moral agents not simply by becoming virtuous but by becoming virtuosos. Moral perfection is the perfection of the set of skills that constitute humanity.

1.4 Skill in Daoist thought

Let us turn now to Daoism. A great deal of Daoist discourse on skill, as we find it in the *Daodejing* and the *Zhuangzi*, is grounded in the idea of *wu wei*, or effortless action (see Sarkissian, Chapter 2 in this volume). Part of the reason for this is deeply metaphysical, reflecting a commitment to a *way* (*dao*) that the universe proceeds, sometimes called the *Great Dao*. Harmony with this way of things is valorized; it ensures success and happiness. It is often reflected in adages to be "like water," flexible, flowing spontaneously in one direction, and effective—not to be inflexible, stationary, obstructive, like rock. The *Daodejing* (Red Pine 1976) observes that "only by doing nothing can everything be accomplished," and that "ruling a great kingdom is like cooking a small fish" (be as light in touch as possible; do as little as possible).

In the context of ethics, we see the disparagement of ritual, of emphasis on rights and duties, in favor of the cultivation of an easy, spontaneous responsiveness to others and to the particulars of situations in which action is necessary. (When the Dao is lost, we find virtue; when virtue is lost, we find filial piety.) Ethical maturity is not, on this view, achieved through the understanding of one's duties, or through internalizing a set of rules or principles; it is achieved through the cultivation of skills of perception and action that are irreducibly particular in their manifestation.

A nice metaphor for this approach is represented in the parable of Butcher Ding, in the *Zhuangzi* (2003). In this parable the king is astonished by the ease and virtuosity of the butcher who carves an ox expertly and without apparent effort. The butcher explains that while in the early stages of his craft he saw oxen, and then parts of oxen, he now sees nothing at all. His blade is thin, and the spaces in the joints are vast, allowing the blade to pass without obstruction, so that it rarely needs sharpening.

The king exclaims that he has learned about life by listening to a butcher. Indeed he has. At the early stages of moral development, we see rules and procedures, proper ways to do things, and we apply these templates to the circumstances in which we find ourselves; later we may come to see exceptions and to treat these rules as merely *prima facie* guides. But we have developed the skills we need for our moral lives only when we respond to situations with effortless spontaneity, doing what is right because we see what is right to do, and know how to do it. Our goal is to become moral virtuosi who can pass without obstruction from situation to action.

This much is a pretty orthodox interpretation of this story in the *Zhuangzi*. And we agree with it. But we also call attention to a small remark near the end of the story that has escaped the notice of commentators, and that we think makes a deep point about the role of conceptual thought and about skill in thinking. The butcher acknowledges that sometimes he comes to difficult places where the meat is knotted. Then he hesitates and his blade slows down. We propose a heterodox reading of this passage: while one aspect of skill is one's ability much of the time to manifest one's skill seemingly effortlessly, spontaneously, *without thought* (*wu wei*), another aspect is to know when to slow down, when to think, when to contemplate; and, when those times come, the expert knows *how* to think, how to contemplate, and how to guide action through that contemplation. Even knots and tangles can be handled if one knows when to slow down and how to consider them. That is, skilled behavior is not, on this view, the complete transcendence of thought and reflection; it is also coming to know when thought and reflection is necessary and when it is not, and when it is, we know precisely how to engage in and to apply the requisite thought. For this reason, higher-order skills, such as the effortless background monitoring of one's own performance, are necessary components of these life-skills.

In the context of ethical skill, this is also important. Part of manifesting moral virtuosity is the ability to see, spontaneously, what a situation demands, and to act appropriately; but another part of moral virtuosity is to know when things are hard, when one has to think, and then to know how to think, what to consider, and how to guide one's action by that thought. Nonetheless, in both kinds of situation, the point that emerges from the *Zhuangzi* and other texts in the Daoist tradition is that it is practical moral skill we develop as we mature, including both that skill that manifests as spontaneous action in which thought is not apparent, and the spontaneous decision to think. Skill is not discursive knowledge: it is the ability to react spontaneously in an appropriate fashion.

While both Buddhism and Daoism valorize spontaneity, and while these streams of thought merge in the Chan/Zen tradition, their accounts of spontaneity are not identical, and it is worth closing this discussion with an observation about the difference between them. Daoists see spontaneity as achieved through an attunement of one's cognition and behavior to the primordial nature of reality, the *Great Dao*, or the way of things. That attunement involves a paring away of the cultural accretions and prejudices that take us away from the *Dao*, and so inhibit our spontaneous action. The *Daodejing* refers to this as "losing day by day," in contrast to training in which one gains day by day.

Buddhists after the second turning of the wheel, on the other hand, argue that there is no fundamental nature of reality, or way the world is, and so nothing like the *Dao* to which one could attune oneself. On a Buddhist view, spontaneity is achieved by study and meditative practices that lead to insight into the emptiness of all phenomena, and the absence of any self. It involves the accumulation of a set of skills, including prominently perceptual and moral skills. It is not so much a whittling away as it is a cultivation. On the other hand, there is also a negative side to this process: the cultivation of these skills is aimed at the elimination of cognitive superimpositions of fixed identity, permanence, essence, and so forth that are obstacles to awakened action. Nonetheless, this is a model of spontaneity through practice and development, not through abandonment. Part of the beauty of the Chinese tradition is that these two streams end up merging in Chan.

1.5 Skill and *karatedō*

In this section, by way or illustrating a number of the themes of the preceding sections we turn to a discussion of *karatedō*.[4] Chan Buddhism—or to give it its Japanese name, Zen Buddhism, will be an important part of our story. One of the notable features of Chan Buddhism is that it is strongly influenced by Daoism.[5] Hence, a number of Buddhist and Daoist themes of previous sections will become apparent in what follows.

First, some history. The origins and early evolution of *karatedō* are not documented.[6] However, fairly uncontroversially, it originated in Okinawa, the largest of the Ryukyu Islands, perhaps about five or six hundred years ago. At that time, Okinawa was not part of Japan. *Karatedō* was a fusion of an old Okinawan martial art, *te* (hand), and Chinese *wushu* techniques. (A number of historically significant masters of *karatedō* either came from China, or trained there.) It was no doubt given a boost after the invasion of Okinawa by the Satsuma Clan from the Japanese mainland in 1609. The Satsuma Clan banned the carrying of traditional weapons, such as swords. The Okinawans responded by developing traditional farming implements into weapons. This became part of traditional *karatedō*, though it has largely disappeared from it now. *Karatedō* migrated to the Japanese mainland at the start of the 20th century, and thence, because of increasing Western involvement with Japan post Second World War, to the West.

Though again, documentation is very hard to come by, it is pretty certain that Buddhism, and especially Zen, had an important influence on *karatedō*. Legend has it that the first patriarch of Zen Buddhism was Bodhidharma, an Indian missionary who took up residence at the Shaolin Temple. Legend has it that the same Bodhidharma was the founder of the Shaolin *wushu*. Whatever the history, the Shaolin Temple is famous for producing Chan Buddhist monks who are also *wushu* practitioners. The connection goes far beyond this, though. Many samurai, such as the legendary Musashi Miamoto (who also practiced Zen calligraphy), were Buddhists, and saw their Buddhism and their martial practice as deeply connected.[7] The Zen Buddhist monk Takuan Sōhō is well known for having written letters to martial practitioners giving them Zen advice.[8] Indeed, in traditional dōjō, training sessions begin and end with short *zazen* (kneeling meditation) sessions. The Buddhist connection is also evident in popular martial arts books,[9] and Buddhist ideas are evident in the thought of many great karate masters.[10]

With this background, let us now turn to *karatedō* itself. Whatever else it is, *karatedō* is a practice of self-defense. Sometimes the best form (and even the only form) of self-defense is attack. So karate skills teach one to neturalize attacks using techniques, some of which can cause the attacker serious injury, and perhaps even death.

Two standard parts of training are *kata* and *kumite*.[11] *Kata* are series of movements. These are something like a dictionary of techniques. They need to be mastered, and their applications understood. *Kata* vary from the very simple to the very complex. They are repeated over and over again until they can be done without thought, though with acute psychological focus. That is, one does not have to think about what to do next. It just happens. There is, however, intense one-pointed attention on the present action, an attention in which all sense of self can disappear. This develops, among other things, powers of intense concentration. *Kumite* is sparring. Again, this may vary from very simple forms, where each person knows exactly what the other is going to do, to free sparring, where each person attacks and defends as best they can. Techniques are pulled just short of the point where they cause serious damage to one's practice partner.

The aim of both *kata* and *kumite* is to develop the skill of self-defense which, if it is deployed, is completely spontaneous and natural (in the sense of being unforced). One does not think about what to do, one just reacts appropriately to the situation. Thinking about matters slows things down and makes one less effective. One aims to develop what Zen Buddhists call *mushin* (no mind) and Daoists call *wuwei* (no—premeditated—action). Of course, this spontaneity is the product of many hours of wiring the brain by constant repetition.

Another thing that a good karate training develops is awareness. In the first instance, this is an awareness of one's opponent. One learns to read them instinctively. But the awareness carries over to one's environment quite generally. One learns how not to put oneself (or others) in harm's way. So, for example, one may see when an interaction with someone (perhaps in a pub) could turn nasty, and take action to defuse the situation. Or when walking, one might perceive possible trouble ahead (perhaps a group of people who could mean no good), and just walk another way. And if trouble does loom, one becomes mindful of exit opportunities, things that might serve as a weapon of self-defense, and so on. In short, one's training affects how one perceives one's environment.

From what we have said so far, it might seem that *karatedō* is simply about the use and avoidance of violence; but when it is taught with a certain (and traditional) spirit it can be much more than this. *Karatedō* is a *dō*, that is, a way. All the Japanese *dō*—*iaidō* (swordsmanship), *shodō* (calligraphy), *chadō* (tea service)—can be seen as practices that inform and develop a way of being in the world. Most of the great *karatedō* masters saw their practices in this way. Not that these things are usually taught in the *dōjō*. It is the practice itself that develops these virtues. A good karate training develops, among other things: perseverance, self-discipline, mindfulness, patience, modesty, a respect for others, a respect for oneself, an awareness of what one owes to others and of what one can give to others.

We might also add to the list non-violence. This may seem a rather odd thing, given that *karatedō* is undoubtedly a training in violence. However, a good *karatedō* training engenders an attitude of peace. Its techniques are only ever to be used for defensive purposes, and then only as a last resort. One should use no more violence than necessary; and it is better to use none at all, simply by avoiding situations where it might be required. It teaches one, so to speak, to win without having to win.

What we have seen in the present section, then, is that and how the Buddhist and Daoist ideas about spontaneity, concentration, and an ethics—a way of being in the world—are integral to the practice of good *karatedō*.[12] We have examined *karatedō* because, like so many specific traditions developed in the Buddhist world (and more specifically in the Daoist-inflected East Asian Buddhist world) its pursuit is in part aimed at cultivating a specific skill—in this case skill in self-defense—but also aimed at cultivating much more general skills, applicable outside the *dōjō*, and particularly the development of spontaneous dispositions to action in the context of highly practiced perception. In this respect, it is not so different from the cultivation of moral skills as adumbrated in texts such as *Bodhicāryāvatāra*, in which practice in perception and practice aimed at the cultivation of spontaneous moral response are both adumbrated.

1.6 Skill, spontaneity and the virtuoso life

As we have seen, the cultivation of skill as it is seen in the Buddhist and Daoist world of East Asia is not understood as restricted to specific domains. Nonetheless, it may be cultivated in a specific domain such as self-defense, tea preparation, calligraphy, gardening, etc. as a more general exercise that enables one to cultivate skill in one's life more broadly. On this understanding of the good life, the good life is a highly skilled life—a virtuoso life, as opposed to a merely virtuous life. That is, the highly skilled *karateka* effortlessly (but as a consequence of the prior exertion of great effort), spontaneously (but only following decades of studied practice) perceives and reacts to those around them as potential threats, allies and so forth. Similarly, the highly skilled calligrapher or gardener effortlessly and spontaneously perceives the affordances for and executes highly skilled actions in the situations appropriate to them. In each case, the relevant spontaneity is achieved through extended practice.

It is often emphasized that these actions are performed without thought (*nirvikapla/mushin*), or without deliberation (*wu wei*). And there is a sense in which this is true: spontaneity and lack of premeditation is essential to skilled action as it is understood in this tradition. This, in turn, is grounded in the nonduality of consciousness that emerges from the lack of thematization of oneself as subject, of one's materials or tools as instruments, and the other as object in such skilled activity, a state referred to in contemporary psychology and sport as *flow*.[13] That nondual experience is important not only because it makes action more fluent, but also because it frees one from the dualism of self and other that distinguishes between subject and the world, occluding one's basic immersion in the world and from the superimposition of conceptual categorization on a world that is primordially uncategorized.

But one should not press this point too far, lest one construct one more duality: that between thought and no-thought. For thinking and deliberating are activities in which one can engage skillfully or unskillfully. Moreover, they are important activities not only in their own right, as so much of our life can only proceed well if it is done with a certain amount of deliberation, but also because, as we have seen, deliberation and thought are required in order even to achieve the ability to engage in thoughtless, spontaneous activity. Thought is hence not a ladder to be discarded, but rather one to be used when necessary, and stored carefully so as to be ready to hand when needed.

As an example of the case in point, consider the skilled mathematician trying to solve a problem, such as proving or rejecting a conjecture. The mathematician will have spent many years honing their skills in focusing on key elements of a situation, making appropriate mathematical constructions, and so on. When faced with a new problem, these skills are deployed. Thought is certainly required in the matter; but the skills are deployed naturally and without being forced—in the way that a skilled jazz musician, but not the novice, plays. Moreover, the phenomenology is quite distinctive. There is no longer a duality of the mind of the mathematician, and the object at which it is directed. There is simply problem-solving going on. The mathematician may, in fact, "awaken" after some time, realizing that they have been "lost in thought."

When we think skillfully, just as when we do anything else skillfully, we do so spontaneously, effortlessly, in a state of flow; if we are truly skilled thinkers, we do not deliberate or think about when or how to deliberate or think, nor in our thought do we thematize the duality of self and object of thought; we just think, paradoxically, in *mushin*. To recognize this fact is to recognize the nonduality of thought and no-thought. That no-thought is not *thoughtlessness*, but simply spontaneous engagement, which can be cognitive as well as physical, and to recognize that skillful activity requires the thorough interpenetration of thought and its transcendence.

We should acknowledge at this point that there is a tension in the Buddhist tradition. Following the metaphor introduced by Candrakīrti in *Introduction to the Middle Way* (*Madhyamakāvatāra*) of the strong potter who sets his wheel in motion and then effortlessly produces pots while it continues to spin without his impelling it, and reflecting the idea that Buddhas have no conceptual thought or explicit intention, some have argued that Buddhas do not act at all, and have no attitudes, and no awareness (see MacKenzie, Chapter 3 in this volume). There is a strain of thought in classical Buddhist literature along these lines (the 15th-century Tibetan philosopher Gorampa Sonam Sengye, for instance defends this view), and it has received endorsement more recently by such philosophers as Dunne (2017) and Siderits (2011), who has characterized Buddhahood as being a zombie-like state of being, the so-called "robo-Buddha" model. On the other hand, other Buddhist philosophers (including the 14th–15th-century Tibetan philosopher Tsongkhapa Lobsang Drakpa) emphasize that the Buddha is aware of all phenomena, and is simultaneously aware of the two truths, that the Buddha constantly acts from care, etc.

Our purpose in this essay is not to adjudicate this dispute. We simply note here that we find the latter proposal more plausible as an account of a soteriological goal, as well as more consistent with the extensive literature on the path to awakening, and the manifold texts that ascribe qualities to Buddhas that require agency, motivation, knowledge, etc. If Buddhahood is to be worth striving for, and if a Buddha is to serve as a moral and epistemological exemplar, the robo-Buddha view seems far too thin, and too much canonical literature requires dismissal if we take that view. We think instead that, while Buddhas are agents and are conscious, their agency and consciousness is nondual, non-conceptual and spontaneous; that is, absolutely skillful. They are thus the kinds of exemplars toward which it is worth striving.

1.7 Conclusion

We have been examining two streams of thought in Asian reflection on skill and spontaneity: one emerging in the Indian Buddhist tradition, and one in the classical Chinese Daoist tradition. These streams converge in Chan and, in turn, feed the developments of the practice and theory of the martial arts. There is an important set of insights about skill carried along these streams: One insight is the sheer ubiquity of skill in our lives. *Upāya* comprises not only physical but hermeneutical and pedagogical skill, as well as moral and perceptual skill. While many might hold that maturation consists primarily in acquiring discursive knowledge, these traditions take it that the practical knowledge embodied in skill is our principal cognitive achievement, and that discursive knowledge may be nothing more than the cognitive equipment we use in manifesting that skill, just as a hammer is important to a carpenter, but only as equipment useful in manifesting her skill in building.

Second, skill is deeply bound up with spontaneity. In learning to lead our lives skillfully we free ourselves from the need to deliberate and from the conceptual mediation between ourselves and our worlds that deliberation entails. We learn to improvise as ensemble players, contributing to the joy and success of social performance. The achievement of that easy but focused and attentive spontaneity, or naturalness in our engagement with the world and with our fellows, is the mark of human maturity.

But finally the nonduality between subject and object, agent and patient, self and world that characterizes the experience of acting without thought also applies to thought and action: skill, as it is understood in these Asian traditions is not the *abandonment* of thought but the skillful use of thought, when, and only when it is appropriate. Just as silence can speak volumes—at the right moment—careful deliberate thought can be a spontaneous response to a situation and can facilitate action—at the right moment. Life is improvisation, and improvisation requires practice.

Notes

1 At least in Indo-Tibetan materials, where the Tibetan *thab mkhas* has a clear positive connotation as a kind of wisdom or knowledge, as opposed to the Chinese tradition where it gets translated as *fangbian*, connoting *expediency*, with a decidedly pejorative connotation. See Garfield (2015).

2 Neither of these sutras is easy to date, but the *Vimalakīrtinirdeśa-sūtra* is generally thought to have been composed in the 1st or 2nd century CE, and the *Saṃdhinirmocana-sūtra* to have been completed in the 3rd century CE, with some fragments dating from the 2nd.

3 This is the root of the Chan/Zen *kōan* of the man hanging by his teeth from the branch of a tree who is asked, "Why did Bodhidharma come from the West?" If he answers, he falls to his death; if he does not answer, he refuses to speak the truth.
4 Much of what follows is developed at greater length in Priest (2014).
5 See Mou (2009), pp. 15–17.
6 Good (objective and reliable) histories of *karatedō* are therefore hard to find. Bishop (1999) is one of the most authoritative we know.
7 See King (1993). On Musashi specifically, see the last chapter of his *Book of Five Rings* (Cleary (1993), 'The Book of Emptiness'.
8 See Cleary (2005).
9 Such as Hyams (1982).
10 See, e.g., Funakoshi (2003).
11 Increasingly, karate is coming to be seen as a sport, where one's aim is simply to win a prize by scoring points in a certain way. However, competition was not a part of traditional *karatedō*, but started only around the middle of the 20th century. With the emphasis on sports training, a number of the more traditional aspects of *karatedō* are, in fact, being lost.
12 Intuitively, it might seem that spontaneity and concentration are incompatible. As we have seen, they are not. The spontaneity of a trained martial artist, jazz musician, rock climber, etc., is possible only because of their total concentration on the "flow" of the moment. It may even be possible to see this in the face: www.youtube.com/watch?v=SPeXVzn-UcI.
13 For further discussion, see Krein and Ilundáin (2014).

References

Bishop, M. (1999) *Okinawan Karate* (revised edition), Boston, MA: Tuttle Publishing.
Cleary, T. (tr.) (1993) *The Book of Five Rings*, Boston, MA: Shambhala.
—— (tr.) (2005) *Soul of the Samurai*, North Clarendon, VT: Tuttle Publications.
Dunne, J. (2017) "Thoughtless Buddha, Passionate Buddha," *Journal of the American Academy of Religion* 64(3): 525–556.
Funakoshi, G. (2003) *The Twenty Guiding Principles of Karate*, Tokyo: Kodansha International Ltd.
Garfield, J. (2015) *Engaging Buddhism: Why it Matters to Philosophy*, New York: Oxford University Press.
Hyams, J. (1982) *Zen in the Martial Arts*, New York: Bantam Books.
King, W. (1993) *Zen and the Way of the Sword*, New York: Oxford University Press.
Krein, K., and Ilundáin, J. (2014) "*Mushin* and Flow: an East-West Comparative Analysis," ch. 9 of G. Priest and D. Young (eds.), *Philosophy and the Martial Arts: Engagement*, Milton Park: Routledge.
Mou, B. (2009) *Chinese Philosophy A-Z*, Edinburgh: Edinburgh University Press.
Powers, J. (1995) *The Wisdom of the Buddha: The Saṃdhinirmocana Sūtra*. Berkeley, CA: Dharma Press.
Priest, G. (2014) "The Martial Arts and Buddhist Philosophy," ch. 11 of G. Priest and D. Young (eds.), *Philosophy and the Martial Arts: Engagement*, Milton Park: Routledge.
Red Pine. (1976) *Lao Tzu's Taoteching*. San Francisco, CA: Mercury Press.
Śāntideva. (1995) *The Bodhicāryāvatāra*. (Crosby and Skilton, trans.). Oxford: Oxford University Press.
Siderits, M. (2011) "Buddhas as Zombies: A Reduction of Subjectivity," in M. Siderits, E. Thompson and D. Zahavi (eds), *Self, No-Self: Perspectives from Analytic, Phenomenological and Indian Traditions*. New York: Oxford University Press, pp. 308–332.
Thurman, R. (1976) *The Holy Teachings of Vimalakīrti*. State College: Penn State University Press.
Zhuangzi (2003) *Zhuangzi*. (B. Watson trans.). New York: Columbia University Press.

2

SKILL AND EXPERTISE IN THREE SCHOOLS OF CLASSICAL CHINESE THOUGHT

Hagop Sarkissian

When reading texts in the classical Chinese philosophical tradition (ca. 6th to 3rd centuries BCE), one is struck by regular celebrations of skill and expertise. Various schools of thought exalt skilled exemplars (whether historical persons or fictional figures) for guiding and inspiring those seeking virtuosity within particular *dao*s (guiding teachings or ways of life), reflecting a shared preoccupation with uncovering and articulating the constituents of an exemplary life. Indeed, there is substantial overlap on some of the core features thought requisite to leading such a life, including spontaneity, naturalness, and effortlessness (e.g. Slingerland 2007). Nonetheless, given the wide array of philosophical thought in this period (later dubbed the *Hundred Schools* period), there was also significant disagreement on what skills were valuable, how one should cultivate them, and who exactly ought to serve as exemplars.

In what follows, I will discuss two prominent types of expertise and their attendant skills. The first is expertise at a particular craft, occupation, or *dao*, which finds its most poignant celebration in the early Daoist anthology *Zhuangzi*. Interest in crafts or skilled occupations was likely motivated by a perceived (or implied) analogy with living a good life more generally. The second is ethical expertise, a prominent and widely held ideal within the Ruist (Confucian) and Mohist schools. Both maintain that ethical expertise consists of an ability to apply past models or precedents to current cases, though they diverge on what those models are and how to properly apply them. The aim is to provide non-specialists an overview of this literature as well as suggestions about further research.

2.1 Skill in craft and performance

Some of the most well-known examples of skill and expertise involve particular crafts, professions, or ways of life. Chapter 19 ("Probing Life" 達生) of the *Zhuangzi*, a compendium of early Daoist thought, contains many such examples. The accounts share a common structure: a member of the societal elite (e.g. a duke or marquis) or a moralizing philosopher (e.g. Kongzi, better known to Westerners as Confucius) encounters a person of lower social status engaged in a mundane activity, yet with such depth of skill, grace, and proficiency, that it startles him. A lesson is thereby seemingly imparted about realms of meaningful human experience that are typically overlooked (see Garfield and Priest, Chapter 1 in this volume).Thus, these episodes both valorize skill while also denigrating the blinkered perspective of the elite.

For example, in a representative passage, Kongzi gazes at a waterfall producing rapids so turbulent that no sea creatures dare swim in it, and foam so abundant that it persists miles downstream. Suddenly, he catches sight of a solitary figure in the water.Thinking this person in mortal danger he dispatches a disciple to render aid, only to see the person emerge from the depths full of song. Amazed, Kongzi asks for his *dao* of swimming.The swimmer claims none. Instead, the swimmer describes his skill as developing naturally out of his having grown up both on land and in water, and thus being adept and at ease in both environments.These were the original circumstances given to him (*gu* 故), and his life course developed naturally therein. He cannot further articulate or illuminate his skill save for thin descriptions (e.g. 'following the current').What was ordinary from his perspective resulted in a way of life seemingly extraordinary to others. Here, Kongzi represents the perspective of a judgmental elite, who claims to possess deep insight on what is proper and improper, admirable and inadmirable, and goes around promulgating his beliefs on the assumption that people require guidance and education. Kongzi assumes the swimmer needs his help, yet he requires none at all. Rather, he has a surety and ease with his own life that Kongzi seems to lack (e.g. Møllgaard 2007: 61).The nameless swimmer is thus a foil to the famous sage, who is characterized as out of touch and out of his depth.

The story of Wheelwright Pian in the same chapter follows this pattern of depicting skill as something learned through practice and hard to convey with words. "Neither slow nor hurried, I feel it through my hand, and it resonates with my mind," explains the wheelwright. "My mouth cannot put it into words.There is a knack in it somewhere that I cannot convey to my son, and which he cannot learn from me" (13/37/16–18).[1]

Here's the general lesson:

> Everyone in the world values *dao* when found in texts. A text does not go beyond its sayings, yet the sayings contain something of value. What is of value in sayings is the impressions they convey.The impressions follow from something else, and these cannot be transmitted with words. Alas, everyone values mere sayings and so transmits texts. Even though everyone values them [i.e. words and books], to me they seem not to obtain value; what everyone values is not what's *really* of value.
>
> *13/37/5–6*

Other stories include further details about the accumulation of skill and how it figures in a satisfying way of life. In one such story, Kongzi runs into a hunchback catching cicadas with amazing dexterity. Kongzi inquires about his skills.The cicada catcher obliges, describing how he hones and sharpens his focus by balancing round pellets on top of one another. "If I can balance two without dropping them, I'll lose a few cicadas; if I can balance three, I'll miss just one in ten; if I can balance five, it will be like gathering them off the ground" (19/50/13–14). He then describes his heightened state of concentration while catching cicada:

> I settle my body like a tree stump, I hold my arm like the branch of a withered tree. Though heaven and earth are vast, though it contains a multitude of things, I am only aware of cicada wings. I don't wander or waver, and I would not trade cicada wings for any other thing. How could it be that I'd fail to succeed!
>
> *19/50/14–15*

Kongzi later tells his disciples: "When the will is undivided, it congeals with the spirit" (19/50/16).

This latter term 'spirit' is a translation of *shen* 神, the source of a person's agency or vitality. It reappears in other discussions of skill in the *Zhuangzi*. In one such story, Kongzi tells his student Yan Hui of a time he encountered a ferryman handling a boat as though he were a spirit (*shen* 神). The ferryman claimed that the secret lay in forgetting what others cannot but bear in mind (i.e. the risk of drowning). He draws an analogy with high-stakes competitions.

> When shooting [your arrow] for earthenware you're skilful; when shooting for fancy belt-buckles you're apprehensive; when shooting for gold you're discombobulated. Your skill is the same as ever, yet there's something that you come to be concerned with—this is attaching weight to what is outside you. Whoever gives weight to what is outside him is being clumsy within.
>
> *19/50/22–23*

Elsewhere, we read of a woodworker named Qing who carved a bellstand so amazing, people thought it was made by a ghost or spirit. A marquis, marveling at his skill, asks his secret. The woodworker claims to achieve heightened focus through fasting and forgetting.

> After fasting three days, I no longer keep in mind congratulations and reward, honors and salary. After five days, I no longer keep in mind blame or praise, skill or clumsiness. After seven days, I am so intent that I forget that I have a body and four limbs.
>
> During this time my lord's court does not exist for me. My skill concentrates, outside distractions melt away, and only then do I go into the mountain forest and observe the nature of the wood. When I see one of perfect form—only then is my vision of the bellstand formed, and only then do I put my hands to it. Otherwise, I'll just give the whole thing up … What people took to be the workings of a spirit in the vessel—could this be it?
>
> *19/52/5–8*

Some have noted similarities between these accounts and the experience of 'flow', as popularized by Mihalyi Csikszentmihalyi (e.g. Barrett 2011; Singh 2014). Consider the following conditions that accompany experiences of flow:

- Perceived challenges, or opportunities for action, that stretch (neither over-matching nor underutilizing) existing skills; a sense that one is engaging challenges at a level appropriate to one's capacities
- Clear proximal goals and immediate feedback about the progress that is being made.

Nakamura and Csikszentmihalyi 2014: 240

There are obvious points of contact here with the skill stories in the *Zhuangzi*, which involve activities that are challenging yet not beyond the skills of the performer, with immediate goals internal to the activity itself. There are further parallels in the phenomenology of flow-type activities:

- Intense and focused concentration on the present moment.
- Merging of action and awareness.
- Loss of reflective self-consciousness (i.e., loss of awareness of oneself as a social actor).

- A sense of control; that one can in principle deal with the situation because one knows how to respond to whatever happens next.
- Distortion of temporal experience (typically, a sense that time has passed faster than normal).
- Experiencing the activity as intrinsically rewarding, such that the end goal is often a mere excuse for the process.

Nakamura and Csikszentmihalyi 2014: 240

Many of these features of flow are noted explicitly in the stories above, while the rest are either consistent with them or can be inferred from them (though cf. Slingerland 2000; Fraser 2014).

I highlighted the use of the term *shen* (spirit/spirited) in the passages above. It is seldom noted, but significant, that in all the cases so far it is a term out-of-touch *observers* use to describe the manifestation of skill (whether in product, performance, or performer). Yet the performers themselves do not use this term, and thus it is difficult to know whether the observers' comments should be read as *veridical*—that is, reflecting the way the author sees these things (as truly spiritual achievements)—or as a *reductio*, reflecting the worthless perspective of the elitist.

The chief passage in support of the former interpretation is also the most famous skill story in the text. It involves a dialogue between a lord and his lowly cook.

> Cook Ding was carving up an ox for Lord Wen-hui. Wherever his hand slapped, wherever his shoulders dipped, wherever his foot braced, wherever his knees pressed, the *thwack!* and *thud!* of flesh falling off and knife penetrating flesh was in perfect cadence, now in time with the Mulberry Forest Dance, now in tune with the Jing Shou Chorus. "Wow! Excellent!" said Lord Wen-hui. "That skill should attain such heights!"
>
> *3/7/30–3/8/2*

These opening lines depict the flow-like state of Cook Ding carving his ox, and the appearance of an elite (Lord Wen-hui) once again signals that he is meant to be a foil. The passage continues with the cook's response:

> "What your servant loves is *dao*; I have advanced past skill. When I first began to carve oxen, I saw nothing but the ox. Three years more and I stopped seeing the ox as a whole. Nowadays, I encounter it with my spirit, and no longer look with my eyes. My overseeing knowledge ceases, and the spirit's impulses proceed. I rely on nature's layering, cleave along the main seams, follow the main cavities, and go by what is inherently so. A ligament or tendon I never touch, not to mention solid bone.
>
> A good cook changes his chopper once a year, because he cuts. A common cook changes it once a month, because he hacks. Now I have had this chopper for nineteen years, and have taken apart several thousand oxen, but the edge is as though it were fresh from the whetstone. The joints have spaces gaps, and the edge of the blade has no thickness. If you insert what has no thickness into a gap, then there's wide open spaces, and of course there is ample room to move the edge about. That's why after nineteen years the edge of my chopper is as though it were fresh from the whetstone.
>
> However, whenever I come to something knotty, I resign to the difficulty ahead. I proceed with caution and halt my gaze. My actions slow, my blade barely flicks and

yet the whole thing crumbles to the ground. I stand, knife in hand, looking round proudly at the results, dawdling to enjoy the triumph until I'm quite satisfied. I then wipe the blade and put it away."

"Excellent!" said Lord Wen-hui. "Listening to the words of this cook, I have learned how to nurture life."

3/8/4–11

Cook Ding's trance-like flow states of engagement while carving oxen are described as going 'beyond skill', and indeed Lord Wen-hui is not only amazed at the cook's performance, but is even more impressed by his *words*. Lord Wen-hui hears the cook discuss his butchery and learns something about *life* and how to nurture it. Presumably, the secret to nurturing life involves analogous engagement with the world through one's spirit (a point that is echoed in the next chapter, *In the World of Men*, though within a political context).

The cook might thus be taken to represent something above and beyond skill. Edward Slingerland, for example, argues that we cannot understand expert skill *per se* to be the ultimate goal of any of the practices above. Skilled mastery in one domain is consistent with being an atrocious human being as a whole (e.g. abusive or malevolent to others). For Slingerland, this is unacceptable. Instead, we must understand such flow states as representing "a perfection of a unique and ultimate skill: the skill of becoming a fully realized human being and embodying the Way in the full range of one's actions." On this reading, the ideal "involved relating the individual to a larger normative cosmic order—as well as presenting an at least implicit picture of human nature as it relates to this order." Thus, this is "first and foremost a *spiritual* ideal ... [with] roots in *archaic Chinese religion*" (Slingerland 2007: 9, emphasis added).

Lee Yearley makes similar arguments. He reads into the text a special notion of drives called 'transcendent' drives, and he sees such drives depicted and celebrated throughout the text of the *Zhuangzi*.

> Transcendent drives generate activities that exceed the normal capacities of the self and seem to arise from beyond it. They produce abilities that surpass normal abilities and transform normal actions ... I find myself able to perform easily and well tasks that previously seemed to be far beyond my normal capabilities. Transcendent drives... allow powers such as the 神 shen, "daemonic" ... to possess a person and therefore they help bring to a person the highest possible spiritual fulfillment.
>
> *Yearley 1996: 154*

Given this latter spiritual dimension, Yearley maintains that skilled activity in the text "transcends what most people would identify as normal skillfulness" (Yearley 1996: 164).[2]

Such religious approaches tend to inflate the wondrous qualities of the skills involved, and advert to extra variables (e.g. the spirit, the 'daemonic', or 'transcendent drives') in order to explain this heightened gap between the ordinary and the extraordinary. But, as noted above, the fact that some of the activities seem rather ordinary (such as swimming, or catching cicadas—something children still do in China today) yet still engendering wonder and awe among the elite, might instead be making light of just how divorced and alienated these elites are. Hans Georg Moeller and Paul J. D'Ambrosio (2017) see both sides at work. However, they believe the fact that the skilled protagonists routinely reject being extraordinary weighs in favor of a more deflationary reading.

The extreme waterfall diver at Lüliang, the nameless drunkard mastering the art of falling off carts unharmed, and Cook Ding, the symphonic slaughterer, are oddly exaggerated "players," partly surreal and partly comical, partly mundane and partly miraculous. They are larger than life and at the same time most average, wonderful, and ordinary. Their stupefying skills are accompanied by the utmost unpretentiousness. These paradoxical artists *disown* their arts ....Thus, both the artisans and their arts are de-idolized and "normalized," and a routine of a paradoxically common and contingent excellence that one may or may not engage in emerges.

Moeller and D'Ambrosio 2017: 183–184

The *Zhuangzi* is not alone in containing noteworthy depictions of skill and mastery. Thinkers and texts we now associate with the Ruist (or Confucian) tradition also invoke examples of skill and expertise across a number of domains, including (and especially) skill at forging human cultural and societal institutions. Exemplars of these kinds are venerated by the Ru for both creating and perpetuating culture through acts of human artifice (*wei* 偽), for it is only through their faithful transmission that culture can persist and thrive, benefiting and beautifying humankind. In the classical text *The Rites of Zhou* (周禮), we find a typical way the Ru saw these things.

The knowledgeable fashion things; the skillful transmit and maintain these things through generations. They are called artisans. The affairs of the hundred artisans are all thus creations of the sages. Some smelt metal to make knives; some harden the earth to make implements; some build chariots to travel over hills; some build boats to travel over water. All of these are things that were created by the sages.

Puett 2001: 77

However, what is most striking from a contemporary perspective is the prevalence of a certain kind of expertise venerated by the Ru and Mohists alike. This is the idea of moral or ethical expertise.

2.2 Ethical expertise

The examples adduced above represent apt domains of expertise. As Christian Helmut Wenzel writes, the invocation of skill in these contexts is apt

because there is a specified range of objects, which corresponds to the specific craftsmanship, and because there are certain criteria of success that are available right from the start. Cook Ting [Ding] does not try to be a good swimmer, and the ferryman does not cut oxen.

Wenzel 2003: 119

By contrast, the idea that one might be an expert (or highly skilled) at ethics seems odd. What does ethical expertise consist of? How is it possible? The criteria themselves are subject to much dispute (should we focus on intent, character, or consequences?), and demonstrating ethical expertise seems problematic. If one were to skeptically interrogate the cicada catcher about whether he really has skill, he can just show the bounty of his hunt, for example. What could be the analogue in the ethical domain? Answering these questions would obviously take us far beyond the scope of this chapter. Nonetheless, some early Ruist texts had answers to these questions.

45

At a basic level, these texts maintained that one can be an expert at ethics because the core of ethics consists of adhering to and exemplifying norms of ritualized propriety (*li* 禮), a set of traditional protocols, ceremonies, rules of etiquette, and other formalized aspects of social interaction that, from their perspective, were honed and perfected by preceding generations of sagacious rulers and ministers, and passed down as a cultural inheritance that could then form the basis of an ethics curriculum.[3] The *li* included detailed and formalized rites and ceremonies keyed to significant life events on one end of a spectrum, with etiquette, manners, and basic courtesy on the other. They were thought to constitute the wisdom of ancient sages of impeccable character, and were revered as holding the key to proper enculturation, humanization, and communication. (A nearby, if imperfect, analogue for modern Westerners might be the norms governing conduct of the nobility in Victorian England.) These norms—the *li*—would apply to most social situations, and could be analogically extended to apply to all facets of life (Sarkissian 2014).

It is important to note just how demanding the *li* were, and how long the Ru thought it would take to gain mastery of them. In the *Analects* (a collection of sayings and anecdotes about Kongzi and his immediate circle of interlocutors), for example, Kongzi claims to have started diligent study and practice at the age of 15, and only at the age of 70 had he internalized these norms and honed his ethical sense such that his immediate inclinations were always correct (*Analects* 2.4). Xunzi (a 3rd-century BCE Ru), takes up this line with vigor, and is at pains to note that skill or mastery at ethics does not consist of mere memorization of rules or rote mimicry of others, but must also involve grace, dignity, and an ability to elicit from others (especially those less conversant in the ceremony) appropriate feelings and attitudes.

Nonetheless, they maintain that ethical expertise is amenable to the kind of sustained, iterative improvement accompanying other forms of skill acquisition noted above, provided one has proper guidance. Justin Tiwald (2012), for example, has explicated Xunzi's model of expertise by noting two kinds of ethical knowledge a student must master. The first is knowledge of general models (*fa* 法) of ethical behavior. Much of this will include knowledge of the *li* as well as paradigmatic instances of right actions, and can be fairly general at their level of description (e.g. one must not address one's parents in a disrespectful fashion). The second kind of knowledge concerns how to apply these models in one's own life. Both kinds of knowledge—though especially the second—require guidance by expert teachers or mentors (*shi* 師). As Xunzi writes,

> Ritual is that by which to correct your person. The teacher is that by which to correct your practice of ritual. If you are without ritual, then how will you correct your person? If you are without a teacher, how will you know that your practice of ritual is right?
>
> *Hutton 2014: 14*

> Anyone on the streets can become a Yu [a sage king]. How do I mean this? I say: that by which Yu was Yu was because he was *ren* [humane], *yi* [right], lawful, and correct. Thus, *ren*, *yi*, lawfulness, and correctness have patterns that can be known and can be practiced. However, people on the streets all have the material for knowing *ren*, *yi*, lawfulness, and correctness, and they all have the equipment for practicing *ren*, *yi*, lawfulness, and correctness. Thus, it is clear that they can become a Yu.
>
> *Hutton 2014: 254*

Teachers help the student to match these models of ethical behavior to particular circumstances. Through such guidance, the student is able to gradually deepen their understanding of the ethical life. They will come to see, for example, how the various models (the first kind of know-ledge) hang together and form a coherent set, and how they instantiate a wider system of goods and values.[4]

Through such direct, personal, and experiential forms of learning, students can begin to note for themselves how various locutions or details of their comportment can signal respect, care, and consideration of others, and how their own conduct impacts and moves them. By noting their successes and failures, those pursuing ethical mastery can eventually achieve a kind of 'deliberative autonomy' whereby they no longer require the aid of teachers or mentors to correct their practices, and can engage in reflection and self-correction in an effective manner themselves. Some have suggested that this overall picture of ethical know-ledge or expertise cannot be readily assimilated into categories such as 'knowing that' or even 'knowing how.' Instead, some early Ruist texts contain a distinctive notion that we might understand as *knowing to*, as in knowing to act in the moment (Lai 2012; Hetherington and Lai 2015). This too can be understood as a kind of expert skill. Others have argued that par-ticular virtues in these classical Ruist texts should be thought of as partially constituted by mastery of a certain set of skills (Stalnaker 2010). Still others have characterized this kind of skill as driven by intuitive inclinations cultivated through the sustained accumulation of a broad range of concrete experiences. Borrowing from Antonio Damasio's *somatic marker* hypothesis (Damasio 2006), the current author has argued that expertise involves the honing of spontaneous inclination. According to Damasio, as one encounters particular situation types, one's mind is full of a diverse repertoire of latent inclinations attuned to the situation at hand via past experience. Each of these has a qualitative feel or valence (e.g. 'that might be good,' 'this might be bad,' etc.), working to limit the possible actions and outcomes to pursue. Sarkissian argues that this

> fine-tunes and *accelerates* the decision-making process; at the limit, the correct course of action would come to mind immediately, with compelling emotional valence.
>
> In completely novel situations, we may be at a loss for an appropriate response, leaving us immobile. Similarly, where social configurations trigger overlapping schemes associated with multiple markers, we may be perplexed and unsure how to react. This can occur, for example, in situations where we find individuals playing roles we are not accustomed to seeing them play or when we encounter individuals acting according to situational norms that conflict with our own. However, familiarity with a *broad* range of emotions, facilitated through exposure to literature, art, and social rit-uals, will allow one to perceive values in a *wide* range of scenarios, thus improving the likelihood of responding appropriately in any *particular* situation.
>
> *Sarkissian 2010a: 7; original italics*

When ethical skill advances sufficiently, and as one becomes recognized as trustworthy and reliable, the Ru maintain that one cultivates a felt presence or personal power (*de* 德), a kind of gravitas or charisma that accompanies one's behavior and judgments, lending one authority and rendering others cooperative and agreeable—disposed to defer to one's ethical expertise (Nivison 2002; Sarkissian 2010b, 2017; Barnwell 2013).

Thus far, the account of ethical expertise has focused largely on two early thinkers in the Ru school—namely, Kongzi and Xunzi. The 4th-century BCE thinker Mengzi (better known to Westerners as Mencius), shares much in common with them. However, his model of expertise departs from theirs in distinct ways. A key passage occurs in *Mengzi* 6A7. There, Mengzi infers that our sensory modalities each have built-in preferences, explaining why expert musicians can produce orchestrations that delight any who hear it, or why expert cooks can produce dishes that delight anyone who taste them. By analogy, the human heart (*xin* 心), the cite of cognition, affect, and volition (thus also translated as heart/mind) must have built-in preferences too. Mengzi claims that the sage kings venerated by the Ru (such as Yao and Shun) discovered what these were, and promulgated ethical standards of order (*li* 理) and rightness (*yi* 義) to others, who similarly delighted in them. In an extended discussion of this passage, Hutton claims that, for Mengzi, "the sages' moral *knowledge* consists in a developed ethical 'taste,' much as Yi Ya's culinary knowledge and Music Master Kuang's musical knowledge consist in a kind of cultivated expertise" (Hutton 2002). On this view,

> the sages are above all *connoisseurs of the human heart.* Their focus is inward, and what their special knowledge concerns is not so much human behavior in general and the way the world at large works *per se*, but rather what sorts of behaviors and states of affairs are most pleasing to the heart, given its innate preferences.
>
> *Hutton 2002: 174*

However, as Dobin Choi (2018) points out, if we take the analogy with Yi Ya and Shi Kuang seriously, it is more likely that Mengzi meant to analogize the sages' morally admirable behavior and personal example to Yi Ya's dishes and Music Master Kuang's compositions. The sages are not merely connoisseurs in the sense of being able to perceive what is morally good; rather, they *enact* moral goodness through their own persons and the virtues and values they exemplify. Upon contemplating the sages' behavior, other people delight in it, just as they do masterful dishes and compositions. This suggests a similar structure to all the analogies above: there is an expert who creates or uncovers something that elicits a sentiment of approval among the people, showing that people have innate preferences; moreover, the sentiment of approval elicited by the people itself instantiates or affirms the excellence of the expert creation.

The Ru were not alone in venerating cultural heroes of the past and holding them up as models of expertise to emulate. This was also the orientation of the Mohists, a rival school of thinkers similarly engaged in the project of social and political reform. They disagreed with the Ru on which figures were worthy of emulation and for what reasons, and their conception of expertise thus adverted to a distinct set of concerns. The Mohists rejected the idea that traditional customs, mores, and ceremonies ought to be taken as reliable guides to what is right. When they look to the sage kings as models, they do not include the sorts of cultural achievements and traditional practices that comprised the Ru curriculum and generally established as customary among the elite (such as lavish funerals for one's deceased parents). Rather, they argued that one must have an objective standard to define which customs are beneficial and ought to be perpetuated, and which are detrimental and ought to be abandoned or reformed. Importantly, they argued that the sage rules of antiquity ought to be followed because they modeled themselves on just such an objective standard—namely *Tian* 天 or Heaven, a supernatural agent of impartial concern.

> It is said that there is no standard like Heaven. Heaven is broad and unselfish in its actions, and is generous in its bestowing without considering itself virtuous. Its radiance is enduring and does not decay. Therefore, the sage kings took it as the standard … Undoubtedly what Heaven desires is that there be mutual love and mutual benefit among people.
>
> *Johnston 2009: 27*

If this is so, Heaven's intentions might be modeled by people directly. And such modeling is depicted as a kind of skill, analogous to those needed in crafts.

> The hundred craftsmen make what is square with a square, make what is round with compasses, use a straight edge to establish what is straight, determine the horizontal with a water level, and the vertical with a plumb line. Whether skilled or unskilled, craftsmen all take these five things as standards. Skilled craftsmen are able to comply with these standards whilst unskilled craftsmen, even if they are unable to comply with them, will still surpass themselves if they follow them in their work. Thus the hundred craftsmen all have standards as a basis for their work. Nowadays, the greatest [achievement] is to bring order to the world and the next greatest is to bring order to a large country, but to attempt these things without reliance on standards is to compare unfavourably in wisdom with the hundred craftsmen.
>
> *Johnston 2009: 25*

Given this general sketch, we can now outline what ethical expertise consists of for the Mohists: an ability (that is, a capability or disposition) to discriminate and apply correct models or paradigms to current circumstances, with these models being the precedents of sage kings guided by, and conforming to, the will of Heaven. In an upshot, expert ethical action should promote the will of Heaven, which is to secure material benefit and care for all. According to Chad Hansen, the Mohists advert to this objective standard, yet remain dependent on teachers to guide one's application of the standard. The Mohists

> take for granted that things really are similar and different. On the basis of objective similarity and difference, we make socially approved distinctions. Once we have achieved virtuosity or competence in discriminating, we assume that our use is correct. Thus it is that Mozi cannot dispense with Confucius' teacher-student method of transmission even though he wants a more objective, realistic content. Our basic linguistic skill in making distinctions requires a string of teacher-student embodiments.
>
> *Hansen 1992: 104*

Similarly, Chris Fraser argues that what drives ethical action for the Mohists "is mainly ability or know-how (*zhi* 知), which is largely the result of skill training. Moral education and cultivation thus are processes similar in important respects to skill development" (Fraser 2016: 23).

> Action is regarded as a skilled response to things or situations. It is triggered by the agent's distinguishing a thing or situation as being of a certain kind and thus invoking a relevant, normatively appropriate response. Instead of tying agency to our capacity for reasoning, this model bases it primarily on our capacity to acquire and exercise skills and virtues.
>
> *Fraser 2016: 76*[5]

The Mohists advocate reforming governing structures and hierarchies so as to promote those who are just so skilled, who they deem the worthy (*xian* 賢). Good government requires this kind of ethical expertise, which in turn demands a degree of individual autonomy, or the ability to make such classifications oneself independent of one's superiors (Brindley 2007). In other words, making correct ethical judgments is a form of skill, and ethical failure results from a lack of such skill.

While diverging in certain important aspects, both the Ru and the Mohist conceptions of ethical expertise presuppose and rely upon the skilled matching of previously learned models to particular cases. Fraser (2009: 76) argues that we can take this general model as paradigmatic of classical conceptions of agency.

2.3 Concluding thoughts/future research

Several classical thinkers in the Chinese tradition thought that central agentic notions such as deliberating, choosing, and acting consisted of a kind of analogical reasoning. When one is deciding what to do or judging right from wrong, one analogizes the current case to a rehearsed set of models or prior examples that comprised one's basic education. Through this process, one sorts objects, actions, or entire states of affairs as falling under one classification or other. Prior learning provides one with response patterns to suit these various classifications. To use an example, coming upon an instance where one might deem a person 'upright' (*zheng* 正) would require a skill to draw analogies between aspects of a person's conduct, reputation, etc., and a past paradigm of 'uprightness.' If the analogies are sufficiently strong, this would trigger relevant attitudes (e.g. admiration or deference) automatically. Judging the strength of analogy may require careful reasoning. Yet with a suitably rich experiential base from which to draw, implicit or explicit comparisons become more and more finely attuned. Over time, this process becomes less demanding and more spontaneous, and one's immediate inclinations to action align with normatively sanctioned responses. The crucial thing for present purposes is that this is a task that one can hone over time, gaining skill and mastery through incessant practice. The current author (Sarkissian 2010a) has suggested a cognitive model that might help to explicate the mechanisms underwriting such a practice. Further research can help to develop and refine this general picture. If true, it suggests that various forms of skill and expertise rest upon shared assumptions about normal, healthy forms of agency.

Put another way, the depictions of skill and expertise above might all be underwritten by a shared capacity for *pattern-recognition*. The cook in the *Zhuangzi* story understands the natural patterns in the ox so as to effectively carve it up without dulling his blade; the skillful ritual expert must understand the patterns of emotional reaction and response in his audience so as to properly execute the rite; and the perspicacious student must come to learn how certain small tokens of behavior or small turns of event routinely unfold and resonate with other phenomena. Future work might examine more carefully the connections between metaphysical notions such as patterning on the one hand, and epistemological capacities such as recognizing and analogizing on the other.[6]

Notes

1 Translations of the *Zhuangzi* are my own, though I consulted Graham (2001) and Ziporyn (2009). The numbering of sections (book/page/line) refers to the standard ICS concordance. Locations of the textual references can also be determined using the Chinese Text Project website: http://ctext.org/ tools/concordance. My thanks to Chris Fraser for numerous suggestions on parsing the original text. Any infelicities are my own.

2 Notwithstanding the prevalence of such interpretations, it remains unclear whether heightened or perfected skill is really different in kind as opposed to mere degree. For discussion, see Wenzel (2003).

3 The traditional 'Six Arts' (六藝) of education included not only the rites (禮), but also music (樂), archery (射), charioteering (御), calligraphy (書), and mathematics (數). We focus on ritual, as it was considered most central.

4 One might wonder *which* of the numerous kings and heroes of antiquity to take as models. Choosing from among them would likely require expertise of its own. Amy Olberding (2012), for example, has

argued that the nature of Kongzi's expertise lay in his ability to identify true exemplars and articulate the coherence among them by developing a shared vocabulary.

5 Fraser argues that Xunzi, builds on the Mohist model by further emphasizing the importance of teachers and mentors in learning how to properly discriminate and apply models (Fraser, 2016: 57). In chapter 8 of his received text ("The Achievements of the *Ru*"), Xunzi claims that what distinguishes the great person from the petty person is precisely this ability to properly discriminate objects and categorize them correctly.

6 My thanks to Chris Fraser, Jing Hu, and David Wong for comments on previous drafts.

References

Barnwell, S. A. (2013) 'The evolution of the concept of de 德 in early China,' *Sino-Platonic Papers*, 235.

Barrett, N. F. (2011) 'Wuwei and Flow: Comparative Reflections on Spirituality, Transcendence, and Skill in the Zhuangzi,' *Philosophy East & West*, 61(4), pp. 679–706.

Brindley, E. (2007) 'Human agency and the ideal of shang tong (upward conformity) in early Mohist writings,' *Journal of Chinese Philosophy*, 34(3), pp. 409–425.

Choi, D. (2018) 'Moral artisanship in Mengzi 6A7,' *Dao*, 17(3), pp. 331–348.

Damasio, A. R. (2006) *Descartes' Error*. New York: Random House.

Fraser, C. (2009) 'Action and agency in early Chinese thought,' 中國哲學與文化. Guangxi Shi Fan Da Xue Chu Ban She (廣西師範大學出版社), 5, pp. 217–239.

—— (2014) 'Heart-fasting, forgetting, and using the heart like a mirror: applied emptiness in the Zhuangzi,' in J. Liu and D. L. Berger (eds) *Conceptions of Nothingness in Asian Philosophy*. New York: Routledge, pp. 197–212.

—— (2016) *The Philosophy of the Mòzǐ: The First Consequentialists*. New York: Columbia University Press.

Graham, A. C. (2001) *Chuang Tzu: The Inner Chapters*. Indianapolis: Hackett Publishing.

Hansen, C. (1992) *A Daoist Theory of Chinese Thought: A Philosophical Interpretation*. New York: Oxford University Press.

Hetherington, S. and Lai, K. L. (2015) 'Knowing-how and knowing-to,' in B. Bruya (ed.) *The Philosophical Challenge from China*. Cambridge: MIT Press, pp. 279–301.

Hutton, E. L. (2002) 'Moral connoisseurship in Mengzi,' in X. Liu and P. J. Ivanhoe (eds) *Essays in the Moral Philosophy of Mengzi*. Indianapolis: Hackett Publishing, pp. 163–186.

—— (2014) *Xunzi: The Complete Text*. Princeton, NJ: Princeton University Press.

Johnston, I. (2009) *The Mozi: A Complete Translation*. Hong Kong: Chinese University Press.

Lai, K. L. (2012) 'Knowing to act in the moment: examples from Confucius' Analects,' *Asian Philosophy*, 22(4), pp. 347–364.

Moeller, H.-G. and D'Ambrosio, P. J. (2017) *Genuine Pretending: On the Philosophy of the Zhuangzi*. New York: Columbia University Press.

Møllgaard, E. (2007) *An Introduction to Daoist Thought: Action, Language, and Ethics in Zhuangzi*. London: Routledge.

Nakamura, J. and Csikszentmihalyi, M. (2014) 'The concept of flow,' in *Flow and the Foundations of Positive Psychology*. Dordrecht: Springer, pp. 239–263.

Nivison, D. (2002) 'De (te): virtue or power,' in A. S. Cua (ed.) *Encyclopedia of Chinese Philosophy*. London: Routledge, pp. 234–237.

Olberding, A. (2012) *Moral Exemplars in the Analects: The Good Person Is That*. New York: Routledge.

Puett, M. (2001) *The Ambivalence of Creation: Debates Concerning Innovation and Artifice in Early China*. Stanford, CA: Stanford University Press.

Sarkissian, H. (2010a) 'Confucius and the effortless life of virtue,' *History of Philosophy Quarterly*, 27(1), pp. 1–16.

—— (2010b) 'Minor tweaks, major payoffs: the problems and promise of situationism in moral philosophy,' *Philosopher's Imprint*, 10(9), pp. 1–15.

—— (2014) 'Ritual and rightness in the *Analects*,' in A. Olberding (ed.) *Dao Companion to the Analects*. Dordrecht: Springer Netherlands (Dao Companions to Chinese Philosophy, 4), pp. 95–116.

—— (2017) 'Situationism, manipulation, and objective self-awareness,' *Ethical Theory and Moral Practice: An International Forum*, 20(3), pp. 489–503.

Singh, D. (2014) 'Zhuangzi, wuwei, and the necessity of living naturally: a reply to Xunzi's objection,' *Asian Philosophy*, 24(3), pp. 212–226.

Slingerland, E. (2000) 'Effortless action: the Chinese spiritual ideal of wu-wei,' *Journal of the American Academy of Religion*, 68(2), pp. 293–327.

—— (2007) *Effortless Action: Wu-wei as Conceptual Metaphor and Spiritual Ideal in Early China*. New York: Oxford University Press.

Stalnaker, A. (2010) 'Virtue as mastery in early Confucianism,' *The Journal of Religious Ethics*, 38(3), pp. 404–428.

Tiwald, J. (2012) 'Xunzi on moral expertise,' *Dao*, 11(3), pp. 275–293.

Wenzel, C. H. (2003) 'Ethics and Zhuangzi: awareness, freedom, and autonomy,' *Journal of Chinese Philosophy*, 30(1), pp. 115–126.

Yearley, L. H. (1996) 'Zhuangzi's understanding of skillfulness and the ultimate spiritual state,' in P. J. Ivanhoe and P. Kjellberg (eds) *Essays on Skepticism, Relativism, and Ethics in the Zhuangzi*. Albany: State University of New York Press, pp. 152–182.

Ziporyn, B. (2009) *Zhuangzi: The Essential Writings with Selections from Traditional Commentaries*. Indianapolis: Hackett Publishing.

3

VOLITION, ACTION, AND SKILL IN INDIAN BUDDHIST PHILOSOPHY

Matthew MacKenzie

There is suffering but none who suffer,
there is action but no agent,
there is *nibbāna* but no one who is released,
there is a Path but no goer on it.

Visuddhimagga

3.1 Introduction

On initial analysis, Indian Buddhist philosophers seem to have an inconsistent set of commitments with regard to the nature of action. First, they are committed to the reality of *karman* (Skt: action), which concerns the moral quality of actions and the short- and long-term effects of those actions on the agent. Skillful or wholesome (*kuśala*) actions will tend to have positive consequences for oneself, while unskillful or unwholesome (*akuśala*) actions will tend to have negative consequences. Second, they are committed to an understanding of karma as deeply connected with intention or volition (*cetanā*). Third, they are committed to the idea that, through Buddhist practice, one may become liberated from the afflictions of craving, aversion, and ignorance and achieve *nirvāṇa*. Thus, it is not surprising that relationship between volition, action, and the results of action for the agent constitutes a central theme of Indian Buddhist philosophy. Yet, fourth, while Buddhist philosophers are committed to the reality of action and its results, they are also committed to the *unreality* of any substantial self or agent of actions. How can one affirm the reality of volition, action, efficacious practice, and liberation, while denying the existence of agents, practitioners, or liberated beings? Reconciling the doctrine of no-self (*anātman*) with an account of agency and karma was a central task of great Buddhist philosophers such as Vasubandhu (fl. 4th to 5th centuries CE). This chapter will discuss Buddhist philosophy of action in the context of their views of the self, general ontology, ethics, and soteriology. After discussing some important preliminaries, section 3.2 will examine the connection between intention, action, and the skillful. Section 3.3 takes up the Buddhist account of agency without agents. Section 3.4 examines the important Buddhist idea of skillful means (*upāya-kauśalya*) in ethics and soteriology. Section 3.5 will discuss the thorny issue of the discontinuity between awakened and unawakened forms of action.[1]

3.2 Volition, action, and the skillful

The Buddhist project centrally concerns understanding and removing the causes and conditions that give rise to and perpetuate suffering (*duḥkha*). Indeed, the basic analysis of the human situation is that we are trapped in *saṃsāra*, a self-reinforcing, self-perpetuating cycle of frustration and dissatisfaction not just within a single lifetime, but across multiple lifetimes. As the Buddhist philosopher Śāntideva, in his *Bodhicaryāvatāra*, memorably characterizes the *saṃsāric* predicament of sentient beings: "Hoping to escape suffering, it is to suffering that they run. In the desire for happiness, out of delusion, they destroy their own happiness, like an enemy" (Śāntideva 1995: 7).[2] *Saṃsāra* here includes a mode of psychological functioning wherein our attempts to attain happiness and avoid suffering are self-defeating.[3] The root causes of this sorry situation are the three poisons of attraction (*rāga*), aversion (*dveṣa*), and delusion (*moha*), which are dysfunctional forms of our basic conative framework, on the basis of which we respond to changing circumstances, seeking happiness and trying to avoid suffering. Because these basic forms of reaction are distorted or dysfunctional, as long as we are bound to them, our attempts to secure the lasting happiness we desire are doomed to fail. And yet, on the Buddhist view, because suffering is dependently originated (*pratītyasamutpanna*)—that is, it arises on the basis of specific causes and conditions—by understanding and removing its causes, one can be free of suffering.

Thus, action (*kriyā, karman*) plays a central role in the classical Buddhist analysis of the human situation and its prescribed path to liberation from *saṃsāra*. In the *Majjhima Nikāya* the Buddha states, "Student, beings are owners of their actions, heirs of their actions; they originate from their actions, are bound to their actions, have their actions as their refuge. It is action that distinguishes beings as inferior and superior" (Bodhi 2005: 166).[4] Individual beings perform actions, but also originate (in part) from their own prior actions. They are bound to their actions both in the sense that they are heirs of their prior actions, and in that they cannot escape the future consequences of their actions. Finally, the moral quality of their actions, rather than social or religious categories such as caste, marks individuals as superior or inferior. Indeed, only in the moral quality of one's actions can one find refuge from the suffering of *saṃsāra*.

The name for this extended feedback loop between the quality of actions and the downstream effects of those actions for the agent is *karma-vipāka* ('action and result'). That is, the Buddhist theory of karma deals with the short- and long-term effects of actions for the agent of those actions. *Kuśala* (skillful, wholesome) actions will tend to have positive consequences for oneself, while *akuśala* (unskillful, unwholesome) actions will tend to have negative consequences. It is thus claimed that there is a reliable causal connection between *kuśala* action and long-term well-being, a claim that is at the center of Buddhist ethics and soteriology. It should be noted here that the term '*kuśala*' (Pāli: *kusala*) is used in a variety of ways in Buddhist texts. The term can mean 'healthy,' 'good,' 'blameless,' 'skillful,' 'conducive to happiness,' 'harmless,' or 'conducive to liberation' (Cousins 1996).[5] Further, both actions and the psychological states that are the roots of action can be *kuśala* or *akuśala*. For instance, in the Pāli canon we see, "whatever action is of the nature (*pakataṃ*) of greed (or hatred, or delusion), born of greed, caused by it, that action is [*akusala*], it is with fault/blameable (*sāvajjaṃ*), it ripens in pain (*dukkhavipākaṃ*)" (Harvey 2010/2011: 178). In contrast, an action that arises from non-greed (etc.) "is [*kusala*], it is faultless/blameless, it ripens in happiness" (Harvey 2010/2011: 178). *Kuśala* roots and actions arise from wise attention (Pāli: *yoniso-manasikāra-hetuka*) which is directly linked to notions of skill and skillfulness. As L. S. Cousins (1996) points out, *kuśala* has as one of its root meanings 'intelligent,' 'produced by skill,' and 'produced from wisdom' and these connotations are included in the moral sense of the term. Wise attention is a trainable quality of mind, indeed a quality that Buddhism is centrally concerned with training. The practitioner can be more or less adept in her deployment of attention and this is directly linked to the moral qualities of her actions and states of mind. Moreover, she can be more or less skillful in her moral discipline (*śīla*), which is again linked to how well trained and controlled is her mind. As Peter Harvey puts it,

> *Kusala* states come from wise skill and contribute to wise skill, and are both morally and spiritually wholesome: morally faultless, nourishing further wholesome states, healthily without greed, hatred or delusion, and contributing to the end of these. They bring no harm to anyone, and lead to happiness for the agent of them.
>
> *Harvey 2010/2011: 207–208[6]*

Furthermore, the Buddhist theory of karma emphasizes the deep interdependence of action and character. *Kuśala* actions plant karmic seeds (*bīja*) in one's psyche that, given the appropriate internal and external conditions, grow into negative consequences (*phala* 'fruit,' *vipāka* 'result') for the agent. That is, one's actions affect one's character, habits, and dispositions over the long term. As a part of Buddhist moral psychology, karma theory focuses on the often subtle and intricate feedback mechanisms in the human psyche, emphasizing the ways in which action, intention, and character are mutually reinforcing (MacKenzie 2013).

Now, as mentioned in section 3.1, a central factor in the Buddhist account of the nature and moral quality of action is *cetanā*, 'intending' or 'volition.' Again, the Buddha states that "Intending (*cetanā*) is *karma* … Having intended, one acts through body, speech, and mind" (Bodhi 2005: 146).[7] Likewise, the Abhidharma philosopher, Vasubandhu, says that *karma* is "*cetanā* and that which arises from it," that is, further actions of body, speech, and mind (Pradhan 1975: 192).[8] What, then, is *cetanā* in Buddhist thought? Most fundamentally, it is the orientation of a mind or mental event (*citta*) toward an object or goal (Meyers 2014: 46). This can include both conscious, reflective goal-orientation as well as more basic appetitive or conative impulses. Thus, both feeling hungry at the sight of an apple and subsequently deciding to take a bite are instances of *cetanā*. Further, in Buddhist Abhidharma, *cetanā* is one of the omnipresent mental factors (*caitta*) alongside hedonic valence (*vedanā*), cognition (*saṃjñā*), attention (*manasikāra*), and sensory contact (*sparśa*). On this view, each moment of experience is grounded in and arises from on-going (somato)-sensory contact between the sentient being and its environment and is structured by affective, cognitive, conative, and attentional factors. These factors, while analytically divisible, are mutually specifying and reinforcing, and typically operate below the level of reflective attention.

When it comes to understanding the nature of action, Abhidharma thinkers distinguished two types. First is the volition or intending itself (*cetanākarman*), seen as a form of mental action. This category of mental actions includes deliberation (*gaticetanā*), decision (*niścayacetanā*), and movement volition (*kiraṇacetanā*). Second is action issuing from volition (*cetanayitvākarman*). This category includes bodily actions (*kāyakarman*) and vocal actions (*vākkarman*). On this account, an individual may find herself, for instance, desiring a mango in a market, but realizing she has no money. She may then consider stealing the mango and, surmising that no one is looking, form the intention to steal it. And yet, perhaps out of fear of being caught, she may not be able to get her hand to reach out and grab the mango. Within a few seconds, however, she has formed a proper movement volition, and her hand darts out, grabs the mango, and she leaves the store having successfully stolen the irresistible fruit. In this scenario, she has experienced a basic attraction to the mango, deliberated, decided, formed an intention to move her body, and engaged in the relevant bodily actions. Moreover, from a Buddhist point of view, her actions have an undeniable moral quality. Her intention to steal is itself morally unwholesome (*akuśala*), as is her subsequent bodily action of stealing. According to the Sautrāntika school of

Abhidharma, both the intending and the subsequent theft plant seeds (*bīja*), which then 'per-fume' or condition (*vāsanā*) her psyche. When the relevant future conditions arise, these karmic seeds will bear fruit (*vipākaphala*) as negative karmic consequences for her as the agent of the unwholesome actions. In effect, what these Buddhist thinkers appear to be describing is a pro-cess of psychological conditioning, whereby an agent's intentions and actions shape her char-acter in positive or negative ways, and which lead her to have certain positive or negative types of experiences (MacKenzie 2013).

A central idea in the Buddhist project is that an understanding of the dependent arising of suffering will allow practitioners to act more effectively so as to reduce or avoid further suffering. In addition, methods of cultivation (*bhāvana*) with regard to one's own mental and bodily states, processes, and habits is thought to increase one's self-awareness and capacity for self-control. On the classical Abhidharma view, the cultivation of mindfulness (*smṛti*) is closely linked to ethical vigilance (*apramāda*) and insight (*vipaśyana*) (Dunne 2011). The basis of the method of mindfulness is the development of attention regulation through the cultivation of *smṛti* (focus or attentional stability) and *samprajanya* (meta-awareness or introspective vigilance). *Smṛti* is the capacity to hold one's attention on an object, such as the breath or bodily sensations. *Samprajanya* is the capacity to monitor the quality of one's focus on the object of attention. In cultivating the joint operation of *smṛti* and *samprajanya*, the practitioner is supposed to develop a calm, focused mind and the increased level of attention to her mental life is supposed to bring a clearer comprehension of her own mental processes. This leads to the cultivation of *apramāda* (ethical vigilance or heedfulness). Here the increased awareness of one's intentions and posi-tive and negative mental states allows one better to keep actions of body, speech, and mind in accord with one's ethical commitments and spiritual goals. Last, one develops penetrating insight (*vipaśyana*) into the impermanent, unsatisfactory, and selfless nature of the phenomena constituting one's mind-body complex (*nāma-rūpa*).

Furthermore, this process of *bhāvana* involves the intentional cultivation of a range of posi-tive traits and capacities, such as mindfulness (*smṛti*), confidence or faith (*śraddhā*), energy (*vīrya*), concentration (*samādhi*), and wisdom (*prajñā*). In addition, increased awareness and self-control are linked to development of the cardinal virtues of benevolence (*maitrī*), compassion (*karuṇā*), sympathetic joy (*muditā*), and equanimity (*upekṣā*). In short, there is fundamental connection between attentional, affective, and conative self-regulation and the cultivation of virtue as well as psychological and spiritual freedom.

3.3 Actions, agency, agents

The above account makes liberal reference to intentions, actions, agents, and various capacities— attention, deliberation, decision, self-control—associated with agency. Yet, this account of the Buddhist path as one in which individuals, through training, come to gain increasing awareness and self-mastery, leading ultimately to awakening (*bodhi*) or spiritual freedom, seems to be in sig-nificant tension with the central Buddhist doctrine of *anātman* or no-self. As the *Vissudhimagga* boldly states, "There is suffering but none who suffer, there is action but no agent, there is *nibbāna* but no one who is released, there is a Path [to release] but no goer on it" (Buddhagosa 1991: 97).

The doctrine of no-self (*anātman*) is perhaps the best known and most controversial aspect of Buddhist thought. The understanding and philosophical deployment of this doc-trine varies significantly in the Buddhist tradition. Here I will focus on what Mark Siderits (1997) terms "Buddhist Reductionism" associated primarily with Abhidharma.[9] First and foremost, the doctrine of no-self is a rejection of the *ātman*, the enduring substantial self. On this view, the 'self' (*ātman*) is not just another term for the empirical person (*pudgala, jīva*), but is rather the substantial, essential core of the person—the inner self whose existence grounds the identity of the person. Within the Brahmanical religious and philosophical traditions, the *ātman* is generally given a strongly metaphysical interpretation. It is the unitary, essentially unchanging, eternal, spiritual substance that is said to be one's true self. However, the ultimate target of the theory of no-self is not just the rarefied spiritual conception of self commonly defended by various Brahmanical schools. It includes any notion of the self as a distinct enduring thing.

Rejecting the existence of the substantial self, "Buddhist Reductionists hold, then, that the existence of a person just consists in the occurrence of a causal series of psycho-physical elements" (Siderits 2016: 265). These psycho-physical elements are grouped into five *skandhas* (bundles or aggregates): material form (*rūpa*), affect (*vedanā*), perception and cognition (*saṃjñā*), conditioning and volition (*saṃskāra*), and consciousness (*vijñāna*). The *skandhas* are not to be taken as independent things, but instead are seen as interdependent aspects of a causally and functionally integrated psycho-physical (*nāma-rūpa*) system or process (*skandhasantāna*, an 'aggregate-stream' or 'bundle-continuum'). The dynamic system of the *skandhas* has no enduring self at its center, and the system itself is not an enduring substance. Rather it is a complex process ultimately composed of ephemeral physical and mental events.

On the Buddhist Reductionist analysis, the existence of the individual person just consists in the existence the right kind of system of subpersonal events. Persons are conventionally real (*saṃvṛtisat*), but not ultimately, irreducibly real (*paramārthasat*). Furthermore, given their rejection of the enduring substantial self and their reductionist account of persons, it should not come as a surprise that Buddhist Reductionists also reject agent causality. Ontologically, there being no enduring substantial entity that could exercise agent-causal power, our naive sense that we and others are such agents is an illusion. Just as Buddhist Reductionist thinkers reject the self and reduce the person to a complex stream of events, so too they will give an account of action, not in agent-causal, but in event-causal terms. For instance, Vasubandhu in chapter 9 of the *Abhidharmakośa-bhāṣya* confronts the objection:

> [Opponent:] If there is no self, who is the agent of an action, and who is the recipient of the consequences of the action?
> [Vasubandhu:] What do you mean by "agent" and "recipient?"
> [Opponent:] He who acts is the agent; he who receives is the recipient ... In common usage, for example, Devadatta is said to have the independent power of bathing, sitting, walking, and so on.
> [Vasubandhu:] What being are you calling "Devadatta?" Is he the self? But that's just what you have to prove! Now, is he the totality of the five aggregates? We would consider that to be the agent. Action is of three types: bodily, vocal, and mental. Bodily action is dependent on the functioning of the mind. The functioning of the mind as regards the body is dependent on its own causes in the same way. Nothing has any kind of independence ... Whatever is the principal cause of an action, that is called the "agent." And the self has no causal efficacy at all. Therefore, the self should not be considered an agent. From memory arises intention; from intention, thought; from thought, exertion; from exertion, a wind in the body; and from this wind comes the action. What does the self do in this process?
>
> *Goodman 2009: 305*

According to Vasubandhu, then, the locus of agency is not an enduring self, but a highly complex psycho-physical system (the 'five aggregates'). Despite our sense that proper names, the first-person pronoun, and terms like 'agent' refer to an enduring self that is the locus of experience and will, these terms in fact refer to an interlocking network of events. In explaining action, we need only refer to the mental and physical events (memories, intentions, bodily impulses) that arise within a relatively causally and functionally integrated system. As Vasubandhu asks, "What does the self do in this process?"

On the Buddhist analysis, the sense of being a stable self arises from and is sustained by a complex set of impersonal causes and conditions, which are not transparent to the system itself. The sense of self functions as a kind of user illusion and it is ultimately maladaptive according to Buddhist thought. The system comes to represent and experience itself as if there were a homuncular, enduring self that is an owner, subject, and agent. Yet, this representation of a self obscures the complex psycho-physical processes that actually drive experience and action.

In this regard, then, Buddhist thinkers like Vasubandhu are similar to contemporary skeptics concerning the experience of agency. For example, Daniel Wegner writes:

> The real causal sequence underlying human behavior involves a massively complicated set of mechanisms … Each of our actions is really the culmination of an intricate set of physical and mental processes … The illusion of conscious will may be a misapprehension of the mechanistic causal relations underlying our own behavior that comes from looking at ourselves by means of a mental explanatory system. We don't see our own gears turning because we're busy reading our minds.
>
> *Wegner 2002: 26–27*

For both Wegner and Vasubandhu, our experience of ourselves as conscious agents obscures the incredibly complex causes and conditions that give rise to our actions. For Vasubandhu, agency is a psycho-physical process with no substance at its base or center. "From memory," he writes, "arises intention; from intention, thought; from thought, exertion; from exertion, a wind in the body; and from this wind comes the action" (Goodman 2009: 305). The self is not the agent. If one wants to use the term 'agent,' on Vasubandhu's account, one can apply the term to the complex system or process as a whole, or to the principal cause of the action. What counts as the agent will be a matter of general usage or explanatory utility, but in either case, there is no substantial thing that is the agent. Furthermore, both thinkers agree that we interpret both others and ourselves through the framework of agency. Our (mis-)interpretation of ourselves and others as enduring, conscious, agential selves is of a piece. Indeed, according to Vasubandhu, the fundamental basis for our false construction of the world of everyday experience is the representational (*vijñapti*) construction of entities (*bhava-kalpanā*) such as the self, others, and objects.

The Buddhist Reductionist account of agentless agency (Repetti 2017) involves a strategy of stepwise reduction. First, the naive experience and discourse of enduring agential selves is reductively analyzed in terms of complex impersonal psycho-physical systems (the five aggregates). On this analysis, there is no enduring self and no centralized locus of agency. Instead, agency is explained in terms of the causal and functional connections within the system and between the system and its environment. Second, the psycho-physical system itself is analyzed into ontologically simple, momentary mental and physical events called *dharmas*. This is the level of fundamental ontology (*paramārthasat*), relative to which categories such as 'person,' 'agent,' 'psycho-physical system,' or 'stream of consciousness' (*cittasantāna*) are treated as pragmatic constructs (*saṃvṛtisat*).

3.4 Wisdom and skillful means

As discussed in section 3.2, on the Buddhist account, a morally fitting action (or habit, trait, etc.) is termed *kuśala*, while an unfitting or inappropriate action is *akuśala*. More specifically, *kuśala* action involves a sensitive responsiveness to the agent's situation and integrates attentional, cognitive, affective, and motivational factors. The morally adept agent is attentive to the morally salient features of the situation, including her own thoughts, feelings, desires, and so on. She has an accurate cognitive grasp of the situation. Her affective response is appropriate and she is motivated to act virtuously in the situation at hand. For instance, the agent senses and attends to her friend's distress, understands the problem, feels compassion, and is motivated to help in a way that will ease her friend's suffering. Moreover, note that the fundamental criterion here is the mitigation of suffering and the facilitation of genuine happiness (*sukha*) and freedom (*mukti*).

In addition, in this account, there is a tight connection between skillfulness and *wisdom* (*prajñā*). Wisdom here is first and foremost deep insight into the impermanent (*anitya*), unsatisfactory (*duḥkha*), and selfless or insubstantial (*anātman*) nature of reality. This wisdom guides and constrains the development and exercise of the cardinal virtues, such as the four immeasurable qualities benevolence, compassion, sympathetic joy, and equanimity mentioned above. Furthermore, in the later Mahāyāna tradition, the ideal agent or *bodhisattva* (being aimed at awakening) is characterized by the perfection of great compassion (*mahā-karuṇā*), and skillful means (*upāya-kauśalya*). Grounded in an altruistic concern to liberate all beings (*bodhicitta*), the bodhisattva path is constituted by the cultivation of the six perfections (*pāramitā*) of generosity (*dāna*), moral discipline (*śīla*), forbearance (*kṣānti*), effort (*vīrya*), meditative stability (*dhyāna*), and wisdom (*prajñā*). The sixth perfection of wisdom is often considered the highest of the virtues and concerns the cultivation and integration of theoretical understanding, experiential insight, and practical wisdom. As in the earlier tradition, wisdom here serves to guide and unify the other perfections. *The Perfection of Wisdom in Eight Thousand Lines* states:

> For this perfection of wisdom directs the six perfections, guides, leads, instructs, and advises them, is their genetrix and nurse. Because if they are deprived of the perfection of wisdom, the first five perfections do not come under the concept of perfections, and they do not deserve to be called "perfections."
>
> *Wright 2009: 218*

Development in wisdom also includes the cultivation of skillful means (*upāya-kauśalya*). The *Vimalakīrti Sūtra* states, "Wisdom not integrated with skillful means is bondage, but wisdom integrated with skillful means is liberation. Skillful means not integrated with wisdom is bondage, but skillful means integrated with wisdom is liberation" (Thurman 1976: 46). *Upāya-kauśalya* (or *upāya* for short) here is a form of practical wisdom, especially concerning how best to facilitate awakening in others. In the ethical context, *upāya* is a sensitive responsiveness to the concrete moral situation. It is a form of moral skillfulness that goes beyond the mere application of rules or precepts, and indeed is the aspect of wisdom needed to discern when rules or precepts are permissibly broken. In the context of teaching the *dharma*, *upāya* involves the ability to find the right teaching and the right method of teaching for the particular needs, temperament, and situation of the students (see Garfield and Priest, Chapter 1 in this volume).

In the *Vimalakīrti Sūtra*, the bodhisattva Vimalakīrti, though a layperson, is depicted as the model of the union of nondualistic wisdom and skillful means. Indeed, his skillfulness is so great that he is able to teach the *dharma* to everyone from prostitutes to highly advanced monks (see Garfield and Priest, Chapter 1 in this volume). In his everyday life, he moves fluidly and effectively in the worlds of business, politics, education, the arts, religion, and even the seedier domains of life. In each context, Vimalakīrti is depicted as flexibly responsive to the situation at hand, the roles of those involved, the needs and interests of others, and the often subtle ways the situation affords opportunities to teach the *dharma* in words or in action. In particular, he encourages others to move beyond the four forms of attachment traditionally delineated in the Buddhist tradition. He encourages laypeople to give up attachment to sensual pleasures. He encourages his fellow spiritual practitioners to let go of attachment to fixed views that hinder their practice or teaching; attachment to ethical precepts and rituals that compromise skillful responsiveness; and attachment to fixed views of self and others that obscure the deeper truth of nonduality. In each case, the unskillful is seen as a form of rigidity or attachment to fixed patterns of thought, perception, or action, while the skillful is seen as a form of flexible responsiveness to the needs of others in the situation at hand.

3.5 Selflessness and liberated action

As we have seen so far in our discussion, in Buddhist thought, the ideal agent's attentional, cognitive, affective, and motivational capacities are so refined that she is able to respond flexibly to the situation at hand with great wisdom and compassion. And this optimal agency is the result of training in the Buddhist eightfold path. That is, through the cultivation of wisdom (*prajñā*), ethical discipline (*śīla*), and meditation (*bhāvanā*), one attenuates *akuśala* states, such as greed or hatred, and develops *kuśala* states such as equanimity or kindness. Indeed, the highly developed agent is said to be spontaneous (*ayatnakṛta*) and effortless (*anābhogaṃ*) in her actions.

Now, given the above description of the ideal agent, it may seem that the Buddhist account involves a fairly straightforward form of cultivated expertise, like the virtuoso musician who has trained diligently for decades and can now 'just play' spontaneously, effortlessly, yet expertly. Things are not so straightforward, however, because on the Buddhist account, awakened or ideal agency is fundamentally different from everyday agency. Awakened action is *radically spontaneous*. An awakened being acts utterly without *cetanā* (volition, intention), without effort, and without discursive-conceptual deliberation (*vikalpa*). As the *Ratnagotravibhāga* puts it, a Buddha's action is "free from constructive thought, without effort, and has nothing on which to stand, inside or out" (Griffiths 1994: 105). On this view, an awakened being does not form an explicit intention or will to benefit other beings. Rather, she spontaneously responds to the needs of other beings. Indeed, it is not just that the awakened individual *need not* act from *cetanā*, she *cannot*. *Cetanā*, recall, drives karma and an awakened one has, by definition, transcended the production of both good and bad karma. On the Buddhist view, awakened activity is *trans-volitional*. But if awakened activity does not arise from *cetanā*, from what does it arise? According to one text, it arises from an "awareness that does what needs to be done" (*kṛtyānuṣṭhānajñāna*) that enacts "what benefits beings in all world-realms" (Griffiths, 1994: 101).

Awakened action is effortless in that, because it is optimally skillful, the action is unforced. Here effort is only required if there is a potential mismatch between the nature of the situation and the response. In the case of ideal action, however, the response fits smoothly with the situation and so the action has an effortless or unforced quality. However, effort here should not be confused with energy or vigor (*vīrya*) which is one of the six virtues the awakened individual has, by definition, perfected. Indeed, a Buddha is traditionally said to display boundless, unimpeded energy directed at the benefit of all sentient beings. Awakened action is free from constructive thought and deliberation, because a Buddha does not need to deliberate or plan the best course of action. Instead she *sees* what needs to be done and does it. On this account, deliberation, thought, and planning are done under conditions of practical uncertainty, whereas the ideal agent always knows the right thing to do. Finally, an awakened agent "has nothing on which to stand, inside or out" (Griffiths 1994: 105). That is, a Buddha does not rely on reified constructions of self, other, or world. Ordinary agents rely on conventional constructions such as 'self,' 'agent,' 'object,' or 'other.' A Buddha, in contrast, sees things as they are (*yathābhūtadarśanam*), and so sees beyond these constructs and does not deploy them as a basis for action.

There is thus a sharp discontinuity between awakened, and even highly skillful yet unawakened action. Recall that, on Vasubandhu's account of agency, there is a gap between an agent's first-person experience and naive understanding of her own agency, and the correct, reductionist explanation of that agency. An individual will typically experience herself as an enduring self, the locus of will. Yet, on the Buddhist Reductionist account, there is no such entity. Instead there is a complex system of momentary mental and physical events unfolding according to the principle of dependent co-arising. Despite how it seems from the first-person point of view, terms such as 'I' or 'agent' do not refer to a self, but rather refer to the impersonal psycho-physical continuum of events. There is thus a gap between the naive first-person experience of agency and the reductionist third-person explanation of it. However, Vasubandhu admits that normal agency might require the naive illusion of the agential self. First, the sense of self (*ahaṃkāra*) arises causally within a particular continuum and tracks the events within that continuum and not those in other continua.[10] A normal agent must be able to tell the difference between 'her own' aggregates and those of 'others,' otherwise coherent action would be compromised. Second, without a sense of diachronic identity, a normal agent would have no basis for prudential concern. Yet, prudential concern over the positive and negative karmic consequences of one's actions, and the promised benefit of the Buddhist path itself seem to require the ability to identify with one's own future. Thus, Vasubandhu argues that this basic sense of self is morally neutral (*avyākṛta*) because it is consistent with and can support skillful conduct (Hanner 2018).

In contrast, for an awakened agent, there is no gap between her experience and how things are. She therefore does not rely on a constructed sense of self and other to underpin skillful agency. In place of a sense of synchronic and diachronic personal identity, there is an awareness of what needs to be done. In place of explicit volition or intention, there is spontaneous wise and compassionate responsiveness. All this, of course, raises a host of interpretive and philosophical problems that are beyond the scope of this chapter (see Griffiths 1994; Garfield 2006; Finnigan 2011). In the present context, the central question concerns what, according to the Buddhist tradition, makes it possible to move from unawakened to awakened agency?

Here the tradition offers a range of positions on a spectrum between what John Dunne calls *constructivist* and *innateist* positions (Dunne 2011). According to the constructivist view, a practitioner must remove negative traits such as greed and ignorance, as well as develop or construct positive traits such as generosity or wisdom. Yet, if sentient beings are so deeply mired in ignorance and maladaptive states, how is this development possible? On this view, human beings possess a set of basic learning and self-regulatory capacities that allow them to both change maladaptive traits and habits and to acquire new more adaptive traits and habits. In this way the transition from normal to awakened agency is consistent with Hubert Dreyfus's account of expertise (Dreyfus and Dreyfus 1999).[11] A novice practitioner will need to deploy explicit rules and precepts (such as the five Buddhist ethical precepts) as a guide and external check on her unwholesome tendencies. Through diligent training, the practitioner is able to attenuate her negative tendencies and internalize and habituate new more wholesome tendencies. Over time the precepts serve less as external checks or guardrails and more as internalized maxims that facilitate skillful coping with complex situations. As the practitioner moves toward expertise, the precepts and other explicit rules recede into the background, now serving primarily as domains of ethical salience, rather than checks on negative tendencies. As Dreyfus and Dreyfus characterize the expert:

> The expert not only sees what needs to be achieved; thanks to a vast repertoire of situational discriminations he sees immediately what to do. Thus, the ability to make more subtle and refined discriminations is what distinguishes the expert from the proficient performer … This allows the immediate intuitive situational response that is characteristic of expertise.
>
> *Dreyfus and Dreyfus 1999: 109*

On the constructivist account, the intuitive situational responsiveness of an awakened agent is a product of long training in which the practitioner develops qualities that were not present in her untrained state. Just as the chess master is not born knowing how to play chess, an individual is not born knowing how to be a Buddha.

In contrast, on the innateist view, the qualities of an awakened agent are thought to be (somehow) already present, even in the unawakened. The movement from unawakened, unskillful agency to awakened, optimally skillful agency does not fundamentally involve the development of new qualities. Rather, it is a matter of progressively clearing away *obscurations* of the incipient awakened qualities present in the agent. As we find in the *Aṅguttara Nikāya* of the Pāli Canon, "Luminous, monks, is this mind. And it is defiled by adventitious defilements" (Bodhi 2012: 97).[12] Hence, on this model, one does not *acquire* qualities such as wisdom and compassionate responsiveness. Rather, one *removes* negative traits such as ignorance and indifference, thereby allowing the innate qualities of awareness and empathy to unfold. Recall that, on the Buddhist account, the individual is a complex psycho-physical system dynamically evolving depending on a complex network of endogenous and exogenous causes and conditions. Below the level of personal self-representation, the system is characterized by awareness and spontaneous perceptual, affective, and cognitive responsiveness. These endogenous capacities are constitutive of the system as a sentient individual and it is these capacities that are developed into awakened forms of agency. On most versions of the innateist view, there is still ample room for development since the innate qualities are understood to be in incipient form. Buddhist practice, then, is a two-pronged process of removing obscurations and cultivating innate positive qualities of mind and heart. Yet, the basic qualities that constitute awakened agency are quite general. When it comes to specific skills, such as the ability to effectively teach a wide range of students, traditional forms of skill acquisition may be required. An awakened being may naturally display her innate qualities of awareness and compassion, but this does not entail that she will know how to perform brain surgery without medical training. Thus, in the context of an innateist view, skillful *means* (*upāya-kauśalya*) may be acquired, but fundamental awakened qualities are only developed and expressed.

3.6 Conclusion

Indian Buddhist philosophers are committed to the reality of karma, the causal efficacy and moral centrality of intending, the effectiveness of sustained long-term practice, and the non-existence of any substantial self as a locus of agency. This seemingly inconsistent set of commitments is reconciled through a rejection of an ontology of enduring substances in favor of an ontology of momentary, dependently originated events. There is no substantial, enduring self or agent, because there are no enduring substances at all. What we think of as selves or agents are then reductively analyzed as highly complex systems of mental and physical events. Among these events are intendings which, when coupled in the right way with other mental and physical events, can serve as the principal causes of subsequent mental and physical events. Mental and physical events caused in the right way by intendings are actions. Therefore, our first-person sense that we are enduring selves and agents is mistaken. Despite this mistaken self-understanding, there are processes that are rightly called actions, and mental events play an ineliminable causal role in these processes. On this account, karma refers to both intendings and to the long-term causal connections between certain types of mental or physical events at one time and those at a future time within the same system. Buddhist practice draws on the basic cognitive, affective, attentional, and self-regulative capacities of human beings in order to transform the functioning of those capacities away from maladaptive, dysfunctional patterns of experience and action, and toward more adaptive and functional patterns. This entails an increase in flexible skillful responsiveness toward an ideal of optimal skillfulness that, according to these thinkers, is in some ways quite different from normal forms of agency.

Notes

1 This work was supported in part by the endowment fund of the Colorado State University Department of Philosophy.
2 *Bodhicaryāvatāra* I.28.
3 Here I am concerned with the psychological dimension of *saṃsāra* in that psychological states such as craving (*tṛṣṇā*) and attachment (*upādāna*) play a crucial role in driving the process of *saṃsāra*. For further discussion of the psychological dimension of *saṃsāra* see Garfield (2015, ch. 9) and MacKenzie (2013).
4 *Majjhima Nikāya* 135: III 202–206.
5 The Pāli English Dictionary defines *kusala* as: "clever, skilful, expert; good, right, meritorious."
6 Damien Keown (1992: 119) distinguishes what he calls the 'technical' and the 'moral' senses of *kusala*. He argues against translating *kusala* as 'skillfull' in a moral context and prefers 'virtuous' or 'good.' He sees little conceptual connection between these two senses. In contrast, I side with Cousins (1996) and Harvey (2010/2011) in seeing these senses as intertwined. At the root of the connection is an appeal to the central importance of wise attention and a well-trained, well-controlled, and wise mind more generally as the root of good action. To call an action *kusala*, then, includes a sense that it is 'intelligent,' 'produced by skill,' or 'produced from wisdom.' Thus my account of the moral sense of *kusala* includes an important conceptual connection to notions of skill and skillfulness that are also reflected in the Sanskirt and Pāli etymologies of the term.
7 *Anguttara Nikāya (AN)* 6.63 (A iii.415).
8 *Abhidharmakośabhāṣya (AKBh)* IV.1b (192.9).
9 Elements of Buddhist Reductionism can be found in both Sarvāstivāda and Sautrāntika schools of Abhidharama. See, for example, Vasubandhu's *Abhidharmakośa-bhāṣya* (Pradhan 1975) for the articulation and defense of a number of ideas associated with Buddhist Reductionism.
10 *AKBh* IX, p. 476.
11 My claim here is not that the Buddhist constructivist account is the same as that of Dreyfus or Heidegger, but only that it is consistent with his general account of the acquisition of expertise.
12 *AN* I. 49 (9). Of course, the proper interpretation of this and other similar passages is a matter of dispute. However, proponents of innateist views often cite them in support of their account.

References

Bodhi, B. (ed.) (2005) *In the Buddha's words: an anthology of discourses from the Pāli Canon*. Boston, MA: Wisdom Publications.
Bodhi, B. (trans.) (2012) *The numerical discourses of the Buddha: a translation of the* Aṅguttara Nikāya. Boston, MA: Wisdom Publications.
Buddhaghosa. (1991) *The path to purification* (*Visuddhimagga*). (Bhikkhu Ñānamoli, trans.) Sri Lanka: Buddhist Publication Society.
Cousins, L. S. (1996) "Good or skilful? *Kusala* in canon and commentary," *Journal of Buddhist Ethics* 3, pp. 136–164.
Dreyfus, H. and Dreyfus, S. (1999) "The challenge of Merleau-Ponty's phenomenology of embodiment for cognitive science," in G. Weiss and H. F. Faber (eds.) *Perspectives on embodiment: intersections of nature and culture* (pp. 103–120). New York: Routledge.
Dunne, J. (2011) "Toward an understanding of non-dual mindfulness," *Contemporary Buddhism* 12(1), pp. 71–88.
Finnigan, B. (2011) "How can a Buddha come to act? The possibility of a Buddhist account of ethical agency," *Philosophy East and West* 61(1), pp. 134–160.
Garfield, J. (2006) "Why did Bodhidharma go to the east? Buddhism's struggle with the mind in the world," *Sophia* 45(2), pp. 61–80.
—— (2015) *Engaging Buddhism: why it matters to philosophy*. Oxford: Oxford University Press.
Goodman, C. (2009) "Vasubandhu's *Abhidharmakośa*: the critique of the soul," in W. Edelglass and J. Garfield (eds.) *Buddhist philosophy: essential readings* (pp. 297–308). Oxford: Oxford University Press.
Griffiths, P. (1994) *On being Buddha: the classical doctrine of Buddhahood*. Albany: SUNY Press.
Hanner, O. (2018) "Moral agency and the paradox of self-interested concern for the future in Vasubandhu's *Abhidharmakośabhāṣya*," *Sophia* 57(4), pp. 591–609.
Harvey, P. (2010/2011) "An analysis of factors related to the kusala/akusala quality of actions in the Pāli tradition," *Journal of the International Association of Buddhist Studies* 33(1-2), pp. 175–209.
Keown, D. (1992) *The nature of Buddhist ethics*. London: Palgrave Macmillan.
MacKenzie, M. (2013) "Enacting selves, enacting worlds: on the buddhist theory of karma," *Philosophy East and West* 63(2), pp. 194–212.
Meyers, K. (2014) "Free persons, empty selves: freedom and agency in light of the two truths," in M. Dasti (ed.) *Free will, agency, and selfhood in Indian philosophy* (pp. 41–67). Oxford: Oxford University Press.
Pradhan, P. (ed.) (1975) *Abhidharmakośabhāṣyam of Vasubandhu* (2nd ed.) Tibetan Sanskrit works series Vol. 8. Patna: K.P. Jayaswal Research Institute.
Repetti, R. (ed.) (2017) *Buddhist perspectives on free will: agentless agency?* New York: Routledge.
Śāntideva. (1995) *The Bodhicaryāvatāra*. (Crosby and Skilton, trans.) New York: Oxford University Press.
Siderits, M. (1997) "Buddhist Reductionism," *Philosophy East and West* 47(4), pp. 455–478.
—— (2016) *Studies in Buddhist philosophy*. Oxford: Oxford University Press.
Thurman, R. (1976) *The holy teachings of Vimalakīrti*. State College: Penn State University Press.
Wegner, D. (2002) *The illusion of conscious will*. Cambridge, MA: MIT Press.
Wright, D. (2009) *The six perfections: Buddhism and the cultivation of character*. New York: Oxford University Press.

4

TECHNĒ IN THE PLATONIC DIALOGUES

Tom Angier

Plato's dialogues are the first systematic philosophical works in the Western tradition, and skill or expertise – or rather the Greek notion of *technē*, from which we derive 'technology', 'technique', etc. – is their central heuristic. When, that is, Socrates[1] sets out – especially in the early dialogues – to test a knowledge-claim, or interrogate some purportedly coherent and well-founded practice, it is usually to the *technē* model that he turns. For instance, the question 'Does the orator know what he is talking about?' is tantamount to asking whether the orator has a *technē*. 'Does the politician know what he is doing?' is tantamount to asking whether the politician has a *technē*. This *technē*-centric approach stands to reason, Socrates maintains, since even at a pre-theoretical level the *technai* (plural of *technē*) constitute an epistemic and practical paradigm. As he remarks to Protagoras:

> When ... the city has to take some action on a building project, we send for builders to advise us; if it has to do with the construction of ships, we send for shipwrights ... But if ... a person not regarded as a craftsman [*dēmiourgon*] tries to advise them, no matter how handsome and rich and well-born he might be, they ... laugh at him and shout him down.
>
> *Protagoras 319b–c*

To contemporary readers, this looks like plain good sense, since as moderns we too are prone to look for the 'experts' when in epistemic or practical difficulty. But Plato's conception and treatment of skill or expertise go against modern expectations in two vital respects.

First, the Greek concept of *technē* has a wider and more diverse extension than any related English concept. It covers the semantic range of 'craft', 'skill', 'art', 'expertise', 'profession', and in fact any ordered, systematic body of knowledge-cum-praxis. True, Socrates often has recourse to crafts that are banausic or artisanal, and that yield a separate, physical product. As Callicles jibes: 'By the gods! You simply don't let up on your continual talk of shoemakers and cleaners, cooks and doctors, as if our discussion were about them!' (*Gorgias* 491a).[2] But Socrates also makes frequent reference to *technai* that go beyond the productive. The dialogues speak often of *technai* whose result (or *ergon*) is either internal to their own activity (such as lyre-playing or dancing), or purely theoretical (such as astronomy or mathematics). Indeed, as I shall document below, it is the purely theoretical *technai* – in particular, mathematics – that function as an epistemic ideal for Socrates. The more a claim or practice approaches the condition of mathematics, the more precise it is, and hence the more reliable – a quality that, as we shall see, is integral to *technē*.[3] In brief, the Platonic dialogues contain an incipient hierarchy of *technai*, which is indexed primarily to the degree of precision and reliability they embody. (I will outline the other generic goods associated with *technē* shortly.)

Second, while ethics and skill or expertise are rarely conjoined in modern philosophy, Plato's interest in *technē* is overwhelmingly ethical. That is, his deployment of the concept is determined largely by his prior interest in virtue (*aretē*, or character excellence). The question which thus preoccupies Socrates throughout the early dialogues, and even later in the Platonic corpus, is: can *aretē* be construed as a *technē*? That is, is there an expertise in virtue? *Prima facie* this is a bizarre question, given the modern tendency to disjoin virtue and skill.[4] But when it is recalled that virtue is Socrates' central concern, the idea of a virtue-*technē* no longer seems so strange. After all, Socrates famously holds that a good man cannot be harmed (*Apology* 30c–d), implying that everyone has overriding reason to be virtuous. He maintains, moreover, that 'with that part [namely, one's soul] corrupted that unjust action harms and just action benefits', one is far worse off than with a corrupted body, since 'the most important thing is not life, but the good life' (*Crito* 47e, 48b). And he holds that '[I] neglected all my own affairs … for so many years while … approaching each one of you like a father or elder brother to persuade you to care for virtue' (*Apology* 31b). Given, then, *aretē*'s overriding value for Socrates, and given that, as we have seen, *technē* is his methodological lodestar, the notion of a *technē* in *aretē* looks eminently attractive: it would, in effect, guarantee the good life. (There remains the prior question of whether such a *technē* is possible: I aim to answer that question over the course of this chapter.)

I have argued, in sum, that although the Platonic dialogues echo modernity's strong affirmation of expertise, they calibrate the latter's nature and role differently. *Technē* picks out a wider range of phenomena than any cognate English concept, and it is subordinated to an ethical project.[5] But why, exactly, is Plato attracted to the *technai* in the first place, especially as a vehicle for exploring the structure of virtue? I have already indicated a partial answer to this: that he saw in them a model of precision [*akribeia*], and that this held out the prospect of virtue approximating an *epistēmē* or 'science'.[6] But this, in turn, needs to be unpacked further: what, exactly, is the good of virtue *qua* science? The answer to this can be elaborated, I think, under five main headings.

First, and at the most general level, a science of virtue would professionalise the ethical life. As Rachana Kamtekar puts matters, 'Describing a new discipline as a *technē* (profession, craft, art) or *epistēmē* (science) is a way of claiming for it a status possessed by better-established practices like medicine' (Kamtekar 2009: 220). Granted, there are passages in the dialogues which caricature the *technai* as merely banausic or artisanal, thereby heaping on them the shame associated with the lower orders and their 'illiberal' pursuits.[7] But these passages are relatively rare, and depend on a tendentious selection of crafts, such as cobbling and blacksmithing. For the most part, acting or speaking *ek technēs* has positive connotations. Well-made products – *technikōs eirgasmena* (*Charmides* 173c) – are to be approved of, and imply approval of their expert makers (cf. *Laws* 921b). As Socrates remarks,

> [I]t is … necessary to investigate first of all whether any one of us is an expert [*technikos*] in the subject we are debating, or not. And if one of us is, then we should listen to him even if he is only one, and disregard the others.
>
> *Laches 184e–5a; cf. Crito 48a–f*

To be *technikos*, moreover, is contrasted in the *Gorgias* with having a mere *empeiria* or 'knack' (see 500a ff., 503c–d): the implication being that a genuine craft or skill is reputable, raising the professional practitioner above the level of a mere amateur. Would it not be good, therefore, if virtue itself were an expert matter, to be taken out of the hands of the mere *empeiros*?

Second, while minimal rational reflection is compatible with practical competence in some areas, the expert or *technikos* still aspires to give a *logos*, or rational account, of his expertise. And the more systematic and precise such an account, the better; hence mathematics is the paradigmatic *technē*. Any *technē* is nonetheless superior to forms of cognition and practice that prescind from rationality altogether. This is why the antithesis of the expert, according to Socrates, is the person who relies solely on a 'divine gift' (*theia moira*). The *enthousiazōn*, or divinely inspired person, finds the rationality and structure of his purported discipline wholly beyond his grasp. In the early dialogue *Ion*, this is characteristic of the eponymous anti-hero, who claims to practise the art of rhapsody, but under Socratic questioning (or *elenchus*) is shown, quite literally, not to know what he is talking about. As Socrates quips, 'that's not a *technē* you've mastered – speaking well about Homer; it's a divine power [*theia dunamis*] that moves you' (533d). And Socrates applies this critique also to the poets: 'none of the epic poets, if they're good', he adjures, 'are so *ek technēs*; they are divinely inspired [*entheoi*], and that is how they utter all those beautiful poems. The same goes for lyric poets' (533e). In fine, the poet 'goes out of his mind and his intellect is no longer in him' (534b), or as the Athenian in the *Laws* charges, 'when a poet takes his seat on the tripod of the Muse, he cannot control his thoughts' (719c). This places poets on the level of 'seers', who, as Socrates asserts in the *Philebus*, 'make their prophecies, not in virtue of any *technē*' (44c; cf. *Apology* 22b–c, *Meno* 99c). Clearly, even if such *enthousiazontes* are capable of impressive results, they do not produce them expertly; they thus make bad models for the virtuous, who should have a rational grasp – akin to the expert – of what they are doing.

Third, and as the above suggests, being able to give a rational account of one's practice – 'And I refuse to call anything that lacks such a *logos* a *technē*', says Socrates (*Gorgias* 465a) – is of a piece with the good of mastery or control. As Martha Nussbaum puts matters, *technē* 'is a deliberate application of human intelligence to some part of the world, yielding some control over *tuchē* [chance]' (Nussbaum 1986: 95). And this contrast between *technē* and *tuchē* occurs often in the Platonic dialogues. As Polus puts it, without any opposition from Socrates: 'experience … causes our times to march along the way of *technē*, where inexperience causes it to march along the way of *tuchē*' (*Gorgias* 448c). In the *Laws*, the Athenian maintains that 'a professional man [*ho echōn tēn technēn*] … could hardly go wrong if he prayed for conditions in which the workings of *tuchē* needed to be supplemented only by his own *technē*' (709d). And Socrates holds that 'it is by virtue of this *technē* [arithmetic] … that a man … has under his control [*hupocheirious*] pieces of knowledge concerning numbers' (*Theaetetus* 198b). It is plain, then, that the rational structure of *technē* is not only a good *per se*, but also a good insofar as it affords the *technitēs* (or expert) mastery over his subject-matter. It thereby affords him, in many cases, mastery over his environment as well. As Socrates summarises things in the *Lysis* (210 a–c):

> In those areas where we really understand something … [t]here we will be free ourselves, and in control of others … But in areas where we haven't got any understanding … there we are going to be subject to the orders of others; there things are not going to be ours.

When it comes, therefore, to the supreme good of virtue, a virtue-*technē* looks highly desirable: for *ex hypothesi* it would enable its practitioners to control the greatest good there is.

Fourth, the above marks of *technē* – namely, professionalism, rationality and control – each undergird a further key value, namely transmissibility. For if *technē* embodies knowledge, and knowledge available to rational reflection, it follows that it can also be transmitted to others – i.e. be both taught and learned. The deep connection between *technē* and education is brought out at many points in the dialogues. Socrates asks, for instance, how one discerns who is most skilled [*technikōtatos*] at gymnastics, and replies: 'Wouldn't it be the man who had studied and practised the *technē* and who had had good teachers in that particular subject?' (*Laches* 185b). He claims that expertise in building requires that 'our teachers have proved to be good and reputable ones' (*Gorgias* 514b–c; cf. *Meno* 90b–c), while at *Phaedrus* 270d, he refers to 'the object regarding which we intend to become *technikoi* and capable of transmitting our expertise'. More famously, during the 'ship of state' passage at *Republic* 488b, Socrates speaks damningly of certain sailors, each of whom thinks that 'he should be the captain, even though he's never learnt the *technē* of navigation, [and] cannot point to anyone who taught it to him'. This internal connection between *technē* and transmissibility is significant, since Socrates repeatedly doubts whether virtue – the most important subject of all – can be taught. As he laments: 'I have often tried to find out whether there were any teachers of [virtue], but in spite of all my efforts I cannot find any' (*Meno* 89e); 'the wisest and best of our citizens are unable to transmit to others the virtues they possess' (*Protagoras* 319e; cf. *Meno* 94b–e). In this context, a virtue-*technē* seems not only desirable, therefore, but also the only real hope of sustaining the ethical well-being of society from one generation to the next.

Fifth and last, the professionalism, rationality, control and transmissibility embodied by the *technai* point to their essential role in securing agreement. Socrates highlights this in the *Euthyphro*, where he cites the *technē* of mathematics as a (if not the) paradigm locus of agreement: 'If you and I', he asks Euthyphro, 'were to differ about numbers as to which is the greater, would this difference make us enemies … or would we proceed to count and soon resolve our difference?' (7b–c). To this rhetorical question he responds: 'if we differed about the larger and the smaller, we would turn to measurement and soon cease to differ … And about the heavier and the lighter, we would resort to weighing and be reconciled' (7c). The implication here is that the more determinate and precise a *technē* is, the more it is a source of consensus. If only, then, the same consensus that reigns in mathematics could be applied to ethics, where dissension and controversy seem most prevalent, and to have the direst effects. And indeed, this appears to be Socrates' own hope, since he poses another rhetorical question shortly afterwards (7d):

> [Are] the just and the unjust, the noble and the shameful, the good and the bad … not the subjects of difference about which, when we are unable to come to a satisfactory decision, you and I and other men become hostile to each other?

The clear upshot is that if virtue were subject to the rigours of a *technē* like mathematics, we would be spared much, even all social disagreement and conflict. While this suggestion is not pursued in the *Euthyphro* itself, it is taken up in the *Protagoras*, whose attempt to construct a virtue-*technē* I will come to next.

All in all, then, I have argued that the great appeal of *technē* lies in its embodiment of a set of epistemic and practical goods – namely, professionalism, rationality, control, transmissibility and agreement – which are both highly prized and not combined elsewhere. The question is whether these goods can be harnessed to virtue itself. This is, after all, Socrates' recurrent and definitive desire. He complains:

> I have had no teacher in this subject … [a]nd yet I have longed after it from my youth
> up … I did not have any money to give the sophists, who were the only ones who
> professed to be able to make a gentleman [*kalos k'agathos*] of me, and I myself, on the
> other hand, am unable to discover the *technē* even now.
>
> *Laches 186c; cf. Apology 20a–c*

The stakes are high, and the resources at hand: what, therefore, is to prevent the construction
of a virtue-*technē*? In what follows, I will outline the Platonic dialogues' two attempts at such
a construction – the first in the *Protagoras*, and the second in the *Republic* – and assess their
respective cogency.

Protagoras is a sophist, i.e. a self-appointed 'wise person', who (as Socrates suggests at *Laches*
186c above) is in business – he charges for his so-called wisdom. The sophists do not claim a
theia moira, or 'divine gift', but are nonetheless pseudo-professionals: they dazzle their customers
with jargon and verbal dexterity, suasive powers that are essentially rhetorical and depend on
flattery.[8] It is against this background that Socrates seeks a truly professional account of virtue
in the *Protagoras*, and its vehicle – following the *Euthyphro*'s propaedeutic account above – is
mathematical. *Contra* the vagaries of sophistic rhetoric, this virtue-*technē* will be impervious to
verbal manipulation, and deliver unimpeachable results by a foolproof method. It is a vision
nicely captured by Nussbaum: '[the] denumerable is the definite, the graspable', she writes,
'therefore also the potentially tellable, controllable; what cannot be numbered remains vague
and unbounded, evading human grasp' (Nussbaum 1986: 107). This vision is echoed, moreover,
in middle and late Plato. In the *Republic*, for instance, Socrates holds that 'the part that puts its
trust in measurement [*metrōi*] and calculation [*logismōi*] is the best part of the soul' (603a). And in
the *Philebus*, he claims that 'The boundless multitude … in any and every kind of subject leaves
you in boundless ignorance … since you have never worked out the amount and number of
anything at all' (17e). Indeed, the *Philebus* even moots the notion that quantification and measurement are essential to *any technē*.[9] Be that as it may, the *Protagoras* places measurement at the
heart of its proposed virtue-*technē*.

What, then, is this *metrētikē technē* or 'measuring expertise' meant to measure? According to
Socrates, it will measure pleasures and pains. It is, in fact, an anticipation of hedonistic utilitarianism, except that its calculus of pleasures and pains operates at an individual, rather than
societal level. The assumption is that pleasure is tantamount to goodness, whereas pain is tantamount to evil; it is virtuous, therefore, to promote the former, and vicious to promote the latter.
Socrates claims, furthermore, that once one knows where the balance of pleasure and pain lies,
one will necessarily act to ensure that pleasure (namely, the good) wins out (or at least, that
pain – the bad – does not). This is because, so he claims, 'knowledge is a fine thing capable of
ruling a person, and if someone were to know what is good and bad, then he would not be
forced to act otherwise than knowledge dictates' (352c). The *metrētikē technē* is, in other words,
a projection of Socratic rationalism, freighted with the high hopes attendant on any form of
rationalism. As Socrates himself puts things, the 'understanding' [*phronēsis*] such a *technē* embodies
'would be sufficient to rescue a person' (352c) – indeed, it would 'save' our lives (356d–e). And
given that this understanding takes a straightforwardly hedonistic (and thus empirical) form, it
will be both transmissible and capable of securing agreement – thereby fulfilling the final two
marks of *technē* outlined above.

Faced with this ambitious project, an immediate objection occurs: surely it is possible, indeed
common, for felt (or merely anticipated) pleasure and pain to overcome knowledge of the
good? We are eminently capable, that is, of opting for pleasures (such as sexual pleasures), even

though we know they will be outweighed by severe pains (such as disease) (see 353c–d). In this way, it is perfectly possible for knowledge to be 'dragged around by other forces, such as desire and pleasure' (352c). And this not only makes a nonsense of Socrates' supposed equation between pleasure and the good, it also scuppers his much-vaunted rationalism. For it seems plain that knowledge *can* be undermined by desire: we are never immune, that is, to *akrasia* or moral 'backsliding', so the kind of motivating power Socrates ascribes to the *metrētikē technē* looks like mere hand-waving. In response to this argumentative assault, however, Socrates makes some deft moves. He denies, crucially, that the purported 'akratic' is overcome by pleasure or pain *simpliciter*. Rather, he is swayed by immediate pleasures and pains, oblivious to or ignorant of the detriment to his overall and long-term pleasure (or at least lack of pain). The good, Socrates holds, is properly equivalent to the latter (354). Hence it is only once one is apprised of such overall and long-term hedonic data that one truly knows where one's good lies. And it is *this* knowledge, Socrates avers, and this knowledge alone, which is proof against *akrasia*. Yet again, we seem back in the rationalist camp: the hedonistic *metrētikē technē* will constitute 'our salvation in life' (356d), jettisoning the 'power of appearance' in favour of the power of truth. Or as Socrates more magniloquently claims, 'What then would save our life? Surely … measurement … In fact, nothing other than arithmetic' (357a).

What are we to make of this proposal? *Prima facie* it appears that Socrates' voice is firmly behind the *metrētikē technē*, and that it constitutes a paradigm case of the professionalism, rationality, control, transmissibility and agreement associated with *technē* in general. But on closer inspection, severe doubts emerge, and on two main fronts. First, hedonism has, both inside and outside the *Protagoras*, only a very dubious Platonic pedigree. Inside the dialogue, Socrates almost always ascribes hedonism to *hoi polloi*, 'the many', or to Protagoras himself (see 353d, 354b–c, 356c). And outside the *Protagoras*, Plato mounts a concerted argument against hedonism. From the early to the late dialogues, he has Socrates deny the identity of pleasure and goodness.[10] Pleasure is consistently characterised either as uniformly bad (e.g., *Philebus* 67a–b; *Laws* 633e, 636c, 714a, 840c), or as evaluatively heterogeneous (e.g., *Phaedo* 83c; *Gorgias* 494e–5a; *Phaedrus* 258e; *Republic* 505b, 509a, 582e; *Philebus* 12c–d, 52c; *Laws* 658e–9a), or as too indeterminate to measure (*Gorgias* 500b, 501a–b, 506d; *Philebus* 31a, 65d). With all this evidence from outside the *Protagoras*,[11] it seems very unlikely – despite some significant dissenting views[12] – that Socrates' voice is genuinely behind the *metrētikē technē*. Its endorsement of hedonism is simply too eccentric in the context of Plato's work as a whole, and hence must find an alternative explanation.

Second, the *Protagoras*' argument against *akrasia* looks not only weak *per se*, but is also superseded, arguably, in the *Republic*. At *Protagoras* 357d–e, Socrates maintains that

> those who make mistakes with regard to the choice of pleasure and pain, in other words, with regard to good and bad, do so because of a lack of knowledge … a lack of knowledge you [namely, Protagoras] agreed was measurement.

Now this position, that knowledge of the good is sufficient for right action, is baseless – unless one also accepts a key tenet of Socratic moral psychology, namely, that all desire is for the good. This tenet is found, for example, at *Meno* 78a and *Gorgias* 468c, and is also enunciated in the *Protagoras*: no one, Socrates asserts, 'willingly makes a mistake or willingly does anything wrong or bad' (345e). This tenet clearly saves a key plank of the *metrētikē technē*, namely, that a correct use of the craft is not only necessary for right action, but also sufficient. The trouble is, however, that we have been given no independent argument for the view that all desire is for the good. Furthermore, this very view may well be abandoned by Plato in the *Republic*. It is here, in book IV, that Socrates' denial of *akrasia* is famously thrown into doubt. For Leontius' perverse desire to look at corpses is presented as forcing him to act 'contrary to rational calculation [*para ton logismon*]' (439e–40b), that is, contrary to what he takes to be right. And this directly impugns Socrates' claim in the *Protagoras* – a claim essential to the success of the *metrētikē technē* – that 'no one who knows or believes that there is something else better than what he is doing, something possible, will go on doing [it]' (358b–c).

So on grounds both of its hedonism, and of its vulnerable stance on *akrasia*, the Protagoras' *metrētikē technē* does not appear to be the virtue-*technē* for which Socrates 'longed after … from [his] youth up' (*Laches* 186c). There is, nonetheless, another candidate for this title, one found in the *Republic*. This is the knowledge-cum-praxis Socrates ascribes to the 'guardian' class, which he refers to explicitly as a *technē*. He speaks, for instance, of 'the *technē* we call justice' (332d), and judges that 'to the degree that the *ergon* of the guardians is most important, it requires … the greatest *technē*' (374e). Sometimes he characterises this expertise simply as 'philosophy', i.e. love of wisdom, but this too is construed as a *technē*: 'Despite her present poor state', he holds, 'philosophy is still more high-minded than these other *technai*' (495d); 'A very few might be drawn to philosophy from other *technai*' (496b). But what, in fine, is this supposed skill? As Rosamund Kent Sprague puts it, it is a 'second-order' skill (Sprague 1976: 68–70, 76), or architectonic *technē*, which takes other *technai* as it object. These latter are the skills practised in Plato's ideal republic, by both the lower orders (the 'provisioners' and 'money-makers'), and the soldier-class of 'auxiliaries'. The virtue of the guardians – namely, justice or *dikaiosunē/dikē* – will consist in arranging the skills of the subordinate classes to achieve a 'kind of consonance and harmony' (430e; cf. 431e–2a). And this harmony will consist, in turn, in each citizen being 'directed to what he is naturally suited for': for it is only given such specialisation – or 'doing the one job [*ergon*] that is his own' – that 'he will become not many but one, and the whole city will itself be naturally one and not many' (423d).

The question remains, however: is this a *technē* specifically of *virtue*? On this score, I submit, there is much room for doubt – and for two main reasons. First, the guardians or 'philosopher-kings' amount to a tiny minority, since not only is their professional training highly demanding, 'they have to have the nature we described, and its parts mostly grow in separation and are rarely found in the same person' (503b; cf. 428e–9a). This goes against the early dialogues' presentation of virtue as universally attainable, or at least as not subject to principled and very severe restrictions. Furthermore, because the *Republic* restricts virtue proper to a small elite, it follows that the vast majority of citizens are effectively the passive objects of the guardians' *technē*. And this too is counter-intuitive: does virtue really consist in treating others *de haut en bas*, as agents most of whom have such limited rational powers that they must be commandeered, and deprived of substantial autonomy? Second and related, the *Republic* does not elaborate virtue *simpliciter*, but rather justice, suggesting that its purpose is not broadly ethical, but instead political. True, Julia Annas argues that we should approach the *Republic* as an ethical work – as many of the ancient commentators did – and bracket the political form of the dialogue.[13] After all, Socrates makes an analogy between the State and the soul, and maintains that the former illustrates the latter (see 368e–9a). But not only does this ignore the points made above, it also fails to acknowledge that the *Republic* never develops the idea of an everyday 'soul-craft' in any detail. Furthermore, it downplays the strong continuities between the *Republic*'s *technē* of justice and the *Statesman*'s 'kingly expertise' [*basilikē technē*], which is clearly political in form.

Even if, however, one thinks the guardians' expertise is genuinely one in virtue, there is reason to think that their education, which includes manifold affective and practical elements – such as listening to the right music, and undergoing the appropriate gymnastic training – cannot properly be understood as a *technē* 'all the way down'. The latter would consist in a cognitive achievement, which, when implemented correctly, would be tantamount to right action (the kind of model of expertise we have seen in the *Protagoras*). But in point of fact, the guardians' *technē* succeeds only on condition that various non-cognitive abilities have already been imparted by early training. Given, furthermore, that the details of how the philosopher-kings grasp the Forms remain notoriously obscure – with Socrates' having to resort to the 'images' of Sun, Line and Cave (see 505–521) – the actual content of their skill seems extremely hard to ascertain. Perhaps that content exists, but so far as the *Republic* is concerned, Socrates never gives it the perspicuous treatment he gives the *metrētikē technē*. At best, and as David Roochnik suggests,[14] the guardians' *technē* appears protreptic, and we will have to look beyond the *Republic* if we want to discover what, exactly, knowledge of virtue consists in.

In the final analysis, therefore, the tantalising prospect of a virtue-*technē* is realised neither in the *Republic*, nor in the *Protagoras*. Despite Socrates' hopes for one in the early dialogues, and the heuristic value he sets on *technē* even as late as the *Statesman*, both the *metrētikē technē* and the guardians' *technē* of justice face too many difficulties to qualify as virtue-*technai*. In the remainder of this chapter, I will argue that this waning of the idea of a *technē* in *aretē* is owing not, however, to peculiarities of either the *Protagoras* or *Republic*. Rather, Socrates' relinquishing of that idea has more to do with structural features of the *technai per se*, features that make them fundamentally inhospitable to virtue. And I will finish by suggesting an avenue for further investigation: namely, that Plato's dialogues do contain material for a systematic knowledge of virtue, but that the latter cannot be construed as a *technē*.

Why, then, might *technē* be essentially the wrong model on which to understand virtue? Three reasons immediately suggest themselves. First, the *technai* are typically narrow in scope, that is, they govern a strictly delimited area of enquiry or practice, and thus have what John Gould calls a 'clearly marked horizon' (Gould 1955: 32). Navigation, for instance, covers sailing ships at sea, while generalship directs armies to victory on land. By contrast, virtue is maximal in scope, since it covers all human activities. This is borne out in early dialogues like the *Laches*, where Socrates concludes that courage involves knowledge of good and evil as a whole – not merely knowledge of some specialism. It is thus difficult to fit virtue into a 'professional' mould, given the latter's narrowness of focus. And this explains, furthermore, why it is hard for virtue to live up to the value of control. For that value presupposes precisely the kind of narrow focus that virtue must forgo. Whereas the well-trained professional can exert a high degree of control over a relatively limited set of variables, the virtuous person must cope with a far more extensive and variegated domain, into which the forces of *tuchē* or chance seem ever likely to insert new variables.[15]

Second, professionals are relatively few in number. We do not expect or need our society to contain numerous cobblers, carpenters, mathematicians, or, for that matter, politicians. They can achieve the goods internal to their respective practices while remaining comparatively rare. By contrast, virtue is a quality both expected and needed in every individual – at least according to Socrates, who, as we have seen, believes that a *technē* of virtue would 'save our lives' (*Protagoras* 356d–e), and that 'it is [not] permitted that a better man be harmed by a worse' (*Apology* 30d). Ideally, then, virtue should be universal, and not restricted to a small pool of experts. But this brings out another and related contrast with *technē*, namely, that the ways virtue and skill are transmitted look markedly different. The typical *technitēs* chooses his profession in early adulthood, dependent on his particular interests and talents, which have developed over time. By contrast, virtue is inculcated from early childhood, whether the individual likes it or not, and is not dependent on his contingent interests or talents.[16] Indeed, if someone thought that virtue were so dependent, they would be guilty of vice.

Third, there is an internal connection between knowledge and action in the case of virtue which seems absent in the case of *technē*. As Laches puts it, the virtuous man has 'render[ed] his own life harmonious by fitting his deeds [*erga*] to his words [*logoi*]' (*Laches* 188d). But this 'fitting' flows from the virtuous man's character; it is not a contingent performance resting on a decision to deploy one's technical know-how. For example, it is perfectly conceivable that an individual both know how to play the flute, and not be motivated to play it most of the time. By contrast, it is untoward, and moreover blameworthy, for a virtuous individual not to instantiate virtue in his actions. Admittedly, Socrates presents those who have mastered the *metrētikē technē* as necessarily motivated to act on it. But this goes against its status as a *technē*, and, as we have seen, such rationalism finds no definitive argumentative support in the *Protagoras*. Similarly, Socrates attributes a *technē* to the guardians in the *Republic*, but what seems to ensure their motivational integrity is precisely the non-cognitive abilities they develop in childhood. Once again, therefore, *technē* is shown to fall short of the knowledge/action holism that is a key mark of virtue.

There are two final, and in my view decisive grounds for the *technai*'s pervasive inhospitability to virtue. First, because the *technai* are narrow or local in scope, they are perforce also narrow in their evaluative purview. As Gould writes, 'the whole horizon of a craftsman is bounded by the limits of his professional occupation: it is not his *business* to be capable of directing what should be done with the product of his skill' (Gould 1955: 32). Indeed, in virtue of this evaluatively limited perspective, an individual *technitēs* may well have to cease practising – at least for a time – in order to ensure the overall or common good. By contrast, it does not make sense for a virtuous individual to put his virtue 'on hold', as it were. Virtue is, as I have outlined, global in scope, and has regard – always and necessarily – for the good *in toto*. Second, whereas *technē* exhibits a subject/object structure – with an individual producing a set of results distinct from himself – virtue exhibits an essentially reflexive structure, where the subject's own soul is at stake. And this shows, perhaps definitively, the inadequacy of the *technē* model: that whereas the *technai* are fundamentally directed outward, virtue is a condition of the subject's own soul, and hence cannot be reified as an object to be 'produced'.[17]

In conclusion, then, I have argued that – despite Socrates' hopes for a *technē* in virtue – neither the *Protagoras* nor the *Republic* manages to supply one. There are at least five substantive reasons for this. The *technai* are too narrow in scope, their practitioners too rare, and their cognition improperly conjoined with their practice. In addition, their evaluative horizon is too limited, and their structure too object-orientated or irreflexive to capture the nature of virtue. Does it follow that the Platonic dialogues simply abandon the project of a knowledge-cum-praxis of virtue? Not so, I would argue. If we leave the *technē* model behind, there are promising vistas ahead. In particular, we should attend to one of Socrates' few claims to knowledge, namely his claim to know 'the erotic things' (*ta erōtika*, mistranslated as 'the art of love').[18] For given Socrates' ideal of virtue as *kalok'agathia* – literally, 'beauty/nobility and goodness' – and given that Plato devotes his great erotic dialogue, the *Symposium*, to the nature of the *kalon* (beauty/nobility), I suggest that eros or love is the best place to start for a true grasp of virtue. It will turn out, indeed, that only *to kalon* – namely, the Form of Beauty/Nobility – has the erotic power to transform the soul, and to convert it to genuine goodness. True, this total transformation excludes the values of professionalism and control, along with the value of transmissibility – for only a direct encounter with *to kalon* can convert the heart. But reason, crucially, has not been jettisoned, since the heart (as Socrates affirms) has its reasons. And mutual acknowledgement of these reasons promises harmony with others.

Notes

1 Socrates was Plato's teacher, and is the principal character in his dialogues.
2 Cf. Alcibiades, Socrates' lover: 'He is always going on about pack asses, or blacksmiths, or cobblers, or tanners' (*Symposium* 221e).

3 David Roochnik dubs the more precise and thus more reliable form of *technē* 'technē1', in contrast to 'technē2', which covers subject-matter that is less fixed and determinate (see Roochnik 1996: ch. 1). Unlike Aristotle, who refers to the former as *epistēmē* ('science'), and only the latter as *technē*, Plato uses *epistēmē* and *technē* almost interchangeably (see Gould 1955: 31; Nussbaum 1986: 94; Roochnik 1996: 90, 113 n. 23, 277; Woodruff 1990: 66). Plato tends to use *dēmiourgia* ('craft', 'handicraft', 'artisanry') to mark out *technai* at the less precise, and typically more manual (or workman-like) end of the spectrum.

4 Julia Annas argues that virtue should be understood as a form of skill (see Annas 2011). But the very fact that her argument is book-length points up their usual estrangement in the modern literature.

5 Plato does speak of the 'craftsman' [*dēmiourgos*] of the universe in the *Timaeus*, thereby deploying *technē* in a grander, metaphysical context. And there is much to be said about why particular practices – especially rhetoric, poetry, prophecy and rhapsody – are suspected of not being *technai* at all. But I cannot address these subsidiary themes in this chapter. On the *Timaeus*, see Carone (2005); on rhetoric as a pseudo-*technē*, see Roochnik (1996: ch. 3). I will touch on the practices of poetry, prophecy and rhapsody (namely, poetry-recitation) below.

6 The English term 'science' is perhaps misleading, since it is often assimilated to the 'hard' sciences (such as physics and chemistry). I intend 'science' in the sense of the German *Wissenschaft*, namely any organised and determinate body of knowledge and practice.

7 It is worth noting that the lower classes in Plato's *Republic* are assigned the menial task of 'provisioning' the *polis* or city-state. For passages that denigrate the relatively unskilled (especially manual) crafts, see *Protagoras* 312b, 318e–f; *Republic* 522b; *Symposium* 203a–f; *Seventh Letter* 341b.

8 The *locus classicus* of sophistic argument in the dialogues is the *Euthydemus*. See the *Gorgias* for an extended argument against rhetoric, to the effect that it aims not at truth or goodness, but rather at pleasure and gratification. See also *Phaedrus* 257c–f, where the tension between rhetoric and truth-seeking is further explored.

9 See, for example, *Philebus* 16c, 55e, 284a–b, 285a. Cf. *Republic* 522c, 526b and *Laws* 645a, 747a–b, 819c. For the connection between measurement and the *technai*, see Roochnik (1996: 195–7, 279); Burnyeat (2000: 20–22, 27); Roochnik (2003: ch. 1). Myles Burnyeat argues that Socrates is drawn to exact measurement because it yields knowledge of 'context-invariant' or 'unqualified' being, rather than belief grounded in individual perspectives.

10 See, for example, *Phaedo* 69a–b; *Gorgias* 499a–b, 500a; *Philebus* 60b; *Laws* 783a.

11 See also Roochnik (1996: 228) and Annas (1999: 157–160, 167–171).

12 See, notably, Irwin (1977: ch. 4) and Irwin (1995: ch. 6).

13 See Annas (1999: 89–91).

14 See Roochnik (1996: 147–150).

15 This variability is analogous to that plaguing the *politikē technē*, though the latter's domain is comparatively limited. Both this variability and consequent lack of control undermine Socrates' precisionist ideal, since the shifting terrain of virtue and vice simply cannot be brought under the kind of determinate and rigid schemas characteristic of mathematics. Hence Aristotle's observation that

> noble and just actions … exhibit much variety and fluctuation … it is the mark of an educated man to look for precision in each class of things just so far as the nature of the subject admits: it is evidently equally foolish to accept probable reasoning from a mathematician and to demand from a rhetorician demonstrative proofs.
>
> Nicomachean Ethics *1094b: 14–27*

16 Granted, these three features – namely, early inculcation, involuntariness and non-relativity to individual interests and talents – *do* characterise the education of the *Republic*'s guardians. But this is exactly what makes it odd to describe their resultant abilities as a '*technē*'.

17 Even the dancer, who does not have an external *ergon*, aims to produce various movements in his *body* – not effects in his soul. One can, of course, 'go to work' on one's own soul, using various self-directed techniques: but a portion of the soul will always have to remain as agent, in order for it to work on the rest. The soul as such, therefore, can never be a pure object to itself. This suggests that virtue can be developed properly and fully only by submitting the whole soul to *external* influence – something that dovetails with my conclusion below.

18 See *Symposium* 177e. Cf. *Symposium* 193e, 198d, 201d, 207a/c, 209e, 211c.

References

Annas, J. (1999) *Platonic Ethics, Old and New*, Ithaca, NY: Cornell University Press.

—— (2011) *Intelligent Virtue*, Oxford: Oxford University Press.

Aristotle (1995) *The Complete Works of Aristotle*, J. Barnes (ed.), Princeton, NJ: Princeton University Press.

Burnyeat, M. (2000) 'Plato on Why Mathematics is Good for the Soul', in T. Smiley (ed.) *Mathematics and Necessity*, Oxford: Oxford University Press, pp. 1–81.

Carone, G. R. (2005) *Plato's Cosmology and its Ethical Dimensions*, Cambridge: Cambridge University Press.

Gould, J. (1955) *The Development of Plato's Ethics*, Cambridge: Cambridge University Press.

Irwin, T. (1977) *Plato's Moral Theory: The Early and Middle Dialogues*, Oxford: Oxford University Press.

—— (1995) *Plato's Ethics*, Oxford: Oxford University Press.

Kamtekar, R. (2009) 'The Politics of Plato's Socrates', in S. Ahbel-Rappe and R. Kamtekar (eds) *A Companion to Socrates*, Oxford: Blackwell, pp. 214–227.

Nussbaum, M. C. (1986) *The Fragility of Goodness: Luck and Ethics in Greek Tragedy and Philosophy*, Cambridge: Cambridge University Press.

Plato (1997) *Plato: Complete Works*, J. M. Cooper and D. S. Hutchinson (eds), Indianapolis, IN: Hackett.

Roochnik, D. (1996) *Of Art and Wisdom: Plato's Understanding of Technē*, University Park, PA: The Pennsylvania State University Press.

—— (2003) *Beautiful City: The Dialectical Character of Plato's 'Republic'*, Ithaca, NY: Cornell University Press.

Sprague, R. K. (1976) *Plato's Philosopher-King: A Study of the Theoretical Background*, Columbia, SC: University of South Carolina Press.

Wolfsdorf, D. (2008) *Trials of Reason: Plato and the Crafting of Philosophy*, Oxford: Oxford University Press.

Woodruff, P. (1990) 'Plato's Early Theory of Knowledge', in S. Everson (ed.) *Epistemology – Companions to Ancient Thought: 1*, Cambridge: Cambridge University Press, pp. 60–84.

5

TECHNÊ IN ARISTOTLE'S TAXONOMY OF KNOWLEDGE

Thomas K. Johansen

5.1 Introduction

Aristotle presents craft (*technê*) as a distinct kind of knowledge. In this chapter I offer first a general outline of his account of craft, as it is presented within his classification of knowledge in the *Nicomachean Ethics* (*EN*). I then analyse this account in view also of other works of his, before homing in on the contrast between *technê* and practical knowledge or *phronêsis*, which is likely to strike readers as the most interesting and problematic aspect of Aristotle's taxonomy.[1]

5.2 The place of *technê* within knowledge

In *EN* VI Aristotle accounts for the intellectual virtues. There are several of these because there are different kinds of intellect. Aristotle (*EN* 1139a9–12) follows the philosophical method described in *De Anima* II.4 (415a18–20) which gives priority in definition to the capacity's object. That is,

P1 A capacity and its activities are determined by its distinctive object.

P1 helps Aristotle distinguish first rational from non-rational capacities: rational capacities are concerned with truths. There are then two kinds of rational capacity: one concerned with necessary and eternal truths, another with contingent truths. The first, theoretical reason, has its virtue theoretical knowledge (*epistêmê*).[2] The contingent truths are the remit of practical and productive reason, the practical sort dealing with action (*praxis*) and the productive with production (*poiêsis*). These two are mutually exclusive, but they do not exhaust the class of contingent truths, since they are restricted to those truths that are under our influence. Contingent truths on Mars are, at least in Aristotle's world, the remit of neither practical nor productive knowledge. Our distinctions give us the picture in Figure 5.1.

Aristotle views the virtues as developed dispositions or states (*hexeis*), so the intellectual virtues are states of the intellectual capacities.[3] As they are states of reason (*logos*), he thinks that they are also accompanied by an account or reason (*logos*).[4] A *logos* could in principle be any statement or verbal expression, but several passages make it clear that Aristotle has in mind an account or explanation of what the *technê* is about.[5] As the virtues are excellences of reason,

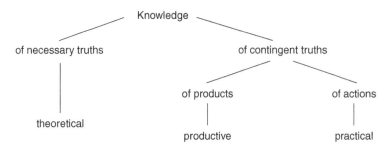

Figure 5.1

the account must also be correct; if the account were false, reason would clearly not have been perfected in possessing this account.

A general formula is then available for all the different virtues of intellect.

P2 A virtue of reason = a state of reason concerned with X accompanied by a true account (*logos*) of X.

P2 will then be differentiated according to the value of X, given **P1**. In this way we arrive at the following characterisations of the three kinds of knowledge:

Theoretical knowledge = a theoretical state of reason concerned with eternal truths accompanied by a true account.
Practical knowledge = a practical state of reason accompanied by a true account.
Productive knowledge = a productive state of reason accompanied by a true account.

5.3 The definition of *technê*

It is in *EN* VI.4 that we learn how **P2** applies to productive knowledge, making it different from both practical and theoretical knowledge:

T1 What admits of being otherwise includes what is produced and what is achieved in action. Production and action are different; about them we rely also on [our] popular distinctions. And so the state involving an account (*logos*) and concerned with action is different from the state involving an account and concerned with production. Nor is one included in the other; for action is not production, and production is not action. Now building, for instance, is a craft (*technê*), and is essentially a certain state involving an account concerned with production; there is no craft that is not a state involving an account concerned with production, and no such state that is not a craft. Hence a craft is the same as a state involving a true account concerned with production. Every craft is concerned with coming to be, and the exercise of the craft is also considering (*theôrein*) how something that admits of being and not being comes to be, something whose principle is in the producer and not in the product. For a craft is not concerned with things that are or come to be by necessity; nor with things that are by nature, since these have their principle in themselves. Since production and action are different, craft must be concerned with production, not with action. In a way craft and fortune are concerned with the same things, as Agathon says: 'Craft was fond of fortune, and fortune of craft'. A craft, then, as we have said, is a state involving true reason concerned with production. Lack of craft is the contrary state involving false reason and concerned with production. Both are concerned with what admits of being otherwise.

EN VI.4 1140a1–23, transl. T. Irwin with alterations[6]

You may ask if *technê* according to this definition is primarily concerned with the production or the product. The Greek word *ergon*, like the English 'work', can be employed for the outcome of the craft (1106b9) but may also indicate the activity of production. Thus we may distinguish between health, for example, and healing, and ask which is the primary concern of medicine. Possibly we could read the definition of *technê* as saying that the state is concerned with the product and the account with the production, or the other way around, or both could be concerned with either the product or the production.

It is plainly implausible to think that the *technê* is concerned exclusively with the product: a state that was able to produce an object and give an account of the product itself but not of how one brings it about would surely not qualify as a craft. Being able to say what a house is as well as being able to conjure one up wouldn't make you an architect: you might be an articulate magician. And when Aristotle says in our passage that 'Every craft is concerned with coming to be, and the exercise of the craft is also considering (*theôrein*) how something that admits of being and not being comes to be', he is surely referring to the craftsman's consideration of how the product comes about. The thought seems to be that since the product is something contingent on the craftsman, he reasons about how to bring it about. Here the craftsman's reasoning would correspond in the ethical realm to the deliberation of the practically wise (the *phronimos*) about how to bring about the desired end. And just as such deliberation is proper to the *phronimos*, so also correct reasoning about how to bring about the product is characteristic of the craftsman.

It would be a mistake, however, to say that the craftsman is concerned with reasoning about the production *rather than* the product itself. For his reasoning is premised on a correct understanding of the product. Just as we deliberate only about the ends that we desire as good, so the craftsman reasons only about how to bring about the product typical of his craft. The *Metaphysics* gives us a clearer picture of how the product works as the starting point for the craftsman's reasoning:

> **T2** From craft come the things whose form is in the soul of the producer – and by form I mean the essence of each thing and the primary substance … For example, health is the account in the soul, the scientific knowledge [of the form]. So the healthy thing comes to be when the doctor reasons as follows: since health is this, necessarily if the thing is to be healthy this must be present – for example, a uniform state – and if the latter is to be present, there must be heat, and he goes on, always thinking like this, until he is led to a final 'this' that he himself is able to make. Then the process from this point onward, toward health, is called production … . Of comings-into-being and processes, one part is called understanding (*noêsis*) and the other producing (*poiêsis*) – what proceeds from the starting-point and form is understanding, what proceeds from the final stage of understanding is producing.
>
> *Metaph. VII.7 1032a32–b17*[7]

Aristotle is clear that the doctor's understanding of health is the starting point of her reasoning. The craft here is the reasoned ability to set in motion changes that lead to the goal of health. In the light of **T2** we might, then, understand the definition in *EN* VI.4 as saying that the craft is the developed ability, hence state, to produce on the basis of reasoning the changes that are instrumental in bringing about a certain goal. We can then understand the proper object of the craft as the production (*poiêsis*) given that the product will be factored into the specification of production. Medicine, for example, will then have healing as its proper object, on the understanding that healing is the process that brings about *health*.

However, a noteworthy feature of the definition of *technê* in **T1** is that Aristotle does not say that craft is a state concerned with production, though it is no doubt also that, as we have just seen. Rather he says that craft is a *productive state*. The difference may reflect a realisation that saying that craft is knowledge of production may not be sufficient to single out an ability to make something. For one might have a theoretical grasp of a kind of production without having the ability oneself to carry it out. As some might say today, having knowledge that this is how to make something may not be sufficient for having the knowledge of how to make that thing oneself.[8] But what Aristotle wants to capture is exactly the sort of knowledge that enables one to make something oneself. 'Productive' therefore qualifies the state rather than (just) the object. The aspect of being able to account for what one is doing, the more 'theoretical' element, comes out rather in the account (*logos*) that accompanies the productive ability.

The question then arises about the relationship between the productive state and the account. Aristotle says that craft is a productive state 'with' (*meta*) a *logos*, but 'with' seems vague enough to allow for anything from conjunction to constitution. So one might take the account to be something merely added to the productive state, which can be understood independently of the account, or one could take the *logos* to be part of what grounds or makes the state the productive state it is. The evidence favours the second option.[9] So in *EN* VI.13 (1144b17–30) Aristotle explains the parallel claim for virtue that it is 'a state *with* the right account' (1144b27). He contrasts the common view that virtue is in accordance (*kata*) with the correct account, arguing that it is possible to act *in accordance* with the correct account without knowingly doing so. Aristotle's choice of *with* (*meta*) is supposed to contrast with 'in accordance with' (*kata*) so understood. The action is *with* a correct account only if it is informed by it. That is to say, to be not just 'in accordance' with the right account but 'with' the right account, the account must be involved in a way that explains how or why the agent acts as he does. Analogously in the definition of craft, the productive state would be 'with' an account in that the craftsman is able to produce as he does because he has an account that tells him how to do so.

A similar picture emerges from Aristotle's discussion of craft in *Metaphysics* IX.2. Here he distinguishes between two kinds of capacity (*dunamis*), those *with* (*meta*) a *logos* and those without (1046b1), all crafts being with an account. He argues that a capacity with an account, a rational (*logikê*) capacity, enables one to bring about opposite results because the *logos* shows the craftsman how to bring about either. So the doctor can kill or cure since the same account which tells her how to cure also incidentally tells her how to kill. Aristotle says that the 'knowledge is a capacity *by having the logos*' (1046b16; emphasis added). It is quite explicit then that it is primarily the account that grounds the craft's characteristic productive ability.

If this is right, and the *logos* is part of what makes the state productive, one might ask, given that the circumstances of production differ from case to case, whether the *logos* is an account of what goes into making a product in particular circumstances or whether it is, rather, a general account of how to go about making a product of a certain sort. **T2** doesn't on its own help us answer this since the example of health and heat could either be taken to refer to a particular case of healing where heat is the way to achieve the aim in this particular situation or to a more general procedure. Aristotle in several places emphasises that a successful craftsman takes account of the particular circumstances. In *Metaphysics* I.1 he says that production concerns the individual, not the universal: for example, the doctor cures the individual human being, not the universal human being (981a17–20). While the craftsman is distinguished from the merely experienced by having an account (*logos*) that enables him to explain and teach how to produce a certain outcome, it is clear that effective production also requires experience. So in *EN* we read that

> **T3** Nor is prudence about universals only. It must also acquire knowledge of particulars, since it is concerned with action and action is about particulars. That is why in other areas also some people who lack knowledge but have experience are better in action than others who have knowledge. For someone who knows that light meats are digestible and [hence] healthy, but not which sorts of meats are light, will not produce health; the one who knows that bird meats are light [and healthy] will be better at producing health. And since prudence is concerned with action, it must possess both [the universal and the particular knowledge] or the [particular] more [than the universal]. Here too, however, [as in medicine] there is a ruling [science].
>
> *EN VI.7 1141b15–23, transl. T. Irwin*

I take Aristotle's point to be not that experience is just added to the account, but that experience affects how the account is pitched. For example, that the account says not just that light meats are easy to digest but that that bird (etc.) meat is such meat. Experience works then to modulate the general information that the account gives the craftsman. An account which also gives us information that bird meat is light will enable us to act appropriately. Similarly, the doctor's account of healing should not just give a general causal description of a disease and its remedies, but also of the stages of the disease and the correct timing and dosage of the administration of the medicine.[10] *Technê* is a *general* disposition to produce things, grounded, as we saw, in a *logos*. So if this account is too specific, its extendability to all relevant cases is threatened. The account needs then to be general in intent, but should still be couched in a manner that is applicable to individual circumstances. If the account is too general it gives insufficient practical information to act on. Experience helps make the account sufficiently fine-grained to be actionable.

5.4 *Technê* and practical wisdom: the distinctions

Much of what I have said so far about the elements of the definition of *technê* in *EN*VI.4 applies *mutatis mutandis* to practical wisdom. But Aristotle uses the definition in **T1** also to distinguish *technê* from practical wisdom (*phronêsis*), as the sort of knowledge that is most similar to *technê*. Indeed, as we saw in the previous chapter, Plato, at least in some of his works, took *phronêsis* to be a kind of craft. Aristotle is keen to correct this mistake, not just from the point of view of getting *technê* right, but also more importantly for the purposes of the *EN*, to become clear about the distinctive features of *phronêsis*.

P1, as we saw, is the primary criterion for distinguishing capacities and their states. But this criterion can be seen to be at work in two different ways, giving us two different contrasts between *technê* and *phronêsis*.

(A) *phronêsis* is of an end without qualification (*telos haplôs*), while *technê* is of 'an end in relation to something and of something' (*telos pros ti* and *tinos*);

(B) *technê* is of production and *phronêsis* is of action.

We have already come across (B) in **T1**. Here is the text in which both (A) and (B) are brought up:

T4 It follows that prudence [*phronêsis*] is not science nor yet craft knowledge. It is not science, because what is achievable in action admits of being otherwise; and it is not craft knowledge, because action and production belong to different kinds. The remaining possibility, then, is that prudence is a state of grasping the truth, involving reason, concerned with action about things that are good or bad for a human being. For production has its end in something other than itself, but action does not, since its end is acting well itself. That is why Pericles and such people are the ones whom we regard as prudent, because they are able to study what is good for themselves and for human beings.

EN VI.5 1140b2–11, transl. Irwin

At first blush, one might have thought that (B) would render (A) superfluous: if *phronêsis* and *technê* have different genera of objects, and so different ends (*telê*), there is no reason to state a contrast between a qualified and an unqualified end. More strongly, one might say that (A) and (B) are in tension with each other: if *phronêsis* and *technê* differ in terms of one dealing with a *telos* unqualified which the other also deals with but in a qualified manner then it can't also be the case that the two are dealing with two generically different ends. Let us, then, consider (A) and (B) in turn and see if these are genuine problems.

5.4.1 Technê, *ends and deliberation*

First (A). One complication is that *phronêsis* does not deal with the good *haplôs* but the good *for man*. Aristotle is clear that this is not the only good, since the good for humans, would be different from the good for fish, just as human health is different from piscine health. Nor is the human good the best good full stop, since man is not the best being in the cosmos; that would be god (*EN VI.7* 1141a22–29). So one might say that *phronêsis* too is about something (*peri tinos* or *tinos*) in the sense of concerning man or being of man, and *phronêsis* for another species, if such a thing is possible, would be about what is good for that species.

In *EN VI.5* Aristotle expresses the difference between the objects of *technê* and *phronêsis* in terms of the part–whole relationship: *phronêsis* deliberates about what as a whole (*holôs*) contributes to the good life, not as a part (*kata meros*), as for example what contributes to health or strength (1140a26–28). However, it is also clear that this notion of the human good in general doesn't preclude deliberating about some human good. The thought would seem to be that deliberation is not just about what the overall human good is, say happiness, but also about some human good in some situation, let's say, whether to have a child or not. A limiting condition here is that there should be no *technê* dealing with the issue. So it would seem right that there is no *technê* for whether or with whom or when to have a child, but there would be a *technê* for how to develop one's strength or attain health, namely, the trainer's or the physician's art. However, there are several further issues arising from this contrast.

(1) Why doesn't deliberating about when to have a child count as deliberation *kata meros*? One reason might be that we can only decide on such issues in relation to the overall human good: you need to think about this decision in relation to the overall happiness and well-being of yourself and others. This suggestion seems to be consistent with the fact that there is no *technê* of such matters. A *technê* can be exercised without regard to whether it contributes to overall human goals. That is why there is a virtue of *technê*, as Aristotle says (*EN* 1140b21–22). The decision whether to exercise the *technê* in a given situation is an ethical one which lies outside the craft's proper remit. So the condition that there should be no *technê* covering the issue is not

ad hoc but touches on the very nature of practical deliberation: even when practical deliberation faces a limited question this question needs, directly or indirectly, to take into account its bearing on the overall human good.

(2) Another issue is whether Aristotle wants to accept that *technê* deliberates at all. In *EN* VI.7 1141b11 Aristotle says that it is the function (*ergon*) of the *phronimos* to deliberate well. This might create the impression that it is not also the function of the craftsman, though what Aristotle says does not exclude that the craftsman might incidentally engage in some deliberation. To be sure, deliberation may not be a feature of craft in the way it is for practical wisdom. However, we cannot ascribe too marginal a role to deliberation in *technê*, since Aristotle repeatedly illustrates ethical deliberation by technical examples. He says, for example, that a doctor does not deliberate whether his patient should be healthy or not, but whether, say, he should take walks or not (*EE* II.11, 1227b25–6; *NE* III.3, 1112b12–13).

The scholarly problem arises because of a claim in *Physics* II.9 (199b28–29) that 'art does not deliberate'. Aristotle is here using an analogy with craft to argue for final causality in nature. He wants to say that it is no objection to this analogy that final causes operate in the arts as objects of a crafting mind, and not so in nature, since also 'art does not deliberate'. Just how to take these words has been much debated. One option is to say that since Aristotle talks about the craft rather than the craftsman, he has in mind the rules and procedures that characterise the craft as such.[11] At this level there is no deliberation, but that does not mean that a craftsman when applying the craft does not deliberate. The problem with this, however, is that Aristotle in *Physics* II.9 has just referred to how we do not in nature 'see *the moving thing* having deliberated'. And here it would seem to be the particular thing that we would or, rather, would not have seen move. If, then, the comparison with craft is to be like for like, we should be thinking of the craftsman, not the craft as such. However, a modified version might be plausible: the craftsman *qua* craftsman does not deliberate since the large majority of cases are routine. Deliberation would then not be involved in what exercising the craft as such would be about, and that might be why Aristotle here chooses to refer to the 'craft' rather than the 'craftsman'.

It is hard, perhaps, to avoid the impression that this is still an idealisation of what craftsmen do.[12] However, what is noteworthy is that when Aristotle acknowledges the importance of the particular circumstances in the exercise of arts such as medicine or navigation, he says that they '*fall under no craft or profession*, but it is necessary for the practitioners themselves to consider what is appropriate (*pros ton kairon*) to the circumstances' (*EN* II.2 1104a7–9). It would appear that Aristotle has in mind here not the sort of means-end reasoning we find described in **T2**. This we might take as a typical case of medical reasoning: when a patient suffers such and such, apply heat, etc. Here the doctor is following a routine procedure rather than deliberating. Rather deliberation would be when the doctor judges in this particular case that the patient's fever is at a point where he has passed the critical stage and therefore this medicine rather than that will be efficacious.[13] Or, in the nautical case, that the clouds are promising a storm of a magnitude that given that the ship's cargo is of this weight and this value means that it is right to jettison this amount of the load. As far as the craft is concerned the practitioner is on his own when reasoning about such particular cases. This is not to say that being able to make such decisions is not part of your development as a craftsman. For example, we may take it that what experience particularly gives the craftsman is this ability to recognise and negotiate the salient features of particular situations. You don't and can't learn this in medical school but a good doctor can do it. There is a sense in which deliberating exceeds what is characteristic of the craft qua craft though it may be presupposed by the successful exercise of the craft in certain circumstances, and more so for some crafts than others. However, compared to practical wisdom, and this is

Aristotle's main point in *EN* II.2, deliberation about particular decisions will play a much more limited role in the exercise of craft. In the same spirit we might take it that Aristotle in *Physics* II.9 wants to say that it is not a general feature of craftsmen *qua* craftsmen that they deliberate (in the way it is for the *phronimos*) and therefore there is no general contrast on this point between the teleology of craft and nature.

5.4.2 Techné, *ends and production*

It is right, Aristotle says in *De Anima* II.4 (416b23), 'to call all things after their end' (*telos*), and it is the ends of production and action that for Aristotle primarily serve to distinguish craft from practical knowledge. This distinction works in two ways for Aristotle in *EN* VI. Already in Chapter 2 he had pointed to the difference between the goals of production and action:

> **T5** Thought by itself moves nothing; what moves us is goal-directed thought concerned with action. For this thought is also the principle of productive thought; for every producer in his production aims at some [further] goal, and the unqualified goal is not the product, which is only the [qualified] goal of some [production], and aims at some [further] goal. [An unqualified goal is] what we achieve in action, since acting well is the goal, and desire is for the goal.
>
> *EN VI.2 1139a37–b3*

Here we might say that the difference lies in the extent to which the goals of production and action actually count as goals. Clearly a craft has a goal which is unqualified in relation to the production itself. Health is the goal of medicine as such, as we saw. Health is not a qualified goal of medicine, but it may be a qualified goal of a human being. We don't produce the goals of production willy-nilly but only when we want to achieve some further goal. We only aim to produce health for example if we want to live or live well. The goal of production points then to a goal outside itself, the goal of *action*.

In reply to our earlier question about the relationship between the two distinctions between *techné* and *phronésis*, (A) and (B), we can say that because the product is not such as to be an end without qualification, the production points to another kind of end, the end of action, which is an end without qualification. Here the craft's end being an end with qualification does not mean being the same sort of end as the end of action, only qualified in a certain way, as one might say for example that a zebra is white only with qualification because it has black stripes whereas a swan is completely white. Rather the difference picks out the end of craft as an objectively different kind of thing from the good of practical wisdom, namely something that is such as to have only instrumental value. It should not surprise us, then, given distinction (A), that distinction (B) points to generically different kinds of objects for productive and practical knowledge.

There is, however, yet another way, way (C), of distinguishing the goals of production and action, which is to see whether the goal is fulfilled in the activity itself or outside of it. Here the concern is not, as earlier, with whether the goal once achieved is a goal unqualifiedly or not. Rather the point is that while the goal of production cannot be achieved (be it an unqualified goal or not) in the production itself, the goal of an action lies in the action itself, namely in the good performance of the action (*eupraxia*). So in **T4** above Aristotle said:

> The remaining possibility, then, is that prudence is a state of grasping the truth, involving reason, concerned with action about things that are good or bad for a

human being. *For production has its end in something other than itself, but action does not, since its end is acting well itself.*

EN VI.5 1140b3–7

The italicised lines can be read as saying that while the end of the production is something other than the production, the end of the action is just the action itself. So house-building aims at a house, which is something other than house-building in the sense explained in *Physics* III.1: while the house-building is ongoing the house is not yet there; when the house is finished the house-building is no longer. Production is a process (*kinêsis*) which is complete only at the end of it. An action meanwhile is an activity (*energeia*) which is complete at each moment it is taking place, that is to say it realises its end while it is happening.[14] The activity of seeing is one example. Aristotle, to be sure, talks here not just of the activity itself as the end but the *good* activity (*eupraxia*), but we may take this to mean that an activity that is fully realised as the activity it is is also a good activity of its kind. Seeing fully is seeing well. In any case, the good activity is not the activity plus some other attribute, but a modality of the activity itself.

While these points are all relevant, it is not yet clear why we should accept the exclusiveness of Aristotle's distinction. In particular, there seems no reason why an action should not also be a production or a production an action. After all, in many cases we act in order to achieve further ends, a point on which Aristotle's account of deliberation is premised. We may act bravely in order to save the nation, or show kindness to make another person happy. Here the mere fact of a means-end relationship doesn't turn our action into a production, though there may also be such cases. For example, you may by eating moderately set an example for your children so that they too become moderate. In this case, it would seem appropriate to judge your action by its effectiveness. On the other hand, we have cases of production that coincide with actions. In John Ackrill's example, mending your neighbour's fence may be returning a favour.[15] Here the production itself constitutes, it seems, the return of the favour. Returning the favour is not a further result of fixing the fence. Given that one and the same activity here can instantiate both an action and a production, it may seem best to take the distinction to be one of how we *describe* activities, and not as a distinction between numerically different activities.[16] We might say today that the same activity is an action *under one description* and a production under another; Aristotle would say that sometimes the production and the action are one in number, but different in being or definition.

In this vein, we could say that production and action pick out different *evaluative* aspects or bases of an activity, using the word 'activity' as neutral between 'production' and 'action'. We evaluate an activity as a production when we focus simply on the value of the product, we assess it as an action by evaluating it in its own right. Take again Ackrill's example: here what you do, fixing the fence, may be described as a production, and as such it is complete when the fence is in fine working order. But the same activity numerically may also be considered an action, returning a favour, which is complete only insofar as the neighbour is satisfied. If the neighbour had changed his mind about having a fence at all, or wanted it somewhere else, or a hedge instead, then we wouldn't say that the favour had been returned, fine as the fence may be. So one and the same activity may be a failed action but a successful production. We might say that the aim of the production is only *per accidens* that of the action, since there is no guarantee that fixing the fence will return the favour. Vice versa, the aim of the action is only *per accidens* that of the production since if some other product had served the action better, returning the favour, we would have chosen to make that thing.[17]

This evaluative difference may be captured by saying that the end of the production is outside, while the end of the action is internal to the activity. We evaluate the production on the basis of the quality of the product. The value of the production lies in the product not in the production as such. In contrast, the value of the action lies in the action itself, that is in the attributes that belong to it as that kind of action, returning a favour, doing a kindness and so on.[18] Nothing here is said about that action not also coinciding with a production or process or some other entity, but that is not the basis on which we evaluate it.

The evaluation of the production in relation to the product seems clear enough. But how we evaluate an action as good or bad is perhaps less clear. In *EN* II.4 Aristotle points to features that we take into account when evaluating an action which don't feature in our assessment of a production:

> **T6** Again, the case of the crafts and that of the virtues are not similar; for the products of the crafts have their goodness in themselves, so that it is enough that they should have a certain character, but if the things that happen in accordance with the virtues have themselves a certain character it does not follow that they are done justly or temperately. The agent also must be in a certain condition when he does them; in the first place he must have knowledge; secondly, he must choose the actions, and choose them for their own sakes, and thirdly his action must proceed from a firm and unchangeable character. These are not reckoned in as conditions of the possession of the crafts, except the bare knowledge; but as a condition of the possession of the virtues knowledge has little or no weight, while the other conditions count not for a little but for everything, i.e. the very conditions which result from often doing just and temperate actions.
>
> *EN 1105a26–b5, transl. after W. D. Ross*

One way of seeing the criteria of a virtuous action is in relation to the idea that the action is a manifestation of a certain character, a term we may here take to refer both to the moral character, that is the emotional dispositions, and the intellectual character, knowledge. A just action follows from a just character and is chosen knowing what is just. While there are ways you can describe an action independently of its relation to the agent, just as there are features of the product you can describe independently of the producer, these are not the features of the action that make it virtuous. That is not to say that the virtuous-making features of the action do not belong to the action as such, since being chosen or manifesting a character clearly are defining features of action, at least if action is taken in the strict sense that Aristotle seems to have in mind here.[19] The contrast with craft is that when we assess the production we look not to the way the production realises the characteristics of the craftsman (except, Aristotle says, for the limited case of knowledge), but simply to the quality of the product. And the product is not the actuality of the craftsman, but that of the materials from which the product has been made, that is the goodness here is predicated of something other than the craftsman.

If this, at least roughly, is Aristotle's account of the difference between production and action, how successful is it? One problem we may have with allowing action and production to be different descriptions of the same activity is that action and production seem to have not just different but mutually incompatible properties. So we might say that a production is necessarily extended in time, an action not so, or that the cause of a production has a cause (namely the goal) that lies outside of it, while the action has an internal goal. As incompatible, these properties seem to point to different subjects or activities. But then we have the problem again of understanding cases like fixing the neighbour's fence. We should note, however, that generally Aristotle does allow things that are one in number to have mutually incompatible descriptions. For example, the same stretch of road goes both from Thebes to Athens and from Athens to

Thebes, the same activity is both teaching and learning, or perceiving and being perceived. It has to be admitted that these cases are not themselves easy to understand, and that the opposition in these cases is not obviously like that between an action and a production. It may be hard in the end to resist Ackrill's verdict that when it comes to the distinction between action and production Aristotle was less clear than one could have wished.[20]

Notes

1 I am grateful to Tom Angier for many helpful comments on this chapter.
2 See *Metaphysics* VI.1.
3 Aristotle will sometimes mention states (*hexeis*) and capacities (*dunameis*) as alternatives. So at *EN* II.5 1105b20 he asks which of state, capacities or affections (*pathê*) virtue is. He clarifies that the capacities (in this context) would be those in virtue of which we are able to suffer affections, while the states are those in virtue of which we are well or ill disposed toward the affections. It is clear then that the states here are states of the capacities.
4 One could imagine a rational state that does not involve being able to give a reason. However, even *nous*, the insight into first principles, grasps a definition, which only contrasts with *logos* in one sense of the word. Contrast *EN* 1142a25–6 and *APo* II.19 100b10 with *Metaph.* 1017b22, *Metaph.* 1030a6–7, and *Metaph.* XII 1075a1–4.
5 So, for example, *Metaphysics* IX.2 discussed below. See further J. Moss (2014: 181–230).
6 Irwin (1999).
7 Translation quoted from Reeve (2013) 147.
8 This being one question at stake in the debate about whether knowledge how can always be analysed in terms of knowledge that.
9 For this interpretation see Johansen (2017).
10 Of the sort we indeed find in the Hippocratic writings, cf. e.g. *Regimen in Acute Diseases* (Lloyd 1978: 20–26) on the administration of gruel.
11 See Sedley (2007: 177–181).
12 As argued by Broadie (1987).
13 So Aristotle uses *kairos* in the quotation, the Hippocratic word for the precise moment in the disease's progression, in relation to which the doctor must judge his treatment.
14 Cf. for this reading, Reeve (2013: 143–144).
15 Ackrill (1978: 596).
16 As suggested by Irwin (1999: 242). For a contrasting view, see Charles (1984: 65–66).
17 As Aristotle says in *Nicomachean Ethics* VII. 9.1: 'if a person chooses or pursues this for the sake of that, *per se* it is that that he pursues and chooses, but *per accidens* it is this. But when we speak without qualification we mean what is *per se*'.
18 See further Charles (1986).
19 Cf. *EN* VI.2 1139a32–36.
20 Ackrill (1978: 601). See also Dunne (1993: Chapter 10).

Further reading

Angier (2010) offers an excellent overview of Aristotle's understanding of *technê* and its importance to his ethics. Johansen (2020) features articles on *technê* by leading scholars covering all periods of ancient philosophy. S. Cuomo, *Technology and Culture in Greek and Roman Antiquity*, Cambridge: Cambridge University Press 2007, puts ancient theories of *technê* in their social and historical context.

References

Ackrill, J. L. (1978) 'Aristotle on Action', *Mind* 87, pp. 595–601.
Angier, T. (2010) *Technê in Aristotle's Ethics: Crafting the Moral Life*, London/New York: Bloomsbury.
Broadie, S. (1987) 'Nature, Craft and *Phronêsis* in Aristotle', *Philosophical Topics* 15, pp. 35–50.
Charles, D. (1984) *Aristotle's Philosophy of Action*, London: Duckworth.

—— (1986) 'Aristotle: Ontology and Moral Reasoning', in Michael Woods (ed.) *Oxford Studies in Ancient Philosophy* Vol. IV, Oxford: Clarendon Press, pp. 119–144.

Dunne, J. (1993) *Back to the Rough Ground: 'Phronesis' and 'Techne' in Modern Philosophy and in Aristotle*, Notre Dame, IN: University of Notre Dame Press.

Irwin, T. (1999) *Aristotle: Nicomachean Ethics*, Indianapolis/Cambridge: Hackett (2nd edition).

Johansen, T. K. (2017) 'Aristotle on the *Logos* of the Craftsman', *Phronesis* 62, pp. 97–135.

—— (ed.) (2020) *Productive Knowledge in Ancient Philosophy*, Cambridge: Cambridge University Press.

Lloyd, G. E. R. (ed.) (1978) *Hippocratic Writings*, London: Penguin.

Moss, J. (2014) 'Right Reason in Plato and Aristotle: On the Meaning of Logos', *Phronesis* 59, pp. 181–230.

Reeve, C. D. C. (2013) *Aristotle on Practical Wisdom*, Cambridge, MA: Harvard University Press.

Sedley, D. (2007) *Creationism and Its Critics in Antiquity*, Berkeley: University of California Press.

6

MENDELSSOHN AND KANT ON VIRTUE AS A SKILL

Melissa Merritt

6.1 Introduction

The idea that virtue can be profitably conceived as a certain sort of skill goes back to the Socratic dialogues of Plato, was developed by competing schools in the Hellenistic era, and has recently attracted renewed attention from virtue theorists.[1] My aim in this chapter is to examine a neglected episode in the history of this idea – one that focuses on the pivotal role that Moses Mendelssohn played in rehabilitating the skill model of virtue for the German rationalist tradition, and Immanuel Kant's subsequent, yet significantly qualified, endorsement of the idea.

I begin with Mendelssohn's place as a critical developer of the German rationalist tradition. Although his rationalist predecessors frequently spoke of virtue as a skill or proficiency, they did so – Mendelssohn contends – without adequately considering what this notion might be good for, what philosophical problems it might help solve. Mendelssohn finds in the concept of skill the resources to meet an objection that might be lodged against the perfectionist and agent-based ethics of his tradition: namely, that a virtuous person would seem to act for the sake of realising his own perfection in everything that he does, thereby taking a morally inappropriate interest in his own character. Since for Mendelssohn the hallmark of skilful activity is unselfconscious automatism, he argues that the expression of skill – and thus virtue, if it is a skill – does not involve thoughts about what one is doing, much less thoughts about one's own dispositions and capacities. The objection can be neutralised, he proposes, with renewed attention to the ancient thesis that virtue is itself a certain sort of skill.

I then turn to Kant, who rejects the automatism featured in Mendelssohn's account, on grounds that it renders virtue mindless and unreflective. But Kant does not reject the skill model wholesale. Rather, he indicates that any successful deployment of it calls for greater clarity about *which* skills can serve as apt models for virtue than Mendelssohn and his cohort offered. To this end, Kant distinguishes between "free" and "unfree" skills, admitting only the former as a possible guide for thinking about virtue as a skill. This move allows Kant to recognise how reflection can be embedded in the expression of free skills, which underwrites in turn his qualified endorsement of the skill model of virtue.

6.2 Mendelssohn and the "modern doctrine of skills"

Mendelssohn discusses the concept of skill, and revives the skill model of virtue, in his *Philosophical Writings* (Mendelssohn 1971: 412–424; 1997: 158–168).[2] This discussion kicks off with a recollection of the Socratic idea that virtue is knowledge (*epistēmē*) as this idea is explored in Plato's *Protagoras*, where it figures – together with the supposition that virtue is also some sort of skill (*technē*) – in a wider debate over whether virtue can be taught.[3] But these Socratic ideas appear to be incompatible with the common experience of knowing what would be good to do, but failing to do it because one has been "overcome" by pleasure or pain, "passion" (*thumos*), and the like.[4] Socrates, however, rejects the psychological assumptions on which the common self-understanding is based, in which separate rational and non-rational powers vie for power over the whole soul and its expression in action. Socratic psychology is monistic: an adult human being is rational through and through – although this rationality is not, for that, very often in a state of excellence or perfection.[5] Our downfall in such cases, Socrates argues, is not that we have been overcome by pleasure, since pleasure does not arise in us independently of our taking some view of what is good. Our error, rather, is originally and fundamentally epistemic.[6]

Mendelssohn explicitly endorses much of this picture. He applauds Socrates[7] for recognising that we can never "want the bad *as* the bad, but only under the appearance of the good", and thus that "the basis of moral evil must always be a lack of insight" (Mendelssohn 1971: 412; 1997: 158).[8] Passions and other affective states make proposals, Mendelssohn elaborates, that we are left to endorse or reject in action: "The passions […] cannot conquer us: for they do not force, but rather persuade, us. They must get us to imagine that the place to which they want to seduce us is good" (Mendelssohn 1971: 412; 1997: 158). He concludes his exposition by nodding to Socrates' view that "virtue is a science" – a *Wissenschaft*, for Plato's *epistēmē* – and thus can be taught (Mendelssohn 1971: 413; 1997: 158). Here we come to a curious wrinkle in Mendelssohn's quick account of the *Protagoras*. Despite his ensuing elaboration upon the skill model of virtue, he in fact pointedly fails to mention that Socrates spoke of virtue not only as *epistēmē*, but also indeed as *technē*. It is not entirely clear what we should make of this, but the silence may be the mark of a modestly lodged complaint: he will pass over in silence Socrates' wisp of a suggestion that virtue must be some sort of skill or know-how, since he neither told us how it is constituted nor how it can develop in us. It is as if he says to his rationalist predecessors: we have already taken this idea on board as the modern inheritors of Socrates, but we have been left to work out our own account of it. For indeed Mendelssohn straightway asserts that "the moderns" have developed "their doctrine of skills" in response to Plato's theory, as well as their division between "*effective* or pragmatic" and "*ineffective* or speculative" modes of cognition (Mendelssohn 1971: 413; 1997: 159). Modern philosophical developments are required, Mendelssohn thereby implies, to answer the question that, by his lights, Plato's dialogue presses most urgently upon us: how can the knowledge of the good be properly efficacious, expressing itself directly in action?

Mendelssohn does not name the "moderns" at issue, but his ensuing exposition of their account of skill makes clear that he is thinking of the German rationalist tradition of Christian Wolff (1679–1754), Alexander Baumgarten (1714–1762), and Georg Meier (1718–1777).[9] Mendelssohn himself worked in this tradition, but he had a unique perspective on it: he was not an academic philosopher, and his remarkable literary prowess made him an important populariser of contemporary work in metaphysics, ethics, and aesthetics from Britain and elsewhere in Europe.[10]

The notion at issue is *Fertigkeit*, which translates the Latin *habitus*, and is plausibly rendered in English as "skill" or "proficiency" – terms I will use interchangeably, depending on what is more suitable in a given context.[11] The notion is introduced in ontology, under the discussion of powers of substances (e.g. Baumgarten 1766: §219), and reappears in empirical psychology, in the elaboration of faculties of mind. Powers of understanding and judgement are presented as proficiencies in this sense, along with their specially cultivated attributes, such as wit, discrimination, and taste.[12] Baumgarten and Meier were particularly interested in the development of such proficiencies and their role in the constitution of epistemic character.[13]

The bare idea of a proficiency is evaluatively neutral: it is literally a "readiness" or habitual disposition to perform an action of a certain type, regardless of whether it is the sort of thing one has good reason to do. Thus virtue and vice are alike deemed acquired proficiencies.[14] But the account of how proficiencies are acquired is not uniform across this tradition: Wolff emphasises that they are acquired through *practice* which he explains as "frequent repetition of a way of thinking, and indeed in frequent repetition of actions of a single kind" – so that the ensuing proficiency is a facility for "having these thoughts, or indeed carrying out those very actions" (Wolff 1752[1712]: §525). Baumgarten and Meier, by contrast, lay greater emphasis on unconscious habit (*Gewohnheit*) in the expression of a proficiency: "Habit (*consuetudo*) is a proficiency so great that it reduces the need to pay attention to the particular actions by which one carries it out" (Baumgarten 1766: §§477, 650). Meier repeats the point, and intensifies the claim: "What flows from habit, flows without consciousness" (Meier 1765: §646).

In order to follow Mendelssohn's exposition of his immediate predecessors, it will help to return to the puzzle left from the *Protagoras*: how can the knowledge in which virtue consists be efficacious, or express itself in action? How could a merely theoretical or scientific grasp of moral principles become genuinely practical, and contribute to the development of good character or virtue? Mendelssohn does not think that his rationalist predecessors adequately confronted these questions, but he credits them with developing some of the resources needed to answer them.

First, they recognise the problem that knowledge *might not* be effective: they distinguish "speculative" cognition from the "pragmatic" cognition that – if nothing else hinders it – expresses itself in action (Mendelssohn 1971: 413; 1997: 159). Second, they recognise that effective cognition differs in quality depending on whether or not it is *distinct*. It is distinct if it involves an articulated view of what one has reason to do – this is a motivating reason, or *Bewegungsgrund*; and *freedom* consists of the capacity to compare such reasons, and decide on the basis of this comparison (Mendelssohn 1971: 414; 1997: 159). Third, they recognise that in most cases deliberation must contend with various kinds of indistinct impulses, which are often more powerful – more *effective* – than any distinctly grasped reason. Sensible affections and emotions are examples of such indistinct effective cognitions: they are "nothing other than an indistinct representation of some *considerable good* or *bad*", which tend to be more effective because they are processed more quickly than their distinct counterparts (Mendelssohn 1971: 416; 1997: 161).[15] But if they are *clear* – directly present to consciousness – then we are in principle able to endorse or reject their suggestions about good and bad. However, action is often influenced by active impulses that are neither clear nor distinct, and thus not open to reflection: "obscure inclinations" (*dunkle Neigungen*) (Mendelssohn 1971: 414; 1997: 159). Finally, the full range of active impulses interact quasi-mechanically, augmenting or lessening one another's power, without the subject's needing to be aware of any "calculation [*Berechnung*]" or comparison of their power (Mendelssohn 1971: 413–414; 1997: 159).

Against this background, the unanswered question from the *Protagoras* becomes: how can clear and distinct knowledge of moral principles be effective, and shape character? Mendelssohn finds his answer in the modern account of skill (*Fertigkeit*), as "a capacity to perform a certain action so fast that we no longer remain conscious of all that we do in carrying it out" (Mendelssohn 1971: 417; 1997: 162). Though he draws this conception of skill directly from Baumgarten and Meier, he stresses that its acquisition comes through *practice* (*Übung*) rather than mere habit. Practice is the intentional and diligent repetition of a certain action (Mendelssohn 1971: 417–418; 1997: 162–163). Practice is conceptually guided, and thus essentially an expression of rationality – whereas habit is not necessarily either of these things. Yet practice, in Mendelssohn's view, renders thinking automatic and unconscious. He finds his paradigmatic examples in a pianist and a typesetter. At first they must deliberately locate each key, each box of type, before striking or selecting. But eventually, with constant practice, their fingers are a blur and the pianist plays "the most splendid music almost without thinking about it" (Mendelssohn 1971: 419; 1997: 163).

It is remarkable that Mendelssohn does not acknowledge how different these examples are from one another, at least if the pianist is to be considered as a musician, not a player-piano. In fact, this oversight turns out to be at odds with Mendelssohn's actual development of the skill model of virtue, at least in the second (1771) edition of *Philosophical Writings*, as I will now explain.

6.3 Mendelssohn on virtue as a skill

Although Mendelssohn takes his own contribution to consist in a detail about the speed of cognitive processing involved in a skill,[16] his recollection of the ancient conception of virtue as a skill or *technē* has more far-reaching significance. For while the modern rationalists speak of virtue as a *Fertigkeit*, they do so in passing – without considering what it might be good for, what philosophical problems it might help us to solve. "Let us apply these remarks [about skill] to ethics generally where they actually belong, and where in fact they appear to have fruitful consequences" (Mendelssohn 1971: 419; 1997: 164), suggests Mendelssohn. For him, the automatism of skill enables virtue-based ethics to respond to the worry that a person must take an objectionable interest in her own ethical perfection in order to acquire, and exercise, virtue at all.[17] For if skilful action is performed without consciousness of what one is doing in the process, then virtue – as a skill – is exercised without needing to think *I want to be virtuous* and *this is what the virtuous person would do*.

> Virtue is indeed a science [*Wissenschaft*], and can be learned; however, it requires not merely scientific conviction if it is to be exercised, but also artful practice and skill. [...] He must continue practicing until he is no longer conscious of his rules in the midst of the exercise, until his principles have transformed into inclinations and his virtue appears to be more natural instinct than reason. Then he has attained the heroic greatness that is far beyond the battle of common passions, and exercises the most admirable virtue without vanity.
>
> *Mendelssohn 1971: 422; 1997: 166*

We first have to make a judgement about appropriate action through deliberate application of principles – the efficacy of this judgement is precisely what remains open to question. However, through practice it becomes one we make without conscious effort, and expresses itself directly in action of the appropriate sort. Mendelssohn's proposal is, in effect, to get principled ethical knowledge down on all fours with obscure inclinations, to meet their force on their own terms. This happens with sufficient practice in making the judgements in question, so that one no longer needs to think about the principles of one's actions and their application: the principles *become* inclinations. This, by corollary, frees one of any need to think of oneself as an agent. Virtue, Mendelssohn concludes, is shown to be something greater than the skill of self-management needed to deal with wayward inclinations, and valuable for more than the tranquillity that comes with it.

Mendelssohn leaves it to his reader to fill in this sketch. The virtuous person must have commitments to something other than his own tranquillity: but to what? Here we need to take up additional clues in the text – clues that, however, cast the automatism that Mendelssohn seems to celebrate in an uncertain light. The first is a footnote that Mendelssohn inserts in the passage just quoted, right at the point where he stresses the unconscious automatism of skilful activity. The note refers the reader back to the beginning of the fourth of the "Letters on Sentiments", where Theocles – Mendelssohn's mouthpiece – presents his maxims for the cultivation of taste.[18] Among other things, these maxims acknowledge that deliberate reflection on principles and their correct application is requisite for the cultivation of good taste; but they also insist that we need to go beyond deliberate reflection in order to "direct [...] attention to the object itself" (Mendelssohn 1971: 18; Mendelssohn 1997: 246) – and *enjoy* the beauty. The footnote directing us to this passage implies that something similar should hold for the cultivation of virtue, the object of which is *action* of the appropriate sort. The upshot is an early modern version of recent discussions of "flow", where the skilled person is freed from the need to think deliberately about what she is doing, and is fully absorbed in the activity itself.[19]

Of course, the bare idea that virtuous activity "flows" does not *ipso facto* support Mendelssohn's apparent readiness to treat the typesetter and the pianist as equally apt guides for elaborating the skill model of virtue. The one suggests a skill that is simply dependent upon brute habit (you can reach, without deliberate thought, for the box that contains the letter you need next). The typesetter might do this with "flow", but it does not seem to be a skill that is indefinitely, or richly, perfectible: he may get faster over time, but the progress will develop mostly along that one track until it reaches a plateau. But the skill of a pianist is multifaceted, and stands to develop in complex ways. There is no reason to suppose that such a skill ever reaches a point beyond which it can develop no further. Aspiration to an ever-receding ideal of perfection seems rather to be part and parcel of what it is to cultivate and express the sort of skill in question – at least at any reasonably high level. Thus, the typesetter and the pianist provide quite different examples of skilful activity; and Mendelssohn appears to have eventually recognised as much. For he added a passage to the second (1771) edition of *Philosophical Writings* that elaborates on the skill model of virtue in ways that would allow the musician, but not the typesetter, to serve as his guide.[20]

In that passage, Mendelssohn begins by asking what composition (*Beschaffenheit*) the principles of virtue must have if they are "to work effectively on the inclinations" (Mendelssohn 1971: 420; 1997: 164). The principle governing such a skill must enable one to sustain one's attention on a worthy object, somewhat as the principles governing harmony might direct one's attention to the notes with which beautiful music can be composed. For virtue, this worthy object is "the true dignity of the human being" (Mendelssohn 1971: 420; 1997: 165). What it is to recognise or be acquainted with this object will take indefinitely many concrete forms: *kennen* is Mendelssohn's verb, implying here a recognition of this dignity in an intuitive judgement of the particulars, rather than a speculative grasp of abstract principle.[21] One must engage with others in a manner that acknowledges their true dignity. The knowledge this involves will naturally admit of degrees of adequacy, inasmuch as it is expressed in what one does and how one is motivated. Further, Mendelssohn continues, one must "regard the sublimity of the human being's ethical nature in the appropriate light" (Mendelssohn 1971: 420; 1997: 165). The human being possesses an *ethical* nature as properly free and self-determined; this nature is "sublime" because it exalts the human being over the rest of creation. One must regard this nature with "true humility", appreciating it as the source of a standard of perfection that is both graspable by us and yet from which we always fall short (Mendelssohn 1971: 420; 1997: 165). This constellation of concerns, Mendelssohn contends, needs to be "before one's eyes in every act that one performs" in order to cultivate a "wholesome enthusiasm for virtue" – that is to say, to develop a more vibrant and effective cognition of the good (Mendelssohn 1971: 421; 1997: 165). Since this cognition is "effective" and properly expresses itself in action, the development of this skill will call for a multifaceted refinement of affective dispositions and perceptual capacities, so that one's attention to what is relevant to acting in the interest of this dignity becomes ever more keen.

This picture of the skill model of virtue does not sit well with the unreflective automatism that Mendelssohn seems initially to celebrate, when he takes the movements of a typesetter to provide an apt example of skilful action for his explanatory purposes. In reaching this conclusion, I have anticipated and partly defended Mendelssohn against Kant's criticisms, to which we turn next.

6.4 Kant's qualified endorsement of the skill model of virtue[22]

Kant's discussion of the skill model of virtue is not a well-known feature of his ethics. The lack of attention it has received might be attributed to two facts. First, it only comes up in the later works, rather than the more frequently studied *Groundwork for the Metaphysics of Morals* (1785) and *Critique of Practical Reason* (1788). Second, his endorsement of the model is highly qualified and, on a superficial reading, the relevant passages may appear to dismiss the idea outright.

The passages on the skill model of virtue that I will focus on here come from the substantial Introduction to the Doctrine of Virtue of the 1797 *Metaphysics of Morals* (Kant 1900–: 6:379–413), where Kant explains the role of the concept of virtue in a broader moral philosophy, and outlines the account of virtue that is developed further in the main text (Kant 1900–, 6:417–474).[23] Kant makes something of (what he takes to be) the etymological roots of the German word for virtue, *Tugend*, in the verb *taugen*, "to be fit for" (Kant 1900–, 6:390) which, as we will see, is conceptually tied to the skill model of virtue. But his initial remarks indicate a departure from his German rationalist predecessors on the matter of virtue as a skill:

> But virtue is not to be explained and valued merely as a *skill* [*Fertigkeit*] and (as the prize essay of Cochius, the court-chaplain, puts it) a longstanding *habit* [*Gewohnheit*] of morally good actions acquired through practice. For if this skill is not the effect of principles that are reflected upon, firm, and continually purified, then it is like any other mechanism of technically practical reason and is neither equipped for all situations, nor sufficiently secure for the altered circumstances that new enticements could bring about.
>
> *Kant 1900–: 6:383–384*

Here Kant tacitly distinguishes two kinds of skill. One is the result of mere habit, the other of some kind of ever-developing critical intelligence. The first cannot provide a viable model for virtue. But the second might. Note that he does not reject the skill model outright: rather, he says that virtue is not to be understood and valued *merely* as a *Fertigkeit*. Virtue could indeed be a *Fertigkeit*, if appropriately qualified: the skill must itself be the "effect" (*Wirkung*) of continually strengthened commitment to, and continually refined grasp of, certain principles.

Let's consider how Kant positions himself against the rationalist tradition here. Kant takes aim at a particular way of working with the skill model of virtue – one that he suggests is exemplified in the prize-winning essay of Leonhard Cochius (1769). The reference is curious for several reasons. First, Cochius's essay does not, in fact, explicitly take up questions about the nature of virtue.[24] The particular passage that Kant appears to have in mind concerns efforts to cultivate character through the habitual imitation of moral exemplars: "By these means the way of thinking [*Denkungsart*] of such persons sneaks unnoticed into the minds of others, and gradually becomes a proficiency [*Fertigkeit*] that adheres there" (Cochius 1769: 85). Kant abhors the suggestion that an unreflective transmission of a "way of thinking" could form genuine character, much less *good* character. Second, if my arguments in the previous section are sound, it was Mendelssohn – and certainly not Cochius – who was chiefly responsible for rehabilitating the skill model of virtue in the German rationalist tradition. Although Wolff and the others spoke of virtue as a *Fertigkeit*, they did not assign particular value to virtue on this basis: after all, Meier spoke of vice as no less a *Fertigkeit* than virtue. Why not pick on Mendelssohn, then, as the chief proximate source of the skill model of virtue? By citing Cochius, Kant indicates a specific target: a conception of virtue as a skill developed through unreflective imitation of exemplars. This is not how Mendelssohn invokes the skill model of virtue – and Kant, who deeply respected Mendelssohn,[25] must have recognised as much. Mendelssohn indicates that the effort to bring oneself closer to the standard of virtue must be grounded in concrete, situation-specific, attention to the "true dignity of the human being" in everything that one does. Although Mendelssohn's remarks are by no means as detailed and explicit as one might like, the result is hardly the virtue-by-osmosis picture that Kant rightly abhors in Cochius.

Kant returns to the skill model later in the Introduction, where he distinguishes between two kinds of skill (*Fertigkeit*) – free and unfree – and indicates that only the former provides a plausible model for virtue. Let's first consider how Kant draws that distinction in the first part of the passage:

> *Skill* [*Fertigkeit*] (*habitus*) is a facility for action and a subjective perfection of choice. But not every such *facility* [*Leichtigkeit*] is a *free* skill (*habitus libertatis*); for if it is a *habit* [*Angewohnheit*] (*assuetudo*), that is, a uniformity in action that has become a *necessity* through frequent repetition, it is not one that proceeds from freedom, and therefore also not a moral skill.
>
> *Kant 1900–: 6:407*

Unfree skills are expressions of *necessitating* habit (*Angewohnheit*, not *Gewohnheit*):[26] given the appropriate stimuli, a certain determinate way of going on has become "a *necessity*" owing to prior repetition. Examples of this sort of skill, which can be cultivated without genuine thought, can be found among the myriad skills of movement and bodily control acquired in the normal course of a young child's development – such as standing, or walking, or being able to grasp objects of a certain size. A one-year-old child who stands has cultivated the requisite resources at great effort, though she never deliberately set herself the task of learning how to stand. And she constantly makes minute adjustments that keep her upright, though she neither has determinate thought about standing as such, nor does she register any explicit attention to the countless little moves that sustain it. This is not, or not simply, because she is an infant: standing adults don't typically consider these constant adjustments either. When I shift my body weight in response to a change in the surface on which I am standing, I am acting on a certain cue: reliably taking perfectly adequate means, in response to this cue, to a certain end (staying upright). What I am *not* doing is considering how I should respond to what I am thereby conditioned to register as a cue, or even whether I should respond: this is the necessitation that Kant takes to be characteristic of an unfree skill.

Since the exercise of any skill has some basis in habit, there is always some way in which one is mechanically disposed to go on, given a certain stimulus. Kant does not spell out exactly how he understands the notion of "a *free* skill (*habitus libertatis*)"; he only says, rather unhelpfully, that it "proceeds from freedom". However, we can suppose that someone exercising such a skill must have something against which to assess the promptings of habit. I take this other thing to be a standard of goodness. A good pianist does not simply hit the right notes, but interprets the score and expresses the music. She wants to play *well*, and both her grasp of what constitutes good playing, and the readiness of her respect for this standard, become more fine-grained, concretely action-guiding, and demanding as she develops greater skill over time.[27]

We can briefly recapitulate Kant's relation to Mendelssohn in light of this distinction between unfree and free skills. Mendelssohn's celebration of automatism in the exercise of a skill only conceivably accords with Kant's notion of an unfree skill. And if a *free* skill can only be "the effect of principles that are reflected upon, firm, and continually purified" as Kant indicates (Kant 1900–: 6:383), then it is presumably a highly refined, and indefinitely perfectible, power of judgement – not an automatism that releases one from any need to think about what one is doing. And since Mendelssohn was the key developer of the skill model of virtue among Kant's immediate predecessors, it is plausible that Kant was thinking of Mendelssohn when he rejected the idea that virtue could be modelled on unfree skill. Yet as we saw, Mendelssohn elaborates his account in the second edition of the *Philosophical Writings* along lines that stand at odds with his initial celebration of automatism. Mendelssohn's account is rich, but muddled   and perhaps for this reason Kant could neither single it out as his target, nor credit it as his inspiration.

But what exactly *does* Kant have in mind when he claims that such a skill "proceeds from freedom"? There is a hint of an answer in the wider context of this passage, where Kant distinguishes duties of right and virtue in a wider moral philosophy. Duties of right are coercively enforceable requirements of conduct, so that one acts in ways that are compatible with "outer freedom" in a political community. These requirements can be met irrespective of one's motivations. Duties of virtue, by contrast, call for the cultivation of a certain mindedness from the free adoption of the morally obligatory ends of one's own perfection and the happiness of others (Kant 1900–: 6:385–388). Resources of attention, judgement, and temperament are the cultivated means to these ends. Virtuous action expresses an intelligent commitment to these ends, and virtue itself must incorporate a readiness to be appropriately motivated.[28] Since no one can be made to adopt an end (Kant 1900–: 6:385), virtue must be the expression of the "inner freedom" of a human being (Kant 1900–: 6:406–407).

When Kant returns to the skill model of virtue in this context, it is to rule out a particular way of taking it up – modelling virtue on unfree skills, which commits one to a conception of virtue as a mechanistic impulse to perform certain actions given the appropriate stimulus. Presumably, virtue is like any free skill in being a mindedness that follows from the free adoption of ends. But since ends can only be freely adopted, this does not tell us much. It also seems to be too thin a notion of the relevant sort of skill: toothbrushing, and myriad other forms of cultivated know-how, fit this description as well. When Kant says that the relevant sort of skill must itself be the effect of "continually purified principles", he suggests that the relevant sort of skill – the one that could provide a model for virtue – is indefinitely perfectible. There is no point at which someone has arrived at a complete and fully adequate grasp of what counts as good piano playing. Likewise there is no reason to suppose that a person's grasp of the value of humanity – the intelligence of a person's commitment to "the human being as such" that unites duties of virtue to self and to others (Kant 1900–: 6:395) – can in principle reach a terminus, a point beyond which it admits of no further augmentation or development.

With this in mind let's consider the qualification under which Kant is prepared to endorse the skill model of virtue:

> Hence one cannot *define* virtue as skill [*Fertigkeit*] in free action in conformity with law unless one adds "to determine oneself through the representation of the law in action", and then this skill is not a property of choice, but rather of *will*, which is a faculty of desire that, in adopting a rule, is at once universally legislative. Only such a skill can be counted as virtue.
>
> *Kant 1900–: 6:407*

A typical free skill is a cultivated fitness for a *discretionary* end, and is thereby deemed "a property of choice". Moral virtue is a perfection of the will, or practical reason. The relevant notion of perfection in this context is the "harmony of a thing's properties with an *end*" (Kant 1900–: 6:386). Kant belongs to a long, and broadly rationalist, tradition that takes reason to be the source of substantive ends. For Kant, the moral law, the constitutive principle of practical reason, yields claims about what we categorically ought to care about: namely, the two morally obligatory ends of one's own perfection and the happiness of others. Therefore, moral virtue *as a skill*, as an acquired perfection of practical reason, can only be a harmony of a person's "properties" with these ends. Like any ends, these ends can only be freely adopted. Thus what marks the difference between virtue and standard free skills is not so much that virtue requires appropriately motivated action and the skill of a musician (say) does not, as it is about the substantive content of the practical commitment in question.[29]

6.5 Conclusion

Let me conclude by acknowledging some of the many questions left open. In the second edition of the *Philosophical Writings*, Mendelssohn revises his account of skill in ways that cast doubt upon his original invocation of the typesetter and the pianist as equally apt guides for thinking about virtue as a skill. But he did not take that opportunity to remove the typesetter example, or otherwise indicate any new preference for the pianist. Thus it remains unclear whether or not Mendelssohn anticipated the problem that Kant later raised when he rejected "unfree" skills – the sort that admit of blind, unreflective automatism – as a guide for thinking about virtue as a skill. One can only speculate about whether the awkward juxtaposition of Mendelssohn's two examples spurred Kant to appreciate the importance of fixing on the right *sort* of skill in the first place. Nevertheless, Mendelssohn's and Kant's quite different ways of taking up the skill model of virtue each merit further attention, and interpretive reconstruction, from philosophers. Such work might allow us to make better sense of Socrates' puzzling but intuitively appealing suggestion that a good human being must be skilled in living.[30]

Notes

1 For a historical perspective on the skill model of virtue see e.g. Annas (1995 and 1993); for contemporary discussion, consider Stichter (2018), Annas (2011), and Bloomfield (2000).

2 The *Philosophical Writings* is a collection of Mendelssohn's earlier writings, which he revised for publication in 1761. The discussion of skill (*Fertigkeit*) is found in an essay new to the 1761 edition called "Rhapsody, or Addition to the Letters on Sentiments". He also made significant changes in the "improved edition" of 1771.

3 See esp. *Protagoras* 357b and 361a–c.

4 *Protagoras* 352b.

5 The Stoics were important developers not only of this psychology but also of the skill model of virtue; it accordingly bears mention that Mendelssohn's discussion of skill concludes with a quotation from the Roman Stoic Seneca.

6 See *Protagoras* 352–357. I am bracketing controversial issues around the proto-utilitarian interpretation of this passage.

7 Actually he attributes this view to *Plato*, when it is more precisely attributed to Plato's portrayal of *Socrates*.

8 Mendelssohn's German rationalist predecessors also endorsed this "guise of the good" thesis: see e.g. Wolff (1752[1712] §§496–506).

9 Scholars debate the debt of these philosophers to Leibniz (with whom Wolff corresponded extensively), and their originality more generally; but the key pieces of what Mendelssohn has in mind as the "modern doctrine of skills" can be traced to their writings without considering those debates.

10 He learned German, Latin, French, English, and Greek within a few years of his arrival in Berlin, as a teenager accompanied by his rabbi from Dessau. His election into the Berlin Academy of Sciences was never ratified by Frederick II, presumably because he was Jewish. See the definitive biography of Altmann (1998 [1973]).

11 Dahlstrom (Mendelssohn 1997) sometimes renders *Fertigkeit* with the full phrase "proficiencies or perfected habits", sometimes just "proficiencies". "Proficiency" provides a more apt rendering for the term in Wolff, Baumgarten, and Meier's writings; but it becomes more strained when Mendelssohn speaks in his own voice, since he is pointedly recalling the Socratic idea of virtue as a skill (*technē*) – which, he implies, his immediate rationalist predecessors have forgotten.

12 On understanding and judgement as proficiencies, see Baumgarten *Metaphysics* §606; G-Met §§467, 473; and on wit, discrimination, and other cultivated proficiencies of judgement, see Baumgarten G-Met §426, §§452–453 and Meier *Metaphysik* §567, §570 (cf. Kant, *Critique of Pure Reason* A654–5/ B682–3).

13 See, e.g., Baumgarten *Metaphysics* §650 and G-Met §475; Meier, *Metaphysik* §644 and *Auszug aus der Vernuftlehre* §§527–563.

14 Note Meier's usage, when he glosses vice as an "proficiency for sinning" and virtue as a "proficiency for free, lawful actions" (*Auszug aus der Vernunftlehre*, §147 and §150).

15 Mendelssohn departs here from the classification offered by Wolff, who takes pleasure, pain, and affective states generally to be indistinct *Bewegungsgründe* (*Vernünftige Gedanken* §506).

16 Mendelssohn endorses the received rationalist view that the efficacy of a cognition will be proportional to the perfection of its object and to the degree of the knowledge of it; he adds that it will also be inversely proportional to the time it takes to consider the perfection thus presented (1972: 414; 1997: 160).

17 Mendelssohn first raises the concern earlier in "Rhapsody", where he gestures towards a somewhat different solution in Stoic cosmopolitanism (1971: 405–406; 1997: 151–152). The complaint that virtue-based moral theories are implicitly egoistic, or call for the wrong sort of attention to be drawn to oneself, has been lodged against contemporary virtue ethics by e.g. Hurka (2001); see Annas (2008) for a response.

18 In *Philosophical Writings*, the discussion of skill in "Rhapsody" follows a piece framed as an epistolary exchange on recent debates in aesthetic theory. See also n2.

19 This idea is associated with the psychological research of Mihaly Csikszentmihalyi, and others; for its deployment in a recent account of virtue as skill, see Annas (2011: 70–82).

20 Cf. Mendelssohn (1761) against (1771); the *Jubiläumsausgabe* and the Cambridge edition follow the 1771 text.

21 Mendelssohn elaborates on speed that "intuitive cognition [*anschauende Erkenntniß*]" brings to the execution of a skill at the very end of "Rhapsody" (422–423/167–168).

22 The account offered in this section is developed and defended more fully in Merritt (2018).

23 A similar passage in the *Anthropology* (7:147) appears rather less open to the skill model of virtue: "one cannot explain *virtue* as the *skill* [*Fertigkeit*] in free lawful actions, for then it would be a mere mechanism of the application of power" (7:147; see also 7:400). In Merritt (2018) I argue that this passage is compatible with the *Metaphysics of Morals* passages, which, as we are about to see, identify two possible kinds of skill or *Fertigkeit* – rejecting one, and accepting the other, as a plausible model of virtue. Another noteworthy passage is found in the records of Kant's lectures on ethics from around this same time (Vigilantius):

> one can find enjoyment in virtue [...] but only when and for the reason that the fulfilling of duty has become a skill [*Fertigkeit*], so that it becomes easy to follow the prescriptions of reason; from this one attains a contentment about one's actions and about the strengthening of one's will for the prescriptions of reason.

27:490–491

24 Cochius (1769) offers an empirical psychological account of the nature of "inclinations" (*Neigungen*) in the early modern rationalist tradition, and takes up the practical problem (set by the Academy of Sciences) of how to alter a person's inclinations, strengthening the good ones and weakening the bad ones.

25 As partial evidence of this, consider Kant's 16 August 1783 letter to Mendelssohn (10:345).

26 *Gewohnheit* in Kant's usage is evaluatively neutral: it is simply a given fact about how our minds work, that habit plays a role in the animation of thought. This is neither good nor bad; nor is it anything for which we can be held responsible. By contrast, Kant claims that "all habit [*Angewohnheit*] is reprehensible" (*Anthropology* 7:149). *Angewohnheit* in Kant's usage consistently implies physical necessitation through the force of habit, that is, as such, at odds with freedom.

27 See Montero (2013) on how certain skills embed such reflective assessment.

28 This is why Kant's own deployment of the skill model of virtue in the main text of the *Doctrine of Virtue* focuses on the cultivation of moral feeling (a readiness to be moved by one's recognition of moral requirement), as I explain in Chapter 7 of Merritt (2018).

29 Stichter (2016) defends the skill model of virtue against the criticism that skills do not require appropriately motivated action, whereas virtue does; his conclusion is similar to mine here.

30 I would like to thank Michael Kremer and Markos Valaris for helpful comments on earlier drafts of this chapter, and Ursula Goldenbaum for discussion.

References

Note on citation of primary texts:

The works of Wolff, Baumgarten, and Meier are cited by section (§). Baumgarten's *Metaphysics* went through multiple editions; I am working with the fourth (1757) edition of the Latin text translated in Baumgarten (2013), as well as Meier's 1766 German translation (abbreviated G-Met) which follows an earlier edition. Mendelssohn's *Philosophische Schriften* is cited first according to the page in the *Jubiläumsausgabe* followed by the page in Dahlstrom's English translation. Kant's texts are cited by volume and page of the German Academy edition, except the *Critique of Pure Reason*, which is cited according to the first (A) and second (B) editions of the text. Translations are my own, though I have consulted the English translations listed below.

Altmann, A. (1998 [1973]) *Moses Mendelssohn: A Biographical Study*, Oxford: Littman Library of Jewish Civilization.

Annas, J. (2011) *Intelligent Virtue*, Oxford: Oxford University Press.

—— (2008) "Virtue Ethics and the Charge of Egoism," in P. Bloomfield (ed.) *Morality and Self-Interest*, New York: Oxford University Press, pp. 205–221.

—— (1995) "Virtue as a Skill," *International Journal of Philosophical Studies* 3: 227–243.

—— (1993) *The Morality of Happiness*, New York: Oxford University Press.

Baumgarten, A. (2013) *Metaphysics: A Critical Translation with Kant's Elucidations, Selected Notes, and Related Materials*, trans. C. Fugate and J. Hymers, London: Bloomsbury.

—— (1766) *Metaphysik*, trans. (Latin to German) G. F. Meier, Halle: Carl Hermann Hemmerde.

Bloomfield, P. (2000) "Virtue Epistemology and the Epistemology of Virtue," *Philosophy and Phenomenological Research* 60: 23–43.

Cochius, L. (1769) *Untersuchung über die Neigungen*, Berlin: Haude and Spener.

Hurka, T. (2001) *Virtue, Vice, and Value*, Oxford: Oxford University Press.

Kant, I. (1900) *Gesammelte Schriften*, edited by Deutschen Akademie der Wissenschaften zu Berlin, Berlin: Walter de Gruyter.

Meier, G. F. (2016 [1752]) *Excerpt from the Doctrine of Reason*, trans. A. Bunch, London: Bloomsbury.

—— (1765) *Metaphysik*, second edition, Halle: Johann Justinus Gebauer.

—— (1752) *Auszug aus der Vernunftlehre*, Halle: Johann Justinus Gebauer.

Mendelssohn, M. (1997) *Philosophical Writings*, trans. D. Dahlstrom, Cambridge: Cambridge University Press.

—— (1971) *Gesammelte Schriften: Jubiläumsausgabe*, Vol. 1: Schriften zur Philosophie und Ästhetik, Stuttgart: Frommann-Holzboog.

—— (1771) *Philosophische Schriften*, second edition ("Verbesserte Auflage"), Berlin: Christian Friedrich Voß.

—— (1761) *Philosophische Schriften*, Berlin: Christian Friedrich Voß.

Merritt, M. (2018) *Kant on Reflection and Virtue*, Cambridge: Cambridge University Press.

Montero, B. (2013) "A Dancer Reflects," in J. Schear (ed.) *Mind, Reason, and Being-in-the-World: the McDowell-Dreyfus Debate*, Abingdon: Routledge, pp. 303–319.

Plato (1992) *Protagoras*, trans. C. C. W. Taylor, Oxford: Clarendon Press.

Stichter, M. (2018) "Virtue as a Skill," in N. Snow (ed.) *Oxford Handbook of Virtue*, Oxford: Oxford University Press.

—— (2016) "Practical Skills and Practical Wisdom in Virtue," *Australasian Journal of Philosophy* 94: 435–448.

Wolff, C. (1752 [1712]) *Vernünftige Gedanken von Gott, der Welt und der Seele des Menschen auch allen Dingen überhaupt*. Halle.

7

GILBERT RYLE ON SKILL AS KNOWLEDGE-HOW*

Michael Kremer

7.1 Introduction

Gilbert Ryle's thought about skill is tied to his famous distinction between knowledge-how and knowledge-that; indeed, as we will see, skill is the paradigm form of knowledge-how for Ryle. His basic view of skill, present in his first writings on knowledge-how (Ryle 1940, 1945, 1949), continued to develop in later work, devoted primarily to the nature of *thinking*. He modeled problem-solving thought on the "self-teaching" in which one might engage to develop or acquire a skill, and repeatedly returned to the topics of skill, learning, and education, in such essays as "Teaching and Training," "Thinking and Self-Teaching," and "Improvisation" (Ryle 1967, 1972, 1976). These writings unfold a picture of skill as a distinctive form of knowledge, inculcated through a distinctive form of teaching, "training." Ryle's thought on skill, and how it is taught and learned, reflect and develop out of his experiences as a teacher of philosophy, rowing coach, and trainer of anti-aircraft gunners, and I will draw on these examples in developing his view in detail.[1] I begin, however, by sketching the background to this discussion, in Ryle's arguments for his knowledge-how/knowledge-that distinction.

7.2 Knowing how and knowing that, "intellectualism," and "practicalism"

Ryle sharply distinguished knowledge-how (to do something) and knowledge-that (something is true). Confusing these forms of knowledge constitutes a *category mistake*, and attempts to explain one in terms of the other must end in absurdity (Ryle 1945, 1949). Recently, however, Jason Stanley and Timothy Williamson (Stanley and Williamson 2001; Stanley 2011) have defended "intellectualism," the view that knowledge-how is a *species* of knowledge-that; knowing how to V is knowing that [W is a way that you yourself can V], for some "way" W with which you are acquainted (Stanley 2011: 122). Carlotta Pavese has modified, elaborated, and defended this position in recent work (Pavese 2015, 2017a, 2017b). Stephen Hetherington takes the opposite, "practicalist" position, that knowledge-that is a species of knowledge-how; knowing that *p* is knowing how "to manifest various accurate representations of *p*" (Hetherington 2011: 42).

Ryle's insights into the nature of skill should interest all parties in this dispute; but Ryle's reasons for his distinction shed light on his own position. He offered two kinds of support: infinite regress arguments, and arguments turning on the "gradability" of knowledge-how.

7.3 The regress

Ryle's famous regress targets "intellectualists," who equate *intelligence* with *intellectual activity*, positing that "practical activities merit their titles 'intelligent', 'clever', and the rest only because they are accompanied by … internal acts of considering propositions" (Ryle 1945: 222). The regress aims to reduce this "intellectualist legend" to absurdity, *thereby* revealing the need to distinguish knowledge-how from knowledge-that. Perhaps the best formulation of Ryle's argument goes:

> The consideration of propositions is itself an operation the execution of which can be more or less intelligent, less or more stupid. But if, for any operation to be intelligently executed, a prior theoretical operation had first to be performed and performed intelligently, it would be a logical impossibility for anyone ever to break into the circle.
>
> *Ryle 1949: 19*

Ryle highlights two "salient points at which this regress could arise": the *selection* of "the one maxim that is appropriate rather than any of the thousands which are not," and its *application* "to the particular situation which my action is to meet." Each of these can be intelligent – or not (Ryle 1949: 19–20; Löwenstein 2017: 276–80; Small 2017: 62–3). Although this argument does not mention knowledge, Ryle concludes: "'Intelligent' cannot be defined in terms of 'intellectual' or 'knowing how' in terms of 'knowing that'" (Ryle 1949: 20).

How does this regress about intelligence support a distinction about knowledge? It is illuminating to see the argument as implicitly *equivocating* between the two forms of knowledge. Two principles, each correct when properly understood, are improperly combined through confusing knowledge-how with knowledge-that. Drawing the distinction saves both principles while avoiding the regress. Thus, the argument shows intellectualism to be *absurd*: a conceptual muddle with no clear meaning.

The crucial principles are:

(I)   An action is intelligent only if it is grounded in knowledge of the agent.
(II) Knowledge can contribute to the intelligence of an action only if it is intelligently selected and applied.

The regress then follows:

Suppose S performs A intelligently.
A was grounded in some knowledge K of S. (I)
K was intelligently selected and applied by S. (II)
The selection and application of K were grounded in further knowledge K_1 and K_2 (I)
K_1 and K_2 were intelligently selected and applied by S. (II)
Etc.

However, if in (I) "knowledge" means knowledge-how, while in (II), "knowledge" means knowledge-that, the regress is blocked. The "intellectualist legend" implicitly equates knowledge-how and knowledge-that; the regress depends on this equivocation.

Properly understood, (I) says that *knowledge-how* accounts for the intelligence of an action. While many intelligent actions involve knowledge-that – we often apply knowledge of truths in deliberation and planning – knowledge-that is insufficient to account for intelligence. Knowledge-how is also needed, at least in the selection and application of the knowledge-that employed. Thus, Ryle recognizes the existence of *intellectual* knowledge-how, intellectual skills.[2]

Similarly, (II) says that the agent must select and apply *knowledge-that*. Stanley objects that this is implausible; Ryle either foists on the intellectualist, or assumes himself, a false picture of knowledge-that as "behaviorally inert." He thus either perpetrates a straw man argument, or reveals his own inadequate conception of knowledge-that (Stanley 2011: 14, 26).[3] In his critique of "intellectualism" Ryle seems to take knowledge-that to involve a "consideration of propositions" that cannot directly influence action. Yet he also asserts that the verb 'to know' is "ordinarily used dispositionally" (Ryle 1949: 32). Hence, knowledge is far from being "behaviorally inert." Perhaps, then, it is Ryle's *intellectualist* who holds the opposite conception. If so, however, Stanley can respond that a "reasonable intellectualist" can embrace a dispositional conception of knowledge-that, leaving the selection and application of knowledge to unintelligent "automatic mechanisms" with no need of a further act of "consideration of propositions" (Stanley 2011: 14, 26). This "reasonable intellectualism" seems invulnerable to the regress.[4]

7.4 Gradability and learning

Hence, we turn to Ryle's second argument for his distinction. This turns on two closely related "non-parallelisms": knowledge-how, but not knowledge-that, comes in degrees; and, more fundamentally, they are *acquired* in different ways. First, "knows how to," but not "knows that," is *gradable*: "we never speak of a person having partial knowledge of a fact or truth … it is proper and normal to speak of a person knowing in part how to do something." Second, "Learning how or improving in ability is not like learning that or acquiring information. Truths can be imparted, procedures can only be inculcated, and while inculcation is a gradual process, imparting is relatively sudden" (Ryle 1949: 46). This second point is more fundamental than the first, because the difference between learning-how and learning-that *explains* the facts about gradability. Knowledge-how must come in degrees, because learning-how brings *improvement* in knowledge-how. There is no parallel phenomenon in learning-that, and so no need for degrees of knowledge-that.[5]

Ryle's regress argument aimed to establish a *categorial* difference between knowledge-how and knowledge-that. Stina Bäckström and Martin Gustafsson argue that we should understand Ryle's talk of *categories* in terms of the idea of *form*, so that the difference between knowledge-how and knowledge-that is *formal*. They see this as "the key to Ryle's dispositional analysis of skill and know-how, and to his specific observations that skill and know-how involve understanding, variability, learning, and so on, as essential characteristics" (Bäckström and Gustafsson 2017: 43). This interpretation allows us to see Ryle's two arguments as internally related. The form of learning that results in each kind of knowledge must reflect the form of that knowledge. Differentiating the two types of learning (the learning argument) and differentiating the two types of knowledge (the regress argument) are then two sides of the same coin. Hence, understanding Ryle's view of skill will go hand-in-hand with understanding his view on the learning of skill.

7.5 Ryle's positive conception of knowledge-how

According to Ryle, skill is a kind of knowledge-how, and so a kind of *knowledge*. Knowledge in general is a *disposition*, and specifically, a *heterogeneous* disposition. Unlike a "single-track disposition," whose manifestations are all of the same type, many different actions manifest knowledge. For example, knowledge that *p* is not a disposition to "judge that *p*," manifested in an action of "internally re-asserting" *p*. Rather, knowledge that *p* manifests itself in a disparate range of actions and behaviors that can only be exhibited in a list ending "and so on" (Ryle 1949: 32).

Ryle's term "disposition" can be misleading, however, since this word is reserved nowadays for what *he* calls "tendencies." For Ryle these constitute *one* kind of disposition, corresponding to conditional statements about what the subject *would* do, *if* such and such were to occur. But, *his* "dispositions" include *capacities*, which correspond to modal statements about what a subject *could* do, rather than *would* do. His category of dispositions is the Aristotelian category of *hexeis*, unified by their general modal character. Ryle places *knowledge* among capacities, while *belief* is a tendency: "'Know' is a capacity verb … used for signifying that the person described can bring things off, or get things right. 'Believe' … is a tendency verb … which does not connote that anything is brought off or got right" (Ryle 1949: 117).[6]

Knowledge-how to *V* is a capacity to "get things right" whose *primary* manifestation is in *V*-ing: "no one would say that I really know how to swim, or that I have swimming-skill, unless when I do it myself I usually succeed" (Ryle 1940: 198). Nonetheless, we cannot *identify* knowledge-how to *V* with the capacity to *V* reliably. That would reduce knowledge-how to a single-track disposition, and equate it with mere ability, which may not exhibit intelligence or knowledge at all. Almost all human beings can digest food, but this involves no knowledge-how (Ryle 1953: 311–12).[7] Ryle accepts that, in order for someone to count as knowing how, it is *necessary* that "they tend to perform … well," satisfying the "standards" or "criteria" which implicitly govern their activity. This is to be "well-regulated," but is compatible with a lack of intelligence – the "regulation" might have an external source, as in the performance of a machine or a trained animal. Therefore, Ryle adds that the intelligent knower-how must not only "satisfy criteria" but "apply them." This is "to regulate one's actions and not merely to be well-regulated." To know how, a person must be "ready to detect and correct lapses, to repeat and improve upon successes, to profit from the examples of others and so forth." Such a person "applies criteria in performing critically, that is, in trying to get things right" (Ryle 1949: 17).

Knowledge-how, then, is a capacity to "get things right," to meet the criteria for success in an activity in a self-regulated, intelligent fashion. This intelligence lies in a disposition for critical scrutiny and correction of one's performances, and those of others. The knower-how is always ready to *learn* and *improve* – in accordance with the gradability and learning arguments discussed above.

Ryle is an empiricist in the minimal sense of holding that there is an internal relation between knowledge and learning. However, he often asserts the stronger view that *all* knowledge, and so all skill, is learned. Bäckström and Gustafsson deploy their idea that Ryle's categorial distinctions have to do with *form*, to defuse this:

> Ryle seems to explain the presence of intelligence in terms of a past history of learning. … Ryle is not making the dubious point that having actually learned the skill is a necessary condition for having the skill." Instead, he "is identifying … a *formal* aspect of skillful behavior … something is a skill only insofar as it is situated in a logical space where questions about learning are *applicable* – where such questions *make sense*."
>
> *Bäckström and Gustafsson 2017: 47*

This is an attractive idea, but it is difficult to fit to Ryle's words. He often equated knowledge with something "learned and not forgotten" (Ryle 1949: 110, 1964: 180), and rejected rationalist talk of innate logical capacities since it entails that "we have masteries of things without ever having mastered them, that is, that we know without having learned, and hence are experts, though totally inexperienced" (Ryle 1960b: 119). Bäckström and Gustafsson's suggestion, then, is perhaps best seen as an amendment, not an interpretation, of Ryle. But in either case, we should expect Ryle's discussions of teaching-how and learning-how to illuminate his view of knowledge-how, and so skill.

7.6 Learning by doing: habits versus intelligent powers, skills versus competences

Knowledge-how is acquired by *learning by doing*, that is, through practice. Practice, however, comes in two types, "drill" and "training." Drill, the repeated performance of the same action, "dispenses with intelligence," yielding "mere habits" (Ryle 1945: 234). The mark of a habit is its "stereotyped," routine nature: "It is of the essence of merely habitual practices that one performance is a replica of its predecessors" (Ryle 1949: 30).[8] Habitual performance is "well-regulated," but acquiring habits is only learning to conform to criteria, not to *apply* them. In contrast, training yields knowledge-how, an "intelligent power."[9] Training involves, but goes beyond, drill. The trainee is not merely habituated to perform, but learns to do so "thinking what he is doing" – "in the right way ... with his head." This does not entail an intellectualist understanding of knowledge-how; rather, "he becomes a judge of his own performances – he learns what mistakes are and how to avoid them" (Ryle 1945: 234). Trainees develop a critical acuity; they learn from both failures and successes, correcting their approach, adopting newly discovered techniques, and testing and practicing them. "It is of the essence of intelligent practice that one performance is modified by its predecessors. The agent is still learning" (Ryle 1949: 30).[10]

The trainer inculcates a capacity for critical scrutiny through teaching *methods* and *techniques*. "It is just here, with the notion of taking care while taking risks, that there enters on the scene the cardinal notion of *method*." A method is a shareable, general, learnable way of doing something. Unlike a stereotyped routine, it calls for attention and care, and involves not just patterns of action, but "systems of avoidances ... patterns of *don'ts*" (Ryle 1967: 473). Learning a method is, in part, learning to recognize and avoid types of mistake. A method has a rational structure; the trainee learns not only what to do, and what to avoid, but *why*. Its application results in "chain-undertakings," in which "infra-actions" stand in "intentional subordination" to a "programme" – whose verbal formulation would display "how the Lower Order actions are tactically subjected to their Higher Order Undertaking" using logical, modal, and temporal vocabulary (Ryle 1974: 336–7). Consequently,

> It is always possible in principle, if not in practice, to explain why he [a knower-how] tends to succeed, that is, to state the reasons for his actions. It is tautology to say that there is a method in his cleverness.
>
> *Ryle 1945: 228*

Ultimately, the trainee should dispense with the trainer, becoming their own "coach." They must improvise and innovate, in two senses. First, the methods they have learned are general, requiring adaptation to changing circumstances (Ryle 1976: 123–6). "What distinguishes ... actions done with method is ... adaptation ... to differences... it is the irregularity of some classes of performances which shows that the author is applying rules" (Ryle 1946: 243). "One main business of a teacher" is to equip students to "think things out for themselves," going beyond their instructions (Ryle 1967: 466). Second, they will sometimes need to come up with new methods, which they must test experimentally to determine their range of usefulness, and reinforce through practice. The "supreme reward of the teacher" is for their students to go beyond "further applications of the established ways of operating," advancing their craft by "discovering new methods or procedures" (Ryle 1967: 466).

Ryle referred to the complex mixture of trials, testing, and practice required for this kind of innovation as "experimental learning." That he thought this form of learning to be essential to acquiring knowledge-how, however, reveals that his argument was not primarily driven by the use of the English expression "knows how to." His discussions of knowledge-how and learning-how fit well to skills, but not so well to many other things we describe using those words. Eventually, he distinguished skills from "mere competences," such as "buttoning up buttons, sloping arms, spelling, counting and reckoning" (Ryle 1993a: 60; cf. Ryle 1964: 180).[11] Unlike skills, competences leave "no room for any improvement, talent, or flair," and do not exhibit gradability: "You can either do it or you cannot." Like habits, they are acquired through drill, and are routine and stereotyped; yet unlike habits, they are capacities, not tendencies. Skills, in contrast, require "craftsmanship," which is "more than mere competence." To possess a skill one must "think for himself – he can't do it in his sleep." Skills are marked by critical performance in trying to get things right; there is "room for praise, etc. in terms of the efficient or inefficient exercise of skills" (Ryle 1993a: 60; cf. Ryle 1964: 180). Thus, Ryle's account of knowledge-how best fits skills.

7.7 The role of the teacher

This account of training in a skill engenders an apparent paradox: learners must be *trained* to be spontaneous, *taught* to do "untaught things" (Ryle 1967: 465). How can a teacher equip their students to go beyond their lessons? Ryle offers no general pedagogical principles, since "different arts and crafts require different disciplines" (Ryle 1967: 475). But mere lecturing will not do; the teacher must get the pupil to *practice*, trying to perform well, perhaps initially by drill in elementary examples. As soon as the student makes the attempt, exhibiting pride in success, envy of others' successes, embarrassment at failure, and contempt for others' failures, they are "co-operating, and so self-moving" (Ryle 1967: 472). The teacher then fosters this through criticism of missteps and praise for correct performance. Suitable phrasing sustains the pupil's interest and response – as Ryle himself coached under-graduate rowers with "a flow of metaphors ranging from reproachful elephants and camels to commendatory swallows" (Mabbott 1986: 224). The pupil begins to make the standards and criteria of the skill their own, imitating their teacher's critical scrutiny of their performance, becoming a self-teacher.

Still, how does the pupil acquire the ability to improvise, in applying learned techniques or devising new ones? Again, Ryle gives no general advice, instead providing a fascinating list of "the teaching-methods, devices, and dodges by which ordinarily good or very good teachers do actually teach things to us" – all "intended … to get us ourselves to do and to say things of our own (as well as very often to undo and unsay things)." Good teachers:[12]

- vary style of presentation, context, emphasis and illustrations
- test for the ability to apply a lesson, join it with other lessons, etc.
- teach by *showing* what to do and what not to do

- ask questions about what we are doing, and further questions about our answers
- impose practice, with variations in situation, speed, and so on
- take us along a familiar path, and "leave us in the lurch" at the end
- exhibit inadequate solutions and ask us to identify their flaws
- give us easier versions of tasks first
- break up complex problems into smaller pieces to solve and join together
- devise analogous problems "to consolidate and limber up our mastery," when we hit upon a solution.

They practice "the art of setting tasks which the pupils have not yet accomplished but are not any longer incapable of accomplishing" (Ryle 1949: 37). Skilled practitioners are equipped to improvise when confronted with new circumstances; teachers must provide opportunities to develop this flexibility in approach.

7.8 A case study

Early in the Second World War, Ryle helped to train soldiers to shoot down enemy aircraft with machine guns. He wrote to his Oxford colleague Frederick Lindemann[13] – Churchill's scientific advisor, responsible for, among other things, work on radar and the atomic bomb – to advocate for a new "hosepipe method" of anti-aircraft fire, in which the gun was held against the hip rather than installed in a mounting. He sent Lindemann a typescript outlining the method, and the training of soldiers in it.[14] Text from this typescript later appeared in official military training manuals (The War Office 1942a, 1942b). It is illuminating to read it in the light of Ryle's thoughts about training and skill.

The typescript outlines in detail the "hosepipe method." Reasons are given for specific instructions, and trainees are told what to avoid as well as what to do. They are instructed that "attacking aircraft are to be engaged at the narrowest possible angle of approach," because the easiest target to hit is head on, planes are most vulnerable in the front, the pilot will be distracted by tracer bullets, and the bullet's penetration will be increased if the plane is flying into it. Similarly, they are told to avoid "going away" shots, because planes are better armored in the rear, and bullets have less force when the plane is moving in the same direction. Thus, trainees are not merely conditioned to shoot, but inducted into a rational structure, a method – they are taught to shoot "with their heads," "thinking what they are doing."

While the typescript does not discuss *practice*, contemporary pamphlets show that training with targets such as hydrogen balloons was common. The typescript emphasizes the importance of selecting personnel "with quick reactions and a natural aptitude," who "can be trained very quickly." It also discusses training for aircraft *recognition*, which was essential if planes were to be engaged before dropping their bombs. For this purpose, the typescript recommends at least one period a day for "practical and not theoretical" instruction, and emphasizes the need for varied methods of instruction, in order to arouse interest in a potentially tedious subject. Techniques mentioned include "the use of Lectures with silhouettes, photographs, playing cards, films, and most important of all, actual observations of planes on the ground and if possible in flight" as well as "Lecturettes by members of the class."

In these and other ways, the typescript matches closely Ryle's account of the teaching of skill. However, one might wonder whether this training left room for that crowning glory of teaching, the discovery of new methods and techniques. Surely, trainees in the anti-aircraft school were to learn the method and apply it, and not try to improvise a different method. Yet the typescript itself advocated a *new method*, since "the present system laid down for engaging

Hostile Aircraft has not proved satisfactory." This method resulted from the crucial form of innovation so prized by Ryle; and it had been tested and refined: "The methods outlined in this pamphlet are those taught at the A.A. (L.M.G.) School, Northolt. They have been altered and improved as a result of the Experience gained at the School."

Ryle's experience in teaching the skill of anti-aircraft gunnery helped shape his views about knowledge-how and skill. Although the topic was briefly raised in (Ryle 1940), his first serious discussion of it was in (Ryle 1945), completed immediately after the war's end. Ryle's wartime experiences are reflected in his use of such examples as sloping arms as a non-skilled competence (Ryle 1945: 30–1, 1993a: 60); marksmanship as a skill (Ryle 1945: 33); and rifle-shooting as a "mundane craft" (Ryle 1972: 65).

7.9 The role of knowledge-that in skill

While Ryle denies that knowledge-how, and so skill, can be reduced to knowledge-that, there is still a place for knowledge-that in skill, in three ways. First, knowledge about the world is essential to success in many skills. For example, if a billiards player

> has any skill in getting the balls where he wishes, he must have knowledge, of a rule-of-thumb sort, of the mechanical principles which govern the accelerations and decelerations of the balls. His knowledge how to execute his intentions is not at loggerheads with his knowledge of mechanical laws; it depends on that knowledge.
>
> *Ryle 1949: 66*

Second, logicians, cookbook writers, and authors of training manuals can describe the methods employed by skilled practitioners. The resulting propositions constitute knowledge-that. They cannot *replace* the knowledge-how they codify, but they have a "pedagogical" and "disciplinary" use for training beginners (Ryle 1945: 232). Ryle recognized the value of inquiry into ways of doing things, which yields "methodology" rather than "methods" (Ryle 1945: 232). Study of this "technical theory" can be valuable even for more advanced practitioners.

> Some people may learn to wrestle well from mere flair, habituation and imitation; but there is much to be learned from the technical theory of wrestling. The same thing is true of medicine and navigation. Rule of thumb is not enough.
>
> *Ryle 1966: 103*[15]

Nonetheless, Ryle denied that knowledge-how amounts to "implicit" knowledge of theoretical propositions. He called this idea a "not unfashionable shuffle," and criticized it as unable to explain why *explicit* affirmation of the same propositions is insufficient for successful performance (Ryle 1945: 227–8).

Third, the need for critical responsiveness entails that skill requires knowledge-that: for the skilled performer to be their own coach, they must know what they are doing, in what circumstances, how well or poorly it is going, and so on. This explains how I can "have knowledge of what I have been non-absent-mindedly doing or feeling" without studying or inspecting my behavior (Ryle 1945: 129). In learning to become my own coach, I learn to *attend* to what I am doing. This yields propositional knowledge that can inform my critical performance in trying to get things right.

Ryle warns against an intellectualist understanding of attention as a separate act of self-monitoring. He thinks of "attend" adverbially – to attend to one's knitting is to knit in a particular manner, *attentively* (Ryle 1949: 130). "To knit attentively" is what Ryle calls a "mongrel categorical-hypothetical" or "semi-dispositional" expression: it reports an occurrence, something that happens, but places it in a larger dispositional pattern – a readiness to react when a stitch is missed or a row is duplicated. The intellectualist goes wrong in thinking of what characterizes the manner of performing one action, in terms of two actions (Ryle 1949: 118).

7.10 Perceptual and intellectual skills

Hence, for Ryle, knowledge-how depends on knowledge-that in important ways. Dependencies also flow in the other direction: we achieve knowledge-that by exercising intellectual and perceptual skills. As we saw, Ryle's regress argument implies the existence of intellectual skills; but they are much more pervasive. Systematic inquirers employ special skills, in arriving at discoveries, and in presenting them in the form of evidence and argument. "Discovering and establishing are intelligent operations," so that even "a scientist or an historian … is primarily a knower-how and only secondarily a knower-that" – they *know how* to achieve *knowledge-that* (Ryle 1945: 234–5).

The dependency of skill on critical awareness, and so on perceptual knowledge-that, also involves acquired skills, for Ryle. There is an echo of his wartime experience here. The anti-aircraft typescript emphasized the importance of training in aircraft recognition. We can almost hear Ryle remembering this work, when he provides "estimating distances by sight, seeing through camouflage, identifying aircraft by sight and sound, and so on" as examples of perceptual skills (Ryle 1993b: 77). Indeed, we have to learn to recognize even the most ordinary objects by deploying "perception recipes."

> There is no more of an epistemological puzzle involved in describing how infants learn perception recipes than there is in describing how boys learn to bicycle. They learn by practice, and we can specify the sorts of practice that expedite this learning.
>
> *Ryle 1949: 209*

For example, feeling, in the sense of tactile detection of things or their properties, is a learned perceptual capacity that we can exercise well or poorly, attentively or carelessly. "To be able to feel things, in this sense, is to have got a certain amount of a specific skill or family of skills." The same is true for the other senses. Success, here, is finding something out – acquiring knowledge-that – "by the exercise of an acquired and perhaps deliberately trained skill" (Ryle 1956: 353). Such skills are involved even when we perceive something with no antecedent task-process of scrutiny. We have a "mastery of the art of recognising on sight the customary occupants of our customary environment"; nonetheless, "the non-occurrence of preliminaries does not entail the non-exercise of a technique" (Ryle 1993b: 77–8).

Ironically, this interdependence of knowledge-how and knowledge-that incurs a threat of regress. If acquiring knowledge-how depends on possessing knowledge-that, and acquiring knowledge-that depends on possessing knowledge-how, how does the acquisition of any knowledge at all get started? Clearly, the answer must be holistic: at some point, we count as possessing both knowledge-how and knowledge-that, when we have accumulated sufficient experience and capacities. But we cannot explore this further here.

7.11 Philosophy as a skill

Historians and scientists are primarily knowers-how, for Ryle; the same is true of philosophers.

> The fact that mathematics, philosophy, tactics, scientific method and literary style cannot be imparted but only inculcated reveals that these too are not bodies of information but branches of knowledge-how. They are not sciences but (in the old sense) disciplines.
>
> *Ryle 1945: 234–5*

In a typescript written shortly after Ryle's death, Julius Moravcsik offered a sketch of Ryle as a teacher of philosophy:

> His method of teaching can be best understood by comparing it to the relation between craftsman and apprentice. What Ryle taught in his tutorials was not theory but activity. For him, philosophy was mainly philosophizing; an art, not a science, to be learned and treasured the way one learns and treasures a craft and the products that genuine craftsmanship can bring into being.
>
> *Moravcsik 1977: 3*

This assessment is borne out by appreciations that Ryle wrote of two important contemporaries on their passing: Austin and Russell. In each case, Ryle focused not on specific doctrines, but on advances in philosophical *method*.

In his *London Times* obituary for Austin,[16] Ryle spoke of his colleague's "vocation," "not to provide philosophical messages, but to give philosophy a discipline." Austin

> drilled himself and others in the guess-free techniques of determining the specific forces of expressions and the interplays of those forces. To have learnt from Austin just how, for example, *negligence* differs from *inadvertence* is to have learnt much more than this; it is to have learnt in part how, in the formulations of very abstract doctrines and questions, to sort out what is girder and what is façade, and more than that, which girders support which parts of the load.
>
> *Ryle 1960a: 13*

Similarly, in a reflection on Russell's career delivered to the Aristotelian Society, Ryle praised the ways in which Russell influenced "the very style of our philosophical thinking" (Ryle 1970: 77). He "taught us a new kind of dialectical craftsmanship," by introducing "aporetic experimentation," testing his theories by puzzles of his own devising, "the self-applied tests by which philosophical thinking can become a self-correcting undertaking" (Ryle 1970: 79–80). In sum, Russell "taught us not to think his thoughts but how to move in our own philosophical thinking" (Ryle 1970: 84).

Thus, Ryle praised Austin and Russell for teaching philosophers *how to* think in new ways. Nonetheless, philosophy, like other higher intellectual disciplines, differs from such mental capacities as calculating or translating simple prose. The latter are more like mere competences: we learn them primarily by rote, and they depend on "knacks, drills and techniques." In philosophizing, as in composing poetry, "the place of drills, wrinkles and prescribable techniques is much smaller," because "to be successful is to advance beyond all beaten tracks." Consequently, "the notion of a well-trained philosopher or poet has something ludicrous in it"; and yet, one can only learn to philosophize through "practice, stimulation, hard work and flair." Therefore, "To teach a student to philosophise, one cannot do much save philosophise with him," in line with Moravcsik's craftsman-apprentice model (Ryle 1953: 312).

An anecdote from Daniel Dennett shows Ryle conforming to this model. Reminiscing about Ryle's supervision of his D. Phil. thesis, Dennett recalls that although "I tried to provoke him, with elaborately-prepared and heavily-armed criticisms of his own ideas," Ryle "would genially agree with all my good points as if I were talking about somebody else, and get us thinking of what repairs and improvements we could together make of what remained." At the time, Dennett felt that "I hadn't learned any philosophy from him." However, just before submitting his final draft, he compared it with an earlier version: "To my astonishment, I could see Ryle's influence on every page. How did he do it?" (Dennett 2008: 26).

Dennett's story shows Ryle exemplifying in his own teaching the spirit of the view of skill and education we have extracted from his writings. Moravcsik averred that his "way of construing the teaching of philosophy is one of the important legacies that Ryle left us" (Moravcsik 1977: 9). I hope to have shown that the same is true of his way of construing skill.

Notes

* A grant from the Franke Institute for the Humanities, University of Chicago, supported work on this chapter. Yuri Cath, Carlotta Pavese, and Will Small provided helpful comments.
1 Recent work on Ryle meshes with my reading, including Hornsby (2011), Bäckström and Gustafsson (2017), Kremer (2017b), Löwenstein (2017), Small (2017), Elzinga (2018), Waights Hickman (2019), and Jackson (2020). The account of the "skill analogy" for virtue in Annas (2011) has resonances with Ryle's account.
2 Weatherson (2017) discusses Ryle's regress and intellectual skill.
3 Kremer (2017a) offers a historical response to the "straw man" charge.
4 See Löwenstein (2017: 284–7), Small (2017: 64–6), and Fridland (2013) for replies.
5 This argument challenges both practicalism and intellectualism. Hetherington defends practicalism, arguing that learning-that can be a gradual process, in which knowledge-that improves (Hetherington 2001: 10–11, 13–16; 2011: 75). Pavese, in contrast, argues that the gradability of knowledge-how is "a rather superficial linguistic phenomenon" (Pavese 2017b: 347) that does not threaten intellectualism.
6 Douskos (2019b) explores the capacity/tendency distinction.
7 Stanley and Williamson (2001) take Ryle to equate knowledge-how with ability. Stanley (2011) corrects this error.
8 While Ryle characterizes habits as "automatic," he also calls this "a metaphorical title." Ryle (1949: 95), Fridland (2017), and Löwenstein (2017) argue against Ryle that automaticity is compatible with intelligence. Understanding habit as characterized by its stereotyped, routine nature, rather than automaticity, may save Ryle from this criticism. However, see footnote 11.
9 Kern (2017: 145) credits Ryle with "summarizing descriptions of ... logical distinctions between habits and rational capacities." She develops a characterization of rational capacities as *constitutive* of the acts in which they are exercised, *normative*, *explanatory*, and *self-conscious*. Ryle's writings hint at these points: "intelligent powers" involve norms and provide distinctive explanations (Ryle 1949: 118); and their exercise requires "heed," and so is self-conscious. However, Ryle would reject Kern's constitutive claim: the "infra-actions" constituting a methodical "chain-undertaking" could occur in other contexts, changing in "tactical subordination" but not intrinsic character (Ryle 1974: 335–6). (I am indebted here to Will Small.)
10 Christos Douskos characterizes habit as "impulsive," and argues against Ryle that the appearance that habitual action is stereotyped depends on the *level of description*. However, his account of skill as "spontaneous" reflects Rylean thoughts about attention, care, and critical scrutiny (Douskos 2019a). Ellen Fridland argues that "control" is essential to skill, in similarly Rylean terms: "the controlled part of skilled action ... that accounts for the exact, nuanced ways in which a skilled performer modifies, adjusts, revises, and guides her performance," is "learned through practice" (Fridland 2014: 2731).

11 Löwenstein (2017: 6–7) takes Ryle to use "competence," "skill," and "know-how" interchangeably. Ryle's occasional talk of "skills and competences" might suggest that he is equating the two; but he may also be referring to his later explicit distinction.

12 I paraphrase Ryle's longer formulations in the list below (Ryle 1972: 68–9).

13 Fort (2003) describes Lindemann's life and career.

14 Ryle's letter and the typescript are F 414/3 and F 414/5 in the Lord Cherwell papers at Nuffield College, Oxford. The letter, dated only "Monday," must antedate Ryle's move to military intelligence in September 1941 (Harrison 2009: 68). Ryle certainly approved the anonymous typescript; he contributed to a second pamphlet "on sights," according to another letter, G 442/56.

15 Ryle himself, as an Oxford rowing coach, owned a manual of rowing technique. Haig-Thomas and Nicholson (1958) was among the books that he donated to Linacre College, Oxford.

16 The obituary is unsigned, but a folder of Ryle materials at the Oxford Philosophy Faculty Library contains a copy. According to Isaiah Berlin, it was "certainly written by Ryle" (Berlin 2009: 720).

References

Annas, J. (2011) *Intelligent Virtue*, Oxford: Oxford University Press.

Bäckström, S., and Gustafsson, M. (2017) "Skill, Drill and Intelligent Performance: Ryle and Intellectualism," *Journal for the History of Analytical Philosophy* 5: 40–55, https://doi.org/10.15173/jhap.v5i5.3205, accessed 17 July 2019.

Berlin, I. (2009) *Enlightening: Letters 1946–1960*, H. Hardy and J. Holmes (eds.), London: Chatto and Windus.

Dennett, D. (2008) "Autobiography: Part 1," *Philosophy Now* 68: 22–6, https://philosophynow.org/issues/68/Daniel_Dennett_Autobiography_Part_1, accessed 17 July 2019.

Douskos, C. (2019a) "The Spontaneousness of Skill and the Impulsivity of Habit," *Synthese* 196: 4305–28, https://doi.org/10.1007/s11229-017-1658-7, accessed 17 July 2019.

—— (2019b) "The Varieties of Agential Powers," *European Journal of Philosophy* 27: 982–1001, https://doi.org/10.1111/ejop.12453, accessed 17 July 2019.

Elzinga, B. (2018) "Self-Regulation and Knowledge-How," *Episteme* 15: 119–40, https://doi.org/10.1017/epi.2016.45, accessed 17 July 2019.

Fort, A. (2003) *Prof: The Life of Frederick Lindemann*, London: Jonathan Cape.

Fridland, E. (2013) "Problems with Intellectualism," *Philosophical Studies* 165: 879–91, https://doi.org/10.1007/s11098-012-9994-4, accessed 17 July 2019.

—— (2014) "They've Lost Control: Reflections on Skill," *Synthese* 191: 2729–50, https://doi.org/10.1007/s11229-014-0411-8, accessed 17 July 2019.

—— (2017) "Automatically Minded," *Synthese* 194: 4337–63, https://doi.org/10.1007/s11229-014-0617-9, accessed 17 July 2019.

Haig-Thomas, P., and Nicholson, M. A. (1958) *The English Style of Rowing: New Light on an Old Method*, London: Faber and Faber.

Harrison, E. D. R. (2009) "British Radio Security and Intelligence, 1939–43," *The English Historical Review* 124: 53–93, https://doi.org/10.1093/ehr/cen361, accessed 17 July 2019.

Hetherington, S. (2001) *Good Knowledge and Bad Knowledge*, Oxford: Oxford University Press.

—— (2011) *How to Know: A Practicalist Conception of Knowledge*, Malden, MA: Wiley-Blackwell.

Hornsby, J. (2011) "Ryle's *Knowing-How*, and Knowing How to Act," in J. Bengson and M. Moffett (eds.) *Knowing How: Essays on Knowledge, Mind, and Action*, Oxford: Oxford University Press, pp. 80–98.

Jackson, G. (2020) "Gilbert Ryle's Adverbialism," *British Journal for the History of Philosophy* 28: 318–35, https://doi.org/10.1080/09608788.2019.1638757, accessed 8 May 2020.

Kern, A. (2017) *Sources of Knowledge: On the Concept of a Rational Capacity for Knowledge*, trans. D. Smyth, Cambridge, MA: Harvard University Press.

Kremer, M. (2017a) "Ryle's 'Intellectualist Legend' in Historical Context," *Journal for the History of Analytical Philosophy* 5: 16–39, https://doi.org/10.15173/jhap.v5i5.3204, accessed 17 July 2019.

—— (2017b) "A Capacity to Get Things Right: Gilbert Ryle on Knowledge," *European Journal of Philosophy* 25: 25–46, https://doi.org/10.1111/ejop.12150, accessed 17 July 2019.

Löwenstein, D. (2017) *Know-How as Competence: A Rylean Responsibilist Account*, Frankfurt am Main: Vittorio Klostermann.

Mabbott, J. D. (1986) *Oxford Memories*, Oxford: Thornton's of Oxford.

Moravcsik, J. (1977) "Gilbert Ryle," unpublished manuscript held at the Oxford Philosophy Faculty Library, dated "2-28-77."

Pavese, C. (2015) "Practical Senses," *Philosopher's Imprint* 15: 1–25, http://hdl.handle.net/2027/spo.3521354.0015.029, accessed 17 July 2019.

—— (2017a) "A Theory of Practical Meaning," *Philosophical Topics* 45: 85–116, https://muse.jhu.edu/article/673029, accessed 17 July 2019.

—— (2017b) "Know-How and Gradability," *Philosophical Review* 126: 345–83, https://doi.org/10.1215/00318108-3878493, accessed 17 July 2019.

Ryle, G. (1940) "Conscience and Moral Convictions," reprinted in Ryle, *Collected Essays 1929–1968: Collected Papers Volume 2*, Abingdon: Routledge, pp. 194–202.

—— (1945) "Knowing How and Knowing That," reprinted in Ryle, *Collected Essays 1929–1968: Collected Papers Volume 2*, Abingdon: Routledge, pp. 222–35.

—— (1946) "Why are the Calculuses of Logic and Arithmetic Applicable to Reality?" reprinted in Ryle, *Collected Essays 1929–1968: Collected Papers Volume 2*, Abingdon: Routledge, pp. 236–43.

—— (1949) *The Concept of Mind*, Abingdon: Routledge.

—— (1953) "Thinking," reprinted in Ryle, *Collected Essays 1929–1968: Collected Papers Volume 2*, Abingdon: Routledge, pp. 307–13.

—— (1956) "Sensation," reprinted in Ryle, *Collected Essays 1929–1968: Collected Papers Volume 2*, Abingdon: Routledge, pp. 349–62.

—— (1960a) "Prof. J.L. Austin: An Influential Philosopher," *The Times* (London, England), 10 February: 13.

—— (1960b) "Epistemology," in J. Urmson (ed.) *Encyclopedia of Western Philosophy*, Abingdon: Routledge, pp. 128–35.

—— (1964) "Thinking," reprinted in Ryle, *Aspects of Mind*, R. Meyer (ed.), Oxford: Blackwell, pp. 146–83.

—— (1966) *Plato's Progress*, Cambridge: Cambridge University Press.

—— (1967) "Teaching and Training," reprinted in Ryle, *Collected Essays 1929–1968: Collected Papers Volume 2*, Abingdon: Routledge, pp. 464–78.

—— (1970) "Bertrand Russell 1872–1970," *Proceedings of the Aristotelian Society* 71: 77–84.

—— (1972) "Thinking and Self-Teaching," reprinted in Ryle, *On Thinking*, K. Kolenda (ed.), Totowa, NJ: Rowman and Littlefield, pp. 65–78.

—— (1974) "Courses of Action and the Uncatchableness of Mental Acts," *Philosophy* 75: 331–44.

—— (1976) "Improvisation," reprinted in Ryle, *On Thinking*, K. Kolenda (ed.), Totowa, NJ: Rowman and Littlefield, pp. 121–30.

—— (1993a) "Our Thinking and Our Thoughts," in Ryle, *Aspects of Mind*, R. Meyer (ed.), Oxford: Blackwell, pp. 51–65.

—— (1993b) "Reason," in Ryle, *Aspects of Mind*, R. Meyer (ed.), Oxford: Blackwell, pp. 66–79.

Small, W. (2017) "Ryle on the Explanatory Role of Knowledge How," *Journal for the History of Analytical Philosophy* 5: 56–76, https://doi.org/10.15173/jhap.v5i5.3206, accessed 17 July 2019.

Stanley, J. (2011) *Know How*, Oxford: Oxford University Press.

Stanley, J., and Williamson, T. (2001) "Knowing How," *Journal of Philosophy* 98: 411–44.

Waights Hickman, N. (2019) "Knowing in the 'Executive Way': Knowing How, Rules, Methods, Principles and Criteria," *Philosophy and Phenomenological Research* 99: 311–35, https://doi.org/10.1111/phpr.12488, accessed 17 July 2019.

War Office (Great Britain) (1942a) *Small Arms Training, Volume I, Pamphlet No. 6: Anti-Aircraft*, London: The War Office, https://vickersmg.files.wordpress.com/2017/07/01-06-42.pdf, accessed 17 July 2019.

—— (1942b) *Small Arms Training, Volume I, Pamphlet No. 6, Supplement No. 1: The Anti-Aircraft Cartwheel Sight*, London: The War Office, https://vickersmg.files.wordpress.com/2017/07/01-06-42-s1-43.pdf, accessed 17 July 2019.

Weatherson, B. (2017) "Intellectual Skill and the Rylean Regress," *The Philosophical Quarterly* 67: 370–85, https://doi.org/10.1093/pq/pqw051, accessed 17 July 2019.

8

ANSCOMBE ON ACTION AND PRACTICAL KNOWLEDGE

Will Small

8.1 Introduction

Elizabeth Anscombe (1919–2001) was one of the most important philosophers of the twentieth century. Her monograph *Intention* (Anscombe 1963[1957]) is a foundational work in analytic philosophy of action from which many now-standard ideas in the field derive (e.g., that there are important conceptual connections between something's being an action and its being done for a reason and between the explanation of action and practical reasoning, and that actions are intentional not simpliciter but *under descriptions*). Less influential, however, was one of *Intention's* central contentions, that an understanding of what Anscombe calls *practical knowledge* must be central to a satisfactory philosophical account of intentional action. This idea was largely ignored by philosophical work on action in the twentieth century (though see Velleman 1989), but it has been a central focus of the twenty-first-century resurgence of interest in Anscombe.[1] However, the 'practical knowledge' that plays a central role in Anscombe's conception of intentional action is not 'knowledge how' in the sense introduced by Ryle (1946, 1949). Whereas the latter—here, *know-how*—is a sort of standing general knowledge that is put into practice on different occasions of action, the former—here, *agential knowledge*—is rather the distinctive knowledge that an agent has of her particular intentional actions.[2]

Anscombe introduces agential knowledge in *Intention* through a negative characterization: what is distinctive about an agent's knowledge of her intentional actions is that it is *non-observational* (§8).[3] But at the culmination of her account (in §48), this is supplanted by a positive characterization of agential knowledge as *practical knowledge*, something that Anscombe thinks "modern philosophy has blankly misunderstood" (§32), and of which she adopts Aquinas's account: "Practical knowledge is 'the cause of what it understands', unlike 'speculative' knowledge, which 'is derived from the objects known'" (§48, citing *Summa Theologiae*, IaIIae, Q3, art. 5, obj. 1). As skill and know-how are often held to be forms of practical knowledge, this raises the following questions: does agential knowledge, as Anscombe understands it, depend on skill/know-how (and if so, how)? And does an Anscombean account of agency incur any commitments about the nature of know-how?

In *Intention* (on which I'll focus), Anscombe says very little about skill, and her remarks about know-how are compressed and present interpretive challenges. Answering our questions is therefore not straightforward; doing so will first require sketching Anscombe's conception of agential knowledge and its place in her account of agency.

8.2 Agential knowledge as *non-observational*

Anscombe introduces agential knowledge in *Intention* in order to break out of a conceptual circle she encounters while undertaking one of the book's first main projects, that of "outlin[ing] the area of intentional actions" (§18). Anscombe is often cited as a source of the popular view that actions are intentional only if performed for reasons. But this misinterprets her famous claim that

> what distinguishes actions which are intentional from those which are not ... is that they are the actions to which a certain sense of the question "Why?" is given application; the sense is of course that in which the answer, if positive, gives a reason for acting.
>
> *§5, p. 9*

First, Anscombe's claim leaves open the possibility (later endorsed, with important qualifications, in §§17–18), that an intentional action may be performed for no reason—i.e. that the question 'Why?' applies but has a negative answer.[4] More importantly, Anscombe thinks attempts to distinguish actions from non-actions, or intentional actions from non-intentional actions, by appeal to the idea of 'reasons for acting' will be perniciously circular:

> Why is giving a start or gasp not an "action", while sending for a taxi, or crossing the road, is one? The answer cannot be "Because the answer to the question 'why?' may give a *reason* in the latter cases", for the answer may "give a reason" in the former cases too; and we cannot say "Ah, but not a reason for *acting*"; we should be going round in circles.
>
> *§5, p. 10*

In order to delimit the "area of intentional actions" (from those of mere events, involuntary bodily movements, involuntary actions, voluntary but unintentional actions, etc.)—and with it the relevant sense of the question 'Why?' (from other senses of that question) and reasons for acting (from reasons, or 'reasons', of other kinds)—Anscombe proceeds negatively, identifying ways of responding to the question 'Why are you X-ing?' that neither answer it positively (by giving a reason for acting) nor answer it negatively ('No reason') but rather show that the question doesn't apply. If the question doesn't apply—if the agent to whom it is put sincerely refuses it application—then the action is not intentional under the description 'X-ing' (though it may be intentional under the description 'Y-ing'). Among the responses that refuse the application of Anscombe's 'Why?'-question, two are especially significant here. First, the question 'Why are you X-ing?' is refused application by the response 'I didn't know I was [X-ing]' (§6). For example, Jones, when asked why he is sawing Smith's plank, might sincerely reply 'I didn't know I was sawing Smith's plank', and this, Anscombe thinks, shows that what he was doing was not intentional under *that* description (though it would presumably have been intentional under such descriptions as 'sawing a plank', 'sawing *this* plank', etc.). Second, the question is refused application by 'I knew I was doing that, but only because I observed it' (§8). For instance, if you noticed that by walking back and forth in front of an automatic door you caused it to keep opening, you might respond in this way if asked why you kept opening the door. By contrast, it would be implausible to think you could have known *only* by observation that you were walking back and forth—and under that description your action was surely intentional.

The claim that agents have non-observational knowledge of their intentional actions (that is, of their actions under those descriptions under which they are intentional) is often, and correctly, attributed to Anscombe. But it is frequently, yet incorrectly, held to be the kernel of her conception of agential knowledge—or worse still, to exhaust it. We have non-observational knowledge of more than our intentional actions: as well as mathematical and metaphysical (and other forms of *a priori*) knowledge, many hold that we have non-observational knowledge of our own minds. And Anscombe contends not only that we "usually know the position of [our] limbs without observation" (§8) but that some of the very things from which she aims to distinguish intentional actions—such as involuntary movements, e.g., the "odd sort of jerk or jump that one's whole body sometimes gives when one is falling asleep" (§7), and involuntary actions, e.g., when "the leap and loud bark of the crocodile made me jump" (§8)—are known without observation, too. Anscombe holds that if someone is X-ing *intentionally*, she knows without observation not only that she is X-ing; she knows without observation *why* she is X-ing (as the subject of an involuntary movement known without observation does not), where this *answers* (positively or negatively) the question 'Why?' in its special sense rather than *refuses it application* (as 'Because of the leap and loud bark of the crocodile' or 'Because I saw a face in the window' refuse, by answering a different sense of, the question 'Why did you jump?', thereby revealing the jumping to be unintentional).[5] Anscombe indeed believes that agents have non-observational knowledge of what they are doing intentionally and why, but it's important that this is a claim she arrives at in giving a negative specification of the "rough outline" of the "area of intentional actions" (§18). The "class of things known without observation" (§8) is a very heterogeneous class indeed; to know simply that intentional actions fall within it is not to know much at all about what it is to be an intentional action, for it is not to know anything about *why* intentional actions fall in that class. The remainder of *Intention* develops a positive account of intentional action and agential knowledge, from which the claim that the latter is non-observational can be expected to *follow*.

8.3 The object of agential knowledge

What exactly is agential knowledge knowledge of? Anscombe insists that it is what is done intentionally. If I'm painting the wall yellow intentionally, then I have agential knowledge that I'm painting the wall yellow. It is a mistake, Anscombe strikingly argues (§§29–30), to hold that the object of agential knowledge is merely what I intend to do, or what I'm trying to do—a fact about the agent's mind, not a fact about the world in which she's actively engaged—or that it is merely what I'm doing with my body in order to (e.g.) paint the wall yellow.[6]

Painting the wall yellow is not something I can do just like that. Executing this task involves doing many things in order to do it: for instance, putting down sheets on the floor, taping off the window frame, opening the can of paint, pouring the paint into a tray, rolling a roller in the tray, and then rolling the roller against the wall by moving my arm up and down. And painting the wall yellow is unlikely to be something I can sensibly claim to be doing for no reason: I'm painting the room yellow as part of a larger redecorating effort, which I'm undertaking in order to make the house more attractive to prospective buyers. What I'm doing intentionally is something with a rich teleological (means-end) structure in it. Anscombe calls this "the A—D order" (§§23–26). If I am doing A in order to do B, B in order to do C, and C in order to do D, then I might answer the question 'Why are you doing A?' by saying that I'm doing it in order to do—or because I want or intend to do, or because I'm doing—B (or C, or D). Doing B is an end relative to doing A, but a means relative to doing C (and D). Thus, while reiterations of the reason-seeking sense of the question 'Why?' move us from A to D ('Why are you doing A?'—'Because I'm doing B'—'And why are you doing B?'—'Because …'), the corresponding means-seeking sense of the question 'How?' (§26) moves us in the opposite direction along the series ('How are you doing D?'—'By doing C'—'And how are you doing C?'—'By …').

Anscombe thus holds that the A—D order, the teleological structure of a complex tract of intentional activity that the question 'Why?' excavates, is the same order as that revealed by considering practical reasoning, in which an agent considers *how* she is going to get what she wants (a house attractive to prospective buyers, for instance). Anscombe's interest in practical reasoning is with this "order which is there whenever actions are done with intentions" and not with any "actual mental processes" that may or may not occur: she thinks "it would be very rare for a person to go through all the steps of a piece of practical reasoning" (§42; cf. Anscombe 1989). Though there will surely have been actual processes of deliberation at the stage of determining how to make the house attractive to buyers and how exactly to redecorate which rooms (etc.), there may not need to be any conscious deliberation about how to open the can of paint, or whether to put down sheets. Nevertheless, Anscombe thinks, the "order which is there"—the order of means and ends—will be *known* by the agent even as it extends beyond any actual mental processes of deliberation that there may have been. Thus the object of agential knowledge will include not simply what the agent is doing intentionally, but how and why she is doing it: she knows that she is doing B, that she is doing B by means of doing A, and that she is doing B because she is doing C.

Agential knowledge is knowledge "in intention", Anscombe says (§32)—i.e. it is not knowledge the vehicle of which is a mental state distinct from the intention involved in acting intentionally. But we intend to do things we are not yet doing. Though most discussions of agential knowledge focus on an agent's knowledge of what she is presently doing intentionally, Anscombe's view can be extended to an agent's knowledge of what she is *going to* do, but is not yet doing (Small 2012). This will be knowledge *in* intention *of* what is going to happen in material reality, not merely knowledge *of* intention (i.e. of a psychological fact):

> If I say I am going for a walk, someone else may know that this is not going to happen. It would be absurd to say that *what* he knew was not going to happen was not the very same thing that I was saying *was* going to happen.
>
> *§52, p. 92*

What an agent knows in intention is something that someone else can know 'in belief' (through perception, inference, testimony, etc.): you can know what I know, namely that I'm painting the wall yellow, though we know this in different ways (perhaps you can see that this is what I'm doing); and you can know what I am going to do, but am not yet doing (e.g., giving a talk at a conference next summer), where this is for you, as it is for me, not simply knowledge of my present state of mind, but knowledge of what is going to happen in the world. For Anscombe, then, the object of agential knowledge is—at least[7]—present and prospective worldly happenings with a rich teleological structure, and not merely the present state of mind (or state of mind and bodily movements) of the agent. Locating practical reason *in* action, rather than in a mind that lies behind and causes action, is one of the distinctive features of an Anscombean approach to agency.[8]

8.4 Agential knowledge as *practical*

Anscombe's discussion of agential knowledge culminates in her claim that "it is the agent's knowledge of what he is doing that gives the descriptions under which what is going on is the execution of an intention," which knowledge is "practical knowledge" (§48). This means more than that it is knowledge *of* practical matters; it is knowledge that is practical in *form* (cf. §33): it relates to its object in a different way from that in which theoretical knowledge relates to its. Theoretical knowledge is "something that is judged as such by being in accordance with the facts. The facts, reality, are prior, and dictate what is to be said, if it is knowledge" (§32); by contrast, practical knowledge is, in Aquinas's phrase, "the cause of what it understands" (§48).

These remarks have led to the accusation that Anscombe leaves agential knowledge "looking not just causally perverse but epistemically mysterious" (Velleman 1989: 103), and authors such as Velleman (1989) and Paul (2009) have offered alternative, deflationary accounts of it. In my view, the best way to understand Anscombe here is that an agent's knowing (practically) what she is doing is *constitutive* of its being the case that she is doing it intentionally: agential knowledge is the *formal cause* of what it understands (Moran 2004). Intentional action is teleologically complex, but the source of that teleological complexity is the agent's practical reasoning. And the very practical reasoning that grounds the status of the events that are transpiring as a teleologically unified course of intentional activity thereby constitutes the agent's knowledge of that order—her knowledge of what she is doing, and how and why she is doing it. Anscombe says that the claim that agential knowledge is practical knowledge—i.e. that it is the cause of what it understands—"means more than that [it] is observed to be a necessary condition of the production of various results; or that an idea of doing such-and-such in such-and-such ways is such a condition" (as someone who held that agential knowledge is an efficient cause of intentional action might maintain); "it means that without it what happens does not come under the description—execution of intentions—whose characteristics we have been investigating" (§48).[9] Agential knowledge is thus non-observational *because* it is practical: what is going on is a case of intentional action, there to be observed, only because it is already known agentially.

8.5 Does agential knowledge depend on know-how?

We can now consider whether agential knowledge (as Anscombe understands it) depends on know-how. This question may be asked in two registers:

(a) Does intentional action (and thus the agential knowledge that is constitutive of it) depend *metaphysically* on knowing how?
(b) Does agential knowledge depend *epistemically* on knowing how?

Two important passages in *Intention* seem to stand in tension, here:

> **(T1)** the topic of an intention may be a matter on which there is knowledge *or opinion* based on observation, inference, hearsay, superstition or anything that knowledge or opinion ever are based on; or again matter on which an opinion is held without any foundation at all. When knowledge *or opinion* are present concerning what is the case, and what can happen—say Z—if one does certain things, say ABC, then it is possible to have the intention of doing Z in doing ABC; and if the case is one of knowledge *or*

if the opinion is correct, then doing or causing Z is an intentional action, and it is not by observation that one knows one is doing Z.

§28, p. 50; my emphases

(T2) Although the term "practical knowledge" is most often used in connexion with specialised skills, there is no reason to think that this notion has application only in such contexts. "Intentional action" *always presupposes what might be called "knowing one's way about"* the matters described in the description under which an action can be called intentional, and *this knowledge is exercised in the action and is practical knowledge.*

§48, p. 89; my emphases

In (T1), Anscombe says that in order to *intend* to do Z by means of doing ABC, an agent needn't *know* that doing ABC is a way to do or effect Z (it is enough that she *believes* this—and the belief seemingly needn't be justified), and that, though true belief that doing ABC is a way to do Z is necessary to *do Z intentionally*, knowledge of that fact is unnecessary (seemingly, true but unjustified belief would suffice). (T1), then, suggests that though intention and intentional action require *beliefs* about means, they do not depend on *know-how*. By contrast, (T2) says that intentional action *always* "presupposes … 'knowing one's way about' the matters described in the description under which an action can be called intentional": e.g., painting a wall yellow intentionally presupposes a certain measure of painting and decorating know-how. There is no suggestion here that correct opinion based on, e.g., superstition would suffice.

One reason to think (T2) represents Anscombe's considered view is that it occurs in §48, where her accounts of agential knowledge and intentional action culminate. By contrast, (T1) occurs in §28, before the introduction of the key idea of practical knowledge (§32) and the discussion of practical reasoning that Anscombe thinks an understanding of practical knowledge presupposes (§33). However, there is independent reason to prefer the view that *knowing* how to do A is a necessary condition of both doing A intentionally and one's having agential knowledge that one is doing A intentionally.[10]

Recall Anscombe's claims (i) that if an agent is intentionally painting the wall yellow, she knows that she is doing so, and (ii) that *what* she knows is that a worldly transaction between her and the wall is taking place in material reality: namely, the wall is being painted yellow by her. That the agent is painting the wall yellow is something that an observer might know by observation. However, this does not mean that the truth value of 'She is painting the wall yellow' can be ascertained simply by attending to what's going on with the wall, perhaps over a period of time. To suppose this would be to suppose that "Knowledge must be something that is judged as such by being in accordance with the facts," which "are prior, and dictate what is to be said, if it is knowledge" (§32)—i.e. to suppose that all knowledge is contemplative or speculative. "She is painting the wall yellow" may be true even though the agent is currently asleep, or at the paint store, or is painting the wall with white primer, or is painting the wall green by mistake. Nevertheless, agential knowledge, to be knowledge, must accord with the facts,[11] even if in determining whether the agent's claim amounts to *knowledge* we must do so by judging whether the facts are in accordance with the claim rather than judging whether the claim is in accordance with the facts: that is, we must interrogate the facts—establish *what is actually going on here*—in the light of the agent's claim to be painting the wall yellow, rather than assume that what is going on here can be understood independently of the agent's claim, which is then assessed for truth against that prior and independent take on what the facts about what's going on are. Thus, if the agent has agential knowledge that she is painting the wall yellow, then it is true that she is painting the wall yellow, where this means more than that she thinks that she is painting the wall yellow (or trying to do so, etc.); it means that, among other things, the wall is becoming yellow—even though that's something that an observer might not be able to tell. So, what *is* required for the truth of 'She is doing A intentionally'?

If an agent *is doing A* intentionally, then she has started doing A and she has not yet done A (on this occasion). Later, it *will* be true that she *was* doing A; it *may* be true that she *did* A. (That she is doing A does not entail that she will succeed.) But if she really is *doing A*—it's really *A*, and not something else, she's doing; and she's really *doing* it, and not just merely trying to do it or playing at doing it—then it must be no accident if she succeeds. If someone who was doing A didn't end up having done A, a special explanation is needed (e.g., something interfered, she changed her mind); no special explanation is needed if she ends up having done what she was doing (Rödl 2012: ch. 6; Small 2012: §4). This suggests that to be doing A intentionally, the agent must not merely intend, but also know how, to do A.[12] For if she intended to do A, but didn't know how to do A, it would surely be some accident if her activity culminated in her having successfully done A.[13]

In addition to this metaphysical role, know-how plays an epistemic role here: what makes the agent's true belief that she is doing A a case of *knowledge* is that she is realizing her intention to do A through good practical reasoning, which involves know-how. Just as the agent's know-how is what makes it true that she is doing A intentionally (by making it no accident that she'll succeed), so it makes her belief that she is doing A non-accidentally true. The answers to our questions (a) and (b) above are thus both: Yes.[14]

8.6 Anscombean commitments regarding know-how

What implications (if any) does an Anscombean conception of agency have for the theory of know-how? In (T1), Anscombe says that "when knowledge or opinion are present concerning what is the case, and what can happen—say Z—if one does certain things, say ABC, then it is possible to have the intention of doing Z in doing ABC." It is clear from this passage, and from her discussion of the A—D order more generally, that Anscombe thinks one can know how to do something by virtue of knowing that one can do it by doing something else. She clearly does not think, as Ryle is sometimes said to, that knowing how to V is wholly disjoint from knowing that p. But there are those—intellectualists—who say that all know-how is knowing that. Should an Anscombean conception of agency incline one to accept or reject intellectualism, or is it neutral?

The following passage, which seems to identify know-how with a *practical capacity*, might suggest that Anscombe is an anti-intellectualist:

> **(T3)** A man has practical knowledge who knows how to do things; but that is an insufficient description, for he *might* be said to know how to do things if he could give a lecture on it, though he was helpless when confronted with the task of doing them. When we ordinarily speak of practical knowledge we have in mind a certain sort of *general capacity* in a particular field; but if we hear of a capacity, it is reasonable to ask what constitutes an exercise of it. ... In the case of practical knowledge the exercise of the capacity is nothing but the doing or supervising of the operations of which a man has practical knowledge; but this is not *just* the coming about of certain effects, like my recitation of the alphabet or of bits of it, for what he effects is formally characterised as subject to our question "Why?" whose application displays the A—D order which we discovered.
>
> §48, p. 88; second emphasis mine

However, though some intellectualists (e.g., Snowdon 2004) deny that know-how consists in practical capacities, others (e.g., Pavese 2015, 2017) hold that the propositional knowledge they take know-how to consist in entails the possession of practical capacities. Moreover, Anscombe's view is incompatible with one prominent form of anti-intellectualism, that of Hubert Dreyfus: Anscombe insists that exercises of know-how are intentional actions (denied by Dreyfus 2001), and that an agent exercising know-how knows that she's doing what she's doing (denied by Dreyfus 2007).

There is, however, some reason to think that an Anscombean conception of action and agential knowledge fits best with a 'bifurcationist' view of know-how on which propositional knowledge that doing A is a way to do B and an intelligent practical capacity to do A are both forms of know-how, each with "its own usefulness and its own purport" (Wiggins 2012: 123). Though many seem to think that 'practical knowledge in Anscombe's sense' just *is* the knowledge agents have of their intentional actions, (T2) and (T3) both say that know-how is *also* practical knowledge: agential knowledge and know-how are, we might say, species of practical knowledge. As noted above, Anscombe insists that "'practical knowledge' can only be understood if we first understand 'practical reasoning'" (§33). And reflection on the structure of practical reasoning ought to lead us to conclude that though much know-how can take the form 'Doing B is a way to do C' (or similar), not all of it can. My knowledge that doing B is a way to do C can figure in *genuine* practical reasoning—i.e. not theoretical reasoning about practical matters, or the "idle" practical reasoning of the classroom example (§33)—only if it is knowledge I can put into practice. If my know-how to do C consists in knowing *that doing B is a way to do C*, then my know-how to do C is practicable only if I have practicable know-how to do B. If I do, then I have derivatively practicable knowledge how to do C. The practicability of my knowledge how to do B might be derivative, too: I might know that doing A is a way to do B. But the structure of practical reasoning (together with the conception, from the previous section, of intentional action as dependent on know-how) demands that there be know-how that is practicable non-derivatively.

Call this *basic know-how*. On the face of it, basic know-how to do A cannot be propositional knowledge of the form '___ is a way to do A.'[15] Moreover, to be consistent with an Anscombean conception of agency, an account of basic know-how must make it clear that its exercises ('basic actions') are genuinely cases of intentional action and that they are agentially (and thus non-observationally) known. This is no mean task: basic know-how is surely ability-entailing, but the sub-intentional or sub-personal abilities and dispositions that figure in familiar accounts of basic action are such that their manifestations can be known—by an Anscombean's lights—only observationally (Lavin 2013; Small 2019). By contrast, if the abilities entailed by basic know-how are *intelligent* abilities, it is unclear that the propositional knowledge that the intellectualist thinks basic know-how consists in has any role to play in the explanation of intentional action (as the Anscombean understands it). For this reason, it seems that the bifurcationist view fits most naturally with the Anscombean conception of agency.

However, it must be admitted that Anscombe has no developed account of skill or know-how, and there are important questions that an Anscombean must answer in this area. Just what sort of a capacity is (involved in) basic know-how? How can we account for agential knowledge of the exercise of basic know-how, given that it will likely be a complex movement the elements of which do not exhibit the "order" of means and ends that is "there whenever actions are done with intentions" (§42)—or at least don't exhibit that order in virtue of practical reasoning? These issues deserve further thought (though see Small 2019), as do the relationships between practical knowledge, know-how, agential knowledge—and any other species of practical knowledge there might be.

Notes

1 See, e.g., Falvey (2000), Moran (2004), Setiya (2008), Paul (2009), Haddock (2011), Rödl (2011), Thompson (2011), Small (2012), McDowell (2013), and Schwenkler (2015).
2 This knowledge is knowledge of action *in progress* and/or *in prospect*; it may thus be unacceptable, ontologically, to characterize it as knowledge of *particular* actions (see Thompson 2008: ch. 8).
3 References in this form are to the numbered sections of *Intention* (Anscombe 1963[1957]).
4 "The question is not refused application because the answer to it says that there is *no* reason, any more than the question how much money I have in my pocket is refused application by the answer 'None'" (§17)—contrast the answer 'I don't have any pockets'.
5 At least, on the most natural interpretation of the scenarios these examples bring to mind.
6 An equally bad mistake, Anscombe thinks, is to hold that the object of agential knowledge is what is done intentionally, but that what I ('really') do intentionally is either whatever I think I am, or intend to be, doing, or what I'm doing with my body in order to bring about further effects.
7 Might there be agential knowledge of what I *have done* intentionally, in addition to knowledge of what I am doing and am going to do intentionally? Setiya (2016) argues that Anscombe thought so; Haase (2018) argues that she didn't, but should have.
8 Anscombe dismisses the claim that the 'because' in 'She X-d because ____' (where '____' gives a reason for acting) is "an ordinary *because* where the *because* clause gives a psychological state" as "lack[ing] acumen" (1989: 110); see also Anscombe (1983). Despite her criticisms of causal theories of action, one should be cautious labeling Anscombe an anti-causalist: she was as critical of modern conceptions of causation as she was of the theories of action that gave it a central role (see, e.g., Anscombe 1963[1957]: §5, 1971).
9 The claim that agential knowledge is necessary for intentional action (under the relevant descriptions) is called into question by Davidson's example of the carbon-copier who is trying to make ten carbon copies at once (and, unbeknownst to him, succeeding) despite doubting that he is achieving his aim. For responses, see Thompson (2011) and Small (2012: §5).
10 The following argument is developed in more detail in Small (2012).
11 Admittedly, Anscombe at one point seems to say that she could have agential knowledge that she is writing 'I am a fool' on a blackboard even though she is not in fact doing so (§45). This seems to be a mis-step; see Moran (2004), Haddock (2011), and McDowell (2013) for discussion.
12 Many hold that it is possible, though perhaps irrational, to intend to do what one doesn't know how to do. The present considerations suggest an argument that one cannot genuinely intend (though one can aspire, hope, or want) to do what one knows not how to do. See Small (2012: §§3–4).
13 This is clearest when the agent has either no idea how to do A or a false conception of how to do A; but even if she has and acts on a true belief, falling short of knowledge, concerning how to do A, her success in action will inherit the luckiness that qualifies the truth of her belief. Like knowledge, intentional action is widely regarded as incompatible with luck. See, e.g., Mele and Moser (1994).
14 Setiya (2012) defends a similar position.
15 Cf. Anscombe's discussion of bodily skill in the physiologist's experiment (§30).

References

Anscombe, G. E. M. (1963[1957]) *Intention*, Oxford: Basil Blackwell.
—— (1971) "Causality and Determination," reprinted in *Metaphysics and the Philosophy of Mind: The Collected Philosophical Papers of G.E.M. Anscombe, Vol. 2*, Oxford: Basil Blackwell, pp. 133–47.
—— (1983) "The Causation of Action," reprinted in M. Geach and L. Gormally (eds.) *Human Life, Action and Ethics: Essays by G.E.M. Anscombe*, Exeter: Imprint Academic, pp. 89–108.
—— (1989) "Practical Inference," reprinted in M. Geach and L. Gormally (eds.) *Human Life, Action and Ethics: Essays by G.E.M. Anscombe*, Exeter: Imprint Academic, pp. 109–47.
Dreyfus, H. L. (2001) "The Primacy of Phenomenology over Logical Analysis," reprinted in M. A. Wrathall (ed.) *Skillful Coping: Essays on the Phenomenology of Everyday Perception and Action*, Oxford: Oxford University Press, pp. 146–67.
—— (2007) "Response to McDowell," *Inquiry* 50: 371–7.
Falvey, K. (2000) "Knowledge in Intention," *Philosophical Studies* 99: 21–44.
Ford, A., Hornsby, J., and Stoutland, F. (eds.) (2011) *Essays on Anscombe's Intention*, Cambridge, MA: Harvard University Press.

Haase, M. (2018) "Knowing What I Have Done," *Manuscrito* 41: 195–253.

Haddock, A. (2011) "The Knowledge That a Man Has of His Intentional Actions," in A. Ford, J. Hornsby, and F. Stoutland (eds.) *Essays on Anscombe's Intention*, Cambridge, MA: Harvard University Press, pp. 147–69.

Lavin, D. (2013) "Must There Be Basic Action?" *Noûs* 47: 273–301.

McDowell, J. (2013) "Zum Verhältnis von Rezeptivem und Praktischem Wissen (How Receptive Knowledge Relates to Practical Knowledge)," *Deutsche Zeitschrift für Philosophie* 61: 387–401.

Mele, A. R., and Moser, P. K. (1994) "Intentional Action," *Noûs* 28: 39–68.

Moran, R. (2004) "Anscombe on Practical Knowledge," in J. Hyman and H. Steward (eds.) *Agency and Action*, Cambridge: Cambridge University Press, pp. 43–68.

Paul, S. K. (2009) "How We Know What We're Doing," *Philosophers' Imprint* 9: 1–24.

Pavese, C. (2015) "Practical Senses," *Philosophers' Imprint* 15: 1–25.

—— (2017) "Know-How and Gradability," *The Philosophical Review* 126: 345–83.

Rödl, S. (2011) "Two Forms of Practical Knowledge and Their Unity," in A. Ford, J. Hornsby, and F. Stoutland (eds.) *Essays on Anscombe's Intention*, MA: Harvard University Press, pp. 211–41.

—— (2012) *Categories of the Temporal*, Cambridge, MA: Harvard University Press.

Ryle, G. (1946) "Knowing How and Knowing That," *Proceedings of the Aristotelian Society* 46: 1–16.

—— (1949) *The Concept of Mind*, London: Routledge.

Schwenkler, J. (2015) "Understanding 'Practical Knowledge'," *Philosophers' Imprint* 15: 1–32.

Setiya, K. (2008) "Practical Knowledge," *Ethics* 118: 388–409.

—— (2012) "Knowing How," *Proceedings of the Aristotelian Society* 112: 285–307.

—— (2016) "Anscombe on Practical Knowledge," in *Practical Knowledge: Selected Essays*, Oxford: Oxford University Press, pp. 156–68.

Small, W. (2012) "Practical Knowledge and the Structure of Action," in G. Abel and J. Conant (eds.) *Rethinking Epistemology Volume 2*, Berlin: De Gruyter, pp. 133–227.

—— (2019) "Basic Action and Practical Knowledge," *Philosophers' Imprint* 19: 1–22.

Snowdon, P. (2004) "Knowing How and Knowing That: A Distinction Reconsidered," *Proceedings of the Aristotelian Society* 104: 1–29.

Thompson, M. (2008) *Life and Action: Elementary Structures of Practice and Practical Thought*, Cambridge, MA: Harvard University Press.

—— (2011) "Anscombe's Intention and Practical Knowledge," in A. Ford, J. Hornsby, and F. Stoutland (eds.) *Essays on Anscombe's Intention*, MA: Harvard University Press, pp. 198–210.

Velleman, J. D. (1989) *Practical Reflection*, Princeton, NJ: Princeton University Press.

Wiggins, D. (2012) "Practical Knowledge: Knowing How to and Knowing That," *Mind* 121: 97–130.

9

HUBERT DREYFUS ON PRACTICAL AND EMBODIED INTELLIGENCE*

Kristina Gehrman and John Schwenkler

9.1 Introduction

If anyone deserves to be called the gadfly of 20th-century analytic philosophy, it is Hubert Dreyfus. Like Socrates, he brought one burning insight to bear in every conversation into which he entered. Like Socrates, with zeal he went repeatedly against the mainstream in a way that could provoke and exasperate his interlocutors, never more so than when he put his finger on a fundamental shortcoming of a cherished theory. Like Socrates, he had a well-deserved reputation as a dragon slayer: his career was bookended by a devastating critique of artificial intelligence (AI) projects in the 1970s and a passionate rejection of John McDowell's conceptualism in the first decade of the 21st century. And it may be that, like Socrates, the profundity of Dreyfus' simple, single-minded philosophy was not fully appreciated during his time.

So what was Dreyfus' fundamental insight? Put simply, it is the thesis that we've been thinking about *ourselves* all wrong. There is, he observed, a "Platonic" conception of human nature so deep to Western analytic philosophy as to be all but invisible (Dreyfus 1979). According to this conception, humans are essentially rational, individual agents. Dreyfus consistently rejected each element of this picture, arguing that rather than being *individual, agential,* and *rational*, human beings are *embedded, absorbed,* and *embodied.* Drawing on Heidegger's conception of lived existence as *Dasein*, Dreyfus argued that the Platonic picture of human nature is a distortion. As Dreyfus saw it, human beings are embedded in our world like a knot in the middle of a fishing net.[1] Human agency, too, is nothing like the Platonic picture would have it. We are rarely—and never ideally—self-directed, explicitly purposive agents. Instead, drawing on Merleau-Ponty's perceptual, body-first conception of action, Dreyfus argued that we are responsive, self-forgetful, "absorbed copers" whenever we function normally (competently) and expertly.

Finally, Dreyfus relied on phenomenology to reject the Platonic picture of human rationality itself, beginning by casting doubt on the role of that picture in early AI research. According to the Platonic picture, human intelligence is fundamentally calculative, computational, or rule-based, involving explicit and codifiable thought, the paradigm of which is inferential reasoning. But Dreyfus argued that this picture construes rationality itself in a rationalistic and thus

123

distorted way. For Dreyfus, human intelligence can be understood only in light of our *embodied* manner of being-in-the-world. When we attend to our characteristic embodiment, we see that human intelligence is first and foremost, and most fundamentally, *practical* as opposed to theoretical. Because of this, the elevation of theoretical rationality that is the bedrock of the Western philosophical tradition is a profound mistake. For theory proceeds from, depends upon, and ultimately is merely one species of—*doing*.

This brings us to the particular focus, and the primary interpretive claim, of the present essay. These three contrasts—individual vs. embedded, agential vs. absorbed, and rational vs. embodied—are closely connected in Dreyfus' thought. And his accounts of each of them, and their relationships to one another, evolved over time. But while it is not feasible here to discuss each of them in depth, we believe that they can be understood in terms of a single underlying conviction. Dreyfus grasped, as very few philosophers do, *the sovereignty of practical intelligence over all other forms of intelligence*. It is this insight that led him to argue in the 1970s and 80s that computers cannot be intelligent because they lack bodies. The same insight led him in the 1990s to develop an account of embodied intentionality that does not presuppose aboutness, or representational content. And it led him, finally, in the early 2000s to develop an account of action and practical wisdom that does not depend on deliberation or purposive agency. Ultimately, Dreyfus' preoccupation with the sovereignty of the practical led him to forsake the contested terminology of practical reason, action, and intention altogether, and he couched his positive views instead in terms of practical skill, practical expertise, phronesis, and skilled, absorbed, or embodied coping.

The remainder of this essay will focus primarily on Dreyfus' late-stage contributions to practical philosophy and philosophy of action, as represented by his engagement with John McDowell and John Searle, and the alternatives that he proposed to their respective theories of mind and action. In our view this portion of his life work constitutes the fruition of Dreyfus' sustained but developing commitment to the sovereignty of the practical. His views in this domain are radical, but also more plausible and much less easily dismissed than they may initially appear.

9.2 Embodied intentionality vs. the "Standard Story"

In his 2005 Presidential Address to the Pacific Division of the American Philosophical Association, Dreyfus advanced the following theses:

- That in skilled action or skilled "coping," human beings respond to relevant features of their situation in a way that does not involve any mental *representation* of these features or the goals in virtue of which they are relevant.
- That skilled action therefore does not depend on any psychologically mediated "causal chain from input to response" (Dreyfus 2005: 107).
- That instead, skilled coping consists in a *direct*, absorbed, and self-forgetful *responsiveness* that depends on our embodied capacities and the features of the physical and social environments we engage with.

These theses were advanced in the context of a criticism of John McDowell's exquisitely nuanced form of conceptualism about the mind. The core claim of McDowell's *Mind and World* is that "conceptual capacities … are already at work in experiences themselves," in an avowedly "demanding" sense of conceptual capacities as ones that "can be exploited in active thinking, thinking that is open to reflection about its own rational credentials" (McDowell 1994: 47). For McDowell, perception and action are permeated with rationality, with understanding, with "logos" as he often calls it—a view that could not be more antithetical to the ideas that Dreyfus had spent his career defending.

Given the influence and stature of *Mind and World*, it must have felt to Dreyfus in 2005 as if he had gained very little ground against the Platonic picture. And in the context of his decades-long struggle to resist "the whole conceptual framework which assumes that an explanation of human behavior can and must take the Platonic form" (Dreyfus 1979: 232), his rather scandalous description of McDowell's grand reconciliation as "a vulture ... feed[ing] off the carcass of the Myth of the Given" (Dreyfus 2005: 53), barely rises to the level of polemic. Yet throughout his exchange with McDowell, Dreyfus was not only playing the role of gadfly, but also continuing to develop a positive philosophy of practice and action that he had already given substantive expression in his earlier work on action theory, especially when discussing his U.C. Berkeley colleague John Searle's theories of mind and action. For example, in "Heidegger's Critique of the Husserl/Searle Account of Intentionality," Dreyfus proposed his own account of absorbed coping, which involves "a kind of intentionality that does not involve content at all" (Dreyfus 2014: 77).

Intentionality that does not involve content? Dreyfus was aware of how strange this would sound. Philosophers of mind use the word "intentional" to refer to the fact that "mental states like perceiving, believing, desiring, fearing, doubting, etc. are always about something, i.e. directed at something under some description" (ibid.). Intentionality is thus normally an intrinsically contentful, mind-involving notion. But absorbed coping, Dreyfus proposed, manifests "a more fundamental sort of intentionality" that is embodied (or bodily) *and yet still intelligent*. It is a sensitive, engaged, dynamic *orientation* of oneself in one's practical and epistemic milieu (ibid.). This kind of embodied intentionality does not admit of a sharp distinction between mind and world at all, let alone one that construes the mind primarily or exclusively in terms of *logos*, or conceptual or rational capacities. Absorbed copers are inextricably embedded in their world. And for that reason, Dreyfus' conception of absorbed coping also does not admit of a distinction between "mind-to-world" and "world-to-mind" directions of fit and causation, as in the account Searle had worked out in his 1983 book, *Intentionality*.

At the core of Searle's theory of intentionality is a parallel between the kinds of representational states and causal transactions involved in perception and action, respectively. According to Searle, a perceptual experience (1) has a *mind-to-world* direction of fit, since it is a state that is accurate insofar as it matches how things are anyway in the world, and (2) is the result of a process with a *world-to-mind* direction of causation, since a person counts as being in a perceptual state only if "the way the world is *makes* [the person] see it that way" (Searle 1983: 96). By contrast, in intentional action (2′) the direction of causation is *mind-to-world*, since in acting a person makes *the world* to be a certain way, and (1′) the direction of fit is *world-to-mind*, since action is successful insofar as its result "fits" the agent's intention. For Dreyfus, by contrast, because the absorbed, expert subject is embedded in the world, she is *pulled* into action by her world as much as she pushes it into this or that shape. The kind of skillful activity found in absorbed coping is not a matter of *making* the world outside so that it accords with an internal representation of it, any more than perception is just a matter of *taking* things in so as to generate an accurate representation of them. Instead, both are reciprocal. Just as perception is an *active* process wherein we explore the world to get it to show up for us, so absorbed coping is *responsive*, attuned; it is a way of being in touch with what one's surroundings call for and afford (see also Gehrman 2014).

We can further clarify Dreyfus' account of skillful, embodied coping by contrasting it with Searle's representational account of intentional action. Searle's account centers, first, on the following pair of theses:

(A) That an action is intentional only if the agent is in a *mental state* that represents the goal of her action;

(B) That this mental state is the *cause* of the bodily movement whereby the agent acts as she intends to.

While the details of Searle's account are controversial, (A) and (B) represent commitments that have been widely accepted by analytic philosophers since the influential work of Donald Davidson. Indeed, David Velleman (1992: 461) has called the picture summed up by (A) and (B) the "Standard Story" of action. Searle also defended three further claims which are, in some version, widely accepted by analytic action theorists:

(C) That the mental state which represents the goal of an agent's action is *internal* to the agent—i.e. it can exist whether or not she acts;

(D) That in acting intentionally, an agent enjoys an *experience* that represents her action as the cause of her bodily movement; and

(E) That "at any point in a [person's] conscious life he knows without observation the answer to the question, 'What are you now doing?'" (Searle 1983: 90)—at least where this concerns the descriptions under which the person's action is intentional.[2]

Dreyfus challenged each one of these claims, arguing that *none* of them are supported by the phenomenology of purposive activity, and that to the extent that they have a basis in the logic of our ordinary action-descriptions or the psychology of "common sense" this is only because our ordinary self-understanding is distorted by the Platonic picture.

Consider first thesis (D). According to Searle (1983: 87–8) there are "characteristic experiences" of an intentional action such as raising your arm, and the intentional content of these experiences has a self-referential character: an experience of acting *represents itself as the cause* of the bodily movement whereby the agent does what she intends. Against this, Dreyfus argues that if we "return to the phenomena" with open minds, we find that "in a wide variety of situations human beings relate to the world in an organized purposive manner without the constant accompaniment of a representational state which specifies what the action is aimed at accomplishing" (Dreyfus 2014: 83). He gives a range of examples:

> skillful activity like playing tennis; habitual activity like driving to the office or brushing one's teeth; casual unthinking activity like rolling over in bed or making gestures while one is speaking; and spontaneous activity such as fidgeting and drumming one's fingers during a dull lecture.
>
> *Ibid.*

All of these activities involve movement that is organized, purposive, and sensitive to environmental contingencies. Yet there is *no* phenomenological support for the claim that there are "characteristic experiences" of acting in any of these ways—let alone experiences that represent themselves as the cause of one's movements. As Dreyfus observed, when these forms of action involve any experience at all, it is not an experience of oneself as *causing* one's activity, but rather of a direct responsiveness to the environment whereby "[o]ne's activity is completely geared into the demands of the situation" (ibid.: 81). Indeed, there is more evidence in the phenomenology of expert action for saying that the world *causes me to act* by eliciting an expert response, than for attributing causality *to me* via my experience of what I do.

Dreyfus' argument against thesis (E) proceeds in a similar way. One often *finds* that one has been gesturing wildly or making the correct turns on a well-learned route, without having known that one was doing these things.[3] And yet there is usually a goal intrinsic to these kinds of activities, which the person who engages in them would treat as her own. One might say, for example, that one was gesturing wildly for emphasis, or that one turned right to avoid the traffic on Sunset, without thereby committing to the self-awareness that (E) stipulates must attend intentional actions. And Dreyfus argued that the same holds for more complex capacities: for example, he loved to cite Larry Bird, who claimed that "[a] lot of times, I've passed the basketball and not realized I've passed it until a moment or so later" (quoted in Dreyfus 1993: 84). This phenomenon supports a construal of an expert's self-knowledge quite at odds with the one that Searle assumes. For Dreyfus, even *without* non-observational knowledge of her own activity, the expert does what she does in precisely the way that her situation demands.

Dreyfus did not claim that purposive activity *never* involves experience of one's movements or non-observational knowledge of what one does. On the contrary, he argued that conscious self-monitoring is necessary in certain situations, including when acquiring a new skill or exercising a well-learned skill in difficult or unfamiliar circumstances. It is primarily in situations like these, he says, that one acts with "a sense of effort with the condition of satisfaction that [this] effort causes the appropriate goal-directed movements"—a way of self-consciously representing our actions that "certainly [has] a place in the overall explanation of how it is that we manage to act in a wide range of situations" (Dreyfus 1993: 89). The mistake of (E) is to conclude that the capacities for self-monitoring that we draw on in these *special* situations are also part of the explanation of purposive activity in the more ordinary situation when there is no particular pressure to attend to the structure of one's action.[4]

Consider finally Searle's thesis (C), which holds that what makes an action intentional must be a representation that can exist independently of her bodily movements and their effects, which in turn can exist without the representation. For Searle (1983: 89–90), this independence of intention from movement is shown by a pair of cases: a person whose arm has been anaesthetized and then held down may, if his eyes are closed, have a mistaken experience as of moving his arm; and a person whose arm is made to move directly by stimulation of his motor cortex will be such that his arm moves without the experience characteristic of *his* moving his arm intentionally.

Against this analysis, Dreyfus would argue that these cases do not present us with the *usual* phenomenon of moving purposively in a world we are "geared into" by our interests. Except in moments where we are forced to adopt an explicitly self-aware, reflexive perspective on what we are doing, in purposive activity we are so thoroughly embedded in the world that what happens "in us" is not a separate domain from what takes place in our "surroundings." The binary subject-object or agent-world distinction that is implied by (C), and which the analytic tradition takes for granted, severely distorts the phenomenology of *everyday* activity, even if we can think of cases where the agent-world contrast has application.

9.3 A Sisyphean task?

Dreyfus (2005) avails himself of resources from "the phenomenology of everyday expertise" to criticize theses (C)–(E) and propose substantive alternative accounts of the relevant phenomena. But are those resources sufficient to ground a substantive alternative to the "Standard Story" of (A) and (B)? When he sought to slay the dragon of the computational theory of mind in

What Computers Can't Do, Dreyfus acknowledged that doing so would (at least at first) be a Sisyphean task:

> [T]he impetus gained by the mutual reinforcement of two thousand years of tradition and its product, the most powerful device ever invented by man [namely, the digital computer], is simply too great to be arrested [or] deflected. ... The most that can be hoped is that we become aware that the direction this impetus has taken ... is not the only possible direction; ... that there may be a way of understanding human reason that explains both why the computer paradigm is irresistible and why it must fail.
>
> *1979: 232*

In the AI context, Dreyfus hoped, not to replace or refute the "computer paradigm," but rather to counteract its distorting effects by giving an *at least equally plausible* phenomenological description of human reason. When it comes to his account of skilled, absorbed coping and practical expertise, we propose that Dreyfus is best understood to have the same aims and priorities. That is, while he argued forcefully against the mentalistic models of action and practical intelligence that he sought to disrupt, Dreyfus was in the end most interested in presenting an *at least equally plausible* phenomenological account of the relevant phenomena, to show that the Standard Story is "not the only possible direction" that an account of human action can take. With this in mind we will devote the present section to motivating Dreyfus' supposedly radical claims about practical intelligence, in order to vindicate them as an intelligible alternative to the Standard Story.

Many of Dreyfus' best-known examples of absorbed, expert coping are things that are already readily understood as primarily embodied: playing soccer, riding a bike, wielding a hammer, and other examples of what Aristotle might have thought of as technical expertise (see Heidegger 1996: 64ff.; Aristotle 2001: 179). But the familiarity of absorbed practical phenomenology in such cases is the thin edge of a wedge that can, if we allow it, separate us gradually from the Platonic conception of ourselves as rational, agential individuals.

To this end, we can begin by observing first that the same absorbed quality that characterizes one's competent use of a hammer or pen also characterizes many activities which, on the Platonic picture, constitutively involve the intellect. While Dreyfus' favorite example was the skillful play of the chess grandmaster, here we will use for illustration some of the activities that are typically part of being a professional academic philosopher: teaching a class, constructing a logical proof, writing a paper, or posing a question following a colleague's oral presentation. These are the kinds of activities with respect to which virtually all academic philosophers are expert. If Dreyfus is right that skilled coping is both *normally* and *ideally* absorbed, then even these paradigmatically intellect-involving activities ought to exhibit the absorbed phenomenology of embodied, engaged intentionality. That is, if Dreyfus is right, then in some real way even these paradigmatically intellectual activities *don't involve the mind* when they are expertly done.

So, consider what you are doing when you are giving a lecture on a familiar topic. (Non-academics can substitute an appropriately intellectual activity at which they have the relevant degree of expertise.) You are, for example, speaking certain words at a certain pace and with a certain pattern of emphasis. You are making eye contact with others in the room. You are using language in a way that aims to communicate clearly and (perhaps) eloquently. You are monitoring the reactions and interactions of the class, and inserting yourself into the developing social events as they take place, in a way that furthers the background objectives that structure and explain your actions in the first place.

Now, in doing all of this, *where is your attention?* Where is your focus? Your focus is on what you are doing. But your focus is not on what you are doing in the way that a peer observer tasked with writing a teaching evaluation would focus on you teaching the class. You are not attending to yourself as agent; you are attending as agent to what you do. Your focus is *in* what you are doing; your attention is taken up by the activity, and other possible candidates for your attention recede.

This focused, active, attuned, attentive, absorbed kind of activity *just is* (Dreyfus might say) what it is to act purposively with skill. To act in this way is to realize absorbed intentionality. In order to be skillfully or expertly teaching purposively, *you have to actually be teaching*—not thinking about teaching, not attending to yourself teaching as an observer might, not describing what it is to teach, not intending to teach, not planning how to teach another person to teach in the way that you currently are. In teaching skillfully you are simply: *teaching.* If you are doing what you do "at someone else's prompting" (Aristotle 2001: 114), under the guidance of a set of rules, or while narrating what you do either to yourself or aloud, you are divided in your purpose, divided in your attention, not "all in" on the action that was ostensibly what you were up to. In the very dividedness of your attention, you would do what you did in a less expert (because less absorbed) way.

9.4 Practical wisdom without rationality

For Dreyfus, absorbed coping is possible only when a skill is fully integrated into the subject's way of being-in-the-world. By contrast, less-than-absorbed, less-than-embodied, less-than-embedded action is not yet truly chosen in this way; it is not yet fully, autonomously purposive or intentional because it has not yet become *part of you.*

This thought may help us to see how Dreyfus could respond to the philosophical orthodoxy that the concept of *acting for a reason* deserves a central place in any philosophical account of what it is to act intentionally. This assumption accounts for the dominance of the Standard Story of intentional action as bodily movement that is caused by an intention: for how can one *act for* a reason without having this reason somewhere "in mind"? And what would it be to act for *this* reason—as opposed to another one that is also in mind—except for this reason to make an appropriate (presumably, causal) difference to what one does?[5]

Dreyfus' account seems at first especially unable to account for these aspects of everyday action-explanation. If a person's mental states are not involved in causing her intentional actions, then there does not seem to be anything there to ground an intention-revealing answer to the question "Why did you do that?" Compounding the problem, Dreyfus frequently presents his views in a way that suggests that he is denying a role to the agent in choosing, causing, or generating her own actions.[6] For example in "A Merleau-Pontian Critique of Husserl's and Searle's Representationalist Accounts of Action," he says:

> Merleau-Ponty argues that what we might call absorbed coping does not require that the agent's movements be governed by an intention in action that represents … what the agent is trying to achieve. Rather, in absorbed coping the agent's body is led to move so as to reduce a sense of deviation from a satisfactory gestalt without the agent knowing what that satisfactory gestalt will be like in advance of achieving it. Thus, in absorbed coping, rather than a sense of trying to achieve success, one has a sense of being drawn towards an equilibrium.
>
> *2000: 293*

In passages like this one, experts start to seem like zombies, or like iron filings in the presence of so many magnets. And if so then the Anscombean question "Why did you do that?" might seem, as she put it, to be appropriately *"refused application"* (Anscombe 1963: 11) in any case of absorbed coping—in which case it is not at all clear that *anything* distinguishes the intentional from the non- or un-intentional on Dreyfus' account.

Let us attempt to address this concern on Dreyfus' behalf. The *phenomena*, he will insist, as opposed to any grammatical test, are the criteria that must distinguish intentional expert coping from other ways of being-in-the-world. And in many cases this is plausible. It is easy, for example, to think of ways in which the actions of an expert differ characteristically from the actions of a novice or an incompetent bungler. For Dreyfus, the real challenge is the automaton. How can we distinguish, *on phenomenological grounds alone*, between the absorbed, expert coper, and the absent-minded person who is operating on autopilot?

Let us consider the question in the context of a specific example. Suppose that on Monday you drive your manual transmission sedan to work along your usual route. You are relaxed and well-slept, and your cell phone is tucked away in your bag. You keep your eyes on the road, you don't grind the gears, and you push it with the yellow lights just as much as you feel is wise, no more, no less. Now it is Tuesday. Overtired and engaged in a voice-texting argument with your spouse, you grind the gears several times getting into second, need to slam on the brakes at least once to avoid running a red, and pull in to your spot with the gas light on only to realize that on Tuesdays you have a standing appointment across town and you ought not to have been driving to work in the first place.

As with Dreyfus' favorite comparison between the deft and sure activity of the expert and the hesitant and fumbling behavior of the novice, there are many familiar differences in the phenomenology of these two scenarios, from both the first- and the third-person perspectives. On Monday, you are coping in an absorbed, expert fashion under a number of descriptions: shifting gears, driving to work, being a defensive driver, etc. Similar to our earlier discussion of the expert philosopher, as you do these things your focus, your attention is on what you are doing under these descriptions. On this particular morning, the focus of your absorbed attention is on navigating the roads, shifting your gears, getting to work in a timely manner. There will be phenomena characteristic of being engaged in doing these things, and ways that another person who is engaged in observing you closely might be able to tell that you are doing them in an absorbed, expert way. Your passenger might notice, for example, that there is never a lurch in momentum when you shift from second to third gear. They may hear a small chuckle or see you lean forward slightly when you hit a yellow light at just the right moment to justify a small burst of speed. They may pick up on the fact that you are relaxed.

On Tuesday, what are you doing? You are certainly absorbed in *something*. But what? Not the same things you were absorbed in the morning before. Instead, your focus is on something else: the voice-texting argument, resentment about your lack of sleep, and the glowing gas light on the dashboard. These things command your attention and assume the place of proximal nodes in your net, embedding you in the world a quite different way as compared to the way you were embedded on Monday, when the gear shifter, the road, the overall drive were your proximal nodes. On Tuesday, distracted and distanced from the driving-related activities, you grind the gears. You fail to time the lights well. You do not drive where you set out to go. And the phenomenology of these activities will be very different from the phenomenology of what were in some sense the same activities during Monday's drive, both from a first-person perspective (the stress, the sweaty palms, the constant guilty peeking to proofread the latest voice-texted zinger before hitting send) and from a third-person perspective (the palpable tension, the vehicular lurches, the conspicuous absence of chuckles, the eyes on the dash and the phone more than the road, etc.).

On the phenomenological account that we have just sketched, it is not as if absorbed, attentive defensive driving is reason-involving in a way that driving distractedly is not. For each of these activities is in its own way embodied and embedded in the world, and thus absorbed in its own set of practical problems. And this similarity is what gave rise to the concern that there is no room within Dreyfus' account for answering Anscombe's "special sense of the question 'Why?'." But the subject in this example is absorbed in very different things on Monday and Tuesday, and the phenomenology of their activities manifests this difference. We can say: the drive on Monday is an example of expert Dreyfusian intentional action; it is expert absorbed coping. The drive on Tuesday is *not* an example of expert Dreyfusian intentional action, though the voice-texting argument might be. We suspect that anybody who thinks that the phenomenology of these two cases will be first- or third-personally indistinguishable has no direct experience of the relevant sort.

We also acknowledge that some reservations about Dreyfus' views will persist to whatever extent his interlocutors remain in the grip of the Platonic picture of humankind (and we include ourselves in this). For if our conception of intentionality is that it is essentially conceptual, representational, and self-aware, then naturally any view to the contrary will seem to lose the phenomenon of intentionality itself. And the same goes for agency, for agents and their purposive activity. But if Dreyfus had meant simply to reject or refute the Platonic picture of human mentality, he would have had no need to recruit the vocabulary and conceptual frames of phenomenology to do so. He could have simply adopted the stance of skeptic, so to speak from *inside* the Platonic tradition, arguing that rationality, individuality, and agency are not characteristics of human beings. Instead, Dreyfus sought to save the practical phenomena, and to focus attention on a very different way of understanding ourselves: as embedded, absorbed, and embodied beings. And this implies that he believed the phenomena of purposive human practical life are there to be saved. The embedded subject still interacts with her world; she is not merely acted upon. The absorbed coper still strives purposively, and can succeed (or fail) to achieve what she aims to achieve. The embodied coper still attends to her world and comports herself in a way that is informed by intelligent appreciation of that world. For Dreyfus, practical intelligence is not an illusion. It is, as we put it earlier, *sovereign* over all other forms of intelligence, and that is why the former cannot be satisfyingly explained in terms of the latter. It remains for us to work with the materials he offered to see whether we can make sense of absorbed intentionality in terms that he would have found acceptable.

Notes

* This chapter is dedicated, with deep gratitude, to the memory of Hubert L. Dreyfus. We are grateful to an audience at the 2017 Southeastern Epistemology Conference, held at Florida State University, for helpful feedback on an earlier draft.
1 See also Dreyfus (1991), (2000), and (2014; especially Chapters 1 and 9). Dreyfus' interpretation of Heidegger is controversial and often idiosyncratic; for more on this see Braver (2011: 145ff.), Wrathall (2014), and Wrathall and Malpas (2000a, 2000b). On the self as a node in a net, compare Arne Naess (1973), who was also influenced by Heidegger.
2 Notably, in her seminal work *Intention* G. E. M. Anscombe flatly rejects each of (A) through (D). The language of *knowledge without observation*, in contrast, is due to her (1963[1957]: 13).
3 However, for some critical discussion of this sort of argument see Schwenkler (2019: 22–4, 44–5).
4 As Sean Kelly puts it,

just as the child assumes that the refrigerator light must always be on, since it is on every time he looks, so too our proposed analyst has claimed that since the intention to type an *f* is explicit when the subject is paying attention to his activity, so too it must have been among the conditions that characterized the content of the activity even when he was not paying attention to it. This is a bad principle in the case of absorbed activity, just as in the case of refrigerator lights.

2005: 20

5 As Davidson famously put it, unless we treat reason-giving explanations as causal "we are without an analysis of the 'because' in 'He did it because ...', where we go on to name a reason" (1980: 11).
6 See Braver (2011), Noë (2013), and Gehrman (2016).

References

Anscombe, G. E. M. (1963) *Intention*, Oxford: Basil Blackwell.
Aristotle (2001) *Nicomachean Ethics*, trans. C. Rowe, Oxford: Oxford University Press.
Braver, L. (2011) "Never Mind: Thinking of Subjectivity in the Dreyfus-McDowell Debate," in J. Schear (ed.), *Mind, Reason and Being-in-the-World: The McDowell-Dreyfus Debate*, London: Routledge, pp. 143–62.
Davidson, D. (1980) "Actions, Reasons, and Causes," in D. Davidson, *Essays on Actions and Events*, Oxford: Oxford University Press, pp. 3–20.
Dreyfus, H. L. (1979) *What Computers Can't Do: A Critique of Artificial Reason*, New York: Harper & Row.
—— (1991) *Being-in-the-World: A Commentary on Heidegger's Being and Time, Division I*, Cambridge, MA: MIT Press.
—— (2000) "A Merleau-Pontian Critique of Husserl's and Searle's Representationalist Accounts of Action," *Proceedings of the Aristotelian Society* 100: 287–302.
—— (2005) "Overcoming the Myth of the Mental: How Philosophers Can Profit from the Phenomenology of Everyday Expertise," *Proceedings and Addresses of the American Philosophical Association* 79: 47–65.
—— (2014) *Skillful Coping: Essays on the Phenomenology of Everyday Perception and Action*, M. Wrathall (ed.), Oxford: Oxford University Press.
Gehrman, K. (2014) "Action as Interaction," *American Philosophical Quarterly* 51: 75–84.
—— (2016) "Practical Wisdom and Absorbed Coping," *The Journal of Value Inquiry* 50: 593–612.
Heidegger, M. (1996) *Being and Time: A Translation of Sein Und Zeit*, trans. J. Stambaugh, Albany: State University of New York Press.
Kelly, S. D. (2005) "Closing the Gap: Phenomenology and Logical Analysis," *Harvard Review of Philosophy* 13: 4–24.
McDowell, J. (1994) *Mind and World*, Cambridge, MA: Harvard University Press.
Naess, A. (1973) "The Shallow and the Deep, Long-Range Ecology Movement," *Inquiry* 16: 95–100.
Noë, A. (2013) *Action in Perception*, Cambridge, MA: The MIT Press.
Schwenkler, J. (2019) *Anscombe's Intention: A Guide*, New York: Oxford University Press.
Searle, J. (1983) *Intentionality: An Essay in the Philosophy of Mind*, Cambridge: Cambridge University Press.
Velleman, J. D. (1992) "What Happens When Someone Acts?" *Mind* 101(403): 461–81.
Wrathall, M. (2014) "Introduction: Hubert Dreyful and the Phenomenology of Human Intelligence", in M. Wrathall (ed.), *Skillful Coping: Essays on the Phenomenology of Everyday Perception and Action*, Oxford: Oxford University Press, pp. 1–22.
Wrathall, M., and Malpas, J. (2000a) *Heidegger, Authenticity, and Modernity: Essays in Honor of Hubert. L. Dreyfus*, Volume 1, Cambridge, MA: MIT Press.
—— (2000b) *Heidegger, Coping, and Cognitive Science: Essays in Honor of Hubert. L. Dreyfus*, Volume 2, Cambridge, MA: MIT Press.

PART II

Skill in epistemology

10

KNOWLEDGE, SKILL AND VIRTUE EPISTEMOLOGY

Duncan Pritchard

10.1 Knowledge, luck and cognitive skill

There is an intimate connection between knowledge and skill, to the extent that it is not seriously in question that the former demands the latter.[1] That is, when a subject has knowledge her true belief is in some significant way due to her exercise of relevant cognitive skills. This is one reason why a subject who gets to the truth in a completely random way—through guesswork, say (assuming that guesswork is ever a genuine route to belief)—doesn't count as having knowledge, since their cognitive agency is not playing any role in producing their cognitive success.[2] Elsewhere I have referred to this widespread intuition in epistemology as the *ability platitude*.[3]

Note that it is useful to keep the ability platitude apart from a second widely held intuition about knowledge. This is the *anti-luck platitude* that knowledge cannot be due to luck.[4] For many cases, a true belief that fails to amount to knowledge runs afoul of both platitudes. In the case just imagined, for example, where the subject's true belief is entirely through guesswork, it is true both that the cognitive success is purely down to luck and that it has nothing to do with the subject's exercise of relevant cognitive skill. Moreover, this doesn't seem to be at all accidental. If one gets to the truth through one's exercise of relevant cognitive ability, then doesn't that exclude the possibility that one got to the truth simply through luck? And if one's cognitive success is not down to luck, then what else could it be attributable to except one's exercise of relevant cognitive ability? On the face of it, then, it does look as if these two platitudes are simply two sides of the same coin.

Interestingly, however, there are also cases that appear to trade on only one of these platitudes. Consider, for example, a belief that is guaranteed to be true, given how it was formed, but where this has nothing to do with the subject's exercise of relevant cognitive agency. Perhaps, for example, there is a divine helper whose sole concern is to ensure that the subject's beliefs about a certain subject matter, formed in this particular way, are sure to be true (to the extent that the divine helper will, if need be, change the facts to conform with what the agent believes). Now imagine that our subject forms her beliefs in this regard in ways that have nothing to do with the exercise of relevant cognitive agency (such as, again, guesswork, say). Since the beliefs are guaranteed to be true, there is no plausible sense in which we can say that they are only true as a matter of luck, and hence the anti-luck platitude should be satisfied. But nonetheless they clearly don't amount to knowledge, and the natural explanation for why this is so is that they don't satisfy the ability platitude.[5]

As we will see shortly, there are also cases that seem to demonstrate that one's belief can satisfy the ability platitude but fail to count as knowledge nonetheless because it fails to satisfy the anti-luck platitude. If that's right, then the two platitudes come apart in extension in both directions. But this second type of scenario is more controversial, for reasons that I will explain. In any case, our interest just now is in the ability platitude and in theories of knowledge which take their lead from this platitude. In particular, there is a way of thinking about knowledge that takes the idea that knowledge involves cognitive skill or ability as primary. We can usefully classify such views as *virtue epistemologies*, even though such a classification covers a very broad spectrum of views. Indeed, there will be positions that fall under this classification where the proponents of these positions would eschew this description (albeit for reasons that don't concern us here).[6]

10.2 Types of virtue epistemology

It will be helpful to differentiate between types of virtue epistemology along two key axes. The first concerns whether the position's appeal to cognitive skills—i.e., cognitive *virtues*, very loosely and broadly conceived (we will comment on this usage shortly)—is meant to offer a complete account of knowledge. Call *robust virtue epistemology* the view that there is nothing more to knowledge than (roughly) virtuously formed true belief—i.e., expressed in terms of skills, specifically, that knowledge is essentially skilfully formed true belief.[7] In contrast, call *modest robust virtue epistemology* the view that virtuous true belief is at most a necessary condition of knowledge.[8] Accordingly, the modest virtue epistemology camp would also include those proponents of virtue epistemology who reject the whole project of analysing knowledge.[9] We will come back to this distinction in a moment.

A second axis along which we can differentiate types of virtue epistemology concerns how broad the class of cognitive traits is that are allowed to count as virtues. On the one hand, we have *virtue reliabilism* which holds that a wide variety of reliable cognitive traits, such as cognitive skills and faculties, can qualify as virtues in the relevant sense, and thus enable a subject to gain knowledge (or at least satisfy the ability epistemic condition relevant to knowledge anyway).[10] In contrast, *virtue responsibilism* holds that only a restricted class of reliable cognitive traits counts as virtues in the relevant sense, and hence is relevant to the acquisition of knowledge. For example, one might hold that it is only the exercise of the intellectual virtues, in the Aristotelian sense, that enables subjects to gain knowledge.[11]

What drives the virtue reliabilism/responsibilism distinction tends to be the epistemic externalism/internalism debate regarding knowledge.[12] All virtue epistemologies are claiming to capture the sense in which a subject's knowledge, on account of it being the significant product of cognitive skill, is thereby a cognitively responsible true belief. But they depart from each other in terms of how much they build into this notion of cognitive responsibility, and that relates to where they stand in the epistemic externalism/internalism debate.

Consider first how virtue reliabilism compares to a simple process reliabilism. Both views focus on reliable belief-forming processes, but what sets virtue reliabilism apart from a simple process reliabilism is the idea that it is not any reliable belief-forming process that matters, but rather those cognitive traits that are stable and integrated aspects of the subject's cognitive character.[13] In short, what matters are the subject's cognitive *skills* (where this category also includes one's innate cognitive skills—i.e., one's cognitive faculties). Mere reliable belief-forming processes, after all, need not have anything to do with the subject's cognitive skills. For example, they can be entirely fleeting belief-forming traits, and hence not represent a subject's cognitive skills for that reason. Or they can be belief-forming traits that are reliable in ways that are contrary to the subject's cognitive character rather than being a manifestation of it, as in cases of reliable malfunctions, and hence do not represent a subject's cognitive skills for that reason.[14]

By focusing on those reliable belief-forming traits that count as cognitive skills, virtue reliabilism is able to directly accommodate the ability platitude. It also enables the view to offer an account of cognitive responsibility. After all, if one's true belief is the product of one's cognitive skills, then there is a clear sense in which one's cognitive success is representative of one's cognitive agency, and hence is something that one can take responsibility for. The contrast is with other kinds of true beliefs that are not due to one's cognitive skills—such as true belief that is the result of guesswork—where one cannot take responsibility for one's cognitive success. Indeed, this contrast will also cover cases of mere reliable true belief too, such as cognitive malfunctions, as these will also be instances where the cognitive responsibility at issue is lacking.

For virtue reliabilism, our concern for cognitive responsibility—especially as regards the kind of cognitive responsibility at issue when it comes to knowledge—is captured by this very broad notion that is in play here. I say broad because it is also relatively undemanding from an intellectual perspective. On this view, a subject might be simply, and unreflectively, manifesting her cognitive skills in circumstances relative to which they are apt and thereby come to have cognitively responsibly true belief (and thereby be in the market for knowledge). In particular, there is no essential reason why the subject should be in a position to offer good reflectively accessible reasons in support of her belief—i.e., a *justification*, as it is normally understood—which is what an epistemic internalist would characteristically demand of a knowing subject.

This is where the contrast between virtue reliabilism and virtue responsibilism comes in, since the latter will insist on a much more demanding conception of cognitive responsibility, one more in keeping with standard forms of epistemic internalism. In particular, they will insist that the relevant notion of cognitive responsibility—at least as it pertains to knowledge anyway—is one that involves a manifestation of cognitive skills in such a manner that the subject is able to offer justifications for their beliefs. In effect, then, they are restricting the way in which cognitive skills can give rise to knowledge, in that they will insist that a mere unreflective exercise of cognitive skill does not suffice for cognitive responsibility (of the relevant kind), and hence does not suffice for knowledge either, *contra* virtue reliabilism.

It will be helpful in this regard to focus on an especially demanding version of virtue responsibilism that insists that it is only intellectual virtues—such as being conscientious or observant—that can generate knowledge.[15] Intellectual virtues are here to be understood along broadly Aristotelian lines, and hence to be contrasted with mere cognitive skills, just as virtues more generally are often contrasted with skills. For example, virtues (and hence intellectual virtues) are acquired and maintained in distinctive ways via emulation of the virtuous combined with a process of habituation so that the target dispositions become second nature. This ensures that intellectual virtues are essentially reflective cognitive traits, in that one needs to engage in relevant reflection in order to acquire them in the first place and then maintain them thereafter. Indeed, in the case of intellectual virtues, even once the target dispositions have become second nature reflection will still be required (perhaps in contrast to virtues more generally). How, for example, could someone manifest conscientiousness in a purely unreflective manner? Skills, on the other hand, can be innate, as cognitive faculties are, or can be acquired in entirely unreflective ways. It's also not necessary to cognitive skills that they require any activity on the part of the subject in order to be maintained—one's faculties, for example, may work perfectly fine without one doing anything (consciously anyway) to ensure their proper function.

There are other differences between virtues and skills, and thus between intellectual virtues and cognitive skills, but the foregoing should suffice to demonstrate that the former is a much more demanding notion.[16] In particular, the notion of cognitive responsibility in play when it comes to the manifestation of intellectual virtues is much more sophisticated than that at issue in virtue reliabilism, and hence much more restrictive as a result. Manifestations of the intellectual virtues essentially involve specifically reflective cognitive skills in ways that are unlike the exercise of mere (unreflective) cognitive skills. They thus bring with them a level of cognitive ownership on the part of the subject that is not demanded by the exercise of mere cognitive skills. This means that there is a very different, and more demanding, notion of cognitive responsibility in play. In short, if knowledge demands the manifestation of intellectual virtue then it will not be enough for knowledge that one's cognitive success be attributable to one's cognitive skills, and thereby one's cognitive character. Instead, one's cognitive success should be attributable to one's reflective employment of one's cognitive skills (e.g., as in the manifestation of an intellectual virtue).

10.3 Robust virtue epistemology

These two ways of distinguishing types of virtue epistemology are completely independent of one another, in that where one stands as regards one of these axes does not determine where one stands as regards the other. For example, one might be a robust virtue responsibilist or a modest virtue responsibilist, or one might be a robust virtue reliabilist or a modest virtue reliabilist.[17] With that in mind, we will now evaluate the merits of robust virtue epistemology while bracketing whether that view should be further allied to virtue reliabilism or virtue responsibilism.

One principal motivation for robust virtue epistemology comes from the idea that knowledge is a particular kind of achievement, a claim that brings with it a distinctive account of the relationship between knowledge and skill.[18] In order to see this, consider what achievements in general involve, taking the case of an archer's achievement at hitting the target as an illustration. Achievements demand success, but mere success does not suffice—it is not enough for an achievement that the archer hits the target through dumb luck. In particular, achievements demand relevant skill, in this case the skills relevant to archery. Interestingly, however, the mere conjunction of success and the exercise of the relevant skill does not suffice for an achievement. This is because one can easily 'Gettierize' such a conjunction, by making the success completely independent of the exercise of skill. So, for example, imagine that the archer skilfully fires the arrow, and that it also hits the target, but that while in flight it is caught by a dog who promptly deposits the arrow in the target. We thus have success and the exercise of relevant skill, but clearly no achievement.

What needs to be added to success and skill in order to get an achievement? Well, at a rough first pass, it seems that what is required is a success that is *because of* one's exercise of the relevant skill, in the sense that one's success is attributable to that exercise of skill. Expressed in sloganizing form, achievements seem to be successes that are because of skill. What's lacking in the archer case just considered is that while there is both success and the manifestation of the relevant skill, the former is not attributable to the latter (but is rather due to the intervention of the helpful dog).

The reason why this is relevant to robust virtue epistemology is that it suggests a fascinating way of thinking about knowledge as a specifically cognitive kind of achievement. That is, knowledge is cognitive achievement, and is thus to be understood as being cognitive successes (i.e., true belief) that is because of cognitive skill. Such a proposal is amenable to robust virtue epistemology precisely because it analyses knowledge exclusively in terms of cognitive skills. The way in which robust virtue epistemology deals with Gettier-style cases should be clear from the toy archery example just offered. Where such cases go awry, according to robust virtue epistemology, is that while one has cognitive success (true belief) and the exercise of relevant cognitive skill, the former is not attributable to, and thus not because of, the latter. So, for example, skilfully examining an instrument that is (unbeknown to one) broken and nonetheless thereby gaining a true belief would be an instance where there is the conjunction of cognitive success and relevant cognitive skill. But since the epistemic luck in play ensures that the former is not because of the latter, it follows that it does not count as an instance of knowledge according to robust virtue epistemology, since it is not a cognitive achievement.

That knowledge is on this view merely the sub-species of an important broader category is clearly an advantage of the proposal. Indeed, this aspect of the position brings with it a notable benefit in that one is now in a position to account for the distinctive value that is often attributed to knowledge by appealing to the value of achievements more generally. Achievements, after all, do seem to have a special kind of value, of a kind that is lacking in mere successes that fall short of achievements (including Gettierized successes). If that's right, then it would hardly be surprising if knowledge, *qua* cognitive achievement, should inherit this distinctive kind of value.[19]

Despite the attractions of the view, it also faces some fairly serious problems. One concern that I want to focus on here is whether robust virtue epistemology can adequately accommodate the anti-luck platitude. I noted above that the ability and anti-luck platitudes seem to come apart in both directions, but I only gave an example of a true belief that satisfied the anti-luck platitude while failing to amount to knowledge because it failed to satisfy the ability platitude (i.e., the case where one's true belief is guaranteed to be true, but in a way that has nothing to do with one's exercise of cognitive skill). The more interesting question right now, however, is how the two platitudes might come apart in the other direction, such that there are true beliefs that satisfy the ability platitude while failing to amount to knowledge because they don't satisfy the anti-luck platitude.

With the ability platitude construed very broadly, the obvious cases that spring to mind in this regard are Gettier-style cases. After all, the subject is manifesting relevant cognitive skill in forming their true belief, but she fails to acquire knowledge nonetheless because of the epistemic luck involved. But the proponent of robust virtue epistemology can argue that what is really being demanded by the ability platitude is not just the exercise of relevant cognitive skill but, more specifically, that one's cognitive success is attributable to that exercise of relevant cognitive skill. And that does appear to be lacking in Gettier-style cases, as we noted above, which is why robust virtue epistemology can seem like such an appealing theory of knowledge.

The problem, however, is that it is fairly straightforward to formulate scenarios where even this stronger conception of the ability platitude is satisfied and yet there is sufficient epistemic luck in play that the true belief in question doesn't seem to amount to knowledge. One way of doing this is by making a distinction between two ways in which a success (cognitive or otherwise) can be lucky. Consider our archer again. In the scenario depicted above where the helpful dog seizes the arrow in flight and places it in the target, what we have is *intervening luck*, in that something actually gets in between the success and the exercise of skill and thereby ensures that the former isn't attributable to the latter (but rather to the intervention of the dog). Intervening luck is clearly incompatible with achievements, as we noted above. Its epistemic variant, *intervening epistemic luck*, is also clearly incompatible with knowledge, as it is the kind of epistemic luck that is standardly found in Gettier-style cases. For example, skilfully forming a belief that there is a sheep in the field by looking at the sheep-shaped object, and happening on a true belief on account of the real sheep hidden from view behind the sheep-shaped object that one is looking at, would fit the bill as a case of intervening epistemic luck.[20]

But there is a different kind of luck that is relevant here that is not of the intervening kind. Imagine our archer scenario but now remove the dog and have the archer skilfully hitting the target unimpeded. The twist in the tale, however, is there are (unbeknown to the subject) wind machines set up to knock the arrow off-target but which narrowly failed to activate at the very last moment. Had they activated, then the archer would not have hit the target. Crucially, what could have easily happened (but didn't) doesn't seem to undermine the subject's achievement. This is important because the success in this scenario does appear to be lucky—i.e., a success that could very easily have been a failure, given how it was brought about. Rather than the luck concerning something that actually intervenes between the exercise of skill and the success, this luck is rather to do with features of the environment itself. Accordingly, it is known as *environmental luck*.

Just as intervening luck has an epistemic variant, there is also *environmental epistemic luck*. Like intervening epistemic luck, environmental epistemic luck is also a form of veritic epistemic luck, in the sense that it involves a belief that is only true as a matter of luck, given how it is formed. Whereas intervening epistemic luck concerns something getting between the subject's exercise of cognitive skill and her cognitive success, and so breaking the explanatory connection between the two that way, environmental epistemic luck concerns broader features of the environment, particularly the modal environment, which nonetheless ensure that the belief is veritically lucky.[21] The barn façade case is often thought to be illustrative in this regard, in that we have a subject whose veritically lucky true belief is not due to a failure to perceive a genuine barn, but rather relates to the fact that in this particular environment what looks like a barn is not a good guide to whether it is a barn.[22] Such cases are held, given the veritic epistemic luck involved, to not be genuine cases of knowledge. And yet, since environmental luck is compatible with achievements, they should be genuine cases of cognitive achievement. That is, in the barn façade case one should be willing to grant that the subject's cognitive success is attributable to her exercise of cognitive skill.

How one should respond to barn façade cases is an increasingly controversial issue. In particular, several commentators have argued that we should treat the subject as having knowledge in this case, even despite the veritic epistemic luck involved. Accordingly, one could stick to the robust virtue epistemology line and treat this case as both being a cognitive achievement and an instance of knowledge.[23] With this in mind, it will be useful to focus instead on a different kind of scenario, which will help us to sharpen up the issues regarding environmental epistemic luck and its relationship to knowledge and cognitive achievements.

Consider the following *epistemic twin earth* case.[24] Imagine two agents who are microphysical duplicates, with causal histories that are also identical in every relevant respect, one on earth, and one on twin earth. Both agents occupy identical causal environments, in that the objects and properties that they are presently causally interacting with, and which are giving rise to their sensory experiences, are the same. It is also true of both agents that their 'normal' environments are the same, in that the kinds of objects and properties that they would normally causally interact with (but which they might not be presently causally interacting with) are the same. Both subjects now form the same true belief on the same basis, say that there is a barn in the field because they are presented with the same perceptual experience as of a barn.

Here is the twist in the tale: the subjects differ in their modal environments. In particular, while for the agent on earth there is no close possible world where she forms the target belief and believes falsely, for the agent on twin earth there is a close possible world where she forms the target belief and believes falsely (presumably because in close possible worlds, but not in the actual world, there are barn façades in her immediate environment). Accordingly, it will follow that while the agent on earth's true belief will not be subject to veritic luck, her counterpart on twin earth's true belief will be veritically lucky (since it will be subject to environmental epistemic luck).

Note that there is nothing in how we have set up this scenario that excludes this divergence in the modal facts regarding the two agents and their beliefs in the respective propositions. Crucially, however, we have kept everything fixed regarding these two agents to ensure that they cannot differ in terms of their manifestation of agency, and in particular their exercise of cognitive skills. Indeed, if anything we have kept more factors fixed than could possibly influence the subjects' manifestation of agency. In any case, if it's true that there can be no difference between the two subjects in terms of their manifestation of agency, then it follows that whether or not a belief is veritically lucky is not to be understood entirely in terms of such a manifestation. Moreover, insofar as one grants that knowledge is incompatible with veritic epistemic luck, then it also follows that we cannot analyse knowledge entirely in terms of true belief that manifests the subject's cognitive agency (and thus skill), as robust virtue epistemology proposes.

10.4 Anti-luck virtue epistemology

Epistemic twin earth cases help us to sharpen the problem posed by environmental epistemic luck to robust virtue epistemology. Inevitably, however, in doing so they also make it clearer how one might go about rejecting such an objection. In particular, once it is clear that veritic epistemic luck can come apart from manifestations of cognitive agency in this manner, then it becomes naturally tempting to question whether knowledge is incompatible with veritic epistemic luck as hitherto supposed.[25]

Rather than take this route, however, I want to close by briefly considering how one might *embrace* the result canvassed, while staying within the virtue epistemology framework. In particular, recall that we have motivated the idea that the anti-luck and ability platitudes are imposing distinct (albeit overlapping) constraints on a theory of knowledge, such that no level of luck-exclusion or cognitive skill manifestation in the relevant senses would suffice by itself for knowledge. This suggests a conception of knowledge that answers to two constraints. Elsewhere I have described the position that fits the bill in this regard as *anti-luck virtue epistemology*, which is a type of modest virtue epistemology.[26] In outline, this holds that knowledge is to be understood as a safe (non-lucky) cognitive success which is significantly attributable to one's manifestation of relevant cognitive skill (and thus one's cognitive agency).[27]

Notice that the explanatory relationship in play in this account of knowledge is both in a sense stronger than that demanded by robust virtue epistemology and also in a sense weaker too. The former, because it is a relation that obtains between one's *safe* cognitive success and one's cognitive agency, rather than just being between one's cognitive success and one's cognitive agency. Anti-luck virtue epistemology is thus not to be understood as the conjunction of an anti-luck and an ability condition on knowledge, as such a view would be easily Gettierizable, and wouldn't in any case capture the interconnected way in which the ability and anti-luck intuitions function. The latter, because it is not demanded that one's safe cognitive success should be primarily attributable to one's manifestation of relevant cognitive agency, but only that it should be significantly attributable (i.e., such that one's manifestation of relevant cognitive agency is an important, but not necessarily the overarching, component of a causal explanation of one's safe cognitive success). This allows us to accommodate cases of knowledge where the subject's cognitive agency is not the primary element in explaining her safe cognitive success, where other factors, such as the epistemically friendly nature of the environment, also carry an explanatory burden. In the right kind of conditions, for example, one can gain testimonial knowledge simply by asking a knowledgeable informant. In such cases, one's safe cognitive success will be at least partly attributable to one's manifestation of relevant cognitive skill (e.g., one wouldn't ask anyone, or believe anything one is told, after all), but it won't be primarily attributable to it. Nonetheless, this can suffice for knowledge on this view, as one's cognitive agency is playing a significant explanatory role in bringing about one's safe cognitive success.

With the anti-luck condition built into the proposal on account of the safety condition, the kinds of scenarios that trade on veritic luck will be immediately dealt with, including cases of environmental epistemic luck. Moreover, with the virtue condition included we can also handle scenarios where the subject's belief is guaranteed to be true, given how it was formed, but where this has nothing to do with her manifestation of cognitive skill. On this view, such cases will not amount to knowledge, just as intuition predicts. Anti-luck virtue epistemology thus has the resources to account for how knowledge demands both the avoidance of high levels of epistemic luck (and thus epistemic risk) and the manifestation of significant levels of relevant cognitive skill, where these are demands that sometimes come apart (in both directions).[28]

Notes

1 I will be focusing on propositional knowledge, specifically. That other forms of knowledge, and ability knowledge in particular, demand skill is also a common motif of contemporary epistemology. For further discussion of the relationship between skill and knowledge, including know-how, see Pavese (2016a; 2016b).
2 I say 'one reason', because in cases like this where there are no cognitive skills in play the lack of knowledge can also be explained by the intuition that knowledge excludes luck. This point will become clearer in a moment.
3 See, for example, Pritchard (2012).
4 See Pritchard (2005) for a systematic defence of this platitude. For a dissenting voice, see Hetherington (2013), which is in turn a response to Pritchard (2013).
5 I present cases of this kind, and discuss their epistemological implications, in Pritchard, Millar and Haddock (2010, ch. 3) and Pritchard (2012).
6 For example, the kind of proper functionalist position defended by Plantinga (1993b) would plausibly count as a virtue epistemology according to the description just offered, though Plantinga himself has distanced his view from this terminology. In particular, he has claimed that any adequate virtue epistemology would need to be supplemented with an account of cognitive proper function, which would make virtue epistemology a variant on proper functionalism rather than vice versa. For more on this point, see Plantinga (1993c).
7 For some of the key defences of robust virtue epistemology (bearing in mind, of course, that there are important differences of detail within these proposals), see Sosa (1991; 2007; 2009; 2011; 2015), Zagzebski (1996; 1999), and Greco (2003; 2007; 2009a; 2009b; 2012).
8 I articulate and explore this distinction between modest and robust virtue epistemology—or as I sometimes express it, 'pure' and 'impure' virtue epistemology—in Pritchard (2009b, chs. 3–4). See also Pritchard (2009c; 2012) and Pritchard, Millar and Haddock (2010, chs. 2–4).
9 For some defences of modest virtue epistemology, see Code (1987), Kvanvig (1992), Montmarquet (1993), Greco (1999; 2000), Hookway (2003) and Roberts and Wood (2007).
10 See Greco (1999), Goldman (1992) and Plantinga (1993b) for examples of virtue reliabilism (though note that this is not a label that they would necessarily apply to their own views).

11 This view is defended by Zagzebski (1996), for example. For some other defences of virtue responsibilism, see Code (1987), Kvanvig (1992), Montmarquet (1993), Hookway (2003) and Roberts and Wood (2007). Note that there are also positions that arguably do not comfortably fall into either camp. Sosa's (e.g., 2007; 2009; 2015) position, for example, seems to incorporate both virtue reliabilist and virtue responsibilist features. For a helpful early articulation of the distinction between virtue reliabilism and virtue responsibilism, see Axtell (1997). For more on the notion of an intellectual virtue, see Battaly (2014).

12 The literature on this debate is now vast. For a useful recent overview of the main contours of this literature, see Pappas (2014).

13 For a very clear expression of this way of thinking of how virtue reliabilism represents a refinement of simple process reliabilism, see Greco (1999).

14 Plantinga (1993a, 195–98 and 205–07) offers a famous example in this regard concerning a brain lesion which reliably leads the subject to believe that she has a brain lesion.

15 Such a proposal is most associated with the neo-Aristotelian epistemology defended by Zagzebski (1996; 1999).

16 For example, there is an axiological aspect to the virtues, on account of how they are held to play a constitutive role in a life of flourishing, unlike mere skills. Relatedly, while it may be sensible to no longer maintain a skill that one no longer needs, it would represent a failing of character to neglect the maintenance of one's virtues.

17 Indeed, there are proposals in the literature that fall under all four headings. For example, Zagzebski (1996) defends a version of robust virtue responsibilism while Hookway (2003) defends a modest form of virtue responsibilism. Along the other axis, in earlier work Greco (2000) defended a modest form of virtue reliabilism, before in later work (e.g., Greco 2009a) adopting a robust variant of the view.

18 For the clearest expression of this way of thinking about robust virtue epistemology, see Greco (2009a).

19 For further discussion of this axiological aspect of robust virtue epistemology, see Greco (2009c). One challenge to the plausibility of this claim is that it isn't clear that our ordinary notion of achievement— at least where this concerns the kind of thing that is of distinctive value to us anyway—is best understood as merely success that is because of one's skill. After all, there are all kinds of trivial, easy and pointless successes that would fulfil these criteria that we wouldn't naturally think of as achievements. But notice that a beefed-up conception of achievements isn't going to suit the purposes of robust virtue epistemology, since knowledge doesn't seem to demand achievement in this sense (and, relatedly, knowledge can certainly be trivial, easy or pointless while being *bona fide* knowledge nonetheless). For more on this point, and on the notion of an achievement more generally, see Pritchard (2010; 2012) and Pritchard, Millar and Haddock (2010, chs. 2–4). For further discussion of the topic of epistemic value more generally, see Pritchard (2007b) and Carter, Pritchard and Turri (2018).

20 This scenario is adapted from a famous case offered by Chisholm (e.g., 1977, 105).

21 I developed the distinction between intervening and environmental epistemic luck, and its implications for virtue epistemology, in a number of places. See, especially, Pritchard (2009a, chs. 3–4; 2009b; 2012) and Pritchard, Millar and Haddock (2010, chs. 2–4).

22 The barn façade case is originally due to Goldman (1976), who credits it in turn to Carl Ginet.

23 See especially Sosa (2007, ch. 5). See Pritchard (2009a) for a critical discussion of Sosa's proposal in this regard.

24 As first described in Kallestrup and Pritchard (2014) with the explicit intention of refining the challenge that environmental epistemic luck poses to robust virtue epistemology. See also Pritchard (2016a).

25 In Pritchard (2015b; 2016b; 2017; 2020), I have argued that shifting our focus from luck to the closely related notion of risk can help us see what would be problematic about this strategy, in that it commits one to holding that knowledge can be compatible with very high levels of epistemic risk, of a kind that we would normally never tolerate. See also endnote 26.

26 Actually, these days I prefer the title *anti-risk virtue epistemology*, though the reasons for the change in title are not relevant here. See Pritchard (2015b; 2016b; 2017; 2020). See also endnote 25.

27 For more on the idea that the anti-luck condition on knowledge should be understood in terms of a safety principle, see Sainsbury (1997), Sosa (1999), Williamson (2000), and Pritchard (2002, 2005, 2007a; 2015a).

28 I am grateful to an anonymous reviewer for detailed comments on an earlier version of this chapter. Thanks also to Ellen Fridland and Carlotta Pavese.

References

Axtell, G. (1997) "Recent Work in Virtue Epistemology," *American Philosophical Quarterly* 34, 410–30.

Battaly, H. (2014) "Intellectual Virtues," (ed.) S. van Hooft, *Handbook of Virtue Ethics*, 177–87, London: Acumen.

Carter, J., Pritchard, D. H., and Turri, J. (2018) "The Value of Knowledge," *Stanford Encyclopedia of Philosophy*, (ed.) E. Zalta, https://plato.stanford.edu/entries/knowledge-value/.

Chisholm, R. (1977) *Theory of Knowledge* (2nd ed.), Englewood Cliffs, NJ: Prentice-Hall.

Code, L. (1987) *Epistemic Responsibility*, Hanover, NH: University Press of New England.

Goldman, A. (1976) "Discrimination and Perceptual Knowledge," *Journal of Philosophy* 73, 771–91.

—— (1992) "Epistemic Folkways and Scientific Epistemology," in *Liaisons: Philosophy Meets the Cognitive and Social Sciences*, 155–78, Cambridge, MA: MIT Press.

Greco, J. (1999) "Agent Reliabilism," *Philosophical Perspectives* 13, 273–96.

—— (2000) *Putting Skeptics in Their Place: The Nature of Skeptical Arguments and their Role in Philosophical Inquiry*, New York: Cambridge University Press.

—— (2003) "Knowledge as Credit for True Belief," in *Intellectual Virtue: Perspectives from Ethics and Epistemology*, (eds.) M. DePaul and L. Zagzebski, 111–34, Oxford: Oxford University Press.

—— (2007) "The Nature of Ability and the Purpose of Knowledge," *Philosophical Issues* 17, 57–69.

—— (2009a) *Achieving Knowledge*, Cambridge: Cambridge University Press.

—— (2009b) "Knowledge and Success from Ability," *Philosophical Studies* 142, 17–26.

—— (2009c) "The Value Problem," in *Epistemic Value*, (eds.) A. Haddock, A. Millar and D. H. Pritchard, 313–21, Oxford: Oxford University Press.

—— (2012) "A (Different) Virtue Epistemology," *Philosophy and Phenomenological Research* 85, 1–26.

Hetherington, S. (2013) "There Can Be Lucky Knowledge," in *Contemporary Debates in Epistemology* (2nd ed.), (eds.) M. Steup and J. Turri, §7, Oxford: Blackwell.

Hookway, C. (2003) "How to Be a Virtue Epistemologist," in *Intellectual Virtue: Perspectives from Ethics and Epistemology*, (eds.) M. DePaul and L. Zagzebski, 183–202, Oxford: Oxford University Press.

Kallestrup, J., and Pritchard, D. H. (2014) "Virtue Epistemology and Epistemic Twin Earth," *European Journal of Philosophy* 22, 335–57.

Kvanvig, J. (1992) *The Intellectual Virtues and the Life of the Mind*, Savage, MD: Rowman & Littlefield.

Montmarquet, J. (1993) *Epistemic Virtue and Doxastic Responsibility*, Lanham, MD: Rowman & Littlefield.

Pappas, G. (2014) "Internalist vs. Externalist Conceptions of Epistemic Justification," *Stanford Encyclopedia of Philosophy*, (ed.) E. Zalta, https://plato.stanford.edu/entries/justep-intext/.

Pavese, C. (2016a) "Skill in Epistemology I: Skill and Knowledge," *Philosophy Compass* 11, 642–49.

—— (2016b) "Skill in Epistemology II: Skill and Know-How," *Philosophy Compass* 11, 650–60.

Plantinga, A. (1993a) *Warrant: The Current Debate*, Oxford: Oxford University Press.

—— (1993b) *Warrant and Proper Function*, Oxford: Oxford University Press.

—— (1993c) "Why We Need Proper Function," *Noûs* 27, 66–82.

Pritchard, D. H. (2002) "Resurrecting the Moorean Response to the Sceptic," *International Journal of Philosophical Studies* 10, 283–307.

—— (2005) *Epistemic Luck*, Oxford: Oxford University Press.

—— (2007a) "Anti-Luck Epistemology," *Synthese* 158, 277–97.

—— (2007b) "Recent Work on Epistemic Value," *American Philosophical Quarterly* 44, 85–110.

—— (2009a) "Apt Performance and Epistemic Value," *Philosophical Studies* 143, 407–16.

—— (2009b) *Knowledge*, London: Palgrave Macmillan.

—— (2009c) "Knowledge, Understanding and Epistemic Value," in *Epistemology (Royal Institute of Philosophy Lectures)*, (ed.) A. O'Hear, 19–43, Cambridge: Cambridge University Press.

—— (2010) "Achievements, Luck and Value," *Think* 25, 1–12.

—— (2012) "Anti-Luck Virtue Epistemology," *Journal of Philosophy* 109, 247–79.

—— (2013) "There Cannot Be Lucky Knowledge," *Contemporary Debates in Epistemology* (2nd ed.), (eds.) M. Steup and J. Turri, §7, Oxford: Blackwell.

—— (2015a) "Anti-Luck Epistemology and the Gettier Problem," *Philosophical Studies* 172, 93–111.

—— (2015b) "Risk," *Metaphilosophy* 46, 436–61.

—— (2016a) "Epistemic Dependence," *Philosophical Perspectives* 30, 1–20.

—— (2016b) "Epistemic Risk," *Journal of Philosophy* 113, 550–71.

—— (2017) "Anti-Risk Epistemology and Negative Epistemic Dependence," *Synthese* [Online First: https://doi.org/10.1007/s11229-017-1586-6].

—— (2020). "Anti-Risk Virtue Epistemology," in *Virtue Epistemology*, (ed.) J. Greco and C. Kelp, 203–24, Cambridge: Cambridge University Press.

Pritchard, D. H., Millar, A., and Haddock, A. (2010) *The Nature and Value of Knowledge: Three Investigations*, Oxford: Oxford University Press.

Roberts R., and Wood, W. J. (2007) *Intellectual Virtues: An Essay in Regulative Epistemology*, Oxford: Oxford University Press.

Sainsbury, R. M. (1997) "Easy Possibilities," *Philosophy and Phenomenological Research* 57, 907–19.

Sosa, E. (1991) *Knowledge in Perspective: Selected Essays in Epistemology*, Cambridge: Cambridge University Press.

—— (1999) "How to Defeat Opposition to Moore," *Philosophical Perspectives* 13, 141–54.

—— (2007) *A Virtue Epistemology: Apt Belief and Reflective Knowledge*, Oxford: Oxford University Press.

—— (2009) *Reflective Knowledge: Apt Belief and Reflective Knowledge*, Oxford: Oxford University Press.

—— (2011) *Knowing Full Well*, Princeton, NJ: Princeton University Press.

—— (2015) *Judgment and Agency*, Oxford: Oxford University Press.

Williamson, T. (2000) *Knowledge and its Limits*, Oxford: Oxford University Press.

Zagzebski, L. (1996) *Virtues of the Mind: An Inquiry into the Nature of Virtue and the Ethical Foundations of Knowledge*, Cambridge: Cambridge University Press.

—— (1999) "What Is Knowledge?," in *Blackwell Guide to Epistemology*, (eds.) J. Greco and E. Sosa, 92–116, Oxford: Blackwell.

11

SKILL AND KNOWLEDGE

Ernest Sosa and Laura Frances Callahan

11.1 Knowledge

1. Knowledge is a form of action, to know is to act, and knowledge is hence subject to a normativity distinctive of action, including intentional action. Some basic elements of this account will be sketched here in part 11.1, setting the stage for a complementary account of justification in the following section.

It may be thought obvious that belief and knowledge are states, and not actions. But, first, we recognize not only consciously intentional judgments, but also functional representations, which are "actions" or "acts" in the extended sense that they are teleological aimings, or dispositions to so aim. Moreover, second, let us focus on the realm of consciously intentional judgments, and dispositions to judge. These dispositions to judge can take the form of policies, which reside in the will, and are thus extended actions, or anyhow actional. Compare one's policies to signal one's turns and to stop at yellow lights, as one drives a car. These are willful extended actions, or anyhow actional states that are sustained by the will.[1]

2. Concerning attempts (whether consciously intentional or functional/teleological), virtue theory distinguishes (a) accuracy or success, where the aim of the attempt is attained, (b) adroitness or competence, and (c) aptness, where the accuracy manifests the adroitness. This is thus an AAA (Accuracy, Adroitness, Aptness) account of performance normativity, as well as an AAA account of knowledge in particular. In identifying knowledge with apt belief, we understand knowledge in terms of skill.[2] A competence is a disposition to succeed when one tries. Whether one is competent to perform on a certain occasion depends not only on one's pertinent skill but also on the shape one is in and on how favorable is one's relevant situation, which gives competences a triple-S (Skill, Shape, Situation) structure.[3] We will return to the relation between skill and competence below.

Functional aims are not consciously intentional, as when our perceptual systems aim to represent our surroundings correctly. Compare the biological function-derived aim of the heart to circulate the blood. Consciously intentional aims can be derived from outright choices or decisions, but might also be acquired without much benefit of deliberation, just through normal human emotions or desires, such as irresistible fear, hunger, thirst, lust, etc. Even if that is its origin, an intention and its corresponding attempts might still be rationally controllable to a great extent, so as to make it rationally assessable. And this would seem prima facie applicable to attempts that are epistemic rather than practical, such as the attempt to get it right on a certain question.

3. Surprisingly, aptness depends not at all on the safety of one's attempt. How apt one's performance is does not depend, without qualification, on how likely one is to succeed if one tries.

Suppose an archer in a windy environment retains her high level of skill and good shape. Suppose her arrow in fact goes straight to the bullseye. However likely a gust may have been, none in fact intervenes. In that case, the archer does deserve credit for that shot's success, surely, no matter how likely a spoiler gust may have been.

At no point in the arrow's actual trajectory from bow to target does a gust impinge. And this is a non-modal property of the trajectory. However, at many points, maybe at all points, it may still be very likely that a gust would take the arrow off course. Yet the pervasive danger of diversion by a gust – that modal property – is irrelevant to the evaluation of the shot. The shot is apt, no matter how unsafe. What is relevant is only that no gust in fact intervenes, so that the speed and direction of the arrow can fully enough manifest archery competence, without intervening luck.

So, safety of situation is inessential for aptness of performance. Neither safety of skill nor safety of shape is essential, either. What matters for aptness is that the relevant skill, shape, and situation be actually in place, no matter how safely or unsafely.

11.2 Justification: the thinker with an envatted brain

1. In what follows we argue for a knowledge-friendly epistemology: not knowledge-first, but knowledge-friendly. Our aim is a theory of knowledge that will fit a unified and wide-scope epistemology. The account to be offered is meant to cover not only knowledge and belief but also epistemic justification, without disjoining knowledge from justification.

What, then, is the place of epistemic justification in the constitution of human knowledge? How do knowledge and justification join together for an overall virtue theory?

In order to answer these questions, we will need to understand – not just how competence can be manifest in the success of a performance – but also how skill is manifest in a skillful performance. And in order to gain this understanding it will be helpful to consider a familiar thought experiment. We mean the envatted brain experiment, which we next try to accommodate within our virtue framework. In the example, a subject's brain is envatted while his course of experience is seamless, since his brain is then stimulated directly, yielding a stream of experience of a sort that one might naturally have. First, however, let us return to our archery example.

2. Our archer's shot can be skillful (or adroit) without being apt. The shot is skillful if and only if it manifests skill. When the shot is also apt, then its success manifests skill (and also competence). But a shot can manifest skill without its success doing so.

Indeed, a shot can manifest skill even when it is not successful at all. The arrow might leave the bow headed straight to the bullseye but be blown off course by a gust of wind. Alternatively, in another shot, the arrow might leave the bow headed straight to the bullseye and go on to hit the target despite being blown about by gusts of wind, because these spoiler gusts combine so as to yield success anyhow, if only by luck. Despite the skill that each shot manifests because of its initial orientation, the success of the second shot might fail to manifest skill nonetheless because of the spoiler gusts.

It is by manifesting a skill that a shot gets to be "a skillful shot," because some quality of it manifests that skill. But this is clearly insufficient for an apt or even successful shot.

3. Take next an archer who not only wishes or hopes but tries to release her arrow here and now. The trying might be constituted by, or might directly yield, a certain brain state that satisfies the following condition: If the subject were in good shape, that state would reliably and generally enough lead to good orientation and speed for the arrow leaving the bow.

Something accidental (gust-like) might intervene within the archer's efferent nerves, however, affecting the outcome at her limbs, so that the shot fails. That subject then manifests her skill in a certain feature of her attempt, despite the lapse in her inner shape. The relevant feature of her attempt is that it is constituted by a certain brain state, which would normally yield success.

4. Suppose a subject with his brain in a vat (a BIV) wishes or hopes to raise an arm here and now, and even decides to do so forthwith, yet akratically fails to try. Of two BIVs, if one tries while the other does not, that can matter for responsibility and proper blame.

When an agent performs a physical act by intentional design, there is an initial physical state (however complex) that would normally bring about the intended outcome. And that brain-involving state is something the agent brings about. She does not bring it about intentionally as such, by design. She is unlikely to be able to specify that particular brain state. But an agent can bring about something attributable to her as her doing even without bringing it about by intentional design. That doing is then a deed. A "deed" is a doing attributable to the agent as her own doing.

For example, when signing a form at a government office, I may bear down so as to sign in one doing a carbon copy of the form. I do not know that I am signing a third copy, as I think there are only two. So, I may take myself not to sign a third copy, and yet may do so anyhow, as my own doing, attributable to me. I sign that third copy even if I do so unintentionally (not by design), unaccompanied by any corresponding intention, either concurrent or aforethought. That doing of mine is then an attributable doing, despite being unintentional (not by design).[4] It is not a mere "doing," as is my squashing of a rabbit by falling on it when pushed unconscious off a cliff.

5. I can bring about a certain brain state, one normally sufficient for the rising of my arm, even if I do not bring it about by intentional design, either concurrent or aforethought. What is more, my doing so may be a deed, an attributable exercise of competence and skill, despite not being an intentional doing (by design).[5]

Exercise of skill requires only that one manifest a disposition to succeed, which one might do through a deed, even one that is not intentional (by design).[6] Here is another example. A pianist in performance may press a certain key with the third finger of her right hand. She does not pick out that particular action as such for that very instant. So, she does not press that key with that finger at that moment by intentional design, either concurrent or aforethought. And yet it is something she does, the doing of which is attributable to her as her deed. Moreover, that deed of hers manifests her skill as a great pianist.[7]

Similarly, we might manifest our competence to raise our arm, and indeed our skill for so doing, when we try to do so through a certain brain state whereby one normally brings about the rising of one's arm. And that is then a way in which a BIV might manifest the skill of a great pianist, even if she fails to exercise the fuller pianistic competence that requires flesh and bone fingers hitting a physical keyboard.

6. An analogy to the BIV who manifests virtuosity in her perceptual judgments is now attractive. That believer seems "justified" in so believing, even if her belief is radically false. She still believes in an epistemically appropriate way, and the belief is still recognizably skillful.

Consider a competence to perceive that one faces something red and round. A certain visual impact on one's eyes leads through the afferent nerves to a corresponding brain-involving state that grounds its visually seeming to the subject as if he faces something red and round. Brain states in a certain range respond respectively to the relevant range of inputs from the vision-involving afferent nerves. Entering such a state is then something agents do as their own attributable doing, even though this outcome is not consciously intentional. That is an essential component of the agent's exercise of competence, and it is something the agent "does" with a teleological purpose, that of correct perceptual representation. That is a performance by that brain and indirectly by that agent. It is not just something that happens to them.

Having entered that afferent state, suppose the agent then tries to get it right on the question whether he faces something red and round. The agent might try judgmentally (intentionally) to get it right on that question. Alternatively, the agent might aim to get it right just functionally through psychological teleology, with no conscious intention. Let us focus, in any case, on the brain state that constitutes visual experience as if one faces something red and round. On the basis of such visual experience, one can then properly try to get it right, which trying might take either a functional (teleological) form or a consciously intentional form. And this attempt (functional or judgmental) can then be justified by being skillfully truth-conducive.

Such "skillful justification" is hence compatible with failure, since one can exercise one's skill while in poor shape or in a poor situation.[8] Clearly, such skillful justification might be attained by a BIV. It is required only that the given perceptual brain state lead competently to the relevant judgmental brain state, the one that underlies the judgment, the attempt to get it right. When normally occurrent in a properly encased brain, such a performance leads reliably enough to true belief.

In suggesting that the BIV has a competence to succeed if they try, we are abstracting from the complete competence. An athletic competence, for example, would require that the BIV's brain be encased in a skull, and properly connected to efferent and afferent nerves, etc. These shape and situation factors are absent when the BIV's brain lies in a vat and is not thus encased. But we assume that there is a deep seat of the disposition nonetheless, something that resides in the brain itself, and lies there when a normal person is even just asleep.

7. In our proposal there is thus a way for a BIV to be epistemically justified. What is that way? It is for his belief to constitute a skillful attempt to get it right, one that can fail miserably to be right while still being a highly skilled attempt. This is because the attempt resides in a deed that is normally very likely to ensure success but fails to have its expected effect only because of the agent's defective shape or situation.

Here we have worked with a broad sense of epistemic justification so as to make room for externalist epistemologies that require no strict deontic sense applicable only to free and voluntary agency. In our broader understanding, a belief can be epistemically justified even if it is not an exercise of free agency, so that it attains no deontic status. Our acceptation is in line with a conception of competence that is, of course, applicable to free attempts but also to deeds. A deed is, again, a doing attributable to a subject as his own doing, one that may or may not manifest competence, despite falling short of free, active agency. Our perceptual competence, for example, resides largely in perceptual mechanisms whose exercise yields passive functionings rather than free actions.

In a narrower sense, only free actions can be justified or unjustified. This, too, can be understood in terms of competence. But now the competence would involve a disposition to succeed when one freely tries intentionally (by design, perhaps consciously so).

Our account of skillful justification is meant to be compatible with the broad sense of justification that admits passive functionings within its scope, and compatible also with the narrower sense restricted to a deontic status that applies only to free actions.

So far, we have discussed central epistemological concepts and corresponding phenomena – knowledge (in part 11.1) and justification (in part 11.2) – employing both the concepts of skill and competence. Next, we turn to considering the implications and commitments of our epistemological account, with respect to understanding skill and competence more generally. We begin in part 11.3 by considering in greater detail the relationship between skill and competence.[9]

11.3 Skill and competence

1. Our epistemological account links knowledge to complete SkShSi (skill, shape, situation) competence and also links justification to skill or Sk competence. Understanding the relationship between complete competence and skill, then, would seem crucial to a proper understanding of our view, and also potentially important for a general understanding of skill. The relationship between skill and competence is our topic for this third section.

2. We begin by noting that skills and competences always co-occur. Any person who has a skill has some competence. That is to say, she has a disposition to succeed when she tries, which is relative to some class of shapes and situations. And any person who has a competence has a skill. She has not only a disposition to succeed relative to certain shapes and situations but also an innermost capacity for performing the quality of actions or deeds that enable her success in such conditions.

Yet, it would be misleading to think of a skill as identical to a complete, SkShSi competence on our account, since as we saw above skill can be manifest in a successful performance when no complete competence is manifest in the success of that performance.

The primary difference between skills and competences is that competences come in three sorts: the complete SkShSi competence, the inner SkSh competence, and the innermost Sk competence, only the last of which plausibly counts as a skill. So, an agent can have and manifest a skill, i.e., an innermost competence, even while being in bad shape and in a bad situation, so as to lack both the corresponding complete competence, and even the inner competence.

Consider again our skilled archer, who enters a proper brain state as she takes her shot and manages to hit the target, despite mutually cancelling interventions in the efferent nerves (or, despite intervening gusts that cancel each other out). The archer's shot does manifest skill insofar as she does perform an attributable deed in entering the proper brain state, whereby she functions properly. Indeed, the success of her shot does seem to depend causally on her skill. After all, given that the interventions in the efferent nerves or the gusts of wind perfectly cancel each other out, she needs to enter a proper brain state in order to hit the target. But the success of her shot does not strictly manifest her skill and does not manifest her competence. Her success does not manifest any competence on her part, whether complete, inner, or innermost.

3. Performance that manifests full SkShSi competence – rather than merely skill – is the more normatively important phenomenon in epistemology. Epistemic success that manifests such

competence is what corresponds to knowledge. One knows if and only if one has a true belief in virtue of one's having exercised skill in an appropriate shape and situation.

On the other hand, as we saw in section 11.2, epistemic performances that manifest skill without aptness are mere justified beliefs, which fall short of knowledge.

It is through our account of knowledge that we attempt to understand epistemic justification. This is an asymmetric explanatory relationship. We do not try to understand or explain knowledge in terms of an independent concept of justification. This approach commits us to thinking that, at least in epistemology, the concept of knowledge has the more basic significance for conceptual explanation. And the concept of skill emerges as that of a disposition to succeed in attaining a given sort of success in the pertinent domain of performance, when one is in a certain range of shapes and in a certain range of situations (ones preselected as the relevant ones in the given domain of performance).

4. It is an interesting question whether the subtle differences between skill and full SkShSi competence might also help in explicating the normativity of performances generally. There seems reason to expect that apt performances – or successes due to competence – are more normatively significant than actions whose quality is due to skill (despite potentially being unsuccessful, or being successful despite the agent's shape or situation).[10]

5. However, we should also consider the possibility that factors are at work in this ordering (of full competence and aptness over skill) that are distinctive of the epistemic domain.

For example, consider two cases of a successful improvisational jazz solo. In each case, the musician brings off the break beautifully, displaying high levels of musical skill. But in the first case, let's suppose, the musician manages to do all this despite being tipsy, and despite the piece being somewhat different from those she normally plays. She could very easily have messed up the piece badly. In contrast, suppose that the musician in the second case was alert and well-rested, and commonly plays similar pieces.

Question: is the first solo worse than the second, as a performance? Not necessarily. We can explain how the first performance may be at least as good as the second (at least in part) within our virtue framework. For, if the first performer retains a reliability of success above the relevant threshold even in her more challenging conditions – i.e., the threshold set in that domain for performances to be competent at all, and not too much due to luck – then her performance too will count as apt and admirable as such.

On the other hand, the tipsy musician's performance may have a standing that depends on respects other than that of its attributability to the agency (functional or intentional) of the agent. The attributability of the performance to the agent is directly proportional to the degree to which it manifests the agent's competence and not sheer luck. Compatibly with this, there may still be other respects in which the performance may gain value and admirability. For example, it may be appropriately risky to make an attempt even if the situation and shape of the agent are abysmal. You may do well to try to jump across a crevasse even if you are tipsy and the distance seems clearly beyond you, so that if you succeed it will be a near-miracle. If you succeed, your success will be minimally creditable to your competence, and yet it might be on the whole an admirable and creditable performance nonetheless. That performance may be admirable and creditable even if it is not apt, even if it is by all accounts really a matter of relevant luck that you succeed. Your jump may miraculously enable you to escape immediate trampling by an elephant.

Similarly, perhaps, even if we imagine that the first jazz performer was not in a shape or situation that her competence included – even if it were a near-miracle that she was able to pull off the break – we might think her pulling it off anyway was rather exciting and even laudable. When the spotlight is on and there's no getting out of an attempt, succeeding beyond one's competences can seem, in its own way, admirable.

Epistemology may be an outlier among domains of performance, if it is less amenable to forms of credit and admirability outside of attributability. We are less inclined to praise one who forms a belief or judgment beyond her competence, even if that belief happens to be true and even if forming such a belief was pragmatically required or appropriate. And in any case, even if a lucky guess attains some such pragmatic success, it would never count as knowledge, so that the virtue-epistemological account of knowledge as apt belief would remain unaffected. So, there is a distinction between judgments and jumps or jazz solos, one important for epistemology.

6. Distinguishing as we do between skill and competence seems clearly valuable in theorizing about performances generally. However, we have noted respects in which domains may differ concerning the place and normative importance of aptness vs. skillful performance.

In the next section, we consider a further question about the relationship between the role of skill in knowledge and its role more generally.

11.4 Possessing vs. manifesting skill (competence)

1. Our account of knowledge and justification is committed to the strong dependence of skillful epistemic performances on the possession of underlying epistemic skills. Crucial to the accounts of knowledge and justification in sections 11.1 and 11.2 was the notion of underlying, dispositional states – epistemic competences, or skills. The possession of these underlying states is, on our account, necessary for knowledge or justification. Here again, it will be interesting to consider the question whether in general, outside of epistemology, we should also think of skillful performances as depending on the possession of an underlying skill.

2. Suppose, for example, one takes a facing bird to be a duck, while lacking the perceptual competence to sort ducks, distinguishing them from the equally numerous geese in that neighborhood. And suppose more specifically that the specific look of the facing bird as often leads one to say goose as duck. In that case, even if one happens to arrive at a true conclusion by basing one's judgment on the bird's duckish look (while in good shape and a friendly situation), our account denies to one's performance the title of knowledge.

3. Similarly, possessing epistemic skill is a necessary condition on performing a skillful epistemic deed. One must have the inner state of skill if this is to be manifest in a particular performance. And, on our account, in order for a belief to be justified, one's performance in having that belief must manifest skill (whether or not one's performance is ultimately successful).

4. These necessary conditions might seem counterintuitive, either as claims about knowledge or justification, or as conflicting with a general principle about skill or competence.

For example, one might think that all that is required for a particular instance of knowledge is that one's attaining a true belief is due to the manner in which one has formed the belief on that occasion, and not also due to the manner in which one is generally disposed to form similar beliefs. Or perhaps all that is required for a particular justified belief is that it be formed some good way (such as being appropriately based on good evidence, or acquired via a reliable method), regardless of whether one generally can form beliefs in good ways.

Considering skill more generally, outside of epistemology: one might also insist that it is not generally true that skills are necessary for skillful performances. After all, it may seem that a poor student can occasionally write a skillful essay, or that a lousy basketball player might occasionally make a skillful pass.

5. However, we can explain the appeal of many such intuitions without admitting their truth. One plausible suggestion is that in such cases truly skillful action is mimicked. The unskilled agent acts much as the skilled agent would. There is in virtue theory a tradition of seeing such actions as good or valuable, despite not being *as* good as actions manifesting inner virtue.[11]

Another possible explanation: sometimes we praise performances as skillful when it would be accurate (using the terms of our virtue account) to say that they are especially successful. So, we can admit that although a tennis ace served by a lucky novice is not exactly skillful, it is skill-level excellent and to be praised as such. (Interestingly, this possibility seems less relevant in epistemology, for reasons we will discuss in the next section.)

6. With respect to epistemology, it is an interesting upshot of our virtue account, that the person without competences cannot have knowledge. This may at first seem a counterintuitive result, but on reflection it seems to resonate with common claims about knowledge and safety. Recall our subject who says duck on the basis of a paradigmatic duck appearance, although he might as easily have said goose. He does base his duck-sorting judgment on a proper perceptual basis, but he still does not know, since his judgment does not manifest a real competence, given how accidental his success turns out to be, despite having the right basis on that occasion.

One reason in favor of evaluating acts of knowing this way is that it allows us to rescue a certain kind of "safety," as a necessary condition on knowledge. In section 11.1, we rejected modal safety as commonly construed as a necessary condition on knowledge. But our position there is a controversial one. There is a deep attraction to the idea that when one knows, one couldn't easily have believed falsely.

We now wish to show how we can partly honor this intuition, in virtue of our commitment to the necessity of underlying dispositional states of competence, for competent performance. Our account guarantees something similar to safety, in virtue of requiring knowers to have broader dispositions to succeed when they try (in situations and shapes similar to those in which they know). For when one knows, our account allows us to say that it is not the case that one easily would go wrong on the question, assuming one were in a similar shape and situation.

Somewhat more carefully: on our account, knowing requires having exercised an underlying skill in an appropriate shape and situation. Whenever one knows, it follows that one would be disposed to believe truly if exercising the same epistemic skill(s) in some similar shapes and situations. So whenever one knows, there will be a modal fact, that not easily could one have gone astray by trying, given the shape and situation one was in. More generally, whenever one performs aptly, one could not too easily have failed, given the shape and situation one was in.

If one removes the condition that skill is necessary for skillful (and competent) epistemic performances and instead says that epistemic performances can be competent and apt in isolation from underlying skillful dispositions, then knowledge loses even this kind of "safety." One might know *p* and yet fail to know any of *q, r, s*, etc., despite any amount of similarity between the propositions and any amount of similarity between the shapes and situations in which one attempts to form beliefs. Since our account can avoid this unseemly conclusion and rescue some very modified form of a "safety" requirement, in virtue of requiring skill for skillful performance, we take the requirement to be well-motivated.

11.5 Gradability

1. In this final section, we wish to reflect on the way that our epistemological account can illuminate the gradability of skills (or competences).

In general, one can be more or less competent, more or less skillful. This is also true in epistemology, with respect to epistemic skills and competences. One's memory can be more or less reliable and extensive, one's sensory perception can be more or less accurate and fine-grained, and one's reasoning can be more or less careful and conscientious.

2. Although our epistemological account relies most explicitly on outright labels such as "competent" and "apt," our approach is compatible with underlying degreed notions. For we can say that there are underlying facts about just how competent or apt a performance is, while also holding that there is some important threshold, determining the answer to the yes/no questions: Is this performance competent? Is it apt? (Justification is another example of a concept like this. Beliefs are either justified or not. But they can also be more or less justified.) So, we can acknowledge that, alongside the yes/no question about whether some agent is competent, there are also important questions about just how competent they are.

3. Moreover, our virtue account can help illuminate some possible dimensions underlying this variability. First, one can be more or less likely to succeed when one tries (relative to the appropriate set of shapes and situations).

Second, one can be likely to succeed when one tries, relative to a wider or narrower set of shapes and situations.

4. There is a third possibility for variation in competence, which interestingly seems different in epistemology compared to other domains of performance. This is the possibility that one can be likely to achieve greater or lesser success.

In epistemology, it is tempting to think that there are no degrees of the "success" one can achieve, with a belief: one's belief is successful if and only if it is true, or "accurate."

On the other hand, in many other domains in which skill is exercised, success is not so seemingly easy to define, and it does plausibly come in degrees. For example, I can "succeed" in pie baking by baking a good apple pie. Or I might succeed by making an even better apple pie, or by making a more creative pear-and-black-walnut pie, etc.

The idea under consideration is that epistemology may be a domain in which skill or competence is less variable in this way.

5. However, we note first that there are competences relevant to inquiry, defined broadly, which do exhibit the kind of variability found in other domains, such as baking. One could be competent in gathering evidence, or selecting research questions. These are not strictly epistemic competences of the sort knowledge constitutively involves, but these auxiliary epistemic competences might help us begin to understand how success in inquiry can be of variable quality.

6. Second, and perhaps more importantly, we have seen that falsehood is not the only kind of "error" or non-success a belief may exhibit, since a judgmental belief fails to succeed if it fails to be apt.

Unlike a guess, a judgment requires aptness and not just truth of affirmation. And the same goes for the dispositional state of judgmental belief. A judgmental belief is apt if and only if the *aptness* (and not just the truth) of its pertinent (first-order) affirmations would be due to the believer's relevant (second-order) competences. One of the present authors has defended such distinctions among higher grades or kinds of knowledge extensively.[12]

If we accept the general possibility of higher grades of knowledge accompanying higher orders of aptness, then this seems to be a dimension along which the success of epistemic performances may vary. And just as there may be no in-principle limitation on the goodness of pies one might bake, there may be no in-principle limitation on the quality of an epistemic performance. For one thing, it may be aptly, aptly, aptly, … apt.

Moreover, although truth does not come in degrees, aptness does; accordingly, the objective attained by a judgment itself comes in degrees, since that objective is (gradable) aptness. Aptness can vary according to the degree to which the success of a performance is due to the competence of the performer.

7. We thus wish partially to resist the appearance that epistemic success and hence also epistemic skill or competence are less gradable than success and skill in other domains. In pie baking and in belief-forming both, it is important that one do well enough. But it may also be desirable to do well indeed, and there may be no in-principle maximum of quality for performances in these domains. In many domains, the objective of a performance is itself gradable. And it turns out that epistemology is not exceptional in this respect.

However, there is something right about the idea that epistemology is a domain where success is rather more limited than in many other domains. Whereas pies (or jazz solos, or thoughtful birthday presents) come in a dizzying variety of successful forms, successful epistemic performances can be arranged in a more regimented hierarchy. It may be that the gradability of epistemic skill or competence is itself, therefore, somewhat more restricted or regimented than the gradability of many other kinds of skills or competences.[13] At the same time, epistemic skill may not be highly exceptional in this respect, when we compare athletic domains generally, especially those that are highly formalized, such as competitive archery.

11.6 Conclusion

Competence and skill are fundamental to understanding how knowledge and justification are acquired and sustained. Knowledge is fully competent, apt belief; justified belief is skillful belief. We understand both claims within a conception of knowledge and belief as action – not necessarily conscious, intentional action, but action more broadly conceived to include not only intentional action but also functional action.

In turn, reflecting on virtue accounts in epistemology can reveal features of skill and competence generally, or else reveal respects in which performances and skills may vary across domains.

Notes

1 See, e.g., Sosa (2015) for a defense of the view that knowledge is a form of action. One might argue instead, e.g., that actions are *events*, whereas knowledge or a disposition to judge is not an event but rather a mental *state*. Both claims are controversial, and rejecting their conjunction would take us too far afield here. See Hyman (2015, pp. 54–74) for an overview of the debate whether actions are events and an argument for a negative conclusion.
2 For views on which we must understand skill itself in terms of knowledge, see, e.g., Stanley and Williamson (2017), Millar (2009).

3 See Sosa (forthcoming, 2017) for extensive recent discussion of the structure of competence in epistemology.

4 Example adapted from Davidson (1978).

5 But the skill exercised need not be the skill to bring about that particular brain state. We need not commit at all on that. The skill exercised may be, e.g., the skill to play a certain concerto, or to tie a knot.

6 Many authors are committed – whether explicitly or tacitly – to the idea that characteristic manifestations of skill are intentional actions. See, e.g., Ryle (1949), Pavese (2016). Pavese (2016, p. 657) argues that since a certain perceptual activity "is not something that a subject can intentionally do or abstain from doing," it cannot therefore be the characteristic manifestation of a skill rather than some other sort of ability. Our account may seem to be at odds with this commitment. But the two are broadly compatible, once one makes a distinction between *consciously* intentional actions and merely intentional actions, and perhaps also between "characteristic manifestations" and deeds that do somehow manifest one's skill. We claim that not every deed that manifests skill is consciously intentional; it may nonetheless be that every characteristic manifestation of a skill is intentional in some sense.

7 The case of the pianist and that of the brain performance reveal a distinction between intentional and ontological "by" relations. Once the pianist knows that in playing a certain phrase she will be hitting a certain key with a certain finger, she can intentionally, by design, bring it about that she does hit that key with that finger. She brings that about intentionally by intentionally playing the relevant phrase. But *ontology* reverses the "by" direction. It is in part by hitting that key with that finger that the pianist ontologically brings about her intentional playing of that phrase. This seems also relevant to the whole "X first" controversy. X could be "first" in ways that do not affect the ontological order of the relevant domain and so do not affect proper *metaphysical* explanation in that domain.

8 In this chapter we consider justification as requiring only the manifestation of innermost competence or skill. See Sosa (forthcoming) for a longer treatment of justification that suggests we may also admit a more demanding form of justification that requires *good shape* in addition to skill.

9 Parts 11.1 and 11.2 above are largely drawn from Sosa (2017), by permission of Princeton University Press, which holds the copyright.

10 Aristotle arguably valued aptness quite broadly, for example, and saw apt performances as central to human flourishing.

11 For a contemporary, albeit Aristotelian, discussion of the value of acting as the virtuous person does, see Hursthouse (2002).

12 Most thoroughly in Sosa (2015).

13 Skills relevant to knowledge-*how* (as opposed to the propositional knowledge that has been our concern) may require a separate treatment; and, as Pavese (2017) has recently argued, they may exhibit the capacity for much less regimented gradability.

References

Davidson, D. (1978) "Intending," *Philosophy of History and Action*, 11, 41–60.

Hursthouse, R. (2002) *On virtue ethics*. Oxford: Oxford University Press.

Hyman, J. (2015) *Action, knowledge, and will*. Oxford: Oxford University Press.

Millar, C. (2009) "What is it that cognitive abilities are abilities to do?," *Acta Analytica*, 24, 223–36.

Pavese, C. (2016) "Skill in epistemology, part II: skill and know how," *Philosophy Compass*, 11, 650–60.

—— (2017) "Know-how and gradability," *The Philosophical Review*, 126(3), 345–83.

Ryle, G. (1949) *The concept of mind*. London: Hutchinson.

Sosa, E. (2015) *Judgment and agency*. Oxford: Oxford University Press.

—— (2017) *Epistemology*. Princeton, NJ: Princeton University Press.

—— (forthcoming) "Competence and justification," in J. Dutant (ed.) *The new evil demon: new essays on knowledge, rationality, and justification*. Oxford: Oxford University Press.

Stanley, J. and T. Williamson (2017) "Skill," *Nous*, 51(4), 713–26.

12

KNOW HOW AND SKILL

The puzzles of priority and equivalence

Yuri Cath

12.1 Introduction

My subject is the relationship between knowledge-how and a family of notions tied to success in action—including skills, dispositions, and intentional actions. The nature of this relationship is puzzling. One reason for this is that while some considerations suggest that knowledge-how is the explanatorily basic notion—that can be used to explain success in action—other considerations suggest exactly the opposite.

It can be natural, for example, to explain Ish Sodhi's haul of five wickets in a cricket match, or his ability to bowl out tailenders, by noting that he knows how to bowl a wrong-un. However, when we ask 'What does Sodhi's knowledge how to bowl a wrong-un consist in?' it seems equally natural to reach for one of these success-in-action notions—suggesting that any explanatory priority here runs in the other direction. More generally, one often finds claims that a given type of knowledge-how is *grounded* or *embodied* in skills, dispositions, or abilities. For example, Sayre-McCord (1996: 137) claims that moral know how is "embodied in a range of capacities, abilities, and skills".

Another reason why this relationship is puzzling has to do with certain equivalence theses linking knowledge-how and success in action. That there are significant connections, of some kind, between knowing-how and intentional action is uncontroversial. Furthermore, there is, I think, an emerging consensus that, when interpreted in the right way, both of the following principles are correct:

(AB→KH): If S has the ability to Φ intentionally then S knows how to Φ.
(KH→AB): If S knows how to Φ then S has the ability to Φ intentionally.

In which case, we can derive the following equivalence thesis:

(KH≡AB): S knows how to Φ if and only if S has the ability to Φ intentionally.

Similarly, Pavese (2016) has identified the following plausible equivalence theses linking knowledge-how with skill:

($\kappa H \equiv s \kappa_1$): *S* knows how to Φ if and only if *S* has the skill to Φ.

($\kappa H \equiv s \kappa_2$): *S* knows how to Φ sufficiently well if and only if *S* is skilled at Φ-ing.

I will simply defer here to existing defences of ($AB \rightarrow KH$) and ($KH \rightarrow AB$),[1] and to Pavese's case for ($\kappa H \equiv s \kappa_1$) and ($\kappa H \equiv s \kappa_2$). For my interest is in what follows if we assume that these theses are true.

One issue here is that it is not easy to see how these equivalence theses can be reconciled with the kinds of *asymmetric* explanations mentioned above, whichever direction they run in. Similarly, these equivalence theses are puzzling for *intellectualists* who not only want to claim that knowledge-how is a kind of knowledge-that, but also that states of knowing-how are explanatorily prior to abilities or skills (e.g., Stanley and Krakauer 2013). And these equivalence theses are also puzzling for theorists who hold that skills are explanatorily prior to knowledge-how (e.g., Dickie 2012; Weatherson 2017). The worry, in both cases, is that these equivalence theses might push us toward simply identifying knowing-how with skills or abilities, in which case neither is prior to the other.

My aim in this chapter is to explore one interesting way in which these issues—concerning equivalence and priority—might be solved by someone who is minimally committed to some form of "weak" (Glick 2011) or "revisionary" intellectualism (Cath 2015), such that knowledge-how is at least some kind of propositional attitude state. In Section 12.2 I will identify certain prima facie concerns one might have with existing ideas that an intellectualist might appeal to in trying to accommodate ($\kappa H \equiv AB$). In Section 12.3 I will sketch a novel version of intellectualism—*practical attitude intellectualism*—and I show how this view can explain ($\kappa H \equiv AB$), and also ($\kappa H \equiv s \kappa_1$) and ($\kappa H \equiv s \kappa_2$), without encountering these same difficulties. And in Section 12.4 I consider how PA-intellectualism might help us to make sense of the priority issues.

12.2 Intellectualism and (K*H*≡A*B*)

If ($\kappa H \equiv AB$) is correct, what does this show us about knowledge-how? An anti-intellectualist might conclude that knowing-how to Φ is nothing more than the ability to Φ intentionally, and not any kind of knowledge-that. The mere assumption that ($\kappa H \equiv AB$) is true does not force us to accept such a position. But, nonetheless, an intellectualist needs to explain how their view can accommodate ($\kappa H \equiv AB$). And this is challenging with respect to both directions of ($\kappa H \equiv AB$).

12.2.1 *Intellectualism and (K*H*→A*B*)*

Starting with ($\kappa H \rightarrow AB$), how might an intellectualist account for the assumption that the ability to Φ is a precondition of knowing how to Φ? One approach would be to endorse the following view from Stanley and Williamson (2001):

> *Practical Mode (PM) Intellectualism*: *S* knows how to Φ iff for some way *w*, (i) *S* knows that *w* is a way for *S* to Φ, and (ii) in possessing this knowledge, *S* entertains *w* under a practical mode of presentation.

Stanley and Williamson (henceforth 'S&W') (2001: 429) suggest that: "thinking of a way under a practical mode of presentation undoubtedly entails the possession of certain complex dispositions." This is not the same thing as saying that it entails the ability to Φ intentionally. But one might hope that, when suitably characterized, this complex of dispositions will be such that possessing it entails that ability.

What exactly is a practical mode of presentation (PMP)? S&W themselves (2001) offered a 'Russellian' account on which it is a special way of being related to the coarse-grained proposition that is the content of one's knowledge. More recently, Stanley (2011) and Pavese (2013, 2015) have developed different 'Fregean' accounts on which a PMP is a special constituent of a fine-grained proposition that is the object of one's knowledge.

This is not the place for a proper evaluation of PM-intellectualism, so I will merely make note of some prima facie concerns. A standard worry about S&W's (2001) account is that it leaves the nature of PMPs mysterious or unmotivated (Noë 2005; Glick 2015). This is because S&W tell us little about the exact natural of the PMPs that they appeal to, beyond a not very filled out analogy with indexical modes of presentation.

One concern about Fregean accounts is that when PMPs are understood in this way it is not clear that a PMP condition would be a genuinely necessary condition on knowing how to Φ. Consider someone who merely knows lots of true propositions about ways for Φ-ing but does not know how to Φ. Hannah might have studied lots of books about riding bicycles, and observed people riding bicycles, etc., but if she has never tried to ride a bicycle she won't know how to do so. The Fregean holds that whenever someone makes the transition from mere knowledge-that to knowing how to Φ there must be a *practical proposition* (Pavese 2015)— which has a PMP as a constituent—that the subject now knows for the very first time. But often the only changes one can clearly point to after a subject makes such a transition is that they have new dispositions related to Φ-ing (to e.g. succeed in Φ-ing when they intend to Φ). The special contents that the Fregean posits might explain the possession of such dispositions in some cases, but are they really necessary for knowing how to Φ? Suppose Hannah merely acquired the new dispositions in some way that didn't involve a PMP, wouldn't she still come to know how to Φ?

There are, of course, lots of things that a PM-intellectualist might say in response to such concerns.[2] My aim here is *not* to try to provide definitive arguments against PM-intellectualism, and the view I will go on to offer is consistent with PM-intellectualism. But I do think the worries that have been raised in the literature about PMPs[3] should at least motivate intellectualists to consider other ways of explaining (KH→AB). In Section 12.3 I will offer my own way of explaining (KH→AB) which does not appeal to PMPs. However, another alternative (suggested by ideas in Brogaard (2009) and Stanley (2011)) is worth considering first.

Intellectualists hold that only one of the four legitimate disambiguations of a 'S knows how to Φ' ascription attributes the practical knowledge that is at stake in the 'knowing how' debates. On this disambiguation, an 'S knows how to Φ' ascription is, roughly, equivalent to the claim 'For some way w, S knows that w is a way that S can Φ in circumstances C'.[4] In which case, given the factivity of knowledge, an 'S knows how to Φ' ascription entails a corresponding 'S can Φ in circumstances C' ascription. This is not the same thing as saying that it entails 'S has the ability to Φ intentionally', but it is close. And an intellectualist might maintain that, rightly interpreted, the relevant 'S can Φ' ascription will entail an 'S has the ability to Φ intentionally' ascription. Could an intellectualist feel satisfied with this explanation of (KH→AB)?

Intellectualism is just the thesis that knowing-how is a kind of knowing-that. However, many intellectualists also want to claim that knowledge-how has some kind of explanatory priority over abilities, or at least deny that the reverse is true. And the ideas just described might seem to be in tension with those assumptions. For the suggestion is that knowledge-how is, roughly, a matter of knowing that one has a certain kind of ability. But then wouldn't one have to, *first*, have this ability in order for one to then, *subsequently*, come to know that one has it? In which case, it would appear that it is abilities that are explanatorily prior to knowledge-how.

The intellectualist seems to face a dilemma. Either the relevant entailed 'S can Φ' ascription is one that itself entails 'S has the ability to Φ intentionally' or it does not. If the latter is true, then the entailment fact cannot explain (KH→AB). On the other hand, if the former is true then the entailment fact can explain (KH→AB) but this explanation seems to commit one to the claim that the ability to Φ intentionally is explanatorily prior to knowing how to Φ, a claim that most intellectualists would reject.

12.2.2 *Intellectualism and (AB→KH)*

What about (AB→KH)? Why is knowing how to Φ a precondition for having the ability to Φ intentionally? Like Kumar (2011), I don't think the role of knowledge-how is to do with the *initiation* of actions. Rather, the role of knowledge-how has to do with actions being under one's *control* or *guidance*. More precisely, (AB→KH) is true because: (i) intentional actions are under one's control or guidance, and (ii) an action is under one's control or guidance only if one knows how to perform it (Gibbons 2001; Cath 2015; Pavese 2015, 2018).

Intellectualists and anti-intellectualists alike can accept these points. Furthermore, an intellectualist can claim that their view offers us a promising explanation of why it is the case that an action is under one's control or guidance only if one knows how to perform it. It is common in the philosophy of action to hold that it is a necessary condition of Φ-ing intentionally that one possess an *action plan* for Φ-ing. And, as Pavese (2018) has shown, an intellectualist can make a reasonable argument that possessing such a plan is a matter of possessing a relevant intellectualist belief of the form '*w* is a way for me to Φ'.

Intellectualists can appeal to an attractive package of views then to help explain (AB→KH). But (AB→KH) is also deeply problematic for intellectualists because, as Cath (2009, 2011) discusses, this thesis can be used to support putative counterexamples to their view. For example, Cath presents three different scenarios each of which is meant to be a case where, intuitively, a subject knows how to Φ but does not know, of the relevant way *w*, that *w* is a way for themselves to Φ.[5] With respect to each case, the denial of knowledge-that is based on the claim that the subject fails to satisfy one of three orthodox constraints on knowledge-that: the anti-luck or 'Gettier' condition, the justified belief condition, or the belief condition. The knowledge-how attribution is based on an appeal to intuition but, as Cath discusses, it can also be supported by (AB→KH). The reason being that, for each scenario, there is a strong case to be made that the subject still has the ability to Φ intentionally on the grounds that they would still succeed in Φ-ing in a controlled manner if they were to try to Φ in the relevant way. And if the subject has the ability to Φ intentionally, and (AB→KH) is true, then it follows that they know how to Φ.

12.3 PA-intellectualism and (KH≡AB)

There are two main theses associated with 'Rylean' or 'anti-intellectualist' views of knowledge-how, one negative and one positive. The negative thesis is that knowledge-how is not a kind of knowledge-that. The positive thesis is that it is a complex dispositional state. The negative thesis is just the denial of intellectualism and, hence, is well deserving of the label 'anti-intellectualism'. But the positive thesis is also associated with 'anti-intellectualism', reflecting the fact that philosophers often assume that intellectualism is inconsistent with the positive thesis.

This assumption is mistaken. An easy way to see this is to note that the thesis that knowing-how is a kind of knowing-that is perfectly compatible with a dispositional account of the nature of propositional attitudes themselves, including the knowledge-that relation. This point has been noted before (see, e.g., Cath 2009, 2015; Stanley 2011; Weatherson 2017) but I think its importance has not been fully appreciated, and it is still easy to find statements of this mistaken assumption. What I want to show now is how an intellectualist can use a dispositional theory of the propositional attitudes to account for (KH≡AB) in ways that avoid the problems identified in Section 12.1.

12.3.1 *Dispositional attitudes*

There have been many dispositional accounts of different propositional attitudes, including, of course, Ryle (1949). I will follow Schwitzgebel's (2002, 2013) 'liberal' or 'phenomenal' view. On Schwitzgebel's account, every propositional attitude toward a given proposition P is associated with a stereotype consisting of a set of different dispositional properties commonly associated with that attitude, and to stand in that attitude to P is for one to have a 'dispositional profile' (that is, a cluster of dispositions) which matches that stereotype to some appropriate degree. And this view is non-reductive, in the sense that the relevant dispositions can include not only behaviourial dispositions but also dispositions to enter phenomenal and cognitive states.

Turning to beliefs specifically, a standard suggestion is that to believe that P is to be disposed to act and react as if P is the case. But, of course, there can be many different ways of acting and reacting as if P is the case. And, if we follow Schwitzgebel, the stereotype for believing that P can include not only dispositions to perform, or manifest, externally observable actions and reactions, but also internal actions and reactions (e.g. affirming in one's mind that P is the case). On a dispositionalist view then, it is natural to think that there will be many different ways of believing that P, related to different subsets of this cluster of dispositions (Hunter 2011: 909).

One kind of distinction we can make of this kind is between more 'intellectual' versus more 'practical' ways of believing that P. For example, the stereotype for believing that the ice on the pond is thin—to borrow a well-known example from Ryle (1949: 134–5)—will include more intellectual or cognitive dispositions (e.g. being disposed to say or think that the ice is thin), but also more action-orientated dispositions (e.g. being disposed to skate warily). Furthermore, on Schwitzgebel's view, our background interests and values can result in one of these subsets of dispositions being more relevant than the other when making an attitude ascription:

> Depending on our interests and values, we might, in attitude ascription, choose to emphasize one aspect of a stereotype relatively more than another. For example, we might be more concerned about a person's patterns of explicit endorsement than about the person's in-the-world lived behavior or vice versa.
>
> *Schwitzgebel 2013: 80*

With these ideas in mind, consider the following analysis of knowing-how:

> S knows how to Φ iff there is some way *w* such that (i) S knows that *w* is a way for S to Φ, and (ii) S possesses that knowledge *in a practical way*.

What is involved in knowing, in a practical way, that w is a way for oneself to Φ? A PM-intellectualist could endorse this analysis and say that it is a matter of one's knowledge involving a PMP. But the suggestion I want to make is that it is a matter of the dispositions, in virtue of which one believes that w is a way for oneself to Φ, including certain "practical" dispositions. The most straightforward way to develop this view would then be to build that requirement into the belief constraint on knowledge-that, like so:

> *Practical Attitude (PA) Intellectualism*: S knows how to Φ iff for some way w, (i) S knows that w is a way for S to Φ, and (ii) in possessing this knowledge, S believes, *in a practical way*, that w is a way for S to Φ.

An intellectual way of possessing the belief that w is a way for oneself to Φ would be, for example, to possess a disposition to verbally affirm such a proposition when asked 'How can you Φ?', or to affirm it in one's head, etc. On the other hand, I will say that to truly believe, in a practical way, that w is a way for oneself to Φ is for one's dispositional profile, in virtue of which one possesses this belief, to include some mix of *success* dispositions (e.g. being disposed to Φ in way w when one intends to Φ in that way) and *guidance* dispositions (e.g. being disposed to make adjustments when faced with obstacles when Φ-ing in way w, and being disposed to perform the next phase of an action of Φ-ing in way w at the right time). And the suggestion is that when we make a knowledge-how attribution we are typically interested in whether the subject has a belief state grounded in these practical dispositions.

12.3.2 PA-intellectualism and (KH→AB)

According to PA-intellectualism, knowing how to Φ is, at least partly, a matter of possessing success and guidance dispositions. In which case, PA-intellectualism can appeal to the practical belief condition to explain why (KH→AB) is true. For the possessing of such dispositions is plausibly a sufficient condition for possessing the ability to Φ intentionally.[6]

PA-intellectualism is consistent with PM-intellectualism but it does not appeal to the notion of a PMP.[7] Furthermore, PA-intellectualism avoids the worries raised for PMP views in Section 12.2. Unlike S&W's (2001) Russellian view, PA-intellectualism avoids the mystery worry because it appeals only to ordinary dispositions that we already have reason to accept, and a well-known theory of the propositional attitudes. And, unlike the Fregean forms of PM-intellectualism, PA-intellectualism does not commit one to the idea that the transition from mere knowledge-that to knowledge-how must always involve some newly known practical proposition. For the PA-intellectualist can account for that transition by appealing just to the new dispositions one acquires when one learns how to Φ, without the involvement of any special constituents of Fregean propositions.

PA-intellectualism can also help us to defuse the priority worries we identified for content-based approaches to explaining (KH→AB). The worry was that if knowledge-how is knowledge of a certain ability, then wouldn't one have to, *first*, have this ability in order for one to then, *subsequently*, come to know that one has it? PA-intellectualism shows how one could block this concern while still maintaining that knowledge-how is a matter of knowing (in a practical way) that one has such an ability. For PA-intellectualism offers us a view on which the very same set of practical dispositions that ground one's state of knowing how to Φ will also ground one's ability to Φ intentionally. In which case, the ability to Φ intentionally would not exist prior to the state of knowing how to Φ and, hence, there would be no pressure to say that the former is explanatorily prior to the latter. (There are more questions to be asked about priority but I will forestall those until Section 12.4.)

12.3.3 PA-intellectualism and (A B →K H)

With respect to (A B →K H), PA-intellectualism also provides us with a promising explanation of why knowing how to Φ is a precondition of having the ability to Φ intentionally. Following Hunter (2012), it is plausible that one Φs intentionally only if one possesses guidance dispositions when one Φs of the kind appealed to earlier. In which case, having the ability to Φ intentionally will plausibly entail having these guidance dispositions. Furthermore, having the ability to Φ intentionally plausibly entails being disposed to Φ in some way *w* when one intends to Φ in that way.

These points together suggest that having the ability to Φ intentionally entails believing, *in a practical way*, that *w* is a way for oneself to Φ (for some way *w* that actually is a way for oneself to Φ). For the very nature of intentional actions themselves is such that the dispositions involved in having the ability to Φ intentionally are the same dispositions involved in possessing such a belief. And, given this belief-entailment, the PA-intellectualist can reasonably claim that their view at least supports a form of weak or revisionary intellectualism according to which knowledge-how is, at least partly, a matter of possessing a true belief of this form.

Furthermore, I think the PA-intellectualist can appeal to these same resources to diagnose what is going on in the supposed counterexamples centred on the belief condition. Cath's (2009, 2011) case is an example where a subject, Jodie, knows how to juggle but then loses her relevant belief of the form '*w* is a way for me to juggle' after she becomes aware of strong (albeit misleading) evidence that her genuine memories of juggling are merely apparent memories that misrepresent the way to juggle. Cath claims that, intuitively, Jodie would not thereby lose her knowledge how to juggle, a claim supported by the fact that if she were to try to juggle in that way, she would still succeed. And Cath notes that (A B →K H) can be used to support this knowledge-how attribution.

In reply, the PA-intellectualist could maintain that, yes, Jodie does not believe, *in an intellectual way*, that *w* is a way for her to juggle, but she does believe, *in a practical way*, that *w* is a way for her to juggle. The suggestion would be that any inclination we have to say that Jodie lacks the relevant belief is driven by our awareness that she lacks the relevant intellectual dispositions (i.e. she is no longer disposed to endorse that proposition in words or thoughts), and the fact that an interest in intellectual dispositions often predominates when we consider bare belief ascriptions. But we are also aware that Jodie still has the relevant success and guidance dispositions,[8] and when we make knowledge-how attributions we are usually interested in whether the subject has a belief based in these practical dispositions. More would need to be said to fully develop this diagnosis of the Jodie case. But I think these points indicate the flexibility that the PA-intellectualist has in replying to examples like this.[9]

What about the supposed counterexamples based on the anti-luck and justified belief conditions? An intellectualist could argue that, despite initial appearances to the contrary, the ability to Φ intentionally is subject to anti-luck and justified belief conditions (Stanley 2011; Pavese 2018). That is, that one has the ability to Φ intentionally only if, for some way *w*, one has a non-Gettierized and justified true belief that *w* is a way for oneself to Φ. My own view, following Cath (2015), is that intellectualists should instead embrace a form of revisionary intellectualism according to which knowledge-how is a true belief state that is not subject to the standard anti-luck and justified belief conditions.

12.3.4 *PA-intellectualism and (Kʜ≡Sᴋ₁) and (Kʜ≡Sᴋ₂)*

Turning to (ᴋʜ≡sᴋ₁) and (ᴋʜ≡sᴋ₂), I think the PA-intellectualist can account for these equivalence theses in the same way as (ᴋʜ≡ᴀʙ). This is because I take it that skilled actions are a species of intentional action (S&W 2001; Noë 2005; Fridland 2010). And, likewise, skills are simply a species of the ability to perform an action intentionally.

What distinguishes a skilled action from a merely intentional action? The key difference is that a skilled action meets a salient threshold of some normative standard of success. As Pavese (2016) discusses, one can know how to Φ without being skilled at Φ-ing but knowing how to Φ *sufficiently well* (i.e. Φ-ing above some contextually salient threshold of success) does plausibly entail being skilled at Φ-ing (with respect to that same threshold). And merely knowing how to Φ still entails having some kind of minimal skill at Φ-ing, even if it is not correct to say that one is skilled at Φ-ing.

With these points in place, the PA-intellectualist can account for (ᴋʜ≡sᴋ₁) and (ᴋʜ≡sᴋ₂). Starting with the left-to-right directions, the PA-intellectualist will appeal, again, to the idea that knowing how to Φ requires the possession of success and guidance dispositions. For the possession of such dispositions will plausibly entail having some minimal skill at Φ-ing, thereby, accounting for (ᴋʜ→sᴋ₁). And if one knows how to Φ *sufficiently well*, then one will possess success and guidance dispositions with respect to the action of Φ-ing *sufficiently well*. And the possession of those dispositions will entail being skilled at Φ-ing, thereby accounting for (ᴋʜ→sᴋ₂).

If we take the right-to-left directions, the intellectualist will face challenges and choices of the same kind as those raised by (ᴀʙ→ᴋʜ). That is, intellectualism seems to conflict with (sᴋ₁→ᴋʜ) and (sᴋ₂→ᴋʜ) if one assumes that one can have a skill at Φ, or be skilled at Φ-ing, without meeting one or more of the standard anti-luck, justification, and belief conditions on knowledge-that. As with (ᴀʙ→ᴋʜ), the intellectualist needs to choose between either arguing that skills are actually subject to the relevant condition, or conceding that they are not, but arguing that this assumption is still compatible with some form of revisionary intellectualism.

12.4 PA-intellectualism and priority

The aim now is to show how PA-intellectualism can help us to untangle some of the issues around apparently competing priority claims. Consider, first, the idea that knowing-how is grounded in dispositions, skills, or abilities. The PA-intellectualist can straightforwardly endorse at least one interpretation of this idea—namely, that knowledge-how is grounded in dispositions—given their commitment to a dispositional analysis of belief.

What about abilities and skills? As noted already, PA-intellectualism offers us a view on which one and the same set of dispositions can ground both one's state of knowing how to Φ, and one's ability to Φ intentionally. I think this suggests that we should adopt a 'no-priority view'[10] with regards to the relationship between knowledge-how and abilities. Rather, knowing how to Φ and possessing the ability to Φ intentionally might be viewed more like two different aspects of one set of dispositions.[11] And the parallel position could be taken with respect to knowing how to Φ sufficiently well and being skilled at Φ-ing.

This is *not* to say though that we should identify knowledge-how with ability. PA-intellectualism tells us that if one knows how to Φ then the set of dispositions in virtue of which one believes that *w* is a way for oneself to Φ must include some success and guidance dispositions. But that requirement does not preclude other kinds of dispositions from forming part of the basis for that belief. It is true that PA-intellectualism also holds that one would know how to Φ even if one only possessed the action and guidance dispositions. But, even so, in most actual cases many other dispositions will be present in the dispositional profile in virtue of which one counts as believing that *w* is a way for oneself to Φ. And these other dispositions may sometimes play a key role in explaining successful and skilled actions.

Back in my glory days of backyard cricket, I used to sometimes struggle to bowl a wrong-un, and would instead end up bowling a standard leg spin delivery. When this happened, I would try to consciously recall the fact that a wrong-un should come out more from the back of one's hand with one's hand pointing toward fine leg, or I would try to visualize an action of bowling a wrong-un. And this would often help me to succeed the next time I tried to bowl a wrong-un.

On the liberal dispositional view, my dispositions to contemplate such propositions, or engage in such imaginings, can constitute part of the dispositional basis for my relevant belief of the form '*w* is a way for me to bowl a wrong-un'. In which case, a PA-intellectualist can still say that my action of bowling a wrong-un is guided by my knowledge of how to bowl a wrong-un, even in these cases where my success is attributable to these more intellectual or cognitive dispositions. And one might also appeal to this point in explaining why it can sometimes be more appropriate, or informative, to explain someone's success in Φ-ing by citing their knowledge-how to Φ, rather than their abilities or skills.

Furthermore, even if we endorse the no-priority idea, we can still allow that there can be lots of true asymmetric explanations of knowledge-how in terms of abilities or skills, or vice versa. For whenever Φ is a non-basic action then there could still be legitimate explanations of S's knowing how to Φ in terms of S's ability to ψ, or S's ability to Φ in terms of S's knowing how to ψ, etc. And this is why we can explain, say, Sodhi's skill at bowling out tailenders in terms of his knowing how to bowl a wrong-un. The no-priority idea does suggest that often it will make little difference whether we explain Sodhi's skill by citing his knowledge how to bowl a wrong-un or, instead, his ability. But that seems to me to be a desirable consequence, because often it seems to make little difference which notion we appeal to when making such explanations.

12.5 Conclusions

I have explored PA-intellectualism, in part, because I think a lot can also be said in support of a dispositional approach to belief. However, I take it to be an open question what the best view of belief is and, hence, on those grounds alone I am unsure myself whether PA-intellectualism is true. That said, I hope to have shown how *if* a dispositional account of belief is correct then that fact might help us to unravel some of the tangled interconnections between knowledge-how and the different success-in-action notions.

Notes

1 For a defence of both theses together, see Pavese (2018). For discussions that support (AB→KH), see, e.g., Hawley (2003), Cath (2009, 2011, 2015), Setiya (2012), Constantin (2018), and Löwenstein (2017). For discussions that support (KH→AB), see, e.g., Hawley (2003), Noë (2005), Glick (2012), Cath (2015), Pavese (2015), and Löwenstein (2017).
2 Pavese (2015: fn. 4) suggests that her Fregean view could be reformulated in a Russellian framework, in which case neither of the above objections would apply to that version of her view. See also Pavese (2019).
3 See Glick (2015) and Mosdell (2018) for further criticisms.

4 On this point see Stanley (2011: 126–8) who appeals to a reading of Hawley's (2003) notion of "counterfactual success". For discussion see Glick (2015) and Cath (2017).

5 For related arguments see Setiya (2008), Wallis (2008), Poston (2009), Carter and Pritchard (2015), and Brownstein and Michaelson (2016).

6 On one prominent view of abilities—the so-called 'simple view'—the ability to Φ is just identified with the disposition to Φ when one intends to Φ.

7 Given the lack of details built into S&W's (2001) notion of a PMP, perhaps one could even regard PA-intellectualism as being a version of Russellian PM-intellectualism. But I don't think this is very important (cf. Bengson and Moffett 2007: fn. 32).

8 And Jodie still has dispositions related to the *seeming analysis* of knowing-how that Cath (2011) discusses.

9 PA-intellectualists could also appeal to Schwitzgebel's (2001) work on 'in-between' beliefs, or Brogaard's (2011) suggestion that knowledge-that, in general, does not entail belief.

10 See Pavese (2016) for a different kind of 'no priority view'.

11 Cf. Hunter's (2012) views on 'practical knowledge' in Anscombe's sense.

References

Bengson, J., and Moffett, M. (2007) "Know-How and Concept Possession," *Philosophical Studies* 136(1): 31–57.

Brogaard, B. (2009) "What Mary Did Yesterday: Reflections on Knowledge-wh," *Philosophy and Phenomenological Research* 78: 439–67.

—— (2011) "Knowledge-How: A Unified Account," in J. Bengson and M. Moffett (eds.) *Knowing How: Essays on Knowledge, Mind, and Action*, 136–60, Oxford: Oxford University Press.

Brownstein, M., and Michaelson, E. (2016) "Doing Without Believing: Intellectualism, Knowledge-How, and Belief-Attribution," *Synthese* 193: 2815–36.

Carter, J. A., and Pritchard, D. (2015) "Knowledge-How and Cognitive Achievement," *Philosophy and Phenomenological Research* 91: 181–99.

Cath, Y. (2009) *A Practical Guide to Intellectualism*, PhD dissertation, Australian National University.

—— (2011) "Knowing How Without Knowing That," in J. Bengson and M. Moffett (eds.) *Knowing How: Essays on Knowledge, Mind, and Action*, 113–35, Oxford: Oxford University Press.

—— (2015) "Revisionary Intellectualism and Gettier," *Philosophical Studies* 172: 7–27.

—— (2017) "Intellectualism and Testimony," *Analysis* 77(2): 1–9.

Constantin, J. (2018) "A Dispositional Account of Practical Knowledge," *Philosophical Studies* 175(9): 2309–2329.

Dickie, I. (2012) "Skill Before Knowledge," *Philosophy and Phenomenological Research* 85: 737–45.

Fridland, E. (2010) *Perception and Skill: Theoretical Foundations for a Science of Perception*, PhD dissertation, CUNY Graduate Center.

—— (2017) "Skill and Motor Control: Intelligence All the Way Down," *Philosophical Studies* 174: 1539–60.

Gibbons, J. (2001) "Knowledge in Action," *Philosophy and Phenomenological Research* 62: 579–600.

Glick, E. (2011) "Two Methodologies for Evaluating Intellectualism," *Philosophy and Phenomenological Research* 83: 398–434.

—— (2012) "Abilities and Know-How Attributions," in J. Brown and M. Gerken (eds.) *Knowledge Ascriptions*, 120–39, Oxford: Oxford University Press.

—— (2015) "Practical Modes of Presentation," *Noûs* 49: 538–59.

Hawley, K. (2003) "Success and Knowledge-How," *American Philosophical Quarterly* 40: 19–31.

Hunter, D. (2011) "Belief Ascription and Context Dependence," *Philosophy Compass* 6: 902–11.

—— (2012) "Guidance and Belief," in D. Hunter (ed.) *Belief and Agency*, 63–90, Calgary: Calgary University Press.

Kumar, V. (2011) "In Support of Anti-Intellectualism," *Philosophical Studies* 152: 135–54.

Löwenstein, D. (2017) *Know-How as Competence: A Rylean Responsibilist Account*, Frankfurt am Main: Vittorio Klostermann.

Mosdell, M. (2018) "Modeling Practical Thinking," *Mind and Language* 34: 445–64.

Noë, A. (2005) "Against Intellectualism," *Analysis* 65: 278–90.

Pavese, C. (2013) *The Unity and Scope of Knowledge*, Ph.D. Dissertation, Rutgers University.

—— (2015) "Practical Senses," *Philosophers' Imprint* 15: 1–25.

—— (2016) "Skill in Epistemology II," *Philosophy Compass* 11: 650–60.

—— (2018) "Know How, Action and Luck," *Synthese.* https://doi.org/10.1007/s11229-018-1823-7.

—— (2019) "The Psychological Reality of Practical Representation," *Philosophical Psychology* 32: 784–821.

Poston, T. (2009) "Know How to Be Gettiered?" *Philosophy and Phenomenological Research* 79(3): 743–7.

Ryle, G. (1949) *The Concept of Mind*, Chicago, IL: Chicago University Press.

Sayre-McCord, G. (1996) "Coherentist Epistemology and Moral Theory," in W. Sinnott-Armstrong and M. Timmons (eds.) *Moral Knowledge?* 137–89, Oxford: Oxford University Press.

Schwitzgebel, E. (2001) "In-Between Believing," *Philosophical Quarterly* 51: 76–82.

—— (2002) "A Phenomenal, Dispositional Account of Belief," *Noûs* 36: 249–75.

—— (2013) "A Dispositional Approach to the Attitudes: Thinking Outside of the Belief Box," in N. Nottelmann (ed.) *New Essays on Belief*, 75–99, New York: Palgrave Macmillan.

Setiya, K. (2008) "Practical Knowledge," *Ethics* 118: 388–409.

Stanley, J. (2011) *Know How*, New York: Oxford University Press.

Stanley, J., and Krakauer, J. W. (2013) "Motor Skill Depends on Knowledge of Facts," *Frontiers in Human Neuroscience* 7: 1–11.

Stanley, J., and Williamson, T. (2001) "Knowing How," *Journal of Philosophy* 98: 411–44.

Wallis, C. (2008) "Consciousness, Context, and Know-How," *Synthese* 160(1): 123–53.

Weatherson, B. (2017) "Intellectual Skill and the Rylean Regress," *Philosophical Quarterly* 67: 370–86.

13

KNOWLEDGE AS SKILL

Stephen Hetherington

13.1 A methodological point

Answering the question 'What is it to know that p?' (for some proposition 'p') can lead us along methodologically disparate paths. Many epistemologists seek a conceptual analysis, aiming to describe necessary and sufficient conditions for the satisfaction of a (or 'the') concept of knowledge. But that familiar path is not the only possible one to follow. We could instead be more metaphysical in thinking about knowledge.[1] This chapter describes a model that is explanatory first and foremost about what we can *do* with knowledge. The result is an interpretation both of knowledge's presence and the correlative potential for action.

This approach is motivated partly by a specific reason to not always reach for 'what we (intuitively) would say' about actual or imagined knowledge-attributions. They might not take us to the heart of what knowledge is.[2] More explanatorily fundamental data might be available. Those linguistic or conceptual reactions amount, even collectively, to one species within a more generic kind—the category of *knowledge-related actions*. So, even at best, those linguistic or conceptual reactions might be reflective of, or revelatory about, only part of what it is to know. I will attend to that potentially wider range of knowledge-related actions.

13.2 A distinction

Consider someone gazing, in normal conditions, at an eagle. She knows that she is seeing an eagle. She also has accompanying skills that we may think of as cases of knowledge-*how*. She knows how to distinguish an eagle from a hawk: she can do this by sight and by sound. *A fortiori*, she knows how to distinguish, by sight and by sound, an eagle from other kinds of bird. This skill of hers is not an expert's—all-but-infallible. Still, it is generally accurate. It could be manifested in several ways. Suppose that she knows how to answer many related questions in a variety of circumstances, and/or knows how to draw some eagle-distinguishing features, and/or knows how to picture to herself an eagle. She has a complex skill—complex knowledge-how—composed of further skills (further instances of knowledge-how). There are further such sub-skills that she might have had, but that she lacks. Nonetheless, she has enough to constitute the relevant knowledge-how.

Now, we expect her knowledge-that ('That's an eagle') and her accompanying knowledge-how (her general eagle-identifying skills) to be inter-related in what they 'say' about her, and about what she might be at this and other moments. *How* are they inter-related, though? To what does 'accompanying' amount in this setting?

Here, we need to reflect upon knowledge and action. Many actions that this person could perform would *reflect* her knowledge-that ('That's an eagle') even while *manifesting* her associated knowledge-how. She might write down some of the bird's identifying characteristics; she might explain to someone else what makes an eagle an eagle; she might form and retain an image of this eagle; she might seek suitable food for the bird; she might muse on its survival prospects; etc. Each such action would manifest or express what are at least this-knowledge-*related* skills—skills related to, or attendant upon, this knowledge-that. But, again, what is the nature of that relation? Are these knowledge-related skills, and actions expressing them, *merely* 'accompanying' the person's knowledge that she is seeing an eagle? Or is there a metaphysically *closer* relationship between the knowledge-how—those skills—and the knowledge-that?

Here is an epistemologically unorthodox answer. Perhaps those actions reflect *and* express or manifest the knowledge; perhaps this is because 'the knowledge' *is* at once the skills (the knowledge-how) and the knowledge-that; and perhaps this is because the skills *are*, collectively, the knowledge-that. This interpretation will be defended in what follows.

Imagine that interpretation's being *false*; and suppose that the person's relevant knowledge-how—her complex skill comprising those sub-skills—*merely* accompanies her knowledge-that. In that case, while those actual or potential actions would be inherently expressive of the knowledge-how (which is the knowledge how to perform such actions), they would not be inherently expressive of the knowledge-that. On the contrary, though, we should insist that those actions *do* express and manifest the knowledge-that. Such actions are distinguishable from other actions in terms that share content (e.g. 'That's an eagle') with how we would distinguish this knowledge-that from other knowledge-that. If we see this as *just* a happening-to-share, we have an 'occasionalist' model of the joint presence of those actions and the knowledge-that. Could we find a stronger model—whereby the actions are *deeply, because metaphysically, linked* to the knowledge?

13.3 Introducing knowledge-practicalism

Let us meet a *practicalist* model of knowledge's nature.[3] This knowledge-practicalism is built around the distinction made in section 13.2 between knowledge-that and knowledge-how. Ryle (1949, 1971/1946), most famously, directed philosophers' attention to that distinction. He argued that it marks the existence of two forms of knowledge.

Knowledge-how is knowledge-how-*to*—knowledge how to perform some action or kind(s) of action (and not knowledge *of* how to perform it). Philosophers often call this *practical* knowledge,[4] which is why I use the term 'practicalism'. Knowledge-practicalism seeks to elide Ryle's distinction, by regarding all knowledge-that *as* knowledge-how. Hence, *if* knowledge is only ever knowledge-that or knowledge-how, practicalism implies that all knowledge is knowledge-how. Practicalism is a form of pragmatism.[5] It aims to understand knowledge's nature by reflecting on what knowledge can *do*. Its focus is on knowledge's actual or possible *uses in action*—actions that are or would be *expressing* or *manifesting* the knowledge-how that (according to practicalism) *is* the knowledge-that.

With the example discussed in section 13.2, of someone's knowing that there is an eagle in front of her, we noted some associated actions that she might perform. We may now distinguish a *causally* constitutive relation between the knowledge and those actions, from a *metaphysically* constitutive relation between them:

> *Causally constitutive.* Knowing can *give* one various skills. *By* knowing that the bird is an eagle, one is enabled—as it happens, perhaps reliably—to perform some or all of those and other actions.

> *Metaphysically constitutive.* Knowing can *include* various skills. *In* knowing that the bird is an eagle, one is enabled—inherently, with no further circumstances needing to cooperate—to perform some or all of those and other actions.

The former links the knowing and the skills in a metaphysically *accidental* or *external* way. The latter links them in a metaphysically *necessary* or *internal* way. The latter is what practicalism advocates.[6]

The practicalist idea is that to know a particular truth *is* to have related skills, natural expressions of which are various actions. Practicalism treats knowledge-that as a kind of knowledge-how. Contrast practicalism with the traditional view that, as a (causal) *result* of having specific knowledge, one might gain such skills yet not *inherently*, not as an 'internal' *part* of the knowing. On that traditional approach, although knowing can be a means, even a reliable means, to having related skills, and thereby to acting or being able to act, this is not metaphysically guaranteed. Possessing those cognitive and behavioural skills would be metaphysically extrinsic to possessing the knowledge. In contrast, practicalism regards knowing as *already and always*—intrinsically—the possessing of such skills.

'Knowledge is power': this beguiling aphorism is generally proffered as a political, pedagogical, and/or social thesis. Still, it remains a causal thesis: possessing knowledge is said (all else being equal) to *lead* to being able to perform socially relevant actions, for example. But when *practicalism* says 'Knowledge is power', the immediate import is metaphysically constitutive, not causally so: possessing knowledge is *already and always, in itself,* one's being able to perform various actions. These actions might be socially significant, politically and/or pedagogically potent. This depends upon the knowledge's content, for a start. Your knowing that there is an eagle in front of you will rarely, if ever,[7] result in socially significant actions.

What would be gained by adopting the causal interpretation—hence by *not* regarding knowledge as in itself a skill? We would lose some explanatory power. We would be saying only 'Knowledge *can give* power', in the sense of knowledge's possibly, even reliably, bestowing power. Whereupon we would struggle to justifiedly interpret that use of '*can give*' so as (i) to do justice to knowledge's potential for generating related actions (this seems to be a datum about why we ever *value* knowledge), while (ii) not also letting knowledge *be* simply that potential (with which move, we would be returning to knowledge-practicalism). The counter-practicalist's need to satisfy (ii), developing a causally constitutive rather than metaphysically constitutive interpretation, threatens to leave us with a less 'intimate' link between knowledge and action. Knowledge-practicalism's availability enables us to regard the knowledge-action link in metaphysically stronger terms.

How have epistemologists recently struggled to justify, in non-practicalist terms, a suitable knowledge-action link? Williamson (2000: ch. 11) has argued that knowing that p is necessary for the normative aptness of asserting that p. In the same spirit, Hawthorne and Stanley (2008) treat knowing as a normative condition for acting. But such talk of normative aptness or normative conditions is less clear than talking, in practicalist terms, of knowledge as a skill at performing related actions. This practicalist option describes a metaphysically shorter path, for knowledge's being 'translated' into action. This need not amount to an empirically shorter path from knowledge to action. The difference reflects what we do *conceptually* in moving from describing knowledge to describing an associated action.

Care is needed, even once we make that conceptual move. Would we—in claiming to lessen that metaphysical distance between knowledge and action—not be doing justice to what knowledge *is*? How should practicalism conceive of the metaphysical relationships between knowledge and its supposedly major components—belief, justification, truth? The rest of this chapter answers that question.

13.4 Knowledge and belief

Plato introduced into philosophy what have remained the two main models of the constitutiveness relation between knowledge and belief (*doxa*—opinion). His *Meno* (97e–98a) uses the idea that any instance of knowledge is a belief (with epistemically salient characteristics). But in his *Republic* (475b–480), it is argued, knowledge and belief are incompatible states, with categorially different objects (contents): knowledge is of what is eternal and unchanging, of what is a fit object only for pure thought; belief is directed at what is transient and contingent, at what is a fit object only for observation.

Contemporary epistemologists standardly describe knowledge as a kind of belief. This portrays the belief as being *what it is* 'within' or about a person that is her knowledge. This treats any instance of knowledge analogously to how a 'concrete' individual might be metaphysically portrayed—as a *substance with attributes*. The belief is the *substance* that is, or is within, the individual instance of knowledge. The belief's being true and epistemically justified (such as by good evidence), along with any additionally needed features, are *attributes* of that substance, insofar as it is an instance of knowledge.

But that metaphysical analogy should prompt us to broaden that standard epistemological thinking. It is a matter of metaphysical contention whether substance-attribute models are correct. For example, are individuals *bundles* of attributes, rather than substances to which attributes adhere? A similar question arises about instances of knowledge, once we acknowledge the conceptual availability of knowledge-practicalism. After all, on practicalism, any instance of knowledge *is*, in effect, a bundle. It is a bundle without a privileged 'centre' or 'core' that is categorially different to whatever features 'attach' to it in constituting an instance of knowledge. It is a bundle of (sub-)skills, amounting to a complex (even if variegated) super-skill that can be expressed or manifested, through the expressing or manifesting—with various actions—of one or more of those sub-skills. On a bundle theory of individuals, no substance is needed as the individual's metaphysical core, being that to which the individual's attributes attach. By analogy, practicalism dispenses with the presumption that each instance of knowledge depends on there being a belief that is the knowledge's metaphysical core, to which the knowledge's epistemic attributes attach. On practicalism, there is no such metaphysical core to an instance of knowledge.

This is not to say that practicalism leaves no conceptual room for belief within knowledge. Practicalism does allow belief to be a part of knowledge, at least sometimes, perhaps even—but not necessarily—always. But practicalism does not *require* belief always to be part of knowledge. Whether each instance of knowing includes a belief is a *contingent* matter.

How does practicalism accommodate that idea? Simple: a belief can *be* one of those (sub-) skills, all or some of which are constituting some instance of knowledge. In one respect, that view is not far removed from epistemological orthodoxy anyway. Many epistemologists think of belief as *dispositional*; and a disposition can be more, or less, reliably expressible or manifestable.

This can itself be thought of as a more, or a less, reliable *skill*. Consider again a belief that one is seeing an eagle. On the present story, this belief could be a more, or a less, reliable skill in representing and/or responding with 'That's an eagle' in appropriate circumstances. We may say 'a more, or a less, reliable skill' because one can believe that one is seeing an eagle, even while being somewhat unreliable in manifesting that belief (in verbal responses). Having a particular belief is compatible with the possibility that sometimes, even in an appropriate circumstance, no suitable representation or response ('That's an eagle') arises. This would not entail the person's lacking the belief. But it would entail something about the belief's *nature*: the belief would have a quality *akin to fallibility*.

This akin-to-fallibility quality is what I have elsewhere (Hetherington 1999, 2001: ch. 2, 2016a: ch. 7) called *failability*. The idea of failability generalises a standard idea of fallibility. The latter envisages there being at least one accessible possible world, say, where a particular belief retains the *justification* supporting it in this world, yet is not *true*.[8] We can generalise that conception, to be talking of epistemic states in general. Here is that 'conception of *epistemic failability* in general' (Hetherington 2016a: 209):

> *EFail* You are failably in an epistemic state ES, if and only if (i) you are in ES but (ii) there is at least one accessible possible world where (even with all else being equal) you are not in ES—because within that world there is at least one component of being in ES that you fail to satisfy.

We could then talk of *failable knowledge*, by conceiving of possible worlds where someone *almost* retains that knowledge—only to lack it by failing *just one* of the conditions jointly constituting her having the knowledge within this world. *One* way to know failably is to know fallibly. When someone knows fallibly that p, the truth condition is the particular '*just one* of the conditions' being failed within another possible world: in at least one accessible world, the person continues satisfying whatever conditions jointly constitute her having the knowledge that p within this world—except for its not being *true* that p within that other world.

Now apply *EFail* to the epistemic state of *believing*. On a dispositional conception, having a belief that p is constituted, for a start, by a range of actual or possible circumstances where one answers appropriately (with 'p'). On that conception, even a person's answering appropriately could be her manifesting or expressing her belief *only failably*, for there could be appropriate occasions where (with all else being equal) she fails to manifest or express the belief.

This description coheres well with the idea, introduced above, that belief is a belief-*skill*—one that can be more, *or* less, reliable in how it is manifested or expressed. Failability admits of degrees or grades: with all else being equal, there being more and closer worlds where the failability is realised (such as worlds where the belief is false, or where it is not generating an appropriate response) either is or models the presence of stronger failability. A particular belief could thus be a more, or a less, failable belief-skill.

And on a given occasion it might contribute *correlatively* to the nature of one's knowing, since a belief-skill can also be regarded as a *knowledge*-skill: we may conceive of the belief-skill as one of the sub-skills that might be present as part of knowing on a particular occasion. Practicalism also allows us to regard the belief as *just* one of those available sub-skills—without requiring that, from among that potentially wide range of available sub-skills, it is *always* present when the knowledge is present. Practicalism allows that on a specific occasion an instance of knowledge might happen not to include that particular sub-skill.

This account also helps to explain a recent argument, by Myers-Schulz and Schwitzgebel (2013), for knowledge's not having to be accompanied by belief. They call upon some experimental philosophy studies: 'the unconfident examinee', 'the absent-minded driver', 'the prejudiced professor', 'the freaked-out movie-watcher', and 'the self-deceived husband'. For each case, respondents were asked to say whether the person being described had knowledge and whether she had belief.

The first case[9] imagines an examinee, Kate, being asked (when the exam period is about to end) the question 'In what year did Queen Elizabeth I die?' Although she has studied, upon hearing the teacher say that the exam's end is imminent Kate starts panicking; she attempts to remember the answer consciously; she fails; whereupon she writes an answer anyway; which happens to be correct; yet she lacks all confidence in its being correct. Is her answer knowledge? Does it reflect belief? A large proportion of respondents surveyed by Myers-Schulz and Schwitzgebel attributed knowledge, but not belief, to Kate. For argument's sake, let us treat this as someone's having knowledge without belief.

Practicalism can accommodate that interpretation. If Kate *was* also to believe her answer, this would make further possible actions available to her as expressions or manifestations of the belief. But they would be expressing or manifesting the knowledge, too. Moreover, this increased range of potential expressions or manifestations would correlatively strengthen or 'expand' her knowledge (that 1603 was when Queen Elizabeth I died). It would give the knowledge behaviourally increased power. For example, Kate would be more confident, within a wider range of circumstances (including ones where her answering is not forced upon her), about answering this question concerning Queen Elizabeth I, and thereby about communicating this belief—which would also constitute her communicating the knowledge. Yet even this does not entail that the belief's presence was essential to the knowledge's presence. Kate's knowledge could be present today as a somewhat extensive range of sub-skills. Tomorrow, it might be present as a *more* extensive range—thanks to her coming to believe tomorrow what today she knows without believing.

13.5 Knowledge and justification

Section 13.4 asked how we might move beyond the thesis that any instance of knowledge must be a belief. What now of knowledge and (epistemic) justification—the latter being another essential element within any instance of knowledge, according to traditional epistemology?

That traditional view—justificationism—is (like the view of knowledge's always being a kind of belief) often traced back to Plato's *Meno* (97e–98a).[10] Justificationism says that any instance of knowledge that p must include something somehow sufficiently generative and/or indicative of p's being true. Many epistemologists (e.g., Conee and Feldman 2004) understand this as requiring the person to have good *evidence* of its being true that p. Alternatively (e.g., Goldman 1979, 1986), we might say that she needs to have formed the belief that p in a truth-conditionally *reliable* way.

Yet practicalism can discard that traditional view, similarly to how section 13.4 dispensed with knowledge's having to include belief. Practicalism allows (as it did, *mutatis mutandis*, for knowledge and belief) that knowledge *can, but need not,* include justification. We can conceive of any justification present within some knowledge as *just another* from the range of available sub-skills that might be jointly constituting the complex skill that is a given instance of knowledge. On this practicalist proposal, justification within knowledge is a justification-*skill*—and so the justification can contribute as a sub-skill within the knowledge, where the latter is a complex skill that might also include belief-skills.

Let us examine that idea more fully. Practicalism allows that knowing *can* include the presence of evidentially supportive skills, or (reliabilist-approved) skills of acquisition. Someone who views knowledge more traditionally might strengthen that '*can*' to a '*must*', a move not discussed here.[11] This section defends only the practicalist thesis that, insofar as knowledge does, can, or must include justification, *what* it would include is a skill. Here is a crucial step in that defence:

> The point of requiring evidence, say, within knowledge was never simply that such evidence *be present*.[12] Nor was the aim just to specify an ideal *location* for the evidence to be present (such as 'it is *in the mind* of the believer'). The deeper point to this traditional requirement on knowing's nature was *action-oriented*.

The underlying point of expecting a knower to have evidence was that it can be *used* by her in appropriate ways. For example, we might think that, *by* being in a believer's mind, evidence is able to be used by her (perhaps because it is relevantly accessible to her) as would be apt if it was to contribute to her knowing.[13]

What are those 'appropriate ways' for evidence to be used, as part of having knowledge? The main idea is that, insofar as knowledge is present (partly by including evidence), the evidence is *ready and able* to be used as continuing support for holding the belief, such as if the person's claim to know is questioned, or if she is wondering whether to retain the belief. The evidence's importance within knowledge is not simply its being present, but rather its being present, whenever it is, as one from a range of *skills* that are, could, or must be present—skills for actually or at least possibly *using* the belief during its continued life.[14] The evidence is available *as* a potential for knowledge-generating or -maintaining action—not merely as an 'item', statically in place. So, *having* evidence is not enough. Nor is one's having *used* evidence. What matters is that there exists an associated evidential *skill*. Having used the evidence to form the belief in such a way that the belief is knowledge is one's having expressed or manifested just such an evidential skill. And once the evidence is present, as part of the resulting knowledge, this is significant only insofar as one is able to call on it, if required by circumstances, in actively supporting the belief, so that the belief is maintained as knowledge. We can parse this in practicalist terms:

> Why we should ever *value* evidence's presence within knowledge (even if we are not always *requiring* its presence there) is that possible actions, expressive of related skills, are thereby available, as ways to use and/or maintain the knowledge.

Those comments have been about evidence-within-knowledge. Their point persists, *mutatis mutandis*, when one's epistemic support for a belief is reliabilist-approved instead—one's having acquired the true belief in a truth-conditionally reliable way. If one has formed a belief reliably, this might be a skilful genesis for the belief. That is less clearly so if the reliable formation occurred at a sub-personal level, such as for a simple perceptual belief, formed via an everyday 'act' of perception. Even here, though, a practicalist may say that, if the belief has been formed skilfully, not only is this a result of action by the believer, but there could remain in place a skilful potential for the belief's future use—being maintained, being defended from doubts, etc. The latter possibility pertains, too, if the belief has been formed reliably but not skilfully (such as sub-personally).

Imagine *lacking* such skills while retaining the evidence, the reliable genesis, and the belief. What would be the point, as a would-be knower, of having this evidence? Practicalism suggests that there is none. Insisting on some such evidence being present would amount to requiring evidence only for the mere *appearance* of having knowledge.

13.6 Knowledge and truth

Non-practicalists might object that, once practicalism ceases requiring knowledge to include belief, we face the possibility of cases of knowledge failing to include *that which is* true. The metaphysical *substance* of knowing would have been thrown away. In which case, does practicalism take us too far away from our quest to understand knowledge?

The worry is misplaced. Practicalism can retain a factivity requirement on knowing. But it does this not merely by requiring that the fact obtain. If there is to be knowledge, what practicalism requires is actual or potential *interaction* between the (known) fact and one or more of the sub-skills constituting the knowledge. For example, the fact that p might play a suitable role in the manifestation or expression of the various sub-skills constituting a given (super-)skill that is the knowledge that p for a particular person at a particular time. Different such sub-skills could involve differently the fact that p. Nonetheless, we may continue insisting that knowledge is somehow answerable to a fact. Practicalism can allow this answerability to take different forms, even for a single instance of knowledge, with each of these involving more than *merely* the fact's obtaining. The answerability is constituted partly by whatever sub-skills are constituting the instance of knowing. There could be skilful representing of the fact, skilful discussing of it, skilful use of one's body in ways that accommodate the fact, etc. In such ways, the fact that p remains implicated in the knowing that p. It plays a part in literally *constituting* the knowing.

13.7 Hyman's narrower knowledge-practicalism

It is rare within contemporary epistemology to encounter knowledge-practicalism. But Hyman (2015: chs. 7, 8) has an elegant version. It embraces the thesis that knowing is not always a form of belief—because knowledge is always an ability or skill. However, Hyman's account is built around an idea that should be seen by practicalists as needlessly restrictive in its conception of knowing.

Hyman conceives of knowledge that p as the ability *to be guided by the fact that p* when acting congruently (in ways expressing that ability). But is that a sufficiently flexible conception? For example, someone's knowing that p could include her being able to *assess detachedly whether* p obtains. She might thereby know that p in a *questioning* way.[15] She could still be respecting her evidence for p, and leaning appropriately toward p's obtaining—even while retaining the ability not to be in *thrall* to that evidence, able to question p's obtaining while knowing that p. Is she being *led* by the fact that p? This is not clear. One can be led by *an interest in whether* p obtains, rather than by *the fact that* p. One might be led *toward* p without being led *by* p.

These are gestural comments, as are Hyman's. He does talk of the impossibility of being led by a guide whom one cannot see. This picture is intended to reinforce his claim that one cannot know that p without always holding in sight—and thus being led by—the fact that p. Yet his picture reinforces the narrowness of his account. Even while holding in sight and following a guide, one might wonder whether to continue doing so: one could be engaging with questions, even doubts, about whether to continue being led by the guide. In which case, it is not clear that one *is* still being guided by her in the trusting way that Hyman apparently has in mind.

13.8 Conclusion

Traditional views of knowledge's nature, this chapter has argued, lack something substantial that is gained by adopting a knowledge-practicalism. They lack something metaphysical. They allow there to be knowledge with no inherent link to action—to actual or possible uses of the knowledge. Knowledge has long been conceived of by epistemologists in ways that leave it in danger of being *useless*, in that metaphysical sense—of not being *inherently* linked to the world of agency and action.

But practicalism deems no knowledge to be inherently useless, in that same sense of being categorially removed from the world of agency and action. Perhaps a given case of knowing is socially useless, or admits only of personally unimportant actions. Even this does not imply that no possible actions could express or manifest that knowledge. Maybe no such actions will occur, for that knowledge and that person; this does not entail that none were possible. Actions need not be publicly observable (as opposed to being 'inner' acts of thought), if they are to satisfy the practicalist conception; nor need they be 'whole body' actions. Practicalism is more generous than that in its conception of knowledge-expressive ways of acting.

And the metaphysical ramifications do not end there. Practicalism promises to render knowing more *inherently* an aspect of being a person. If knowledge is power (in the sense described by practicalism), having knowledge is expressive of being inherently a thing with powers—expressive of person-powers, we might say. In contrast, on more traditional views whereby knowledge is *not* inherently tied metaphysically to action, in principle there could be knowledge within someone possessing no related powers. Do those traditional theories of knowledge allow that in theory a person might come into existence and later go out of existence, never possessing powers, while nevertheless having knowledge? Seemingly so. But seemingly *not* so, on knowledge-practicalism. In principle, practicalism conceives of knowledge as *inherently*—not extrinsically, accidentally, or contingently—a bridge between states of being and actions.[16] This is accomplished by the central practicalist move: we need only conceive of knowledge from the outset as *being* a power.[17]

Notes

1 Another option involves being *less* metaphysical in thinking about knowledge. See, for example, Williamson's (2000) 'knowledge-first' research programme.
2 For a case study in applying this thought, see Hetherington (2016a: ch. 6).
3 Superficially, it is a view with precedent. Hartland-Swann (1958: 10–14) claimed to argue that knowing is a kind of skill. But he meant only that *claims* to knowledge—the *actions* of making such claims—are skilful. He was not arguing that underlying states of knowing are skills. That thesis, however, will be this chapter's. For a fuller defence, see Hetherington (e.g., 2011a, 2011b, 2013, 2015, 2018a, 2019). It has also been defended by Hyman (2015: chs. 7, 8): see section 13.7.
4 Knowledge-that is often called *theoretical* or *contemplative* knowledge (even though it need not be contemplative in mood of mind or theoretical in content).
5 It is to be contrasted with intellectualism, which implies that all knowledge—including knowledge-how—is knowledge-that. For defences of intellectualism, see Stanley and Williamson (2001), Stanley (2011), and Pavese (2015a, 2015b, 2017). For anti-intellectualist arguments, see Fridland (2012, 2013). For further critical discussion, see Carter and Poston (2018: ch. 2).
6 The former—the accidentalist interpretation—should not be read as saying that the knowing is linked with the skills only *luckily*. 'Accidental' is being contrasted with 'essential'. The point here is metaphysical, using this traditional pair of ideas.
7 Well, it depends on where you are. See the 2016 Kazakh-language documentary *The Eagle Huntress*, about traditional hunting practices with eagles in part of Mongolia.
8 For discussion of fallibility and fallible knowledge, see Hetherington (1999, 2001, 2005, 2016a: ch. 5, 2016b, 2018c, 2018d).
9 It is inspired by Radford's (1966) famous case.
10 For discussion of this linking, see Hetherington (2020a).
11 But see Hetherington (2001: ch. 3, 2011a: ch. 3, 2018b, 2018d).
12 The same is true, as we will see, about requiring a belief to be formed *reliably* if it is to be knowledge.

13 For more on this—amounting, respectively, to an *active*-internalism and an *active*-externalism about justification—see Hetherington (2020c).

14 'What about how the belief ever arrived? Epistemologists devote much energy to understanding how a belief has been formed, usually aiming to tell us why it is knowledge only if it was formed appropriately (such as by not being formed too luckily).' Up to a point, that is fine. Elsewhere (Hetherington 2020b), I show how knowledge-practicalism can accommodate the idea of a belief's arriving in an appropriate way. But elsewhere (Hetherington 2016a: ch. 3) I describe a limitation upon the explanatory power of talking of a belief's not being formed too luckily.

15 For more on how knowledge can literally include questioning of itself as knowledge, see Hetherington (2008, forthcoming).

16 Does practicalism thereby become a virtue epistemology? Potentially, there is overlap between the two approaches, as I discuss elsewhere (Hetherington 2017: secs. 1, 10), focusing on some of Sosa's recent work (e.g., 2011, 2015, 2016). For him, knowing is an epistemic performance, and so can be judged on virtue-theoretic criteria. I have elsewhere (Hetherington 2011b) distinguished, in practicalist terms, between *knowledge* and *knowing*. But Sosa's discussions seem not to include that distinction; in which case, presumably he also treats *knowledge*—in virtue of his talk of *knowing*—as an epistemic performance. I allow that knowing can be an epistemic performance—without the knowledge as such (able to be manifested in that action of knowing) being so. The knowledge itself remains a *skill*, able to be manifested in epistemic performances. Some of these are what I have elsewhere (Hetherington 2013) termed *knowing actions*.

17 Thanks to an anonymous referee for very thoughtful comments on a draft of this chapter.

References

Carter, J. A., and Poston, T. (2018) *A Critical Introduction to Knowledge-How*, London: Bloomsbury.

Conee, E., and Feldman, R. (2004) *Evidentialism: Essays in Epistemology*, Oxford: Clarendon Press.

Fridland, E. (2012) "Knowing-How: Problems and Considerations," *European Journal of Philosophy* 23: 703–27.

—— (2013) "Problems with Intellectualism," *Philosophical Studies* 165: 879–91.

Goldman, A. I. (1979) "What Is Justified Belief?" in G. S. Pappas (ed.) *Justification and Knowledge: New Studies in Epistemology*, Dordrecht: D. Reidel, pp. 1–23.

—— (1986) *Epistemology and Cognition*, Cambridge, MA: Harvard University Press.

Hartland-Swann, J. (1958) *An Analysis of Knowing*, London: George Allen & Unwin.

Hawthorne, J., and Stanley, J. (2008) "Knowledge and Action," *The Journal of Philosophy* 105: 571–90.

Hetherington, S. (1999) "Knowing Failably," *The Journal of Philosophy* 96: 565–87.

—— (2001) *Good Knowledge, Bad Knowledge: On Two Dogmas of Epistemology*, Oxford: Clarendon Press.

—— (2005) "Fallibilism," *The Internet Encyclopedia of Philosophy*, www.iep.utm.edu/f/fallibil.htm.

—— (2008) "Knowing-That, Knowing-How, and Knowing Philosophically," *Grazer Philosophische Studien* 77: 307–24.

—— (2011a) *How to Know: A Practicalist Conception of Knowing*, Malden, MA: Wiley-Blackwell.

—— (2011b) "Knowledge and Knowing: Ability and Manifestation," in S. Tolksdorf (ed.) *Conceptions of Knowledge*, Berlin: De Gruyter, pp. 73–100.

—— (2013) "Skeptical Challenges and Knowing Actions," *Philosophical Issues* 23: 18–39.

—— (2015) "Technological Knowledge-That as Knowledge-How: A Comment," *Philosophy & Technology* 28: 567–72.

—— (2016a) *Knowledge and the Gettier Problem*, Cambridge: Cambridge University Press.

—— (2016b) "Understanding Fallible Warrant and Fallible Knowledge: Three Proposals," *Pacific Philosophical Quarterly* 97: 270–82.

—— (2017) "Knowledge as Potential for Action," *European Journal of Pragmatism and American Philosophy* 9, http://journals.openedition.org/ejpap/1070.

—— (2018a) "Knowledge and Knowledge-Claims: Austin and Beyond," in S. L. Tsohatzidis (ed.) *Interpreting Austin: Critical Essays*, Cambridge: Cambridge University Press, pp. 206–22.

—— (2018b) "Knowledge as Simply Being Correct," in B. Zhang and S. Tong (eds.) *A Dialogue between Law and Philosophy: Proceedings of the International Conference on Facts and Evidence*, Beijing: Chinese University of Political Science and Law Press, pp. 68–82.

—— (2018c) "Skepticism and Fallibilism," in D. Machuca and B. Reed (eds.) *Skepticism: From Antiquity to the Present*, London: Bloomsbury, pp. 609–19.

—— (2018d) "The Redundancy Problem: From Knowledge-Infallibilism to Knowledge-Minimalism," *Synthese* 195: 4683–702.

—— (2019) "Creating the World: God's Knowledge as Power," *Suri* 7: 1–18.

—— (2020a) "Knowledge-Minimalism: Reinterpreting Plato's *Meno* on Knowledge and True Belief," in S. Hetherington and N. D. Smith (eds.) *What the Ancients Offer to Contemporary Epistemology*, New York: Routledge, pp. 25–40.

—— (2020b) "The Epistemic Basing Relation and Knowledge-That as Knowledge-How," in P. Bondy and J. A. Carter (eds.) *Well-Founded Belief: New Essays on the Epistemic Basing Relation*, New York: Routledge, pp. 305–23.

—— (2020c) "The Grounds of One's Knowledge Need Not Be Accessible," in S. B. Cowan (ed.) *Problems in Epistemology and Metaphysics: An Introduction to Contemporary Debates*, London: Bloomsbury, pp. 107–18.

—— (forthcoming) "Some Fallibilist Knowledge: Questioning Knowledge-Attributions and Open Knowledge," *Synthese*.

Hyman, J. (2015) *Action, Knowledge, and Will*, Oxford: Oxford University Press.

Myers-Schulz, B., and Schwitzgebel, E. (2013) "Knowing That P without Believing That P," *Noûs* 47: 371–84.

Pavese, C. (2015a) "Knowing a Rule," *Philosophical Issues* 25: 165–88.

—— (2015b) "Practical Senses," *Philosophers' Imprint* 15: 1–25.

—— (2017) "Knowledge and Gradability," *The Philosophical Review* 126: 345–83.

Radford, C. (1966) "Knowledge: By Examples," *Analysis* 27: 1–11.

Ryle, G. (1949) *The Concept of Mind*, London: Hutchinson.

—— (1971/1946) "Knowing How and Knowing That," in his *Collected Papers*, Vol. II, London: Hutchinson, pp. 212–25.

Sosa, E. (2011) *Knowing Full Well*, Princeton, NJ: Princeton University Press.

—— (2015) *Judgment and Agency*, Oxford: Oxford University Press.

—— (2016) "Knowledge in Action," in A. Bahr and M. Seidel (eds.) *Ernest Sosa: Targeting his Philosophy*, Dordrecht: Springer, pp. 1–13.

Stanley, J. (2011) *Know How*, Oxford: Oxford University Press.

Stanley, J., and Williamson, T. (2001) "Knowing How," *The Journal of Philosophy* 98: 411–44.

Williamson, T. (2000) *Knowledge and Its Limits*, Oxford: Clarendon Press.

PART III

Skill, intelligence, and agency

14

CONSCIOUSNESS AND SKILL

Barbara Gail Montero

[A]rt demands above all the full consciousness of the artist
Igor Stravinsky, An Autobiography, *1962: 100*

14.1 Introduction

The conscious mind is sometimes seen as getting in the way of doing things well. In the popular press, consciousness is frequently vilified, whereas, automatic, unconscious action is prized: "*Thinking* about an action," we are told, "is the sign of a novice, or a key to transforming an expert back into an amateur" (Epstein 2013), whereas "playing unconscious[ly]" leads to excellence (Brennan 2007). Similar, though more nuanced, views are expounded by researchers who argue that skills falter when attention is focused on the lower level components of a skill (Papineau 2013) or when attention is directed toward the body (Wulf 2013) or when one is performing a skill in a situation free from unusual interferences (Beilock and Gray 2012). But are there compelling reasons to believe that the conscious mind is necessarily or even generally a nuisance in such situations?

Let me call the view that conscious attention to performance impedes skill in situations free from unusual interferences, "the *just-do-it principle.*" According to this principle, barring injuries or uncommon environmental hinderances, experts—by which I mean professional level athletes, dancers, musicians and others who have not only reached professional status, but are keen on improving—perform best when their conscious minds are disengaged from their actions, when, as I shall also put it, they are performing "automatically." Although the idea that automatic actions proceed without conscious attention has been questioned (Fridland 2015), I follow my interlocutors and use the phrases "automatic action" and "proceduralized action" to refer to actions that lie outside the realm of conscious control, attention, working memory and, (for the most part) introspection. Furthermore, I take a rather broad view of what counts as conscious thought. For as I understand it, although consciously thinking in action is often verbalizable, I also maintain that one can consciously reason spatially and proprioceptively about one's actions (which, as I use the term, includes reasoning about one's movements, the effects of one's movements and the environment in which one's movements occur) without being able to verbalize or at least readily verbalize this reasoning. For example, though sometimes one might be able to describe the arc of a tennis ball in flight and how one plans to respond to it, I suggest that it may be possible to be consciously reasoning about the ball in flight without being able to (readily) describe what you are conscious of.

So much for terminological niceties. My aim in this chapter is to lay out and, to the best of my ability, knock down what I see as the three central reasons wielded in support of just-do it: experimental data indicates that conscious attention to skill precipitates choking under pressure, certain actions proceed too quickly for conscious thought, and experts are frequently unable to recall what they do in their domain of skill. I conclude by offering some reasons to accept that online conscious thought about what you are doing is compatible with expertise, or, to put it in Igor Stravinsky's stronger manner, expert skill demands the full consciousness of the expert. This is what I refer to as "the beauty of consciousness."

14.2 Choking under pressure

Choking under pressure occurs when an individual performs significantly worse than would be expected in a high-pressure situation, such as when a tennis player on the verge of an important victory begins to double-fault every serve (Hill et al. 2009). Choking under pressure is relevant to the role of consciousness in expert skill because choking episodes are thought to arise because the anxiety such situations can produce lead one to focus on skills that should proceed without conscious attention (Baumeister 1984; Masters 1992; Beilock and Carr 2001; Ford et al. 2005; Jackson et al. 2006; Gucciardi and Dimmock 2008). Although proponents of this account of choking under pressure—the "explicit monitoring hypothesis" (EMH)—don't deny that experts may consciously monitor their movements when something has gone drastically wrong, they maintain that in normal circumstances conscious monitoring interferes with high-level performance.

If EMH is correct, conscious attention is pretty much the bugbear it is made out to be. But is it correct? Support for the hypothesis is largely based on "varied-focus experiments," in which two groups of participants—individuals experienced at a task and novices—are asked to perform a task under various conditions: as they normally perform it (the single-task, or control condition), while directing their attention to a specific aspect of their own movement (the skill-related supplemental task condition), and while engaging in an extraneous task (the skill-unrelated supplemental task condition). What has been found is that, relative to the control condition, the more highly skilled participants perform significantly worse in the skill-related condition yet only marginally (or negligibly) worse in the skill-unrelated condition, whereas novices, relative to the control condition, perform significantly worse in the skill-unrelated condition and, if anything, slightly better in the skill-related condition. In other words, the more highly skilled participants perform worse when consciously attending to what they are doing than when they are consciously attending to an extraneous task. For the less skilled participants, however, conscious attention does not interfere with performance while focusing on an extraneous task does. Such studies are seen as substantiating the precept, as Beilock et al. (2002) put it, that "skill-focused attention benefits less practiced and less proficient performances yet hinders performance at higher levels of skill execution" (14).

Although EMH garners substantial support in the psychology literature on choking under pressure, the strength of this support has been questioned. For example, Christensen et al. (2015) have argued that the type of foci usually elicited in the experiments are highly artificial, and thus the conclusions drawn from them may not generalize to real-life situations. Furthermore, it has been pointed out that many experiments testing EMH fail to produce the high-stakes situations athletes find themselves in when they are playing a real game, which leaves open the possibility that even if attention to a secondary task does not degrade performance in an experimental setting, it might degrade performance in the wild since performance in the control condition is already degraded due to lack of full attention and motivation (Montero 2016).

That said, it is perhaps too easy to question the ecological validity of such experiments. Experimental conditions are always going to differ from real-life conditions and it is an open question what counts as too much of a difference (Schmuckler 2001). Moreover, it is not clear how much the artificiality of the tasks impinges on the results since both the less and more experienced participants perform the same tasks, yet ability is differentially affected. Why is this, if not for the reason, as Beilock et al. (2002) conclude, that "well learned performance may actually be compromised by attending to skill execution" (9)? If one wants to counter just-do-it, something needs to be said about why skill-focused tasks skew the more experienced participants' performance but not the less experienced participants' performance.

And something can be said. To start, when success at a task is measured in terms of speed, a skill-related supplementary task may create comparatively more drag on the higher-skilled participants' performance. For example, in one experiment, participants are asked to dribble a soccer ball through a slalom course. During the skill-related condition, participants are asked to identify, at the sound of a tone, which side of their foot was most recently in contact with the ball and, because under normal conditions the more experienced soccer players are faster than the less experienced players, thinking back to the most recent contact with the ball may be more distracting for them (because they have moved further ahead in the course) than for the less skilled players, thus slowing them down relatively more than the less skilled players. In another experiment, participants, while swinging at a virtual baseball, are requested to report at the sound of a tone whether their bats are moving up or down at that moment (Castaneda and Gray 2007) and it could be that the quicker you can perform such a task, the more detrimental it is to report on your movement, for reporting might slow you down to, or pull you toward, the tempo of the report, which is a greater reduction of speed for those who are quicker at performing a task than those who are slower at it.

Beyond this, because experts are better than novices at attending to their own movements, it could be that when asked to do so, they can do so with a vengeance; thus, the request to monitor an aspect of their movement that they normally would not monitor (or would not monitor exclusively) will be more distracting for experts than for novices. If recalling which side of the foot was most recently in contact with the ball is not relevant to their skill, this focus may interfere with their performance more than with novices' performance, as novices are not able to monitor the details of their movements as well. For novices, the skill-related supplementary task generally resulted in a slight improvement over how they perform without any additional task. And this makes sense if one thinks that focusing on a skill can be beneficial, for it could be that since novices have not developed the ability to focus on any aspects of their movements intently, the skill-related supplementary task, which encourages such focus— even if the target of such focus is not ideal—results in a better trial than one without any bodily focus.

Finally, if we assume that some type of bodily focus is beneficial at high levels of performance and that distractions closer to or more similar to your intended focus impede performance more than distractions dissimilar to your intended focus, the skill-related supplementary task may have degraded the skilled participants' performance more than the skill-unrelated supplementary task since it induced a type of focus that was close to, but not the same as that which the more highly skilled players have found beneficial. In other words, because the skill-related supplementary task brings about a type of focus that is close to but not exactly the type of focus most beneficial for experts, it distracts experts more than the skill-unrelated task which, arguably, still allowed for some optimal conscious attention. Again, for novices, who may not have developed this important aspect of skill, there is nothing to be distracted from, and any improvements could be explained in terms of the task prompting a beneficial type of attention (cf. Bermudez 2017).

Thus, there are interpretations of the varied-focus experiments that are consistent with the view that consciousness is beneficial to skill. Should we nonetheless simply accept EMH as the best explanation for choking under pressure? It's not clear that we should. Though most varied-attention experiments support EMH, not all do. For example, Suss and Ward (2010) asked expert shooters to monitor the action of their trigger finger while shooting and found that relative to a situation where the shooters were asked to focus on a skill-unrelated task, the shooters performed just as well (Sutton et al. (2011) present a theory that aims to account for such data). Furthermore, there is a competing account of the relationship between anxiety and choking, which, far from supporting the just-do-it principle, runs counter to it. On this view, referred to as the "distraction hypothesis," high pressure draws attention away from the task at hand and to irrelevant aspects of performance, such as worries over how performance will be judged or the possibility of failure (Wine 1971; Gucciardi et al. 2010; Hill et al. 2010; Oudejans et al. 2011; Mesagno et al. 2011). Both the distraction hypothesis (DH) and EMH attribute choking under pressure to misplaced attention. Yet, to put the contrast in the starkest terms, EMH implies that the misplaced attention is directed toward the action while DH implies that the misplaced attention is directed away from the action.

The DH of choking under pressure turns on the idea that the enactment of expert skill draws heavily on working memory and is cognitively demanding. Extraneous thoughts, according to DH, coopt attention and thus interfere with one's ability to store task-related information in working memory. Accordingly, studies supporting DH often investigate tasks that are thought to place high demands on working memory, such as solving math problems (Ashcraft and Kirk 2001; Beilock et al. 2004). However, the support for DH is not exclusively based on such skills, as it also reaps support from a number of studies, typically based, at least in part, on verbal reports of thoughts during competitions. These studies tend to indicate that task-irrelevant worries flood athletes' minds during choking episodes (see, for example, Hatzigeorgiadis and Biddle 2000, 2001; Hatzigeorgiadis 2002; Lane et al. 2005; Gucciardi et al. 2010; Oudejans et al. 2011. Both Gucciardi et al. (2010) and Oudejans et al. (2011) seem to indicate that not only are task-irrelevant worries present during choking episodes but that they are far more common than task-related thoughts).

That said, just as there is room to doubt the results of the experiments that support EMH, there is also room to question the experiments that support DH. While the explicit monitoring theory, as we saw, is bolstered mainly by the results of controlled experiments, DH is bolstered mainly (though not exclusively) by studies that draw data from surveys, concept maps, or diaries, and such methods may also be subject to confounds. For example, there is usually a high drop-out rate in diary studies and memory is not perfectly reliable, perhaps especially in cases of extreme anxiety (Beilock et al. 2003). Ideally a robust theory of choking would emerge from a convergence of the two approaches. As things stand, however, it seems that the experimental data leaves open the question of whether conscious attention to skill precipitates choking under pressure.

14.3 Lightning-fast actions

In addition to leaning on the empirical data on choking under pressure, proponents of the just-do-it principle sometimes point out that certain skills proceed so quickly that they preclude conscious thought. I take it for granted that some components of expert actions occur without conscious attention. For example, focusing on any one of the "three H's" of the backstroke (hips, hands, head), might preclude focusing on either of the other two, which, if you are a proficient swimmer, will nonetheless do their part in propelling you through the water. However, I question whether experts initiate actions in response to cues that are processed entirely nonconsciously. Although I make no claim to prove that experts never process movement cues entirely nonconsciously, I argue that we lack compelling evidence for the view that some expert skills must be initiated so quickly that one can only react without consciously attending to what one is reacting to. More specifically, I question whether two examples often used to illustrate the impossibility of consciously processing movement cues—that of returning a tennis serve and that of making a move in speed chess—actually do illustrate this impossibility and argue that after the onset of a cue to act (such as a serve in tennis or a move in chess) there may be time to process the cue consciously.

Some philosophers, however, think otherwise. In sports such as tennis, David Papineau (2013) tells us, "there is not time to think once the ball has been released. You can only react" (177). And according to Jeffrey Gray (2004), a served ball is travelling so fast and the distance it needs to travel is so short that players must strike it back before they consciously see the ball leave the server's racket. When Roger Federer serves to Rafael Nadal, Papineau (2017) explains, "he hits the ball at around 135 miles per hour from about 78 feet away," which means, he continues, that there is "less than half of a second for the ball to reach Nadal. (Around 400 milliseconds, to be specific)" (21). Because it takes, Papineau tells us, 500 milliseconds for the receiver to become conscious of the ball and then another 175 milliseconds to execute the shot, "these numbers don't add up" (23).[1] Thus, according to both Gray and Papineau, rather than consciously registering how the ball is leaving the server's racket and subsequently deciding, tennis players use anticipatory cues based on the server's bodily movements prior to hitting the ball, which, they both hold, are also not processed consciously: thus, as Papineau puts it, "hitting balls in fast-reaction sports happens below the level of conscious awareness" (26). Nadal, as charming as he may be during interviews, is a zombie when it comes to returning serves.

That players rely on anticipatory cues is undeniable (see, for example, Williams et al. 2002).[2] Whether such cues are processed entirely unconsciously is another matter (see Montero (2016) for some reasons to think that they may not be). However, let us put that issue aside and address the question of whether the receiver has time to consciously process the movement of the ball after it leaves the server's racket. Do the numbers really not tally? Is it really true that "athletes [do not] consciously decide what to do once they see how the ball is coming at them [since] there's no time for that" (Papineau 2017: 33)?

The numbers Papineau uses don't tally since dividing distance (78 feet) by rate (135 mph or 712,800 feet per hour) gives us 394 milliseconds. Yet a smaller divisor seems called for. Courtside digital displays of serve speed, from which Papineau presumably gleans the 135-mph figure, are measured immediately after the ball ricochets off the racket. Yet tennis is not played in a vacuum: air resistance coupled with the friction of the court surface slow the ball down so that, on average, by the time the ball hits the opponent's racket, its speed is roughly half of what it started out as (Yandell 2005). Tennis balls are fuzzy not to be cute, but to create drag. How do we figure out how long a receiver has then? Since spin of the ball, court speed (clay surfaces slow the ball down more than other surfaces) and, especially, the precise distance the ball travels should all be taken into account, there is no one simple equation. However, as with so many things these days, rather than painstakingly reasoning it out, it is easier to watch the video, and high-speed video analyses suggest that the amount of time receivers have to return 120-mph serves (on a medium hard court with the returner three feet or so behind the baseline) is around 660 milliseconds (Yandell 2005). Sometimes, of course, there is even less time; for example, data from Hawk-eye, a computer system widely used in numerous sports to track and predict ball trajectories, reveals that in the Wimbledon 2016 match between Andy Murray and Milos Raonic, Murray returned Raonic's (initially) 147-mph serve in an unbelievable 577 milliseconds (Pickup 2017). So, the divisor Papineau plugs into his equation is too large. Nonetheless, if we accept that the rest of his equation is correct, zombie actions are still required.

But is the rest of the equation correct? That it takes around 175 milliseconds after players have determined which shot to make to execute it is, I gather, accurate enough.[3] However, that it takes 500 milliseconds to become conscious of an input is, as far as I can tell, not. Although Papineau tells us that this number "is generally agreed [upon] by vision scientists," there is, from what I gather, quite a bit of controversy over how to set up experiments investigating when consciousness kicks in during perceptual tasks (see Wiens 2007; Sandberg et al. 2010; Peters et al. 2017). Some researchers find their way through this controversy. David Eagleman and Terrence Sejnowski (2000) suggest an 80-millisecond time lag, with Eagleman emphasizing in an interview that this is only an average, commenting that for all he knows "perhaps fighter pilots live less in the past than the rest of us" (Salk Institute 2000). And although more recent work points to a longer lag—proponents of the so-called "local recurrence theory" argue that consciousness of visual stimuli takes between 100 and 200 milliseconds after stimulus onset (Lamme and Roelfsema 2000; Lamme 2010) while proponents of the "global workspace theory" maintain that it takes between 300 and 400 milliseconds after stimulus onset (Dehaene and Changeux 2011; Del Cul et al. 2007)—none report 500 milliseconds.

That said, the window for thinking is not large. It may not be literally true that "we're talking about eye-blink-fast" reactions (Papineau 2017: 32). The mean duration of a blink, from the point at which the eyelid begins to close to the point at which it is fully open again seems to be around 400 milliseconds, with only a fraction of a millisecond of that time being taken up by the period during which the eyelids are closed (Espinosa et al. 2018). Nonetheless, tennis players must react quickly, but, for all we know, perhaps not so quickly that conscious thought is precluded.

The amount of time one has to respond in lightning chess, which allows one minute per player per game, is also extremely short. But is there no time for conscious thought? The philosophers John McDowell and Herbert Dreyfus, as different as their views are in many respects, nonetheless agree the speed at which players must react in lightning chess precludes conscious thought, or at least that conscious thought—and in particular "explicit commentary (on the passing scene or on what one is doing)" (McDowell 2007)—would significantly hinder one's skill at the game.

An experiment I conducted to probe the speed limits of conscious thought in lightning chess, however, fails to support the Dreyfuss/McDowell view (Montero 2019). I had four accomplished chess players—two masters, one national master and one (retired) international master—think aloud, saying what came into their minds, if anything, as they were playing a game of lightning chess with a similarly ranked opponent on an online chess site. All were able to do this and the results were what would be expected given the pairings: when paired against slightly weaker players, they won; against slightly stronger ones, they lost, making for three wins and one loss. This suggests that thinking aloud while playing does not significantly hinder chess performance. However, given the small number of trials and given my coarse-grained means of evaluating their level of skill (which took into account only outcomes of the games and did not also employ an independent analysis of the quality of the moves) it was not possible to determine whether the wins were due to the players playing as they normally would or whether the skill differential permitted them to win despite playing slightly worse than normal. Indeed, as Grandmaster Michael Rhode commented when I explained the experiment to him, they likely did perform slightly worse than normal since "doing anything extra is going to take attention away from the game … [the participants' skill will be impacted since] saying your thoughts out loud is extra." Vocalizing their thoughts may have hindered the games slightly, but there is no reason to believe that conscious attention, itself, did.

14.4 Post-performance amnesia

The final pillar of support for the just-do-it principle that I want to question is motivated by the fact that highly skilled individuals—professional ballet dancers, tennis players, musicians and others—sometimes perform optimally yet shortly afterwards report not remembering anything about what they did. For example, in an interview with Alex Zolbert (2012), tennis champion Maria Sharapova claims that she had no idea what happened when she beat Martina Navratilova; after Zolbert commented that without such knowledge, she is lucky that her groundstrokes didn't go into the net, she countered, "maybe they were in the net." Apparently, her memory was so impoverished, she couldn't tell.

The standard explanation of such "post-performance amnesia" is that expert actions are performed without conscious attention, they are, as Beilock and Carr (2001) put it, "controlled in real time by procedural knowledge" (702). Procedural knowledge couples well-worn neural programs—programs that run without the intervention of conscious control, programs that run *autonomously*—with action. And since an automated action, as it is generally understood, "requires little attention, operates largely outside of working memory, and is substantially closed to introspection" (Beilock and Carr 2001: 702), and since long-term conscious memory formation requires attention (Schacter 1996; Fernandes et al. 2005), it follows that high-level skills ought to leave impoverished consciously accessible memory traces.

Does post-performance amnesia occur? It seems to. It has anecdotal support and Simon Høffding's (2015) qualitative study of the performing experiences of members of the Danish String Quartet indicates that, though rare, the quartet members had periods of time performing or rehearsing that failed to leave long-term memory (i.e. longer than 30 secs) traces. In any event, I accept that post-performance amnesia sometimes occurs. What I question, however, is the idea that the best way to explain such memory blanks is always in terms of the conscious mind going on holiday. Sometimes the conscious mind does go on holiday, but if conscious attention to action is an important component of expert skill, then such vacation-performances should be sub-optimal.

Although I can only speculate, I think that there are two other possible explanations for post-performance amnesia that do not turn on the idea that such performances are automatic. One possibility is that post-performance amnesia may occur when performers are focusing so intently on their actions that each moment of attention interferes with long-term memory formation of what was previously attended to. It is known that a distraction task immediately following a memory task, interferes with long-term memory formation. An early illustration of this comes from Müller and Pilzecker's (1900) pioneering study in which participants, after they attempted to memorize a list of syllables, were presented with a new syllable list either 17 seconds or six minutes later. In the 17-second condition, participants recalled 28% of the syllables whereas in the six-minute condition this increased to 49%. This and numerous recent studies of both humans and non-human animals, using both behavioral and neuroimagining approaches, are thought to support the idea that distraction immediately following a memory task can serve as a "retroactive interference" impeding long-term memory formation (see, for example, Dewar et al. 2009; for a review, see Wixted 2004).

On the automaticity account (Beilock et al. 2002), post-performance amnesia is explained in terms of expert actions being so fully automated that the conscious mind is not present during performance. My proposed alternative, "deep engagement," is consistent with the view that expert actions are proceduralized to a large degree. A selective focus on one aspect of a skill is only possible if the other aspects of the skill proceed automatically. However, it does not require the type of full proceduralization of action that is required to explain post-performance amnesia on the automaticity account. Rather, the deep engagement account maintains that when challenges are present and surmounted with aplomb, yet rapidly forgotten, conscious attention is so keenly focused on the moment that each subsequent period of attention impedes memory formation of the previous period.

Another possibility is that post-performance amnesia may occur when performers are highly focused on aspects of their bodily skills that are not readily expressible in words. When you close your eyes and feel your right arm extend so that it forms a 90-degree angle with your torso, your sense of proprioception along with a declarative conceptualization of your position, helps you to judge the angle formed by your torso and arm; you might think, "my arm is at a 90-degree angle from my body." And if you conceive of your arm position in this way, you will likely be left with a declarative memory of having assumed that position. If someone later asked you what position you were in a few minutes ago, barring intervening distractions (for example, barring situations where you continually moved into other angles) you would be able to report that you had assumed the position in question. But if conscious awareness of our movements and positions outstrips what we can presently put into words, it may be that an exclusive focus on nondeclarative elements or qualities of our movements and positions will result in our inability to say anything, or at best very little about what had just transpired.

If conscious attention to skill is beneficial, then such attention should enable one to do certain actions that otherwise one would not be able to do or not be able to do as well. In other words, such attention must be a form of practical reasoning outside of language. Yet it is difficult to see how this could occur. As Michael Devitt (2006) points out, "we still have very little idea of how thinking could proceed if thoughts were not language-like" (147).

Admittedly, the idea that one can reason outside of language is controversial (Buckner 2019). However, it has been argued that humans engage in nondeclarative spatial reasoning in navigating (Camp 2007), in playing chess (Montero 2016) and in some forms of mathematical thinking (Montero 2016). Might tennis players, when running to return a serve, engage in conscious nonverbal spatial reasoning? If they do, and if this were their sole conscious focus, they might be left without any declarative memory of what they had done.

I would also like to suggest that enacting a skill sometimes involves conscious, proprioceptive reasoning. What is proprioceptive reasoning? Proprioceptive reasoning, as I see it, is reasoning about the moving body. It can involve conscious reasoning about tempo, force, shape, quality of movement (smooth, sharp, etc.). It may be remembered when it can be expressed in words (tempo, force, etc.). However, the type of proprioceptive reasoning that would result in post-performance amnesia (if it exists—for, remember, this is speculative) would be reasoning about qualities of the moving body that cannot readily or perhaps at all be put into words (see also Montero 2019; Høffding and Montero 2019).

On the standard account, post-performance amnesia results when experts' conscious minds are not engaged during performance. In contrast, according to the two alternative explanations I've just tendered, post-performance amnesia occurs when the nature of the performers' conscious experience leaves them unable to recall what they have done (cf. Bermudez 2017).

14.5 The beauty of consciousness

Consciousness is sometimes seen as detrimental to expert performance because it is thought that experimental data indicates that conscious attention to skill precipitates choking under pressure, that certain actions proceed too quickly for conscious thought, and that experts are occasionally unable to recall what they do in their domain of skill. I have attempted to counter these three reasons to doubt the relevance of consciousness to expert-level skill. Although my criticisms fall short of providing a reason to think that conscious attention is beneficial or even compatible with expert performance, I think that it is both of these things: even when there is nothing out of the ordinary that would demand an expert's attention, expert skills generally proceed best when the conscious mind is in control.[4] This is "the beauty of consciousness."

My most salient motivation for thinking that experts consciously attend to their skills comes from first-person experience. I was a professional ballet dancer, and I recall (it seems to me) consciously thinking during performances. Of course, memory is labile, but I have recently taken up dancing again (in part to be my own research subject) and during both performance and practice, it at least seems to me that I frequently focus on the aspects of my skill that I want to work on or play with and that this object of my focus can be anything from the rise and fall of an emotion to the rise and fall of my pinkie finger. And I am not alone among dancers in adopting this type of focus: When Guss-West and Wulf (2016) surveyed 53 international professional ballet dancers to identify what these performers focused on or imagined when preparing and executing a variety of actions, they found that 72% of responses related to body movements.

But is such attention beneficial? I think that there is an argument based on Anders Ericsson and colleagues' research into what he refers to as "deliberate practice" (Ericsson et al. 1993) that suggests that it is at least compatible with optimal performance. Deliberate practice, as opposed to mere repetition, is practice with the specific aim of improvement, often involving focusing on aspects of a skill that are most challenging. According to Ericsson, those who excel engage in deliberate practice. And according to most everyone, improvement requires conscious thought. Now, performance is different from practice as one can't stop and do something again and one might also be more risk-averse. Nonetheless, I think it is reasonable to maintain that if an athlete or performer engages in conscious thought during practice, then some level of conscious attention will be compatible with performance.

Beyond this, consciousness attending to one's actions can be engaging. The cellist Ivan Luza told me that he never performs the Bach cello suites the same way twice because he is always trying to discover something new. And, when Luza is playing Bach, such fun often does lead to beauty, both in the standard use of that word and in my ideocratic sense of improvement of skill since, as he explained, playing is a form of experimental investigation into what works and what doesn't.

Of course, when the aim is to win, one might not have the luxury to experiment. But, arguably, one does not always play exclusively to win; sometimes, even during a tournament, one aims at improvement. Finally, one also typically wants to do better than ever, not only next time, but also this time. And consciousness would play a role in achieving this aim since automaticity leads to stagnation (Ericsson et al. 1993).[5]

14.6 Concluding cerebrations on the philosophical import of conscious skill

What is the philosophical relevance of the research into the role of conscious attention during the execution of skill? I would like to suggest that it has a rare philosophical implication: it illustrates how consciousness—a feature of the world that philosophers sometimes claim resists scientific explanation—can be, and is, studied scientifically. To be sure, the scientific investigation into the role of consciousness in skill may not fall under that heading of what philosophers such as David Chalmers (1996) refer to as "the hard problem," which is the problem of explaining how a mere physical machine, such as the brain, can produce conscious experience. But the way to solve the hard problem might be both to accept that physical machines like our brains are not so mere as philosophers sometimes make them out to be, and also to let science tackle the available problems of consciousness until the hard problem fades away, if not entirely, then at least into that isolated corner of inquiry filled with philosophical conundrums that merely reveal something about our cognitive capacities. In other words, perhaps it's time to move on.

Notes

1 In this passage, Papineau actually says that it takes 500 milliseconds for the ball "to come into clear focus." Because his conclusion to this "no time" argument is that "athletes [do not] consciously decide what to do once they see how the ball is coming at them" (33), I'm interpreting "clear focus" to mean "conscious focus." With such an interpretation, his argument is valid (but, as I later argue, not sound).
2 And such anticipatory cues might be conscious (Montero 2016).
3 There is some indication that a reaction to an auditory stimulus can be under 85 milliseconds (Pain and Hibbs 2007), and it is sometimes speculated that tennis players grunt to cover up the auditory cues. Yet disagreement exists over the proper method for measuring reaction time (Wickens and Hollands 2000).
4 The view I am advocating resonates with Shepherd (2015).
5 This is all assuming consciousness is not epiphenomenal, which I think is a reasonable assumption (Montero 2007 and in progress).

References

Ashcraft, M. H., and Kirk, E. P. (2001) "The Relationships Among Working Memory, Math Anxiety, and Performance," *Journal of Experimental Psychology: General* 130: 224–37.
Baumeister, R. F. (1984) "Choking Under Pressure: Self-Consciousness and Paradoxical Effects of Incentives on Skillful Performance," *Journal of Personality and Social Psychology* 6: 610–20.
Beilock, S. L., and Carr, T. H. (2001) "On the Fragility of Skilled Performance: What Governs Choking Under Pressure," *Journal of Experimental Psychology* 130: 701–25.
Beilock, S. L., and Gray, R. (2012) "Why Do Athletes Choke Under Pressure?" in G. Tenenbaum and R. Eklund (eds.) *Handbook of Sport Psychology: Third Edition*, John Wiley and Sons, https://doi.org/10.1002/9781118270011.ch19.
Beilock, S. L., Wierenga, S. A., and Carr, T. H. (2002) "Expertise, Attention, and Memory in Sensorimotor Skill Execution: Impact of Novel Task Constraints on Dual-Task Performance and Episodic Memory," *Quarterly Journal of Experimental Psychology: Human Experimental Psychology* 55: 1211–40.
—— (2003) "Memory and Expertise: What Do Experienced Athletes Remember?" in J. L. Starkes and K. A. Ericsson (eds.) *Expert Performance in Sports: Advances in Research on Sport Expertise*, 295–320, Champaign, IL: Human Kinetics.
Beilock, S. L., Kulp, C. A., Holt, L. E., and Carr, T. H. (2004) "More on the Fragility of Performance: Choking Under Pressure in Mathematical Problem Solving," *Journal of Experimental Psychology: General* 133: 584–600.
Bermudez, J. P. (2017) "Do We Reflect While Performing Skillful Actions? Automaticity, Control, and the Perils of Distraction," *Philosophical Psychology* 30: 896–924.
Brennan, C. (2007) "Lack of Marquee Teams Doesn't Mean Viewers Can't Watch," *USA Today*, 17 October 2007, http://usatoday30.usatoday.com/sports/columnist/brennan/2007-10-17-baseball-tv_N.htm, accessed 4 November 2015.

Buckner, C. (2019) "Rational Inference: The Lowest Bounds," *Philosophy and Phenomenological Research* 98: 697–724.

Camp, E. (2007) "Thinking with Maps," *Philosophical Perspectives* 21: 145–82.

Castaneda, B., and Gray, R. (2007) "Effects of Focus of Attention on Baseball Batting Performance in Players of Differing Skill Levels," *Journal of Sport and Exercise Psychology* 29: 60–77.

Chalmers, D. J. (1996) *The Conscious Mind: In Search of a Fundamental Theory*, Oxford: Oxford University Press.

Christensen, W., Sutton, J., and McIlwain, D. J. (2015) "Putting Pressure on Theories of Choking: Towards an Expanded Perspective on Breakdown in Skilled Performance," *Phenomenology and the Cognitive Sciences* 14: 253–93.

Dehaene, S., and Changeux, J. P. (2011) "Experimental and Theoretical Approaches to Conscious Processing," *Neuron* 70: 200–27.

Del Cul, A., Baillet, S., and Dehaene, S. (2007) "Brain Dynamics Underlying the Nonlinear Threshold for Access to Consciousness," *PLoS Biology* 5: e260.

Devitt, M. (2006) *Ignorance of Language*, Oxford: Clarendon Press.

Dewar, M., Garcia, Y. F., Cowan, N., and Sala, S. D. (2009) "Delaying Interference Enhances Memory Consolidation in Amnesic Patients," *Neuropsychology* 23: 627–34.

Eagleman, D. M., and Sejnowski, T. J. (2000) "Motion Integration and Postdiction in Visual Awareness," *Science* 287: 2036–8.

Epstein, D. (2013) "Why Pujols Can't (and A-Rod Wouldn't) Touch This Pitch," *Sports Illustrated*, 29 July 2013, www.si.com/vault/2013/07/29/106348951/why-pujols-cant-anda-rod-wouldnt-touch-this-pitch, accessed 7 November 2015.

Ericsson, K. A., Krampe, R. T., and Tesch-Romer, C. (1993) "The Role of Deliberate Practice in the Acquisition of Expert Performance," *Psychological Review* 100: 363–406.

Espinosa, J., Domenech, B., Vazquez, C., Perez, J., and Mas, D. (2018) "Blinking Characterization from High Speed Video Records: Application to Biometric Authentication," *PloS One* 13: e0196125, https://doi.org/10.1371/journal.pone.0196125.

Fernandes, M. A., Moscovitch, M., Ziegler, M., and Grady, C. (2005) "Brain Regions Associated with Successful and Unsuccessful Retrieval of Verbal Episodic Memory as Revealed by Divided Attention," *Neuropsychologia* 43: 1115–27.

Ford, P., Hodges, N. J., and Williams, A. M. (2005) "Online Attentional-Focus Manipulations in a Soccer-Dribbling Task: Implications for the Proceduralization of Motor Skills," *Journal of Motor Behavior* 37: 386–94.

Fridland, E. (2015) "Automatically Minded," *Synthese* 194: 4337–63.

Gray, J. A. (2004) *Consciousness: Creeping Up on the Hard Problem*, Oxford: Oxford University Press.

Gucciardi, D. F., and Dimmock, J. A. (2008) "Choking Under Pressure in Sensorimotor Skills: Conscious Processing or Depleted Attentional Resources?" *Psychology of Sport and Exercise* 9: 45–59.

Gucciardi, D. F., Longbottom, J. L., Jackson, B., and Dimmock, J. A. (2010) "Experienced Golfers' Perspectives on Choking Under Pressure," *Journal of Sport and Exercise Psychology* 32: 61–83.

Guss-West, C., and Wulf, G. (2016) "Attentional Focus in Classical Ballet: A Survey of Professional Dancers," *Journal of Dance Medicine & Science* 20: 23–9.

Hatzigeorgiadis, A. (2002) "Thoughts of Escape During Competition: Relationships with Goal Orientations and Self-Consciousness," *Psychology of Sport and Exercise* 3: 195–207.

Hatzigeorgiadis, A., and Biddle, S. J. (2000) "Assessing Cognitive Interference in Sport: Development of the Thought Occurrence Questionnaire for Sport," *Anxiety, Stress and Coping* 13: 65–86.

—— (2001) "Athletes' Perceptions of How Cognitive Interference During Competition Influences Concentration and Effort," *Anxiety, Stress and Coping* 14: 411–29.

Hill, D. M., Hanton, S., Fleming, S., and Matthews, N. (2009) "A Re-Examination of Choking in Sport," *European Journal of Sport Science* 9: 203–12.

Hill, D. M., Hanton, S., Matthews, N., and Fleming, S. (2010) "A Qualitative Exploration of Choking in Elite Golf," *Journal of Clinical Sport Psychology* 4: 221–40.

Høffding, S. (2015) *A Phenomenology of Expert Musicianship*, PhD dissertation, University of Copenhagen.

Høffding, S., and Montero, B. (2019) "Not Being There: An Analysis of Expertise-Induced Amnesia," *Mind & Language*, https://doi.org/10.1111/mila.12260.

Jackson, R. C., Ashford, K. J., and Norsworthy, G. (2006) "Attentional Focus, Dispositional Reinvestment, and Skilled Motor Performance under Pressure," *Journal of Sport and Exercise Psychology* 28: 49–68.

Lamme, V. A. (2010) "How Neuroscience Will Change Our View on Consciousness," *Cognitive Neuroscience* 1: 204–20.

Lamme, V. A., and Roelfsema, P. R. (2000) "The Distinct Modes of Vision Offered by Feedforward and Recurrent Processing," *Trends in Neurosciences* 23: 571–9.

Lane, A. M., Harwood, C., and Nevill, A. M. (2005) "Confirmatory Factor Analysis of the Thought Occurrence Questionnaire for Sport (TOQS) Among Adolescent Athletes," *Anxiety, Stress, and Coping* 18: 245–54.

Masters, R. S. W. (1992) "Knowledge, (K)nerves, and Know-How: The Role of Explicit versus Implicit Knowledge in the Breakdown of a Complex Motor Skill Under Pressure," *British Journal of Psychology* 83: 343–58.

McDowell, J. (2007) "Response to Dreyfus," *Inquiry* 50: 366–70.

Mesagno, C., Harvey, J. T., and Janelle, C. M. (2011) "Self-Presentation Origins of Choking: Evidence from Separate Pressure Manipulations," *Journal of Sport and Exercise Psychology* 33: 441–59, https://doi.org/10.1123/jsep.33.3.441.

Montero, B. (2007) "Physicalism Could Be True Even If Mary Learns Something New," *Philosophical Quarterly* 57: 176–89.

—— (2016) *Thought in Action: Expertise and the Conscious Mind*, Oxford: Oxford University Press.

—— (2019) "Chess and the Conscious Mind: Why Dreyfus and McDowell Got It Wrong," *Mind & Language* 34: 376–92.

—— (in progress) *Mind without Matter: Post Physicalism and the Mind-Body Problem*, Oxford: Oxford University Press.

Müller G. E., and Pilzecker A. (1900) Experimentelle Beiträge zur Lehre vom Gedächtnis. *Z. Psychol. Ergänzungsband* 1: 1–300.

Oudejans, R. R., Kuijpers, W., Kooijman, C. C., and Bakker, F. C. (2011) "Thoughts and Attention of Athletes under Pressure: Skill-Focus or Performance Worries?" *Anxiety, Stress, and Coping* 24: 59–73.

Pain, M. T., and Hibbs, A. (2007) "Sprint Starts and the Minimum Auditory Reaction Time," *Journal of Sports Sciences* 25: 79–86.

Papineau, D. (2013) "In the Zone," *Royal Institute of Philosophy Supplement* 73: 175–96.

—— (2017) *Knowing the Score: What Sports Can Teach Us About Philosophy (And What Philosophy Can Teach Us About Sports)*, New York: Basic Books.

Peters, M., Kentridge, R., Phillips, I., and Block, N. (2017) "Does Unconscious Perception Really Exist? Continuing the ASSC20 Debate," *Neuroscience of Consciousness* 3: nix015, doi: 10.1093/nc/nix015.

Pickup, O. (2017) "Rapid Response: The Art of Returning Serve," *The Telegraph*, www.telegraph.co.uk/tennis/wimbledon-reaction/how-to-return-a-serve/.

Salk Institute (2000) "We Live in the Past, Salk Scientists Discover," *Salk News*, 16 March 2000, www.salk.edu/news-release/we-live-in-the-past-salk-scientists-discover/.

Sandberg, K., Timmermans, B., Overgaard, M., and Cleeremans A. (2010) "Measuring Consciousness: Is One Measure Better Than the Other?" *Consciousness and Cognition* 19: 1069–78.

Schacter, D. L. (1996) *Searching for Memory: The Brain, the Mind, and the Past*, New York: Basic Books.

Schmuckler, M. (2001) "What Is Ecological Validity? A Dimensional Analysis," *Infancy* 2: 419–36.

Shepherd, J. (2015) "Conscious Control over Action," *Mind and Language* 30: 320–44.

Suss, J., and Ward, P. (2010) "Skill-Based Differences in the Cognitive Mechanisms Underlying Failure Under Stress," *Proceedings of the Human Factors and Ergonomics Society Annual Meeting* 54: 1062–6.

Sutton, J., McIlwain, D., Christensen, W., and Geeves, A. (2011) "Applying Intelligence to the Reflexes: Embodied Skills and Habits between Dreyfus and Descartes," *The Journal of the British Society for Phenomenology* 42: 78–103.

Wickens, C., and Hollands, J. (2000) *Engineering Psychology and Human Performance*, Upper Saddle River, NJ: Prentice Hall.

Wiens, S. (2007) "Concepts of Visual Consciousness and Their Measurement," *Advances in Cognitive Psychology* 3: 349–59, doi: 10.2478/v10053-008-0035-y.

Williams, A. M., Ward, P., Knowles, J. M., and Smeeton, N. J. (2002) "Anticipation Skill in a Real-World Task: Measurement, Training, and Transfer in Tennis," *Journal of Experimental Psychology: Applied* 8: 259–70.

Wine, J. (1971) "Test Anxiety and Direction of Attention," *Psychological Bulletin* 76: 92–104.

Wixted, J. T. (2004) "The Psychology and Neuroscience of Forgetting," *Annual Review of Psychology* 55: 235–69.

Wulf, G. (2013) "Attentional Focus and Motor Learning: A Review of 15 Years," *International Review of Sport and Exercise Psychology* 6: 77–104.

Yandell. J. (2005) "Ball Speed in Pro Tennis," www.tennisplayer.net/public/mystheavyball/john_yandell/ball_speed_pro_tennis/ball_speed_pro_tennis_page1.html?format=print.

Zolbert, A. (2012) "Interview with Women's Tennis Champion Maria Sharapova," *CNN*, 19 October 2012, www.cnn.com/TRANSCRIPTS/1210/19/ta.01.html.

15

EMBODIED EXPERIENCE IN THE COGNITIVE ECOLOGIES OF SKILLED PERFORMANCE

John Sutton and Kath Bicknell

15.1 Real experts

Research on expert skills is harder than studying particular cognitive processes – remembering, hearing, grieving, and so on – because its domain is less neatly bounded. Skill and expertise are multi-level, composite phenomena: multi-level in that they involve neural, cognitive, affective, motor, social, technological, and cultural processes and resources all at once, composite in that expert musicians or sportspeople are deploying many integrated psychological, bodily, and social capacities all at once, from perception and attention through emotion and memory to precise movement coordination and interactive communication.

In a provocative paper for the new *Journal of Expertise*, Fernand Gobet laments that 'the current state of research into expertise is problematic as knowledge is currently fragmented and communication between disciplines is poor'. This is 'regrettable, as many contradictions between the disciplines have been ignored and many opportunities for cross-fertilization missed' (2018: 1, 5).

We embrace Gobet's challenge: 'the way forward for the field of expertise is to join forces and carry out multi-disciplinary research' (2018: 5). We highlight skill phenomena much discussed by expert practitioners, specialist applied researchers, and philosophers influenced by phenomenology and ethnography, which have received less attention in cognitive neuroscience and philosophy of mind. We focus on (a) the embodied experience of (b) real expert performers in (c) real domains of practice, as they deploy (d) richly embedded strategies in (e) full and challenging ecological settings.

This should not be a surprising 'turn' in the field: while there are many reasonable ways to study skill, one useful path is to find, track, closely observe, and listen to experts. This is a natural route to striking case studies, new puzzles, suggestive angles on existing questions, mature empirical traditions, and rich bodies of theory. While here we take the arts and, primarily, sport as our core domains, this kind of naturalistic or natural philosophy of expertise also operates in other fields, from medical diagnosis and surgery to emergency response, from aviation to software engineering, from teaching to science. These fields have long been investigated empirically, from controlled experiment to immersed ethnography. We can tap and critically engage with research on such experts not only in cognitive psychology and neuroscience, not only in the social sciences, but also in the applied sciences of each domain – music, sport, or organisational psychology of various stripes – which integrate distinct levels of analysis, to inform and assist the professions and practitioners themselves.

We focus on experts, those who devote significant time and effort to 'deliberate practice of their skill, which is practice with the specific aim of improving, and [are] still intent on improving' (Montero 2016: 10). In some domains, objective or intersubjective standards serve to compare or rank experts; in others, social or reputational factors influence attributions of expertise alongside performance history (Goldman 2018). In other contexts, we argue for more continuity than Montero between everyday and elite skill (Christensen et al. 2016; Christensen et al. 2019): but the features of skill we address show up more clearly in looking at higher or extraordinary, rather than ordinary or dysfunctional, levels of performance.

We consider the embodied experience of experts in skilled performance domains such as sport and the arts in two compatible ways – over time, and at a time. Experts are, as we say, *experienced* performers who hone their skills *over time*, through long and arduous training regimes which directly alter and shape their bodies, tuning perceptual, cognitive, emotion-regulation, and motor capacities which continue to improve and knit together in action. Alongside physical and technical development, experts develop effective strategies for shaping mood and motivation, for detecting salient changes in the environment or in an opponent's response repertoire, and for building problem-solving capacities to help recovery from trouble. In this sense, the embodied experience of experts is their history of practice. They then deploy their skills *at a time* in performance, and we can enquire into the nature of their experience in doing so. Research on skill and expertise can fruitfully address these two – diachronic and synchronic – aspects of embodied experience together.

Some researchers deliberately avoid the complex and messy contexts of expert action, abstracting away from the ecologies of performance, to focus on single or general features of skill. In different ways, this is true both of the conceptual methods characteristic of philosophical work on know-how (e.g., Stanley 2011; Pavese 2015), and in the isolation of controllable variables for laboratory experiments on the neuroscience of expertise (Bilalić and Campitelli 2018). Such mainstream approaches play important, if rather disconnected, roles in the multidisciplinary field. But given how little we really know about the nature, components, and bases of skill, it also makes sense to seek more in-situ access to what happens when all the integrated features of expert performance are operating together.

The ongoing rebirth of skill as a central topic in philosophy should be informed by close examination of experts' embodied experience in the cognitive ecologies of skilled performance. There are a number of ways to do this effectively, and we survey methods for tapping experts' experience, from more tightly controlled procedures for self-report which deliberately exclude background knowledge and personal insight, to practitioner-driven research and qualitative case studies drawing on participation, interviews, or materials generated by athletes. We hope to encourage an expansion of standard sources for skill research, to incorporate attention to the embodied experience of real experts in uneven and heterogeneous ecologies of practice. In an extended case study from elite road cycling, with which we end, we show that athletes can tell us much about their successful decision-making in dynamic environments. We triangulate one competitor's reports against a diverse range of sources to suggest how rich and flexible experts' speedy thoughts and feelings can be in dynamic decision environments.

15.2 Research on embodied expertise

Expertise researchers have long grasped opportunities to study embodied skills in their natural or home communities and settings. Even historians, for whom musical or other skilled performances are distant in time, address challenges posed by the ephemeral nature of skilled action to analyse particular historical forms of 'kinesic intelligence' (Le Guin 2006; Tribble 2017; Pearlman et al. 2018). For contemporary skilled practices, the multi-disciplinary research that Gobet recommends needs to stretch from biology and neuroscience to the sociology and politics of expertise. Integrating such disparate research enterprises, philosophers of cognition, mind, and action can create important niches in multi-disciplinary applied sciences of skill. The last 30 years of cognitive theory have highlighted enactive and phenomenological, ecological and dynamical, embodied and distributed perspectives on cognition and action which align closely with applied concerns. '4E cognition' (Newen et al. 2018) is changing relations with applied skill domains: we focus again on sport, though similar accounts hold for music, dance, and performance research.

Many philosophers in the 1990s, picking up on and contributing to internal developments in the cognitive sciences, rejected a picture of cognition as an inner process 'sandwiched' between information pick-up and behavioural output. In making the alternative case that flexible intelligent action involves continuous coupling of perception and action, with mutually modulatory dynamics operating between brain, body, and world, some introduced analogies with jazz improvisation, sport, and circus performance (Clark 1997: 165; Hurley 1998: 2).

Nonetheless, suggestions that many aspects of embodied mental life might be better modelled on dynamic, improvisatory, collaborative forms of active expertise than on isolated rational deliberation were developed only in general terms, without sustained attention to these domains of practice. Little engagement with applied research took philosophers of mind beyond casual anecdote. The instructive book *Visual Perception and Action in Sport* (Williams et al. 1999), for example, structured in impressive detail around the contrast between indirect/cognitivist and ecological/dynamical perspectives on perception and action, was barely cited in philosophy. At that stage, little work in the specialist fields of 'philosophy of sport' and 'philosophy of music' made contact with empirical studies or with cognitive theory, focusing instead on ethics, metaphysics, or aesthetics. In turn, discussion of sporting or musical traditions in social science often tended, as Downey (2010) noted, to address ideology and politics to the neglect of embodied expert practice and experience itself.

While applied researchers have contributed to cognitive science and philosophy of mind, relatively few philosophers of mind and cognitive theorists over the last 30 years demonstrated equivalent interest or respect in return. Researchers on skilled action in philosophy and cognitive science alike often advocate more phenomenological and ethnographically informed accounts to further understanding of performance in real-world contexts. Yet until recently they rarely acknowledged the extent to which researchers and researcher-practitioners have been doing just that, as we illustrate below. But perhaps we are now entering a more integrative, pluralist phase of expertise research. Alongside attempts to bring cognitive and phenomenological philosophy into contact with sports psychology (Kretchmar 1982; Moe 2005; Aggerholm et al. 2011; Ravn and Christensen 2014; Toner et al. 2015; Kimmel and Rogler 2018), a clear sign of change is MIT's grand-scale *Handbook of Embodied Cognition and Sport Psychology* (Cappuccio 2018), with many chapters co-authored by philosophers and sports scientists, moving multi-disciplinary skill and expertise research along substantially. We can build on this momentum.

Before surveying methods for tapping into expert practice, we point to two key research targets for the ecological or distributed approach we're developing.

15.3 Ecologies and cues

Alongside the embodied experience of expert performers in real domains of practice, we need to study the full, challenging settings in which they attend to particular cues and deploy particular strategies for maintaining or improving performance. Such settings are hard to simulate. Professional athletes regularly navigate factors as various as changing weather conditions, unfamiliar locations or terrain, equipment and new technologies, fatigue, injury, pain, risk, the sounds and expectations of crowds and supporters as well as media, self-imposed or career-threatening pressure, interaction with peers or team-mates under varying constraints, the actions of opponents and other competitors, and strong personal emotions. A number of these factors are in play in our case study from cycling below.

Challenging ecological factors are par for the course, and not outside what we have called 'the conditions of expected skill' for expert performers, to be expected and prepared for even if not encountered frequently from a statistical point of view (Christensen et al. 2016: 52–4). Navigating such aspects of the bodily, motivational, collaborative, and environmental settings of performance, while maintaining or intensifying the highest levels of technical competence in skill execution, is utterly unlike reproducing a single isolated component of one's overall skill set in simplified training or laboratory settings, no matter how useful such repeated performance might be for other purposes (Christensen et al. 2015b). Professional musicians and dancers face different, but often no less challenging, variations in the settings and contexts of practice and performance. Because experts' work is thus dependent on often unpredictable changes in the distributed ecologies of skilled performance, they deliberately get (as they say) out of their comfort zone, to stay fresh and ready to innovate or improvise. They do not rest easy with repetition of prior actions. To respond to challenge, athletes attune to a range of cues, which help them attend, anticipate, and act appropriately as situations shift.

Sports psychologists have focused on the advance pick-up of perceptual and kinematic cues, which grounds expert advantage in interceptive tasks such as hitting a ball (Abernethy et al. 2018). We'll note below complementary recent work on the role of contextual cues, when experts access and deploy relevant situational knowledge to influence and adjust their well-honed embodied skills in real time. Verbal cues, in the form of self-talk as well as input from team-mates and coaches, often function less as direct instructions than as compressed, context-sensitive nudges to adjust action tendencies (Sutton 2007). Other sets of cues, across skill domains, may be multimodal and overlapping. The roles of multimodal cues in instruction and performance have been studied most thoroughly in other professional fields, including archaeological practice and courtroom debate (Goodwin 1994), agriculture (Grasseni 2004), architecture and design (Rietveld and Brouwers 2017), navigation (Hutchins 2010), and aviation (Hutchins et al. 2013). Using microanalytic methods, such research in interaction studies and cognitive ethnography traces the developmental processes of embodied apprenticeship which ground skilled vision, practical know-how, and insiders' context-sensitive banter (Streeck et al. 2011). With new mobile recording and analysis techniques, such methods will increasingly influence integrative multi-disciplinary research in the arts (Kirsh 2010; Waterhouse et al. 2011; Geeves et al. 2014a) and sport (King and de Rond 2011; Collins 2015; Muntanyola-Saura and Sánchez-García 2018), and offer rich pickings for philosophers and cognitive theorists.

15.4 Methods

Methods from interaction studies and cognitive ethnography, like those mentioned above, involve probing, listening to, and analysing what experts say about their domain, their activities, and their decisions. They are not vulnerable to the critiques of self-report which have long stopped many philosophers and psychologists from working closely with experts' own accounts of their skilled practice. Poorly controlled collection of verbal report data, it is feared, leaves us with confabulated accounts of cognitive processes, arising from implicit culturally sanctioned theories, involving causal claims disconnected from the true springs of action. The resulting lack of interest in what experts tell us chimes with longstanding philosophical assumptions that higher levels of skilled performance are intuitive and 'mindless', and therefore cannot be accessed or articulated, assumptions we criticise elsewhere (Sutton et al. 2011; Geeves et al. 2014b; Christensen et al. 2016).

Discomfort with self-reports also arises within the relevant sciences. In one trenchant critical review of the use of verbal reports in sport science, Eccles (2012) found that many studies employ overly directive probe questions, tap only general states rather than particular episodes, and involve long delays between action and report. Yet, as Eccles acknowledged, there are methods for tapping experts' embodied experience that do not rely on problematic, theory-infected self-reports. Expert accounts can be treated as further explananda rather than as potential causal explanations. In the interaction research mentioned above, verbal reports are triangulated against arrays of other data on the same events. Most directly, clearer methods for accessing expert reports are available. Participants can be trained to report only on what they have just been thinking, rather than offering interpretations of their cognitive processes. They can be asked to think aloud during performance or, in dynamic sports, to provide immediately retrospective reports on specific episodes.

Protocol analysis of concurrent or retrospective verbalisation is widely used in expertise research (Fox et al. 2011; Ericsson 2018). In impressive longitudinal studies of memory and cognition in professional musicians' rehearsals and performances, Roger Chaffin and colleagues record reports by expert pianists, cellists, or singers of their decisions, feelings, and thoughts during practice, sometimes spread over years. They code changes over time and across distinct rehearsal phases in musicians' attention to distinct basic, technical, structural, interpretative, and expressive performance cues. They match these verbal reports against a range of behavioural data, for example identifying the precise points within a score at which musicians stop and start during practice, or quantifying hesitations and the exact tempo profiles of phrases which constitute musical gestures (Chaffin et al. 2002; Noice et al. 2008; Lisboa et al. 2018). First-person perspectives on the stages of practice and the challenges of the musical material are checked against large bodies of longitudinal third-person data, producing powerful multi-level accounts of the roles of different forms of memory in experts' musical practice, and of the nature and role of spontaneity and creativity in highly prepared music performance (Chaffin et al. 2009).

Likewise, recent research in sport deploys thought sampling and verbal protocol analysis, in iterative, mutually informing interaction with behavioural methods. McPherson and colleagues find significant differences between the immediately retrospective reports given by experts and novices across sports, in the breadth, depth, and diversity of detailed tactical plans and adjustments in response selection as game situations change (McPherson 2008; Sutton and McIlwain 2015). McRobert's mixed method studies show that experts across a range of sports are thinking more about task-relevant options, and engaging in more prediction and more planning than less skilled performers (McRobert et al. 2011; Ward et al. 2013). Experts often effectively integrate broader contextual information – about opponents, past performances, the competitive situation, and the time remaining, for example – with immediate and changing kinematic information, to anticipate and shape appropriate actions. This deployment of contextual information has been confirmed by Runswick and colleagues, who interpret controlled verbal report data gathered immediately after cricket batting tasks in light of independent measures of performance (Runswick et al. 2018). Coding the content of these retrospective verbal reports is not the sole source of evidence, but when matched against data on the accuracy of players' anticipation and action strongly suggests that – in addition to any technical advantage – experts surpass less skilled players cognitively, in their capacity for fast and effective access to and deployment of relevant contextual information.

While there are legitimate concerns about some uses of verbal reports in expertise research, there are also proven, rigorous methods for gathering and analysing them effectively. Yet such controlled procedures do not exhaust appropriate ways of tapping the embodied experience of experts. If our goal is to seek explanatory causal accounts of specific mechanisms underlying skilled performance, we may need that specific kind of verbal report. But because we know so little about the richer cognitive ecologies of performance, the admirably narrow conception of self-report advocated by Eccles and implemented in the research just described will not satisfy all our theoretical needs. Experts' personal meanings, contexts, individual and shared performance histories, and their long-term experience of embodied action, all which are excluded in the formal protocol analyses described above, might be relevant to other questions. As we have suggested,

> if certain components of expert knowledge are thus more or less accessible, they are likely also to be shareable with researchers as well as with coaches and peers, provided the researcher establishes a situation of sufficient rapport, asks the right questions, and the practitioner is appropriately motivated and has no reason not to share.
>
> *McIlwain and Sutton 2015: 223*

We advocate a broader range of qualitative, phenomenological, interview-based, and participatory ways of getting nearer to embodied experience. Where possible these can be matched against and meshed with quantitative and nomothetic research, but we should not rush to premature hypotheses and experiments in domains where extraordinary levels of skilled performance may first need to be identified and described in sufficient richness. Phenomenological traditions in philosophy are being creatively adapted in this spirit, for example in Høffding's development of the phenomenological interview for music and sport (Ravn and Høffding 2017; Høffding 2018). We now discuss more complete immersion in the expert's world, seeking to access embodied experience in full cognitive ecologies either by ethnographic participation, or by listening closely to an expert's own account. We look in turn at two ways of approaching skilled action from the inside out.

15.5 Researcher-practitioners on expert embodied experience

Experts' embodied experience unfolds, over time and in the moment, in rich and strange cognitive ecologies. Some researchers are also practitioners, and generate sustained, phenomenologically informed investigations of skilled action. Researcher-practitioners aim to speak 'with and for us' in tapping and articulating embodied processes. We are not thinking here of academics discussing their casual explorations of skilled action, because novice or recreational performers cannot always access the embodied experiences of experts, and thus cannot go beyond anecdote to offer rich detail in reports. Apprenticeship-based study requires persistence, whether through immersive fieldwork to 'dive into the stream of action' and report back (Wacquant 2015), or to draw on embodied practical knowledge in interpreting others' accounts.

Through long-term immersion in the rich ecologies of expert activity, researcher-practitioners can feel and evoke the distributed but integrated webs of bodily, cognitive, affective, techno-logical, and cultural resources and strategies that characterise their domains. Doris McIlwain draws on years of experience in two yoga traditions to analyse their very distinctive norms for sculpting embodied habits, involving different kinds of cue and instruction, and different ways of dealing with emotion, bodily tension, or 'silent zones', as different metaphorical and meta-physical systems pervade bodily practice over time (McIlwain and Sutton 2014). In exploring the way men experience, or do, masculinity in surfing, Clifton Evers (2009) shows how multiple interacting forces – sand, wind, water, affect, behavioural codes, skill, perception, equipment, cul-tural histories, shared embodied practice – together shape social experiences, identity, and bodily movement. Ian Maxwell's (2016) thick descriptions of the embodied experience of being at sea likewise reveal the dynamic, co-constitutive ecology of bodies, environment, and equipment in sailing: no element of the experience can be adequately described in isolation from its relation-ship to the others. Kath Bicknell draws on her embodied experiences in mountain biking over two decades to unpack performance processes and strategies in herself and others. Addressing distinctive aspects of embodied expertise, she describes mutually beneficial audience-spectator relationships in racing contexts (Bicknell 2010, 2011), the behavioural and social implications of technological trends for women's experiences in mountain biking (2016), and how increases in skill retune experts' sense of agency and perception of affordances (Christensen et al. 2015a; Christensen and Bicknell 2018). We add pointers to practitioner-based studies of sport and movement expertise through autoethnography (Allen-Collinson 2009), apprenticeship and neuroanthropology (Downey 2005, 2010; Downey et al. 2015), and carnal or enactive sociology (Wacquant 2014, 2015). These approaches, making contact variously with 4E cognitive theory, seek experientially grounded paths to richer understandings of skill. By inhabiting a world and at least partially setting aside the spectatorial posture of the researcher, these phenomenological and ethnographic projects approach expert action in the making.

15.6 Case study: Chloe Hosking's winning sprint

Another way to prioritise insider perspectives is through data produced by and for people within the expert subculture, such as interviews, social media, video footage, or post-event blogs. Unprompted athlete reports can counteract the pervasive assumption that experts cannot articulate or explain what they did in performance, or how they did it. Our final case study, built around Chloe Hosking's blog on her winning ride in the 2016 La Course by Le Tour de France (Hosking 2016), shows the range of embodied experiences some athletes can articulate. It goes some way toward elucidating the calculations and fine-grained tactics in road cycling that intrigue and mystify fans and commentators, who can only wonder why 'some riders are better at these computations than others' (Papineau 2017: 128–9). Bicknell's expertise as cyclist, researcher, and cycling journalist helps us interpret Hosking's report. It was published four days after Hosking won La Course, at the time the highest profile event, globally, in women's road cycling.

The delayed and self-reported nature of a blog post raises questions about the reliability and validity of Hosking's recall. But examined with a critical eye, such sources provide insight into expert embodied experience which may be unavailable by other means. Hosking's blog relays her *experience* of the race, from inside the peloton, where video cameras were absent, thought-sampling methods impractical, and the actions of over a hundred other athletes too variable to simulate with intensity in a lab. We can supplement and triangulate her blog post against independent sources, including video footage of the race and Hosking's own initial reactions after winning (Voxwomen 2016). The blog elaborates or unpacks Hosking's decision-making processes during the event. Athletes frequently recall in considerable detail significant moments and decision-making processes as critical moments unfold. We suggest not that Hosking's report is unflinchingly accurate, but that it does reflect factors that inform decision-making during performance.

La Course by Le Tour de France was a 13-lap race on the Champs-Élysées. Each lap was just under seven kilometres, and each took the leading riders between nine and ten minutes. In Hosking's team, Wiggle High5, she was the protected rider if the finish became a bunch sprint. This was one of the team's several strategies for the race depending on how it unfolded (Wiggle High5 2016).

As you read Hosking's description of the race's closing phases, note how she quickly accounted for the tactical decisions and anticipated movements of her competitors in relation to her own abilities as she decided who to follow and when.

> [A]ll of a sudden Ellen van Dijk shot out of the peloton and down the ramp into the tunnel faster than you backtrack when you say you'll come to something with your family and then find out you have to pay. She obviously hadn't read the script, this was meant to be a bunch sprint.
>
> I literally thought, 'oh shit'. I had no one left, they had done their jobs already, and I learnt after the race, had all been caught in crashes. I couldn't chase Ellen myself. I had to wait.
>
> The Canyon-SRAM team obviously felt the same sense of urgency as I did and flicked out of the compact group in pursuit of Ellen who had already established a solid gap with about 1.5kms to go.
>
> The issue was there was only two left in the Canyon train – Alena Amialiusik and Tiffany Cromwell – and one of them had to sprint leaving only one to chase Ellen, a former world time trial champion. Positioned third and glued to Tiffany's wheel as we powered towards the final kilometer I was willing Alena to keep going but I could see her starting to rock on her bike. We weren't going to catch Ellen.

While this move may not have been in Hosking's script, van Dijk revealed in a post-race interview that it was her plan to attack at this point in the race all along (UCI Women's World Tour 2016). Hosking's report does not describe one single decisive moment that won the race, but reflects a series of decisions and moments that added up to her navigating the final moments of the race most successfully. She had to flexibly adapt her strategy for sprinting to the line without her team for support. She chose not to chase van Dijk solo as it would have used up too much energy. The blog reveals clear appreciation of what she *can* do (draft on the wheels of other riders), *cannot* do (chase van Dijk solo and hold off the chasing peloton for over a kilometre) and *might* be able to do (adapt again if circumstances change). Her rapid assessment of the unfolding situation drew not only on years of experience as a professional cyclist, but on strong contextual knowledge of the capabilities of her rivals. Hosking was aware van Dijk had the capacity to pedal away given her time trial credentials. Hosking was also observing her rivals for cues and clues about their form in the moment: Amialiusik's rocking body revealed she was struggling and would be unlikely to sustain her power output.

Then as we rode under the 1km to go banner I could feel riders coming up on the right hand side. I started to move out and somehow found myself on Pauline Ferrand-Prevot's wheel. She was flying. She took it through the two last corners but Ellen still had twenty meters on the peloton with 350 meters to go.

And then Pauline swung to the right. She was done. I was on the front. This is way too early.

According to the website Strava, where some athletes make their GPS data public, the final 400 metres of La Course took 2014 winner Marianne Vos approximately 28 seconds (Strava 2016). While Hosking didn't share her own data from the 2016 race, 15th place finisher Sarah Roy, who rode across the line with the bunch just behind Hosking, took 30 seconds. A lot can happen in those final critical seconds. With Prevot gone, van Dijk in front, and a motivated peloton behind her, Hosking was on her own.

It is amazing how much actually goes through your head in a sprint, it seems like you have minutes to make decisions but really it's milliseconds. I decided to go. I figured I could jump and maybe hang on for a podium or get swamped and come away with nothing.

Hosking obviously wanted to win, but made the decision that gave her the best chance of a podium position rather than focusing exclusively on the win. She didn't take the shortest route to the line. She rode tactically given the wind and the brief respite she might get before kicking again. She continued to monitor the situation, and other riders, all the way to the line. She also monitored parallel experiences of time: the gap to van Dijk, her sense of pace and of how long she could hold it given the two hours racing already, and the anticipated time to the finish line.

With Pauline in the middle of the road and Ellen glued to the barriers on the left hand side of the road I put the power to the pedals and steered my bike for Ellen's back wheel. I figured I could run at her wheel and maybe use her as a wind break to close the last few meters. I must have passed her with 200 meters or so to race. Then I just had to keep going.

With my elbows out and head down I just tried to put everything through the pedals. I was looking under my arms to see if any wheels were creeping up behind me but nothing came. The finish line kept getting closer and no one was coming around me, 'this can't be real'.

Then I won La Course by Le Tour de France.

15.7 Learning from the cognitive ecologies of experts

To win a sprint in a bike race requires considerable strength to ride harder and faster than the competition, especially when they are the best in the world. Hosking's report shows that it also involves finely tuned cognitive capacities to mediate between distinct aspects of embodied expertise in the race's crucial final minutes. She drew on a range of anticipatory cues to time the release of energy, to monitor the wind, ground surface, other riders, and her internal state. Then she narrowed down alternate courses of action as the race became (predictably) unpredictable. We see evidence of previous experiences at different timescales informing the decisions she made in high-pressure moments. Hosking's focus was so heavily on how to *tactically* navigate the final two laps of the race that she barely even mentioned controlling her bike on the uneven cobbled surface of the Champs-Élysées, save for putting power through the pedals and steering it toward van Dijk.

Reports like Hosking's are not unusual in cycling. Alongside other sources, athlete-generated accounts help researchers explore and tap into the mechanisms informing embodied expertise. Hosking's description helps us appreciate that it's not simply that some riders are better at computing real-time decisions on when to go hard and when to wait. She lets us in on her ongoing assessment of this situation and these specific competitors (their histories, strengths, and current form), in this specific place (slightly uphill, cobbled road, into a headwind). When the way the race unfolded meant Hosking had no team-mates to lead her out for the sprint as planned, she solved problems on the fly under pressure, making quick choices based on the best chance of finishing well.

In this engaging case study, individual history and embodied experience matter, as the basis of adaptability in the moment. Here we prioritise expert insight into the settings where the relevant skillsets are regularly deployed. As researchers interpreting Hosking's words, we co-construct an account, letting the athlete speak for herself from her integrated world of practice. This serves our multi-disciplinary agenda, as the expert's perspective guides us in exploring the idiosyncratic, context-specific ways that the features of the cognitive ecology of performance operate together. Being open to athletes' communications from within their sporting worlds, to audiences familiar with the subtleties of performance in these contexts, is one effective way among others of understanding the embodied experience of expert performers in real domains of practice, as they deploy richly embedded strategies in full and challenging ecological settings, where multiple stimuli, plans, tasks, and pressures compete for attention. We can learn much about skill and expertise if we work with real experts in the environments to which their expertise is so intelligently attuned.

Acknowledgements

Our collaborators Wayne Christensen, Greg Downey, Andrew Geeves, and Doris McIlwain have strongly influenced our approach: thank you. We're grateful to our colleagues in CEPET, the Macquarie University Centre for Elite Performance, Expertise, and Training; and our colleagues in ASAN, the Australian Skill Acquisition Network. This research is funded by the Australian Research Council's Discovery Project grant DP180100107, 'The Cognitive Ecologies of Collaborative Embodied Skills: a philosophical study'.

References

Abernethy, B., Farrow, D., and Mann, D. L. (2018) "Superior Anticipation," in K. Ericsson, R. Hoffman, A. Kozbelt, and A. Williams (eds.) *The Cambridge Handbook of Expertise and Expert Performance*, 677–95, Cambridge: Cambridge University Press.

Aggerholm, K., Jespersen, E., and Ronglan, L. T. (2011) "Falling for the Feint: An Existential Investigation of a Creative Performance in High-Level Football," *Sport, Ethics and Philosophy* 5: 343–58.

Allen-Collinson, J. (2009) "Sporting Embodiment: Sports Studies and the (Continuing) Promise of Phenomenology," *Qualitative Research in Sport and Exercise* 1: 279–96.

Bicknell, K. (2010) "Feeling Them Ride: Corporeal Exchange in Cross-Country Mountain Bike Racing," *About Performance* 10: 81–91.

—— (2011) "Sport, Entertainment and the Live(d) Experience of Cheering," *Popular Entertainment Studies* 2: 96–111.

—— (2016) "Equipment, Innovation, and the Mountain Biker's Taskscape," in H. Thorpe and R. Olive (eds.) *Women in Action Sport Cultures: Identity, Politics and Experience*, 237–58, London: Palgrave.

Bilalić, M., and Campitelli, G. (2018) "Studies of the Activation and Structural Changes of the Brain Associated with Expertise," in K. Ericsson, R. Hoffman, A. Kozbelt, and A. Williams (eds.) *The Cambridge Handbook of Expertise and Expert Performance*, 233–54, Cambridge: Cambridge University Press.

Cappuccio, M. L. (ed.) (2018) *Handbook of Embodied Cognition and Sport Psychology*, Cambridge, MA: MIT Press.

Chaffin, R., Imreh, G., and Crawford, M. (2002) *Practicing Perfection: Memory and Piano Performance*, Mahwah, NJ: Lawrence Erlbaum Associates.

Chaffin, R., Logan, T. R., and Begosh, K. T. (2009) "Performing from Memory," in S. Hallam, I. Cross, and M. Thaut (eds.) *The Oxford Handbook of Music Psychology*, Oxford: Oxford University Press.

Christensen, W., and Bicknell, K. (2018) "Affordances and the Anticipatory Control of Action," in M. Cappuccio (ed.) *Handbook of Embodied Cognition and Sport Psychology*, 601–21, Cambridge, MA: MIT Press.

Christensen, W., Bicknell, K., McIlwain, D. J. F., and Sutton, J. (2015a) "The Sense of Agency and Its Role in Strategic Control for Expert Mountain Bikers," *Psychology of Consciousness: Theory, Research, and Practice* 2: 340–53.

Christensen, W., Sutton, J., and Bicknell, K. (2019) "Memory Systems and the Control of Skilled Action," *Philosophical Psychology* 32: 693–719.

Christensen, W., Sutton, J., and McIlwain, D. J. F. (2015b) "Putting Pressure on Theories of Choking: Towards an Expanded Perspective on Breakdown in Skilled Performance," *Phenomenology and the Cognitive Sciences* 14: 253–93.

—— (2016) "Cognition in Skilled Action: Meshed Control and the Varieties of Skill Experience," *Mind & Language* 31: 37–66.

Clark, A. (1997) *Being There: Putting Brain, Body, and World Together Again*, Cambridge, MA: MIT Press.

Collins, R. (2015) "Visual Micro-Sociology and the Sociology of Flesh and Blood," *Qualitative Sociology* 38: 13–17.

Downey, G. (2005) *Learning Capoeira: Lessons in Cunning from an Afro-Brazilian Art*, Oxford: Oxford University Press.

—— (2010) "'Practice Without Theory': A Neuroanthropological Perspective on Embodied Learning," *Journal of the Royal Anthropological Institute* 16: S22–S40.

Downey, G., Dalidowicz, M., and Mason, P. H. (2015) "Apprenticeship as Method: Embodied Learning in Ethnographic Practice," *Qualitative Research* 15: 183–200.

Eccles, D. W. (2012) "Verbal Reports of Cognitive Processes," in G. Tenenbaum, R. Eklund, and A. Kamata (eds.) *Measurement in Sport and Exercise Psychology*, Champaign, IL: Human Kinetics.

Ericsson, K. A. (2018) "Capturing Expert Thought with Protocol Analysis: Concurrent Verbalizations of Thinking During Experts' Performance on Representative Tasks," in K. Ericsson, R. Hoffman, A. Kozbelt, and A. Williams (eds.) *The Cambridge Handbook of Expertise and Expert Performance*, 192–212, Cambridge: Cambridge University Press.

Evers, C. (2009) "'The Point': Surfing, Geography and a Sensual Life of Men and Masculinity on the Gold Coast, Australia," *Social & Cultural Geography* 10: 893–908.

Fox, M. C., Ericsson, K. A., and Best, R. (2011) "Do Procedures for Verbal Reporting of Thinking Have to Be Reactive? A Meta-Analysis and Recommendations for Best Reporting Method," *Psychological Bulletin* 137: 316–44.

Geeves, A., McIlwain, D. J. F., and Sutton, J. (2014a) "The Performative Pleasure of Imprecision: A Diachronic Study of Entrainment in Music Performance," *Frontiers in Human Neuroscience* 8: 863.

Geeves, A., McIlwain, D. J. F., Sutton, J., and Christensen, W. (2014b) "To Think or Not to Think: The Apparent Paradox of Expert Skill in Music Performance," *Educational Philosophy and Theory* 46: 674–91.

Gobet, F. (2018) "The Future of Expertise: The Need for a Multidisciplinary Approach," *Journal of Expertise* 1: 1–7.

Goldman, A. (2018) "Expertise," *Topoi* 37: 3–10.

Goodwin, C. (1994) "Professional Vision," *American Anthropologist* 96: 606–33.

Grasseni, C. (2004) "Skilled Vision: An Apprenticeship in Breeding Aesthetics," *Social Anthropology* 12: 41–55.

Høffding, S. (2018) *A Phenomenology of Musical Absorption*, London: Palgrave.

Hosking, C. (2016) "My Le Course by Le Tour," 28 July 2016, http://chloehosking.wordpress.com/2016/07/28/my-la-course-by-le-tour-2/.

Hurley, S. (1998) *Consciousness in Action*, Cambridge, MA: Harvard University Press.

Hutchins, E. (2010) "Cognitive Ecology," *Topics in Cognitive Science* 2: 705–15.

Hutchins, E., Weibel, N., Emmenegger, C., Fouse, A., and Holder, B. (2013) "An Integrative Approach to Understanding Flight Crew Activity," *Journal of Cognitive Engineering and Decision Making* 7: 353–76.

Kimmel, M., and Rogler, C. R. (2018) "Affordances in Interaction: The Case of Aikido," *Ecological Psychology* 30: 195–223.

King, A., and de Rond, M. (2011) "Boat Race: Rhythm and the Possibility of Collective Performance," *British Journal of Sociology* 62: 565–85.

Kirsh, D. (2010) "Thinking with the Body," in S. Ohlsson and R. Catrambone (eds.) *Proceedings of the 32nd Annual Conference of the Cognitive Science Society*, 2864–9, Austin, TX: Cognitive Science Society.

Kretchmar, R. S. (1982) "'Distancing': An Essay on Abstract Thinking in Sport Performances," *Journal of the Philosophy of Sport* 9: 6–18.

Le Guin, E. (2006) *Boccherini's Body: An Essay in Carnal Musicology*, Berkeley and Los Angeles: University of California Press.

Lisboa, T., Demos, A. P., and Chaffin, R. (2018) "Training Thought and Action for Virtuoso Performance," *Musicae Scientiae* 22: 519–38.

Maxwell, I. (2016) "12 Hours Before the Mast," *Performance Research* 21: 58–62.

McIlwain, D. J. F., and Sutton, J. (2014) "Yoga from the Mat Up: How Words Alight on Bodies," *Educational Philosophy and Theory* 46: 655–73.

—— (2015) "Methods for Measuring Breadth and Depth of Knowledge," in J. Baker and D. Farrow (eds.) *Routledge Handbook of Sport Expertise*, 221–31, London: Routledge.

McPherson, S. (2008) "Tactics: Using Knowledge to Enhance Sport Performance," in D. Farrow, J. Baker, and C. MacMahon (eds.) *Developing Sport Expertise*, 155–71, London: Routledge.

McRobert, A. P., Ward, P., Eccles, D. W., and Williams, A. M. (2011) "The Effect of Manipulating Context-Specific Information on Perceptual-Cognitive Processes During a Simulated Anticipation Task," *British Journal of Psychology* 102: 519–34.

Moe, V. F. (2005) "A Philosophical Critique of Classical Cognitivism in Sport: From Information Processing to Bodily Background Knowledge," *Journal of the Philosophy of Sport* 32: 155–83.

Montero, B. (2016) *Thought in Action: Expertise and the Conscious Mind*, Oxford: Oxford University Press.

Muntanyola-Saura, D., and Sánchez-García, R. (2018) "Distributed Attention: A Cognitive Ethnography of Instruction in Sport Settings," *Journal for the Theory of Social Behaviour* 48: 433–54.

Newen, A., de Bruin, L., and Gallagher, S. (eds.) (2018) *The Oxford Handbook of 4E Cognition*, Oxford: Oxford University Press.

Noice, H., Jeffrey, J., Noice, T., and Chaffin, R. (2008) "Memorization by a Jazz Musician: A Case Study," *Psychology of Music* 36: 63–79.

Papineau, D. (2017) *Knowing the Score*, New York: Basic Books.

Pavese, C. (2015) "Practical Senses," *Philosophers' Imprint* 15: 1–25.

Pearlman, K., MacKay, J., and Sutton, J. (2018) "Creative Editing: Svilova and Vertov's Distributed Cognition," *Apparatus: Film, Media, and Digital Cultures in Central and Eastern Europe* 6, http://dx.doi.org/10.17892/app.2018.0006.122.

Ravn, S., and Christensen, M. (2014) "Listening to the Body? How Phenomenological Insights Can Be Used to Explore a Golfer's Experience of the Physicality of Her Body," *Qualitative Research in Sport, Exercise and Health* 6: 462–77.

Ravn, S., and Høffding, S. (2017) "The Promise of 'Sporting Bodies' in Phenomenological Thinking," *Qualitative Research in Sport, Exercise, and Health* 9: 56–68.

Rietveld, E., and Brouwers, A. A. (2017) "Optimal Grip on Affordances in Architectural Design Practices: An Ethnography," *Phenomenology and the Cognitive Sciences* 16: 545–64.

Runswick, O. R., Roca, A., Williams, A. M., McRobert, A. P., and North, J. S. (2018) "The Temporal Integration of Information During Anticipation," *Psychology of Sport and Exercise* 27: 100–8.

Stanley, J. (2011) *Know How*, Oxford: Oxford University Press.

Strava (2016) *0.4 km Ride Segment in Paris, Île-de-France, France on Strava*, accessed 23 October 2018, www.strava.com/segments/15569027?filter=overall&gender=F.

Streeck, J., Goodwin, C., and LeBaron, C. (eds.) (2011) *Embodied Interaction: Language and Body in the Material World*, Cambridge: Cambridge University Press.

Sutton, J. (2007) "Batting, Habit and Memory: The Embodied Mind and the Nature of Skill," *Sport in Society* 10: 763–86.

Sutton, J., McIlwain, D. J. F., Christensen, W., and Geeves, A. (2011) "Applying Intelligence to the Reflexes: Embodied Skills and Habits between Dreyfus and Descartes," *Journal of the British Society for Phenomenology* 42: 78–103.

Sutton, J., and McIlwain, D. J. F. (2015) "Breadth and Depth of Knowledge in Expert Versus Novice Athletes," in J. Baker and D. Farrow (eds.) *Routledge Handbook of Sport Expertise*, 95–105, London: Routledge.

Toner, J., Montero, B., and Moran, A. (2015) "Considering the Role of Cognitive Control in Expert Performance," *Phenomenology and the Cognitive Sciences* 14: 1127–44.

Tribble, E. B. (2017) *Early Modern Actors and Shakespeare's Theatre*, London: Arden.

UCI Women's World Tour (2016) "UCI Women's World Tour / La Course (FRA)," *YouTube*, 25 July 2016, www.youtube.com/watch?v=0IvxxjTGpJ4.

Voxwomen (2016) "La Course Winner Chloe Hosking," *YouTube*, 24 July 2016, www.youtube.com/watch?v=TNuToc8gEo4.

Wacquant, L. (2014) *Body and Soul: Notebooks of an Apprentice Boxer*, Oxford: Oxford University Press.

—— (2015) "For a Sociology of Flesh and Blood," *Qualitative Sociology* 38: 1–11.

Ward, P. R., Ericsson, K. A., and Williams, A. M. (2013) "Complex Perceptual-Cognitive Expertise in a Simulated Task Environment," *Journal of Cognitive Engineering and Decision Making* 7: 231–54.

Waterhouse, E., Watts, R., and Bläsing, B. E. (2014) "Doing *Duo*: A Case Study of Entrainment in William Forsythe's Choreography '*Duo*'," *Frontiers in Human Neuroscience* 8: 1–16.

Wiggle High5 (2016) "Wiggle High5 at La Course," *YouTube*, 25 July 2016, www.youtube.com/watch?v=TOt-FQLN-0g.

Williams, A. M., Davids, K., and Williams, J. G. (1999) *Visual Perception and Action in Sport*, London: Spon.

16

AUTOMATICITY, CONTROL, AND ATTENTION IN SKILL

Wayne Wu

16.1 Introduction

Skill emerges from a shifting balance between automaticity and control over time as a result of learning and practice. Accordingly, explaining the dichotomy between automaticity and control is essential to an adequate characterization of skill. These notions are inextricably intertwined with agency. So, if automaticity and control are to be applied to agentive phenomena, we must understand the phenomena within which the notions get a grip, agency itself. I present a framework that locates *both* automaticity and control in the structure of intentional agency, and suggest how the balance between them changes as agency develops. My analysis pulls together disparate and opposing tendencies in theoretical work on these topics such that the concepts of automaticity and control can be consistently applied to every skilled behavior.

In what follows, I identify two different levels of analysis of these concepts. The first is at a coarse grain that focuses on the structure of action to ground a notion of automaticity and control in terms of a basic executive attitude, an agent's *intention*.[1] This level of analysis is as abstract as the content of the agent's motivational attitude and fixes a causal structure that yields a sharp boundary between automaticity and control. We can think of this as a synchronic, or at least temporally narrow view of agentive control. Then, at a second, finer grained analysis, one sensitive to the diachronic aspects of skill acquisition and performance, I examine the specific features or properties of a concrete action that are identified as controlled or automatic given the content of the agent's intention. At this second level, a "gradualist" aspect of automaticity and control can emerge in two ways: First, in how the membership of the sets of properties identified as automatic or as controlled for a given action changes over time, and second, in the tuning of specific action properties over time. I then use this account to provide a framework for experimental work on overt attention in batting sports and to formulate sharper questions to understand that form of skilled agency.

16.2 The psychology of automaticity and control

There have been extensive discussions of automaticity and control in psychology, and as there are various comprehensive reviews available, I shall highlight a few salient points in the history of this dialogue (Bargh 1994; Logan et al. 1999; Moors 2016). What one finds in this literature is a tug of war between *dichotomous* approaches that sharply distinguish automaticity from control and a contrary pull toward *gradualist* conceptions that take the notions to lie on a continuum or to come in degrees. I shall argue that the two approaches can be unified in a conceptually rigorous way by appealing to the structure and dynamics of human agency. This unification is one reason to endorse the approach to be offered.

In psychology, initial theories endorsed what I call the *Simple Connection*, namely that automaticity and control are incompatible. Theorists began by defining one notion in terms of the absence of the second and the second in terms of a distinct feature such as attention or consciousness. In Schneider and Shiffrin's seminal work (Schneider and Shiffrin 1977; Shiffrin and Schneider 1977), automaticity was defined in terms of the absence of control and control defined as requiring the involvement of top-down attention. LaBerge and Samuels (1974) argued that when reading becomes fluent, this involves the automatization of decoding of language so that attention is no longer required for that purpose and can be redeployed for comprehension.[2]

Other views appealed to distinct features tied to behavior including the speed of processing (efficiency), the involvement of different aspects of consciousness, the lack of task interference, the presence of an intention or goal and so on (Moors and De Houwer 2006). Thus, Posner and Snyder (1975) emphasized three features tied to automaticity: the lack of intention, of consciousness, and of task interference. Bargh (1994) emphasized four features of automatic processes: they are efficient, uncontrolled, unintentional, and unconscious. More recent discussions have identified even more features. Palmeri (2006) lists 13 paired features that characterize automaticity versus controlled process while Schneider and Chein (2003) list no fewer than 17.

The ever-expanding list of individuating features exemplifies the pull away from strict dichotomies and was motivated by empirical evidence against that approach. If a theorist claimed that automatic processes are to be identified by feature F (or some subset of features), then assuming a dichotomous relation to control processes, the presence of F should be necessary and sufficient to pick out an automatic process, or alternatively, its absence should be necessary and sufficient to pick out a controlled process. Yet for any F proposed to individuate (say) automatic processes, experimental work consistently showed that F was found in pretheoretically accepted controlled processes. For example, initially, attention was taken to be necessary and sufficient for controlled processes, and yet it was demonstrated that there are automatic processes that are dependent on attention (e.g., the Stroop effect).

Theorists began looking to other features or to combine features, but no solution was found. Bargh (1992: 183) claimed that all approaches were faced with internal inconsistency in the following sense:

> The problem with the unitary, all-or-none definitions of automaticity and controlled processing is that they have been repeatedly disconfirmed empirically over the past 10 years. The defining features just do not hang together in an all-or-none fashion, but rather seem to be able to co-occur in just about any combination.

Currently, for many theorists, talk of automaticity and control is linked to a set of features which correlate with but do not provide necessary or sufficient conditions for those processes. That is, they moved away from a simple dichotomous conception of automaticity and control to viewing those terms as describing ends of a continuum characterized by a variety of features.

It is possible, however, to incorporate disparate insights regarding automaticity and control as found in much of the past work on the topic. First, the Simple Connection can be maintained by drawing on the philosophically explicated causal structure of intentional action. The analysis identifies sets of features that are either controlled or automatic but never both simultaneously. Thus, a strong division between automaticity and control can be established. Second, these sets of features exhibit relevant gradations across time as an expression of the development of skill during learning, practice, and performance. Recognizing this is fully consistent with dividing automaticity from control. There need be no tug of war. We are all pulling in the same direction.

16.3 The coarse grain: an analysis of automaticity and control

Descriptions of skilled agency advert to automaticity and control. On the one hand, experts in their skilled actions exert an exemplary capacity for control. On the other hand, their expertise is exemplified in pervasive automaticity due to training and practice. Part of the point of this acquired automaticity is to disengage control from certain aspects of behavior so that it is free to exert influence elsewhere. A theory of skilled agency must capture this give and take between automaticity and control within action. Skilled agency is, of course, a form of agency, so we might hypothesize that the basis of automaticity and control as central aspects of skill will be explicated in the structure of human agency. Irrespective of any additional usage in cognitive science, say in the description of subsystems in the agent's brain/mind as involving control and automaticity, an *agentive* construal of automaticity and control is primary. It links discussions of agents in philosophical, empirical, and folk theories of mind.[3]

Accordingly, the primary motivation for a philosophical account of automaticity and control is in making sense of human agency. This means that the account must clarify central claims that invoke the notions. Consider three claims that seem to be jointly inconsistent and yet each of which seems to be true:

1.   Intentional action expresses agentive control: we exert control in acting intentionally.
2.   Human actions involve substantial automaticity.
3.   Simple Connection: If something is controlled, it is not automatic and vice versa.

Proposition 1 is central, and it motivates our approach. In thinking of skilled behavior, agentive control is tied to intentional agency as its fundamental expression. If agents exert any control, it is through their intentional action. That is, if we provide analyses of control that cannot make sense of how intentional agency exemplifies it, then our theories will have missed the central case. Yet when we consider any instance of intentional agency, we find it imbued with automaticity as per Proposition 2. We might walk intentionally to the store or drive there in our car, but many of our movements are automatic: the way we shift our legs, the sequence of joint movements, our speed, the way we flick on the turn signal, and so forth.

The first two propositions express basic truths about human action (see Wu 2013 for an initial discussion), where the notions of control and automaticity are part of a conception of human agency as a subject-level phenomenon. No doubt the notion of *control* has its place in other theories concerned with mechanisms that might explain agency or other behaviors, but *agentive control* as given in Proposition 1 is fundamental from a philosophical conception of actions as what people do. I start here rather than, say, with optimal control theory (Fridland 2017b), because my level of analysis is that of the subject-agent and not the motor control systems that contribute to explaining aspects of her agency. This is where the notion "control" needs to be used with care since it crosses levels of analysis (similar worries apply to "attention" as used in philosophy and cognitive science, see Wu 2014).

The problem arises when we add the Simple Connection which animated psychological approaches to automaticity and control, for now, it looks like an action that is controlled cannot be automatic, so Propositions 1 and 3 seem to imply the negation of Proposition 2. If so, we have an inconsistent triad. The resolution might seem obvious: reject Proposition 3 given the history of work on automaticity and control in psychology. The problem, however, is not the Simple Connection but how it was implemented in psychology, with its focus on specific experimental tasks, rather than the basic structure of intentional action. If it turns out that a way of making the propositions consistent was missed, one that is compatible with the fruits of empirical labor, then we have good reason to endorse the resulting analysis. We will see how to save a simple idea that motivated empirical research on automaticity and control in respect of tasks by merging it with philosophical propositions about action. We render the three propositions consistent. I submit that a sufficient condition of adequacy for a theory of automaticity and control as agentive phenomena is that it shows how the inconsistent triad is in fact consistent, and in a way that does not run roughshod over relevant empirical work, but links it to philosophical concern.

To do this, we reinterpret the Simple Connection to focus on a *feature* of a process as either automatic or controlled but not, at the same time both. This relativization of control and automaticity to action *properties* allows us to render the three claims consistent. That is the motivation for this shift in conceptualization, away from the standard scientific conceptualization of processes themselves as simply automatic or controlled. For if a feature of a process is either controlled or automatic at a time (or stretch of time) but not both at that time (or stretch of time), then when considering an action, we can describe it as controlled and automatic relative to specific features. Processes can be both automatic and controlled, relative to their features. There is then nothing odd about intentional action being controlled and yet also exemplifying much automaticity as per Propositions 1 and 2. Thus, the proposed schema resolves the seeming paradox we have noted.

With this in place, we define automaticity in terms of the absence of control, as per the Simple Connection, and then control in terms of some individuating feature. At this point, the first proposition indicates how we should analyze control since the relevant form of control is exemplified in intentional action. Specifically, we find control in the structure of intentional action, and the salient aspect of that structure is the role of the agent's intention in action. Although one can say more about the details of that structure, it suffices for our present purposes simply to recognize the executive role of intention which allows us to pin control to it (for more detailed unpacking of the structure of intentional action, see Wu (2016)). To find control in action is to understand it in the influence of an agent's intention.

An intention represents a type of action to be done, say when one intends to F, and when the intention performs its functional role, it generates an action that is an F. Thus, when one intends to pick up that mug to drink from, then the intention generates an action which is a picking up of that mug. We can treat the action kind intended, namely F, to specify a set of properties such that if the resulting action has those properties, then the intention is satisfied in that the resulting action is intentional under the relevant description (Anscombe 1957). We can then say that a property F of an action A is controlled relative to an intention if and only if the intention's representing an F-action as to be done brings about the action A's having F.[4] Otherwise, the property is automatic. Simply put, an action is controlled relative to F iff its having F is a result of the agent's doing F given an intention to do so (doing F is part of the content of the intention). Not surprisingly, the bulk of the properties of an action are automatic in the *technical* sense just specified.

This leads to the following analyses:

S's doing an action A with property F is agentively controlled with respect to F iff A's having F is the result of S's intention to A in an F way.

An action instance A with property F is automatic with respect to F iff A's having F is not agentively controlled [i.e. the revamped Simple Connection].

An action instance A is passive (fully automatic) iff for all properties F of A, F is automatic.

An action instance A is fully controlled iff for all properties F of A, F is controlled.

Clearly, only an omniscient being could fully control A, this requiring that the agent has cognized *every* feature of action in a corresponding intention and brings about those features because they are intended. Only God could do that. In contrast, there are instances of (defective) human action that are plausibly passive, say passivity phenomena in schizophrenia (Cho and Wu 2013).

Ellen Fridland (2017a) asks why we should emphasize intention in the analysis rather than some other feature such as consciousness or dual task interference. I hope the answer is now clear: control must be rooted in our conception of the structure of human agency as a subject-level phenomenon. Intentional action is at the core of that conception. So, I take Proposition 1 to be a conceptual truth that provides the motivation for starting with intention in understanding agent-level control. Further, the specific analysis is motivated precisely because it resolves the paradox generated by the three putative truths that we noted earlier. We have maintained the Simple Connection and shown it to be consistent with two truths about human agency.

That said, it is important to note that the analysis I have provided, though focused on the subject level, identifies a basic schema for discussion of control in other domains such as empirical discussions of *systems* within the mind or brain (e.g., top-down modulation of attention, see Wu (2017)). It is, then, of general use to cognitive science. In the case of intention, we envisioned a structure where intentions represent an action to be done and then influence the agentive capacities whose expression yields the action. Thus, there is a general *control structure*, a representation of some feature such that this representation generates a process with that feature. I have focused on intentions as the relevant action representations as first in the order of philosophical analysis, but the structure can be iterated for any representation that plays a causal role in influencing behavior in light of that representation's content.

Assume that we are interested in a hierarchically organized system where a top-level T plays a role in modulating the activity of a bottom-level B. We can then speak of B-type processes as controlled relative to some feature F if T plays the appropriate role in bringing about F, namely by representing the B-process to be produced as having F.[5] For example, if one wished to speak of goals as mental states that represent ends which are to be reached by implementing specific intentions, then to the extent that the goals play a role in shaping behavior so that, when successful, the resulting behavior satisfies the goal, we can speak of *teleological* control, namely control by the goal. Thus, we can say that an action instance A with property F is *teleologically* controlled with respect to F iff A's having F is the result of a goal to achieve F.

Consider also the case where a subject knows that a certain undesirable outcome will obtain in doing something intentionally. Thus, one wants to achieve some action X but recognizes that the undesirable outcome Y will also obtain. Thus, one might be said to intentionally bring about X and Y. Still, talk of intention doesn't quite separate two different aspects of the control structure.

The primary form of control is agentive control that is tied to an intention to X. Still, as we saw for goals, knowledge and other higher order states might play a role so that we can use them to render salient in our descriptions of an action certain of its features. If we wish to highlight known but undesirable outcomes, then we could in principle speak of *knowledgeable control*: an action instance A with property F is *knowledgeably* controlled with respect to F iff A intends to do A knowing that F will result. In this case, it need not be true that one's knowledge brings about A's having F in the way that an intention might have brought F about. Nevertheless, knowledgeable control makes F salient in the sense that the agent is aware of it, and this can engage with concerns about responsibility and blame. In any event, different notions of control draw on the basic schema I have provided, namely relating higher level representations to action *features*. The usefulness of these further distinctions will rely partly on their highlighting different forms of top-down influences on action that are theoretically salient.[6]

There can be as many different notions of control as there are hierarchical structures in the generation of a process, these structures exemplifying an interaction between representations and the processes they influence. This proliferation need not be problematic so long as we are *clear* which structure we are interested in, say the influence of memory, desires or emotions on action or in the generation of processes at lower levels of analysis. What matters will then be fixed by our theoretical concerns. Yet what fixes the idea of control is the schema revealed in reflecting on intentional control of action, that structure which is first in the order of explanation if we are interested in human agency, a subject-level phenomenon. Correspondingly, any talk of automaticity will, given the Simple Connection, also need to be relativized to the control structure with which it is contrasted. For most philosophical purposes, and related empirical approaches, intentional control will be primary.

16.4 The fine grain: gradations in automaticity and control

As I noted earlier, there were severe pressures on attempts in psychology to draw a sharp division between automaticity and control, and these led to a more gradualist approach, or at least to the emphasis of correlated features, many of which are graded (e.g., response measures such as reaction time, speed, or efficiency). It is an advantage of the current approach that it allows one to draw a sharp distinction between automaticity and control and also to take on board the gradualism that has saturated current theoretical discussions. This section shows two ways that a gradual approach is consistent with drawing a sharp dichotomy.

As I have implemented the Simple Connection, control and automaticity are fixed relative to a set of features of a given action in light of a background intention that generates that action. So, let the features of action represented by an intention be captured in the set $\{F, G, H, \ldots\}$ and the features of action not represented be the set $\{X, Y, Z \ldots\}$. We can say, if we wish, that automaticity always swamps control in that the number of controlled properties will be limited by what the agent can represent in an intention, something not true of automatic properties.[7] That is a clear type of capacity limitation, rooted in representational capacity limits of a finite mind. Accordingly, at any point in time in the performance of an action kind, there will be a balance between control and automaticity tied to the agent's representational capacity. This is a synchronic perspective on how automaticity and control are "graded."

If we take a diachronic view of behavior, given that we are interested in the development of a skill, then we can see a shift over time in the membership of the set of controlled properties. This dynamic is simply a function of how intentions change over time. A basic intuition is that initially when first carrying out an action, many basic facets of the behavior must be explicitly kept in mind as part of what we intend to do. As skill increases, what we must keep in mind moves to higher level properties (or indeed, given specific situations, to fine-grained lower level properties). This shift in intention thereby changes which features of the action are controlled and which are automatic. Thus, as one is first learning a piece on an instrument, one might be explicit in one's intention of certain basic movements, say a tough fingering in a tricky passage, but as one practices, the need to think of the sequence of movement disappears. When one reaches that passage, one just plays the notes. Consequently, one can now think about how to play that sequence of notes, say at what speed, intensity, and so forth. Thus, the first diachronic gradation in automaticity and control will lie precisely in this push and pull of the members of the set of relevant properties over time.[8]

Second, we can see gradations within automatic and controlled properties. Of most interest are the properties that have been traditionally correlated with automaticity. On these, Logan (1985: 373) notes that "each of the properties of automaticity change more or less continuously as a function of practice." We can understand his reference to properties of automaticity as meaning those properties that traditionally are associated with automaticity: speed, diminishing of dual task interference, load effects (e.g., attention understood as a limited resource). Note that the Simple Connection does not see any of these as individuating automatic processes, nor would most empirical theorists of automaticity. Rather, these are features of an action that can become, or are, automatic in the technical sense defined, but also are features that change their profile over time. For this reason, we can take on board the empirical results concerning automaticity and affirm the Simple Connection as explicated earlier.

To take an example, the speed of response is not always something we intend. When learning to play a difficult passage, the goal is not to play the passage quickly (at least initially), but to play it correctly. But as one focuses on ordering one's fingers in the correct way, as defined by the music score, it also happens that one's playing of the passage increases in speed. At some point, the playing of the passage becomes automatic in that our intentions are not so fine-grained as to be concerned with representing the exact sequence of finger movements. At the same time, that exact sequence of finger movements becomes faster in execution over time. So, we have two transitions: the automatization of the finger movements in that the intention no longer is fine-grained in representing them and the changes in the quality of this specific automatic feature of the action, one's fingers moving in that way, which increases in speed over time with practice. The same can be true of many features that cognitive scientists have associated with automaticity. We can speak of this change in specific properties that reflects practice and training as a type of *tuning* which does not define the action as automatic or controlled, but reflects the ongoing dynamics of automaticity and control.

As theorists (and indeed, as teachers or coaches), which properties we choose to focus on will depend on our interests, but no matter what the given theoretical context renders salient in respect of automaticity and control, the analysis of this section shows how we can maintain a sharp boundary between automaticity and control while also allowing for talk of gradation. This is the first way that we can accommodate both the original insight of the Simple Connection and later empirical concerns with gradualism in automaticity and control, one that respects a philosophical theory of action.

16.5 Skill as such

Assessments of skill are relational: we pinpoint skilled behavior by contrasting it with some relevant contrast class. The contrast class I shall focus on is that generated by looking at the agent's history, following the agent's *developmental* trajectory in learning an action and examining how the action changes in profile over time. The first dimension focuses on how the agent conceptualizes the target action in the initial intention, as she first learns the skill, and how this conceptualization, which fixes the initial controlled features of the action, changes over time, and consequently, how the features that are identified as controlled or automatic change over time. Again, an intuitive shift is from the initial explicit representation in one's intention of low-level features of the action (e.g., in learning a musical piece, representation of finger movements and sequences) to an intention that no longer needs to represent these features, but shifts to higher level features (e.g., in representing the intensity or speed at which the piece should be played, and perhaps later, in representing higher level aesthetic properties of the performance). The shift in the content of the intention then fixes, at the relevant points, the sets of properties that count as automatic and as controlled.

Drawing on this intuitive starting point, when we look at the skilled agent, we consider the way she conceives of her action, especially in higher level features that are made available precisely because many lower level features have become automated, freeing up conceptual space. Thus, automatization opens up other avenues for control and the possibilities of control not only are indicative of her expertise, but also differentiate her from other highly skilled agents. For example, in music, we reflect not just on her technique, which reflects the automatization and tuning of basic skills, but on the subject's artistic choices in how the piece is played. In speaking of performance as cerebral, spontaneous, inspired, programmed, etc., we can map these intuitive notions on the action. We need only understand the structure of acquired skilled agency in respect of automaticity and control, synchronically and diachronically.

Concomitant with these global changes in automaticity and control, the action properties made salient to the theorist in the automaticity-control context also change their character over time. This is clearest for automatic properties. Thus, we can see changes along a continuum in terms of measured features such as reaction time, load effects, interference effects, and so on. One measure of the subject's increased efficiency is a change over time as we compare performance now to past performance. Thus, even if the agent does not intend to be able to play a passage faster and faster, over time, this sharpening of motor capacities might happen automatically (as we normally say). This would constitute a change in her skill, but not one brought about intentionally even if brought about by intentional practice.

This leads to a schema where we assess the skill of an agent *diachronically* to the agent's past performance, if we are interested in the agent's learning, or *synchronically* relative to the performance of others if we are interested in an *intersubjective* assessment of skill level. This assessment then draws on two levels of analysis:

1. The shift in properties in the set of controlled and of automatic features.
2. The shift in the character of those properties, typically as measured in performance.

How we assess skill will be contingent on the properties that we think salient to the skill in question.

16.6 Skill in attention

The theoretical should engage the practical. A theoretical apparatus used in characterizing skilled behavior should engage with understanding actual expert behavior. We are only at the beginning of merging these perspectives, and there are substantial challenges. I shall illustrate this by examining overt visual attention in cricket batters, and recent experimental work probing such attention. Regarding attention, I work with a notion central to the science of attention which yields a basic *guidance condition*: if a subject selects X to inform their performance of a task T, then the subject thereby attends to X (Wu 2014). The hypothesis is that as batters become more skilled, their visual attention to the ball will change character, a shift from control to more automatic and tuned attention. Unfortunately, the experimental results are noisy. There is much to be done including systematization of results under a theory of batting action as well as probing skilled batting in more natural contexts.

A coaching adage regarding attention in batting is to "keep your eye on the ball." It might seem difficult to do so with projectiles at high speed such as a ball delivered by a fast bowler in cricket, a fastball in baseball, or a first serve in tennis. In cricket, ball speeds can range from 17–25 m/s (slow to medium bowlers) to up to 44 m/s (fast bowlers). When facing a fast bowler, the time from ball release to its reaching the interception point with the bat can be shorter than the time required to execute a batting movement, so batting expertise involves gathering prelease information to aid *prediction* of the flight of the ball. Again, we have a demand for appropriate attention: what aspects of the bowler's delivery provide information relevant to increasing performance and can the batter efficiently select that information to guide behavior? How does one learn this? There is positive correlation between the number of structured hours spent in batting practice and the level of expertise (Weissensteiner et al. 2008; Ford et al. 2010).

Still, uniformity in the data is somewhat elusive. An initial notable study by Land and McLeod (2000) identified a consistent pattern of eye movement across three cricket batters of different skill levels. Balls were delivered by a bowling machine at 25 m/s. All three batters initially tracked the flight of the ball at its release but then made a *predictive* saccade to the bounce point of the ball. Land and McLeod observed that the more skilled batters made *earlier* saccades. One hypothesis is that with more skill, batters are better at extracting information. Croft et al. (2010) worked with sub-elite to elite batters below the age of 19 in New Zealand at slow to medium ball speeds (17–25 m/s). They observed a variety of eye movements. Some batters were able to maintain fixation on the ball throughout the duration of the flight; some tracked the ball initially, broke off foveation, and then caught up with the ball to maintain fixation; some only tracked the ball near the end of the flight while some did not track the ball by fixation but kept the ball in a parafoveal region. Clearly, the data is noisy. Mann et al. (2013) studied the batting of two elite batters ("two of the most accomplished cricket batters to have played the game") with a machine delivering balls at speeds of 33 m/s, faster than the previous two studies. Strikingly, these batters were able to keep the ball at a constant egocentric position relative to the head and they were consistently able to direct their gaze at the contact point between bat and ball:

> the elite batters appeared to do whatever was necessary to ensure that their gaze was directed towards the location of bat-ball contact: usually they made two predictive saccades, but even when they produced only one, they shifted gaze to the anticipated location of bat-ball contact rather than to ball-bounce.
>
> *Mann et al. 2013: 8*

One challenge to all of these studies is the low number of subjects as well as non-natural conditions since balls were delivered straight at consistent speeds making prediction easier. Sarpeshkar et al. (2017) attempted to reproduce earlier results as well as introduce more uncertainty in ball trajectory by mixing curved with straight deliveries and contrasting elite with competent batters. They were unable to replicate some earlier observations: They did not observe earlier saccades in any of their subjects, even in the condition where balls were consistently delivered straight at about 33 m/s, one of the central findings in the Land and McLeod (2000) study. They did replicate the finding that elite batters initiate more saccades toward bat-ball contact and orient their gaze in the direction of the ball at the moment of contact. Club batters' gaze was more likely to lag relative to elite batters, perhaps the result of less efficient prediction. What is clear is that there are different patterns of attention within each paradigm in relation to the ball and to bodily movements. In several of the studies, expert behavior differs from less skilled behaviors in respect of attention-based tracking of the ball. For example, the Land and McLeod study demonstrates that under conditions of fairly high predictability at low to medium ball speeds, expert ability correlates with predictive saccades. The results of Mann et al. need not contradict this, since they used faster ball speeds, but their concern about ecological validity is well taken.

How does one learn to be an expert? How does effective training in batting make salient aspects of the information available to the batter? Given our discussion about automaticity and control, we can formulate a set of experimental questions that can be generalized to other skilled behaviors and which draws on the definition of automaticity and control I have given:

1.   What visual information is necessary to bat effectively?
2.   What is the pattern of attention in a novice?
3.   What instructions help the novice to shift attention so as to acquire more skill?
4.   What are the patterns of attention at different skill levels and how are instructions tailored to tune attention?
5.   How do the intentions shift over periods of training, and thus what features become automatized over time?
6.   How are the automatic and controlled features tuned over time?

The framework presented provides a uniform structure to apply to any skilled activity, helping us formulate sharper questions. One goal of philosophers in this area should be to work with the experimentalist in constructing hypotheses and theories, a merging of the theoretical with the practical. In doing so, a harmonious philosophical and empirical picture of skill at a time and over time will emerge.[9]

Notes

1 Or more broadly, states that motivate actions by representing the action kind in question as to be done, say a belief-desire pair.
2 This issue is complicated by evolving conceptions of attention at that time, from Broadbent's (1958) "single channel" view, where attention acted as a filter, to a shift to a conception of attention as a limited resource or capacity. I set aside these complications here.
3 See also the recent literature on know-how for related discussion (Hawley 2003; Pavese 2015a, 2017, 2018). I hope to engage this link more fully elsewhere.
4 For an echo of this idea in the empirical literature, see Moors (2016) who writes of control: "*A* has control over *X* when *A* has a goal about *X* and the goal causes fulfillment of the goal" (265). Carlotta Pavese reminds me that this presumes that the causal links are not deviant. On how to deal with causal deviance in action by appeal to attention, see Wu (2016).
5 This concurs with Moors and De Houwer (2006) when they claim that intentional actions are a subset of controlled behaviors.
6 The issues regarding knowledgeable control will intersect intellectual positions regarding know how. These are important matters to take up elsewhere. See, among others, Stanley and Williamson 2001; Stanley and Krakauer 2013; Pavese 2015b, 2017, 2018, 2019.
7 In principle, the set of automatic properties is an infinite set while the set of controlled properties is, given our finite minds, finite. Our explanatory interest restricts the set of automatic properties that we dissect experimentally or theoretically.
8 Ellen Fridland suggests to me that skilled action involves *more* control. I think that skilled action involves a *different kind* or *pattern* of control (vs unskilled action). Training changes the nature of one's control.

Novices exert control of a certain kind, focused on some features that become automatized. That said, if one wanted to quantify control, the theory offered does provide a way to do so.

9 I am grateful to the editors for their encouraging and helpful comments.

References

Anscombe, G. E. M. (1957) *Intention*, Oxford: Blackwell Publishers.

Bargh, J. A. (1994) "The Four Horsemen of Automaticity: Awareness, Intention, Efficiency, and Control in Social Cognition," *Handbook of Social Cognition: Basic Processes* 1: 1–40.

—— (1992) "The Ecology of Automaticity: Toward Establishing the Conditions Needed to Produce Automatic Processing Effects," *The American Journal of Psychology* 105: 181–99, https://doi.org/10.2307/1423027.

Broadbent, D. E. (1958) *Perception and Communication*, New York: Pergamon Press.

Cho, R., and Wu, W. (2013) "Mechanisms of Auditory Verbal Hallucination in Schizophrenia," *Schizophrenia* 4: 155, https://doi.org/10.3389/fpsyt.2013.00155.

Croft, J. L., Button, C., and Dicks M. (2010) "Visual Strategies of Sub-Elite Cricket Batsmen in Response to Different Ball Velocities," *Human Movement Science*, Human Movement across the Lifespan: Learning, Synergies and Disease 29: 751–63, https://doi.org/10.1016/j.humov.2009.10.004.

Ford, P. R., Low, J., McRobert, A. P., and Williams, A. M. (2010) "Developmental Activities That Contribute to High or Low Performance by Elite Cricket Batters When Recognizing Type of Delivery From Bowlers' Advanced Postural Cues," *Journal of Sport and Exercise Psychology* 32: 638–54, https://doi.org/10.1123/jsep.32.5.638.

Fridland, E. (2017a) "Automatically Minded," *Synthese* 194: 4337–63.

—— (2017b) "Skill and Motor Control: Intelligence All the Way Down," *Philosophical Studies* 174: 1539–60, https://doi.org/10.1007/s11098-016-0771-7.

Hawley, K. (2003) "Success and Knowledge-How," *American Philosophical Quarterly* 40: 19–31.

LaBerge, D., and Samuels, S. J. (1974) "Toward a Theory of Automatic Information Processing in Reading," *Cognitive Psychology* 6: 293–323, https://doi.org/10.1016/0010-0285(74)90015-2.

Land, M. F., and McLeod, P. (2000) "From Eye Movements to Actions: How Batsmen Hit the Ball," *Nature Neuroscience* 3: 1340–45, https://doi.org/10.1038/81887.

Logan, G. D. (1985) "Skill and Automaticity: Relations, Implications, and Future Directions," *Canadian Journal of Psychology/Revue Canadienne de Psychologie* 39: 367–86.

Logan, G. D., Taylor, S. E., and Etherton, J. L. (1999) "Attention and Automaticity: Toward a Theoretical Integration," *Psychological Research* 62: 165–81, www.springerlink.com/index/TP8LNL6QPQHJCY01.pdf.

Mann, D. L., Spratford, W., and Abernethy, B. (2013) "The Head Tracks and Gaze Predicts: How the World's Best Batters Hit a Ball," *PloS One* 8: e58289, https://doi.org/10.1371/journal.pone.0058289.

Moors, A. (2016) "Automaticity: Componential, Causal, and Mechanistic Explanations," *Annual Review of Psychology* 67: 263–87, https://doi.org/10.1146/annurev-psych-122414-033550.

Moors, A., and De Houwer, J. (2006) "Automaticity: A Theoretical and Conceptual Analysis," *Psychological Bulletin* 132: 297–326, https://doi.org/10.1037/0033-2909.132.2.297.

Palmeri, T. J. (2006) "Automaticity," in L. Nadel (ed.) *Encyclopedia of Cognitive Science*, 290–301, New York: John Wiley & Sons.

Pavese, C. (2015a) "Knowing a Rule," *Philosophical Issues* 25: 165–88.

—— (2015b) "Practical Senses," *Philosophers' Imprint* 15: 1–25.

—— (2017) "Know-How and Gradability," *Philosophical Review* 126: 345–83.

—— (2018) "Know-How, Action, and Luck," *Synthese*: 1–23.

—— (2019) "The Psychological Reality of Practical Representation," *Philosophical Psychology* 32: 784–821.

Posner, M. I., and Snyder, C. R. R. (1975) "Attention and Cognitive Control," in Robert L. Solso (ed.) *Information Processing and Cognition: The Loyola Symposium*, 55–85, Hillsdale, NJ: Erlbaum.

Sarpeshkar, V., Abernethy, B., and Mann, D. L. (2017) "Visual Strategies Underpinning the Development of Visual–Motor Expertise When Hitting a Ball," *Journal of Experimental Psychology: Human Perception and Performance* 43: 1744–72, https://doi.org/10.1037/xhp0000465.

Schneider, W., and Chein, J. M. (2003) "Controlled & Automatic Processing: Behavior, Theory, and Biological Mechanisms," *Cognitive Science: A Multidisciplinary Journal* 27: 525–59, https://doi.org/10.1207/s15516709cog2703_8.

Schneider, W., and Shiffrin, R. M. (1977) "Controlled and Automatic Human Information Processing: I. Detection, Search and Attention," *Psychological Review* 84: 1–66.

Shiffrin, R. M., and Schneider, W. (1977) "Controlled and Automatic Human Information Processing: II. Perceptual Learning, Automatic Attending and a General Theory," *Psychological Review* 84: 127–90, http://eric.ed.gov/ERICWebPortal/recordDetail?accno=EJ161631.

Stanley, J., and Krakauer, J. W. (2013) "Motor Skill Depends on Knowledge of Facts," *Frontiers in Human Neuroscience* 7: 503, https://doi.org/10.3389/fnhum.2013.00503.

Stanley, J., and Williamson, T. (2001) "Know How," *Journal of Philosophy* 98: 411–44.

Weissensteiner, J., Abernethy, B., Farrow, D., and Müller, S. (2008) "The Development of Anticipation: A Cross-Sectional Examination of the Practice Experiences Contributing to Skill in Cricket Batting," *Journal of Sport and Exercise Psychology* 30: 663–84, https://doi.org/10.1123/jsep.30.6.663.

Wu, W. (2013) "Mental Action and the Threat of Automaticity," in A. Clark, J. Kiverstein, and T. Vierkant (eds.) *Decomposing the Will*, 244–61, Oxford: Oxford University Press.

—— (2014) *Attention*, Abingdon, UK: Routledge.

—— (2016) "Experts and Deviants: The Story of Agentive Control," *Philosophy and Phenomenological Research* 92: 101–26.

—— (2017) "Shaking up the Mind's Ground Floor: The Cognitive Penetration of Visual Attention," *Journal of Philosophy* 114: 5–32.

17
AUTOMATIZING KNOWLEDGE
Confusion over what cognitive neuroscience tells us about intellectualism

John W. Krakauer

17.1 Introduction

In 2013, Stanley and Krakauer (S&K) made the intellectualist case for knowledge-how by arguing that practical knowledge is in part propositional, using the example of motor skill. They suggested that findings from cognitive neuroscience have been misinterpreted as evidence for the anti-intellectualist position; that practical knowledge is different from theoretical knowledge and is non-propositional, when in fact experimental findings support the opposite (Stanley and Krakauer 2013). Stanley and Williamson (2001) have also made a parallel intellectualist case for practical knowledge via a theory of semantics, which will not be addressed here, other than to note that some commentators have argued that the semantic argument contaminated and was used to bolster our purportedly independent evaluation of the neuroscientific evidence (Springle 2019; Schwartz and Drayson 2019). Here I will take the opportunity to further elaborate our argument and to address this criticism and some of the others that have appeared since S&K was published.

17.2 Amnesia and automatization

S&K discussed the case of patient HM and other amnestic patients in significant detail based on the widespread assumption that the scientific evidence for a dissociation between procedural and declarative memory provides empirical support for the anti-intellectualist position, which considers there to be a fundamental difference between knowing-*how* and knowing-*that* (Ryle 1949; Dreyfus and Dreyfus 1984; Wallis 2008; Devitt 2011). HM was a patient who underwent bilateral medial temporal lobectomy in an attempt to control his intractable epilepsy. The unforeseen consequence of the surgery was that he was left with life-long profound anterograde amnesia; he forgot events or facts within minutes of their occurrence or exposure to them. In a seminal experiment, it was shown that HM was nevertheless able to learn, improve and retain a mirror-drawing ability across three days even though he had no recollection or even familiarity with the task when re-encountering it on days two and three (Milner 1962). This genuinely profound result has been taken as strong evidence that a motor skill can be learned solely procedurally without the need for a declarative component. More importantly, for our purposes it was taken as evidence that learning to mirror draw, like learning to ride a bike or play the piano, is non-propositional practical knowledge (know-how) that can survive loss of the ability to learn new propositional knowledge.

S&K pointed out that HM needed instruction, i.e., propositional knowledge, each day in order to begin to mirror draw. In other words, picking up the pencil, looking in the mirror and beginning to draw the perimeter of the star required instruction, even though the improved ability that subsequently ensued did not. This led S&K to suggest that all motor (know-how) skills, such as piano playing and bike riding, are likely to require a similar combination of the propositional and the non-propositional. They then went on to discuss a paper written by psychologists Shumita Roy and Norman Park (Roy and Park 2010), in which they describe experiments done on amnestic patients that required them to learn how to use complex novel tools. The key finding was that the patients were never able to learn to use the tool properly over consecutive days; a result in direct contrast with mirror drawing. S&K concluded that the total skill of using a new tool could not be learned by these amnestic patients because propositional knowledge about its parts was needed to bring their hands into the correct position in order to express their non-propositional ability to use the tool faster and more accurately. Interestingly, all sorts of explanatory contortions have ensued to explain this clear fact away. One is to say that this is just a semantic issue, Felipe De Brigard in a recent article (De Brigard 2019: 748) states:

> After all, both Milner and Corkin repeatedly acknowledged that HM needed to be reminded of the nature of the task immediately prior to testing, which clearly indicates that they did not consider this explicit, task-related information to be constitutive of the performance they were trying to measure.

This is like saying that walking over to a bike, sitting on it and adjusting the gears properly does not count as part of knowing how to ride a bike. This is critical because the examples of practical tasks dating back to Ryle are precisely about real-world skills like riding a bike; thus contrived attempts to peel away the non-practical bits play right into S&K's hands because they a clear admission that the practical task *in toto* is indeed made up of two components. In a sense, the intellectualists and anti-intellectualists are both wrong as there are propositional and non-propositional components in motor skills.

The undeniable fact is that as soon as the number of propositional components of a "know-how" practical task increases beyond a certain level then patients like HM are rendered utterly incapable. For example, a patient might indeed get better with practice at hitting a billiard ball with a cue, but not be able to express this in a game because they can't remember what the ball colors mean or what the rules are. We shall unpack this point below. It should also be said that the distinction between propositional and non-propositional components of a practical task is not affected in any way by evidence showing that patients such as HM are not as pure when it comes to the declarative/procedural divide as was initially thought (De Brigard 2019). All that needs to be shown is *relative* experimental dissociation of these two components in either patients or healthy subjects when performing a practical task. In this way, experiments remain of great value in the intellectualist/anti-intellectualist debate as long as they are conducted and interpreted carefully.

Another argument against S&K's two-component argument for practical skills is to say that in the experiments described the purported propositional component is not long-term knowledge but just fleeting short-term or working memory. For example, in an article by Arieh Schwartz and Zoe Drayson (2019: 677), it is stated that it's not clear that the ephemeral nature of the information in short-term memory qualifies it to count as knowledge, where the latter is generally assumed to be a stable and longlasting state…there is a clear difference between the sort of knowledge that amnesia subjects receive in the form of external instruction and the ever-accumulating repertoire of knowledge that enables someone to manifest skilled behavior.

Similarly, in an article discussing a result in the complex tool study alluded to above, in which a patient was able to use a tool when the receptacle was placed in the right position but when distracted and the receptacle put in the wrong position, he was again unable to use it, Felipe De Brigard concludes that he was just using working memory rather than knowledge (De Brigard 2019). The authors of these two articles are mistaken. In the first case, the authors state that the evidence works against S&K because the very fact that amnestic patients *can* learn motor skills but do not have declarative memory lends the lie to the S&K position. It is an odd objection because they seem to agree with S&K when they talk about the need for an accumulation of knowledge but then say the neuroscience says that this is not necessary; they should have instead questioned the lab-based tasks that have been assumed to capture skill learning. Had they done so they would see that their argument is untenable. I, along with my colleagues, have shown how the mirror-drawing task is anomalous as a motor learning task precisely *because* it can be learned without needing long-term storage of knowledge. In recent experiments, we have shown how this can happen through incremental automatization of *within*-day knowledge (Huberdeau et al. 2019). In this way, what is *known* on day 1; that there is a mirror inversion and that a strategy can be used, is forgotten but not before the strategy for mirror drawing has been automatized. It is the automatization of the knowledge held in short-term memory on each day that is carried across days. Schwartz and Drayson's claim that when HM was told there was a mirror inversion, this was not knowledge for the 10–20 minutes that he knew it before forgetting it is simply wrong. As we state in our recent experimental paper on this issue (Huberdeau et al. 2019: 1057):

> Thus, individuals with amnesia could have been able to gradually learn new skills by caching fragments of deliberate behavior within each session of practice. Iterating this fragmentary process could ultimately allow a new, cached association mediating a newly learned skill to be gradually acquired and retained across sessions, even though the skill initially depended on deliberate processes.

It should be apparent here that one must not confuse the process of deliberating itself with forgetting that one has deliberated. So, in the case of HM, he received instruction each day and deliberated as to how one should move one's hand under a mirror transformation and how to respond to errors. What happened is he forgot that he deliberated, but not before some of the things he did got cached. The critical point here is that practical tasks need deliberation; one must possess belief and knowledge about how to perform the task – in this case it is propositional knowledge about what a mirror does to visual feedback and how to counter it. That the memory of such deliberation is lost is important, but it certainly does not mean it did not happen. Indeed, the crucial aspect of our recent experiment cited above is that we demonstrated that the memory across days in a practical task is, in fact, attributable to the initially deliberative component. An intuitive way to understand this experiment is to again think about how you learn a six-figure PIN – at first of course you *know* it but then with practice your finger learns it and you can in fact forget it. This indeed led to difficulties for me when I went overseas to countries where the keyboard configuration at ATMs was different. My cached finger policy no longer worked but I no longer knew my number. I would have to look up a picture of an American ATM keypad – imagine typing and get my number back. This is a very vivid demonstration of caching knowledge; a propositional representation has become non-propositional. Another example of this change in representation is learning multiplication – one can at first actually compute $4 \times 8 = 32$ but soon it becomes memorized in a look-up table. Mirror drawing and other simple lab-based motor learning tasks are also just like this and can be solved by patients like HM because the propositional component can become procedural before it is forgotten.

The crucial point for the S&K argument arises when the knowledge component of a practical task gets to be so large that it cannot be cached within the time-frame of short-term memory. This is how to think about the complex tool task by Roy and Park. In this case, the patients failed because you can't learn all that is needed to be known fast enough to usefully automatize it, even in pieces, and so without the ability to carry that deliberative knowledge over to subsequent days and weeks in long-term memory one is forever starting again. Felipe De Brigard's comment that the only way the patient can use the novel tool is through affordance but then quickly forgets it, simply confirms the fact that without long-term memory the patients can't learn the novel tools across days. As practical tasks become more complex along the spectrum from mirror drawing to the Roy and Park tools to tennis and bike riding the need for long-term memory just rises exponentially. Indeed, once one gets to real-world practical tasks, which were the very ones used by Ryle and others as examples, they no longer map onto practical and theoretical knowledge in a useful way. As I state in a recent article titled "The Intelligent Reflex" (Krakauer 2019: 828):

> [A]ll tasks that require weeks, months, and years of practice are like this, whether they be tennis, chess, or French. They will always have deliberative and automatic pieces that are hierarchically assembled in task space and in the neuroaxis … The longstanding intellectualist/anti-intellectualist debate originated before there was scientific evidence showing that almost any deliberative propositional content can be automatized.

17.3 Intelligent control policies

The philosopher Ellen Fridland objected to the S&K framework for a different reason, namely that the non-propositional component, what we called motor acuity, was unintelligent. She states: "In short, for S&K, skill combines intelligent guidance by propositional knowledge with the noncognitive, basic, subpersonal, low-level motor and perceptual abilities. The propositional bit of skill is knowledge involving while the motor acuity bit is not" (Fridland 2016: 1542–3). Now I can see how Fridland could have gotten this impression from the S&K article. This is because we barely discussed the topics of automatization and control policies. Instead, we discussed explicit propositional knowledge and motor acuity – in a sense the two book-ends of a practical or a motor skill. That said, at the end of the S&K article, we do state that skills are composite states, requiring both increasing knowledge of required actions, and practice-related improvement in the *selection* and acuity of these actions. This admittedly all too brief mention of practice-related improvement in selection is exactly what Fridland is alluding to. Ironically, Fridland refutes our alleged position by quoting liberally from another paper that I co-authored with Adrian Haith, which was published the same year as S&K, in which we explain optimal feedback control (Haith and Krakauer 2013). That said it must be admitted that the link between them could have been laid out better, which I attempted to do when I recently wrote "The Intelligent Reflex" (Krakauer 2019).

The key concept, as already alluded to in the previous section, is that propositional knowledge, can through practice, be cached as a movement control policy, which is to say that declarative knowledge can be *proceduralized*. A control policy is a goal-dependent mapping or set of rules between the state of body or environment and motor commands. For example, when you first learn about traffic lights as a child, you are informed explicitly that red means stop and green means go. Over time, with practice, this knowledge is automatized and cached as a control policy (an intelligent reflex) – a red light triggers braking at a latency too short for deliberation. Indeed, if there were a planet where you were now informed that green meant stop and red meant go, this would represent new propositional knowledge that would come into conflict with the older propositional knowledge that has since been cached or proceduralized, i.e., it is no longer propositional. As I argue in "The Intelligent Reflex" – real-world skills are always a composite of propositional and procedural knowledge. One can now understand the limited motor skill learning abilities of patients such as HM – they can't hold onto the propositional knowledge long enough to proceduralize into control policies over days, weeks, months of practice.

Thus, we are not and were never in disagreement with Fridland, with the exception of a concern that she has a somewhat vague and overly porous view of how control policies can be altered by ongoing intentionality. Reconciliation is possible by saying that a given policy can be selected quickly, for example a passing shot versus a lob, but how each policy runs is *not* so easily interrupted. I can choose a swallowing policy over a spitting-out policy when I have a pill in my mouth but a given policy cannot itself be easily modified by intentionality – start swallowing and try to stop it. The philosophers Carlotta Pavese and Neil Levy also picked up on the lack of discussion of what amounts to intelligent control policies in S&K. Control policies can be considered a kind of rule that, with practice, automatizes and is cached. For example, the policy for mirror drawing is to go left rather than right after making a leftward error; with practice this policy gets cached, which is why it no longer had to be explicitly remembered by HM. I wrote about the notion of control policy in this context, along with my colleagues, before, at the same time and after S&K (Shmuelof et al. 2012; Haith and Krakauer 2013, 2018).

It is important to briefly discuss Carlotta Pavese's notion of "practical representation" (Pavese 2013, 2015, 2019) and Neil Levy's "motor representations" (Levy 2017). I agree that there are explicit representations that are not conceptual/propositional but are nevertheless intelligent. We have recently written about the ability to explicitly represent the shapes of movements, for example when we trace the letter S in the air with our arm, consider how a tool should be moved in space, or plan a trajectory around obstacles (Wong et al. 2015, 2016, 2019). Fascinatingly, patients with the condition called ideomotor apraxia can have great trouble with such tasks, for example they are very poor at pantomiming how to use a hammer despite knowing exactly what a hammer is; a clear demonstration of the dissociation between a practical representation and a conceptual one (see Pavese, Chapter 18 in this volume). Again, we under-emphasized such non-propositional representations in S&K. The intelligence in these practical representations, just like propositional ones, can with practice become "baked-in" as cached policies, which are by definition non-representational. The S&K position more properly and clearly stated is that any motor skill is the combination of overt representations, propositional and motor, automatized former representations (cached policies), and hard-wired policies. Levy, in his critique of S&K, is incorrect, however, to consider motor acuity a motor representation – it is a capacity that never has to go through a representational phase any more than a stretch reflex does. One can consider stretch reflexes intelligent from the standpoint of evolution but not from the point of view of the organism that possesses them. Thus ironically, Levy is right about representations but picked on an aspect of motor behavior, motor acuity, that does not need their invocation.

17.4 Conclusions

I have addressed two kinds of criticism here of S&K. The first kind centered around claims that we were misunderstanding HM and HM-like observations and using them to make the intellectualist case when they in fact support the opposite. We were also accused of smuggling in the semantic argument for intellectualism to bolster our weak naturalistic metaphysical argument. I hope that I have now made it clear that these claims are unfounded and are in fact incorrect on the scientific evidence. The second set of criticisms was correct in so much that we were indeed remiss in not giving sufficient attention to automatization of propositional knowledge or movement representations. This is especially unfortunate as these are areas that I had done extensive work in. Indeed, had we dealt with these topics in the depth they deserved in S&K then perhaps our treatment of HM would have also been better understood. On balance, it is clear that a composite view of practical skills is the most plausible. Once this is accepted it is a short hop, skip and a jump to the realization that this is true of *all* skills – cognitive, perceptual and motor. The perceived difference between motor and cognitive skills and their purported mapping onto the anti-intellectualist/intellectualist distinction can be blamed in part on the impoverished "skill" tasks used to study patients with amnesia.

References

De Brigard, F. (2019) "Know-How, Intellectualism, and Memory Systems," *Philosophical Psychology* 32: 719–58.
Devitt, M. (2011) "Methodology and the Nature of Knowing-How," *Journal of Philosophy* 108: 205–18.
Dreyfus, H. L., and Dreyfus, S. E. (1984) "From Socrates to Expert Systems: The Limits of Calculative Rationality," *Technology in Society* 6: 217–33.
Fridland, E. (2016) "Skill and Motor Control: Intelligence All the Way Down," *Philosophical Studies* 174: 1539–60.
Haith, A. M., and Krakauer, J. W. (2013) "Theoretical Models of Motor Control and Motor Learning," in A. Gollhofer, W. Taube, and J. B. Nielsen (eds.) *Routledge Handbook of Motor Control and Motor Learning*, 16–37, New York: Routledge.
—— (2018) "The Multiple Effects of Practice: Skill, Habit and Reduced Cognitive Load," *Current Opinion in Behavioral Sciences* 20: 196–201.
Huberdeau, D., Krakauer, J. W., and Haith, A. M. (2019) "Practice Induces a Qualitative Change in the Memory Representation for Visuomotor Learning," *Journal of Neurophysiology* 122: 1050–9.
Krakauer, J. W. (2019) "The Intelligent Reflex," *Philosophical Psychology* 32: 823–31.
Levy, N. (2017) "Embodied Savoir-Faire: Knowledge-How Requires Motor Representations," *Synthese* 194: 511–30.
Milner, B. (1962). "Les Troubles de la Memoire Accompagnant des Lesions Hippocampiques Bilaterales," in P. Passouant (ed.) *Physiologie de L'hippocampe* (257–72). Paris: Centre National de la Recherche Scientifique.
Pavese, C. (2013) *The Unity and Scope of Knowledge* (PhD thesis), Rutgers University.
—— (2015) "Practical Senses," *Philosophers' Imprint* 15: 1–25.
—— (2019) "On the Psychological Reality of Practical Representation," *Philosophical Psychology* 32: 784–821.
Roy, S., and Park, N. W. (2010) "Dissociating the Memory Systems Mediating Complex Tool Knowledge and Skills," *Neuropsychologia* 48: 3026–36.
Ryle, G. (1949) *The Concept of Mind*, London: Hutchinson's University Library.

Shmuelof, L., Krakauer, J. W., and Mazzoni, P. (2012) "How Is a Motor Skill Learned? Change and Invariance at the Levels of Task Success and Trajectory Control," *Journal of Neurophysiology* 108: 578–94.

Schwartz, A., and Drayson, Z. (2019) "Intellectualism and the Argument from Cognitive Science," *Philosophical Psychology* 32: 661–91.

Springle, A. (2019) "Methods, Minds, Memory, and Kinds," *Philosophical Psychology* 32: 634–60.

Stanley, J., and Krakauer, J. W. (2013) "Motor Skill Depends on Knowledge of Facts," *Frontiers in Human Neuroscience* 7: 503.

Stanley, J., and Williamson, T. (2001) "Knowing How," *The Journal of Philosophy* 98(8): 411–44.

Wallis, C. (2008) "Consciousness, Context, and Know-How," *Synthese* 160: 123–53.

Wong, A. L., Goldsmith, J., and Krakauer, J. W. (2016) "A Motor Planning Stage Represents the Shape of Upcoming Movement Trajectories," *Journal of Neurophysiology* 116: 296–305.

Wong, A. L., Haith, A. M., and Krakauer, J. W. (2015) "Motor Planning," *The Neuroscientist* 21: 385–98.

Wong, A. L., Jax, J. A., Smith, L. L., Buxbaum, L. J., and Krakauer, J. W. (2019) "Movement Imitation via an Abstract Trajectory Representation in Dorsal Premotor Cortex," *Journal of Neuroscience* 39: 3320–31.

18

PRACTICAL REPRESENTATION*

Carlotta Pavese

We know facts in a variety of ways. For example, one may know a fact perceptually or by mere testimony. Compare an instance of *perceptual knowledge*—e.g., the knowledge that one acquires when one sees that there is a table in front of oneself—to an instance of non-perceptual knowledge with the same content—e.g., the knowledge that one acquires by mere testimony when one is told that there is a table in front of one. It is natural to distinguish between these two types of knowledge in terms of *the modes of presentation* under which they represent the state of affairs that there is a table in front of one. In the former case (when one sees the table), one knows that there is a table in front of oneself under a visual mode of presentation, whereas in the latter case (when one is merely told that there is a table), one comes to know that proposition under a non-visual mode of presentation.

According to a prominent view of know-how—known as *intellectualism about know-how*—knowing how to perform a task is a matter of being in a propositional knowledge state about how to perform the task under a *distinctive* mode of presentation. The relevant mode of presentation is neither testimonial nor merely perceptual. Rather, it is distinctively practical. Knowing how to perform a task, and being skilled at performing a task, such as swimming, is a matter of knowing facts about how to perform a task under a practical representation of that task. As I understand it, the view is motivated by a variety of considerations coming from action theory and cognitive sciences that strongly suggest that the intentionality and intelligence of our actions is to be explained in terms of propositional knowledge about the means to achieve certain goals.[1]

This chapter will not rehearse those motivations here. Rather, it will focus on the question: what does it mean to represent a task under a practical mode of presentation? The chief challenge for proponents of intellectualism is to spell out in clear and independently motivated terms what it means to represent something practically. This chapter discusses recent attempts to clarify the notion of practical representation and its theoretical fruitfulness. The ultimate goal is not just to show that intellectualists are on good grounds when they appeal to practical representation in their theories of know-how. Rather, it is to argue that *any* plausible theory of skill and know-how has to appeal to the notion of practical representation developed here.

Section 18.1 explains the notion of a mode of presentation and introduces practical modes of presentation. Section 18.2 illustrates practical representation by discussing models of motor control in current theories of sensori-motor psychology; Section 18.3 puts forward an argument for positing practical representation. Section 18.4 goes from practical non-conceptual representations to practical *conceptual* representations—to practical concepts. Section 18.5 concludes.

18.1 What is a mode of presentation?

We are accustomed to the idea that the same individual might be represented under different *conceptual* modes of presentation. For example, one might think of Venus *as the morning star*; one might think of Venus *as the evening star*. In this case, the different modes of presentation specified by the "think of *x* as *y*" locution correspond to different *concepts* that one possesses and under which one might group individuals. Had one grouped Venus under yet different concepts, one would be in a position to think of it under yet different conceptual modes of presentation.

Many authors also argue for the existence of *perceptual* (and non-conceptual) modes of presentation (Evans 1982; Block 1990; Peacocke 1992, 2001; Bermudez 1995; Burge 2010; Neander 2017; Lande 2018). Block (1990) argues that inverted spectrum subjects with phenomenally distinct color experiences in different environments might represent the same external colors. Peacocke (1992: 73–8) argues that perceptual representations can stand in many-to-one relations to their content, as in the Mach diamond's case, where a square is perceived as a diamond instead of as a square. Burge (2010) mounts a sustained argument for perceptual modes of presentation starting from the phenomenon of *perceptual constancy*. In perceptual constancy of, say, a rectangular object, the representation of its rectangularity from different angles happens via an egocentrically anchored spatial coordinate system due to the spatial layout of light registration by retinal receptors. Differences in the spatial format of sensory cues and processing *can* determine differences in our abilities to perceive a given attribute, such as the rectangularity of an object, by affecting our accuracy and precision of representation. This is because how we represent is a function of our representational abilities which are determined by the differences in sensory cues and processing. Therefore, differences in representational abilities determine differences in modes of presentation—e.g., *rectangular at specific tilt Tn* and *rectangular at specific tilt Tm* may therefore represent the very same attribute (e.g. *rectangularity*).

Representations might be classified by their distinctive modes of presentation. Say that a representation is *conceptual* if it represents what it does *via* a conceptual mode of presentation; and *perceptual* if it represents what it does *via* a perceptual mode of presentation. The nature of the relevant perspective depends on the relevant *representational abilities*. In the conceptual case, the different ways in which we might conceptually represent the world depend on the *basic conceptual abilities* that we possess—i.e., the most basic abilities for thinking and reasoning (Rosch 1978; Jackendoff 1989; Laurence & Margolis 1999; Prinz 2004: Chapter 1; Machery 2009: 7–51; Margolis & Laurence 2019). Perceptual modes of presentation, on the other hand, depend on basic representational abilities that do not need to be conceptual. For example, consider the ability of the visual system to locate objects in two-dimensional space relative to a viewpoint. This ability to locate objects in two-dimensional space is not a conceptual ability—it is not an ability to think and to reason. Rather, it is a *tracking* ability because it is an ability to vary states that are two-dimensionally structured in accordance with the varying of objects and their features in three-dimensional space (Dretske 1988; Stalnaker 1999: 347; Neander 2017: 152–3).[2] The auditory and the touch systems' ways of tracking features in the environment do not need to be of the same kind as the visual system's ability to locate objects in two-dimensional space. Their modes of presentation are correspondingly different. If we have had yet different tracking abilities, such as bats' echolocation, we would perceptually represent the world under still different modes of presentation.

This discussion puts us in a position to introduce *in abstracto* the notion of *practical representation*. Suppose our minds could represent the world or some aspect thereof, in a way that is a function *not* (or not just) of our conceptual abilities, and not even (or not just) of our perceptual abilities, but rather of abilities that are neither (merely) perceptual nor (merely) conceptual and instead are practical, in some sense to be made precise. By representing (some aspect of) the world in a way that is function of their practical abilities, there would be a good sense in which our mind could represent things via a practical mode of presentation.[3] Different minds, or the same mind at different times, might even differ in their practical abilities and henceforth in how they practically represent the world. A representation is practical if it represents what it does via a practical mode of presentation, and it represents via a practical mode of presentation if it represents as a function of the representor's most basic practical abilities.

This section has provided an initial abstract characterization of practical representation. Section 18.2 discusses in some detail an example of practical representation, posited by *sensori-motor psychology*.

18.2 Sensori-motor psychology and the Casio metaphor

Suppose I form the intention to grasp a bottle of wine within my visual field. How does that intention translate into the corresponding intentional movement of grasping the bottle?

According to prominent psychological theories of motor control (e.g., Schmidt 2003; Jeannerod 1997: 11–55, 2006; Arbib 1985; Wolpert 1997; Wolpert & Kawato 1998), building on the insights of Helmholtz (1867) and Bernstein (1923, 1930, 1967), the motor system translates that intention into a *motor command*, prescribing to one's muscles and nerves the relevant movement. *Contemporary sensori-motor psychology* studies how this translation happens.[4] Figure 18.1 illustrates one prominent model of motor control, due to Wolpert (1997).

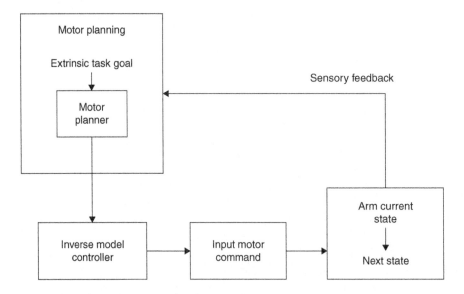

Figure 18.1 The motor system (cf. Wolpert 1997)

According to this model, the agent's intention is an input to the motor planner which uses sensory stimulations, including stimulations of the retina, the inner ear, muscle spindles and so on, to make an estimate of the environmental conditions, of the location of the goal and the relative location of the limbs. Based on these estimates, the motor planner issues a *motor command* to execute the intended task. On this model, the translation from intention to a motor command involves various sorts of representations—some merely perceptual, some more distinctively motoric. Among the motoric representations, there are motor schemas, which I will return to later. Now, I'd like to start focusing on the outputs of this model—i.e., on the motor commands. How are we to think of them?

To answer this question, it is helpful to compare the motor system to a Casio electronic keyboard (Figure 18.2). In such a keyboard, pressing each white and black piano-style key activates the switches, which triggers the electronic sensors to generate a sound—i.e., a musical note (Figure 18.3). So, each key is a *command* that, when executed, generates a note. Because each key is a command that is not made out of other commands, it is structurally simple or primitive. Let us call it an *elementary command*. A sequence or a configuration of keys is a *non-elementary command*.

Compare playing on the keyboard to executing a motor task—e.g., the task of grasping a bottle within one's visual field. And compare the music produced by means of the keyboard to the motor task executed—to having grasped the bottle.

Figure 18.2 A Casio keyboard

Figure 18.3   Key = elementary command

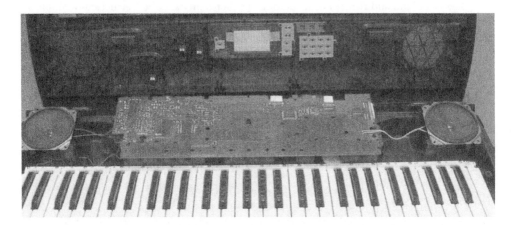

Figure 18.4   The matrix

The comparison runs deeper: the matrix circuits are neural paths from motor cortex to spinal cord; the wires to the speakers are the spinal cord; the speakers themselves are the efferent nerves and muscles (Figure 18.4).

Typically, a motor command issued by the motor system will be a *sequence* of instructions, like complex configurations of keys on the keyboard. This realization goes back to Lashley (1951). He noted that fast movements such as those required, for example, for playing the piano, are performed too quickly to rely on feedback about one movement shaping the next movement. The time required to receive feedback about the first movement, combined with the time needed to develop a plan for the subsequent movement and send a corresponding message to muscles, was simply too long to permit piano playing. Movements are performed as motor sequences, with one sequence being ready, while another ongoing sequence was being completed. Hence motor commands issued by the motor system will typically be *complex instructions*, like complex configurations on the keyboard.

Now, different motor systems might prescribe the same motor task in different ways, depending on the primitive abilities of the system. To see this, compare again a motor system to a Casio keyboard. A keyboard may use different sequences of keys to play the same sequence of sound. Consider the sort of commands that some keyboards possess—or *chunked commands*— which, when pressed, play at once a whole soundtrack (Figure 18.5). These commands enable

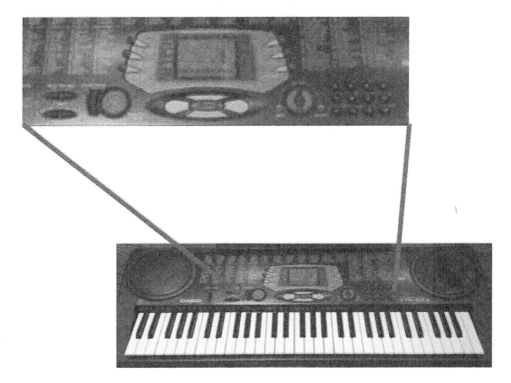

Figure 18.5 Elementary but chunked commands

to execute not just one note but a sequence of notes *at once*. Chunked commands are also not structured, just like the main white and black keys; so in this sense, they are as structurally simple as elementary commands. They differ from elementary commands as their content is complex, and therefore, the instructions they issue are complex.

Now, as illustrated in Figure 18.6, we might imagine different keyboards with a different repertoire of commands. For example, Keyboard #1 only possesses the main keys as commands. Keyboard #2 possesses a chunked command—a green button—that plays a sequence of two notes in addition to the main keys. Keyboard #3 possesses the main keys and a blue button, that plays a sequence of three notes. Keyboard #4 possesses the main keys and a red button that plays at once the whole sequence of four notes. The execution of these four different configurations of commands brings about the same sequence of sounds.

The motor system and motor commands are similar to a Casio keyboard and its configurations in some key respects. Similar to how Casio keyboards might differ in the set of their chunked commands, different motor systems might differ in their set of elementary commands. That might happen, for example, if two motor systems have undergone different "*chunking processes.*" A chunking process is the process through which complex operations become elementary for a system. A variety of experimental studies have demonstrated the existence of *motor* chunking (Newell 1990: 8–10; Sakai et al. 2003; Verwey 2010; Verwey et al. 2011: 407; Fridland 2019; Pavese 2019). Motor chunking is believed to occur as a result of practice and to make the execution of a task more efficient as a result. This efficiency can be explained by modeling the result of motor chunking in terms that are analogous to what I have called a "chunked command" on a keyboard. Just like Keyboard #2 has a specialized

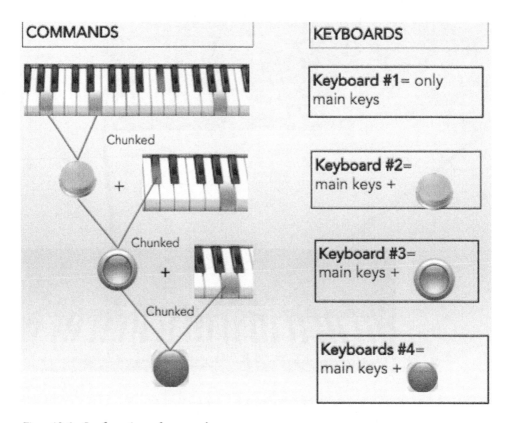

Figure 18.6 Configurations of commands

instruction (the green button) to execute a sequence of two notes, the motor system can chunk a sequence of commands to develop a specialized new elementary command that can execute that whole sequence at once.[5] Because of chunking, the set of elementary operations of a motor system can vary through time as practice occurs and can vary across motor systems at the same time.

Since motor systems can have different elementary commands, they can differ in their abilities in ways that are neither conceptual nor merely perceptual. To see this, consider again the Casio keyboard. Recall that the four keyboards differ in their elementary commands. This difference in their elementary commands corresponds to a difference in the keyboards' abilities. For example, Keyboard #1 can play a sequence of two sounds only by pressing two keys; by contrast, Keyboard #2 can execute the same sequence at once, by pressing a single command. Hence, Keyboard #2 and Keyboard #1 differ in their elementary abilities. The abilities to execute different elementary commands are neither merely perceptual nor merely conceptual abilities.[6] Imagine that we endow a Casio keyboard with a sub-system—system Perc—that tracks the frequencies of the sounds in the environment with an oscilloscope showing the result of the tracking, like a sound frequency meter (Figure 18.7). System Perc would be akin to our perceptual system because the display would represent sounds in the environment in accordance with the keyboard's tracking abilities, which are frequencies tracking. Or imagine we equipped the Casio keyboards with an additional sub-system—system Conc—that classifies sounds in the environment according to their pitch or their rhythm by mapping them

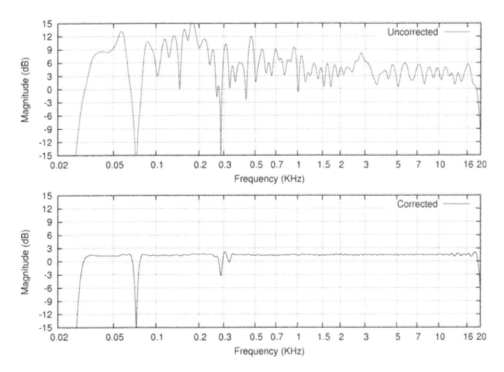

Figure 18.7 Sound frequency meter

into the label of the corresponding musical note, in a way analogous to *a note recognition device or app*. Imagine the system is sophisticated enough that it can draw simple inferences—e.g., from the fact that the note is a C to its not being a D. System Conc would be akin to our conceptual system because it would represent in accordance with the keyboard's classificatory, reasoning, and thinking abilities (e.g., which sounds it can not only tell apart but also label and reason about).

The main keyboard's system, including both black and white keys and chunked commands, is distinct from both system Perc and system Conc, because the main keyboard's abilities include neither system Conc's conceptual abilities nor system Perc's perceptual abilities, and differ from both in their direction of fit (Platts 1979: 257; Anscombe 1957: 56). Conceptual abilities are abilities to conceive—i.e., to be in a certain conceptual state, to output conceptual representations; perceptual abilities are abilities to perceive—i.e., to output perceptual representations. Practical abilities are abilities to execute instructions. In conclusion, the different configurations of commands in the four keyboards above stand for the same sequence of sounds but in different *ways* that depend on the elementary practical abilities of the relevant keyboards.

A configuration on a Casio keyboard is a metaphor for practical representation (Figure 18.8). We can think of each key, and each configuration of keys, to *stand* for (and in this sense, *to represent*) the note, or the sequence of notes, that pressing that key will result in playing. In this sense, those different configurations of keys stand for the same sequence of sounds in different *practical* ways, in terms of different primitive commands and abilities to execute those commands.[7] In the same way, different motor systems that have undergone different chunking processes will differ in their primitive commands and in their practical abilities.

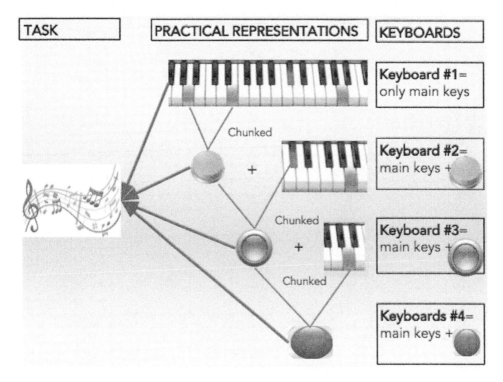

Figure 18.8 Different practical representations

Similar to configurations of keys on different keyboards, motor systems that have undergone different practice and therefore have different chunking processes, might differ in their set of primitive abilities. Because the set of a system's primitives can vary through time, a motor system might prescribe the same task in different ways at different times. They will break down the task into a different set of elementary commands depending on the set of their primitive abilities at that time.

In conclusion, the analogy between the motor system and the Casio keyboard is instructive for it highlights in what ways motor commands are functions of the practical abilities of their system. Predictably, the analogy is not perfect. Let me highlight two important differences. First, motor commands (though not merely perceptual) are perceptual because they are the output of perceptual processes and take into account the environment's features where the task takes place. Hence, if motor commands count as representations, they must be *hybrid* representations, both perceptual and practical. Second, although configurations on a keyboard are played one after the other, they are in an important sense *static*: they "stay there" waiting to be executed. By contrast, motor representations are *dynamic* because they are issued in furtherance of the task goal as the task unfolds (cf. Rescorla 2018).

A final difference between configurations on a Casio keyboard and motor commands is the following. The status of Casio configurations as representations is questionable, because it is not clear that we *need* to think of those configurations as representations. When explaining the functioning of the keyboard, representation-talk is dispensable. By contrast, as I argue in the next section, it is explanatorily helpful to think of motor commands, as well as other motoric prescriptive representations to be discussed later, as *bona fide* representations.

18.3 Why posit practical representation?

Cognitive scientists definitely speak of motor instructions as if they are *bona fide* representations (e.g., Winograd 1975; Tulving 1985; Anderson 1982; Stevens 2005; Knowlton & Foerde 2008; Tankus & Fried 2012). More generally, it is common to find cognitive scientists talking as if procedural systems such as the motor system are representation-based. For example, Tulving tells us that "[t]he representation of acquired information in the procedural system is prescriptive rather than descriptive" (Tulving 1985: 387–8). Many philosophers follow motor scientists in allowing these sorts of unconscious representations that are not necessarily available at the personal level (e.g., Butterfill & Sinigaglia 2014; Mylopoulos & Pacherie 2017; Rescorla 2016; Pavese 2017; Levy 2017; Fridland 2017).

There are, indeed, excellent empirical reasons for thinking that the procedural system encodes information about the task to be performed. However, as Dretske (1988) teaches us, carrying information and representing are a different matter. For example, tree rings carry information about the tree's age, without representing it. So, why think that we are dealing with *bona fide* representations when we are dealing with practical representations?[8] Following a recent argument by Ramsey (2007: section 2.2), some might argue that talk of practical representation is *dispensable* (see also Shea 2018).[9] Consider a rifle that responds to a finger movement by discharging a bullet from the muzzle. There is an internal mechanism whereby the movement of the trigger causes the movement of the firing pin, which causes the ignition of the primer in the cartridge, which causes the explosion of the propellant, which causes the bullet to travel down the barrel and exit at speed. This explanation of the behavior of the rifle does not need to appeal to *any* representation: the description of the mechanism of the trigger will satisfactorily explain the rifle's firing. Motor commands are not *that* different from the command issued when pulling the trigger. If so, why think of motor commands in representational terms and of the motor system as a representational system? Doing so might seem explanatorily idle. Call this the *objection from the rifle*.

Skepticism about positing practical and procedural representation is often voiced even by those philosophers who are convinced that representation-talk in cognitive science can sometimes be explanatorily helpful. Because what is at stake here is whether practical representation is real, as opposed to whether *any* representation is real, I will assume that representation-talk is explanatorily helpful *at least in some cases*. In particular, I will assume that there are personal-level representations such as intentions and beliefs. Then, the question becomes: Why think that, when explaining motor behavior, we need to posit motor and procedural representation in addition to intentions, beliefs, and desires?

In order to show that positing practical representation is not explanatorily idle, what has to be shown is that the constitutive aspect of representation—what distinguishes representation from information carrying, for example—enters essentially in our explanations of motor behavior. What is distinctive of representation is that it is normatively assessable as accurate or inaccurate: a representation can *misrepresent* (e.g., Brentano 1874; Dretske 1988; Neander 2017). What has to be shown is that this normative aspect of representation is explanatorily helpful when it comes to explaining motor behavior.

The normative aspect of representation is helpfully modeled by the so-called "content-target" model (Cummins 1996; Greenberg 2019). According to this model, a representation *aims at its target*—a representation that is meant as a representation of Obama *aims* at Obama—and *expresses/denotes its content*—the set of properties that the representation ascribes to Obama (Figure 18.9). For example, the picture of Obama aims at Obama if that is what the painter wanted to paint; and the picture expresses certain properties if it portrays Obama as having

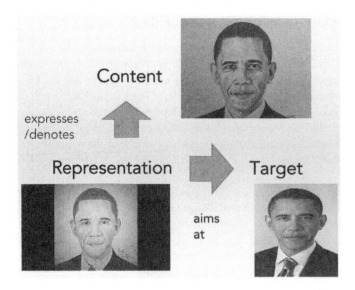

Figure 18.9 The content-target model of representation
Source: Cummins 1996; Greenberg 2019

certain properties. A representation is *correct* when the content matches its target—if the properties expressed match those that Obama actually has—and incorrect otherwise.

Appealing to the content-target model of representation, we can reframe the question of whether positing practical representation is explanatorily helpful in the following terms. Motor commands (and motor schemas) are genuine representations if they can be explanatorily helpful to appeal to the content-target model of representation with respect to motor commands and, in particular, to talk as if motor commands misrepresented their target.

At first, one might reasonably wonder whether talk of misrepresentation applies to motor commands. After all, imperatives do not represent accurately or not, they are not true or false. However, note that there is an important sense in which motor commands *can* be correct or incorrect: a motor command can prescribe the execution of a certain task correctly or incorrectly *with respect to the original intention of the agent.* The standards of correctness here are imposed by the intentions of the agent, which fix the target task to be executed.

Appealing to the agent's intention in fixing the target of the motor commands enables the extension of this three-part model to the notion of practical representation. On this model, a practical representation (say, a motor command) *aims at its target* (the task that the agent intends to execute) and *expresses its content* (the set of properties that the command prescribes the task to be executed to have). Thus, if an agent wants to dance, *ceteris paribus*, the motor system will produce a motor representation that aims at the task of dancing and represents it as having certain properties. The representation is correct if it represents the task that the agent wanted to execute—i.e., when its content matches the target (Figure 18.10). When the motor commands incorrectly prescribe the target task that the agent intends to execute, the three-part model licenses us to say that the motor command misrepresents that task.

So, it does make sense to talk of misrepresentation for motor commands. But is it ever explanatorily helpful to talk of *mis*representation when it comes to motor behavior? As a case study, consider Ideomotor Apraxia (henceforth, "IA") (Geschwind 1965a, 1965b; Heilman & Rothi 1993; Macauley & Handley 2005; Jeannerod 2006; Wheaton & Hallett 2007; Krakauer

Extending the model to practical representation

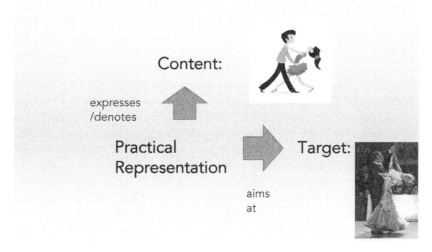

Content:

expresses
/denotes

Practical
Representation

Target:

aims
at

Figure 18.10 The content-target model of practical representation

& Shadmehr 2007; Gross & Grossman 2008; Vanbellingen & Bohlhalter 2011; Sathian et al. 2011). IA is a motor deficit that is not due to paralysis, muscle weakness, or even sensory loss.[10] Rather, it is a deficit in the ability to *plan* motor actions in the following sense. Patients affected by it are perfectly able to explain how a certain task is performed. However, strikingly, they are unable to imagine, act out, or pantomime the correspondent movement on demand, such as "pretend to brush your teeth" or "pucker as though you bit into a sour lemon" or "pick up a phone." Often their pantomime reflects improper orientation of their limbs and impaired spatio-temporal organization. Remarkably, however, they are often able to perform an action when environmentally cued. For example, while they may not be able to pick up the phone when asked to do so, they might be able to perform the action when the phone rings. Although, for a while, IA has been thought to be due to a deficit in semantic knowledge, recent findings suggest otherwise. Some patients affected by IA might perform well when it comes to correctly identifying the correct hand postures in observational tasks or to verbally describing how to use the tool and to position their limb (Hayakawa et al. 2015). This suggests that the deficit is not due to defective semantic understanding of what subjects are asked to do.

IA is an example of dissociation between the declarative knowledge system and the procedural system. But it also provides an exemplary illustration of the explanatory advantage of practical representation. For how do we go about explaining IA? Talking simply about the motor system not functioning, as when the rifle fails to shoot despite the shooter wanting it to, would not distinguish apraxic patients from subjects who simply lack the ability to perform the relevant motor task. As mentioned, many apraxic patients *can* perform the relevant tasks at least in some circumstances. Rather, what is distinctive to the IA patients is that the motor system is not "hooked up" to the high-level personal representation of the task command *in the right way* and the motor behavior ends up diverging from the request that the agent intends to execute. Note that it is not simply that the intention does not succeed at causing the motor behavior. The motor behavior *is* issued in this case. Moreover, the motor behavior issued by apraxic subjects is not random, as if it resulted from *some* sort of planning. What is distinctive about IA is that there seems to be a mismatch between the task the agent represents as being required and the task that is prescribed by the motor system: the task that the motor commands prescribe does not match the task that the agent intended to perform upon request. This description of apraxic behavior essentially appeals to the *content* of the motor commands and essentially appeals to the fact that the target of the motor representation (in this case, what task the agent is asked to perform) does not match the actual content of the motor representation.

Hence, talk of practical representation gains us the most natural and empirically supported psychological description of what goes distinctively wrong in patients with IA and in other similar dissociations between one's personal-level intentions and one's motor system.[11] The *objection from the rifle* fails to establish that practical representation is explanatorily dispensable. Although the behavior of the motor system, like the mechanism of the rifle, might be described without representation-talk, as soon as we aim at describing how the motor system interacts with the agent's intentions and at explaining in what ways the motor system fulfills them, we are led back to talking as if the motor system correctly represented or misrepresented those intentions—i.e., we are back to exploiting the normative dimension of representation.

18.4 From practical representations to practical concepts: the hierarchy of practical representation

In the literature on action and know-how, practical modes of presentation are discussed as pertaining in the first instance to *conceptual representation*. Peacocke (1986: 49–50) talks of "action-based ways of thinking." Stanley and Williamson (2001) draw an analogy between practical modes of presentation and *first personal* modes of presentation (Perry 1993). Stanley (2011: 98–110) identifies practical modes of presentations with practical ways of *thinking*. Bengson and Moffett (2007) talk of "ability-entailing concepts." Pavese (2015a) talks of "practical concepts." Pavese (2015b) talks about *practical senses* and Fregean senses are typically assimilated to concepts. Mylopoulos and Pacherie (2017) talk of "action-executable concepts."

Prima facie, the discussion in this chapter might seem to substantially diverge from these discussions of practical modes of presentation in that practical modes of presentation have been defined by contrast to conceptual modes of presentation and ways of thinking. Despite this apparent discrepancy, the current discussion is compatible with and a desirable development of those earlier views of practical modes of presentation.

First, some practical representations are, like perceptual representations, non-conceptual: for example, motor commands are non-conceptual practical representations. But the present proposal is compatible with there being hybrid representations, for it is compatible with there being representations that represent both as a function of practical abilities and as a function of conceptual and perceptual abilities. So, it is compatible with there being practical representations that are also conceptual or even both conceptual and perceptual.

Now, consider the sort of motoric representations involved in the translation of intentions into motor commands: motor schemas (Bernstein 1967; Schmidt 1975, 2003; Arbib 1985; Jeannerod 1997). Motor schemas are less context-specific and more enduring motor representations that mediate between intentions and motor commands. For example, Arbib (1985) talks of motor schemas as a predetermined set of commands, often characterized as a "control program." This suggests that like motor commands, motor schemas are also prescriptive representations, only more general and less context-dependent. They are supposed to be

Non-practical concept	Non-observational concept
Motor schema (or practical concept)	Observational concept
Motor command	Percept

Figure 18.11 The hierarchy of practical representation

revisable through trial and error and able to store information about the invariant aspects of an action (Arbib 1992; Jeannerod 1997: 51–5). There seems to be some evidence for thinking that motor schemas can be refined through focus and mental rehearsing of the motor task, which would suggest that they are accessible to the personal level (e.g., Feltz & Landers 1983; Sherwood & Lee 2003).

Motor schemas are better candidates for being a conceptual, albeit practical, sort of representation. For they are akin to "object schemas" that some identify with conceptual representation of objects. They interface between motor commands and the semantic representations of an action, in a way similar to how, in the theory of perceptual representations, *observational concepts* are supposed to mediate between percepts and non-perceptual conceptual representations (Weiskopf 2015; Pavese 2020b).[12] These representations can be modeled by Pavese's (2015b) practical senses. Like a program, a practical sense breaks down a task into a different sequence of instructions, depending on the system's most basic practical abilities. For example, if multiplying is an elementary operation for the system, it does not break down the task of multiplying into subtasks. But if multiplying is not elementary, then it might break it into subtasks that include adding. So, a practical sense can play the role of interfacing between semantic concepts of a task and a motor command by mapping the semantic representation of a task into different motor commands, depending on the basic abilities of the system. In this sense motor schemas can be modeled as practical senses (Figure 18.11).

The conceptual nature of motor schemas is, however, debatable. Whether or not motor schemas are best thought of as conceptual sort of representations, it is nonetheless true that distinctively practical and person-level conceptual representations mediating between semantic representations of a task and motor representations might be needed, in order to overcome some puzzles that arise when understanding the relation between intentions and motor representations (cf. Pacherie 2000; Sinigaglia & Butterfill 2014; Mylopoulos & Pacherie 2017) and in order to provide a complete explanation of IA. Indeed, the best explanation of what goes on with IA might be that the subjects affected by this deficit cannot think of the task practically—that is, they cannot engage in a distinctively *productive* kind of reasoning—and because of that, are incapable of forming the correct motor representations (Pavese 2020b, manuscript).[13]

18.5 Conclusions

Intellectualists have first introduced the notion of a practical mode of presentation in the debate about know-how (Stanley & Williamson 2001; Stanley 2011; Pavese 2015b, 2017). Earlier discussions of intellectualism have assumed that practical modes of presentation ought to be *conceptual* modes of presentation. In this chapter, I have presented a taxonomy of modes of presentation according to which modes of presentation can be conceptual, perceptual, practical, or a combination thereof (Section 18.2). The notion of practical representation has been illustrated with the case of motor commands and motor schemas in sensori-motor psychology and its distinctive practical dimension has been explained via the Casio keyboard metaphor (Section 18.3). Although the notion of a practical mode of presentation has faced a lot of criticisms (Schiffer 2002; Noe 2005; Glick 2015), it is perfectly intelligible, as it is a matter of representing as a function of one's practical abilities. Moreover, practical representation is psychologically real: a variety of representations posited by cognitive scientists when explaining motor skillful behavior represent practically. In Section 18.4, I have reviewed some reasons for thinking that the existence of practical representation is motivated not by mere reliance on the current scientific practice but by a more principled argument for the explanatory helpfulness of this notion when it comes to describing the interplay of the motor system with the agent's intentions. This picture is not meant to rule out the possibility of *practical concepts*—i.e., concepts that one comes to possess by virtue of practically representing the world in a certain way, just like one comes to possess observational concepts in virtue of perceptually representing the world a certain way. In fact, a complete theory of know-how and skill might ultimately have to appeal to practical concepts (Section 18.5).

If that is right, practical representation—whether conceptual practical representation or non-conceptual practical representation—is not an unwelcome commitment that intellectualists about know-how face; it is a necessary posit for any theory of know-how and skills.

Notes

* For discussion that helped me with this material, I am particularly grateful to Todd Ganson, Gabriel Greenberg, and John Krakauer.

1 See e.g., Pavese (2013, 2018, 2020a). For the role of propositional knowledge in skillful action, see also Stanley & Krakauer (2013), Christensen et al. (2019), and see Wu, Chapter 16 in this volume.

2 Not everybody thinks of perception in terms of tracking. Cf. Lupyan and Clark (2015) who defend a view of perception as a *predictive process*.

3 As this informal gloss gives out, the notion of practical representation introduced in this essay is very different from Nanay's (2013) notion of "pragmatic representation" (cf. Pavese 2019: 801–3 for extended comparison). For a different notion of practical modes of presentation, one according to which practically representing something is a matter of representing it in terms of one's practical interests, see Weiskopf (2020).

4 See Rescorla (2016) for a helpful review of this literature.

5 An important difference between the motor system and a normal Casio keyboard is that once a motor system has chunked a sequence [A][B][C] into [A, B, C], the motor system will not be able to execute the very same sequence by executing the commands [A][B][C] sequentially. By contrast, Keyboard #2, for instance, can still play the first two notes by using instead of the green button the two original black and white keys.

6 There are two distinguishable senses in which the Casio keyboard's ability to execute a command has a mind-to-world direction of fit. In the first sense, it has a mind-to-world direction of fit because executing a primitive command results in a change in the world. In the second sense, it has a mind-to-world direction of fit because it enables the keyboard to represent a note with a single command, and a command has a mind-to-world direction of fit.

7 It is worth noting that on a view on which representation requires agency, of the sort defended by Burge (2010: chapters 8–9), there is no sense in which a Casio keyboard can represent perceptually, conceptually, let alone practically. By contrast, on a more permissive notion of representation, broadly teleosemantic, on which any system that has been assigned a certain function is in position to represent in virtue of being assigned that function (Dretske 1988; Neander 2017), a configuration on a Casio keyboard could be a representation. In this case, the relevant function is the function to activate the switches to generate the production of the sounds. Here, I wish not to take a stance on this thorny issue.

8 As many scholars have emphasized, there are many "intra-theoretical" reasons for positing motor representations. As Sinigaglia & Butterfill (2014: 122–13) and Pavese (2017) notice, the *functional*

role of motor representations within computational models of motor behavior seems to be that of a representation: motor representations are the outputs of a computational process, motor planning. Motor planning takes a representation as input (an intention) and returns a representation as output. Moreover, they are inputs to monitoring, which are internal predictive models that estimate likely effects of actions (Miall & Wolpert 1996). And, as Fodor (1998) would put it, no computation without representation! This argument for positing representation, however, requires granting a lot: that certain computational models of motor behavior are correct, for example, in describing the motor system as planning an action or monitoring it. The "intentionality" of this way of speaking already presupposes that it makes sense to posit representations for the motor system. But this is exactly what is at stake.

9 I am grateful to Ganson for discussion here.
10 Neuroscientists routinely describe IA as a defect in "motor programming" or in "selecting the right motor program." Cf. Macauley & Handley (2005: 30–1). Jeannerod (2006: 12) describes the phenomenon as the consequence of a "disruption of the normal mechanisms for action representations."
11 Another example of the explanatory helpfulness of practical representations is the case of motor adaptations, (e.g. Mazzoni & Krakauer 2006), where the motor system adapts to a strategy that does not necessarily align with the agent intentions. Cf. also Gallistel (1999). See Pavese (2020b) for more discussion.
12 With respect to these sorts of motor schemas, also Pacherie (2006) talks of "executable concepts," that one can possess only by virtue of possessing the lower level motor representation.
13 Pacherie (2006) makes a similar point about IA. Pavese (2020b) develops it and extends by looking at the most recent findings concerning IA.

References

Anderson, J. (1982) "Acquisition of Cognitive Skill." *Psychological Review* 89(4): 369–406.

Anscombe, E. (1957) *Intention*. Oxford: Blackwell.

Arbib, M. A. (1985) "Schemas for the Temporal Organization of Behavior." *Human Neurobiology* 4: 63–72.

—— (1992) "Schema theory." *The Encyclopedia of Artificial Intelligence* 2: 1427–1443.

Bengson J. and M. Moffett (2007) "Know-How and Concept Possession." *Philosophical Studies*, 136(1):21–57.

Bernstein, N. (1923) "Studies on the Biomechanics of Hitting Using Optical Recording" *Annals of the Central Institute of Labor* 1: 19–79.

—— (1930) "A New Method of Mirror Cyclographie and Its Application Towards the Study of Labor Movements During Work on a Workbench." *Hygiene. Safety and Pathology of Labor* 56:3–11.

——, (1967) *The Coordination and Regulation of Movements*. Oxford: Pergamon.

Bermúdez, J. L. (1995) "Nonconceptual Content: From Perceptual Experience to Subpersonal Computational States." *Mind & Language* 10.4: 333–369.

Block, N. (1990) "Inverted Earth." *Philosophical Perspectives* 4: 53–79.

Brentano, F. (1874) [1911, 1973]) *Psychology from an Empirical Standpoint*. London: Routledge and Kegan Paul.

Burge, T. (2010) *Origins of Objectivity*. Oxford: Oxford University Press.

Butterfill, S. A., & Sinigaglia, C. (2014) "Intention and Motor Representation in Purposive Action." *Philosophy and Phenomenological Research* 88(1): 119–145.

Christensen, W. D., Sutton, J., & Bicknell, K. (2019). "Memory Systems and the Control of Skilled Action." *Philosophical Psychology* 32(5): 693–719.

Cummins, R. (1996) *Representations, Targets, and Attitudes*. Cambridge, MA: MIT Press.

Dretske, F. I. (1988). *Explaining Behavior: Reasons in a World of Causes*. Cambridge, MA: MIT Press.

Evans, G. (1982) *The Varieties of Reference* (published posthumously, edited by J. McDowell). Oxford: Oxford University Press.

Feltz, D. L., & Landers, D. M. (1983) "The Effects of Mental Practice on Motor Skill Learning and Performance: A Meta-analysis." *Journal of Sport Psychology* 5(1): 25–57.

Fodor, J. A. (1998) *Concepts: Where Cognitive Science Went Wrong*. Oxford: Oxford University Press.

Fridland, E. (2017) "Skill and Motor Control: Intelligence All the Way Down." *Philosophical Studies* 174(6): 1539–1560.

—— (2019) "Longer, Smaller, Faster, Stronger: On Skills and Intelligence." *Philosophical Psychology* 32(5): 759–783.

Gallistel, R. (1999) "Coordinate Transformations in the Genesis of Directed Action." In B. M. Bly & D. E. Rumelhart (eds.) *Cognitive Science* (pp. 1–42). San Diego, CA: Academic Press.

Geschwind, N. (1965a) "Disconnexion Syndromes in Animals and Man." Part I. *Brain* 88: 237–294.

—— (1965b) "Disconnexion Syndromes in Animals and Man." Part II. *Brain* 88: 585–644.

Glick, E. (2015) "Practical Modes of Presentation." *Noûs* 49(3): 538–559.

Greenberg, G. (2019) "Content and Target in Pictorial Representation." *Ergo* 5(33): 865–898.

Gross, R. G., & Grossman, M. (2008) "Update on Apraxia." *Current Neurology and Neuroscience Reports* 8(6): 490–496.

Hayakawa, Y., Fujii, T., Yamadori, A., Meguro, K., & Suzuki, K. (2015) "A Case with Apraxia of Tool Use: Selective Inability to Form a Hand Posture for a Tool." *Brain and Nerve* 67(3): 311–316.

Heilman, K. M., & Rothi, L. J. G. (1993) "Apraxia." In K. M. Heilman & E. Valenstein (eds.) *Clinical Neuropsychology* (3rd ed., pp. 131–149). New York: Oxford University Press.

Helmholtz, H. von (1867) *Handbuch der Physiologischen Optik.* Leipzig: Voss.

Knowlton, B. J., & Foerde, K. (2008) "Neural Representations of Nondeclarative Memories." *Current Directions in Psychological Science* 17: 62–67.

Krakauer, J. W., & Shadmehr, R. (2007). Towards a Computational Neuropsychology of Action. *Progress in Brain Research*, 165: 383–394.

Jackendoff, R. (1989) "What Is a Concept, that a Person May Grasp It? *Mind & Language* 4(1–2): 68–102.

Jeannerod, M. (1997) *The Cognitive Neuroscience of Action.* Oxford: Blackwell Publishers, Inc.

—— (2006) *Motor Cognition: What Actions Tell the Self* (No. 42). Oxford: Oxford University Press.

Lande, K. (2018) "The Perspectival Character of Perception." *The Journal of Philosophy* 115(4): 187–214.

Lashley, K. S. (1951) *The Problem of Serial Order in Behavior* (Vol. 21). Oxford: Bobbs-Merrill.

Laurence, S., & Margolis, E. (1999) "Concepts and Cognitive Science." In E. Margolis & S. Laurence (eds.) *Concepts: Core Readings* (pp. 3–81). Cambridge, MA: MIT Press.

Levy, N. (2017) "Embodied Savoir-faire: Knowledge-how Requires Motor Representations." *Synthese* 194(2): 511–530.

Lupyan, G., & Clark, A. (2015) "Words and the World: Predictive Coding and the Language-perception–Cognition Interface." *Current Directions in Psychological Science* 24(4): 279–284.

Macauley, B. L., & Handley, C. L. (2005) "Gestures Produced by Patients with Aphasia and Ideomotor Apraxia." *Contemporary Issues in Communication Science and Disorders* 32: 30–37.

Machery, E. (2009) *Doing without Concepts.* Oxford: Oxford University Press.

Margolis, E., & Laurence, S. (2019) "Concepts." In E. Zalta (ed.) *The Stanford Encyclopedia of Philosophy* (Summer Edition), https://plato.stanford.edu/archives/sum2017/entries/perceptual-learning/.

Mazzoni, P., & Krakauer, J. W. (2006) "An Implicit Plan Overrides an Explicit Strategy during Visuomotor Adaptation." *Journal of Neuroscience* 26(14): 3642–3645.

Miall, R. C., & Wolpert, D. M. (1996) "Forward Models for Physiological Motor Control." *Neural Networks* 9(8): 1265–1279

Nanay, B. (2013) *Between Perception and Action.* Oxford: Oxford University Press.

Neander, K. (2017) *A Mark of the Mental: In Defense of Informational Teleosemantics.* Cambridge, MA; London, England: MIT Press.

Newell, A. (1990) *Unified Theories of Cognition.* Cambridge, MA: Harvard University Press.

Noë, A. (2005) "Against Intellectualism." *Analysis* 65(4): 278–290.

Pacherie, E. (2000) "The Content of Intention." *Mind and Language* 15: 400–432.

—— (2006) "Towards a Dynamic Theory of Intentions." In S. Pockett, W. Banks, & S. Gallagher (eds.) *Does Consciousness Cause Behavior? An Investigation of the Nature of Volition* (pp. 145–167). Cambridge, MA: MIT Press.

Pavese, C. (2013) *The Unity and Scope of Knowledge.* Ph.D. dissertation, Rutgers University.

—— (2015a) "Knowing a Rule." *Philosophical Issues*, a supplement to *Noûs* 25(1): 165–178.

—— (2015b) "Practical Senses." *Philosophers' Imprint* 15(29): 1–25.

—— (2017) "A Theory of Practical Meaning." *Philosophical Topics* 45(2): 85–116.

—— (2018) "Know-how, Action, and Luck." *Synthese*: 1–23.

—— (2019) "The Psychological Reality of Practical Representation." *Philosophical Psychology* 32(5): 784–821.

—— (2020a) "Knowledge, Action, and Defeasibility." Forthcoming in M. Simion & J. Brown (eds.) *Reasons, Justification, and Defeaters.* Oxford: Oxford University Press.

—— (2020b) "The Empirical Case for Practical Concepts." Forthcoming in *Synthese*, Special Issue on Mind in Skilled Performance.

—— Manuscript. "Might there be practical thoughts?"

Peacocke, C. (1986) *Thought: An Essay on Content.* Oxford: Basil Blackwell.

—— (1992) *A Study of Concepts.* Cambridge, MA: MIT Press.

—— (2001) "Does Perception Have a Nonconceptual Content?" *The Journal of Philosophy* 98(5): 239–264.

Perry, J. (1993) *The Problem of the Essential Indexical: And Other Essays.* Oxford: Oxford University Press.

Platts, M. (1979) *Ways of Meaning.* London: Routledge and Kegan Paul.

Prinz, J. (2004) *Furnishing the Mind: Concepts and their Perceptual Basis.* Cambridge, MA: MIT Press.

Ramsey, W. M. (2007) *Representation Reconsidered.* Cambridge: Cambridge University Press.

Rescorla, M. (2016) "Bayesian Sensorimotor Psychology." *Mind & Language* 31(1): 3–36.

—— (2018) "Motor Computation." In Matteo Colombo & Mark Sprevak (eds.) *The Routledge Handbook of the Computational Mind* (pp. 424–435). Abingdon: Routledge.

Rosch, E. (1978) "Principles of Categorization." in E. Rosch & B. Lloyd (eds.) *Cognition and Categorization* (pp. 27–48). Hillsdale, NJ: Lawrence Erlbaum Associates.

Sakai, K., Kitaguchi, K., & Hikosaka, O. (2003) "Chunking during Human Visuomotor Sequence Learning." *Experimental Brain Research* 152(2): 229–242.

Sathian, K., Buxbaum, L. J., Cohen, L. G., Krakauer, J. W., Lang, C. E., Corbetta, M., & Fitzpatrick, S. M. (2011) "Neurological Principles and Rehabilitation of Action Disorders: Common Clinical Deficits." *Neurorehabilitation and Neural Repair* 25: 21S–32S.

Schiffer, S. (2002) "Amazing Knowledge." *The Journal of Philosophy* 99(4): 200–202.

Schmidt, R. A. (1975) "A Schema Theory of Discrete Motor Skill Learning." *Psychological Review* 82(4): 225–260.

—— (2003) "Motor Schema Theory after 27 Years: Reflections and Implications for a New Theory." *Research Quarterly for Exercise and Sport* 74(4): 366–375.

Shea, N. (2018) *Representation in Cognitive Science.* Oxford: Oxford University Press.

Sherwood, D. E., & Lee, T. D. (2003) "Schema Theory: Critical Review and Implications for the Role of Cognition in a New Theory of Motor Learning." *Research Quarterly for Exercise and Sport* 74(4): 376–382.

Stalnaker, R. (1999) *Context and Content: Essays on Intentionality in Speech and Thought.* Oxford: Oxford University Press.

Stanley, J. (2011) *Know How.* Oxford: Oxford University Press.

Stanley, J., & Williamson, T. (2001) "Knowing How." *Journal of Philosophy* 98(8): 411–444.

Stanley, J., & Krakauer, J. W. (2013) "Motor Skill Depends on Knowledge of Facts." *Frontiers in Human Neuroscience* 7(503): 1–11.

Stevens, J. A. (2005) "Interference Effects Demonstrate Distinct Roles for Visual and Motor Imagery during the Mental Representation of Human Action." *Cognition* 95(3): 329–350.

Tankus, A., & Fried, I. (2012) "Visuomotor Coordination and Motor Representation by Human Temporal Lobe Neurons." *Journal of Cognitive Neuroscience* 24(3): 600–610.

Tulving, E. (1985) "How Many Memory Systems Are There?" *American Psychologist* 40(4): 385–398.

Vanbellingen, T., & Bohlhalter, S. (2011) "Apraxia in Neurorehabilitation: Classification, Assessment and Treatment." *NeuroRehabilitation* 28(2): 91–98.

Verwey, W. B. (2010) "Diminished Motor Skill Development in Elderly: Indications for Limited Motor Chunk Use." *Acta Psychologica* 134: 206–214.

Verwey, W. B., Abrahamse, E. L., Ruitenberg, M. F., Jiménez, L., & de Kleine, E. (2011) "Motor Skill Learning in the Middle-aged: Limited Development of Motor Chunks and Explicit Sequence Knowledge." *Psychological Research* 75(5): 406–422.

Weiskopf, D. A. (2015) "Observational Concepts." In E. Margolis & S. Laurence (eds.) *The Conceptual Mind: New Directions in the Study of Concepts* (pp. 223–247). Cambridge, MA: MIT Press.

—— (2020) "Anthropic Concepts." *Noûs* 54(2): 1–18.

Wheaton, L. A., & Hallett, M. (2007) "Ideomotor Apraxia: A Review." *Journal of the Neurological Sciences* 260(1–2): 1–10.

Winograd, T. (1975) "Frame Representations and the Declarative/Procedural Controversy." In Daniel Bobrow & Allan Collins (eds.) *Representation and Understanding: Studies in Cognitive Science* (pp. 185–210). New York: Academic Press Inc.

Wolpert, D. M. (1997) "Computational Approaches to Motor Control." *Trends in Cognitive Sciences* 1(6): 209–216.

Wolpert, D. M., & Kawato, M. (1998) "Multiple Paired Forward and Inverse Models for Motor Control." *Neural Networks* 11: 1317–1329.

19

THE NATURE OF SKILL

Functions and control structures

Ellen Fridland

19.1 Introduction

To identify the nature of skill, I'd like to avoid two extremes that strike me as equally tenden-tious. These two extremes can be seen clearly in debates concerning the relationship between know how and ability. Though know how is not always obviously identical to skill (see for instance Stanley and Williamson (2017) on know how vs. skill; also see Fields, Chapter 26 in this volume), the connection between the two is naturally close and many of the issues that arise in the realm of know how have parallels in considerations of skill.

On one side of the debate about the relationship between know how and ability there is the position that is usually identified as anti-intellectualist—a position, rightly or wrongly, attributed to Gilbert Ryle,[1] that know how is a kind of intelligent ability. According to this view,[2] knowing how to *phi* just is being able to *phi*, or having the ability to *phi*.[3] On the opposing side of the debate is a position that is often endorsed by intellectualists, a position that holds that knowing how to *phi* is a matter of possessing or being disposed to acquire some relevant state of propos-itional knowledge. On this view, being able to *phi* or having the ability to *phi* is not necessary for know how, since one may possess a standing state of knowledge but lack the ability to put that knowledge into action. According to such a position, knowledge is primary and action is secondary.[4] It strikes me that both the intellectualist and anti-intellectualist get something right and something wrong and, in developing a theory of skill, I'd like to do justice to the insights of both positions while avoiding the mistakes of each.

First, let's take a look at what anti-intellectualism gets wrong. It seems to me that there are two major reasons why we should want to avoid identifying skills with abilities. The first reason is that such a position lacks the ability to explain why an agent is able to successfully instantiate her skills on various occasions. Second, it has the odd consequence of seeming to imply that the only time that people have skills is when they are able to perform them.

Let's take the second problem first. It should be obvious that agents possess skills even when they are not performing them and even when they are in situations where they are unable to perform them. But if skills just are abilities to instantiate skilled actions then it seems that we are in an odd position of denying this. On such an account, it will turn out that no one has reading skills in a dark room and no one has swimming skills in the desert, no one has cooking skills in a swimming pool, and no one has dancing skills with a twisted ankle.[5]

Now, one might think ascribing skills to an agent just amounts to *predicting* that they'll perform successfully or reliably in appropriately related circumstances. But in the same way as above, this gets things the wrong way around. The reason why we can predict that skilled agents will perform successfully in various circumstances is because they have accumulated, through experience, the control and knowledge necessary to perform skills on various occasions. Their possession of skill accounts for their successful instantiation of skilled actions. At bottom, then, if we look exclusively at actual abilities or instantiations of skilled actions, we lose the power to predict and explain why different instantiations of action have the features that they do. That is, we lose the power to see what it is about the agent that makes her able to perform skillfully. This is the second and perhaps more critical problem with the anti-intellectualist position. Possession of skills should account for successful performances of skilled actions on various occasions. Focus on performance loses sight of the underlying conditions or standing states of the agent that explain, unite, and account for the abilities to *phi* when those abilities are manifest.

On the other side of things, however, we have what the anti-intellectualist gets right—and that's the fact that skills and implementations, instantiations or abilities to perform skills are naturally and essentially connected. That is, the anti-intellectualist's emphasis on abilities to *phi* gets right the necessary connection between skills or know how and action. If we give up the centrality of action in an account of skill or know how then we aren't giving an account of skill anymore (see Shepherd, Chapter 21 in this volume). We are giving an account of something else. We have lost the thread.

And this brings us to the main problem with an intellectualist account of skill or know how. Such an account, in emphasizing the possession of knowledge or the disposition to acquire states of knowledge, makes action or guiding action not only secondary but contingent to skill. This can be seen clearly in discussions where intellectualists insist that an agent can possess know how but lack the ability to put that know how into action. For instance, in their defense of intellectualism, Stanley and Williamson (2001: 6) write:

> [I]t is simply false that ascriptions of knowledge-how ascribe abilities. As Ginet and others have pointed out, ascriptions of knowledge-how do not even entail ascriptions of the corresponding abilities. For example, a ski instructor may know how to perform a certain complex stunt, without being able to perform it herself. Similarly, a master pianist who loses both of her arms in a tragic car accident still knows how to play the piano. However, she has lost her ability to do so.[6]

The main problem with the intellectualist account of know how or skill is that action or instantiation of skill becomes demoted to contingent status. That is, intellectualism focuses almost exclusively on the internal standing psychological and epistemic states of skilled agent and loses the centrality of action in an account of skill.[7] Intellectualism, it seems, attempts to give an account of know how but not an account of *intelligent, controlled, skilled action*. But this is exactly what needs to be accounted for if we want an adequate account of skill. Giving an account of skill in terms of knowledge, where skilled, successful action or ability becomes contingent, betrays a fundamental misunderstanding of the kind of thing that skill is. This misunderstanding will become clear once my account is on the table.

On the other hand, however, we should note what intellectualism gets right: the insistence that we have to do justice to the underlying, internal, cognitive, and epistemic states of the agent if we are to give an adequate account of skill. That is, intellectualism, even though it identifies the wrong sort of psychological state, is right to hold that states or conditions of the agent are required to explain, unify, and account for the various occasions on which skills are successfully instantiated in action.

Overall then, my take on the philosophical debate between possessing skills and the ability to perform them is as follows: if anti-intellectualists think knowing how is simply the instantiation of know how in action, they are wrong. Skills critically involve internal, learned, control states that account for the ability to implement skilled actions at different times. But anti-intellectualists are right to think that skills and instantiations of skilled actions are necessarily and intimately connected. That is, anti-intellectualists are right that action is at the heart of skill. Intellectualists, on the other hand, are right that skill is not identical to the ability to instantiate skill on any particular occasion or group of occasions. But they are wrong if they conclude from this that skill and instantiations of skill in action are only contingently related. They are also wrong to conceive of the standing states of a skilled agent in terms of propositional knowledge, but they are right to insist that the internal standing states are central to the possession of skill. In sum, then, the account of skill that I will offer will do justice both to the centrality of action on an account of skill and to the fact that skilled actions need to be explained and accounted for by the internal conditions of the agents that possess them.

19.2 Skills as functions

I suggest that we think of skills as functions. Namely, as functions from intentions to controlled, successful actions, where the functional transformations from intention to action are implemented by control structures that have been developed through practice. Coming from the philosophy of mind, this is a natural way to think of actions in general, but it is an especially apt way to think of skills. This is because skills, in virtue of their peculiar learning histories, rely on control structures that give rise to characteristic, controlled, intelligent actions. Identifying these control structures gives us a way to identify the cognitive processes at the heart of skilled action.

A major benefit of thinking of skills as functions stems from the fact that such a conception allows us to naturally integrate several essential features of skill that on other accounts appear contingent or peripheral. By identifying skills with input, output, and the control structures that are responsible for transforming the one into the other, we group together conceptually disparate but actually essential aspects of skill. In thinking of skills as functions from intentions to controlled actions, however, we are well positioned to naturally unify these disparate aspects of skill in a way that is clear, motivated, and powerful. Moreover, we also retain an explanation of why it is that skills, when instantiated, are a species of intentional action—a characterization of skill that has been accepted by intellectualists and anti-intellectualists alike.[8]

To make clear how the function of skill is to be characterized, we can think of the more familiar example of visual perception. The functional characterization of vision, of course, is in terms of the transformation of visual stimuli (inputs) into visual experiences of discrimination and identification (outputs). Analogously, but in the opposite direction, we can think of skills as transforming intentions (inputs) into controlled actions (outputs). In the case of vision, these transformations are implemented by visual processes that take place largely in the visual cortex. In contrast, in the case of skill, the function is carried out by control structures of at least three kinds: strategic, attention, and motor, which I'll flesh out below. Accordingly, the control structures of skill are not realized by a single set of neural mechanisms or regions in the brain. The lack of a single brain area or region should not, however, by itself make us think that control structures do not comprise a robust, unified functional category. After all, it certainly is not the case that all or even most functional phenomena are realized by a single area of the brain. Think, for instance, of the motor control system which is composed not only of the motor cortex but also the cerebellum, basal ganglia, thalamus, brainstem, and spinal cord. At bottom, then, the suggestion on the table is this: we should think of skills as functions that transform intentions or goals into controlled actions. And control structures of at least three kinds, all of which are developed through practice, are responsible for the relevant functional transformations.

Now, of course, we *could* simply identify skills with their manifestations in action just like we *could* identify vision with visual experience or with the discrimination and identification of visual objects. But in both these cases, in looking exclusively at the manifest phenomenon we lose the underlying processes that unify, explain, and make these kinds of episodes possible. In the case of vision, after all, we learn a lot about its nature by looking at the way in which visual inputs are transformed into visual experiences. The hope is that in the case of skill, we can learn about its nature by examining the control structures that are responsible for implementing intentions into skilled actions. Of course, we *could* also identify skill with control structures just as we *could* identify vision with visual processing in the visual cortex. But lacking the functional connection to behavior would make such an identification meaningless—we would lose the manifest phenomenon that we are trying to explain in the first place. The other option, but one that has very little going for it, is to identify skills with intentions. This seems about as attractive an option as identifying vision with visual stimuli, which is to say, not very attractive at all.

At this point, we can return to the discussion of intellectualism above and see why skills do not have only a contingent connection to skilled action or abilities. That is, we can now see why skills are not just the internal conditions of the agent that have a merely contingent connection with actual performances. We can now see that pure intellectualism misidentifies the nature of skill. And this misidentification betrays a fundamental misunderstanding of the nature of functions. As is well known, in biology, psychology, and the cognitive sciences, the nature of a phenomenon is often distinguished and identified according to what it has the function of doing. Of course, independent instances of the function are not identical to the function itself. Likewise, simply because skills are not identical to skillful instantiations does not mean that the two are somehow only contingently connected. After all, we wouldn't say that visual perception is not for discriminating and identifying visual features of a visual array simply because the function of visual perception is not identical to any one instance or set of instances of actually discriminating or identifying visual features of a visual array. Likewise, even if skills do not always manifest in the ability to put the skill into action this does not mean that skilled action is secondary, contingently, or peripherally related to the internal conditions that make such action possible. As such, we can see why focus on internal conditions alone is insufficient for providing an account of skill.

The talk of skill as functions isn't a familiar way of thinking about skills, I understand, but I think the view has a lot going for it. When we think of skills in this way, we see immediately why the internal standing conditions of the agent are essential to our account of skill—because they are responsible for implementing the function. And we also see why both intentions and practical instantiations of skilled actions are centrally implicated by our theory—because they are the inputs and outputs of the function.

Further, we learn why it is that control structures develop and work the way they do—because their role is to produce the control that skilled actions exhibit, something that they acquire as a result of deliberate, directed practice. But we should also note that control structures, even though they may involve knowledge, are not simply states of propositional knowledge—they are transformational mechanisms that guide and control actions. Thinking of control structures in these terms has the potential to cast the intelligence of skill at the right level, neither fully conceptual or rational nor brute causal, but interestingly intermediate between the two.

19.3 Kinds of control

As I've indicated above, control structures are not meant to pick out any one type of state or structure but to identify a set of relevant representations which are responsible for the flexible modification, adaptation, and adjustment of action in order to reach a goal (see Wu, Chapter 16 in this volume). Importantly, these structures are learned through practice. When it comes to embodied skills, control structures are hierarchically organized and function on at least three levels. I will discuss the relevant types of control and how to understand them below.

19.3.1 Strategic control

On my account, intentions are themselves a kind of control structure governing skilled action.[9] Accordingly, I'll maintain that practice is required not only for automatizing certain motor components of skilled action but for refining and structuring the practical plans that specify and organize the instantiations of those skilled actions. As such, skilled agents uniquely possess strategic, practical, organizing intentions that structure their skilled actions in appropriate and effective ways. In this way, part of being skilled is knowing and planning, in a practical manner, what one is going to do. I'll refer to this sort of *knowledge in action*, that is, to the plans and goals that are learned as a result of practice and directly involved in guiding skilled actions, as *strategic control*.[10]

When I discuss strategic control, I have in mind the practical goals, plans, and strategies that skilled agents use in order to specify, structure, and organize their skilled actions. The idea is that skilled agents are better than novices not only at implementing the intentions that they have but also at forming the right intentions. More specifically, skilled agents are able to formulate and modify, adjust, and adapt their practical intentions in ways that are appropriate, effective, and flexible given their more distal, overall goals. In this way, through practice, an agent develops strategic control by developing the right kinds of practical intentions to guide her action effectively.[11]

But what kind of thing are practical intentions, you might be wondering? On the account I'm offering, practical intentions should be understood as higher-order, perceptual-motor structures that encode specific invariant features of actions and guide actions in virtue of encoding this information. These invariant features are usually combinations of complex action elements, which are specified in terms of motor commands and expected sensory outcome pairs. What I have in mind is very much in line with what Mylopoulos and Pacherie (hereafter M&P; 2017, 2019), following Schmidt (1975, 2003) have called "motor schemas."[12] As they explain:

> According to schema theory, motor schemas are both repositories of information and control structures. They are internal models or stored representations that represent generic knowledge about a certain pattern of action and are implicated in the production and control of action … . The generalized motor program is thought to contain an abstract representation defining the general form or pattern of an action, that is the organization and structure common to a set of motor acts (e.g., invariant features pertaining to the order of events, their spatial configuration, their relative timing and the relative force with which they are produced).
>
> *M&P 2017: 330*

There is one significant difference between motor schemas and embodied practical intentions, or as I call them, "action schemas." Most importantly, the informational states that I suggest are involved in strategic control are personal-level representations that an agent can access, manipulate, commit to, and use for planning, decision-making, and reasoning.[13] That is, they are agent-level structures, whereas M&P's motor schemas are subpersonal, unconscious states that are not directly responsive to or involved in practical reasoning and agent-level thinking. Instead, for M&P motor schemas are triggered, or activated by their associated executable action concept (M&P 2017, 2019).[14]

This difference makes all the difference since on the account I am forwarding, perceptual-motor control structures—that is, action schemas—can themselves function as practical intentions when they are tokened. That is, action schemas can function as states that we can commit to and with which we can plan and guide action in virtue of their informational relations (spatial, temporal, biomechanical, and predicted). That is, action schemas are not merely associated or triggered by propositional thought but, rather, are themselves, in virtue of their structural and informational relations, involved in thought and reasoning.

A second point I'm concerned to emphasize is that action schemas encode not only features such as sequence, timing, relative force, etc. but also prediction or anticipation of expected sensory outputs. This forward-looking aspect of action schemas not only forges a connection between strategic control and ideomotor theories of action (Prinz 1997; Hommel 2009, 2015) and predictive accounts of cognition in general (Clark 2013; Hohwy 2013), but also sets the stage for a substantive explanation in the next section of how attention and strategic control are related.

Finally, it is important to see why we should think of practical intentions as somewhat intermediate between high-level abstract, amodal representations and low-level sensorimotor processes. My claim is that practical intentions involve structures grounded in perception and action but that these are not low-level, subpersonal, associative states. In the way I am conceiving of the practical intentions involved in strategic control, they are personal-level, higher-order, perceptual-modal structures. Further, they can be targeted by deliberate manipulation and conscious control and they can be involved in agent-level processes such as counterfactual reasoning, and decision-making. In this way, action schemas are grounded, perceptual or imagistic structures with which real thinking and planning can be done.[15]

We should notice that practical intentions are rational states insofar as they are means-ends coherent, and consistent with beliefs and desires. For all that, they remain representations of perceptual and motor systems. I should add that I am not simply asserting here that practical intentions involve embodied concepts (Prinz 2004; Barsalou 2008, 2010). I am claiming that the intentions that we use to plan, specify, and guide skilled actions are effective in virtue of the shape and configuration of their grounded, informational structures. That is, the claim here is not that we use concepts to reason and those concepts happen to be modal. The claim is that, at least sometimes, we reason by manipulation, perhaps via simulation (Currie and Ravenscroft 1997; Prinz 2004), of the structural relations that constitute action schemas. That is, we use the information gathered through the manipulation of action schemas to guide decision-making, counterfactual reasoning and, most importantly, action.

19.3.2 Attention

Of course, to account for skill, we need to explain not only how intentions or action schemas are formulated or represented by the agent but also how those practical intentions are implemented in actual action—in a way that is controlled, accurate, and reflective of those intentions. To understand this, we need to account not only for an abstract cognitive representation of some complex action, even an embodied, grounded one, but also an explanation of how that intended action can be performed right here and now with this particular body in this particular context. That is, we need to move from a more abstract embodied conception of action to acting in this exact world as it is right now. We need to situate and ground our actions. For this to happen, an agent has to be sensitive to both what she wants to do, that is, the practical plan that she has formulated, and also to the state of her body and the state of the world in which she will be performing it. This, I think, is where attention comes in.

On the theory of skill as I am developing it, attention selects relevant perceptual features of the action environment and acting agent in order to both constrain and guide action execution. In this way, attention is a form of selection for action (Allport 1987; Wu 2011a). This means that attention is conceived of, first and foremost, as selecting perceptual information that contributes to the instantiation of successful skilled action.

Though attention likely plays several roles at different levels of skill (e.g., selecting intentions or providing sensory information for online sensorimotor control), I will focus on what I'll call attention's rational integration function. Specifically, I'll claim that attention selects relevant perceptual information about the environment and agent, under the direction of practical intentions, which then gets passed to the motor system for planning. In selecting this information, attention rationally constrains the goal that the motor system receives.

We should notice that though attention is required for settling on a practical intention for skilled action in the first place, it is the attention that is necessary for deciding what happens *after* one has formulated a practical intention that I will focus on here. That is, once an intention has been settled, attention then has the role of providing the relevant, intention-sensitive perceptual information about the conditions of the actual world to the motor system, such that a coherent, rational, and successful motor response can be planned and initiated.[16]

I maintain that an explanation of the rational integration role of attention can be spelled out by appeal to action schemas (instantiated practical intentions) if we take seriously the predictive component of the schema and connect selection of perceptual features, that is, attention, to that anticipatory representation. In short, intention can structure complex skilled motor behavior, if attention is tied to the predictions or prospections of action schema and if attention can thus select action-specific information based on those predictions. If attention selects situation-specific perceptual information under the direction of the anticipatory predictions of action schemas, then such attention can establish the complex plan of the agent in the motor system by structuring the goals that the motor system receives. Importantly, once we see top-down attention as directed by the forward predictions of a personal-level action schema, we can revise our view of the function of attention from merely informing motor reactions to guiding and shaping movement organization in a robust, systematic, and rational way.

My main claim, then, is that the role of attention in skill should be identified not merely with selection of relevant input, which then informs motor behavior in order to satisfy intentions but with anticipatory selection of relevant perceptual information to organize and direct skilled motor behavior according to the strategic plan of the agent. In this way, attention not only provides information for action but shapes and structures the unfolding action based on the practical intentions that an agent has formed. That is, the form of the movements instantiated during skilled action is organized by practical intentions and integrated with motor control via anticipatory attention. And this can be achieved if the intention guiding skill is conceived of properly, specifically, as encoding a prediction of sensory outcome that attention can then use in anticipatory selection. Of course, the more refined the action schema the more accurate the prediction and this helps us to understand why it is that attention improves as a result of skill learning.[17] That is, this helps us to see why it is that practice produces more accurate, organized, and effective selective attention.

19.3.3 Motor control

The last kind of control that develops in skill as a result of practice is motor control. The motor level of control is obviously crucial for bodily skills, since the way in which an action is performed is critical to its skill or lack thereof. That is, for a truly skilled action, we want not only a sophisticated conception of the action, and not only that the conception of the action involves perceptual selection, but that the intention actually gets implemented into a controlled, successful action.

I'll maintain that motor control develops as a result of practice in two ways that highlight the intelligence of this level of control. Both aspects of motor control are worth discussing briefly here: first, there is the diachronic shaping of motor schemas—where the internalized model of motor output becomes automatized and internalized into the motor system in a way that reflects the particular guiding and shaping power of deliberate practice (see Wu, Chapter 16; Krakauer, Chapter 17 both in this volume). Second, motor control develops in the responsiveness of motor schemas to the goals that the motor system inherits via the selection mechanisms of attention. That is, motor representations become more responsive to the goals of the agent.

As with action schemas, the view of motor representation that I endorse is one where motor schemas are both representational and control mechanisms that consist of structured complexes of invariant action elements and which involve predictive components anticipating sensory outcomes (M&P 2017, 2019). Unlike action schemas, however, motor schemas are internal to the motor system and thus cannot be used in practical reasoning or in the formation of practical intentions.[18] We should note, however, that though motor schemas are not themselves personal-level states, they still reflect agent-level processes in their shape and structure. That is, motor schemas reflect the technique-oriented, deliberate practice through which they were formed.

To understand how personal-level states shape and structure motor schemas, we can look at the process of motor chunking. As a result of practice, motor chunking restructures individual action elements into larger units that can be implemented in fast, accurate, effective, and automatic ways. Importantly, empirical evidence concerning motor chunking indicates this kind of unitization proceeds as a result of two different, likely hierarchical processes (Hikosaka et al. 1999, 2002; Verwey 2001; Sakai et al. 2003; Wymbs et al. 2012; Fridland 2019). As Wymbs et al. (2012) describe these processes they are:

a. Concatenation: the formation of motor-motor associations between elements or sets of elements.
b. Segmentation: parsing of multiple contiguous elements into shorter action sets.

Concatenation is best thought of as an associative learning process where individual action elements are combined into wholes (Verwey 2001; Wymbs et al. 2012). So, individual elements of an action sequence or task are fused or bound together into larger combined units. In brief, individual elements in a series develop stronger connections to the other elements in the sequence through the process of concatenation. This allows for more fluid and automatic execution of the whole (see Pavese, Chapter 18 in this volume).

However, if concatenation were the only process involved in the automatization of motor schemas then we'd expect to see the connection between all elements in a sequence increase to form a large single unit or motor plan. That is, if only concatenation were involved in the unitization or shaping of motor routines then we should see an undifferentiated associative increase in the connection between all the motor elements in a sequence, at least until the relevant limit on working memory was reached. For example, if concatenation was alone responsible for motor learning, then with a sequence like "A B C A B C" we should see a stronger connection between all the elements in the series, such that the entire succession of elements could be executed faster. We could represent such an increase in associative strength as follows: [ABCABC]. In contrast, however, in healthy individuals, motor chunking actually looks more like this: [ABC] [ABC].

As such, we can conclude that motor chunking is not simply the result of a concatenation process. Rather, motor chunking manifests in a strong connection between a set of elements in an action sequence, and that set is separated from other sets of very well-integrated elements in a larger series or structure. This strategy of cutting down and organizing action sequences into shorter segments is called parsing (Wymbs et al. 2012). Crucially, parsing is an executive or control-level process (Kennerley et al. 2004; Verwey 2010; Verwey et al. 2011; Pammi et al. 2012). Groupings are not simply the result of limitations on working memory but, rather, an efficient strategy for structuring the sequence in a logical, rational way—*according to the agent's own lights.*

It should be clear from this brief overview that the automatized motor schemas that are internalized in the motor system as a result of deliberate practice are a kind of, as Krakauer (2019) has eloquently put it, "intelligent reflex." They are the automatic structures that can be deployed without cognitive effort or explicit attention to performing a specific action in a specific way. But even if they are automatic, they are not in any way brute, basic, or unintelligent.

Importantly, motor schemas do not become more rigid or inflexible as a result of deliberate practice and automaticity. In fact, the refined sensitivity of motor schemas to the practical demands of the task ensures that they continue to function in adaptable, flexible, and modifiable ways. The claim then is that motor control not only develops internal to the motor system but also in its integration with the agent's particular practical goals for implementing a task. Motor schemas, in this way, though not globally integrated with the beliefs and desires of the agent are still sensitive specifically to the practical intentions that the agent herself (and not the motor system) is committed to implementing.

The goal sensitivity of motor representations to practical intentions is well documented and can be illustrated briefly by appeal to the minimum intervention principle. According to this principle, agents

> only correct perturbations that interfere with the achievement of task goals. If a perturbation is irrelevant to the task, for instance, if your elbow is knocked during a reaching movement without affecting your hand position then there is no need to correct for it—just maintain the new elbow posture during the rest of the movement.
> *Haith and Krakauer 2013: 16*[19]

Crucially, however, if the motor system only corrects those movements that are relevant to task success then it must be able to differentiate between task-relevance and task-irrelevance. However, to do this, the system must be sensitive to success and failure at the task or goal level. After all, the motor system has to understand the task goal and not simply a motor or sensory goal to differentiate between task-relevance and task-irrelevance—as it is related to task success and failure.[20] It would seem then that motor control is sensitive to a semantically construed goal of action (even though it is not sensitive globally to the epistemic and psychological states of the agent) (see Pavese, Chapter 18 in this volume).

Presumably, with practice, motor states can become more appropriate and accurate by becoming more sensitive to the particular demands of the particular circumstances and particular goals of the agent. That is, the integration between action schemas and motor schemas can become more accurate and appropriate through practice. As such, we see another aspect of motor control that is crucial to understand when it comes to bodily skill: not only is the motor system better able to accurately and effectively implement some predetermined task but the motor system is more sensitive to the constraints of the task itself as it is formulated by the practical intentions of the agent. That is, motor schemas become more effectively integrated with the goals of the agent—calculating and selecting more appropriate motor commands for the task at hand. It is both of these ways that motor control develops through practice and, thus, becomes able to more appropriately adapt, adjust, modify, and correct the motor implementation of a skill.

Notes

1 It isn't clear what exactly Ryle's position here really was. Stanley and Williamson (2001) attribute Ryle this position: "According to Ryle, an ascription of the form 'x knows how to F' merely ascribes to x the ability to F." See also Bengson et al. (2009) who claim that anti-intellectualism or neo-Ryleans hold that "x knows how to ψ if and only if x possesses a certain sort of ability to ψ." And Glick (2012) who attributes to Ryle a strong version of the ability thesis. Others disagree, see, for instance, Noë (2005), Hornsby (2011: 82), and see also Kremer, Chapter 7 in this volume.
2 See, for instance, Setiya (2012).
3 See Millikan (2000: 51–68) and also Noë (2005: 283–4) for a distinction between being able to and possessing an ability.
4 Stanley and Williamson's (2017) more recent explication of skill as a disposition to know (that manifests in knowledge states poised to guide action) is making a similar error in putting knowledge at the center of skill and making action secondary.
5 This criticism isn't meant to imply that no decent solutions to this problem have been offered. See, for instance, Hawley's (2003) account which characterizes know how as ability under normal counterfactual conditions.
6 See also Bengson et al. (2009) who argue that their experimental philosophical evidence supports the claim that folk judgments are consistent with this kind of intellectualism.
7 More recent developments of the intellectualist view, for instance Pavese (2015) and Stanley (2011), have insisted that knowing how to *phi* entails the ability to *phi* (intentionally). However, these ability-entailing views are not purely intellectualist as they require that the intelligence of know how be accounted for in not exclusively propositional terms. In this way, these views can be seen as more hybrid than intellectualist.
8 See, for instance, Stanley and Williamson (2001); Stanley (2011); Setiya (2012); Fridland (2014); Pavese (2017, 2018).
9 Practical intentions then are both inputs that are implemented into action by other control structures and control structures themselves that improve via recurrent cycles of practice, feedback, and consideration.
10 This notion of strategic control is similar in important respects to Christensen et al.'s (2016) notion of cognitive control.
11 The effectiveness of mental practice (Landers 1983; Driskell et al. 1994; Jeannerod and Decety 1995; Hanakawa et al. 2003, 2008; Guillot et al. 2009; Madan and Singhal 2012; Schack et al. 2014) helps us to appreciate the importance of strategic control for skill. This is because, presumably, it is the more strategic components of skill that are enhanced via mental practice. After all, since motor learning is reliant on actual feedback for improvement, mental practice's benefits cannot be at the motor level since no actual physical feedback is present.
12 See also Arbib (1992) and Jeannerod (1994).

13 This type of state is in close proximity to both what M&P have called "executable action concepts (EACs)" (2017) and what Pavese (2015, 2019) has called a "practical sense." However, unlike EACs and practical senses, the action schema, as I envision it, is not simply a concept that is associated with a control mechanism but is itself a control structure.

14 As M&P describe motor schema, they are

> the inputs and outputs of practical reasoning processes, they [motor representations] are the inputs and outputs of rapid sensorimotor computations. Rather than being subject to norms of practical reasoning they are subject to a set of biomechanical and motor rules. Rather than being personal-level representations, they are subpersonal representations. Rather than functioning under conscious control, they function largely automatically.
>
> *M&P 2017: 322–3*

15 As Gauker (2011), van Leeuwen (2011), Langland-Hassan (2011), and Nanay (2016) have emphasized, perceptual states like those involved in imagination can serve as an important epistemic tool for gaining knowledge.

16 See Wu (2011b) for more on this "non-deliberative" many-many problem.

17 See Mann et al. (2007) for meta-analysis and Davids et al. (1999) for review. See also Fridland (2017).

18 For evidence that motor control processing is isolated from the personal-level states of the agent see, for instance, Fourneret and Jeannerod (1998) or Aglioti et al. (1995).

19 See also Bernstein (1967); Cole and Abbs (1986); Scholz and Schöner (1999), Scholz et al. (2000); Domkin et al. (2002); Todorov and Jordan (2002); Nagengast et al. (2009).

20 As Taylor and Ivry (2011) explain,

> A key insight of the model is that implicit and explicit learning mechanisms operate on different error signals. Consistent with previous models of sensorimotor adaptation, implicit learning is driven by an error reflecting the difference between the predicted and actual feedback for the movement. In contrast, explicit learning is driven by an error based on the difference between feedback and target location of the movement, a signal that directly reflects task performance.

See also Mazzoni and Krakauer (2006); Day et al. (2016); McDougle et al. (2016).

References

Aglioti, S., DeSouza, J. F., and Goodale, M. A. (1995) "Size-Contrast Illusions Deceive the Eye but Not the Hand," *Current Biology* 5: 679–85.

Allport, D. A. (1987) "Selection for Action: Some Behavioral and Neurophysiological Considerations of Attention and Action," *Perspectives on Perception and Action* 15: 395–419.

Arbib, M. A. (1992) "Schema Theory," *The Encyclopedia of Artificial Intelligence* 2: 1427–43.

Barsalou, L. W. (2008) "Grounded Cognition," *Annual Review of Psychology* 59: 617–45.

—— (2010) "Grounded Cognition: Past, Present, and Future," *Topics in Cognitive Science* 2: 716–24.

Bengson, J., Moffett, M. A., and Wright, J. C. (2009) "The Folk on Knowing How," *Philosophical Studies* 142: 387–401.

Bernstein, N. (1967) *The Coordination and Regulation of Movements*, New York: Pergamon Press.

Christensen, W., Sutton, J., and McIlwain, D. J. (2016) "Cognition in Skilled Action: Meshed Control and the Varieties of Skill Experience," *Mind & Language* 31: 37–66.

Clark, A. (2013) "Whatever Next? Predictive Brains, Situated Agents, and the Future of Cognitive Science," *Behavioral and Brain Sciences* 36: 181–204.

Cole, K. J., and Abbs, J. H. (1986) "Coordination of Three-Joint Digit Movements for Rapid Finger-Thumb Grasp," *Journal of Neurophysiology* 55: 1407–23.

Currie, G., and Ravenscroft, I. (1997) "Mental Simulation and Motor Imagery," *Philosophy of Science* 64: 161–80.

Davids, K., Williams, A. M., and Williams, J. G. (1999) *Visual Perception and Action in Sport*, London: Routledge.

Day, K. A., Roemmich, R. T., Taylor, J. A., and Bastian, A. J. (2016) "Visuomotor Learning Generalizes Around the Intended Movement," *eNeuro* 3: e0005–16, doi: 10.1523/ENEURO.0005-16.2016.

Domkin, D., Laczko, J., Jaric, S., Johansson, H., and Latash, M. L. (2002) "Structure of Joint Variability in Bimanual Pointing Tasks," *Experimental Brain Research* 143: 11–23.

Driskell, J. E., Copper, C., and Moran, A. (1994) "Does Mental Practice Enhance Performance?" *Journal of Applied Psychology* 79: 481.

Fourneret, P., and Jeannerod, M. (1998) "Limited Conscious Monitoring of Motor Performance in Normal Subjects," *Neuropsychologia* 36: 1133–40.

Fridland, E. (2014) "They've Lost Control: Reflections on Skill," *Synthese* 191: 2729–50.

—— (2017) "Motor Skill and Moral Virtue," *Royal Institute of Philosophy Supplements* 80: 139–70.

—— (2019) "Longer, Smaller, Faster, Stronger: On Skills and Intelligence," *Philosophical Psychology* 32: 759–83.

Gauker, C. (2011) *Words and Images: An Essay on the Origin of Ideas*, Oxford: Oxford University Press.

Glick, E. (2012) "Abilities and Know-How Attributions," in J. Brown and M. Gerken (eds.) *Knowledge Ascriptions*, 120–39, Oxford: Oxford University Press.

Guillot, A., Nadrowska, E., and Collet, C. (2009) "Using Motor Imagery to Learn Tactical Movements in Basketball," *Journal of Sport Behavior* 32: 189–206.

Haith, A. M., and Krakauer, J. W. (2013) "Model-Based and Model-Free Mechanisms of Human Motor Learning," *Advances in Experimental Medicine and Biology* 782: 1–21.

Hanakawa, T., Immisch, I., Toma, K., Dimyan, M. A., Van Gelderen, P., and Hallett, M. (2003) "Functional Properties of Brain Areas Associated with Motor Execution and Imagery," *Journal of Neurophysiology* 89: 989–1002.

Hanakawa, T., Dimyan, M. A., and Hallett, M. (2008) "Motor Planning, Imagery, and Execution in the Distributed Motor Network: A Time-Course Study with Functional MRI," *Cerebral Cortex* 18: 2775–88.

Hawley, K. (2003) "Success and Knowledge-How," *American Philosophical Quarterly* 40: 19–31.

Hikosaka, O., Nakahara, H., Rand, M. K., Sakai, K., Lu, X., Nakamura, K., et al. (1999) "Parallel Neural Networks for Learning Sequential Procedures," *Trends in Neurosciences* 22: 464–71.

Hikosaka, O., Nakamura, K., Sakai, K., and Nakahara, H. (2002) "Central Mechanisms of Motor Skill Learning," *Current Opinion in Neurobiology* 12: 217–22.

Hohwy, J. (2013) *The Predictive Mind*, Oxford: Oxford University Press.

Hommel, B. (2009) "Action Control According to TEC (Theory of Event Coding)," *Psychological Research PRPF* 73: 512–26.

—— (2015) "The Theory of Event Coding (TEC) as Embodied-Cognition Framework," *Frontiers in Psychology* 6: 1318.

Hornsby, J. (2011) "Ryle's Knowing-How, and Knowing How to Act," in J. Bengson and M. Moffett (eds.) *Knowing How: Essays on Knowledge, Mind, and Action*, 80–98, Oxford: Oxford University Press.

Jeannerod, M. (1994) "The Representing Brain: Neural Correlates of Motor Intention and Imagery," *Behavioral and Brain Sciences* 17: 187–202.

Jeannerod, M., and Decety, J. (1995) "Mental Motor Imagery: A Window into the Representational Stages of Action," *Current Opinion in Neurobiology* 5: 727–32.

Kennerley, S. W., Sakai, K., and Rushworth, M. F. (2004) "Organization of Action Sequences and the Role of the Pre-SMA," *Journal of Neurophysiology* 91: 978–93.

Krakauer, J. W. (2019) "The Intelligent Reflex," *Philosophical Psychology* 32: 822–30.

Landers, D. M. (1983) "The Effects of Mental Practice on Motor Skill Learning and Performance: A Meta-Analysis," *Journal of Sport Psychology* 5: 25–57.

Langland-Hassan, P. (2011) "A Puzzle About Visualization," *Phenomenology and the Cognitive Sciences* 10: 145–73.

Madan, C. R., and Singhal, A. (2012) "Motor Imagery and Higher-Level Cognition: Four Hurdles Before Research Can Sprint Forward," *Cognitive Processing* 13: 211–29.

Mann, D. T., Williams, A. M., Ward, P., and Janelle, C. M. (2007) "Perceptual-Cognitive Expertise in Sport: A Meta-Analysis," *Journal of Sport and Exercise Psychology* 29: 457–78.

Mazzoni, P., and Krakauer, J. W. (2006) "An Implicit Plan Overrides an Explicit Strategy During Visuomotor Adaptation," *Journal of Neuroscience* 26: 3642–5.

McDougle, S. D., Ivry, R. B., and Taylor, J. A. (2016) "Taking Aim at the Cognitive Side of Learning in Sensorimotor Adaptation Tasks," *Trends in Cognitive Sciences* 20: 535–44.

Millikan, R. G. (2000) *On Clear and Confused Ideas: An Essay About Substance Concepts*, Cambridge: Cambridge University Press.

Mylopoulos, M., and Pacherie, E. (2017) "Intentions and Motor Representations: The Interface Challenge," *Review of Philosophy and Psychology* 8: 317–36.

—— (2019) "Intentions: The Dynamic Hierarchical Model Revisited," *Wiley Interdisciplinary Reviews: Cognitive Science* 10: e1481.

Nagengast, A. J., Braun, D. A., and Wolpert, D. M. (2009) "Optimal Control Predicts Human Performance on Objects with Internal Degrees of Freedom," *PLoS Computational Biology* 5: e1000419.

Nanay, B. (2016) "The Role of Imagination in Decision-Making," *Mind & Language* 31: 127–43.

Noë, A. (2005) "Against Intellectualism," *Analysis* 65: 278–90.

Pammi, V. C., Miyapuram, K. P., Samejima, K., Bapi, R. S., and Doya, K. (2012) "Changing the Structure of Complex Visuo-Motor Sequences Selectively Activates the Fronto-Parietal Network," *Neuroimage* 59: 1180–9.

Pavese, C. (2015) "Practical Senses," *Philosopher's Imprint* 15: 1–25.

—— (2017) "A Theory of Practical Meaning," *Philosophical Topics* 45: 65–96.

—— (2018) "Know-How, Action, and Luck," *Synthese*: 1–23.

—— (2019) "The Psychological Reality of Practical Representation," *Philosophical Psychology* 32: 784–821.

Prinz, J. J. (2004) *Gut Reactions: A Perceptual Theory of Emotion*, Oxford: Oxford University Press.

Prinz, W. (1997) "Perception and Action Planning," *European Journal of Cognitive Psychology* 9: 129–54.

Sakai, K., Kitaguchi, K., and Hikosaka, O. (2003) "Chunking During Human Visuomotor Sequence Learning," *Experimental Brain Research* 152: 229–42.

Schack, T., Essig, K., Frank, C., and Koester, D. (2014) "Mental Representation and Motor Imagery Training," *Frontiers in Human Neuroscience* 8: 328. doi:10.3389/fnhum.2014.00328.

Schmidt, R. (1975) "A Schema Theory of Discrete Motor Skill Learning," *Psychological Review* 82: 225–60.

—— (2003) "Motor Schema Theory After 27 Years: Reflections and Implications for a New Theory," *Research Quarterly for Exercise and Sport* 74: 366–75.

Scholz, J. P., and Schöner, G. (1999) "The Uncontrolled Manifold Concept: Identifying Control Variables for a Functional Task," *Experimental Brain Research* 126: 289–306.

Scholz, J. P., Schöner, G., and Latash, M. L. (2000) "Identifying the Control Structure of Multijoint Coordination During Pistol Shooting," *Experimental Brain Research* 135: 382–404.

Setiya, K. (2012) "XIV—Knowing How," *Proceedings of the Aristotelian Society* 112: 285–307.

Stanley, J. (2011) *Know How*, Oxford: Oxford University Press.

Stanley, J., and Williamson, T. (2001) "Knowing How," *The Journal of Philosophy* 98: 411–44.

—— (2017) "Skill," *Noûs* 51: 713–26.

Taylor, J. A., and Ivry, R. B. (2011) "Flexible Cognitive Strategies During Motor Learning," *PLoS Computational Biology* 7: e1001096.

Todorov, E., and Jordan, M. I. (2002) "Optimal Feedback Control as a Theory of Motor Coordination," *Nature Neuroscience* 5: 1226.

Van Leeuwen, N. (2011) "Imagination Is Where the Action Is," *The Journal of Philosophy* 108: 55–77.

Verwey, W. B. (2001) "Concatenating Familiar Movement Sequences: The Versatile Cognitive Processor," *Acta Psychologica* 106: 69–95.

—— (2010) "Diminished Motor Skill Development in Elderly: Indications for Limited Motor Chunk Use," *Acta Psychologica* 134: 206–14.

Verwey, W. B., Abrahamse, E. L., Ruitenberg, M. F., Jiménez, L., and de Kleine, E. (2011) "Motor Skill Learning in the Middle-Aged: Limited Development of Motor Chunks and Explicit Sequence Knowledge," *Psychological Research* 75: 406–22.

Wu, W. (2011a) "Attention as Selection for Action," in C. Mole, D. Smithies, and W. Wu (eds.) *Attention: Philosophical and Psychological Essays*, 97–116, Oxford: Oxford University Press.

—— (2011b) "Confronting Many-Many Problems: Attention and Agentive Control," *Noûs* 45: 50–76.

Wymbs, N. F., Bassett, D. S., Mucha, P. J., Porter, M. A., and Grafton, S. T. (2012) "Differential Recruitment of the Sensorimotor Putamen and Frontoparietal Cortex During Motor Chunking in Humans," *Neuron* 74: 936–46.

20

THE INTELLIGENCE OF MOTOR CONTROL

Myrto Mylopoulos

20.1 Introduction

A highly skilled tennis player—let's call her Bianca—intends to return her opponent's serve. Her opponent fires the ball to the side opposite to the one that Bianca occupies. Bianca powers her way toward the ball, and in a lightning sequence, swings her arm back, rotates her shoulder, tightens her grip on her racquet, extends her elbow, swings her arm forward with a precise force, speed, and direction, and makes contact with the ball.

Few would disagree that skilled action like this involves the exercise of a high degree of *intelligence* within a certain domain. In the course of skilled performance, an agent executes the correct actions, at the correct time, and in the correct way. Likewise, many would accept that skill in some domain is acquired by way of extensive practice and training and that, as a result, the bulk of the behaviour involved in skilled action is executed *automatically* and *without thought or explicit intention*.[1] But now consider this: automatic, unthinking behaviours are often assumed to be reflexive and paradigmatically *unintelligent*. They are viewed as lacking the flexibility and sophistication of behaviours that are the product of varieties of thought such as deliberation, problem-solving, and reflection.

These seemingly plausible assumptions together give rise to what I call *the puzzle of skilled action*. The puzzle is this: How is it that skilled action can exhibit such a high degree of intelligence, when so much of it is performed (seemingly) unintelligently and automatically? (For similar concerns, see Wu, Chapter 16 in this volume). In this chapter, I'll offer a solution to this puzzle. The solution will take the form of an extension to existing *hybrid views of skilled action*, according to which its intelligence is to be accounted for in terms of the combined contributions of intentions and other propositional attitude states, as well as the representations and processes involved in motor control (see, e.g., Fridland 2014, 2017a; Christensen et al. 2016; Levy 2017; Shepherd 2017; Pavese 2019). I argue that, though such views are on the right track, they sometimes take an overly narrow view of the motor system's intelligence, such that it must be *derived* from intention, rather than inherent in its own operations. I further argue that in order to properly understand the intelligence of the motor system, we must recognize the complexity of the representational structures it utilizes in the control of skilled behaviour, and that this complexity forms the basis for the difference in intelligence between expert and novice performance, and points us toward a solution to the puzzle of skilled action.

20.2 Motivating the hybrid approach

Not all would agree that the activities of the motor system have any role to play in an explication of the intelligence of skill. In order to see what I take to be the limitations of such an approach, and reasons for preferring a hybrid view that countenances the involvement of motor representations in the intelligence of skill, it will be useful to consider an instance of it defended by Stanley and Krakauer (2013) in a paper titled "Motor Skill Depends on Knowledge of Facts".

On their view, for an agent S to have skill at Φ-ing, S must possess propositional knowledge about the activity of Φ-ing. In elaborating on what type of propositional knowledge is relevant, Stanley and Krakauer place a special emphasis on knowledge of what to do to initiate an action, claiming that "[k]nowing what to do to initiate an action is clearly factual knowledge; it is the knowledge that activities x1 … xn could initiate that action" (Stanley & Krakauer 2013: 4). This type of knowledge is especially important for explaining what they take to be a central feature of skill, namely that its "manifestations […] are intentional actions" (Stanley & Krakauer 2013: 6). Skills are not like reflexes, e.g., withdrawing one's hand from a hot stove; rather, they are such that an agent has direct control over whether and how they are manifested.

Stanley and Krakauer allow that in addition to propositional knowledge, skilled action involves a second component that they refer to as *motor acuity*. They understand this as "practice-related reductions in movement variability and increases in movement smoothness" (Stanley & Krakauer 2013: 8). But according to them, improvements in motor acuity do *not* contribute to the intelligence of skill. This is because they view the kind of learning that results in the sharpening of such acuity to be driven by purely bottom-up, low-level motor mechanisms that are not themselves intelligent (see Krakauer, Chapter 17 in this volume). In support of this claim, they point to empirical findings that "healthy subjects will adapt to perturbations like a mirror despite it being contrary to their own intention" (Stanley & Krakauer 2013: 8). "Such adaptations," they go on to say, "are not the acquisition of something that characteristically manifests in intentional action, i.e., they are not the acquisition of skill" (Stanley & Krakauer 2013: 8).

Stanley and Krakauer are surely right to point out that skills are intentional actions, so any ability that manifests in skill must also be one that manifests in intentional action. But why deny that the adaptations involved in improvements of motor acuity are themselves intentional? The key move here is the claim that they are "contrary" to the agent's intention. And since, on a standard view of intentional action, an action is intentional only if it is suitably caused by an agent's intention, activity that is causally independent of such a state does not thereby qualify.

Reflected in their claim that motor acuity proceeds independently of intention, is a view on which the motor system is *modular* and informationally encapsulated, at least to an important extent. A system is informationally encapsulated to the degree that it lacks access to information stored outside of it in the course of processing its inputs (Fodor 1983). When a system is informationally encapsulated with respect to the states of the central system—those states familiar as propositional attitude states—this is referred to as *cognitive impenetrability* or *cognitive impermeability*. Pylyshyn (1999) provides a fairly standard characterization of this notion, according to which,

> if a system is cognitively penetrable then the function it computes is sensitive, in a semantically coherent way, to the organism's goals and beliefs, that is, it can be altered in a way that bears some logical relation to what the person knows.
>
> *Pylyshyn 1999: 343*

For instance, in the famous Müller-Lyer illusion, the visual system fails to be sensitive to the content of the belief that the two lines are identical in length, so it is cognitively impermeable relative to that belief.

Is it true that the motor system is cognitively impermeable in this way relative to an agent's intentions? First, it is clear that there must be *some* degree of permeability, since otherwise no intentional action would ever be successfully performed. Still, the degree to which the motor system is sensitive to the content of intention might be limited in a way that prevents us from ascribing to it a role in underpinning the intelligence of skill. Stanley and Krakauer seem to think so on the basis of experimental work employing visuomotor rotation tasks. In such tasks, the participant is instructed to reach for a target on a computer screen. They do not see their hand, but they receive visual feedback from a cursor that represents the trajectory of their reaching movement. On some trials, the visual feedback is rotated relative to the actual trajectory of their (unseen) hand during the reaching task. This manipulation allows experimenters to determine how the motor system will compensate for the conflict between the visual feedback that is expected on the basis of the motor signals it is executing, and the visual feedback it actually receives. The main finding is that the participants' reaching movements "drift" in the direction *opposite* to the rotation. So, for example, if the rotation is 45 degrees clockwise, participants' movements will show drift 45 degrees *counter*clockwise. This is thought to be the result of an implicit learning strategy that the motor system adopts in order to reduce the conflict between expected and actual sensory feedback from the reaching movement it programs.

For their claim that motor adaptation—which they view as an aspect of motor acuity—does not constitute intentional action, Stanley and Krakauer (2013: 8) focus on a variant of this paradigm devised by Mazzoni and Krakauer (2006), wherein participants are instructed to adopt an explicit "cheating" strategy—that is, to form intentions—to counter the perturbation. This is achieved by placing facilitating targets at 45 degree angles from the proper target (Tp), such that if participants aim to hit those neighbouring targets (Tn), the cursor will hit the Tp, thus satisfying the primary task goal. Initially, reaching errors related to the Tp are almost completely eliminated. The cursor hits the Tp as a result of the explicit strategy to hit the Tn. But as participants continue with further trials, their movements *once again* start to drift toward the Tn and *away* from the Tp, despite their intention to hit it. Stanley and Krakauer (2013) take this to be evidence that motor acuity can develop contrary to an agent's intentions, and thus does not manifest in intentional action.

Is this correct? I think some care is needed in interpreting the results. The important thing to note is that there are *two* task goals in this context, *both* of which have corresponding intentions. There is the primary task goal of hitting the Tp and the secondary task goal of hitting the Tn in order to hit the Tp. Likewise, there is the primary intention to hit the Tn, and a secondary intention, the satisfaction of which serves as a means to the satisfaction of the primary one. Importantly, in order to satisfy the secondary intention, it is not enough that the agent merely intend to *aim* for the Tn. The trajectory of the cursor is determined by the actual trajectory of their arm. The participant must thereby intend to *hit or reach for* the Tn. What's more, this is the most proximal intention of the agent, i.e., the intention that directly initiates and guides the relevant action, and not the one that corresponds to the primary task goal of hitting the primary target.

The upshot here is that, though Stanley and Krakauer are correct that the kind of motor adaptation exhibited in the task occurs independently of *some* intention that the agent possesses, i.e., the primary intention to hit the Tp, it does not occur independently of *all* intentions, i.e., the secondary intention to hit the Tn. And this consideration is enough, I think, to undermine their denial that motor acuity manifests in intentional action. Motor acuity is indeed driven by an agent's intention—the most proximal one they have formed—though it is not always sensitive to or cognitively permeable by all of an agent's intentions, including the ones that those proximal intentions serve.

A more general worry for the type of approach that Stanley and Krakauer defend is that it would seem that what a skilled agent gains as they progress from novice to expert in Φ-ing, and the intelligence of their performances increases in some domain, is primarily knowledge what to do to initiate a wide variety of actions relevant to that domain. But this does not seem sufficient to account for the difference between a novice and expert's skilled behaviour. Both may know how to initiate some action or set of actions, but it is the expert's *implementation* of these actions after initiation that sets them apart from the novice—and in particular the *way* that they guide their movements. Granted, we are told by Stanley and Krakauer that

> [t]he same kind of knowledge that is used to initiate an activity can also be injected at anytime in the ongoing course of that activity. For example, a tennis player changes her mind and switches from a groundstroke to a drop shot based on the position of the opponent.
>
> *Stanley & Krakauer 2013: 5*

But once again this tells us nothing about the way the expert guides her drop shot to completion. An appeal to motor acuity will not even help here, since it can only illuminate differences in movement variability and smoothness, but not differences in the implementation of the action itself, having to do with its functional and temporal organization. At best, then, the type of account defended by Stanley and Krakauer (2013) seems incomplete when it comes to explaining the difference between the kind of intelligent guidance that an expert deploys and that which a novice does. For this, we must look downstream of action initiation at the psychological processes that implement the movement.

Before moving on, it is important to acknowledge a view that is more nuanced than that of Stanley and Krakauer (2013) with respect to the role that propositional knowledge might play in skill, and indeed *links* an agent's propositional knowledge pertaining to a certain skill to the motor representations that they deploy in the service of said skill. This is the view defended by Pavese (2019), according to which skill requires knowledge of a proposition *under a practical mode of presentation*, and on which such modes of presentation are, in turn, to be understood in terms of motor representations (see Pavese, Chapter 18 in this volume). Pavese argues that the motor representations available to an individual agent for performing a certain task do not just represent those tasks or the action outcomes that are associated with them, but rather the *method* by way of which they are to be performed in accordance with the agent's practical abilities. Think of the different *ways* in which one might perform the task of kicking a ball, for example, in terms of the exact path one's leg takes and the exact angular arrangements of the different joints involved. These all correspond to the different methods that one can deploy in order to kick the ball. On Pavese's account, these methods, in turn, constitute the practical mode of presentation under which the propositions underlying skill are known. So on this view, "knowing a proposition about, say, how to grab a bottle using a motor representation of that task is just one way of knowing a proposition under a practical mode of presentation" (Pavese 2019: 804).

While I am highly sympathetic to Pavese's (2019) careful account of motor representations as a type of practical representation—indeed, it is consistent with what I go on to say in this chapter—the main difference between our views is that I do not commit myself to the claim that the type of knowledge one possesses in skill that is secured by one's possession of the ability to deploy relevant motor representations is best understood as knowledge of a proposition under a practical mode of presentation. There may be other reasons to hold that knowledge of a proposition is required for skill (see, for instance, those discussed by Pavese (2018) pertaining to a belief requirement on intentional action), but I do not commit myself to holding that the acceptance of those reasons entails that the role of motor representations in the possession of a skill must also be understood in terms of propositional knowledge.

Regardless of this particular point of disagreement, given that Pavese's view countenances a role for both propositional attitude states and motor representations in the intelligence of skill, I take it to be an instance of the type of hybrid view of skill that I endorse. In short, hybrid accounts are not incompatible with a role for propositional knowledge in skill, so long as there is also a role for motor representations (see Pavese, Chapter 18 in this volume).

In what follows I want to make a case for an additional dimension of the intelligence of motor control that sometimes gets overlooked in hybrid accounts. On *one way* of understanding the intelligence of motor control, it *derives* from its sensitivity to the content of intention or other propositional attitude states, so that it may be viewed as a form of "trickle down" intelligence. As an articulation of this view, consider Fridland's claim that "some automatic processes are not unintelligent *since they bear robust, systematic relationships to personal-level intentional contents*" (Fridland 2017b: 4339, emphasis mine; but cf. Fridland 2013: 884; Fridland 2017a). If this is correct, then it is solely by virtue of being sensitive to personal-level intentional contents that the motor system is intelligent. But I think we can say more than this. In particular, I will argue that the intelligence of the motor system goes beyond that which is derived from intention, or other personal-level states. Once we properly understand the types of representation that the motor system employs to perform its tasks, we can better see that the motor system is intelligent in its own right (see Fridland, Chapter 19 in this volume).

20.3 Intelligence as flexibility

First, let me briefly say more about the notion of "intelligence" at work here. Along with others (see, e.g., Levy 2017; Shepherd 2017; Fridland 2014, 2017a), I suggest that a central feature of intelligent behaviour is its *flexibility*. This seems to capture our commonsense ways of thinking about intelligent action. When one thinks of a paradigmatically *un*intelligent response, one often thinks of a reflex. Reflexes are rigid stimulus-response pairings with a highly limited range of available mappings from stimulus to response. Intelligent behaviour, on the other hand, is sensitive to a wide range of information, both external to the agent and internal to its psychology. This is especially apparent in the case of skilled action. As Fridland has persuasively argued, at the heart of skilled action control is "an agent's ability to guide and modify her actions appropriately" (Fridland 2014: 2732), such that the processes underlying such control are "flexible, manipulable, subject to learning and improvement, responsive to intentional contents at the personal-level, and holistically integrated with both cognitive and motor states" (Fridland 2014: 2732). So, if we want to account for the intelligence of motor control in skill, we must account for its flexibility. No doubt some of this flexibility will come from its top-down sensitivity to the content of an agent's intentions. But as Levy (2017), correctly to my mind, points out, motor mechanisms also flexibly adapt to ongoing changes in the environment in a way that does not conform to a pattern of brute reflexes. By way of illustration, he asks us to consider the motor representations of a skilled jazz pianist:

> She may respond to a broad variety of cues *online*; that is, without requiring (or having time for) top-down deliberation. An improvising pianist may respond to subtle cues

from the bass player, to changes in the ambiance of the room and the expectations of the audience, to feedback from her instrument and the proximity to the next break in the performance. Famously, her exquisite sensitivity to a broad range of cues may extend to some cues of which she lacks personal-level awareness. Jazz musicians, for instance, regularly report that they are surprised by their own playing, indicating a lack of personal level awareness of information to which they respond. The kind of flexibility and ongoing responsiveness to variations in the conditions under which the action unfolds is the mark of skill (Fridland 2014) but *it is the motor mechanisms that intelligently adjust to these variations.*

Levy 2017: 520, emphasis mine

According to Levy, the motor system is thus intelligent since "[t]he genuine mark of intelligence […] is the capacity to flexibly adapt in an appropriate manner to environmental perturbations. It is this kind of flexibility that distinguishes the intelligent mechanism—or agent—from the unintelligent" (Levy 2017: 518).

I think Levy gets this point exactly right. Even if the pianist has certain general intentions to "read the room" or to "go with the flow" of the performance, the subtle variations that their playing exhibits in response to the environment are not primarily guided by such intentions, but by downstream representations of the motor system. But in order to see how this might be, we need a more robust understanding of just what these representations are like.[2] Once we have this, we can see that motor acuity involves more than simple reductions in movement variability and smoothness, but also the fine-tuning of an action in terms of its functional and temporal organization. To see this, it will be useful to start by highlighting two main features of motor representations.

First, there are good reasons to think that they are not propositionally formatted. Elisabeth Pacherie and I have argued for this conclusion elsewhere (Mylopoulos & Pacherie 2017: 321–323). The propositional format of beliefs, desires, and intentions, underlies the types of inferential transitions and rationality constraints that are characteristic of practical reasoning. Given an agent's desire that some state of affairs obtain, and their belief that performing some action A will result in that state of affairs, it is rational for them to form the intention (here the conclusion of practical reasoning) to A. Moreover, it is irrational for them to form the intention to B, if they believe that B-ing is not compatible with A-ing. But we plainly do not ascribe irrationality to an agent who makes an error in action execution, say failing to accurately reach for some target. The constraints governing the motor system are not the norms of rationality. Rather its computations are governed by biomechanical constraints and learning mechanisms that aim to reduce sensory feedback error. And there is good reason for this. As Butterfill and Sinigaglia point out, "[t]he many requirements on motor planning cannot normally be met by explicit practical reasoning, especially given the rapid and fluid transitions involved in many action sequences. Rather they require motor processes and representations" (Butterfill & Sinigaglia 2014: 123).

Second, motor representations are not limited to specifying the detailed kinematic features of bodily movement, such as force, direction, and speed. Rather, they also seem capable of specifying what some have called "action outcomes" (Butterfill & Sinigaglia 2014), that is, action types that might vary in their specific kinematic features while still preserving the same functional organization.

In the next section, I fill in this picture by appeal to an influential theory in the motor control literature. I argue that a proper understanding of the nature of motor representations offers us a clearer account of the ways in which the motor system implements the flexibility required of it for intelligent action.

20.4 Two types of motor representation: motor programs and motor commands

The key to understanding the intelligence of the motor system, and of skilled action more generally, lies in recognizing that motor control involves rich representational control structures that are intermediate between intention and behaviour (Schmidt 1975, 2003; Arbib 2003; Jeannerod 1997; Mylopoulos & Pacherie 2017). This intermediate level of representation contributes to the sensitivity and thereby flexibility and intelligence of motor control in ways that outstrip the contribution of intention.

On my view, motor representations are the psychological states that mediate between intention and behaviour, and encode the goals specified in an agent's intention and the means to those goals in a motoric format. By appeal to an influential theory within the cognitive psychology of motor control known as *schema theory* (Schmidt 1975), we can further develop this line by introducing two different types of motor representation that are hierarchically related. These are (i) *motor programs*, which specify the general form of an action type, and (ii) *motor commands* computed on the basis of motor programs, which specify the detailed kinematics of the action given the condition of the agent (e.g., current bodily position) and the present context (e.g., distance from target objects).

Importantly, and as others have done (e.g., Pavese 2017), it is useful to divide into two phases the computation between the input of the proximal intention and the output of corresponding behaviour. In the first phase of computation, the motor system takes as input the proximal intention to Φ, and outputs a motor program that corresponds to Φ-ing. In the second phase, the motor program is taken as input, and the details of the motor program are computed, yielding the output of motor commands that specify the fine-grained aspects of the movement, such as its force, direction, and velocity. In order to better understand this process, we must better understand the nature of motor programs and motor commands, respectively.

I start with the notion of a motor program, as described by schema theory. According to schema theory, a motor program is a stored representation in long-term memory (LTM) of the invariant features of an action type. The invariant features of an action type are those that remain the same—or with negligible differences—across several token performances of it. There is much ongoing debate as to which precise features are invariant, but two proposed features are (i) an action's relative timing, and (ii) its functional organization. The relative timing of an action refers to the set of ratios that define the temporal structure of the action. Each of these ratios is calculated by taking the duration of some part of the action and dividing it by the total duration of the action sequence as a whole. Thus, we can "stretch out" and "compress" various action types (e.g., extending one's elbow, raising one's arm), by increasing or decreasing the total duration of the movement, while keeping the ratios fixed. Next, functional organization refers to the spatial configuration and temporal ordering of the movements that define the functional structure of the action. For instance, a reaching-and-grasping movement typically has the following functional organization: elevation of the acting limb, extension of the elbow, and forward movement toward the target. Together, the relative timing and functional organization of an action serve as "blueprints" for that action type.

In addition to invariant features, action types also have what are known as *surface features*, which are those that change across token performances. The surface features are represented in the motor program by open parameters, the values of which are assigned through a process of *parameterization*, in accordance with the situation of action and feedback during execution. This parameterization thus plays the role of "scaling" the action to the present context. For example, while the action of throwing an object has invariant features invoking specific shoulder and elbow mechanics, it also has surface parameters corresponding to, e.g., which limb to use, what object to throw, how fast and far to throw it, and in what direction to throw it (Schmidt & Lee 2014). Once the parameter values have been selected, the specific movement can be executed in a way that is tailored to the situation of action. This explains why, each time we perform some action, we do not perform it in the exact same ways we have before, nor do we perform it in an entirely novel way. Motor programs allow for the storage of a stable representational structure corresponding to a general action type, as well as the scaling of the action to the present context (see Pavese, Chapter 18 in this volume).

Within this framework, motor learning is understood both as a process by which the general form of a motor program is acquired, as well as a process by which parameterization of a given motor program is fine-tuned. There is evidence that these two aspects of the learning process can be differentially affected by learning conditions. For instance, using randomized learning trials (vs. blocked learning trials) facilitates the learning of the motor program, but degrades the learning of parameterization. The explanation for this is that randomized learning prevents the agent from responding in the same way from trial to trial, requiring them to reconstruct the motor program "from scratch" each time. At the same time, reducing how much feedback the agent receives during practice also facilitates the learning of the motor program, but degrades the learning of parameterization. This is because no sensory feedback is available in order to determine whether parameterization was successful on that trial (Schmidt 2003).

In order to explain how motor programs for action types are acquired and fine-tuned, schema theorists posit two types of *schema* that are stored in LTM and developed across a lifetime of practice and experience. The so-called *recall schema* stores mappings between parameter values (e.g., force and speed) of a general motor program and specific action outcomes resulting from executing that program with those parameters (e.g., distance thrown) given the present context. The recall schema contributes heavily to the process of parameterization. The so-called *recognition schema* stores mappings between past action outcomes generated by executing the motor program (e.g., distance thrown), and the outcome of executing the program (e.g., distance thrown).

We can further introduce a distinction between basic and complex motor programs corresponding to basic and complex action types. Basic action types (e.g., bending of knees, swinging of arm, straightening of elbow) are those that the agent can perform without doing something else first.[3] Complex action types (e.g., jump shot, tennis serve, volleyball spike, cartwheel) are constituted by a structured set of functionally and temporally organized basic action types. Basic motor programs correspond to basic action types, while complex motor programs correspond to complex action types. So, for example, the complex motor program for a cartwheel might be constituted by a set of basic motor programs corresponding to the preparatory phase, movement phase, and follow-through phase. The preparatory phase might include basic motor programs for planting the dominant foot, and raising one's arms above one's head. The movement phase might include basic motor programs for the rotation of each arm and bending of the torso. And the follow-through phase might include basic motor programs for the flexing of the shoulders, and tightening of the abdominal muscles. In executing this complex motor program, each of these basic motor programs would be parameterized given the present condition of the agent, the context of action, and past learning experience.

I take the framework provided by schema theory to be a highly promising candidate for understanding the nature of the motor representations and structures that mediate between intention and action. Taking this framework on board, we can revisit our previous question of what accounts for the difference in skill and intelligence between the novice and the expert performer. A credible answer now presents itself: differences in the intelligence of performances by novices and experts are marked by differences in flexibility. And differences in flexibility are supported by differences in the complexity, organizational structure, and fine-tuning of an agent's motor programs underlying skilled behaviour.

Indeed, we have empirical evidence that this is a central difference between experts and novices. The evidence derives from the application of a method known as the *structural dimensional analysis of mental representation* (SDA-M). The aim of this method is to map "mental representations as integrated networks of [basic action concepts] across both individuals and groups, by providing information on relational structures in a given set of concepts with respect to goal-oriented actions" (Schack et al. 2014: 2).

The first step of this method is to select a complex action type (e.g., tennis serve) and then, with the help of experts, coaches, and non-experts, break it down into basic action types and determine their correct functional and temporal sequencing. Next, participants are grouped into novices and experts, and presented with an "anchor" basic action concept corresponding to a basic action type (e.g., bending of the knees). They are asked to perform a series of pairwise comparisons between that concept and the basic action concepts corresponding to all the other basic action types in the set. Participants must judge whether the given basic action concept is functionally related to the anchor concept in movement execution. They perform this task until all basic action concepts in the set have been compared to all other basic action concepts in the set, and a distance scaling is available between each one. A hierarchical cluster analysis then structures the set of basic action concepts into a hierarchy, and a factor analysis is performed to reveal the dimensions in the hierarchy. Finally, the degree of invariance in judgements within each group of experts and novices, as well as between the groups, is determined. The result of this procedure is a "dendogram", which is thought to depict the structure of motor programs stored in LTM that corresponds to a complex action type for novices and experts, respectively.

In a recent study, this method was applied in a structural analysis of the motor representations underlying the tennis serve for novices and experts (see Fig. 1 from Schack et al. 2014). There were three main findings when it came to the dendograms of experts. First, they were organized in hierarchical tree-like structures. Second, they had a high degree of similarity across individuals. Third, there were no significant differences between the structure depicted in the dendograms of the experts and that of the predetermined functional and temporal sequencing of the tennis serve. For novices, however, the dendograms displayed less hierarchical structure, a higher degree of variance across individuals, and were more poorly matched with the functional and temporal organization of the tennis serve.

The picture that emerges from these studies is that the motor system has a complex store of information that is derived from practice and experience, and that it is this resource that allows for the kind of sophisticated flexibility that we see in the case of skilled action, and that thereby accounts for a significant portion of its intelligence, in a way that goes beyond the contributions of an agent's intentions.

20.5 Conclusion

To take stock, I've presented a view on which we cannot account for the intelligence of skilled action without taking as central—as other hybrid views do—the coordination between an agent's intentions and their motor system. Importantly, I've further argued that the intelligence of the motor system is not exhaustively derived from that of intention, but rather resides in its access to rich representational structures that are built up from experience and training. In proposing this view, I agree with other hybrid theorists that motor control is "intelligent all the way down" (Fridland 2017). What I hope to have done is offered a credible way of illuminating an important aspect of just what this means.

Notes

1 This is supported by two popular considerations. First, there is what Montero (2016) calls the *just-do-it principle*: the widely appealed to idea that experts perform best when they're not thinking about or focused on what they are doing. Second, there are real-time constraints on skilled action that prevent experts from thinking about what to do next. For instance, cricket batsmen must select a shot based on the trajectory of a ball which may travel at up to 160 km per hour (Yarrow et al. 2009). Similarly, elite chess players can play at a rate of 5 to 10 seconds per move (Dreyfus 2002: 372).
2 I do not here make a case for thinking that the motor system carries out its computations by way of representations in the first place. For convincing support, see Pavese (2017) and Butterfill and Sinigaglia (2014).
3 I take the notion of a basic action type appealed to here to be synonymous with Pavese's (2017, 2019) notion of *elementary operations*.

References

Arbib, M. A. (2003) "Schema Theory," in *The Handbook of Brain Theory and Neural Networks* (2nd ed.), Cambridge, MA: The MIT Press, pp. 993–998.
Butterfill, S. A., & Sinigaglia, C. (2014) "Intention and Motor Representation in Purposive Action," *Philosophy and Phenomenological Research*, 88, 119–145.
Christensen, W., Sutton, J., & McIlwain, D. J. (2016) "Cognition in Skilled Action: Meshed Control and the Varieties of Skill Experience," *Mind & Language*, 31(1), 37–66.
Dreyfus, H. (2002) "Intelligence without Representation: Merleau-Ponty's Critique of Mental Representation," *Phenomenology and the Cognitive Sciences*, 1, 367–383.
Fodor, J. (1983) *The Modularity of Mind: An Essay on Faculty Psychology*, Cambridge, MA: The MIT Press.
Fridland, E. (2013) "Problems with Intellectualism," *Philosophical Studies*, 165(3), 879–891.
—— (2014) "They've Lost Control: Reflections on Skill," *Synthese*, 91(12), 2729–2750.
—— (2017a) "Skill and Motor Control: Intelligence All the Way Down," *Philosophical Studies*, 174(6), 1539–1560.
—— (2017b) "Automatically Minded," *Synthese*, 194, 4337–4363.
Jeannerod, M. (1997) *The Cognitive Neuroscience of Action*, Oxford, UK: Blackwell Publishers, Inc.
Levy, N. (2017) "Embodied Savoir-Faire: Knowledge-How Requires Motor Representations," *Synthese*, 194(2), 511–530.
Mazzoni, P., & Krakauer, J. W. (2006) "An Implicit Plan Overrides an Explicit Strategy During Visuomotor Adaptation," *The Journal of Neuroscience*, 26(14), 3642–3645.
Montero, B. (2016) *Thought in Action*, Oxford, UK: Oxford University Press.
Mylopoulos, M., & Pacherie, E. (2017) "Intentions and Motor Representations: The Interface Challenge," *Review of Philosophy and Psychology*, 8(2), 317–336.
Pavese, C. (2017) "A Theory of Practical Meaning," *Philosophical Topics*, 45(2), 65–96.
—— (2018). "Know-how, action, and luck", *Synthese*, online first: https://doi.org/10.1007/s11229-0181823-7
—— (2019) "The Psychological Reality of Practical Representation," *Philosophical Psychology*, 32(5), 784–821.
Pylyshyn, Z. W. (1999) "Is Vision Continuous with Cognition?," *Behavioral and Brain Sciences*, 22(3), 341–365.
Schack, T., Essig, K., Frank, C., & Koester, D. (2014) "Mental Representation and Motor Imagery Training," *Frontiers in Human Neuroscience*, 8(328), 1–10.
Schmidt, R. A. (1975) "A Schema Theory of Discrete Motor Skill Learning," *Psychological Review* 82(4), 225–260.
—— (2003) "Motor Schema Theory after 27 Years: Reflections and Implications for a New Theory," *Research Quarterly for Exercise and Sport*, 74(4), 366–375.
Schmidt, R., & Lee, T. (2014) *Motor Learning and Performance, 5th Edition. With web study guide: From Principles to Application*, Champaign, IL: Human Kinetics.

Shepherd, J. (2017) "Skilled Action and the Double Life of Intention," *Philosophy and Phenomenological Research*, doi:10.1111/phpr.12433

Stanley, J., & Krakauer, J. W. (2013) "Motor Skill Depends on Knowledge of Facts," *Frontiers in Human Neuroscience*, 7(503), 1–11.

Yarrow, K., Brown, P., & Krakauer, J. W. (2009) "Inside the Brain of an Elite Athlete: The Neural Processes that Support High Achievement in Sports," *Nature Reviews Neuroscience*, 10(8), 585–596.

21

THE TARGETS OF SKILL, AND THEIR IMPORTANCE

Joshua Shepherd

21.1 Introduction

Skill essentially involves an agent's being excellent in some way. The skilled agent is skilled – possesses an excellence, exercises an excellence – at something. What is the thing at which agents become skilled? Call this something the target of skill.[1]

Normal talk is permissive about the nature and boundaries of skill's targets. Agents display skill at actions, at games, and at a wide range of practices and activities. Such talk suggests pluralism about the targets of skill. But understanding what we are committing to when (or if) we commit to pluralism here requires more attention to the targets of skill, for philosophers have said very little about this topic.

In this chapter I hope to illustrate the importance of clarity regarding the targets of skill. Among other things, attention to the targets of skill suggests that skills display variable structure, depending upon the target. In addition, attention to the targets of skill suggests that antecedent commitment to some account of some target provides motivation for certain specific accounts of skill.

Here is the plan. In Section 21.2, I discuss action as a target for skill. In Sections 21.3 through 21.5, I discuss games as a target for skill. In Section 21.6, I suggest that the most general target for skill is what I call an action-domain, and I offer some reflection regarding the nature of action-domains.

21.2 Skill at action

Philosophers often talk as though action is the primary target of skill. We read of skill at A-ing, where A is an action-type. This makes decent sense. One can be skilled at baking, throwing, or telling a joke. Baking, throwing, and telling a joke are all types of (intentional) actions.

What is an action? That's a pretty spicy one. There are lots of views. All of them, I wager, have some commitment to the general view that action is a kind of success. To have acted is to have done something that rises above the level of abject failure. So action, like skill, displays a kind of excellence.

Beyond this, disagreement is rife. For the purposes of an account of skill, does it matter which view is right? Let's see.

Consider a view – really a family of views – that makes knowledge necessary in some way for (intentional) action (Anscombe 2000; Gibbons 2001; Pavese 2018). There are different ways of fleshing the idea out. Gibbons states one of them when he asserts that 'the role of knowledge in the explanation and production of intentional action is as indispensable as the roles of belief and desire' (Gibbons 2001: 580).

On such a view, an agent's behavior does not qualify as an action unless that agent has a certain kind of knowledge of what she is doing, as she does it. (There could be different accounts of the kind of knowledge the agent needs.) If action is knowledge-involving in this way, one might think it plausible that an account of skill should give a central role to knowledge, perhaps explaining features of skill in terms of features of knowledge. The idea would be that what makes action excellent qua action – in this case, knowledge – might help explain what makes skilled action excellent qua skilled.

Two recent philosophical accounts of skill do appeal to knowledge, each in different ways. Carlotta Pavese (2016a, 2016b) proposes that an agent is skilled at A-ing if and only if that agent knows how to A sufficiently well. There are two components to this kind of account. The first involves a particular view of knowledge how. It is distinctive of Pavese's approach that knowledge how is a kind of propositional knowledge – 'S's knowing how to phi is a matter of S's knowing, for some way w to phi, that w is a way he himself could phi' (Pavese 2016a: 650). For Pavese, then, skill at action is explained in part by the kind of propositional knowledge agents possess regarding ways to act.

The second component arises in the transition from non-skilled to skilled action. The skilled agent not only knows how to A, she knows how to A well. What's that? It turns out that knowing how to A sufficiently well is a difficult notion to explicate. Pavese has made good progress here, however, in a recent paper that explores different ways knowledge how may come in degrees (Pavese 2017). Examining her proposals is beyond the present scope. But I offer an example that gives some of the flavor. Consider Pavese's discussion of degrees of qualitative knowledge how – a kind of knowledge how that involves knowing qualitatively better answers to questions regarding how to A.

> Suppose Carla and Ale both know several practical answers to the question How to make ravioli but one of the answers known by Carla is better than any of those known by Ale. One way that answer may be better is by being more detailed and precise; or it may be better by being about a better way of making ravioli (a better recipe); a further way her practical answer may be better is by practically presenting a recipe for making ravioli in a better way than any of Ale's answers … a practical sense may be better by being more efficient or simpler, just as certain computer programs can be more efficient than others; or it may be better by being more reliable, just like programs can be more or less likely than others to enable the successful execution of the task.
>
> *Pavese 2017: 377*

Stanley and Williamson appeal to knowledge, but in a very different way than Pavese. They argue that skill is 'a kind of disposition to know' – in other words, 'to be skilled at the action type of Φ-ing is to be disposed to form knowledge appropriate for guiding tokens of Φ-ing' (Stanley & Williamson 2017: 715). This appeal to dispositions and knowledge that guides sets up a distinction between manifestations of skill. For Stanley and Williamson, skill's direct manifestation is knowledge appropriate for guidance. The indirect manifestation of a skill is the action guided by acquired knowledge states: 'any skilled action is guided by knowledge that manifests [in the direct sense] possession of skill at that activity' (Stanley & Williamson 2017: 718).

One awkwardness for this kind of account is that agents could be disposed to acquire guidance-apt knowledge despite qualifying as skilled at an action. Stanley and Williamson might respond that such a case represents a failure to indirectly manifest skill – the essence of skill is the acquisition of the knowledge. Even so, such an account requires an account of skill's gradability. Stanley and Williamson offer some thoughts on this matter, in one place endorsing Pavese's account of knowledge how's gradability. So it may be that both accounts come closer together when attempting to explain the range of excellence that different skills display.

It is not my aim to assess either of these accounts in this chapter. Just here I wish to trace the connection between an account of action as requiring knowledge, and an account of skill as doing the same. If one favors the knowledge-involving account of action, one might see motivation for a knowledge-involving account of skill. After all, if action does not require knowledge, one might expect to find at least some instances of excellently performed action that also do without knowledge. That would be awkward for a knowledge-involving account of skill.

But now consider causalist views that understand the nature of action not in terms of knowledge, but in terms of relationships of (non-deviant) causation between mental states like intentions (or events of intention acquisition and persistence) and behavior (Goldman 1970; Brand 1984; Mele & Moser 1994; Shepherd forthcoming). On these views, much of the explanatory work is done by those capacities, dispositions, or whatever, that explain how intentions manage to non-deviantly cause behavior.

An account of skill at actions construed in this causalist way might make no reference to knowledge. Consider the following kind of view, which I float in my (forthcoming). I suggest that in order to possess skill regarding some action A, the agent needs only (a) a set P of success-conducive plans for behavior, (b) high levels of control regarding the behaviors in the plans such that attempts to execute (most) members in P reliably leads to successful A-ing, where the successes occur in virtue of control the agent exercises (that is, occur non-deviantly).

Such an account has obvious work to do. The notion of non-deviant causation may be thought problematic (see, e.g., Williamson 2017). Note, though, that I offer a novel account of non-deviant causation in Shepherd (forthcoming). Or, given the recent acceleration of work on control (Fridland 2014; Shepherd 2014; Wu 2016; Buehler 2019), one could find fault with the notion of control in operation here. But even if the notion of control can be satisfyingly specified, there is work to do in specifying how an account without knowledge can properly explain the successes. But if such work can be done, proponents of action that do without knowledge may prefer the account.

A still different view of action does not explain action in terms of any other notion. Action-first views take action as primitive, and use action to explain other features of agency (Levy 2013; O'Brien 2017). This is a research program that, as Levy explains, 'reverses the explanatory order of the standard reductionist programme by casting intentional action in the role of *explanans* rather than *explanandum*' (Levy 2013: 712).

How might such an account explain skilled action? One option would be to take skilled action as primitive, and think of non-skilled action as somehow derivative. It is not clear how such an account would go. In any case a view that takes action as primitive will likely need additional resources to explain what separates the skilled from the unskilled actions. Each theorist can chart for herself the best available routes. But it looks like the action-first theorist has options.

She might explain skilled action in terms of higher degrees of control over action and better quality of plans for action – retaining the commitment, of course, to action as primitive. Or she could follow a knowledge-involving account, maintaining that action plus knowledge, suitably mixed, yields a satisfying account of skilled action. Or, following the action-first manifesto, she could try to use the notion of action itself to explain skill. How that might go remains to be seen.

It emerges, then, that distinct views on the nature of action provide motivation, at the very least, for distinct views of skill at action. Might the same be true of other targets of skill? Perhaps that question is too quick. A prior question: is action the only target of skill?

21.3 Moving beyond action

Consider developing skill at a simple computer game, such as the game Infinite Stairs.[2] This game is straightforward. Using a customizable avatar, one is supposed to climb an ascending set of stairs. There are only two buttons, each on the bottom of one's tablet screen. One button moves the avatar up the stairs to the right. One button moves the avatar up the stairs to the left. So one furiously taps the screen in accordance with the moves the ascending staircase requires.

There are a finite series of stair combinations that can appear. So one can master, relatively quickly, the relevant combinations – left/right/right/left, or right/left/right/left, etc. One other relevant parameter involves the speed with which one can repetitively hit a single button. And, reporting from practice, a final parameter involves attention. Some of the avatars are shaped differently, and some move in annoying ways. So it is sometimes necessary to direct attention away from distractors and only to the upcoming stair combinations.

Pretty quickly, one acquires skill at Infinite Stairs. But Infinite Stairs is not an action-type. Infinite Stairs is a game. The game has a certain structure. And this structure calls forth more than one kind of behavior, and more than one kind of action from the skilled agent. One needs to master capacities to recognize stair sequences. One needs to master capacities to direct attention within the limited space of the screen. One needs to master capacities to sequence button combinations, at various speeds.

This example, and many more besides, suggest that agents become skilled not just at actions, but at clusters of actions (and other behaviors). One way actions cluster together is via games. Indeed, some of the clearest and cleanest examples of skill we have involve gameplay. These examples drive the psychology of skill and inform philosophical reflection. Agents spend large parts of their lives practicing at games. So it seems games are legitimate targets of skill.

21.4 Games

What is a game?

Chess is a game, Stratego is a game, Freezetag is a game, rugby is a game, baseball is a game, netball is a game, Capture the Flag is a game. It is not difficult to point to examples. But what holds these together? This is a notoriously difficult question to answer, and some – e.g., Wittgenstein (1953) – have suggested that attempting to define 'game' is a mistake.

Bernard Suits' (2014) influential suggestion was that a game involves taking up unnecessary obstacles for the sake of the behaviors – actions, activities – doing so makes possible. It is an interesting view, though few have followed Suits in the specifics.

A leading tradition in the philosophy of sports makes central appeal to rules. In a review paper, Nguyen describes formalism as the view that 'the essential nature of a game is its ruleset' (Nguyen 2017: 9). This is coupled with a view that 'proper play involves obeying the rules' (Nguyen 2017: 9).

It is difficult to deny that games involve rules in some way. Perhaps they do so essentially. But even if rules are essential to the nature of games, it is difficult to accept that this is all there is to it. Many have pointed out problems. To name just one, noticed by Williamson, 'in the ordinary sense of "game", games such as tennis gradually change their rules over time without losing their identity' (Williamson 1996: 490).

It would take us far afield to consider in detail the best available accounts of games. One suggestion, however, is fruitful for our purposes. Some have suggested that in addition to rules, games are governed by an ethos (Morgan 2004; Russell 2004; Simon 2000). Russell argues that 'games create opportunities for developing certain human excellences by presenting obstacles that must be mastered and overcome in order to achieve the goal set by the game' (Russell 2004: 146). He further proposes a principle according to which '[t]he practice of any game should be undertaken in such a manner that the excellences embodied in achieving the elusory goal of the game are not undermined but are maintained and fostered' (Russell 2004: 146).

One can find much of value in the notion of an ethos even of one thinks of the ethos as deriving not from duties or anything committing one to normative realism, but rather as deriving from agreements or tacit contracts players enter into in specific contexts (Ciomaga 2013). Nor need one commit to the idea that it is excellences that the ethos makes central. It could very well be goals, or specific actions, or other zones of value, depending on the case.

Some games are fantastic because they are so silly. They seek to promote, not excellences so much as humorous moments, awkward situations, or whatever. This seems to be the case with many party games. (No one likes the guy who plays a game to win when winning is beside the point.) It might be the case with Calvinball – a game played by the two star characters, Calvin and Hobbes, in Bill Watterson's comic of the same name. In Calvinball the players change the rules constantly. One rule is excepted from constant change – all players must wear masks. Beyond this, there does appear to be a structure, provided by two meta-rules. First, one can never play the same way twice. Second, one must accept the introduction of new rules. (It does not appear that one must always announce the introduction of new rules. Sometimes previously existing rules are only revealed when a new rule comes to bear on their zone of influence.) Is it possible to be skilled at Calvinball? It seems so. Calvin and Hobbes seem very adept. But it is unclear what one means in saying this unless one is appealing to something like an ethos – something like a commitment to absurdity and fun-promotion in rule-changes coupled with a deference to following existing rules.

I think we can be pluralists about the ethos of games while agreeing with Russell that the structure of games involves rules as well as a background normative notion.

To say this is to stop far short of an account of the nature of games. But we have enough to consider whether consideration of games as a target for skill generates any interesting thoughts about skill.

21.5 Skill at games

One thing that is interesting about games as targets of skill is that their structure seems to transmit a structure to the skill one develops. There is a relationship between target and the capacities that (at least partially) constitute skill. One's skill at some game is not just skill at an action-type, but rather skill at a cluster of behaviors and actions.

Now games display a wide range of differences in complexity. Some games are simple. Infinite Stairs is an example. Some are not. At more complex games, the skill agents develop takes on a more complicated structure. The rugby player needs to be good at relatively technical aspects of the game, depending on her position. She needs to know how to enter into a tackle safely, and how to tackle safely. She needs to become comfortable with the rugby ball and its odd patterns of movement, and the ways one might throw, kick, and catch it. She might need to learn special techniques – what some call the dark arts – for surviving the scrum. She probably needs to acquire a series of expectations and finely honed predictions regarding the intentions of her teammates and her opponents – how they are likely to move given the circumstance, what they are trying to do, what broad patterns of coordinated movement are evolving, and how she might tweak this evolution in advantageous ways.

Given their sometimes complicated structure, the development of high levels of skill at some games can take years even for very advanced players. (In part this is because one plays the game against highly intelligent opponents who anticipate one's moves and plan counters.) Consider the basketball writer Zach Lowe's analysis of the growth displayed by a young professional player (Jaylen Brown). In the following passage Lowe is discussing how Brown has begun to display a special kind of shot – a floater – useful in the rare circumstance that one is on the run at a certain specific place on the court, and to integrate this shot into the broader ability to generate offense for his team.

> Brown is trying the right stuff, and you see some nascent feel – the instinct to change pace, keep his defender on his hip, Chris Paul-style, and manipulate the defense. That floater is a handy break-in-case-of-emergency weapon. Most players don't develop a bunch of high-level offensive skills at once. They build brick-by-brick, using one skill to enable another. Once you can shoot 3s, you can drive around defenders who run you off the arc. The leap from there to functional pick-and-roll work might be the hardest for wing players. It can take years. Some guys never make it. Brown entering the early stages already is a huge win for Boston.
>
> *Lowe 2018*

Lowe's analysis makes an interesting point about skills in general, namely, that they often display a kind of compositionality and structure, and that fine-graining this structure allows one to think fruitfully about differences in levels of skill. Most basketball analysts would, of course, say that Jaylen Brown is already skilled at basketball. He is a professional player, after all. Lowe's point is that developing high-level skills of the sort the best players possess – involving a kind of flexibility of ways to achieve common goals such as scoring or finding one's teammates an open shot against world-class defenses – often takes several years of play at the professional level. This is because one must not only develop a range of abilities and master a range of actions. One must develop abilities to deploy these abilities and actions flexibly and appropriately across a range of challenging circumstance-types.

The more complicated structure displayed by skill at some games raises issues for a general account of skill.

Suppose that one begins with a success-based account of skill at action. All that one needs to be skilled is to have high levels of control regarding high-quality plans. One might worry that this does not cleanly transfer to skill at complex games. What's left out? It looks like such a view has to take for granted the skilled agent's capacity to routinely, reliably slot the right plans in at the right moment. That is, the constitution of skill at sophisticated games may require the fine-tuning of capacities to form, revise, and deploy plans for action.

There are different ways one may flesh this out. A natural suggestion is that we turn here to the agent's knowledge base. So, for example, Stanley and Krakauer construe the kind of learning that supports flexible plan formation in terms of knowledge.

Typically, the process of becoming more skilled involves learning about multiple actions involved in success at the activity, in addition to their initiation conditions. The same kind of knowledge that is used to initiate an activity can also be injected at anytime in the ongoing course of that activity. For example, a tennis player changes her mind and switches from a groundstroke to a drop shot based on the position of the opponent. Such cases of learning are also knowledge.

Stanley & Krakauer 2013: 5

But there are other options. In forthcoming work Ellen Fridland points to the ways that practice not only develops an agent's practical representations – her intentions and motor schemata – but also adds organizational structures that connect practical representations with perceptual representations in ways that assist on-line planning and enhance strategic control (see Fridland (forthcoming) for development of this notion).

John Bengson (2017) emphasizes the close relationship between understanding – here conceived as a cognitive, epistemically evaluable state distinct from knowledge – and skill. For Bengson, skillful activity is a paradigmatic manifestation of practical understanding. And practical understanding is a standing cognitive state characterized by a number of interesting features. Among others, practical understanding is: objective, in that it 'involves genuinely grasping some portion of reality' (Bengson 2017: 19); intelligent, as opposed to mindless reflex; coherent, in that it does not display inconsistency. Bengson argues that the kind of state that qualifies as understanding is a noetic conception: a conception of the activity in question the content of which is (at least) (a) correct regarding the activity's features, (b) complete in adequately characterizing the activity's central features, (c) internally coalescent in identifying pertinent substantive connections between the activity's central features, (d) externally coalescent in being rationally consistent with alternative conceptions of the activity, and (e) content over which the agent displays mastery. Such a conception, Bengson asserts, is guiding for the agent: 'an individual who has practical understanding will be in a state that is action-guiding, poised to underlie and explain the intentional execution of intelligent action' (Bengson 2017: 43).

Bengson's account of practical understanding is, obviously, subtle. I am not here aiming to assess it. But it is a candidate for explaining the subtle structure skill at games comes to take.

It is worth noting that incorporating a central role for understanding or skill at some games need not undermine a central role for control. Consider the following kind of case, which I discuss in Shepherd (forthcoming). It involves two agents, J and K. Assume that both know the same propositions regarding how to play some game. And assume that both have the same grasp – the same understanding – regarding how to play the game. It might still arguably be the case that J is more skilled than K. How? J may display higher levels of control at executing the actions favored by her knowledge or understanding. So J's actions may more frequently meet with higher levels of success.

It is, of course, possible to construe J's control over her action partially in terms of additional knowledge how, or perhaps in terms of qualitatively better. Perhaps J knows when and where to execute her actions. But it is an open question whether a knowledge-involving or an understanding-involving account can get by without incorporating a notion like control.[3]

So it looks like consideration of a more complex target for skill motivates an account that weds elements that are easier to keep separate when the target of skill is relatively unsophisticated. We may neglect the role of understanding when focusing on skill at simple actions. Or we may be happy with an account of a primitive notion of action, plus the addition of knowledge, without needing any explicit mention of control. Such moves are less plausible when the target of skill is more sophisticated. Perhaps skill at basketball requires control, knowledge, and understanding, in a way that skill at kicking (or some other simple action-type) does not.

Once we allow that actions and games are both legitimate targets of skill, a question arises about further targets. It seems unlikely that games are the most general target of skill. In the next section I consider some examples.

21.6 Action-domains

Agents develop skill at targets not best thought of as games.

Consider, as targets of skill, various practices: weaving, knitting, painting, driving. All of these go beyond skill at action, since these practices consist at least partially of structured clusters of behaviors and actions. And none of these are easily construed as games.

Consider, as targets of skill, various professions: law, medicine, philosophy. It does seem that some people develop skill at these professions. And all of these go well beyond what is easily captured in terms of action-types or games.

I propose that the most general target of skill is an action-domain. As I employ it, action-domain is a technical term. It is, however, familiar from normal talk about skills. It is possible to think of Infinite Stairs, rugby, neurosurgery, philosophy, and knitting as kinds of action-domain. The same is true of action-types, although this is somewhat artificial. But one can restrict one's action-domain to the case of a single action – juggling, baking, knitting, kicking, whatever.

What is an action-domain? I develop an account in Shepherd (forthcoming). I am not sure it is the best possible account. Indeed, given that very few have theorized regarding the targets of skill, it is unlikely that I have hit upon the best account. But I offer it here as a way forward.

The chief constituent of an action-domain is an ideal of success. Sometimes the ideal can be cashed out in terms of a goal. If the domain in question is a sport, the chief goal might be to win games, or championships. If the domain in question revolves around some social good, the chief goal might be to further the more abstractly characterized ideal. The defense lawyer, for example, has a goal of defending her clients. But the broader aim may be to further an ideal of justice.

The ideal of success can be more or less complex. There may be more than one way to succeed. The ideal of stand-up comedy might be in part to perform in a way that is funny. But maybe that's not all there is to it. Some might value an element of insightfulness about society or the human condition. If so, success at stand-up comedy might not be entirely about getting laughs. The point is simply that domains exist which contain complex ideals of success.

Indeed, domains exist in which the ideals of success are contested, and perhaps even shifting, as the agents who act and compete in these domains explore the space.

In more regimented cases, ideals of success become adumbrated – sometimes explicitly, via rules, and sometimes implicitly, via agreements among sets of agents – by various constraints. For example, we sometimes find constraints on permissible behavior-types. In hockey, you cannot take a golf club onto the ice rink.

Further, we sometimes find constraints on permissible circumstance-types. How I make breakfast for my kids has nothing to do with the level of skill I exercise at chess. When playing chess only a strictly regimented set of circumstances are relevant.

In virtue of the constraints that adumbrate a domain's ideal of success, we often find an ordering over the goals common to agents in terms of centrality-to-success. In some games, this ordering remains largely informal, but most agents are aware of it because most agents know the rules and can see the broad means-ends structure the rules set up. Goals related to hitting the baseball are more important than goals related to running the bases. Both are important, but if you had to choose, you would rather be an excellent hitter than an excellent runner. This is because hitting well is a more effective means to scoring runs. In some domains, disagreement regarding the complex ideal of success can lead to disagreements regarding which goals are more important. I would like to develop skill as a philosopher. Should I spend my time immersed in imaginative science fiction? Should I memorize all the key distinctions charted by recent analytic philosophy? Or should I read the classics instead? Should I immerse myself in politics and culture? Should I rigorously study various logics? Maybe I should do all of these. But reasonable people can disagree about which ones are more important for the development of skill at philosophy.

Action-domains are a very general category. Almost anything can be a domain. Domains can be constructed on the fly. Does this generality pose a problem for an account of skill?

I think not. This is just the nature of the case. There are many degrees of freedom regarding how human agency is structured, and regarding our rationale for constructing any particular domain. Sometimes we select structured domains for the development of excellence, or for other reasons (see Nguyen 2019). Recall Calvinball – an absurd fictional game, created for laughs by a genius comic writer. But there are humans who play it, as the internet will confirm.

What is the upshot for skill? It seems the structure of skill can vary in terms of its sophistication. This is because the targets of skill vary widely in terms of their sophistication. Indeed, in Shepherd (forthcoming), I discuss the notion of partial skill that falls out of this point. The idea is that in some complex domains one way to succeed is to specialize at one important thing. In rugby, one may specialize as a kicker. In basketball, one may specialize as a long-range shooter. In philosophy, one may specialize in modal logic. In many domains, if one is good enough at one thing, the absence of skill at other elements within the domain can be forgiven.

If the structure of skill is variable, one might naturally ask for an account of the lowest common denominators of skill. Perhaps such an account can be provided – it might include elements such as control and knowledge how. But there may be a difference between this account and an account of some more specific skill whose target is sophisticated. Thus, clarity regarding a skill's target is important for understanding the nature of that skill.

21.7 Conclusion

An account of the nature of skill provides an explanatory and conceptual architecture for inquiry into the shape skills often take, and for philosophical inquiry into connections between skill and other important phenomena – for example, control, intentional action, and knowledge. The perspective I have pushed in this chapter is that these questions about skill's nature and structure will be impacted by one's assumptions regarding the targets of skill, and the way skill's targets set up constraints for skill's honing through practice and its expression in behavior.

Reflection on skill's variety suggests skills often run wider and deeper than talk of action-types alone can capture. A skilled debater is good at various kinds of reasoning, at listening, at a way of speaking, at synthesizing information, at presenting information. A skilled surgeon possesses a high degree of dexterity of hand and fingers, coupled with a refined understanding of the function of some part of the body, the ways this function may break down, the ways it may be repaired, as well as an ability to apply this understanding to a variety of case-types: to micro-differences in injury and damage and body-type. I have argued that the skilled agent is sometimes skilled at actions, and sometimes skilled at games. But more broadly, she is skilled at action-domains.

Notes

1 The author acknowledges two generous sources of support. First, funds from European Research Council Starting Grant 757698, awarded under the Horizon 2020 Programme for Research and Innovation. Second, the Canadian Institute for Advanced Research's Azrieli Global Scholar Programme on Mind, Brain, and Consciousness.
2 Here I draw on my description of Infinite Stairs in Shepherd (forthcoming).
3 And it is, further, an open question whether skill qua skill is always constituted (even in part) by knowledge or understanding. It might be that while most skills depend upon knowledge and/or understanding, some skills are entirely a matter of (a) possession of good plans for success in the relevant game, and (b) high levels of control regarding the plans.

References

Anscombe, E. (2000) *Intention*. Cambridge, MA: Harvard University Press.
Bengson, J. (2017) The unity of understanding. In Grimm, S. R. (ed.) *Making Sense of the World: New Essays on the Philosophy of Understanding*. Oxford: Oxford University Press, 14–53.
Brand, M. (1984) *Intending and Acting: Toward a Naturalized Action Theory*. Cambridge, MA: MIT Press.
Buehler, D. (2019) Flexible occurrent control. *Philosophical Studies*. DOI: 10.1007/s11098-018-1118-3.
Ciomaga, B. (2013) Rules and obligations. *Journal of the Philosophy of Sport*, 40(1), 19–40.
Fridland, E. (2014) They've lost control: Reflections on skill. *Synthese*, 191(12), 2729–2750.
Fridland, E. (forthcoming) *Skill in Action*. Oxford: Oxford University Press.
Gibbons, J. (2001) Knowledge in action. *Philosophy and Phenomenological Research*, 62(3), 579–600.
Goldman, A. I. (1970) *Theory of human action*. Princeton, NJ: Princeton University Press.
Levy, Y. (2013) Intentional action first. *Australasian Journal of Philosophy*, 91(4), 705–718.
Lowe, Z. (2018, Feb. 16) Ten things I like and don't like, including the NBA tank battle. Espn.com, www.espn.com/nba/story/_/id/22459076/zach-lowe-10-things-like-including-great-nba-tank-race, accessed Feb. 17, 2018.
Mele, A. R., & Moser, P. K. (1994) Intentional action. *Nous*, 28(1), 39–68.
Morgan, W. J. (2004) Moral antirealism, internalism, and sport. *Journal of the Philosophy of Sport*, 31(2), 161–183.
Nguyen, C. T. (2017) Philosophy of games. *Philosophy Compass*, 12(8), e12426.
—— (2019) Games and the art of agency. *Philosophical Review*, 128(4), 423–462.
O'Brien, L. (2017) Actions as prime. *Royal Institute of Philosophy Supplements*, 80, 265–285.
Pavese, C. (2016a) Skill in epistemology I: Skill and knowledge. *Philosophy Compass*, 11(11), 642–649.
—— (2016b) Skill in epistemology II: Skill and know how. *Philosophy Compass*, 11(11), 650–660.
—— (2017) Know-how and gradability. *Philosophical Review*, 126(3), 345–383.
—— (2018) Know-how, action, and luck. *Synthese*, 1–23.
Russell, J. S. (2004) Moral realism in sport. *Journal of the Philosophy of Sport*, 31(1), 142–160.
Shepherd, J. (2014) The contours of control. *Philosophical Studies*, 170(3), 395–411.
—— (forthcoming) *The Shape of Agency: Control, Action, Skill, Knowledge*. Oxford: Oxford University Press.
Simon, R. L. (2000) Internalism and internal values in sport. *Journal of the Philosophy of Sport*, 27, 1–16.
Stanley, J., & Krakauer, J. W. (2013) Motor skill depends on knowledge of facts. *Frontiers in Human Neuroscience*, 7, 503.
Stanley, J., & Williamson, T. (2017) Skill. *Noûs*, 51(4), 713–726.
Suits, B. (2014) *The Grasshopper: Games, Life and Utopia*. Peterborough, Canada: Broadview Press.
Williamson, T. (1996) Knowing and asserting. *The Philosophical Review*, 105(4), 489–523.
—— (2017) Acting on knowledge. In J. A. Carter, E. C. Gordon, & B. Jarvis (eds.) *Knowledge First: Approaches in Epistemology and Mind*. Oxford: Oxford University Press, 163–183.
Wittgenstein, L. W. (1953) *Philosophical Investigations*, G. E. M. Anscombe and R. Rhees (eds.), G. E. M. Anscombe (trans.), Oxford: Blackwell.
Wu, W. (2016) Experts and deviants: The story of agentive control. *Philosophy and Phenomenological Research*, 93(1), 101–126.

PART IV

Skill in perception, imagination, and emotion

22

EMBODYING EXPERTISE AS A PERFORMER AND PERCEIVER

Insights from the arts and robotics

Emily S. Cross

22.1 Linking action with perception

The ability to use perceptual information about another individual's or one's own movements to inform subsequent movements is essential for successful interactions with the environment, and thus, for survival. Consequently, it is no surprise that inquiry into how the human brain negotiates the path between action execution and perception has intrigued venerable thinkers throughout the millennia, including Aristotle, Descartes, and William James. Until the mid-19th century, prevalent thinking on this relationship was dominated by the Cartesian sensori-motor view, which advanced the idea of independence between the perceptual and production domains (Descartes 1664, as discussed in Prinz 1997). As knowledge about the capabilities of the human brain continued to accrue, pioneering scholars began to explore the idea that perceptual processes might indeed converge or overlap to some extent with motor perform-ance (James 1890). Empirical investigation into the brain's ability to use perceptional infor-mation to shape movement began in the mid-20th century, during which time information processing explanations proposing complex transformations from perception to the organisa-tion and execution of action gathered momentum (Sanders 1967, 1983; Welford 1968; Massaro and Friedman 1990).

In the 1990s, research into the intersection of action perception and production experienced an extraordinary renaissance that was due in large part to the discovery of mirror neurons in the ventral premotor cortex of the monkey brain. Remarkably, these neurons discharge in a similar manner both when a monkey performs an action and when it observes another monkey or human perform the same action (di Pellegrino et al. 1992; Gallese et al. 1996; Rizzolatti et al. 1996a). As such, these specialized neurons have prompted these researchers and others to propose that action perception and production processes form a bidirectional, interactive loop within the primate brain, and that action recognition might be explained by the observer's brain simulating the observed movements of another individual (Fadiga et al. 1995, 1999; Grafton et al. 1996; Rizzolatti et al. 2001).

This hypothesis has sparked lively debate among researchers regarding the specific parameters, scope, and limitations of such an action simulation system. From this debate, multiple theories

281

have emerged that are motivated by action-perception interactions, such as simulation theory (Gallese and Goldman 1998), the dual route theory (Tessari and Rumiati 2007), and the action hierarchy theory (Grafton and Hamilton 2007). However, many of these theories do not make specific predictions and consequently collapse under empirical scrutiny. The theory that has been the subject of the most empirical investigation over the past several decades is simulation theory (sometimes referred to as the direct matching hypothesis). Simulation theory maintains that human sensorimotor cortices become active under a broad array of action-related activities, ranging from executing planned, overt movements to observing or imagining actions that are never executed. According to this theory, we represent another individual's actions by matching their movements with resonating, covert movements of our own (Gallese and Goldman 1998; Jeannerod 2001; Goldman, 2005), perhaps by using mirror neurons (Gallese and Goldman 1998; Goldman 2005). A striking and consistent result from neuroimaging studies (Grafton et al. 1996; Rizzolatti et al. 1996a; Iacoboni et al. 1999, 2005; Buccino et al. 2001; Grèzes and Decety 2001; Grèzes et al. 2001), and transcranial magnetic stimulation studies (Fadiga et al. 1995, 1999; Strafella and Paus 2000; Gangitano et al. 2001; Patuzzo et al. 2003) is that motor and premotor areas that are classically associated with movement preparation are also active when simply observing the actions of others.

Behavioural psychophysics studies have demonstrated interactions between action perception and execution (Brass et al. 2000, 2001a, 2001b; Kilner et al. 2003; Hamilton et al. 2004, 2005) and lend additional credence to the notion of overlapping neural processes for action observation and execution. However, although quantifiable overlap exists between different action activities, there is not a 1-to-1 correspondence between primary motor, premotor, and parietal cortical regions active during action observation, simulation, and execution. This is clear from meta-analyses of functional neuroimaging studies on shared representations across these action domains (Grèzes and Decety 2001).

Important for considerations of the role played by expertise in shaping the relationship between action and perception, a wealth of literature demonstrates that the more familiar an action is, the stronger the response is within these core sensorimotor regions (Buccino et al. 2004; Calvo-Merino et al. 2005; Cross et al. 2006; Shimada 2010; Gardner et al. 2015). These studies and others thus lend support to experience-driven simulation accounts of action perception (Sinigaglia 2013), which form the foundation of the direct matching hypothesis of action understanding (Gallese and Goldman 1998; Rizzolatti et al. 2001; Wolpert et al. 2003; although see Csibra 2005 and Kilner 2011 for alternative accounts). In terms of familiarity (for which expertise can be considered an extreme example), a linear relationship between magnitude of sensorimotor activity and familiarity would be consistent with this hypothesis: as familiarity or expertise increases, the simulation of how an action might unfold over time becomes more accurate and resonance between an observer's motor system and an observed action is maximized.

While this linear relationship between an observer's expertise or familiarity with an action and sensorimotor cortical activity has found support within the empirical literature and certainly has intuitive appeal, an increasing number of studies report findings demonstrating that this relationship is likely not that straightforward (Gazzola et al. 2007; Cross et al. 2012; Liew et al. 2013; Tipper et al. 2015; Gardner et al. 2017). These studies have all reported greater activity within sensorimotor cortices when participants observe actions that are unfamiliar or with which they have very little expertise (compared to more familiar actions), a finding that appears at odds with a simulation-based account of how the brain negotiates the link between action and perception. The findings from these studies suggest that a linear relationship between sensorimotor activity and familiarity is likely too simplistic. In terms of the direct matching hypothesis, this theory would struggle to explain why an *unfamiliar* action that is *not* in the observer's repertoire would elicit greater action observation network (AON) activity. Predictive coding models of AON function (Keysers and Perrett 2004; Kilner et al. 2007a, 2007b; Gazzola and Keysers 2009; Schippers and Keysers 2011; Tipper et al. 2015), predicated on the use of perceptuomotor maps to predict and interpret observed actions (Lamm et al. 2007; Schubotz 2007; Urgesi et al. 2010), may potentially help to resolve these seemingly discrepant findings concerning the relationship between familiarity of an observed movement and engagement of sensorimotor cortices (cf. Gardner et al. 2017).

In order to explore some of the theoretical ideas introduced above in more detail, the following two sections highlight a number of empirical studies from two distinct but complementary avenues. First, I discuss work performed with expert and novice dancers, and then I examine how our understanding of a system that has evolved to code action and perception information within a common space might be co-opted for skillful interactions with artificial agents. Together, these examples should reinforce how a better understanding of the neurocognitive mechanisms and consequences of expertise help us to navigate a complex social environment in a skillful manner.

22.2 Expertise, embodiment, and the performing arts

In the past decade and a half or so, the number of researchers using performing arts experts or contexts to explore the relationship between expertise, embodiment, and perception has continued to grow. The empirical work in this domain has primarily followed one of two routes: either recruiting and examining performing arts experts (such as dancers) who have built up motoric expertise over many years of training or recruiting naive participants and training them how to perform a particular set of movements and examining the mechanisms and consequences of de novo expertise. In a chapter co-authored by Beatriz Calvo-Merino and myself, we examine in detail a broad range of studies that fit into these two categories (Cross and Calvo-Merino 2016). Rather than simply repeating what we have already covered in this previous chapter, in the following I present a brief overview of major studies and seminal findings that fit within these two primary domains, and then include some considerations regarding the relationship between expertise, embodiment, and aesthetic preference, another research area that is rapidly gaining momentum (cf. Kirsch et al. 2018).

22.2.1 *Longstanding expertise*

The very first study to draw upon expertise from the performing arts domain to examine how years of practice to hone a particular motor vocabulary shapes how we see the world was run by Beatriz Calvo-Merino and colleagues (Calvo-Merino et al. 2005). In this study, the authors recruited a sample of male participants from three groups: one group comprised professional ballet dancers, another group comprised expert capoeira[1] performers, and a third group included men who had no particular expertise in either ballet or capoeira. All participants underwent functional magnetic resonance imaging (fMRI), a type of brain scanning that requires participants to lie still in a supine position with the head immobilized, while watching and/or listening to stimuli of the experimenter's choosing via fMRI compatible audiovisual equipment. In this study, participants watched short, silent film clips that featured an expert male ballet dancer performing a number of ballet movements and an expert capoeira performer performing capoeira movements. Strikingly, Calvo-Merino and colleagues reported the most robust engagement of sensorimotor cortices, including dorsal and ventral premotor cortices, superior parietal lobe extending along the intraparietal sulcus, and the superior temporal sulcus, when ballet dancers watched ballet (but not capoeira) and when capoeira performers watched capoeira (but not ballet).

This dissociation of sensorimotor engagement based on longstanding expertise provided striking evidence in support of simulation theory, and inspired an innovative follow-up study by the same group of authors (Calvo-Merino et al. 2006). In this study, the authors sought to further examine the role of embodied expertise on perception, and to determine whether physical experience per se was necessary to shape perceivers' brain responses when watching others in action (or whether it was perhaps possible that extensive visual experience alone could shape responses in a similar way). To address this question, Calvo-Merino and colleagues recruited professional male and female ballet dancers for an fMRI study, during which the dancers watched video clips of male and female gender-specific movements (i.e., movements that are only present in the repertoire of one gender), as well as movements that are performed by both male and female dancers. In order to determine the role of embodied expertise per se, the authors evaluated dancers' brain activity when they watched movements that were specific to their gender compared to movements performed by the opposite gender (i.e., movements they had extensive visual familiarity with, but never performed). The authors found more robust engagement of premotor, parietal, and cerebellar cortices when dancers watched movements they had extensive familiarity performing (as well as seeing) compared to those movements that were every bit as visually familiar, but for which they were not motorically familiar (Calvo-Merino et al. 2006).

These two studies have sparked a number of follow-on studies that have continued to investigate how longstanding expertise shapes the brains and behaviour of perceivers, with subsequent work showing that trained dancers are better than non-dancers at discriminating pairs of point-light displays of dance movements (Calvo-Merino et al. 2010), and people can accurately recognize point-light displays of their friends versus strangers dancing (Loula et al. 2005). Together, this field of work demonstrates that longstanding expertise in the visual and especially the motor domain shapes how we perceive others moving around us.

22.2.2 De novo (laboratory) expertise

A useful counterpoint for examining how expertise changes how we see others' actions is provided by studies that train participants to become experts with specific actions. As with investigations into longstanding expertise, in this domain as well researchers have enlisted the help of dancers and used dance learning paradigms to provide new insights on these questions. One of the first studies to do this was performed by my colleagues and myself, and involved tracking the brain activity of a company of professional contemporary dancers as they learned a complex new dance work (Cross et al. 2006). Across six weeks of the rehearsal period, we invited dancers into the laboratory to undergo an fMRI scan while they watched two types of choreography: a number of movements that they were currently in the middle of learning as part of their new choreography, and a group of kinematically similar "control" movements that the dancers never actually learned or rehearsed. Following each short video clip, the dancers were asked to rate how well they thought they could perform the movement they had just watched. Behaviourally, we found that the dancers unsurprisingly rated their own performance of the rehearsed (but not control) movements as improving across the course of the study. More strikingly, the brain imaging findings showed that as dancers watched movements they rated their ability to perform as increasingly better, clusters of activity within left ventral premotor and inferior parietal lobule showed increasingly robust responses. My colleagues and I interpreted this as evidence that the better you are at performing an action that you have been learning in the recent past, the more you simulate that action. Here again, the simulation theory of action perception appears to be theoretically consistent with this finding.

Since this initial study, my colleagues and I performed a number of other studies involving laboratory-based dance training paradigms to address in more depth the relationship between quantifiable experience and how we perceive others in action. In one subsequent study, we examined how visuomotor and visual experience alone among novice dancers learning to play a dance video game shaped engagement of sensorimotor cortices. This study showed that both visual and visuomotor experience shaped parietal and premotor engagement in a similar manner (Cross et al. 2009). A more recent follow-up study also performed with novice dancers learning hip-hop dance sequences in the context of a popular video game probed this relationship in more depth, and found that the more sensory modalities through which one acquires experience with a new action, the more strongly sensorimotor cortices are engaged during action observation (Kirsch and Cross 2015). We have also examined how visual experience alone shapes perception of actions that are beyond observers' motor abilities (such as mechanical movements made by wind-up toys, or complex gymnastic passes performed by expert rhythmic gymnasts), and report that visual training results in decreased recruitment of particularly visual regions associated with action observation (such as the extrastriate and fusiform body areas (Cross et al. 2013)). Even though such pre- and post-training fMRI experiments are costly in a number of ways, this research approach provides a useful counterpoint to longstanding expertise in building our understanding of how our experiences shape how we see others.

22.2.3 Expertise, embodiment, and aesthetics

One final research area that draws together action expertise and the performing arts that merits discussion here concerns how this relationship influences an observer's aesthetic or affective responses. This research area continues to attract increasing research attention (Orgs et al. 2013, 2016; Kirsch et al. 2015, 2016a; Christensen et al. 2016a), not least because of various international initiatives that seek to bring together artists and scientists to generate truly interdisciplinary research from the ground up (such as the Dance Engaging Science initiative). Studies have shown that not only are sensorimotor cortices engaged when we observe dance movements we find pleasurable to watch (Calvo-Merino et al. 2008), but also that these brain regions can show increasingly robust responses the more we like watching a movement, and the less we can embody it (Cross et al. 2011).

Specifically, this latter study asked dance-naive participants to watch a series of short video clips depicting ballet and contemporary dance movements, as performed by members of the Leipzig Ballet, and found that participants rated the movements they found most pleasing to watch as the most difficult to perform (a somewhat intuitive finding when one considers that patrons of the arts often pay substantial sums of money to watch expert artists perform physical feats they could never imagine doing themselves). According to simulation theory (and based on the studies reviewed in the previous sections), one might expect sensorimotor cortices to respond most robustly when observers watch things they can physically execute themselves; instead, we found robust engagement of the right intraparietal sulcus (as well as visual regions) when participants watched movements they rated as nearly impossible to perform (such as a male dancer performing a triple rotation jump or a female dancer performing a perfect split leap), but highly enjoyable to watch.

Subsequent work shows that dance expertise also leads to greater somatic manifestations of affect, as shown by implicit facial responses (Kirsch et al. 2016b), and a general measure of arousal revealed by galvanic skin responses (Christensen et al. 2016a). In addition, training studies document that when dance-naive participants spend time coming to the laboratory each day and practising learning new dance sequences, their aesthetic preferences for these movements increase with increasing embodiment and ability to perform (Kirsch et al. 2013, 2015), and this relationship is present from early adolescence through to older age (Kirsch and Cross 2018). As discussed in a review article on this topic (Kirsch et al. 2016a), the relationship between an observer's body, his or her motor skills, and how this shapes aesthetic preferences is only just beginning to be explored, and given the biological and evolutionary value of the human body, a more developed understanding of this relationship is likely to yield important insights into how we create and appreciate art as well.

22.3 Skill and expertise insights to optimize human–robot interactions

Another burgeoning area of inquiry greatly informed by research into skill and expertise is that of human–robot interaction. At first blush, this topic might seem remote from the theoretical underpinnings discussed in the first section of this chapter, and the insights gained from expert dancers in the second section. However, a growing number of laboratories are tackling challenges regarding designing socially engaging robots and how to optimize human–robot interaction by taking a social cognition-based approach that very much draws upon core ideas advanced by simulation theory. More specifically, a dominant view in social cognition states that throughout phylogeny and ontogeny, humans have developed to seek out self–other equivalences, which form the foundation of social cognition (Meltzoff and Prinz 2003; Meltzoff 2007). This account, known as the 'like me' hypothesis and consistent with simulationist accounts of action perception (cf. Gallese and Goldman 1998), further proposes that actions performed by oneself and another are represented in supramodal cognitive codes (Meltzoff 2007). Much of the literature covered in the first section of this chapter provides support for the 'like me' hypothesis, in that it demonstrates evidence of behavioural facilitation (Press et al. 2005; Catmur et al. 2007) and increased engagement of sensorimotor brain regions when individuals observe familiar actions or those with which they have expertise performing, or interact with agents similar to themselves (Buccino et al. 2004; Tai et al. 2004; Cross et al. 2006, 2009; Shimada 2010).

In addition to sensorimotor brain regions' involvement in sharing experiences between actor and observer, successful interaction with others also entails taking an interaction partner's perspective. A part of the brain known as the right temporoparietal junction (TPJ) is implicated in this process (Saxe and Kanwisher 2003; Apperly et al. 2004), and neuroimaging findings support the 'like me' nature of TPJ engagement when interacting with socially similar others (Klapper et al. 2014; Takahashi et al. 2014). Sensorimotor cortices along with TPJ are components of a broader network of cortical regions collectively called the 'social brain' (Frith 2007; Pelphrey and Carter 2008), and are involved in how we perceive, learn from, and interact with other agents we encounter in our social environments.

22.3.1 From social cognition to social robotics

Over the past decade, individuals working to develop socially interactive robots are taking an increased interest in the social cognition and social neuroscience research reviewed above (Asada 2001, 2014; Breazeal 2007; Ishiguro 2013). An ongoing goal for robotics designers has been to maximize the similarity of artificial agents to humans, in terms of appearance and movement (while perhaps attempting to circumnavigate the uncanny valley; see Mori 2005), in an aim to make particular artificial agents as 'like me' as possible (Coradeschi et al. 2006). This idea also fits nicely with the notion that the expertise we have as being humans ourselves, and interacting with others like us, should be capitalized upon when creating artificial agents. In an elegant review paper, Press details many examples from behavioural psychology and cognitive neuroscience studies that support the notion that social brain regions are biologically tuned, demonstrating the most robust responses when viewing or interacting with other agents who look or move like us (Press 2011).

As compelling as the data and arguments supporting this idea that our experience of being human and interacting with other humans means that robots should be designed to be as human-like as possible are, it is important to note that a steadily growing body of research continues to call into question whether this relationship is really so straightforward. For example, my colleagues and I demonstrated that watching a human or robot perform actions that were robotic led to far more engagement of sensorimotor/social brain regions than smooth, familiar actions that participants had far more experience performing (Cross et al. 2012). These findings, as well as those reported by a number of other laboratories (Gazzola et al. 2007; Ramsey and Hamilton 2010) call for a far more systematic evaluation of the limits of neurocognitive plasticity when interacting with unfamiliar agents, in order to better understand how malleable social cognition is, the actual value of embodied expertise in shaping human–robot interactions, and the role that learning or longer-term exposure plays in shaping perception. As enthusiasm builds among the robotics community for incorporating social cognition and neuroscience research into robotics design (Hashimoto et al. 2006; Belpaeme et al. 2012; Lakatos et al. 2014; Henschel et al. 2020), future research examining the role of expertise should benefit the development of socially engaging and compatible robots by more clearly establishing the extent to which an artificial agent must be perceived as 'like me' in order to elicit a social response in a human interaction partner's brain or behaviour (Hortensius and Cross 2018; Cross et al. 2019).

22.4 Conclusions

The aim of this chapter was to provide an overview of how embodying expertise as a performer or observer shapes our perception of others, and how research exploring this relationship is helping to spur developments in both arts and aesthetics as well as development of robots designed to socially engage with people. As stated previously, this chapter did not attempt to exhaustively cover all issues related to these domains, but instead aimed at providing the reader with a taste of the theoretical history and underpinnings for these questions, and some of the research approaches and findings that drive this field forward. Naturally, many exciting opportunities exist for follow-up work in both the performing arts and robotics domains. For example, future work in the arts domain could examine how the relationship between physical or embodied expertise and aesthetic preferences changes across time, either with the accumulation of additional skill, or with repeated exposure to the same stimuli over a longer time course than the studies described here (for example, many weeks or months rather than several days). It seems likely that the benefits that embodied expertise afford aesthetic preferences will only last up until a certain point, after which observers will become bored, no matter how much skill they have to perform the action they are observing. In the robotics domain, here as well great scope exists for the type of training studies described in the dance section, examining how the accumulation of social experience or interactive expertise with robots changes how people perceive these machines. Moreover, it will be illuminating to examine the extent to which social similarity or expertise influences the utility of robots used in social contexts. In sum, both areas are ripe for future exploration, and a clear understanding of the theoretical and empirical foundations of embodied expertise will bolster progress in these domains.

Note

1 Capoeira is an Afro-Brazilian martial art that draws on elements of dance, self-defence, music, and acrobatics.

References

Apperly, I. A., Samson, D., Chiavarino, C., and Humphreys, G. W. (2004) "Frontal and Temporo-Parietal Lobe Contributions to Theory of Mind: Neuropsychological Evidence from a False-Belief Task with Reduced Language and Executive Demands," *Journal of Cognitive Neuroscience* 16: 1773–84.
Asada, M. (2001) "Cognitive Developmental Robotics as a New Paradigm for the Design of Humanoid Robots," *Robotics and Autonomous Systems* 37: 185–93.
Asada, M. (2014) "Development of Artificial Empathy," *Neuroscience Research* 90: 41–50.
Belpaeme, T. et al. (2012) "Multimodal Child-Robot Interaction: Building Social Bonds," *Journal of Human-Robot Interaction* 1: 33–53, doi:10.5898/JHRI.1.2.Belpaem.
Brass, M., Bekkering, H., and Prinz, W. (2001a) "Movement Observation Affects Movement Execution in a Simple Response Task," *Acta Psychologica* 106: 3–22.
Brass, M., Bekkering, H., Wohlschlager, A., and Prinz, W. (2000) "Compatibility between Observed and Executed Finger Movements: Comparing Symbolic, Spatial, and Imitative Cues," *Brain and Cognition* 44: 124–43.
Brass, M., Zysset, S., and Von Cramon, D. Y. (2001b) "The Inhibition of Imitative Response Tendencies," *Neuroimage* 14: 1416–23.
Breazeal, C. (2007) "Sociable Robots," *Journal of the Robotics Society of Japan* 24: 591–3.
Buccino, G., Binkofski, F., Fink, G. R., Fadiga, L., Fogassi, L., Gallese, V., et al. (2001) "Action Observation Activates Premotor and Parietal Areas in a Somatotopic Manner: An fMRI Study," *European Journal of Neuroscience* 13: 400–4.
Buccino, G., Lui, F., Canessa, N., Patteri, I., Lagravinese, G., Benuzzi, F., et al. (2004) "Neural Circuits Involved in the Recognition of Actions Performed by Nonconspecifics: An fMRI Study," *Journal of Cognitive Neuroscience* 16: 114–26.
Calvo-Merino, B., Glaser, D. E., Grèzes, J., Passingham, R. E., and Haggard, P. (2005) "Action Observation and Acquired Motor Skills: An fMRI Study with Expert Dancers," *Cerebral Cortex* 15: 1243–9.
Calvo-Merino, B., Grèzes, J., Glaser, D. E., Passingham, R. E., and Haggard, P. (2006) "Seeing or Doing? Influence of Visual and Motor Familiarity in Action Observation," *Current Biology* 16: 1905–10.
Calvo-Merino, B., Jola, C., Glaser, D. E., and Haggard, P. (2008) "Towards a Sensorimotor Aesthetics of Performing Art," *Consciousness and Cognition* 17: 911–22.
Calvo-Merino, B., Urgesi, C., Orgs, G., Aglioti, S. M., and Haggard, P. (2010) "Extrastriate Body Area Underlies Aesthetic Evaluation of Body Stimuli," *Experimental Brain Research* 204: 447–56, doi:10.1007/s00221-010-2283-6.
Catmur, C., Walsh, V., and Heyes, C. (2007) "Sensorimotor Learning Configures the Human Mirror System," *Current Biology* 17: 1527–31.
Christensen, J. F., Gomila, A., Gaigg, S. B., Sivarajah, N., and Calvo-Merino, B. (2016a) "Dance Expertise Modulates Behavioral and Psychophysiological Responses to Affective Body Movement," *Journal of Experimental Psychology: Human Perception and Performance* 42: 1139–47.
Christensen, J. F., Pollick, F. E., Lambrechts, A., and Gomila, A. (2016b) "Affective Responses to Dance," *Acta Psychologica* 168: 91–105.
Coradeschi, S., Ishiguro, H., Asada, M., Shapiro, S. C., Thielscher, M., Breazeal, C., and Mataric, M. (2006) "Human-Inspired Robots," *IEEE Intelligent Systems* 21: 74–85.
Cross, E. S., and Calvo-Merino, B. (2016) "The Impact of Action Expertise on Shared Representations," in S. S. Obhi and E. S. Cross (eds.) *Shared Representations: Sensorimotor Foundations of Social Life.* Cambridge: Cambridge University Press, pp. 541–62.
Cross, E. S., Hamilton, A. F., and Grafton, S. T. (2006) "Building a Motor Simulation De Novo: Observation of Dance by Dancers," *Neuroimage* 31: 1257–67.

Cross, E. S., Hortensius, R., and Wykowska, A. (2019) "From Social Brains to Social Robots: Applying Neurocognitive Insights to Human-Robot Interaction," *Philosophical Transactions of the Royal Society of London. Series B, Biological Sciences* 374: 20180024, https://doi.org/10.1098/rstb.2018.0024.

Cross, E. S., Kirsch, L., Ticini, L. F., and Schutz-Bosbach, S. (2011) "The Impact of Aesthetic Evaluation and Physical Ability on Dance Perception," *Frontiers in Human Neuroscience* 5: 102.

Cross, E. S., Kraemer, D. J., Hamilton, A. F., Kelley, W. M., and Grafton, S. T. (2009) "Sensitivity of the Action Observation Network to Physical and Observational Learning," *Cerebral Cortex* 19: 315–26.

Cross, E. S., Liepelt, R., Hamilton, A. F., Parkinson, J., Ramsey, R., Stadler, W., and Prinz, W. (2012) "Robotic Movement Preferentially Engages the Action Observation Network," *Human Brain Mapping* 33: 2238–54.

Cross, E. S., Stadler, W., Parkinson, J., Schutz-Bosbach, S., and Prinz, W. (2013) "The Influence of Visual Training on Predicting Complex Action Sequences," *Human Brain Mapping* 34: 467–86.

Csibra, G. (2005) "Mirror Neurons and Action Observation: Is Simulation Involved? Available at: www.interdisciplines.org/mirror

Di Pellegrino, G., Fadiga, L., Fogassi, L., Gallese, V., and Rizzolatti, G. (1992) "Understanding Motor Events: A Neurophysiological Study," *Experimental Brain Research* 91: 176–80.

Fadiga, L., Buccino, G., Craighero, L., Fogassi, L., Gallese, V., and Pavesi, G. (1999) "Corticospinal Excitability Is Specifically Modulated by Motor Imagery: A Magnetic Stimulation Study," *Neuropsychologia* 37: 147–58.

Fadiga, L., Fogassi, L., Pavesi, G., and Rizzolatti, G. (1995) "Motor Facilitation during Action Observation: A Magnetic Stimulation Study," *Journal of Neurophysiology* 73: 2608–11.

Frith, C. D. (2007) "The Social Brain?" *Philosophical Transactions of the Royal Society B: Biological Sciences* 362: 671–8.

Gallese, V., Fadiga, L., Fogassi, L., and Rizzolatti, G. (1996) "Action Recognition in the Premotor Cortex," *Brain* 119: 593–609.

Gallese, V., and Goldman, A. (1998) "Mirror Neurons and the Simulation Theory of Mindreading," *Trends in Cognitive Sciences* 2: 493–501.

Gangitano, M., Mottaghy, F. M., and Pascual-Leone, A. (2001) "Phase-Specific Modulation of Cortical Motor Output during Movement Observation," *Neuroreport* 12: 1489–92.

Gardner, T., Aglinskas, A., and Cross, E. S. (2017) "Using Guitar Learning to Probe the Action Observation Network's Response to Visuomotor Familiarity," *NeuroImage* 156: 174–89, doi:10.1016/j.neuroimage.2017.04.060.

Gazzola, V., and Keysers, C. (2009) "The Observation and Execution of Actions Share Motor and Somatosensory Voxels in All Tested Subjects: Single-Subject Analyses of Unsmoothed fMRI Data," *Cerebral Cortex* 19: 1239–55.

Gazzola, V., Rizzolatti, G., Wicker, B., and Keysers, C. (2007) "The Anthropomorphic Brain: The Mirror Neuron System Responds to Human and Robotic Actions," *Neuroimage* 35: 1674–84.

Goldman, A. (2005) *Mirror Systems, Social Understanding and Social Cognition*, www.interdisciplines.org/mirror/papers/3/6/1.

Grafton, S. T., Arbib, M. A., Fadiga, L., and Rizzolatti, G. (1996) "Localization of Grasp Representations in Humans by Positron Emission Tomography," *Experimental Brain Research* 112: 103–11.

Grafton, S. T., and de C. Hamilton, A. F. (2007) "Evidence for a Distributed Hierarchy of Action Representation in the Brain," *Human Movement Science* 26: 590–616, doi:10.1016/j.humov.2007.05.009.

Grèzes, J., and Decety, J. (2001) "Functional Anatomy of Execution, Mental Simulation, Observation, and Verb Generation of Actions: A Meta-Analysis," *Human Brain Mapping* 12: 1–19.

Grèzes, J., Fonlupt, P., Bertenthal, B., Delon-Martin, C., Segebarth, C., and Decety, J. (2001) "Does Perception of Biological Motion Rely on Specific Brain Regions?" *Neuroimage* 13: 775–85.

Hamilton, A., Wolpert, D., and Frith, U. (2004) "Your Own Action Influences How You Perceive Another Person's Action," *Current Biology* 14: 493–8.

Hamilton, A., Wolpert, D., Frith, U., and Grafton, S. T. (2005) "Where Does Your Own Action Influence Your Perception of Another Person's Action in the Brain?" *Neuroimage* 29: 524–35.

Hashimoto, T., Hiramatsu, S., and Kobayashi, H. (2006) "Development of Face Robot for Emotional Communication between Human and Robot," in *Proceedings of the IEEE International Conference on Mechatronics and Automation* (Luoyang), 25–30.

Henschel, A., Hortensius, R., and Cross, E. S. (2020) "Social Cognition in the Age of Human-Robot Interaction," *Trends in Neurosciences*, https://doi.org/10.1016/j.tins.2020.03.013.

Hortensius, R., and Cross, E. S. (2018) "From Automata to Animate Beings: The Scope and Limits of Attributing Socialness to Artificial Agents," *Annals of the New York Academy of Sciences* 1426: 93–110.

Iacoboni, M., Molnar-Szakacs, I., Gallese, V., Buccino, G., Mazziotta, J. C., and Rizzolatti, G. (2005) "Grasping the Intentions of Others with One's Own Mirror Neuron System," *PLoS Biology* 3: e79.

Iacoboni, M., Woods, R. P., Brass, M., Bekkering, H., Mazziotta, J. C., and Rizzolatti, G. (1999) "Cortical Mechanisms of Human Imitation," *Science* 286: 2526–8.

Ishiguro, H. (2013) "Studies on Very Humanlike Robots," in International Conference on Instrumentation, Control, Information Technology and System Integration, Nagoya University, Aichi.

James, W. (1890) *Principles of Psychology*, New York: Holt.

Jeannerod, M. (2001) "Neural Simulation of Action: A Unifying Mechanism for Motor Cognition," *Neuroimage* 14: S103–9.

Keysers, C., and Perrett, D. I. (2004) "Demystifying Social Cognition: A Hebbian Perspective," *Trends in Cognitive Sciences* 8: 501–7.

Kilner, J. M. (2011) "More Than One Pathway to Action Understanding," *Trends in Cognitive Sciences* 15: 352–7.

Kilner, J. M., Friston, K. J., and Frith, C. D. (2007a) "Predictive Coding: An Account of the Mirror Neuron System," *Cognitive Processing* 8: 159–66.

—— (2007b) "The Mirror-Neuron System: A Bayesian Perspective," *Neuroreport* 18: 619–23.

Kilner, J. M., Paulignan, Y., and Blakemore, S. J. (2003) "An Interference Effect of Observed Biological Movement on Action," *Current Biology* 13: 522–5.

Kirsch, L. P., and Cross, E. S. (2015) "Additive Routes to Action Learning: Layering Experience Shapes Engagement of the Action Observation Network," *Cerebral Cortex* 25: 4799–811.

—— (2018) "The Influence of Sensorimotor Experience on the Aesthetic Evaluation of Dance Across the Life Span," *Progress in Brain Research* 237: 291–316.

Kirsch, L. P., Dawson, K., and Cross, E. S. (2015) "Dance Experience Sculpts Aesthetic Perception and Related Brain Circuits," *Annals of the New York Academy of Sciences* 1337: 130–9.

Kirsch, L. P., Drommelschmidt, K. A., and Cross, E. S. (2013) "The Impact of Sensorimotor Experience on Affective Evaluation of Dance," *Frontiers in Human Neuroscience* 7: 521.

Kirsch, L. P., Urgesi, C., and Cross, E. S. (2016a) "Shaping and Reshaping the Aesthetic Brain: Emerging Perspectives on the Neurobiology of Embodied Aesthetics," *Neuroscience & Biobehavioral Reviews* 62: 56–68.

Kirsch, L. P., Diersch, N., Sumanapala, D. K., and Cross, E. S. (2018) "Dance Training Shapes Action Perception and Its Neural Implementation within the Young and Older Adult Brain," *Neural Plasticity* 2018, https://doi.org/10.1155/2018/5459106.

Kirsch, L. P., Snagg, A., Heerey, E., and Cross, E. S. (2016b) "The Impact of Experience on Affective Responses during Action Observation," *PloS One* 11: e0154681.

Klapper, A., Ramsey, R., Wigboldus, D., and Cross, E. S. (2014) "The Control of Automatic Imitation Based on Bottom-Up and Top-Down Cues to Animacy: Insights from Brain and Behaviour," *Journal of Cognitive Neuroscience* 26: 2503–13.

Lakatos, G., Gacsi, M., Konok, V., Bruder, I., Bereczky, B., Korondi, P., and Miklosi, A. (2014) "Emotion Attribution to a Non-Humanoid Robot in Different Social Situations," *Plos One* 9: e114207.

Lamm, C., Batson, C. D., and Decety, J. (2007) "The Neural Substrate of Human Empathy: Effects of Perspective-Taking and Cognitive Appraisal," *Journal of Cognitive Neuroscience* 19: 42–58.

Liew, S.-L., Sheng, T., Margetis, J., and Aziz-Zadeh, L. (2013) "Both Novelty and Expertise Increase Action Observation Network Activity," *Frontiers in Human Neuroscience* 7: 541.

Loula, F., Prasad, S., Harber, K., and Shiffrar M. (2005) "Recognizing People from Their Movement," *Journal of Experimental Psychology: Human Perception and Performance* 31: 210–20. doi:10.1037/0096-1523.31.1.210.

Massaro, D. W., and Friedman, D. (1990) "Models of Integration Given Multiple Sources of Information," *Psychological Review* 97: 225–52.

Meltzoff, A. (2007) "'Like Me': A Foundation for Social Cognition," *Developmental Science* 10: 126–34.

Meltzoff, A., and Prinz, W. (2003) *The Imitative Mind: Development, Evolution, and Brain Bases*, Cambridge: Cambridge University Press.

Mori, M. (2005) "On the Uncanny Valley," in *Proceedings of the Humanoids 2005 Workshop: Views of the Uncanny Valley*, Tsukuba, Japan.

Orgs, G., Casperson, D., and Haggard, P. (2016) "You Move, I Watch, It Matters: Aesthetic Communication in Dance," in S. Obhi and E. S. Cross (eds.) *Shared Representations: Sensorimotor Foundations of Social Life*, Cambridge: Cambridge University Press.

Orgs, G., Hagura, N., and Haggard, P. (2013) "Learning to Like It: Aesthetic Perception of Bodies, Movements and Choreographic Structure," *Consciousness and Cognition* 22: 603–12.

Patuzzo, S., Fiaschi, A., and Manganotti, P. (2003) "Modulation of Motor Cortex Excitability in the Left Hemisphere during Action Observation: A Single- and Paired-Pulse Transcranial Magnetic Stimulation Study of Self- and Non-Self-Action Observation," *Neuropsychologia* 41: 1272–8.

Pelphrey, K. A., and Carter, E. J. (2008) "Brain Mechanisms for Social Perception: Lessons from Autism and Typical Development," *Annals of the New York Academy of Sciences* 1145: 283–99.

Press, C. (2011) "Action Observation and Robotic Agents: Learning and Anthropomorphism," *Neuroscience & Biobehavioral Reviews* 35: 1410–18.

Press, C., Bird, G., Flach, R., and Heyes, C. (2005) "Robotic Movement Elicits Automatic Imitation," *Cognitive Brain Research* 25: 632–40.

Prinz, W. (1997) "Perception and Action Planning," *European Journal of Cognitive Psychology* 9: 129–54.

Ramsey, R., and Hamilton, A. (2010) "Triangles Have Goals Too: Understanding Action Representation in Left aIPS," *Neuropsychologia* 48: 2773–6.

Rizzolatti, G., Fadiga, L., Gallese, V., and Fogassi, L. (1996a) "Premotor Cortex and The Recognition of Motor Actions," *Cognitive Brain Research* 3: 131–41.

Rizzolatti, G., Fadiga, L., Matelli, M., Bettinardi, V., Paulesu, E., Perani, D., and Fazio, F. (1996b) "Localization of Grasp Representations in Humans by PET: 1. Observation versus Execution," *Experimental Brain Research* 111: 246–52.

Rizzolatti, G., Fogassi, L., and Gallese, V. (2001) "Neurophysiological Mechanisms Underlying the Understanding and Imitation of Action," *Nature Review Neuroscience* 2: 661–70.

Sanders, A. F. (1967) "Some Aspects of Reaction Processes," *Acta Psychologica* 27: 115–30.

—— (1983) "Towards a Model of Stress and Human Performance," *Acta Psychologica* 53: 61–97.

Saxe, R., and Kanwisher, N. (2003) "People Thinking about Thinking People: The Role of The Temporo-Parietal Junction in 'Theory of Mind'," *Neuroimage* 19: 1835–42.

Schippers, M. B., and Keysers, C. (2011) "Mapping the Flow of Information within the Putative Mirror Neuron System during Gesture Observation," *NeuroImage* 57: 37–44.

Schubotz, R. I. (2007) "Prediction of External Events With Our Motor System: Towards a New Framework," *Trends in Cognitive Sciences* 11: 211–18.

Shimada, S. (2010) "Deactivation in the Sensorimotor Area during Observation of a Human Agent Performing Robotic Actions," *Brain and Cognition* 72: 394–9.

Sinigaglia, C. (2013) "What Type of Action Understanding Is Subserved by Mirror Neurons?" Neuroscience Letters 540: 59–61.

Strafella, A. P., and Paus, T. (2000) "Modulation of Cortical Excitability during Action Observation: A Transcranial Magnetic Stimulation Study," *Neuroreport* 11: 2289–92.

Tai, Y. F., Scherfler, C., Brooks, D. J., Sawamoto, N., and Castiello, U. (2004) "The Human Premotor Cortex Is 'Mirror' Only for Biological Actions," *Current Biology* 14: 117–20.

Takahashi, H., Terada, K., Morita, T., Suzuki, S., Haji, T., Kozima, H., et al. (2014) "Different Impressions of Other Agents Obtained through Social Interaction Uniquely Modulate Dorsal and Ventral Pathway Activities in the Social Human Brain," *Cortex* 58: 289–300.

Tessari, A., and Rumiati, R. I. (2004) "The Strategic Control of Multiple Routes in Imitation of Actions," *Journal of Experimental Psychology: Human Perception and Performance* 30: 1107–16.

Tipper, C. M., Signorini, G., and Grafton, S. T. (2015) "Body Language in the Brain: Constructing Meaning from Expressive Movement," *Frontiers in Human Neuroscience* 9: 450. https://doi.org/10.3389/fnhum.2015.00450.

Urgesi, C., Maieron, M., Avenanti, A., Tidoni, E., Fabbro, F., and Aglioti, S. M. (2010) "Simulating the Future of Actions in the Human Corticospinal System," *Cerebral Cortex* 20: 2511–21.

Welford, A. T. (1968) *Fundamentals of Skill*, London: Methuen.

Wolpert, D. M., Doya, K., and Kawato, M. (2003). "A Unifying Computational Framework for Motor Control and Social Interaction," *Philosophical Transactions of the Royal Society of London. Series B: Biological Sciences* 358: 593–602.

23

MOTOR REPRESENTATION AND KNOWLEDGE OF SKILLED ACTION

Corrado Sinigaglia and Stephen A. Butterfill

23.1 Introduction

Most of the chapters in this volume concern the role of skill in doing. Our focus is on its role in observation. Why consider observation? Much evidence suggests that skill is every bit as important for observing as for doing. It is no exaggeration to say that your skills are a foundation of your ability to observe and acquire knowledge about others' actions.

Start with an illustration. A commentator and a former player are at a basketball match observing a player taking a free shot, potentially winning the match. Just as the ball leaves the player's hands, the lights go out and the stadium is in complete darkness. So information about the early part of the player's kinematics is available to the two observers whereas they have little or no information about the ball's trajectory. Each observer, the commentator and former player, is asked to predict whether the ball went into the basket. Who would you bet is more likely to be right? Betting on the commentator might seem safe: she has years of experience watching shots taken from this perspective, while the former player, although skilled, has comparatively rarely observed the action from this perspective. Yet it is the former player, not the commentator, who is more likely to make the correct prediction.[1] As this illustrates, being skilled in performing actions of a certain type can enable you to acquire observational knowledge about others' actions of that type. But why? Why are those more skilled in performing certain actions (sometimes, at least) better able to acquire knowledge when observing those actions?

Our chapter aims to answer this question. Before facing it directly, in Section 23.2, we shall first review further evidence for the premise that those more skilled in performing certain actions are, at least sometimes, better able to acquire knowledge when observing those actions. We shall then elaborate a conjecture which, if correct, would answer the question. Our conjecture is that performing and observing actions involves a common element, namely motor representations of outcomes to which the actions are directed. It is this common element that explains why skills matter not only for performing actions but also for gaining knowledge in observing actions. While a body of evidence supports this conjecture (see Section 23.3), it faces an objection. The double life motor representations lead appears to require that they have two, incompatible directions of fit. After answering this objection (in Section 23.4), we find ourselves confronted with a further challenge. If our conjecture is right, whether we know something

292

about the goals of an action sometimes depends on how we represent that action motorically. That is, motor representations can have content-respecting influences on knowledge states. The challenge, which we call the Interface Problem, is how there could be such influence. At present many candidate answers are available, as we shall see in Section 23.5. In our view, neither any available evidence nor narrowly theoretical considerations are likely to yield decisive reasons in favour of any one answer. A deeper understanding of how expertise matters for gaining knowledge of observed actions ultimately requires new discoveries on how motor representations and knowledge states interface.

23.2 That skills matter for observational knowledge

The premise of our question is that those more skilled in performing certain actions are, at least sometimes, better able to acquire knowledge when observing those actions. This is illustrated by Aglioti et al.'s (2008) basketball study, as we have seen. But this is much too bold a premise to accept on the basis of a single study. What further evidence supports it?

The method of Aglioti et al.'s (2008) study relied on correlation as there was no intervention on the subjects' level of skill. By contrast, Urgesi et al. (2012) included a training component. They studied volleyball fans and players, replicating and extending Aglioti et al.'s (2008) findings. They then studied two groups of nonplayers, giving one observational training and the other training in playing volleyball. They found that those trained in playing volleyball also acquired observational skills not found in those given observational training only. Specifically, only those trained became able to use bodily movement in predicting whether a shot would be in or out.[2]

Acquiring a skill through training usually involves observing actions, even if only one's own. Could it be observational experiences associated with training, rather than the acquired skills to act, which explain improved observational abilities? To answer this question, Casile and Giese (2006) investigated the effects of training blindfolded subjects to acquire a new skill. (The blindfold ensured they could not visually observe the actions they were being trained to perform.) When walking, people typically swing their arms in phase with their legs. It is surprisingly difficult to adopt different phase relations between arms and legs, although this can be learnt (Chapman et al. 1970). Importantly, it can also be difficult to identify walking actions involving unusual phase relations between arms and legs through observation. Exploiting these facts, Casile and Giese (2006) trained subjects in performing a silly walk while blindfolded. Before training, and again after training, each subject was tested on her ability to visually identify walks that differed in the phase relation between arms and legs. The found not only that training improved accuracy (see Casile and Giese 2006: figure 2 on p. 70), but also that how well a subject could perform a novel walk after training was correlated with how accurately she could visually identify it after (but not before) training (pp. 71–2). This is evidence that the effects of having skills to act on your abilities to observe actions does not, or does not always, depend on gaining sensory experience in observing actions acquired as a side-effect of training.

Further evidence for the effect of skills to act on acquiring knowledge of others' actions through observation comes from research with human infants. When observing a hand that is approaching some objects and about to grasp one of them, infants will, like adults, often look to the target of the action in advance of the hand arriving there (Falck-Ytter et al. 2006). As in adults, this proactive gaze indicates that the infants are tracking the goals of the observed actions.[3] Critically, though, the occurrence of this proactive gaze in infants is related to their acquisition of the skills needed for performing the actions. For those infants who are as yet less good at reaching and grasping, their eyes do not arrive on an object to be grasped in advance of the hand grasping it (compare Kanakogi and Itakura 2011). Further, if we consider pro-active gaze for different kinds of observed actions (such as putting objects into containers or various kinds of grasping actions), we find that infants' gaze to the target of an action becomes more proactive as they become better able to perform the particular kind of action observed (Cannon et al. 2012). Ambrosini et al. (2013) extended this finding by exploiting the fact that grasping skill can be measured by the minimum number of digits used to grasp from ten to two. Remarkably, they found that this fine-grained measure of skill in performing actions correlated with infants' abilities to track the goals of observed actions.[4]

What happens if we intervene on infants' skills? Sommerville et al. (2005) put 'sticky mittens' on three-month-old infants and allowed them to play with objects. This allowed them not exactly to grasp objects but to manipulate them with their hands, which likely boosted their skills. Following the training (but, in other studies, not mere observation: see Sommerville et al. 2008; Gerson and Woodward 2014; Bakker et al. 2015), infants manifested abilities to track the goals of simple object-directed actions which untrained infants appeared to lack.[5] This indicates that, as with adults, boosting an infant's skill in performing an action can have a corresponding effect on the infant's abilities to track the goals of actions of that type. The link between skills and action observation is present even as humans are first acquiring skills to manipulate worldly objects.

In this section we have seen evidence from a range of studies covering a diversity of skilled actions which supports our premise that those more skilled in performing certain actions are, at least sometimes, better able to acquire knowledge when observing those actions (for a longer review and some bolder claims, see Shiffrar and Heinen 2011).

This premise requires qualification. The cases of skill we have considered all involve very small-scale bodily actions: they are skills such as throwing a ball, walking, and grasping an object. These examples of skill contrast with, say, the skill that a successful politician exercises in winning an election for the fifth time despite having caused several disasters and being transparently corrupt. We should not generalise from one kind of skill to another without evidence.

23.3 The effects of skill depend on having capacities to represent actions motorically

Why should having a skill required for the performance of an action ever enhance your ability to observe and acquire knowledge about actions of that type? It is, sometimes or always, because there is an element common to having skill in performing an action and being able to acquire knowledge about that action through observation: both involve abilities to represent outcomes motorically. Or so we conjecture.

In this section our aim is to elucidate and support this conjecture. Let us start by further specifying the conjecture as the conjunction of three subclaims:

1. exercising skills in performing very small-scale bodily actions involves representing certain outcomes motorically;
2. motor representations of these very outcomes sometimes occur when you are merely observing the actions; and
3. the occurrence of these motor representations can enhance your ability to acquire knowledge about the actions when observing them.

In what follows we review evidence for each of the three subclaims in turn.

Skill in performing an action often depends in many subtle, ordinarily unnoticed ways on anticipating its consequences. For instance, to open a sliding drawer with any kind of finesse, you need to make anticipatory postural adjustments in order to maintain your balance, and these adjustments need to be tightly coordinated with the timing of your action. The difficulty, and the importance, of such anticipatory adjustments can be made vivid by considering developmental changes in infants' abilities to perform actions such as reaches. Infants' initial anticipatory postural adjustments are not well timed and only gradually develop adult-like temporal precision over a period of around seven months (Witherington et al. 2002; see also von Hofsten 1991). These and other minute observations of the development of abilities to perform very small-scale actions reveal that, often enough, the early parts of a skilled action anticipate the future parts in ways that cannot be determined from environmental constraints alone.

Adult-like skill in performing an action also involves anticipatory adjustments related to goals of later parts of the action (rather than merely to side-effects of action such as changes in posture). To illustrate, consider arranging some new books (the old-fashioned, paper kind) on your shelves. You take them out of a box on the table and place them on different shelves depending on where they belong in your collection. Some go on to high shelves, some are placed low down. Although mundane, this is a highly skilled activity. One aspect of the skill concerns how you grasp each book. Typically, the higher the shelf for which a book is destined, the lower on its spine you will grasp it (Cohen and Rosenbaum 2004). The lower grip is initially more awkward but makes things easier when you come to finally placing the book.[6] As this illustrates, some skilled actions unfold in ways that anticipate the goals of later parts of the action (see Kawato 1999 for another example).

Given that skilled performance of very small-scale actions requires anticipation, including anticipation reflecting the goal's future actions, how is such anticipation achieved? Many researchers hold that control of very small-scale actions involves motor representations.[7] These representations specify outcomes that are quite abstract relative to bodily configurations and joint displacements. They may represent the movement of a book from one place to another, for example; or they may represent the securing of an object in a way that is neutral as between manual grasping, oral grasping and grasping with a tool (e.g., Rizzolatti et al. 2001; Umiltà et al. 2008; Cattaneo et al. 2009). By representing outcomes, motor representations enable some forms of anticipatory control in performing very small-scale bodily actions.

A further reason for postulating motor representations of outcomes arises from the need to understand how action control can be computationally tractable given the many degrees of freedom, even after taking bodily synergies into account, afforded by the body's joints (Tessitore et al. 2013). Representing actions in terms of outcomes and the means by which they are achieved contributes to making anticipatory control tractable.

So much for the first of the three subclaims of our conjecture (item 1 in the list above). What about the second subclaim? This is the idea that motor representations lead a double life, for they sometimes occur not only when you are performing an action but also when you are merely observing another performing that action. Perhaps the most direct evidence in humans for this subclaim comes from measuring motor evoked potentials on the muscles of an observer. Several investigations have revealed that when motor activity is amplified in the brain of an observer using transcranial magnetic stimulation, there are minute indicators of muscle activation in the observer in the right muscles at the right time (e.g., Fadiga et al. 1995, 2002; Cattaneo et al. 2009; Cavallo et al. 2011). This is one indication that observing an action can trigger motor representations that would occur in you if you were not merely observing but actually performing the action. Further evidence for the occurrence of motor representations in action observation has been obtained from many scenarios using a wide variety of neurophysiological and behavioural measures in both human and monkey subjects (Rizzolatti and Sinigaglia 2016 provides reviews; see also Rizzolatti and Sinigaglia 2008, 2010).

Importantly for our purposes, what is represented motorically in action observation includes outcomes to which actions are directed. We know this thanks to experiments that (a) vary features of the action such as kinematics and context while keeping the outcome constant (e.g., Rizzolatti et al. 1988; Umiltà et al. 2008); and (b) vary the outcome while meticulously exploiting video editing to keep all other features of the action as constant as possible (e.g., Fogassi et al. 2005). The findings from these experiments suggest that there are motor representations whose occurrence in an observer varies specifically with the outcome of the action observed (see Pavese, Chapter 18 in this volume).

Further, the degree to which motor representations are involved in observation depends on the level of your skill in performing the action (see Cross, Chapter 22 in this volume). Or at least this is suggested by comparing pianists with nonpianists (Haslinger et al. 2005), and ballet with capoeira dancers (Calvo-Merino et al. 2005). In each case, observers skilled in performing the particular kind of action showed stronger brain activation in areas that would be involved in performing that action. This indicates that they represent the observed actions motorically in ways that the unskilled do not.

But what are those motor representations of outcomes doing in you when you are merely observing another's actions? The answer, we suggest, is that they are enhancing your ability to acquire knowledge about the observed actions. Or, if not the whole answer, this is at least one thing those motor representations are doing. Hence, the third subclaim of our conjecture (item 3 in the above list). But why accept this?

Evidence for this subclaim comes from experiments in which subjects' abilities to represent actions motorically are momentarily impaired. This can be done indirectly by constraining body parts, which is thought to impair abilities to represent motorically actions involving those body parts. Or it can be done more directly using transcranial magnetic stimulation (TMS) pulses. However it is done, the findings are broadly similar. The proactive eye movements which indicate goal tracking are less likely to occur (Ambrosini et al. 2012; Costantini et al. 2014), and your judgements about the goals of actions are slower (D'Ausilio et al. 2009) or less accurate (Urgesi et al. 2007; van Kemenade et al. 2012; Michael et al. 2014) when your ability to represent actions motorically is momentarily impaired.

If the effect of performance skills on action observation is sometimes or always mediated by motor representations as we are suggesting, then we might guess that how accurate your observations are would depend on how closely you and the agent observed are matched in skill. You would be best at using observations to predict outcomes of actions performed by someone very like you in skill. Accordingly, Knoblich and Flach (2001) and Knoblich et al. (2002) tested how matches in skill between observer and agent influence predictions. They had subjects watch videos of actions and predict their outcomes, where the agent in the video could be either a stranger or the subject herself (thus ensuring an ideal match in skill between observer and agent). They found that, for throwing darts and also for handwriting, subjects could best predict the outcomes of their own actions, even when not informed that the observed actions were their own.[8]

The subclaim that motor representations can enhance your ability to acquire observational knowledge of actions needs further specification. For it should not be assumed that the influence of motor representations on knowledge states is a matter of one-off triggering: it may be more plausible to suppose that motor representations dynamically influence processes by which knowledge states are arrived at and maintained (as Fridland 2016 suggests in a parallel case). And, further, the influence of motor representations on these epistemic processes should probably not be understood as a matter of determining their outcomes in the sense that you could predict exactly which knowledge states will be arrived at from knowledge of what is represented motorically (compare Burnston 2017). Finally, note that we are here offering no suggestions about how motor representations may enhance abilities to acquire knowledge: the view defended so far is silent on processes.

So why are those more skilled in performing certain actions (sometimes, at least) better able to acquire knowledge when observing those actions? In this section we have elaborated and defended our conjecture that it is sometimes or always because both involve abilities to represent outcomes motorically (see Shiffrar 2010 for a broader review). Your skills matter for action observation because you exercise these skills in observing much as you do in performing an action.

While a body of evidence appears to support this conjecture (as we have just seen), there is an objection to its coherence. The objection concerns the idea that motor representations both control actions (so must have a world-to-mind direction of fit) and are involved in tracking the goals of others' actions (which requires a mind-to-world direction of fit).

23.4 An objection: motor representation and direction of fit

Our conjecture entails that there is a single kind of representation, motor representation, which features both in performing actions and in gaining observational knowledge of them. Let us take a further step and suppose that this is no accident but, rather, reflects the functions motor representations serve. It appears to follow that representations of this kind have different directions of fit. Apparently, some are world-to-mind insofar as they are supposed to lead to performing actions, while others are mind-to-world insofar as they are supposed to enable predictions of others' actions.

This objection arises from the idea that motor representations lead a double life. On the view introduced earlier, what is represented motorically in action observation includes outcomes to which actions are directed. Further, these representations have the function of enhancing your ability to acquire knowledge about the observed actions. It seems, therefore, that these representations must be mind-to-world. That is, their function depends on the motor representation representing only outcomes that are actually goals of the observed action. Because the idea that motor representations lead a double life involves saying that there is just one kind of representation here and in action control, it appears to entail that different instances of a single attitude can have different directions of fit: some are world-to-mind, others are mind-to-world. But this is arguably incoherent. So the objection.

One response to the objection would be to embrace the idea that a single representation can have multiple directions of fit, as others have done (see, for example, Millikan 1995; Shea 2018: Section 7.2). As not everyone accepts this,[9] we propose a reply to the objection that does not depend on contradicting it.[10]

As a preliminary to replying to this objection, consider an analogy. There is a rotary dial on your oven that enables you to initiate and control the oven's activity. We might think of the dial as having an oven-to-instrument direction of fit: the oven temperature is supposed to adjust to the setting on the dial. But now suppose, further, that there is an indicator light on your oven that is illuminated unless the oven has reached the temperature specified by the dial. This enables you to use the dial to discover the temperature of the oven: if the light is on, you turn the dial down until just the point where the light goes off. Now the setting on the dial tells you the temperature of the oven. So, we might think of the dial as having an instrument-to-oven direction of fit.

This analogy will guide our response to the objection. The key point can be put like this. There is a core system featuring the dial, thermostat, heating element and oven. Relative to this core system, the dial always has an oven-to-instrument direction of fit. However, there is a larger system which embeds the core system and exploits it for novel ends. This larger system includes you and your capacity to temporarily prevent significant changes in the temperature of the oven (perhaps by moving the dial between settings too quickly for the heating element to respond). Relative to this larger system the dial has an instrument-to-oven direction of fit. So, to understand the dial's functions, we do need two directions of fit, oven-to-instrument and instrument-to-oven. But this is not quite to say that the dial has both directions of fit. For something has a direction of fit only relative to a particular system. Which direction of fit we see depends on which system we are considering. Understanding the dial does not require supposing that anything has two directions of fit relative to a single system.

Our response to the objection is similar. If we consider planning-like motor processes only (the core system), then each motor representation's function is linked to initiating and controlling action. From this perspective, only a world-to-mind direction of fit is in view. But these planning-like motor processes can occur in the context of a larger system, one that involves something that somehow prevents performance of action. The functions of this larger system concern predicting which outcomes actions will be directed to. If we consider this larger system, it is natural to describe the motor representations as having a mind-to-world direction of fit. So, as in our analogy, which direction of fit we see depends on which system we are considering. We need never have two directions of fit in view simultaneously. Our reply to the objection, then, is that our conjecture involves no incoherence when properly understood.

So much for the objection. From here on we will assume that it is at least coherent to conjecture, as we have, that having skills enhances your observational abilities wholly or in part because it enables you to better represent the goals of others' actions motorically. But the truth of this conjecture would raise a theoretical challenge. The challenge concerns how motor representations could have content-respecting influences[11] on knowledge states. We call meeting this challenge the Interface Problem.

23.5 How do motor representations influence knowledge states?

Suppose, as we have been considering, that having skills enhances your observational abilities because it enables you to better represent the goals of others' actions motorically. Then we are sometimes in this situation: in observing an action, we represent a certain outcome motorically; and partly in virtue of this motor representation, we come to know that this outcome or a matching[12] outcome is a goal of the observed action. It is not just that motor representations influence knowledge states: whether we know something can depend, in some way, on what we represent motorically. That is, motor representations can have content-respecting influences on knowledge states. How is this possible?

There have been millennia of discussion about knowledge and, more recently, quite a bit of research on motor representation. By contrast, there is comparatively little written on how the two might be connected. For this reason, it seems to us worthwhile to consider a range of candidate answers at this stage. As the question is ultimately a scientific one, our hope is that some or all of the rough candidate answers reviewed in this section can be turned into hypotheses generating readily testable predictions.

One candidate answer—'Identity', as we shall call it—involves identifying motor representations with knowledge states. Perhaps, for example, motor representations that occur in action observation are one kind of knowledge state. This candidate answer implies that there is no issue concerning how motor representations can have content-respecting influences on knowledge states; or, if there is, it is just a special case of the more general issue of how knowledge states can have content-respecting influences on each other.

An alternative candidate answer is that motor representations are connected to knowledge states via inferential processes. There is no mystery about how one knowledge state can have content-respecting influences on another knowledge state: inference is paradigmatically a process by which mental states have content-respecting influences. It might, in principle, be that motor representations can similarly lead to knowledge states via a process of inference combining the two kinds of state. One attraction of this candidate answer (call it 'Inference') is that, if correct, it would appear to solve the Interface Problem without conceptual novelty or reliance on untested conjectures.

How can we determine the correctness of these views, Identity and Inference? Suppose you represent the goal of some observed action motorically. Then you should be in a position to know what the goal of the action is. How could you not? Given Identity, motor representations that occur in action observation are one kind of knowledge state, so failure to know would presumably involve having inconsistent beliefs or some other knowledge-preventing failure of rationality. And given Inference, only this or failure to make a simple inference could preclude you from knowing. So, if it turned out that humans can represent the goals of observed actions motorically while lacking corresponding knowledge despite there being no inconsistency or failure to make a simple inference, then we would have evidence against both Identity and Inference.

Is this prediction testable? Consider that there are parallels to Identity and Inference for a question about how motor representations relate to intentions rather than knowledge states. One consideration against these parallel views arises from ways motor representations and intentions can fail to match, as illustrated by Anarchic Hand Syndrome (compare Mylopoulos and Pacherie 2017: 323). Subjects with Anarchic Hand Syndrome, which usually follows lesions of the anterior part of the corpus callosum and of the supplementary motor area, perform actions incompatible with their avowed intentions. These patients may also refer to their anarchic hand as having a mind of its own (Della Sala et al. 1994). Consider a subject with Anarchic Hand Syndrome who intends not to drink some hot tea until it cools. As one hand attempts to pick up the cup and bring it to her mouth, she needs to intervene with her other hand to put the cup back onto the table (Della Sala et al. 1991: 1114). There is clearly some mismatch between her intentions and her motor representation. But there is no reason independent of accepting Identity to suppose that the mismatch involves anything like the kind of irrationality that occurs when one knowingly has incompatible intentions. And since Anarchic Hand Syndrome is not specifically linked to failures in reasoning, nor is there reason independently of accepting Inference to conjecture that the mismatch is due to failure to make a simple inference. Our suggestion is that parallel considerations could be used to show that any discoverable mismatches between knowledge (rather than intention) and motor representation provide evidence against Identity and Inference. If so, the striking prediction is readily testable.

A third candidate answer, due to Mylopoulos and Pacherie (2017), involves the notion of an executable action concept.[13] This is a concept that 'could guide the formation of a volition, itself the proximal cause of a corresponding movement' (Mylopoulos and Pacherie 2017: 324). To illustrate, in humans MANUAL REACH would typically be an executable action concept whereas WAG TAIL would not typically be. Further, they propose that concepts are executable action concepts in virtue of an association between the concept and a motor schema[14] such that when a thought involving the concept occurs, the associated motor representation is activated.

We might suppose that the converse also occurs. That is, when a motor representation occurs in action observation, any associated executable action concepts are somehow activated, biasing the observer to think about the corresponding action.

Could this idea explain, in principle, how motor representations have content-respecting influences on knowledge states without there being any inference or translation process? Suppose that the concept MANUAL REACH is associated with a motor schema for manual reaching. Then when observing someone reach for a cup, this outcome is represented motorically. Such a motor representation involves both the specific outcome involving this particular cup and a motor schema. Because the motor schema is associated with the concept, activation of the motor schema increases the probability that the concept will be activated too.

Our fourth (and last) candidate answer invokes experience. When observing an action you may have an experience that provides you with reasons for a judgement about the goals of that action. Call this an *experience revelatory of action*. Now we know that motor representations can influence perceptual processes (Bortoletto et al. 2011), and there is even some evidence that motor expertise may influence whether an experience reveals an action (Funk et al. 2005). To make a leap, we might guess that which outcomes are represented motorically can influence which goals are revealed in experiences revelatory of action: that is to say, motor representations can *shape* experiences revelatory of action. Perhaps this is how motor representations can have content-respecting influences on knowledge states.

This candidate answer, call it Experience, suggests a rough parallel between two interface problems. One concerns representations that feature in perceptual processes, the other motor representations. In both cases, the question is how these representations can have content-respecting influences on knowledge states. And in both cases the answer is that the representations shape experiences, which in turn provide reasons for judgements. There is a reason why some animals have experiences: it provides a link between representations with different kinds of formats in cases where binding things together with inferential processes would be suboptimal (perhaps because it would break otherwise useful encapsulation, for example).

Of course, the parallel needs careful development. Whereas there are perceptual modalities, it is perhaps unlikely that there is also a motor modality. So the closest parallel for motor representations' influence on knowledge states may be with amodal perceptual representations such as object indexes (as Sinigaglia and Butterfill 2015: 12 suggest). It would also be possible to develop Experience while rejecting the parallel with a perceptual interface problem entirely (see Sinigaglia and Butterfill 2016: 156–8).

However exactly it is developed, Experience faces a methodological objection. As a candidate answer to a question about one problem (How can motor representations have content-respecting influences on knowledge states?) it raises two questions that appear no less puzzling. After all, it seems no easier to understand how motor representations can have content-respecting influences on experiences, nor how experiences can have content-respecting influences on knowledge. Our view is that such objections carry little weight when we are so far from understanding how to solve the Interface Problem. Any candidate answer that can be turned into a hypothesis capable of generating readily testable predictions is worth considering.

But could Experience really be turned into a testable hypothesis? We know that motor representations can influence judgements about the trajectories of bodies in motion (Shiffrar and Freyd 1990; Blake and Shiffrar 2007). But how? The Visual Hypothesis says these judgements are based are visual experiences of movements only. By contrast, the Action Hypothesis says that motor representations can influence experiences associated with bodily trajectories in ways that are not exhaustively visual. Note that the Action Hypothesis does not flow directly from Experience (which is, strictly speaking, consistent with the Visual Hypothesis). However, the Action Hypothesis could be regarded as one way of developing Experience. If the Action Hypothesis is right, there should be situations in which subjects can rationally distinguish bodily trajectories in ways not fully explained by their visual experiences of movements. To illustrate, consider placing a solid barrier somewhere along a possible hand trajectory. Suppose (as might in principle happen) that subjects were to judge, on the basis of observation, that the hand follows this trajectory and that they also report not seeing the hand pass through the solid barrier. If the same combination were not obtained concerning the movements of mere shapes (rather than hands), we might conclude that the judgement about the hand trajectory is not, or is not entirely, a consequence of visual experiences of movement. This would be evidence for the Action Hypothesis. Of course, it is unlikely that things would turn out so neatly. We mention the possibility merely to illustrate one virtue of the fourth candidate answer, Experience: although perhaps implausible and complicated, it is a source of hypotheses that generate readily testable predictions.

23.6 Conclusion

We started with the discovery that those more skilled in performing certain very small-scale bodily actions are sometimes better able to acquire knowledge when observing those actions (Section 23.2). But why? We conjecture that it is because performing and observing actions involves a common element, namely motor representations of outcomes to which the actions are directed. This conjecture is supported by a range of evidence (23.3). It is also theoretically coherent (23.4). However, its correctness would leave us with a deeper and more puzzling question than the one it aims to answer.

If our conjecture is right, whether we know something about the goals of an action sometimes depends on how we represent that action motorically. That is, motor representations can have content-respecting influences on knowledge states. How is this possible? As we have seen in Section 23.5, there are at least four distinct candidate answers to this question. Further, at least three of these are consistent with each other in the sense that, in principle at least, any combination of them could be correct. There is a gap in our understanding of how expertise matters for gaining knowledge of observed actions.

In our view, progress could be made in two ways. The first is to explore links between different interface problems. An interface problem arises wherever it is challenging to explain how representations of one kind can have content-respecting influences on representations of another kind. This is challenging not only for how motor representations influence knowledge states but also, moving in the opposite direction, for how intentions influence motor representations (Butterfill and Sinigaglia 2014). And, more broadly, there appear to be related challenges for understanding how perceptual representations can influence knowledge states (e.g., Jackendoff 1996). Of course, the solutions to different interface problems may turn out to have little in common. But our guess is that good solutions will be reused. Linking different interface problems may therefore constrain the range of candidate solutions that need be considered. This is likely to leave several candidates in play, of course. After all, the interface problem is a question about how minds work and so not one that could be answered on the basis of narrowly theoretical considerations. We therefore need a second way of making progress: we need to turn rough ideas into hypotheses and to test their predictions.

Notes

1 Aglioti et al. (2008: experiment 1) compared three groups: one group of players, one of coaches and sports journalists ('expert watchers') and one of novices. Each was shown clips of the early stages of a player taking a shot and tasked with predicting whether the shot would land in or out. The players made correct predictions significantly more often than the expert watchers did, and the expert watchers were no more likely to be correct than the novices (p. 1111; see figure 1). Modelling the impact of shorter and longer clips on correct responses suggests that only the players were able to make full use of bodily information, while expert watchers and novices may have relied more on information about ball trajectory (p. 1111).

2 Urgesi et al. (2012: experiment 2) studied three groups who all took part in 12 two-hour sessions over three weeks. The three groups' sessions differed in how subjects were taught about floating serves: one group was shown videos and given verbal instructions ('observation training'); another group was given training that required them to perform floating serves ('execution training'); and the control group was given training that did not involve floating serves at all. Before the training, and then again after the training, each subject was tested on how accurately they were able to predict whether a shot would be in or out. Subjects made predictions after watching two kinds of clips. One kind of clip showed bodily movement only (stopping at just the point where the hand contacts the ball); the other kind of clip showed the ball's trajectory (starting at just the point where the hand contacts the ball). Only execution training resulted in significantly more accurate predictions on the basis of bodily movements; and only observation training resulted in significantly more accurate predictions on the basis of ball trajectories (Urgesi et al. 2012[BIB-062]: see figure 3 on p. 533).

3 For an infant to *track the goal of an action* is for there to be a process in the infant such that how this process unfolds nonaccidentally depends, perhaps within limits, on which goal the action is directed to. We take no view on whether or not the infants have knowledge about the goals of actions. Research on their abilities is relevant given that, as we suppose, the goal-tracking processes infants manifest somehow matter for knowledge.

4 Note that our suggestion is not that infants cannot track the goals of observed actions they cannot perform. The key claim for us is that infants are like adults insofar as those more skilled in performing certain actions are also better at extracting information when observing them.

5 Infants' goal-tracking abilities were measured using the much-replicated habituation paradigm introduced by Woodward (1998).

6 This is an instance of what is usually called the 'end-state comfort effect' (Rosenbaum et al. 1992, 1993). While it is important not to conflate end-states with goals, in this instance there is a connection. Sensitivity to the end-state of the action implies sensitivity to the goal of the last part of the action (the placing of the book) since it is this goal that determines the end-state.

7 On what motor representations are and why they are necessary, key sources include Prinz (1990); Wolpert et al. (1995); Jeannerod (2006); Rizzolatti and Sinigaglia (2008); Rosenbaum (2010).

8 In Knoblich and Flach (2001), the subjects were informed about the identity of the agent observed; in Knoblich et al. (2002) they were not.

9 For example, Artiga (2014: 546) argues that 'the main motivation for embracing the Pushmi-Pullyu account is flawed'.

10 Our reply to the objection also indicates a way of defanging some of Millikan's (1995) original arguments for the existence of representations with both directions of fit.

11 For one state's influence on another to be *content-respecting* is for whether or how the first influences the second to nonaccidentally reflect some relation between the two state's contents.

12 Two outcomes *match* in a particular context just if, in that context, either the occurrence of the first outcome would normally constitute or cause, at least partially, the occurrence of the second outcome or vice versa.

13 Mylopoulos and Pacherie (2017) focus on how motor representations relate to intentions rather than to knowledge states; however, their view can be generalised in a natural way. The notion of an executable action concept may be related to Pavese's (2015: 19) suggestion that 'operational semantic values are kinds of practical senses' (Pavese, personal communication): in both cases, a key idea is that entertaining propositions or possessing concepts concerning ways of acting enable agents to act in those ways.

14 Motor schema 'are internal models or stored representations that represent generic knowledge about a certain pattern of action ... that is the organization and structure common to a set of motor acts' (Mylopoulos and Pacherie 2017: 330).

References

Aglioti, S. M., Cesari, P., Romani, M., and Urgesi, C. (2008) "Action Anticipation and Motor Resonance in Elite Basketball Players," *Nature Neuroscience* 11: 1109–16. https://doi.org/10.1038/nn.2182.

Ambrosini, E., Reddy, V., de Looper, A., Costantini, M., Lopez, B., and Sinigaglia, C. (2013) "Looking Ahead: Anticipatory Gaze and Motor Ability in Infancy," *PLoS One* 8: e67916. https://doi.org/10.1371/journal.pone.0067916.

Ambrosini, E., Sinigaglia, C., and Costantini, M. (2012) "Tie My Hands, Tie My Eyes," *Journal of Experimental Psychology: Human Perception and Performance* 38: 263–6. https://doi.org/10.1037/a0026570.

Artiga, M. (2014) "Teleosemantics and Pushmi-Pullyu Representations," *Erkenntnis* 79: 545–66. https://doi.org/10.1007/s10670-013-9517-5.

Bakker, M., Sommerville, J. A., and Gredebäck, G. (2015) "Enhanced Neural Processing of Goal-Directed Actions After Active Training in 4-Month-Old Infants," *Journal of Cognitive Neuroscience* 28: 472–82. https://doi.org/10.1162/jocn_a_00909.

Blake, R., and Shiffrar, M. (2007) "Perception of Human Motion," *Annual Review of Psychology* 58: 47–73. https://doi.org/10.1146/annurev.psych.57.102904.190152.

Bortoletto, M., Mattingley, J. B., and Cunnington, R. (2011) "Action Intentions Modulate Visual Processing During Action Perception," *Neuropsychologia* 49: 2097–104. https://doi.org/10.1016/j.neuropsychologia.2011.04.004.

Burnston, D. C. (2017) "Interface Problems in the Explanation of Action," *Philosophical Explorations* 20: 242–58. https://doi.org/10.1080/13869795.2017.1312504.

Butterfill, S. A., and Sinigaglia, C. (2014) "Intention and Motor Representation in Purposive Action," *Philosophy and Phenomenological Research* 88: 119–45. https://doi.org/10.1111/j.1933-1592.2012.00604.x.

Calvo-Merino, B., Glaser, D. E., Grèzes, J., Passingham, R. E., and Haggard, P. (2005) "Action Observation and Acquired Motor Skills: An FMRI Study with Expert Dancers," *Cerebral Cortex* 15: 1243–9. https://doi.org/10.1093/cercor/bhi007.

Cannon, E. N., Woodward, A. L., Gredebäck, G., von Hofsten, C., and Turek, C. (2012) "Action Production Influences 12-Month-Old Infants' Attention to Others' Actions," *Developmental Science* 15: 35–42. https://doi.org/10.1111/j.1467-7687.2011.01095.x.

Casile, A., and Giese, M. A. (2006) "Nonvisual Motor Training Influences Biological Motion Perception," *Current Biology* 16: 69–74. https://doi.org/10.1016/j.cub.2005.10.071.

Cattaneo, L., Caruana, F., Jezzini, A., and Rizzolatti, G. (2009) "Representation of Goal and Movements Without Overt Motor Behavior in the Human Motor Cortex: A Transcranial Magnetic Stimulation Study," *The Journal of Neuroscience* 29: 11134–8. https://doi.org/10.1523/JNEUROSCI.2605-09.2009.

Cavallo, A., Becchio, C., Sartori, L., Bucchioni, G., and Castiello, U. (2011) "Grasping with Tools: Corticospinal Excitability Reflects Observed Hand Movements," *Cerebral Cortex* 22: 710–16. https://doi.org/10.1093/cercor/bhr157.

Chapman, G., Cleese, J., Idle, E., Jones, T., Palin, M., and Gilliam, T. (1970) *Monty Python's Flying Circus, Series 2*, London: British Broadcasting Corporation.

Cohen, R. G., and Rosenbaum, D. A. (2004) "Where Grasps Are Made Reveals How Grasps Are Planned: Generation and Recall of Motor Plans," *Experimental Brain Research* 157: 486–95. https://doi.org/10.1007/s00221-004-1862-9.

Costantini, M., Ambrosini, E., Cardellicchio, P., and Sinigaglia, C. (2014) "How Your Hand Drives My Eyes," *Social Cognitive and Affective Neuroscience* 9: 705–11. https://doi.org/10.1093/scan/nst037.

D'Ausilio, A., Pulvermüller, F., Salmas, P., Bufalari, I., Begliomini, C., and Fadiga, L. (2009) "The Motor Somatotopy of Speech Perception," *Current Biology* 19: 381–5. https://doi.org/10.1016/j.cub.2009.01.017.

Della Sala, S., Marchetti, C., and Spinnler, H. (1991) "Right-Sided Anarchic (Alien) Hand: A Longitudinal Study," *Neuropsychologia* 29: 1113–27. https://doi.org/10.1016/0028-3932(91)90081-I.

Della Sala, S., Marchetti, C., and Spinnler, H. (1994) "The Anarchic Hand: A Fronto-Mesial Sign," in F. Boller and J. Grafman (eds.) *Handbook of Neuropsychology Vol. 9*, 233–255, Amsterdam: Elsevier.

Fadiga, L., Craighero, L., Buccino, G., and Rizzolatti, G. (2002) "Speech Listening Specifically Modulates the Excitability of Tongue Muscles: A TMS Study," *European Journal of Neuroscience* 15: 399–402.

Fadiga, L., Fogassi, L., Pavesi, G., and Rizzolatti, G. (1995) "Motor Facilitation During Action Observation: A Magnetic Stimulation Study," *Journal of Neurophysiology* 73: 2608–11.

Falck-Ytter, T., Gredeback, G., and von Hofsten, C. (2006) "Infants Predict Other People's Action Goals," *Nature Neuroscience* 9: 878–9.

Fogassi, L., Ferrari, P. F., Gesierich, B., Rozzi, S., Chersi, F., and Rizzolatti, G. (2005) "Parietal Lobe: From Action Organization to Intention Understanding," *Science* 308: 662–7.

Fridland, E. (2016) "Skill and Motor Control: Intelligence All the Way Down," *Philosophical Studies* 174: 1539–60. https://doi.org/10.1007/s11098-016-0771-7.

Funk, M., Shiffrar, M., and Brugger, P. (2005) "Hand Movement Observation by Individuals Born Without Hands: Phantom Limb Experience Constrains Visual Limb Perception," *Experimental Brain Research* 164: 341–6. https://doi.org/10.1007/s00221-005-2255-4.

Gerson, S. A., and Woodward, A. L. (2014) "Learning from Their Own Actions: The Unique Effect of Producing Actions on Infants' Action Understanding," *Child Development* 85: 264–77. https://doi.org/10.1111/cdev.12115.

Haslinger, B., Erhard, P., Altenmüller, E., Schroeder, U., Boecker, H., and Ceballos-Baumann, A. O. (2005) "Transmodal Sensorimotor Networks During Action Observation in Professional Pianists," *Journal of Cognitive Neuroscience* 17: 282–93. https://doi.org/10.1162/0898929053124893.

Jackendoff, R. (1996) "The Architecture of the Linguistic-Spatial Interface," in P. Bloom et al. (eds.) *Language and Space*, 1–30, Cambridge, MA: The MIT Press.

Jeannerod, M. (2006) *Motor Cognition: What Actions Tell the Self*, Oxford: Oxford University Press.

Kanakogi, Y., and Itakura, S. (2011) "Developmental Correspondence Between Action Prediction and Motor Ability in Early Infancy," *Nature Communications* 2: 341. https://doi.org/10.1038/ncomms1342.

Kawato, M. (1999) "Internal Models for Motor Control and Trajectory Planning," *Current Opinion in Neurobiology* 9: 718–27. https://doi.org/10.1016/S0959-4388(99)00028-8.

Knoblich, G., and Flach, R. (2001) "Predicting the Effects of Actions: Interactions of Perception and Action," *Psychological Science* 12: 467–72. https://doi.org/10.1111/1467–9280.00387.

Knoblich, G., Seigerschmidt, E., Flach, R., and Prinz, W. (2002) "Authorship Effects in the Prediction of Handwriting Strokes: Evidence for Action Simulation During Action Perception," *The Quarterly Journal of Experimental Psychology Section A* 55: 1027–46. https://doi.org/10.1080/02724980143000631.

Michael, J., Sandberg, K., Skewes, J., Wolf, T., Blicher, J., Overgaard, M., and Frith, C. D. (2014) "Continuous Theta-Burst Stimulation Demonstrates a Causal Role of Premotor Homunculus in Action Understanding," *Psychological Science* 25: 963–72. https://doi.org/10.1177/0956797613520608.

Millikan, R. G. (1995) "Pushmi-Pullyu Representations," *Philosophical Perspectives* 9: 185–200. https://doi.org/10.2307/2214217.

Mylopoulos, M., and Pacherie, E. (2017) "Intentions and Motor Representations: The Interface Challenge," *Review of Philosophy and Psychology* 8: 317–36. https://doi.org/10.1007/s13164-016-0311-6.

Pavese, C. (2015) "Practical Senses," *Philosopher's Imprint* 15: 1–25.

Prinz, W. (1990) "A Common Coding Approach to Perception and Action," in O. Neumann and W. Prinz (eds.) *Relationships Between Perception and Action*, 167–201, Berlin: Springer.

Rizzolatti, G., Camarda, R., Fogassi, L., Gentilucci, M., Luppino, G., and Matelli, M. (1988) "Functional Organization of Inferior Area 6 in the Macaque Monkey," *Experimental Brain Research* 71: 491–507. https://doi.org/10.1007/BF00248742.

Rizzolatti, G., Fogassi, L., and Gallese, V. (2001) "Neurophysiological Mechanisms Underlying the Understanding and Imitation of Action," *Nature Reviews: Neuroscience* 2: 661–70.

Rizzolatti, G., and Sinigaglia, C. (2008) *Mirrors in the Brain: How Our Minds Share Actions, Emotions, and Experience*, Oxford: Oxford University Press.

—— (2010) "The Functional Role of the Parieto-Frontal Mirror Circuit: Interpretations and Misinterpretations," *Nature Reviews: Neuroscience* 11: 264–74. https://doi.org/10.1038/nrn2805.

—— (2016) "The Mirror Mechanism: A Basic Principle of Brain Function," *Nature Reviews Neuroscience* 17: 757–65. https://doi.org/10.1038/nrn.2016.135.

Rosenbaum, D. A. (2010) *Human Motor Control*, 2nd ed., San Diego, CA: Academic Press.

Rosenbaum, D. A., Vaughan, J., Barnes, H. J., and Jorgensen, M. J. (1992) "Time Course of Movement Planning: Selection of Handgrips for Object Manipulation," *Journal of Experimental Psychology: Learning, Memory, and Cognition* 18: 1058–73. https://doi.org/10.1037/0278-7393.18.5.1058.

Rosenbaum, D. A., Vaughan, J., Jorgensen, M. J., Barnes, H. J., and Stewart, E. (1993) "Plans for Object Manipulation," in D. E. Meyer and S. Kornblum (eds.) *Attention and Performance XIV: Synergies in Experimental Psychology, Artificial Intelligence, and Cognitive Neuroscience*, 803–20, Cambridge, MA: The MIT Press.

Shea, N. (2018) *Representation in Cognitive Science*, Oxford: Oxford University Press.

Shiffrar, M. (2010) "People Watching: Visual, Motor, and Social Processes in the Perception of Human Movement," *Wiley Interdisciplinary Reviews: Cognitive Science* 2: 68–78. https://doi.org/10.1002/wcs.88.

Shiffrar, M., and Freyd, J. J. (1990) "Apparent Motion of the Human Body," *Psychological Science* 1: 257–64. https://doi.org/10.1111/j.1467-9280.1990.tb00210.x.

Shiffrar, M., and Heinen, T. (2011) "Athletic Ability Changes Action Perception: Embodiment in the Visual Perception of Human Movement," *Zeitschrift für Sportpsychologie* 17: 1–13.

Sinigaglia, C., and Butterfill, S. A. (2015) "On a Puzzle About Relations Between Thought, Experience and the Motoric," *Synthese* 192: 1923–36. https://doi.org/10.1007/s11229-015-0672-x.

—— (2016) "Motor Representation in Goal Ascription," in M. H. Fischer and Y. Coello (eds.) *Conceptual and Interactive Embodiment: Foundations of Embodied Cognition, Volume 2*, 149–64, London and New York: Routledge.

Sommerville, J. A., Hildebrand, E. A., and Crane, C. C. (2008) "Experience Matters: The Impact of Doing Versus Watching on Infants' Subsequent Perception of Tool-Use Events," *Developmental Psychology* 44: 1249–56. https://doi.org/10.1037/a0012296.

Sommerville, J. A., Woodward, A. L., and Needham, A. (2005) "Action Experience Alters 3-Month-Old Infants' Perception of Others' Actions," *Cognition* 96: B1–B11. https://doi.org/16/j.cognition.2004.07.004.

Tessitore, G., Sinigaglia, C., and Prevete, R. (2013) "Hierarchical and Multiple Hand Action Representation Using Temporal Postural Synergies," *Experimental Brain Research* 225: 11–36. https://doi.org/10.1007/s00221-012-3344-9.

Umiltà, M. A., Escola, L., Intskirveli, I., Grammont, F., Rochat, M., Caruana, F., et al. (2008) "When Pliers Become Fingers in the Monkey Motor System," *Proceedings of the National Academy of Sciences* 105: 2209–13. https://doi.org/10.1073/pnas.0705985105.

Urgesi, C., Candidi, M., Ionta, S., and Aglioti, S. M. (2007) "Representation of Body Identity and Body Actions in Extrastriate Body Area and Ventral Premotor Cortex," *Nature Neuroscience* 10: 30–1. https://doi.org/10.1038/nn1815.

Urgesi, C., Savonitto, M. M., Fabbro, F., and Aglioti, S. M. (2012) "Long- and Short-Term Plastic Modeling of Action Prediction Abilities in Volleyball," *Psychological Research* 76: 542–60. https://doi.org/10.1007/s00426-011-0383-y.

van Kemenade, B. M., Muggleton, N., Walsh, V., and Saygin, A. P. (2012) "Effects of TMS over Premotor and Superior Temporal Cortices on Biological Motion Perception," *Journal of Cognitive Neuroscience* 24: 896–904. https://doi.org/10.1162/jocn_a_00194.

von Hofsten, C. (1991) "Structuring of Early Reaching Movements: A Longitudinal Study," *Journal of Motor Behavior* 23: 280–92. https://doi.org/10.1080/00222895.1991.9942039.

Witherington, D. C., von Hofsten, C., Rosander, K., Robinette, A., Woollacott, M. H., and Bertenthal, B. I. (2002) "The Development of Anticipatory Postural Adjustments in Infancy," *Infancy* 3: 495–517. https://doi.org/10.1207/S15327078IN0304_05.

Wolpert, D. M., Ghahramani, Z., and Jordan, M. (1995) "An Internal Model for Sensorimotor Integration," *Science* 269: 1880–2. https://doi.org/10.1126/science.7569931.

Woodward, A. L. (1998) "Infants Selectively Encode the Goal Object of an Actor's Reach," *Cognition* 69: 1–34.

24

SKILL AND EXPERTISE IN PERCEPTION*

Susanna Siegel

24.1 Introduction

We can distinguish theses that connect skill with perception in general from theses that connect skill with perceptual experience in particular. Perceptual experiences are the conscious states and episodes that are characteristic of perception. These experiences are sensitive to how one's attention is distributed. One can undergo perceptual experiences both in cases when the experience leads to knowledge, or in hallucination or illusion. By contrast, perception in general includes both perceptual experiences and the unconscious information processes that give rise to them via the perceptual system. So there is more to perception than perceptual experience. The focus of this chapter is the relationship of skills to perceptual experience.

How are perceptual experiences related to skills? According to some researchers, skills can be exercised only in intentional actions. But when discussing the relationship between skills and perceptual experience, it's useful to work with a broader notion of skill that could count as skilled behavior the exercise of some recognitional abilities that don't involve intentional action, such as visually recognizing avocadoes, or your favorite sheep in the flock, or the sound of A-flat, without antecedently intending to do any of these things. The broader notion of skill includes these forms of expertise.

It's clear that perceptual experience plays a central role in skilled behavior of all kinds. It is difficult (if not impossible) to catch a football if you can't see or otherwise feel it coming, or to play chess while blindfolded, or to recognize your favorite sheep without getting any sensory input. At a minimum, perceptual experience enables these forms of skilled action. Some philosophers go farther and suggest that perceptual experience is itself a kind of skilled action, or that it constitutively involves skilled actions of various kinds. Whether or not any version of this further claim is true, there are several important ways in which perceptual experiences might be thought to manifest a subject's skills. This chapter focuses on three of them. Section 24.1 discusses the idea that perceptual experience consists in motor skills. Section 24.2 focuses on the idea that perceptual experience can consist partly in skilled mental actions of recognition, such as recognizing a particular animal scurrying past as a mouse. Section 24.3 reviews some of the main ways that various kinds of expertise or cultural understanding manifest themselves in patterns of perceptual attention.

24.2 Are motor skills constitutive of perceptual experience?

The 20th-century French phenomenologist Maurice Merleau-Ponty analyzed perceptual experience as necessarily engaging motor skills. In Merleau-Ponty's paradigmatic cases of perception, the flow of information taken in by perceivers is inseparable from the way they move through a scene. On this view, even superficially static perceptions engage motor skills, such as seeing the color of a table as uniform when different parts of it are differently illuminated. By analogy, in a dance, the dancers' movements are unified in their intake of kinesthetic, tactile, visual and auditory information to such an extent that any purely sensory dimensions of the dancing process would be hard to factor out from motor dimensions. Merleau-Ponty's focus on roles of the body in perceptual experience has inspired some contemporary thinkers to construe the sensory and motor dimensions of perceptual experience as best understood as a unit, just as they are in dancing (Hurley 1998; Kelly 1999; Noë 2004).

How far could this model plausibly generalize? Watching a sunset or examining the colors of paint are other paradigms of perception, but they apparently need not involve doing much with one's body. Because one is just looking, these experiences are more like taking in a spectacle than actively creating one. Some followers of Merleau-Ponty try to make the case that even color perception involves the bodily activity of finding what Merleau-Ponty called the optimal point of view from which the color – or anything – should be viewed.[1] According to these interpreters, we gravitate toward optimal viewpoints, and finding these optima is a skill on par with knowing how to walk: it is a learned skill that we are innately disposed to develop.

What kind of evidence could support the idea that we are sensitive to visual optima? The main evidence would seem to be behavioral dispositions to gravitate toward optimal viewpoints and feel uncomfortable with suboptimal ones. But if perceptual experience in general consists in exercising the skill of finding optimum viewpoints, and if different qualities (color, shape, motion and so on) each have their own optimum, then we will often have competing dispositions. And if that's our situation, or if for all we know it is our situation, then we cannot straightforwardly take the behavior we find in others, or the discomfort we feel in ourselves, to be the manifestation of dispositions to move toward the optimum. There is no obvious feedback that indicates which behavior meets the optima. And if there are neither phenomenological nor behavioral markers of such optima, for many forms of perception there are no obvious success conditions for perceiving optimally. So even if Dreyfus and Kelly's approach captures an aspect of some perceptual experiences when they are deeply integrated with bodily action, the analysis of these aspects may not support the broader idea that perceptual experience is constitutively an exercise of skilled bodily action. Here's a case where skills are construed as manifesting in dispositions to navigate the social and physical environment in a way that would be legible to others in that environment, rather than as an intentional action.

Dreyfus and Kelly focus on the optimal viewpoints in analyzing Merleau-Ponty's idea of the intentional arc. In developing this idea, Merleau-Ponty brings into focus a whole range of mental states that situate us in social and physical environments. As he puts it, the intentional arc is that set of representations by which we "project around us our past, our future, our human milieu, our physical situation, our ideological situation, and our moral situation, or rather, that ensures that we are situated within all of these relationships".[2]

Merleau-Ponty construes the intentional arc as an embodied mode of intentionality. According to him, our motor dispositions embody a kind of understanding of the things we perceive (perhaps optima would be but one example). For example, in the social realm, the culturally specific boundaries of personal space regulate how close we stand to one another, and how far we can squish together on a subway without feeling that boundaries have been violated

(Kelly 2005). Our bodily stances also communicate cues of social status and relationships, such as authority, deference and confidence. Exhibiting and interpreting these cues is a form of cultural literacy, expressed through the body, and it constitutively engages perceptual experience.

On this analysis, perceptual experience constitutively includes skills of navigating the social and physical environment, rather than being a representation that mediates between subpersonal perceptual inputs and behavioral outputs, in conjunction with other beliefs, desires and preferences. The unit of analysis here is something that both has a phenomenological feel and consists in a set of dispositions to respond to cultural and physical environments in culturally recognizable ways.[3]

If Merleau-Ponty is correct, then cultural literacy is mediated by attention, including joint attention. This prediction of Merleau-Ponty's is independently plausible. Like other primates, humans follow the gaze of their con-specifics to direct their attention across all sorts of scenarios.[4] Gaze-following is part of joint attention, in which person A can tell by perception what person B is attending to, and person A goes on to attend to it as well. In this way, person B's attention directs person A's attention. Joint attention is a fundamentally social form of perception and it provides a basis for human cooperation. Just think of how your attention has to be coordinated with another person's, if you are going to carry a table down a flight of stairs, or pass each other a narrow path, or carry on a conversation. Actors in cooperative human activities typically have to presume that they can direct their cooperants' attention to the relevant part of the flow of information. For these reasons, joint attention is part of the basis on which Merleau-Ponty's intentional arc could unfold.

Independently of the picture inspired by Merleau-Ponty on which perceptual experience is infused with motor skills, we can also zoom in on more piecemeal recognitional abilities and consider their relationships to perceptual experience. This brings us to the idea that perceptual experience could be constituted wholly or in part by exercising abilities to recognize things, where recognition is construed as a mental action.

24.3 Are recognitional dispositions ever constitutive of perceptual experience?

Chances are good that you can recognize avocados by sight, or your housemate's footsteps on the stairs by the patterns of sound, or coffee brewing by its smell. What kind of knowledge do you have, when you know what avocados look like, or when you know what someone's footsteps sound like, or what coffee smells like?

A first possibility is that you have some articulable knowledge detailing the features by which you can recognize avocados. Even if you had never seen avocados before, someone could describe them to you, and you could learn from them that avocados are oval, and that depending on the variety they have either blackish thick skin with knobby texture, or greenish thin skin that's relatively smooth. In this way, you could know this is what avocados look like, even if you had never actually seen one.

A second possibility is that your knowledge of what things look like could consist ultimately in an ability to recognize them (as per Lewis 1990). For instance, if housemate Jack has a bad knee, it might give his gait a distinctive rhythm that you can recognize when you hear it. A rhythmic sophisticate might know that the interval in between the sound of the left foot stepping and the sounds of the right foot landing is one-and-a-half times longer than the interval between right foot stepping and left foot landing, and might be able to describe the sound of Jack's steps to you even if neither of you had ever heard any gait like that. But let's suppose that you're not a rhythmic sophisticate, and that no one has ever described anyone's gait to you before. You still might simply know how to identify Jack on the basis of the sound of his footsteps. Your knowledge would consist in an ability to recognize Jack. If you lacked the ability, then on this analysis, you would lack the knowledge as well.

Let's focus on this second option and call it the purely practical one.[5] Is perceptual experience then constituted either by acquiring or by exercising such abilities? If so, then that may be because perceptual experience is partly constituted by having these abilities, in which case we have an example of the thesis that perceptual experience is constituted by a type of mental action.

Alternatively, what if perceptual experience is purely an occasion for exercising recognitional abilities? Sometimes we have a concept, such as rose, and we have the disposition to recognize roses, but we fail to apply the concept to a rose we encounter. Kant described this type of situation when discussing a physician who sometimes makes errors of judgment.[6] If this situation can arise with every concept we have, then recognition and perceptual experience are only contingently connected.

This type of contingency can occur in different strengths. Its strongest form allows that perceptual experience never constitutively involves the application of any recognitional dispositions at all. In that case, perceptual experience enables recognition of things, but is not constituted by recognitional abilities, even in part. In a weaker form, in every perceptual experience, some recognitional dispositions are exercised, but no recognitional disposition is guaranteed to be exercised on every occasion on which it would be fitting to do so. This weak form reintroduces a type of constitutive link between perceptual experiences and recognitional dispositions.

Just as we can ask how perceptual experience relates to practical ability to recognize things like roses, we can ask a parallel question about the relationship between perceptual experiences and introspection. When you know what it's like to see red, you know something about the character of a type of visual experience. In Frank Jackson's thought experiment, a neuroscientist Mary who is said to know all the physical facts sees red for the first time after living in a black and white room. What does Mary come to know when she learns what it's like to see red? According to some philosophers, knowing what it's like to see red is ultimately a kind of ability to self-ascribe a phenomenal type of experience.[7] If they are right, then knowing what it's like to have this type of color experience is an irreducibly practical ability.

24.4 How can perceptual attention reflect the subject's skill?

There are many ways in which specialized expertise including modes of being culturally embedded can manifest itself in patterns of attention.

When you perceive a scene, your attention is always distributed in a way that puts some things into the foreground and other thing into the periphery. How your attention is distributed can depend on other factors as well, including whether the scene contains the types of stimuli that "grab" your attention, such as a sudden movements, bright flashes, loud bangs, or unexpected behavior.

It can also depend on what you're already in the midst of doing, and on how well you know how to do it. For instance, a softball player at the bat knows where to look to figure out what kind of pitch is coming and how best to hit it. A pickpocket observing a potential victim knows which gestures indicate where the victim keeps his wallet, and whether he is sufficiently distracted not to notice a hand reaching in to take it out. Someone lacking expertise in thievery who is watching the very same man could easily have no idea where his wallet is, let alone how to snatch it.

Distributions of attention can also depend on scientific expertise. Faced with the same sequence of X-ray images, a radiologist and a novice will parse each image differently. To the radiologist, some patterns of lines and light contrast stand out from others, whereas the novice finds no difference in kind between them. The radiologist's expertise allows her to find the tumours in the image. She knows what to look for, and she knows when she has found it. And moving down a continuum from scientific expertise to expertise gained merely by exposure, someone used to seeing toads is better than someone with less exposure at finding a toad camouflaged on a tree.[8]

The 18th-century Scottish philosopher Thomas Reid observed that patterns of exposure to things could lead perceivers to differentiate between properties that previously were indistinguishable to them. For example, a wine ignoramus may taste no difference between five different wines, whereas a wine expert can tell them apart. A birder can see the visible differences between two kinds of ducks, whereas a duck novice can't tell them apart.[9] Pairs of phonemes that sound different to speakers of a language sound the same to people who don't understand that language. In these ways, expertise can improve perceptual acuity (see Stokes and Nanay, Chapter 25 in this volume).

Expertise in birds, wine and language improves the overall epistemic position of the experts in these examples. But in other contexts, selective improvement in acuity introduces perceptual asymmetries that highlight epistemic limitations. The prime example is facial differentiation. In racially segregated parts of the United States, the most lengthy and socially valued interactions occur primarily among people who share a socially designated "race". People who are designated regularly as belonging to a racial category, such as white, and who interact mainly with the same are much better at visually discriminating between different white faces, and much worse at visually discriminating between faces of people belonging to other races.[10] This pattern of interaction has an adverse effect on the ability to discriminate between faces of the people belonging to the socially designated "races" with whom they do not interact.

When new abilities to differentiate within a category (such as faces, wines, or birds) emerge from a long pattern of exposure to instances of that category, the process is known as perceptual learning.[11] Perceptual learning differs from perceptual development, which is a matter of brain maturation. Even the most mature perceptual systems can undergo perceptual learning.

When a perceiver's acuity within a category increases due to perceptual learning, her perceptual experiences reflect both her ability to differentiate and her past pattern of exposure to instances of the category.

Perceptual learning is most often illustrated by improved acuity in categorization. But the general idea that long-term changes in acuity can result from practice and experience applies to perception of structures as well. Gaining practice and expertise in music, for example, can improve the ability to find the beat in a piece of music and keep track of it. A beat is the temporal structure of a piece of music. It may or may not have an audible expression (for instance in the pattern of sounds made by a drumbeat). A long-term change in sensitivity to this kind of temporal structure due to patterns of exposure or practice trying to find the beat belongs to the same family of perceptual influences as improvements in acuity within a category.[12]

Aside from categorization and differentiation, perceptual learning in an extended sense can take the form of social facility in a culture. In any human interaction among adults, some possibilities of interaction are foregrounded and others are backgrounded, and normally it is commonly known what the main options are for how the situation is likely to unfold. For instance, it is possible to learn the social cues that someone wants to shake your hand, catch your eye, talk to you, or avoid you, and these possibilities of interactions are learned and can be culturally specific.

Another way for cultural embeddings to shape perceptual experience brings us back to joint attention. Alongside its role in social coordination, joint attention is also a means by which people develop sensitivity of social value. Adams and Kveraga (2015) present experimental evidence that in the United States, the extent of gaze-following behavior is sometimes sensitive to race and social power. To a statistically significant degree, Americans of European descent (white participants) followed the gaze of white faces but did not follow the gaze of Americans of African descent (black participants), whereas black participants followed the gaze of both groups of faces. To the extent that gaze-following indicates confidence that the followed-person's object of attention, or experience of it, is epistemically valuable, it is reasonable to hypothesize that this result reflects an underlying pattern of social valuation, and specifically the epistemic under-valuation of black adults by white adults.

Merleau-Ponty would predict that a person's cultural embedding can affect distributions of attention, and this prediction too is borne out. Eberhardt et al (2004) found that the cultural stereotype that associates black men and crime becomes a "visual tuning device" that directs attention in toward stereotype-congruent information, and away from stereotype-incongruent information.[13] For instance, in one experimental paradigm, participants were primed with the face of a man and then shown a series of images that gradually morphed into a clear image from a noisy one. Participants find crime-related objects such as guns and knives at a lower threshold after seeing the face of a man who is black, compared to the threshold at which they report such objects after seeing the face of a man who is white. And when the primed face is black, participants find crime-related objects at a lower threshold than they find non-crime-related objects such as watches or bugles.

In another experimental paradigm involving a "dot-probe" task, participants are first quickly shown a subliminal crime-related prime, such as a picture of a gun, fingerprint, police badge, or handcuff. The image is flashed too quickly for them to report what they see. They are then shown two male faces, one black and one white, and after the faces disappear, a dot appears in the place where one of the two faces was shown. With a crime prime, participants find the dot more quickly when it replaces a black male face, compared to when it replaces a white male face, and compared to when there is no prime at all. Eberhardt takes this experiment to show that crime prime directs attention to black male faces. Here, culturally entrenched stereotypes produce associations that in turn facilitate patterns of attention that reflect those stereotypes.

Finally, both ethical and aesthetic engagement can take the form of patterns of attention as well, and in these ways, perceptual skills are central to both ethics and aesthetics (see Stokes and Nanay, Chapter 25 in this volume). Consider a long and complicated piece of classical music. Musically engaged people can direct their attention to structures within the music, distinguishing a theme from its development, and finding other aesthetically relevant features of the music. When attention is distributed this way, the musically important features of the symphony are made salient (a point emphasized by Nanay 2015). In ethics, as philosopher and novelist Iris Murdoch emphasized, in some cases, acting well consists in part in noticing the good-making or bad-making features of a scene, or the features that call for specific kinds of moral action, such as giving up one's seat on a bus for someone who needs it more badly. One could see these dispositions as a kind of moral skill in the form of perception, an idea developed at length in a quite different ways by Mandelbaum (1955), Murdoch (1967), Fridland (2017), and Bengson et al. (forthcoming).[14]

Notes

* Thanks to Kevin Connolly, Kati Farkas, Ellen Fridland, Zoe Jenkin, Samantha Matherne, Matthew McGrath, Jessie Munton and Carlotta Pavese for criticism and discussion.
1 Kelly (1999, 2005); Dreyfus (2002, 2005).
2 Merleau-Ponty (2013: 137). For further analysis, see Matherne (2017) on Merleau-Ponty's notion of style.
3 O'Regan and Noë (2001).
4 Eilan et al. (2015).
5 Matherne (2014) argues that this position is found in Kant. Pavese (2015, 2019) defends a mixed view. For useful discussion of perceptual recognition in general, see Brewer (2011), McGrath (2017) and Millar (2019).
6 Kant imagines a physician, judge or statesman who

> can have many fine pathological, juridical, or political rules in his head, of which he can even be a thorough teacher, and yet can easily stumble in their application, either because he is lacking in the natural power of judgment (though not in understanding), and to be sure understands the universal *in abstracto* but cannot distinguish whether a case *in concreto* belongs under it, or also because he has not received adequate training for this judgment through examples and actual business.
>
> *Kant 1781/1998 A134/B173*

Matherne (2014) discusses this example in connection with perceptual experience.
7 Lewis (1990).
8 This observation about toads is an instance of the general claim that being used to seeing F's gives you a facility at perceptually distinguishing F's from their background. For discussion, see Goldstone (2015) and Connolly (2019).
9 Pylyshyn (1999), Goldstone (2015), and Connolly (2019).
10 This effect is known as the cross-race effect. For an overview see Meissner and Brigham (2001).
11 Goldstone (2015) and Connolly (2017).
12 On rhythm perception, see Boll-Avetisyan et al. (2017).
13 For some criticisms of statistical analysis in Eberhardt's study, see Francis (2016).
14 For more on these ideas, see Mandelbaum (1955), Murdoch (1956) and Bengson (forthcoming).

References

Adams, R., and Kveraga, K. (2015) "Social Vision: Functional Forecasting and the Integration of Compound Social Cues," *Review of Philosophy and Psychology* 6: 591–610.

Bengson, J., Cuneo, T., and Shafer-Landau, R. (Forthcoming) *Grasping Morality: Moral Intuitionism*, Oxford: Oxford University Press.

Boll-Avetisyan, N., Bhatara, A., and Höhle, B. (2017) "Effects of Musicality on the Perception of Rhythmic Structure in Speech," *Laboratory Phonology: Journal of the Association for Laboratory Phonology* 8: 9.

Brewer, B. (2011) *Perception and its Objects*, Oxford: Oxford University Press.

Connolly, K. (2017) "Perceptual Learning," in E. Zalta (ed.) *The Stanford Encyclopedia of Philosophy* (Summer 2017 Edition), https://plato.stanford.edu/archives/sum2017/entries/perceptual-learning/.

Dreyfus, H. L. (2002) "Intelligence Without Representation: Merleau-Ponty's Critique of Mental Representation," *Phenomenology and the Cognitive Sciences* 1: 367–83.

—— (2005) "Merleau-Ponty and Recent Cognitive Science," in T. Carman and M. Hansen (eds.) *The Cambridge Companion to Merleau-Ponty*, 129–50, Cambridge: Cambridge University Press.

—— (2019) *Perceptual Learning: The Flexibility of the Senses*, Oxford: Oxford University Press.

Eberhardt, J. L., Goff, P. A., Purdie, V. J., and Davies, P. G. (2004) "Seeing Black: Race, Crime, and Visual Processing," *Journal of Personality and Social Psychology* 87: 876.

Eilan, N., Hoerl, C., McCormack, T., and Roessler, J. (eds.) (2005) *Joint Attention: Communication and Other Minds*, Oxford: Oxford University Press.

Francis, G. (2016) "Implications of 'Too Good to Be True' for Replication, Theoretical Claims, and Experimental Design: An Example Using Prominent Studies of Racial Bias," *Frontiers in Psychology* 7: 1382.

Fridland, E. (2017) "Motor Skill and Moral Virtue," *Royal Institute of Philosophy Supplement* 80: 139–70.

Goldstone, R. (2015) "Perceptual Learning," in M. Matthen (ed.) *Oxford Handbook of the Philosophy of Perception*, 812–32, Oxford: Oxford University Press.

Hurley, S. (1998) *Consciousness in Action*, Cambridge, MA: Harvard University Press.

Kant, I. (1781/1998) *Critique of Pure Reason*, Cambridge, MA: Cambridge University Press.

Kelly, S. D. (1999) "What Do We See (When We Do)?" *Philosophical Topics* 27: 107–28.

——— (2005) "Seeing Things in Merleau-Ponty," in T. Carman and M. Hansen (eds.) *The Cambridge Companion to Merleau-Ponty*, 74–110, Cambridge: Cambridge University Press.

Lewis, D. (1990) "What Experience Teaches," in W. Lycan (ed.) *Mind and Cognition*, 499–519, New York: Blackwell.

Mandelbaum, M. (1955) *The Phenomenology of Moral Experience*, Baltimore, MD: Johns Hopkins Press.

Matherne, S. (2014) "Kant and the Art of Schematism," *Kantian Review* 19: 181–205.

——— (2017) "Merleau-Ponty on Style as the Key to Perceptual Presence and Constancy," *Journal of the History of Philosophy* 55: 693–727.

Merleau-Ponty, M. (2013) *Phenomenology of Perception*, New York: Routledge.

McGrath, M. (2017) "Knowing What Things Look Like," *Philosophical Review* 126: 1–41.

Meissner, C. A., and Brigham, J. C. (2001) "Thirty Years of Investigating the Own-Race Bias in Memory for Faces: A Meta-Analytic Review," *Psychology, Public Policy, and Law* 7: 3–35.

Millar, A. (2019) *Knowing by Perceiving*, Oxford: Oxford University Press.

Murdoch, I. (1956) "Vision and Choice in Morality," *Aristotelian Society,* Supplementary volume 30: 14–58.

——— (1967) *The Sovereignty of Good*, New York: Routledge.

Nanay, B. (2015) "Aesthetic Attention," *Journal of Consciousness Studies* 22: 96–118.

Noë, A. (2004) *Action in Perception*, Cambridg, MA: MIT Press.

O'Regan, K., and Noë, A. (2001) "A Sensorimotor Account of Vision and Visual Consciousness," *Behavioral and Brain Sciences* 24: 939–73.

Pavese, C. (2015) "Practical Senses," *Philosophers' Imprint* 15: 1–25.

——— (2019) "The Psychological Reality of Practical Representation," *Philosophical Psychology* 32: 784–821.

Pylyshyn, Z. (1999) "Is Vision Continuous with Cognition? The Case for Cognitive Impenetability of Visual Perception," *Behavioral and Brain Sciences* 22: 341–65.

25

PERCEPTUAL SKILLS

Dustin Stokes and Bence Nanay

25.1 What are perceptual skills?

Skills are abilities we can be better or worse at and that characteristically manifest in actions (Ryle 1949; Pavese 2016).[1] Juggling skills are abilities related to keeping three or more balls in the air and we can be better or worse at this. Similarly, perceptual skills are abilities we can be better or worse at and that typically manifest in various perceptually guided actions. Here are some examples of perceptual skills: distinguishing pinot noir and cabernet sauvignon, spotting Waldo in the picture, and recognizing a dominant chord.

These examples may immediately raise eyebrows – are they really *perceptual* skills? Are they genuinely perceptual or are they post-perceptual cognitive skills? After all, however rich the concept of our perceptual experience may be, it clearly does not attribute properties such as "dominant chord" or "pinot noir" (see Siegel, Chapter 24 in this volume). So, the question is whether these skills are perceptual or cognitive (or, in some sense, both). Before we address this question, here are some more examples standardly given of perceptual skills (starting with the ones we mentioned in the first paragraph):

(a) *Perceptual discrimination*: Distinguishing pinot noir and cabernet sauvignon is an example of this. Note that perceptual discrimination does not entail that we can conceptualize the stimuli perceptually discriminated. You may not know what pinot noir or cabernet sauvignon are, but you could still reliably distinguish two kinds of red colored liquids by flavour or smell.

(b) *Perceptual recognition*: Spotting Waldo and identifying a dominant chord are instances of recognition. Also, most of the examples in the perceptual expertise literature would fall under this heading: recognizing certain bird or plant species, recognizing an original Matisse, and so on. Perceptual skills of this kind (unlike (a)) require conceptualization of some sort.

(c) *Picture perception*: Richard Wollheim often referred to picture perception ability as "the perceptual skills of seeing-in" (Wollheim 2003: 5). And there is a rich literature in art history about how perceptual skills of looking at pictures influence our experience of these pictures.

(d) *Speech perception*: the perception of everyday speech is often also taken to be a form of perceptual skill. As Casey O'Callaghan writes: "the capacity to perceive speech in a manner that enables understanding is an acquired perceptual skill. It involves learning to hear language-specific types of ethologically significant sounds" (O'Callaghan 2015: 475).

How could we decide whether these skills would be perceptual or post-perceptual cognitive skills? None of these skills involve only the perceptual system. Recognition of Waldo requires knowing what Waldo looks like, and it leads to a belief that Waldo is hiding behind the garbage truck, and this leads to the action of pointing out Waldo. Restricting perceptual skills to skills that are performed by the perceptual system only would be nonsensical: the perceptual system does not do much by itself (not much that is observable, in any case).

We propose the following as a straightforward and not particularly controversial way of keeping apart perceptual and post-perceptual cognitive skills: if the perceptual system works in the same way in the case of two very different skills, it is not a perceptual skill. If having different skills entails that the perceptual system works differently during the execution of these skills, it is a perceptual skill. Remember that we defined perceptual skill as something the perceptual system does. If we have acquired a new perceptual skill, this implies that the perceptual system works differently.

Let's consider the example of perceptual discrimination. Fingerprint experts can differentiate two very similar fingerprints quickly and reliably – in a way novices cannot. Before undergoing extensive forensic fingerprint training, the expert did not have this skill, after that training she did. If this change entails a change in the way her perceptual system works (and we know it does, see Busey and Parada (2010); Jarodzka et al. (2010); see also Matthen (2015) for a philosophical summary), then this perceptual discrimination skill is a genuine perceptual skill.

One may worry that by identifying perceptual skills with the help of the changes in the functioning of the perceptual system, we have not made real progress, as it is notoriously unclear where perceptual processing ends and cognitive processing begins (see Teufel and Nanay (2017) for a summary). However, we can use the outlined way of identifying perceptual skills in a pro tanto manner. Some parts of mental processing are very clearly perceptual: it is uncontroversial that processing in the primary visual cortex, in the cortical brain regions V4/V8 or in MT is perceptual processing. So, if it turns out to be the case that changes in a skill entail changes in these cortical areas, then the skill in question is unquestionably a perceptual skill. The examples in (a), (b) and (c) are unequivocally perceptual skills according to these criteria (example (d) is a bit less unequivocal (see, e.g., O'Callaghan 2011), so we leave the discussion of it for another occasion).

25.2 Perceptual expertise

This section explores (a) perceptual discrimination and (b) perceptual recognition through the lens of perceptual expertise. Empirical research on perceptual expertise can mostly be traced to research on face perception in the 1990s. With certain qualifications, all humans with normally functioning vision are expert face perceivers. By contrast to equally complex visual stimuli, we are extremely adept at both discriminating and recognizing individual faces.[2] Research on this undeniably perceptual phenomenon has led to research in specialized domains – from birds to cars to fingerprints to radiographic images – and whether and how individuals can become experts at perceiving objects within those domains.[3] That these experts are better at domain-specific tasks is uncontroversial. But an interesting question concerns whether that performance is partly constituted by better perceptual performance. Perceptual experts are thus plausible candidates, and a useful testbed, for possession of exceptional perceptual skills.

Behavioural measures for expertise typically concern diagnostic or categorization tasks. Thus the radiologist is asked to identify tumours in sometimes rapidly presented mammograms; a fingerprint examiner is asked to identify a target fingerprint in an array. Expert birdwatchers or dog show judges are asked to make fine-grained category-sensitive discriminations, as well as recognize previously viewed individuals. One robust finding across these disparate domains is an "entry-level shift": as expertise is acquired, the category invoked for various tasks shifts from basic (e.g., bird) to subordinate (e.g., kingbird) or sub-subordinate (e.g., eastern kingbird) (Tanaka and Taylor 1991). These experts, within their domains, perform both more accurately and more rapidly. For example, expert radiologists can, above chance, identify an anomaly in a radiographic image in 200 ms (Evans et al. 2013). Subjectively, these subjects report pop-out visual phenomenology, often claiming to "just see" the relevant item, performing without felt cognitive effort.

More complicated behavioural measures highlight this apparent automaticity and corroborate subjective reports. Interference effects suggest that the expert enjoys more holistic perceptual processing of objects of expertise, where incongruence between an irrelevant-to-task object component (e.g., the bottom half of an object) interferes with rapid judgements about the relevant-to-task object component (e.g., the top half of an object). This effect is modulated by alignment of the two components (experts suffer less interference from the irrelevant object half when it is misaligned with the target object half), and this does not occur in non-experts (Richler et al. 2011). Experts are more sensitive to spatial changes between features than stand-alone featural changes (Bukach et al. 2006). And experts, but not non-experts, suffer inversion effects. For example, performance on dog or car identification is significantly hindered in the dog show judge and car expert, respectively, but not the novice, when images of dogs or cars are perfectly inverted (Diamond and Carey 1986; McKeeff et al. 2010). The explanation for these effects is that experts rely on holistic, configural processing of objects of expertise and this is what is thwarted by stimulus inversion. All of these effects are found in lab-trained experts for artificial lab-created classes of objects, for example, with "Greebles". Here subjects undergo a training period after which they can make fine-grained categorical and individual-level judgements, where behavioural performance enjoys all the same markers: interference effects, greater sensitivity to configural features, inversion effects. This paradigm allows researchers to follow the behavioural trajectory of expertise acquisition, and further clarify some of their neural-physiological correlates (Gauthier et al. 1998).

A standard EEG measure for face perception is the N170 ERP component: this component responds at higher amplitudes, 150–200 ms post-stimulus onset, to faces. Across a variety of domains, and for both "real-world" and lab-trained experts, researchers find an enhanced N170 response for experts (Tanaka and Curran 2001; Rossion et al. 2002; Busey and Vanderkolk 2005). Another standard, but relevantly controversial, neural measure for face perception is activity in the FFA and the OFA. Here again researchers find enhanced FFA and OFA activity for experts when viewing objects of expertise, and this is true for natural objects (birds), artificial objects (cars) and lab-created artificial objects (Greebles) (Gauthier et al. 1999, 2000). Eye tracking measures reveal distinctive saccadic eye movement and fixation patterns for experts, again relative to their domain of expertise, from radiologists to persons with training in the visual arts (Kundel and La Follette 1972; Vogt and Magnussen 2007). Although there is space for (and is) debate in the vicinity, these neural and physiological patterns are taken by relevant empirical scientists to correlate with visual experience and/or visual attention. So while they may not serve, in isolation, as conclusive evidence, they converge with the behavioural measures discussed just above and in a way that makes a strong case: perceptual expertise is a genuinely perceptual phenomenon involving enhanced, domain-sensitive perceptual skill.

In the face of this convergence of data, one may still wonder how or whether any such skills are grounded in cognitive learning or experience. Maybe perceptual experts just enjoy some kind of low-level perceptual enhancement or development, or perhaps they entered into a domain having already possessed a higher degree of perceptual acuity. Both interpretations, however, are easily dispelled: acquisition of expertise is highly sensitive to the information and category information within that domain, and does not transfer to similarly complex extra-domain performance. Researchers find that regular, mere exposure to a stimulus type does not suffice for behavioural success (e.g., identifying a tumour in a mammogram), and moreover that achievement and persistence of task success (and neurological changes that correlate with that success) require both explicit feedback, and learning of subordinate-level categories (e.g., the make and model of a car) (Scott et al. 2008). And while expertise generalizes to discrimination of novel exemplars within the domain of expertise (Gauthier et al. 1998), experts perform no better at equally complicated perceptual tasks, such as visual search over complicated images (e.g., Where's Waldo puzzles) (Nodine and Krupinski 1998).

Perceptual expertise is thus a well-studied example, perhaps an extreme case of, perceptual skill. As a result of domain-specific, cognitive learning, the perceptual systems of experts plausibly work differently.

25.3 Picture perception

We want to spend some more time on (c), on the perceptual skills involved in picture perception, for two reasons. First, these perceptual skills are very widely discussed not just in philosophy of mind or in philosophy in general, but also in art history, film studies, cultural studies and a number of other disciplines. The second reason is that most alleged reasons for taking (c) to be a perceptual skill are based on phenomenology, which leads to some methodological complications, as we shall see.

A good starting point for discussing perceptual skills of kind (c) is the history of vision debate. A recurring theme in art history, film studies, cultural studies and related disciplines is that vision has a history. Hence, understanding the art of foregone ages requires understanding how people in these ages perceived art. This idea was very central to the German formalist tradition (Riegl 1901/1985; Wölfflin 1915/1932) but it is also an important premise of recent post-formalist art history (Summers 2003; Davis 2011, 2015; see also Nanay 2015).

There are stronger and weaker versions of this history of vision claim. According to the stronger version (Riegl 1901/1985; Benjamin 1936/1969), our vision of anything and everything has a history: medieval people saw a birch tree or the Moon differently from the way we do. A more modest version of the history of vision claim is that our perception of pictures has a history (Wölfflin 1915/1932; Baxandall 1972). So, when our ancestors looked at a birch tree or the Moon, their visual experience was the same as ours. But when they looked at a painting, their experience was very different from ours when we are looking at the very same painting. What is of interest for the purposes of this chapter is the more modest (and less problematic) version.

If vision has a history, what is it really that changes in the course of history? Presumably not the retinal stimulation or the way in which retinal stimulation is transmitted to the lateral geniculate nucleus. But then what? A number of different philosophers and art historians independently suggested that what changes is the set of perceptual skills people have. When people looked at a painting in the 15th century and when we do it now, the retinal stimulation is the same, but we have different perceptual skills and, as a result, our perceptual phenomenology is also different. Some versions of this general claim have been held by Ernst Gombrich, Michael Baxandall, David Bordwell and Tom Gunning (Gombrich 1960/1972; Baxandall 1972; Bordwell 1997; Gunning 1986).

Michael Baxandall's version is the most developed. Baxandall did extensive research on various texts from 15th-century Italy about how observers at that time looked at pictures. His conclusion is that the visual skills of 15th-century Italian observers were very different from ours and, as a result, their experiences were also different (they included, for example, the visual skill of volume estimation as well as of recognizing various dance moves).

Baxandall coined the term "period eye" to refer to this phenomenon (Baxandall 1972: 29), but he is very clear that it is the visual skills that change, not the retinal image. Tom Gunning has a very similar argument about the history of the perception of film. He argues that there was a radical change in the way people perceived films around 1908 as a result of the emergence of montage, which made people develop very specific visual skills that allowed them to piece the different intercut scenes together. They did not have these skills before, and the acquisition of these skills changed their phenomenology significantly.

Baxandall and Gunning took these skills that vary in history to be visual skills. But what makes them visual? It seems that their main evidence is phenomenological: having these skills makes a difference in our perceptual phenomenology – not our non-perceptual (say, cognitive) phenomenology. Noel Carroll (2001) has a structurally very similar solution to understanding how our experience of artworks may have changed throughout history, one that does not allow for the history of vision.

According to Carroll what changes are our skills, but not our visual skills. He makes a distinction between seeing and noticing and argues that noticing changes in the course of history whereas seeing does not (Carroll 2001: 15). Carroll takes noticing to be a post-perceptual process, hence, vision itself does not have a history. And as noticing is a *skilful* activity, this would be a view according to which picture perception involves not perceptual but cognitive skills (and it is these cognitive skills that change).

All of this raises a crucial question: how can we decide whether the skill involved in picture perception is perceptual or post-perceptual/purely cognitive? We do not think that the traditional reliance on perceptual phenomenology is decisive here, as it is notoriously difficult to settle disagreements about what kind of phenomenology would count as perceptual (Siegel 2006; Bayne 2009; Nanay 2012). Luckily, we have a wide range of experimental findings about how the different pictorial perception skills involve different behavioural patterns.

One particular study compared performance of trained visual artists and non-artists (Kozbelt 2001). Tasks included both an array of drawing tasks, as well as visual tasks – identifying a depicted object in out-of-focus pictures, gestalt completion tasks, mental rotation tasks. Not surprisingly, the artists perform better than the non-artists on the drawing tasks. More surprisingly, they also perform better than non-artists on all the strictly visual tasks, and performance here positively co-varies with drawing skill. Given that these are tasks that require specific performance for success – for example, rotating a geometrical figure in mental imagery to determine if it is the same or different from a target image – it is less natural to describe the artist's performance as mere noticing.

Further, different pictorial perception skills also involve different patterns of eye movements (Vogt and Magnussen 2007). The eye movement patterns of art experts when they look at a novel picture are very different from eye movement patterns of novices. Novices tend to look at the most salient features of the picture – for example a central figure or a face. The eye movements of art experts, in contrast, are much more distributed and involve longer saccades. Whatever one thinks about perceptual phenomenology, eye movement is something the visual system does – so different patterns of eye movements would be an indicator that the skills involved are perceptual skills (and not cognitive skills).

25.4 The mechanisms of perceptual skills

We said that perceptual skills are abilities of the perceptual system that we can be better or worse at. But how does one get better at these perceptual skills? In some cases, especially cases of expertise, explicit or implicit effort is involved. The perceptual skills of the fingerprint expert get better as a result of repeated trying.

Is repeated trying a necessary condition on acquiring perceptual skills then? Mohan Matthen thinks so, when he characterizes skills in general as "abilities that are acquired by repeated trying" (Matthen 2015: 184). Hence, perceptual skills would come out as perceptual abilities that are acquired by repeated trying. We consider this characterization far too strong. Many perceptual skills are not acquired by repeated trying. One can come to have the perceptual skill of differentiating between pinot noir and cabernet sauvignon by being exposed to the two substances a lot, without trying to categorize them in any way whatsoever.

And the same is true of some of the perceptual skills in picture perception. Some perceptual skills are acquired as a result of extensive training or repeated trying. In the empirically studied cases of expertise, exposure appears to be insufficient for expert perceptual performance, but some other perceptual skills are acquired as a result of mere exposure. This just highlights that not all cases of perceptual skill are cases of perceptual expertise (see Matthen 2015). Accordingly, we could weaken Matthen's way of characterizing skills in general and perceptual skills in particular as "abilities that are acquired by repeated trying or exposure".

We have considered some examples of perceptual skills and argued that they are in fact perceptual. But what are these perceptual skills – what does the perceptual system do that could be considered to be the basis of these perceptual skills? Of the many activities involved, we will focus on two particularly important ones, attention and the forming of mental imagery.

As discussed in the previous section, one thing that we know changes with the acquisition of a perceptual skill is eye movement patterns. This is true of radiologists, and it's true of people with training in the visual arts. The eye movement patterns of art experts when they look at a novel picture are different from eye movement patterns of novices.

It is important not to confuse eye movements with attention. We can shift our attention without moving our eyes – this is called a covert shift of attention. So even if your eyes are fixating on the same point, you could move your attention around. As a result, we need to be careful in interpreting these results about eye movements in order to talk about the role of attention in perceptual skills.

Nonetheless, a straightforward explanation of the differences in eye movements between experts and novices is that they allocate their attention differently (Connolly 2014). And this should not really come as a surprise. What you attend to will often depend on what you know (or value or expect or intend to find, and so on). If you know that Waldo is dressed in red and white stripes, you attend to those parts of the picture where there are red and white stripes. This consists not in a difference in moving a "spotlight" of attention, but of certain behaviourally relevant features being highlighted or made more salient – the red and white stripey ones. Feature or object-based attention of this kind is importantly modulated by higher-level cognition (see Fridland, Chapter 19 in this volume). The ignorant viewer of the Where's Waldo puzzle will not experience attentional selection of red and white stripey things; those features pop out only if one has some belief or understanding that Waldo's features are the target of one's visual search). Analogously, experts in various domains, from fingerprints to radiology to visual art, know more about the task at hand than novices. Just like the compliant Where's Waldo puzzler, the expert's attention is informed by these pieces of knowledge, whereas the novice's is not.[4] And this different allocation of attention is what explains the different eye movement patterns.

Perceptual attention is a genuine perceptual phenomenon. We can be better or worse at attending to a specific kind of perceptual stimulus. Sometimes it is an action in the philosopher's sense: behaviour appropriately captured by at least one description that requires attribution of an intention to the agent. In other words, it can be something we *do* as psychological agents. But it is also something that can be done by our perceptual systems, without our intending or trying, even if it depends upon personal-level states or attitudes. What is crucial is that enhancement of either controlled or automatic attention varies with what we have done as agents: what we have learned about a domain such as radiology or art or ornithology. In such cases, we are partly responsible for the etiology of the acquired perceptual skill, even if that skill sometimes deploys automatically (see Wu, Chapter 16 in this volume). In this regard, attentional differences that come with expertise are attributable to the agent and so are, in this regard, skilful. So, attending can be a skill – a perceptual skill.[5]

The other mediator of perceptual skill is less obvious: mental imagery. Closing your eyes and visualizing an apple is a form of exercising your mental imagery. But so is looking at a floor plan and visualizing the building, or looking at a patient's body and visualizing their inner organs.

Conjuring up mental imagery is something we do. As in the case of attention, often forming mental imagery is an action in the literal philosophical sense – we count to three and visualize an apple. And we know a fair amount about the mechanisms of how we form mental imagery – how this happens in very early perceptual areas – as early as the primary visual cortex (Kosslyn et al. 1995; Pearson et al. 2015; see also Nanay 2018, forthcoming). And mental imagery is something we can be better or worse at. When architects see a floor plan, they can have mental imagery of the building that is much more detailed and much more accurate than the novice's. And training mental imagery can help surgeons be more precise with their procedure (Sanders et al. 2004, 2008; Immenroth et al. 2007).

So, forming mental imagery is something we do and do with varying degrees of success. In short, it is a skill. And it is a perceptual skill as the processes involved in creating mental imagery are low-level perceptual processes (see the references above as well as Tartaglia et al. (2009)). Forming mental imagery is a perceptual skill and mental imagery also underlies other perceptual skills (such as the architect's skills of getting a sense of the spaciousness of a building on the basis of a floor plan or the surgeon's skill of finding the right place to cut the skin).

Attention and mental imagery often interact. The architect's attention is at least partly driven by what she visualizes and vice versa, mental imagery is constructed by perceptually attending to some features and ignoring others and forming images on the basis of those materials. And while they are two important mechanisms of perceptual skills they are by no means the only ones.

Importantly, both attention and mental imagery can be and often are sensitive to top-down information (see Stokes 2013, 2018; Mole 2015; Teufel and Nanay 2017). And, as we have seen in Section 25.2, the same is true of some of the remarkable cases of perceptual skill – perceptual expertise cases: they are also highly dependent upon the semantic and categorical information specific to the domain of expertise. Therefore, at least some perceptual skills are causally dependent upon non-perceptual mechanisms, whatever mechanisms allow experts to learn category information, diagnostic goals and relevant technologies. Hence, whatever perceptual mechanisms are responsible for these perceptual skills, be it attention or mental imagery or something else, these skills are also causally dependent on our knowledge, belief and other cognitive states.

25.5 Conclusion

We conclude with provocation for future research. Although not widely discussed, perceptual skills are no mere peripheral aspect of human perception, and so should be no mere niche market for philosophical and cognitive scientific theories of perception. This is true for at least two reasons.

The first concerns experience: perceiving the world skilfully is plausibly to experience it differently. What it's like to perceive an impressionist painting, or a mammogram, or an eastern screech owl is different for one who is skilled in these domains, by contrast to one who is not. This is a point about phenomenology, but not only a point about phenomenology. We have identified plausible mechanisms – attention and mental imagery – that contribute generally to the phenomenology of perception and would do so no less in cases of perceptual skill. Empirical researchers have identified physiological and neural differences between experts and novices that, again, would make a difference in the functioning in perceptual processing and so, when taken together, imply differences in experience.

The second reason is epistemic. To acquire a perceptual skill is to actively engage and navigate one's environment, and sometimes to do so with expert levels of success. This highlights both how perception is active, and how it can be improved. And importantly, in many of the cases discussed, the improvement is a credit to the perceiving agent: it is something that the skilled or expert perceiver *does* (or a result of training she has done). Perceptual skills are thereby epistemic virtues; they are truth-conducive dispositions, either acquirable or improvable *by the agent* and, thereby, values attributable to the agent. Surprisingly, the philosophy of perception talks very little about potential for perceptual improvement, but an emphasis on perceptual skill reveals that, and how, we can become better perceivers.

Our view is that these reasons, among others, yield a prescription: we can't achieve a rich understanding of how we perceive the world without understanding perceptual skills.

Acknowledgement

Thank you to Carlotta Pavese and Mohan Matthen for helpful comments on an earlier draft. This work was partially supported by the ERC Consolidator grant [726251] and the FWO research grant [G0C7416N].

Notes

1 Some philosophers insist that the actions skills typically manifest in must be an *intentional* action (see Ryle 1949: 33 for the locus classicus). We want to leave open the possibility that skills manifest in non-intentional actions. A more thorough discussion of this point would lead to a detailed treatment of the distinction between intentional and non-intentional actions, which is not something we can do here.

2 The important qualification is this. While individuals within a race are exceptional (relative to other similarly complex stimuli) at recognizing, identifying and recalling individual faces from within their "same race" or their "ingroup", subjects fail or frequently err along the same measures with respect to "cross race" our "outgroup" faces. See Meissner and Brigham (2001) for a review piece.

3 Particular studies are cited below. For two review pieces, see Bukach et al. (2006) and Scott (2011). For philosophical analysis, coupled with empirical review, see Stokes (forthcoming-a).
4 Given the variety of domains of possible perceptual expertise and skill, and the variety of tasks and stimulus types that come with those domains, we want to be pluralist about the kind of knowledge involved. Sometimes an expert will enjoy relevant propositional knowledge (knowing *that* a target stimulus has such-and-such features); sometimes an expert will enjoy relevant procedural knowledge (knowing *how* to distinguish one individual from another). Very plausibly, many cases of expertise will involve both.
5 Indeed, one may go further and characterize some cases of perceptual skill as exceptional cases of intellectual (and, therefore, epistemic) virtue. See Stokes (forthcoming-b).

References

Baxandall, M. (1972) *Painting & Experience in Fifteenth-Century Italy*, Oxford: Oxford University Press.
Bayne, T. (2009) "Perception and the Reach of Phenomenal Content," *Philosophical Quarterly* 59: 385–404.
Benjamin, W. (1936/1969) "The Work of Art in the Age of Mechanical Reproduction," in *Illuminations*, trans. Harry Zohn, New York: Schocken Books, pp. 217–52.
Bordwell, D. (1997) *On the History of Film Style*, Cambridge, MA: Harvard University Press.
Bukach, C. M., Gauthier, I., and Tarr, M. J. (2006) "Beyond Faces and Modularity: The Power of an Expertise Framework," *Trends in Cognitive Science* 10: 159–66.
Busey, T. A., and Parada, F. J. (2010) "The Nature of Expertise in Fingerprint Examiners," *Psychonomic Bulletin and Review* 17: 155–60.
Busey, T. A., and Vanderkolk, J. R. (2005) "Behavioral and Electrophysiological Evidence for Configural Processing in Fingerprint Experts," *Vision Research* 45: 431–48.
Carroll, N. (2001) "Modernity and the Plasticity of Perception," *Journal of Aesthetics and Art Criticism* 59: 11–17.
Connolly, K. (2014) "Perceptual Learning and the Contents of Perception," *Erkenntnis* 79: 1407–18.
Davis, W. (2011) *A General Theory of Visual Culture*, Princeton, NJ: Princeton University Press.
—— (2015) "Succession and Recursion in Heinrich Wölfflin's *Kunstgeschichtliche Grundbegriffe*," *Journal of Aesthetics and Art Criticism* 73: 157–64.
Diamond, R., and Carey, S. (1986) "Why Faces Are and Are Not Special: An Effect of Expertise," *Journal of Experimental Psychology: General* 115: 107–17.
Evans, K. K., Georgian-Smith, D., Tambouret, R., Birdwell, R. L., and Wolfe, J. M. (2013) "The Gist of the Abnormal: Above-Chance Medical Decision Making in the Blink of an Eye," *Psychonomic Bulletin & Review* 20: 1170–5.
Gauthier, I., Skudlarski, P., Gore, J. C., and Anderson, A. W. (2000) "Expertise for Cars and Birds Recruits Brain Areas Involved in Face Recognition," *Nature Neuroscience* 3: 191–7.
Gauthier, I., Tarr, M. J., Anderson, A. W., Skudlarski, P., and Gore, J. C. (1999) "Activation of the Middle Fusiform 'Face Area' Increases with Expertise in Recognizing Novel Objects," *Nature Neuroscience* 2: 568–73.
Gauthier, I., Williams, P., Tarr, M., and Tanaka, J. (1998) "Training 'Greeble' Experts: A Framework for Studying Expert Object Recognition Processes," *Vision Research* 38: 2401–28.
Gombrich, E. (1960/1972) *Art and Illusion*, Princeton, NJ: Princeton University Press.
Gunning, T. (1986) "The Cinema of Attractions: Early Cinema, Its Spectator, and the Avant-Garde," *Wide Angle* 8: 63–70.
Immenroth, M., Burger, T., Brenner, J., Nagelschmidt, M., Eberspacher, H., and Troidl, H. (2007) "Mental Training in Surgical Education: A Randomized Controlled Trial," *Annals of Surgery* 245: 385–91.
Jarodzka, H., Scheiter, K., Gerjets, P., and van Gog, T. (2010) "In the Eyes of the Beholder: How Experts and Novices Interpret Dynamic Stimuli," *Learning and Instruction* 20: 146–54.
Kosslyn, S. M., Behrmann, M., and Jeannerod, M. (1995) "The Cognitive Neuroscience of Mental Imagery," *Neuropsychologia* 33: 1335–44.
Kozbelt, A. (2001) "Artists as Experts in Visual Cognition," *Visual Cognition* 8: 705–23.
Kundel, H. L., and La Follette Jr, P. S. (1972) "Visual Search Patterns and Experience with Radiological Images," *Radiology* 103: 523–8.
Matthen, M. (2015) "Play, Skill, and the Origins of Perceptual Art," *British Journal of Aesthetics* 55: 173–97.

McKeeff, T., McGugin, R., Tong, F., and Gauthier, I. (2010) "Expertise Increases the Functional Overlap Between Face and Object Perception," *Cognition* 117: 355–60.

Meissner, C. A., and Brigham, J. C. (2001) "Thirty Years of Investigating the Own-Race Bias in Memory for Faces: A Meta-Analytic Review," *Psychology, Public Policy, and Law* 7: 3–35.

Mole, C. (2015) "Attention and Cognitive Penetration," in J. Zeimbekis and A. Raftopoulos (eds.) *The Cognitive Penetrability of Perception: New Philosophical Perspectives*, Oxford: Oxford University Press, pp. 218–37.

Nanay, B. (2012) "Perceptual Phenomenology," *Philosophical Perspectives* 26: 235–46.

—— (2015) "The History of Vision," *Journal of Aesthetics and Art Criticism* 73: 259–71.

—— (2018) "Multimodal Mental Imagery," *Cortex* 105: 125–34.

—— (forthcoming) *Mental Imagery*, Oxford: Oxford University Press.

Nodine, C. F., and Krupinski, E. A. (1998) "Perceptual Skill, Radiology Expertise, and Visual Test Performance with Nina and Waldo," *Academic Radiology* 5: 603–12.

O'Callaghan, C. (2011) "Against Hearing Meanings," *Philosophical Quarterly* 61: 783–807.

—— (2015) "Speech Perception," in M. Matthen (ed.) *The Oxford Handbook to Philosophy of Perception*, Oxford: Oxford University Press, pp. 475–94.

Pavese, C. (2016) "Skill in Epistemology 1: Skill and Knowledge," *Philosophy Compass* 11: 642–9.

Pearson, J., Naselaris, T., Holmes, E. A., and Kosslyn, S. M. (2015) "Mental Imagery: Functional Mechanisms and Clinical Applications," *Trends in Cognitive Sciences* 19: 590–602.

Richler, J., Wong, Y., and Gauthier, I. (2011) "Perceptual Expertise as a Shift from Strategic Interference to Automatic Holistic Processing," *Current Directions in Psychological Science* 20: 129–34.

Riegl, A. (1901/1985) *The Late Roman Art Industry*, Rome: Giorgio Bretschneider Editore.

Rossion, B., Gauthier, I., Goffaux, V., Tarr, M. J., and Crommelinck, M. (2002) "Expertise Training with Novel Objects Leads to Left-Lateralized Facelike Electrophysiological Responses," *Psychological Science* 13: 250–7.

Ryle, G. (1949) *The Concept of Mind*, Chicago, IL: University of Chicago Press.

Sanders, C. W., Sadoski, M., Bramson, R., Wiprud, R., and van Walsum, K. (2004) "Comparing the Effects of Physical Practice and Mental Imagery Rehearsal on Learning Basic Surgical Skills by Medical Students," *American Journal of Obstetrics and Gynecology* 191: 1811–14.

Sanders, C. W., Sadoski, M., van Walsum, K., Bramson, R., Wiprud, R., and Fossum, T. W. (2008) "Learning Basic Surgical Skills With Mental Imagery: Using the Simulation Centre in the Mind," *Medical Education* 42: 607–12.

Scott, L. (2011) "Face Perception and Perceptual Expertise in Adult and Developmental Populations," in A. Calder et al. (eds.) *Oxford Handbook of Face Perception*, Oxford: Oxford University Press, pp. 195–214.

Scott, L., Tanaka, J., Sheinberg, D. L., and Curran, T. (2008) "The Role of Category Learning in the Acquisition and Retention of Perceptual Expertise: A Behavioral and Neurophysiological Study," *Brain Research* 1210: 204–15.

Siegel, S. (2006) "Which Properties Are Represented in Perception?" in T. Gendler and J. Hawthorne (eds.) *Perceptual Experience*, Oxford: Oxford University Press, pp. 481–503.

Stokes, D. (2013) "Cognitive Penetrability of Perception," *Philosophy Compass* 8: 646–63.

—— (2018) "Attention and the Cognitive Penetrability of Perception," *Australasian Journal of Philosophy* 96: 303–18.

—— (forthcoming-a) "On Perceptual Expertise," *Mind & Language*.

—— (forthcoming-b) *Thinking and Perceiving*, London: Routledge.

Summers, D. (2003) *Real Spaces*, London: Phaidon.

Tanaka, J. W., and Curran, T. (2001) "A Neural Basis for Expert Object Recognition," *Psychological Science* 12: 43–7.

Tanaka, J. W., and Taylor, M. (1991) "Object Categories and Expertise," *Cognitive Psychology* 23: 457–82.

Tartaglia, E. M., Barnert, L., Mast, F. W., and Herzog, M. H. (2009) "Human Perceptual Learning by Mental Imagery," *Current Biology* 19: 2081–5.

Teufel, C., and Nanay, B. (2017) "How To (and How Not To) Think About Top-Down Influences on Perception," *Consciousness and Cognition* 47: 17–25.

Vogt, S., and Magnussen, S. (2007) "Expertise in Pictorial Perception: Eye-Movement Patterns and Visual Memory in Artists and Laymen," *Perception* 36: 91–100.

Wölfflin, H. (1915/1932) *Principles of Art History*, New York: Dover.

Wollheim, R. (2003) "In Defense of Seeing-In," in H. Hecht, R. Schwartz, and M. Atherton (eds.) *Looking into Pictures: An Interdisciplinary Approach to Pictorial Space*, Cambridge, MA: MIT Press, pp. 3–15.

26

SKILL, VISUAL PREJUDICE, AND KNOW-HOW

Keota Fields

26.1 Introduction

Zack harbors an implicit bias that black men are typically violent. Malik, a black man, is holding a cellphone. When Zack sees this, his implicit bias permeates the perceptual processing that produces Zack's visual experience. As a result, Zack sees Malik's cellphone as a gun.[1] Zack's visual experience is an instance of cognitive penetration of perception.[2] Following Jessie Munton (2019), let's call Zack's experience *visual prejudice*, a *prejudicial experience*, or *biased seeing*.

A compelling epistemological question is whether Zack's prejudicial experience justifies him in believing that Malik is holding a gun.[3] Given recent philosophical work on skill, I want to ask a different question. Is Zack's prejudicial experience skillful? I argue for an affirmative answer. Yet, Zack's case presents a puzzle. It is not uncommon for philosophers to suppose that skills are instances of know-how. I argue that Zack's case is *not* an instance of know-how because it does not manifest knowledge of facts. The result is a counterexample to a guiding principle in much of the literature that skills are instances of know-how.

In what follows, I present reasons to think that instances of cognitive penetration in general and cases of visual prejudice in particular are skilled performances.[4] But since Zack's prejudicial experience does not manifest knowledge of facts, I argue that it cannot be an instance of know-how. To make the discussion manageable, I focus on a recent account of skill as know-how defended by Jason Stanley and Timothy Williamson (2017; see also 2001). I conclude that some skilled performances are epistemically deviant or pathological. This result broadens our understanding of skills and their epistemic impact.

In Section 26.2, I briefly discuss cognitive penetration of perception. Section 26.3 reviews philosophical approaches to skill that emerge from the need to reconcile agential control with automaticity. I use that literature to identify some characteristic features of skilled performance. In Section 26.4, I use the example of Memory Color to argue that cognitively penetrated visual experiences exhibit the characteristic features of skilled performances identified in Section 26.3. Section 26.5 rehearses Stanley and Williamson's approach to skill in terms of know-how. In Section 26.6, I reply to an objection that cognitive penetration and visual prejudice do not exhibit the intentional control required by skill. Following Wayne Wu's chapter in this volume (see Chapter 16), I argue that cognitively penetrated visual experiences can exhibit intentional control. I conclude in Section 26.7 by replying to further objections.

I pause for preliminary remarks about implicit bias and intentional control before continuing. One might think that implicit biases are unconscious or uncontrolled in a way that rules out skillful execution. Thus, some clarification is necessary before considering whether Zack's visual prejudice is skillful.

The empirical and philosophical literature on implicit bias is ambiguous as to what is picked out by 'implicit'. Mental states that are explicitly disavowed by agents are sometimes called implicit. Elsewhere, 'implicit' is used to refer to instruments for measuring such mental states, such as Implicit Association Tests (IATs). I follow Michael Brownstein (2019) in using 'implicit' to refer to measures. As a result, I need not take a stand on whether mental states themselves are implicit.[5]

This is useful for the present discussion because implicit measures predict behavior by estimating the contents of mental states that cause the measured behavior. Assuming that mental states in the causal history of behavior constitute intentions, properties of φ-ing can be predicted by identifying properties represented by an intention to φ. In this way, prediction by implicit measures serves as evidence of intentional control.

I take the fact that an agent explicitly disavows the mental states measured by implicit instruments as evidence that the agent intends not to harbor those mental states (i.e., they do not intend to *have* certain beliefs or attitudes). I distinguish that from the intention to perform actions that are measured by implicit instruments. Similarly, I distinguish between the intention to φ and the intention to cause harm by φ-ing. Lack of the latter is often taken for lack of the former, which is clearly not the case. I can intend to serve my friend food which, unbeknown to me, will cause a violent allergic reaction, but I do not intend to harm my friend by serving her that food. Of course, I can intend both. My point is that intentions are fine-grained enough to draw such distinctions.

When considering whether Zack intends to see Malik's cellphone as a gun, I understand Zack's bias to be implicitly measured and not necessarily an unconscious mental state. I assume that implicit measures of Zack's bias predict his prejudicial experience by estimating the contents of causally efficacious mental states; and that such predictions, when correct, are evidence of an intention to produce a prejudicial experience rather than an intention to harbor the causally efficacious mental states; or an intention to cause harm by having a prejudicial experience.

26.2 Cognitive penetration of vision

A cognitive state permeates a perceptual experience when the former changes the phenomenal character of the latter from what it otherwise would have been. Such changes in phenomenal character are semantically linked to the permeating cognitive state, so that the latter explains modulation of the former. Zack's implicit bias explains why he sees Malik's cellphone as a gun, and it plays an etiological role in the phenomenal content of Zack's visual experience. That content represents a symbol of violence – a gun – and associates it with Malik.

The proposal to treat visual perceptions as skilled has at least two benefits. First, it takes advantage of the explanatory power and empirical strength of Constructivist models of visual perception. Such models treat visual perceptions as the conclusions of Bayesian probabilistic inferences. Constructivist models imply that the visual system learns how to produce a visual representation of a distal stimulus by deploying stored information about environmental regularities. Treating visual processing as a skill explains how the visual system learns to do this. On my proposal, the visual system learns how to see a perceiver's environment in roughly the same way that a person learns how to swim.

A second benefit of treating visual perceptions as skilled achievements is that it explains the mechanism of cognitive penetration.[6] Philosophical models of skilled action typically treat them as automatic sensorimotor routines guided by cognitive states. Skilled performances are manifestations of the cognitive states that guide sensorimotor execution. Likewise, Zack's visual prejudice is produced by automatic visual processes permeated by a cognitive state. When Zack sees Malik's cellphone as a gun, Zack's visual experience is a manifestation of the implicit bias that permeates his visual processing.

When combined with Constructivism, an account of Zack's visual prejudice is fairly straight-forward. Zack's implicit bias permeates his visual processing by influencing the unconscious Bayesian inference that produces his visual experience. It is, of course, an empirical question how this influence occurs.

The suggestion to treat visual perception as skilled Bayesian inference is generally applicable. It explains the mechanism of commonplace instances of skilled seeing, such as perceptual con-stancies. The capacity to produce a visual percept that represents distal stimuli as having constant color, size, shape or motion despite wide variations in retinal stimulation requires expert execu-tion of Bayesian inferences. Such performances are properly construed as skilled. But the present suggestion also explains deviant instances like Zack's visual prejudice.

26.3 Control vs. automaticity

A fundamental challenge for understanding skills is that they are both controlled and auto-matically implemented. Recent work on skilled action seeks to overcome this challenge by integrating the cognitive and intentional aspects of skills with the automaticity of their imple-mentation. One result has been a variety of hierarchical accounts of skill. Papineau (2015), for instance, argues that in skilled action the expert exhibits conscious cognitive control over high-level executive functions whereas the basic actions that are the components of skills are implemented by automatic motor routines. On Papineau's account, cognitive states indirectly influence automatic motor routines (2013). Christensen et al. (2016) also propose a hierarchical model. But in a departure from Papineau, Christensen et al. argue that "cognitive control dir-ectly influences motor execution" (2016: 43).

Other work has specified mechanisms of cognitive control of automatic motor routines. Fridland (2017a, 2017b), for instance, argues that the influence of cognitive control allows fine-grained adjustments to automatic sensorimotor routines so that motor control is flexibly responsive to task goals. According to Fridland, this requires selective attention to target features of perceptual inputs and behavioral outputs, which is achieved through diachronic training. Common to all of these accounts is the notion that skilled action involves both cognitive con-trol and automaticity.

These hierarchical accounts suggest that skilled actions have the following characteristic features: automaticity; diachronic refinement (i.e., training); intelligent task sensitivity; selective attention; and control. I do not claim that these are necessary or sufficient conditions for skill. Rather, I suggest only that expert performances exhibit some subset of these features in some degree. Moreover, there is some overlap between these features (e.g., automaticity and selective attention) that becomes evident when their mechanisms are specified.

Automaticity is perhaps the most difficult notion to explicate because, it seems, for many features typically associated with automaticity there is empirical evidence of automatic processes that lack those features. For instance, automatic processes are sometimes characterized as unin-tentional, unconscious, uncontrolled, and attention-independent. Yet none of these features is true of all automatic processes. As a result, the dichotomy between automatic and controlled processes has been superseded by a notion of automaticity as a cluster of characteristic features exhibited in varying degrees by different automatic processes at different times.

It's clear that developing a skill requires practice. Whether it's typing, swimming, or playing the guitar, expertise is developed by sustained effort over a large number of trials. What explains improvement in performance over these trials, according to Fridland (2017a), are intentional states that diachronically shape the automatic motor routines through which skilled actions are executed. Fridland argues that the structure and shape of automatic motor routines that implement skilled action are diachronically refined "under the guidance of higher-order intentions" (2017a: 4357).

But these automatic motor routines are not uniform or undifferentiated. Rather, Fridland cites empirical findings suggesting that automatic motor routines develop in ways that differentiate "between task-relevant and task-irrelevant dimensions of movement." This suggests that an automatic motor routine constitutive of a skilled action is flexibly sensitive to the semantic contents of higher-order intentions rather than a brute causal routine (2017a: 4358).

Selective attention requires determining relevant properties of perceptual inputs and behavioral outputs in order to expertly execute an action given the agent's goals. To borrow Wu's (2011: 56) example, if I wish to grab a hammer on a cluttered table I must visually select the hammer (ignoring other objects in my visual field) and also select those properties relevant to my grasping it (ignoring, say, the hammer's color and texture). According to Fridland, selective attention "improves with training, is often automatic, and is directly sensitive to the semantic contents of intentional states at the personal-level" (2017a: 4354). The finding that selective attention improves with training suggests that it, too, undergoes diachronic refinement. As with motor routines, the automaticity of selective attention also exhibits flexible sensitivity to the semantic contents of higher-order intentions.

Wu (2016) argues that selective attention is indispensable to control because attention "is a crucial ingredient needed to explain how intention 'guides' action" (p. 112). Elsewhere, Wu (2011, 2013) argues that agentive control is implementation of a solution to what he calls the Many-Many Problem. The problem is that there are many possible inputs and outputs for a given course of action. Agency requires "selection of a specific linkage between input and output" by "reducing the set of many possible inputs to a single relevant input" (Wu 2011: 53). Likewise, the agent must select a behavioral output from among many possible outputs. In other words, the agent must select a path in a space of possible inputs and behavioral outputs. To repeat Wu's example, in order to grasp a hammer I must visually select target inputs relevant to the hammer and my grasping it; and in order to grasp it I must select sensorimotor outputs (reach, hand position, etc.) relevant to my goal. Wu argues that implementation of a selected path through a behavioral space of possible actions constitutes agentive control of bodily action. This is the case even though the motor routines that implement the selected path are themselves automatic.[7]

26.4 Skilled seeing

As with skilled action, I argue that skilled perception involves a hierarchical relation between executive states and lower-level visual processes that include the following features: automaticity; diachronic refinement; intelligent task sensitivity; selective attention; and control. In what follows, I take a paradigm case of cognitive penetration – Memory Color – and argue that it possesses these characteristic features of skill. Aside from differences in mechanisms (e.g., skilled perception involves visual processes rather than motor routines), the obvious difference between skilled action and skilled perception is that the former outputs bodily behavior whereas the latter outputs perceptual experience.

A large series of experiments shows top-down influence on perceived color. In early versions (see Duncker 1939; Bruner et al. 1951; Delk and Fillenbaum 1965), subjects are shown silhouettes of objects with characteristic colors (*color-diagnostic* objects) such as lips, hearts, and apples (red), as well as color-neutral objects (circles, ovals, etc.) and sometimes color-incongruent objects (horse, bell, mushroom). All silhouettes are cut out of orange-red cardboard and presented on an illuminated background. Subjects are asked to adjust the color of the background to match the color of the object (so that the object disappears). When completing this task with color-diagnostic objects, subjects adjust the background so that it is redder than the object, implying that they see the object as redder than it is. More recent versions (Ling et al. 2008; Witzel et al. 2011) present subjects with images of color-diagnostic objects (bananas, lemons, etc.) against an achromatic (gray-scale) background and ask subjects to adjust the image so that it matches the background. But when adjusting a banana image to appear achromatic, for instance, subjects over-adjust so that the resulting image is slightly blue (the chromatic opposite of yellow). This suggests that subjects saw the banana as slightly yellow when it was in fact gray. These findings suggest that subjects' beliefs about color-diagnostic objects (e.g., that bananas are yellow) permeate their color experiences.

A top-down influence on perceived color entails a hierarchical relation between color-diagnostic beliefs and low-level visual processing. In Memory Color, the content of the perceiver's perceptual experience occurs automatically. Perceivers automatically see the gray banana as yellow. It also seems clear that Memory Color requires selective attention to color and shape, and that this attention is automatically implemented. Olkkonen et al. (2008) and Witzel et al. (2011) show that Memory Color effects strengthen when the perceptual targets have more features (e.g., complete images rather than silhouettes). This suggests that Memory Color effects involve automatically implemented selective attention to features of the perceptual target.[8]

Memory Color is also learned through training. Witzel et al. (2011) found Memory Color effects for man-made objects such as Smurfs, the Nivea tin, the German cartoon character Die Maus, the Pink Panther, and so on. They conclude, "Since these objects are tied to a particular cultural context, their association with a typical colour must have been learned in everyday life" (2011: 44). Perceivers learn to see artificial and culturally specific objects as color-diagnostic, producing a measurable Memory Color effect.

Intelligent task sensitivity is evident in recent experiments showing Memory Color effects to be robustly illumination-independent (Olkkonen et al. 2008). That is, Memory Color effects persist despite changes in illumination. The perceiver's visual system does not correct for changes in illumination. This is presumably because illumination is irrelevant to the perceiver's goal of color constancy of the color-diagnostic perceptual target. These results show that Memory Color effects exhibit semantic sensitivity of automatic low-level visual processes to the perceiver's permeating cognitive state. Those processes bypass semantically irrelevant perceptual perturbations when generating a permeated perceptual experience.

The remaining feature of skill is control. On Wu's model of skilled action, implementing a solution to the Many-Many Problem constitutes agentive control. An analogous account of control for cognitive penetration attributes selection of a path through a manifold of multiple possible perceptual inputs and outputs to the visual system. Moreover, that path must be semantically coherent in order for the output of the selected path to be explicable in terms of a permeating cognitive state. In Memory Color, it seems clear that a color-diagnostic belief guides selection of path through a manifold of multiple possible inputs (e.g., the banana region of the image is modulated rather than the background), and multiple possible outputs (e.g., the output color is yellow rather than pink or blue). Given that the visual system solves a Many-Many Problem when producing a cognitively penetrated percept, the production of that percept is controlled rather than reflexive.

26.5 Skill and know-how

The features of skill outlined in Section 26.3 are also generally attributed to know-how. Knowing how to ride a bike requires training, control, selective attention, intelligent task sensitivity, and automatic sensorimotor routines. Accordingly, Stanley and Williamson write, "Skill is intimately connected to a kind of knowledge which philosophers have typically, though misleadingly, called 'knowing how'" (2017: 714). What's 'misleading' about this, they go on to argue, is the notion that know-how is distinct from propositional knowledge – a notion attributed largely to Ryle.

Ryle (1949/2009: 17) describes know-how in terms of learning, flexible control, detection and correction of errors, and improving upon past successes. But Ryle argues that none of these features of intelligence entails propositional knowledge. Ryle's argument takes the form of an infinite regress. Suppose that knowing how to swim requires considering some propositions. Considering is itself an act, so it must be something we know how to do. But then knowing how to consider propositions about swimming requires considering some further propositions (about considering). But we must also know how to consider those propositions. And so on *ad infinitum*. For this reason, Ryle rejects Intellectualism – that view skill presupposes propositional knowledge.

Another intuition motivating Anti-Intellectualism is that the automaticity of skilled performance rules out propositional knowledge as a component of skill. The idea seems to be that considering a proposition or being sensitive to its semantic content requires cognitive resources unavailable to automatic processes. A dog knows how to catch a frisbee, but the dog does not consider propositions in order to do so.

Intellectualist replies often take know-how to be *manifestations* of propositional knowledge (Ginet 1975; Stanley and Williamson 2001, 2017; Stanley 2011), which are contrasted with considerations of the relevant propositions. Since know-how requires only manifesting propositional knowledge without considering the proposition known, Ryle's regress is halted. Furthermore, such manifestations are understood to be automatic actions that express knowledge of a proposition under what Stanley and Williamson call a practical mode of presentation (2001: 429). To borrow Ginet's much-discussed example, I manifest my knowledge *that* there is a door in front of me, and *that* the door can be opened by turning the knob and pushing, simply by turning the knob and pushing the door open (Ginet 1975: 7). The action that manifests this knowledge is automatic, and I needn't consciously consider any of the propositions that I know.

Stanley and Williamson (2001, 2017) and Stanley (2011) offer further evidence that know-how manifests propositional knowledge by considering various other kinds of knowledge – knowing when, knowing where, knowing what, knowing which, knowing whether, etc. – and their relation to knowing how. Let's call these other types of knowledge 'knowledge-wh' states. They argue that know-how typically entails knowledge-wh states, and that knowledge-wh states are propositional knowledge. Know-how, then, is a form of propositional knowledge.

Visual processing manifests knowledge-wh states when solving underdetermination problems. There are many different distal stimuli compatible with such-and-such retinal inputs.

Yet the visual system reliably produces a perception of the most likely distal stimulus given retinal inputs and stored information about environmental regularities. The visual system knows whether to interpret retinal stimulation as originating from a convex object reflecting light from overhead, or a concave object reflecting light from below; or whether the distal surface is white and bathed in red light or red and bathed in white light (Rescorla 2015: 694). The visual system knows how to produce a percept of constant surface color from retinal stimulation of diverse color-producing properties; and it does so under varying conditions by knowing which surface colors are most likely; knowing whether the light source is uniform; and knowing when a retinal stimulus is produced by background illumination. As a result, the visual system knows how to see a distal stimulus. For similar reasons, the visual system knows how to see constant size, constant shape, and constant motion. It does so despite ambiguous retinal stimulation manifesting knowledge-wh states.

Yet the same can be said of Memory Color. The visual system knows which regions of the percept to modulate in order to be semantically consistent with color-diagnostic beliefs (the banana, not the background). It knows what color is the target of the color-diagnostic belief (yellow, not pink or blue). It knows whether to correct for changes in illumination. Given all of this, Memory Color effects manifest propositional know-wh states indicative of skill. But can a Memory Color effect be rightly considered an instance of know-how? None of the know-wh states manifested by a Memory Color experience entail knowledge that the banana image is yellow. It seems that some instances of cognitive penetration present a challenge to Stanley and Williamson's view that skill manifests know-how and know-how is a disposition to know facts.[9] Although dispositions can be manifested in a variety of situation-specific ways, a disposition to know a fact cannot be manifested by not knowing that fact.

As with Memory Color, Zack's visual prejudice manifests a variety of knowledge-wh states. It knows which region of the percept to modulate (the cellphone, not Malik's hands or clothes). It knows what modulations are semantically consistent with depictions of violence (weapons rather than wallets or toys). Let's suppose that it knows whether to correct for changes in illumination, occlusions, and so forth. Since Zack's visual prejudice manifests a variety of knowledge-wh states, it is skilled on Stanley and Williamson's account.

But considered as an instance of know-how, Zack's visual prejudice is epistemically worse than Memory Color. The color-diagnostic belief that bananas are typically yellow might plausibly count as a knowledge state. But Zack's implicit bias is not a knowledge state at all. Thus, whereas one might be tempted to say that the disposition to know that bananas are typically yellow is *improperly* manifested in a Memory Color effect, something similar cannot be said of Zack's implicit bias simply because implicit biases are not knowledge states.

26.6 Intentional control

It might be objected that cases of cognitive penetration such as Memory Color are not skills because they do not exhibit intentional control. Wu's chapter in this volume proposes an account of intentional control that, I think, is consistent with cognitive penetration. Following Anscombe, Wu argues that intentions represent a type of action to be done. Those representations "specify a set of properties such that if the resulting action has those properties, then the intention is satisfied in that the resulting action is intentional under the relevant description," (Wu, Chapter 16 in this volume: [page number]). Control is then defined over properties of an intended action-type. A property of an action, "is controlled relative to an intention if and only if the intention's representing [that property] as to be done brings about the action's having [that property as represented in the content of the intention]" (Wu, Chapter 16 in this volume: [page number]).

The perceptual analogue is that an intention represents a type of visual output to be experienced. Those representations specify a set of properties such that the output is intentional under the relevant description if it has those properties. Control is then defined over properties of the intended visual output type. A property of the visual output is controlled relative to an intention if and only if the intention's representing that property as to be experienced brings about the visual output's having that property as represented by the content of the intention.

What's more, Wu's analysis suggests that we can individuate intentions from non-intentional mental states by identifying a link between properties represented in the content of mental states and properties of an action (or output) etiologically downstream from those mental states. If the latter has properties represented in the content of the former *because* those properties are represented by those mental states (and this relation can be identified through counterfactual truths – e.g., if the mental states had not represented those features, then the action would not have those properties), then those mental states are intentions. The resulting action is controlled with respect to those properties.

It's fairly easy to see how the merger of Wu's Many-Many Problem and his account of intentional agential control might work. An agent solves the Many-Many Problem by selecting a representation of an action with a certain set of features as 'to be done' from among multiple such representations. If the resulting action has those features because they are contents of the selected representation, then the action is intentionally controlled. This can provide an analysis of task sensitivity in representational terms. Task sensitivity requires semantic coherence with a representation of a type of action to be done, or a type of visual output to be experienced.

For instance, in Memory Color cases beliefs about color-diagnostic objects represent a type of visual output to be seen. As a result, predictions can be used to measure intentional control in Memory Color cases. Consider Witzel et al.'s (2011) findings of Memory Color effects for man-made culturally specific objects. Based on these findings we can plausibly predict that subjects whose color-diagnostic beliefs are shaped by a specific cultural context will demonstrate particular Memory Color effects. We can predict, for instance, that subjects who grew up in Germany will demonstrate Memory Color effects specific to images of Die Maus, but other subjects will not demonstrate such effects. This prediction estimates the contents of those subjects' color-diagnostic beliefs. Insofar as properties of a visual output can be predicted by identifying properties of a permeating color-diagnostic belief, and insofar as that belief represents properties as to be seen in a target percept, such predictions are evidence of intentional control.

Similarly, Zack's bias specifies representations of violence or aggression as properties of the visual output that includes a black male face, and since Zack's visual experience has those properties it is plausibly intentional under the relevant description. Zack's prejudicial experience has the property represented by his bias (i.e., violence) and *would not have that property* had that bias not permeated his visual experience. Zack's prejudicial experience is intentionally controlled with respect to that property.

It might be wondered whether this is sufficient to establish person-level intentional control. (Wu is explicit that his account of intentional control is *agential* or person-level.) As far as I can tell, what's needed to establish person-level intentional control is that a person-level representation of a target action specifies a set of properties such that the resulting action has those properties because they are specified by the relevant person-level representation. Color-diagnostic beliefs and implicit biases are person-level representations that, in the context of a permeated perceptual experience, specify sets of properties of target visual experiences such that the resulting experiences have those properties because they are specified by permeating person-level representations. That is sufficient, on this analysis, to establish person-level intentional control.

26.7 Conclusion

It might be objected that cognitive penetration is an *ability* of the visual system rather than a skill. In reply, consider that Zack's visual prejudice exhibits modal properties that are closely associated with know-how rather than ability. Stanley and Williamson (2001: 416) and Stanley (2011: 126) reject the ability view of know-how by arguing that there is a modal difference between ability and know-how. They consider the case of a pianist who loses her arms. She knows how to play piano but loses the ability to do so. Stanley and Williamson conclude that know-how does not entail ability. The reason the armless pianist knows how to play piano despite lacking the ability to do so is that there is a close possible world in which she *has* that ability – a world in which she has arms.

Zack's case can be given a modification to show that it exhibits similar modal properties. Suppose that Zack's visual processing is disrupted by a sudden flash of bright light. Zack is unable to see either Malik's face or his cellphone. But in a close possible world (i.e., one without the flash of light), Zack has the same instance of biased seeing as in the original case. Zack's visual processing has modal properties associated with know-how in this modified version of the case even though it lacks the ability to produce a prejudicial experience. Zack's visual processing is more than just an ability.

Zack does not know whether Malik is holding a gun. The Memory Color patient does not know whether *this* banana is yellowish *now*. What this suggests is that manifesting situation-specific know-wh states is not sufficient for manifesting knowledge of facts. But Stanley and Williamson take know-how to be a disposition to know facts. Memory Color and visual prejudice are skilled but not instances of know-how on their analysis.

The hierarchical models of skill discussed in Section 26.3 are helpful for understanding where Stanley and Williamson's account goes astray. In Memory Color and visual prejudice, lower-level visual processes manifest situation-specific know-wh states. But the higher-level intentional states that guide those lower-level visual processes do not manifest knowledge of facts. For that reason, these performances are skilled in the sense that the features of skill identified in Section 26.3 (automaticity, control, selective attention, diachronic refinement, task sensitivity) are instantiated by the relation between higher-level intentional states and lower-level visual processes.

But whether a performance manifests knowledge of facts seems to be determined by whether the higher-level intentional state that guides it expresses knowledge of facts. In Memory Color, the guiding higher-level intentional state arguably *does* express knowledge of facts, but this is not sufficient for the performance to manifest *situation-specific* knowledge of facts. In visual prejudice, the guiding higher-level intentional state does not express knowledge of facts at all, explaining why the performance does not manifest knowledge of facts.

Stanley and Williamson might object that I have overlooked their distinction between two senses of 'manifest'. Skilled actions are manifestations$_2$ of knowledge states; and knowledge states are manifestations$_1$ of dispositions to know. But in Memory Color and visual prejudice, lower-level visual processes manifest$_1$ task-sensitive know-wh states. The resulting visual experiences manifest$_2$ the knowledge states manifested$_1$ by low-level visual processes. The issue isn't that I have overlooked two senses of 'manifest'. The issue is that task sensitivity requires that low-level states are guided by higher-level intentions that either are not knowledge states or are not sufficient for manifesting situation-specific knowledge states.

Notes

1 See Payne (2001); Correll et al. (2002); Hugenberg and Bodenhausen (2003, 2004); Stokes and Payne (2011).
2 Cognitive penetration is also sometimes referred to as a top-down effect on perception. The phenomenon has been defined in several different ways depending on a range of variables (e.g., Macpherson 2012; Siegel 2012). Siegel (2017) has introduced the additional phrase 'perceptual hijacking' to identify instances of cognitive penetration that are epistemically bad in some way (e.g., Zack's biased seeing).
3 For detailed discussion, see Siegel (2012, 2017).
4 Munton (2019) also proposes to treat visual perceptions as skilled. Unfortunately, a detailed discussion of Munton's approach would take us too far afield.
5 I can also sidestep the issue of how to categorize implicit biases.
6 Macpherson (2012) argues for an indirect model of the mechanism of cognitive penetration. I think an indirect model is compatible with the Constructivist account suggested here, but there is insufficient space for a detailed discussion.
7 Wu contrasts selection of a path through behavioral space of multiple possible actions with reflexes, wherein the behavioral space is limited to "a single one-one link between stimulus and response at a time" (Wu 2011: 53). Implementation of this reflexive one-one link requires no selection of a path through behavioral space by the agent, and so no solution to the Many-Many Problem. For this reason, reflexes are uncontrolled on Wu's account.
8 It also explains some of the inconsistencies of earlier Memory Color effects observed by Duncker (1939), Bruner et al. (1951), and Delk and Fillenbaum (1965), which used silhouettes having fewer properties to which a perceiver could attend.
9 See also Stanley and Krakauer (2013).

References

Brownstein, M. (2019) "Implicit Bias," in E. N. Zalta (ed.) *The Stanford Encyclopedia of Philosophy*, https://plato.stanford.edu/archives/fall2019/entries/implicit-bias/.
Bruner, J. S., Postman, L., and Rodrigues, J. (1951) "Expectation and the Perception of Color," *The American Journal of Psychology* 64: 216–27.
Christensen, W., Sutton, J., and McIlwain, D. J. F. (2016) "Cognition in Skilled Action: Meshed Control and the Varieties of Skill Experience," *Mind & Language* 31: 37–66.
Correll, J., Park, B., Judd, C. M., and Wittenbrink, B. (2002) "The Police Officer's Dilemma: Using Ethnicity to Disambiguate Potentially Threatening Individuals," *Journal of Personality and Social Psychology* 83: 1314–29.
Delk, J. L., and Fillenbaum, S. (1965) "Differences in Perceived Color as a Function of Characteristic Color," *The American Journal of Psychology* 78: 290–3.
Duncker, K. (1939) "The Influence of Past Experience upon Perceptual Properties," *The American Journal of Psychology* 52(2): 255–65.
Fridland, E. (2017a) "Automatically Minded," *Synthese* 194: 4337–63.
—— (2017b) "Skill and Motor Control: Intelligence All the Way Down," *Philosophical Studies* 174: 1539–60.
Ginet, C. (1975) *Knowledge, Perception, and Memory*, Dordrecht: D. Reidel Publishing Company.
Hugenberg, K., and Bodenhausen, G.V. (2003) "Facing Prejudice: Implicit Prejudice and the Perception of Facial Threat," *Psychological Science* 14: 640–3.
—— (2004) "Ambiguity in Social Categorization: The Role of Prejudice and Facial Affect in Race Categorization," *Psychological Science* 15: 342–5.
Ling, Y., Allen-Clarke, L., Vurro, M., and Hurlbert, A. C. (2008) "The Effect of Object Familiarity and Changing Illumination on Colour Categorization," *Perception* 37: 149.
Macpherson, F. (2012) "Cognitive Penetration of Colour Experience: Rethinking the Issue in Light of an Indirect Mechanism," *Philosophy and Phenomenological Research* 84: 24–62.

Munton, J. (2019) "Perceptual Skill and Social Structure," *Philosophy and Phenomenological Research* 99: 131–61.

Olkkonen, M., Hansen, T., and Gegenfurtner, K. R. (2008) "Colour Appearance of Familiar Objects: Effects of Object Shape, Texture and Illumination Changes," *Journal of Vision* 8: 1–16.

Papineau, D. (2013) "In the Zone," *Royal Institute of Philosophy Supplement* 73: 175–96.

—— (2015) "Choking and the Yips," *Phenomenology and the Cognitive Sciences* 14: 295–308.

Payne, B. K. (2001) "Prejudice and Perception: The Role of Automatic and Controlled Processes in Misperceiving a Weapon," *Journal of Personality and Social Psychology* 81: 181–92.

Rescorla, M. (2015) "Bayesian Perceptual Psychology," in M. Matthen (ed.) *The Oxford Handbook of Philosophy of Perception*, 694–716, Oxford: Oxford University Press.

Ryle, G. (1949/2009) *The Concept of Mind*, New York: Routledge.

Siegel, S. (2012) "Cognitive Penetrability and Perceptual Justification," *NOÛS* 46: 201–22.

—— (2017) *The Rationality of Perception*, Oxford: Oxford University Press.

Stanley, J. (2011) *Know How*, Oxford: Oxford University Press.

Stanley, J., and Krakauer, J. W. (2013) "Motor Skill Depends on Knowledge of Facts," *Frontiers in Human Neuroscience* 7: 1–11.

Stanley, J., and Williamson, T. (2001) "Knowing How," *The Journal of Philosophy* 98: 411–44.

—— (2017) "Skill," *NOÛS* 51: 713–26.

Stokes, M. B., and Payne, B. K. (2011) "Mental Control and Visual Illusions: Errors of Action and Construal in Race-Based Weapon Misidentification," *The Science of Social Vision* 7: 295.

Witzel, C., Valkova, H., Hansen, T., and Gegenfurtner, K. R. (2011) "Object Knowledge Modulates Colour Appearance," *i-Perception* 2: 13–49.

Wu, W. (2011) "Confronting Many-Many Problems: Attention and Agentive Control," *NOÛS* 45: 50–76.

—— (2013) "Mental Action and the Threat of Automaticity." in A. Clark, J. Kiverstein, and T. Vierkant (eds.) *Decomposing the Will*, 255–61, Oxford: Oxford University Press.

—— (2016) "Experts and Deviants: The Story of Agentive Control," *Philosophy and Phenomenological Research* 93: 101–26.

27

THE SKILL OF IMAGINATION

Amy Kind

In a memorable scene from the 1984 film *Amadeus*, Mozart imperiously dictates various instructions to Salieri while at work composing the Requiem. But Salieri cannot easily follow Mozart's instructions. Why not? As the film depicts things, it seems that Mozart's powers of musical imagination far outrun those of Salieri. Salieri simply can't imagine the music as well as Mozart can; Mozart can hear the music in his head in a way that Salieri cannot.[1]

In ordinary life, as in film, we generally accept the claim that imaginative abilities vary from one person to the next. We accept that some people are better at imagining than others – whether it's auditory imagining, as in the case from *Amadeus*, or some other kind of imagining, as in many other cases. On this folk view of imagination, imagination is viewed as a skill.

Of course, folk views are notoriously problematic in all sorts of respects, but when it comes to imagination, I think we find at least one instance in which the folk have got things right. Imagination is indeed a skill. Unfortunately, this pre-theoretical insight about imagination seems to have been largely lost in the contemporary philosophical investigation of imagination. Amid the explosion of philosophical interest in imagination in the last three or four decades, while we can find occasional passing references to the fact that imagination is a skill, this fact has not played a significant role in philosophical treatments of imagination and the implications of it remain almost entirely unexplored.[2]

In an attempt to rectify this omission, this chapter undertakes a preliminary investigation into the categorization of imagination as a skill. In Section 27.1, I develop a rough framework for characterizing skills. In Section 27.2, I apply that framework to imagination. In Section 27.3, I consider three objections to considering imagination to be a skill and show how each can be answered. Finally, I close the chapter with some concluding remarks that focus on the philosophical payoffs that come from the recognition that imagination is a skill.

27.1 What is a skill?

The philosophical inattention to treating imagination as a skill is perhaps at least partly explained by a more general philosophical inattention to the notion of skill. As Jason Stanley and Timothy Williamson have noted, "analytic philosophers have shown little or no interest in the analysis of skill" (Stanley and Williamson 2017: 714). Carlotta Pavese makes a similar assessment, noting that the topic "has been marginalized" in analytic epistemology (Pavese 2016: 642). While there are a couple of contexts in which the notion of skill has played a key role – more specifically, it features in discussions of virtue epistemology and in discussions of the intellectualism/anti-intellectualism debate – there isn't a general philosophical consensus on what exactly skill is.

In what follows, however, I'll extract a rough analysis of skill from some recent work by Stanley in a paper coauthored with John Krakauer. While discussing the pre-theoretic notion of skill, Stanley and Krakauer (2013) mention three different components that are central to this notion.[3]

First, when someone is skilled at an activity, they are "better than baseline" at that activity; they have crossed certain performance thresholds with respect to the activity. What exactly will be involved in the relevant performance threshold will vary with the activity. Some performance thresholds relate to speed: the skilled crossword puzzle solver completes the puzzle more quickly than an average puzzle solver, and the skilled sprinter covers the distance more quickly than the average sprinter. Others relate to the complexity of the activity: the skilled juggler juggles more balls, and throws them in more elaborate patterns, than the unskilled juggler. Yet others relate to aesthetic characteristics: the skilled ballroom dancer moves across the dancefloor with more grace and elegance than the unskilled ballroom dancer. And so on.

Second, when someone is skilled at an activity, the activity is under their intentional control.[4] An unskilled crossword puzzle solver may sometimes solve a difficult puzzle, and an unskilled juggler might occasionally manage to keep the balls in the air for several tosses, but if their successes arise from guesswork or luck, their performances don't count as skilled. Along these lines, consider Gilbert Ryle's discussion of the skilled clown: the clown "trips and tumbles just as clumsy people do, except that he trips and tumbles on purpose and after much rehearsal and at the golden moment and where the children can see him and so as not to hurt himself" (Ryle 1949: 33). Unlike the clumsy person's stumbles, the clown's stumbles are deliberate and controlled.

Third, the skilled person maintains and/or increases their skill by way of practice. This practice may involve explicit instruction via a trainer, or it may involve observation. Either way, however, repetitive efforts will be involved.

Having laid out these central features that characterize when someone can be said to be skilled at a certain activity, we are led directly to a corresponding list of the central features of activities that can be generally classifiable as skills. When an activity is a skill, it:

1. can be done more or less well;
2. is under one's intentional control;
3. can be improved via practice/training.

When we think about the many different sorts of varied activities that are usually classified as skills – from juggling and ballroom dancing to playing chess, solving crossword puzzles, and performing mental calculations – this list seems to be suitably inclusive.[5] Moreover, it does a nice job of excluding activities that are usually not classified as skills; activities such as blinking or raising one's arm or shutting a window. But does it capture all and only activities commonly thought of as skills? Probably not. Consider pattern recognition, an activity often referred to as a perceptual skill. Pattern recognition is a subpersonal activity of the perceptual system, done without any intentional guidance by the agent. Thus, on the analysis of skill we are extracting from Stanley and Krakauer, it does not seem that pattern recognition can count as a skill, since it is not under the intentional control of the person performing the action. For this reason, we should probably not think of the list as providing a set of necessary and sufficient conditions for skill, but rather as a list of central features of skill.[6] For our purposes here, this will be enough. Given that the list provides us with a robust sense of how skills can be classified, capturing paradigm cases of skills and not capturing paradigm cases of non-skills, we have an adequate framework to apply to the case of imagination. Doing so will be the main concern of the rest of this chapter.

27.2 Treating imagination as a skill

In order to see whether and how the framework developed in the previous section can be applied to the case of imagination, we need first to briefly explore what imagination is and how it has been typically characterized by philosophers. In doing so, it will be helpful to have an example before us. Here I'll utilize a case that I've used before, a case of two young boys playing a game of make-believe:

> "Let's imagine that a scary monster is chasing us," Max says.
> "What does it look like?" Sammy asks.
> Max scrunches up his face, picturing the monster, before answering: "It's 20 feet tall, green with orange spots; it has huge claws, spikes on its tail, and big crooked teeth."
> Sammy shudders as he imagines seeing such a monster. "I'd be really scared if I ever ran into that monster in real life," he tells his brother. "Let's hide behind that mountain," he adds, pointing to the living room sofa.
> Later that night, while lying in bed, Sammy finds himself worrying that the monster has snuck into the closet and is waiting to attack the boys as they sleep. No matter what he tries, he can't stop himself from imagining it.[7]

Games of make-believe are just one context of many in which imagining plays a key role. Imagining also seems to be involved when we daydream, when we engage with thought experiments or with fiction, when we attempt to understand the thoughts and feelings of others (a process usually referred to as *mindreading*), and when we're involved in creative endeavors. It is also often involved in cases of problem-solving, decision-making, and planning. But attending to this specific example allows us to tease apart several different activities that go under the heading of imagining:

- *Propositional imagining.* When the boys imagine that a scary monster is chasing them, they engage in what philosophers typically call *propositional or attitudinal imagining.* Here imagining is likened to other propositional attitudes such as belief and desire.
- *Sensory imagining.* When the boys imagine the scary monster itself, and it's almost like they are seeing the monster before them, they are engaged in what is usually called *sensory* or *imagistic imagining.* When philosophers talk of imagistic imagining, they typically want the notion of imagery to be understood in a broad sense so that it means something like "sensory presentation." In this sense, we can have auditory imagery just as we can have visual imagery, and likewise for all of the other senses.
- *Experiential imagining.* When the boys imagine feeling scared, they are engaged in what philosophers tend to call *experiential imagining.* Experiential imagining is very similar to sensory imagining and in fact, if we were to take the notion of "imagistic" or "sensory presentation" even more broadly than was just suggested, we might be able to capture emotional presentations under this heading and thereby capture experiential

imagining under the heading of sensory imagining. Perhaps better, however, we can collapse imagistic and experiential imagining into a broader category that we might call *phenomenological imagining*.

Having distinguished these different types of imagining, the question now arises: When we think of imagination as a skill, which type of imagining do we have in mind? Just one type or all three? Though I think a case can be made that all three types of imagining can be brought under the framework of skill that we developed in the previous section, I also think the case seems to be clearest with respect to sensory and experiential imagining.

Generally speaking, propositional attitudes such as belief and desire do not seem to be the sort of things that are appropriately characterized as skills. Believing and desiring are not the kinds of things that are done more or less well. Though some people may be better at forming *true* beliefs than others, and some people may be better at forming *satisfiable* desires than others, this doesn't really make them better at believing or desiring in and of themselves. Believing and desiring also don't seem to be the sorts of things that you learn how to do via experiential techniques such as learning and observation, nor are they the sorts of things that you can get better at with practice. Part of the problem here is that believing and desiring (and, more generally, the having of propositional attitudes) are not really activities at all; they are not things we do. But if they are not things we do, then they cannot be things we do skillfully.[8]

Insofar as propositional imagination is like these other propositional attitudes, it seems that it too would not be properly characterized as a skill. Of course, there may be reasons to think that propositional imagining is relevantly different from these other propositional attitudes. For example, though belief may be best thought of as the *having* of an attitude toward a proposition, imagining may be best thought of as the *taking* of an attitude toward a proposition. That makes propositional imagining sound considerably more like an activity than believing. Even so, however, it is not clear that propositional imagining can be done more or less well or that it is improvable via practice and training.

When it comes to sensory and experiential imagination, these problems do not arise. When Max and Sammy are playing make-believe, one of them might be better at imagining the monster than the other is, and likewise, one of them might be better at imagining the fear that they'd feel if the monster were really chasing them. These kinds of imagination also seem like the kinds of activities that one could improve by way of practice. The more the boys play make-believe, the better they might become at imagining the various elements of their games.

What about the fact that skills are generally characterized as being under one's intentional control? Here a worry might arise since there are many examples of sensory and experiential imagination that belie this claim. As I presented the case of Max and Sammy, when Sammy is in bed at night after having played monsters with his brother all afternoon, he finds himself unable to stop imagining the scary monster from the game. We can find many similar examples in the literature on imagination, e.g.:

> Often after seeing a particularly gruesome murder scene in a horror movie, I keep imagining the murder again and again. In such a case, I usually want the imagining to stop, I might even will myself to stop it, but I typically find myself quite powerless to stop the imagining. Analogously, after awakening to a catchy tune on the radio, the tune often runs through my head for quite a while; I might even be unable to keep from imagining it, in this way, all day long.
>
> *Kind 2001: 91*

These sorts of examples seem to set imagining apart from other skilled activities. We don't find ourselves powerless to stop ballroom dancing or juggling. But, in fact, this conclusion is a bit too quick. For consider another activity that's typically classified as a skill: remembering. We see a similar kind of "powerless to stop" phenomenon with respect to memory as we do with imagining. We might just find ourselves remembering an event from our past, or find ourselves powerless to stop remembering an embarrassing moment.

In fact, once we think more carefully about the notion of intentional control relevant to skill, we see that we need to refine our understanding of exactly what this condition involves. Consider a skilled activity such as skiing. Even someone who is a very skilled skier might find herself at times having lost control of what she's doing. But even if there are times while skiing that the activity is not under the skier's intentional control, skiing is still the kind of activity that *can* be under one's intentional control. And likewise for imagining. Though there might be times while imagining that the activity is not under the imaginer's intentional control – as when Sammy can't stop himself from imagining the scary monster, or when I find myself powerless to banish a gruesome movie scene from my mind – imagining is still the kind of activity that *can* be under one's intentional control.

At least on an initial assessment, then, imagination – or more specifically, sensory and experiential imagination – seems to fit the framework developed in Section 27.1.[9] As we will see, however, further exploration suggests that there are several important objections that might be raised to this assessment. In the next section of this chapter, I will consider three such objections. Though I think the objections deserve to be taken seriously, the defender of the claim that imagination is a skill has plausible lines of response to each one.

27.3 Objections

The first of the three objections we will consider arises from thinking about two very different uses to which imagination might be put. When we imagine in contexts of daydreaming or make-believe, we are using imagination to move beyond the world in which we live. But when we imagine in contexts of thought experimentation, decision-making, and mindreading, we are typically trying to learn something about the world in which we live. In previous work, I have referred to these two uses of imagination, respectively, as the *transcendent* and *instructive* uses of imagination (Kind and Kung 2016). That imagination has two such different uses suggests that there would be two very different kinds of skills associated with imagination, a skill of transcendence and a skill of instruction. Someone who is very skilled at imagination in the first sense is good at unshackling her imagination and letting it roam free of reality, disconnecting from it. Someone who is very skilled at imagination in the second sense is good at tethering her imagination to reality in just the right way that she can learn from it. That there might be two such different skills associated with imagination shouldn't itself worry us. After all, when we consider marathon running vs. sprinting, we can see that there are two very different kinds of skills associated with running. But noticing these two different kinds of uses to which imagination is put might lead us to a deeper worry about whether both such uses of imagination really correspond to skilled activities.

Consider an objector who reasons as follows:

> Transcendent imagination, insofar as it corresponds to creativity, might be a skill. Since we see lots of people who are more creative than other people, it makes sense to think that some people are better transcendent imaginers than others. But how

could instructive imagination be a skill? If it were, then we should see some obvious examples of skilled imaginers. But we don't, so it's not.

Let's call this *the Socratic objection* since it seems to have faintly Socratic overtones: Just as Socrates brought Meno to see that we should expect to be able to find expert teachers of virtue if virtue is really the kind of thing that can be taught, our objector here is arguing that we should expect to find expert imaginers if imagination is really the kind of thing at which one can be an expert.

To respond to this objection, it's helpful first to recall that when someone is putting imagination to an instructive use, they are using their imagination to try to figure out how the world works, or at least, how some aspect of the world works. Once we put things this way, I think it's pretty easy to see that we do find experts at this. Consider interior decorators who are especially good at using imagination to figure out which curtains will best match the sofa. Or consider workers for a moving company who are especially good at using imagination to figure out how to make a large load of furniture fit into a relatively small truck.

Here it might be worth pausing over a couple of examples in a little more detail.[10] First, consider inventor Nikola Tesla. Although he's probably best known for his work on alternating current electricity, he also experimented with wireless technology and remote controls, X-ray imaging, and mechanical oscillators, and over the course of his life he patented about 300 of his inventions worldwide. In autobiographical works, Tesla explicitly credits his imaginative capacities as being responsible for his success. As he describes his design process:

> Before I put a sketch on paper, the whole idea is worked out mentally. In my mind, I change the construction, make improvements, and even operate the device. Without ever having drawn a sketch, I can give the measurement of all parts to workmen, and when completed these parts will fit, just as certainly as though I had made accurate drawings.
>
> *Tesla 1921*

If we take Tesla at his word, and we have no reason not to, he provides us a notable example of someone who learns via imaginative exercises how various devices can be best constructed.

My second example comes from a very different domain. Consider master origamist Satoshi Kamiya. In 2006, Kamiya produced "what is considered the pinnacle of the field, an eight-inch tall Eastern dragon with eyes, teeth, a curly tongue, sinuous whiskers, a barbed tail, and a thousand overlapping scales" (Kahn 2006: 60). Just the folding process itself took over 40 hours. Unlike other origamists, however, Kamiya produces his creations without the help of any software or computer aid. When asked how he can achieve such elaborate design without digital assistance, a feat that seems almost incomprehensible to his competitors, Kamiya's answer indicates the importance of imagination: "I see it finished. And then … I unfold it. In my mind. One piece at a time" (Kahn 2006: 63). Though Kamiya's imaginative efforts are aimed at a very different kind of result from that of Tesla, here too we have an example of someone who learns via imaginative exercises how a certain result can best be obtained.

Though these examples should put the Socratic objection to rest, another objection is lurking in the vicinity. Given that the imaginative skills of Tesla and Kamiya seem so out of reach to those of us who are not expert imaginers, it's tempting to think that they must simply have been born great imaginers. If this were right, then we would have good reason to think that imagination isn't a skill. Lots of recent work suggest that imaginative capacity differs from person to person, for example, that there are significant interpersonal variations in one's capacity for mental imagery.[11] But if this capacity is simply inborn, that is, if imagination were not the kind of activity that can be improved or maintained by training, then it wouldn't fit very well within the framework that we developed in Section 27.1. Let's call this *the nativist objection.*

To respond to this objection, I want to suggest that it is simply wrong about imagining. Just as one can become a better ballroom dancer or juggler via training and practice, so too can one become a better imaginer via training and practice. But before I address the issue of imaginative training directly, I want to consider a related skill to which one might think the same kind of objection would apply: memory. Someone who thinks that some people are just born with better imaginations than others will likely also think that some people are just born with better memories than others. Sure, perhaps we do some small things to improve our memories a little bit here and there, says this objector, but is memory really the kind of thing that can be improved with training?

Here, however, the answer is most definitely "yes." There have been various empirical studies that are relevant, but I'll here just mention one. This study, conducted by a team of researchers led by Anders Ericsson (Ericsson et al. 1980), aimed to see what kinds of improvements in memory could be achieved via a regular routine of practice sessions. The subject of the study was S.F., an undergraduate with average memory abilities and average intelligence. Over the course of 20 months, S.F. participated in hourlong practice sessions about three to five times a week. At the start of the study, S.F. could recall random sequences of digits from lists that were seven digits in length. At the end of the 20 months, S.F. was able to recall random sequences of digits from lists that were 79 digits in length. His ultimate performance compares favorably to known memory experts, e.g., the mnemonist S famously described by A.R. Luria (1968).

With respect to memory, then, performance can be massively improved by serious training.[12] What, then, about imagination? Is there reason to think that differences in imaginative capacity, unlike differences in memory capacity, must be simply innate and not the result of training?

I can't speak to this issue with respect to Kamiya. I simply haven't been able to find information one way or the other. But with respect to Tesla, we have testimony that suggests that his gifted imagination owes in large part to deliberate training. In his autobiographical essay "My Inventions," Tesla describes how he successfully developed his imaginative capacities as a child. The process started when, as part of an effort to rid himself of some "tormenting" images from experiences in his past (such as when he'd witnessed a funeral), he would concentrate on something else he had seen. While this would work temporarily, he soon realized that he needed to conjure up new and more interesting images to focus his mind. As he notes:

> I instinctively commenced to make excursions beyond the limits of the small world of which I had knowledge, and I saw new scenes. These were at first very blurred and indistinct, and would flit away when I tried to concentrate my attention upon them, but by and by I succeeded in fixing them; they gained in strength and distinctness and finally assumed the concreteness of real things. I soon discovered that my best comfort was attained if I simply went on in my vision farther and farther, getting new impressions all the time, and so I began to travel – of course, in my mind. Every night (and sometimes during the day), when alone, I would start on my journeys – see new places, cities and countries – live there, meet people and make friendships and acquaintances and, however unbelievable, it is a fact that they were just as dear to me as those in actual life and not a bit less intense in their manifestations.
>
> *Tesla 1919*

Of special interest to us is the fact that he was able to improve his imaginative abilities via effort and repetition. What was at first "blurred and indistinct" would eventually become strong and concrete.

Granted, the fact that these imaginative efforts began because he was afflicted by tormenting images suggests that he might have had some inborn capacity for imagination. But other activities typically thought of as skills have genetic components, and this does not count against their classification as cases of skills. No one denies that Michael Phelps is a very skilled swimmer, for example, but his genetics play a key role in making him so accomplished. He was born with an arm span longer than his height (unlike most people who have arm spans equal to their height), with the ability to hyperextend his joints, with a muscular system that produces only a low quantity of lactic acid, and so on. Likewise, sprinters tend to have more fast-twitch muscle fibers compared to marathon runners who have more slow-twitch muscle fibers. Even given these inborn advantages, however, swimmers and runners still need to train and practice to develop and maintain their skills.

The examples we have seen so far are probably enough to show that the nativist objection should be rejected, but there are two more classes of examples that it will be useful to have before us. Further evidence for the ability to train one's capacity for imagination can be found in the use of guided imagery in meditation practices and from the use of visualization techniques in sports. Alongside their physical training, many of the world's most highly skilled athletes have trained themselves to become highly skilled imaginers. At the 2016 Olympic games in Rio de Janeiro, the U.S. Olympic team brought along eight sports psychologists who specialize in visualization exercises. Such exercises involve the athletes visually imagining themselves achieving an intended outcome, a particular movement, or an entire routine. Some athletes go even further by imagining not only the actions that they want to perform but the overall context and scene in which they will be performing it, from the surrounding sights to surrounding sounds and smells. In an effort to become better at the actions they will need to perform, they work hard to become better at visualizing those actions.[13]

With the nativist objection overturned by this discussion of training, we are now brought to the third and final objection that I'll here consider – what I'll call the *no feedback objection*. In answering the nativist objection, we discussed various examples where people seem to have improved their imaginative capacities by way of training. But as the proponent of the no feedback objection will say, however that training proceeded, it seems to be a weird and nonstandard kind of training. Normally in training the trainee gets some kind of feedback that enables them to see whether they are doing better or worse. For example, when S.F. was being trained to memorize digits, he received feedback when he made mistakes, and in the next trial following a mistake, the sequence he was given went down by a digit. With respect to imaginative training, it is not clear how any such feedback could be given. How, then, can we ever tell that someone's imaginative capacities are actually improving? How can we have any criterion of success?

While this objection has more force than the previous two, I think that it too can be answered. With a little thought, we can see that there are ways to develop relevant training exercises with respect to imagination that would allow for the trainee to receive direct feedback. One possibility comes from image rotation tests of the sort that were done by Shepard and colleagues. In these tests, subjects were shown pairs of figures and asked to determine whether the second figure in the pair was identical (except for its rotation) to the first figure in the pair. While the experiments were initially designed for another purpose, they could easily be retooled into a slightly different experimental paradigm to work as training exercises for imagination.[14] Working with pairs of figures and asked to mentally rotate them to determine whether they were the same or different, subjects could be given direct feedback on whether their answers were correct. Moreover, when they can consistently make such determinations with figures of a certain degree of complexity, they could then be exposed to ones of greater complexity.

There are lots of similar kinds of experimental paradigms we might set up. An imagination trainer might buy a picture book of monsters and describe one to the trainee verbally and ask them to imagine what it looks like. The trainer could then show the trainee the picture and they could assess how well they did. Together they could go through the whole book. In this case, the trainee would be self-assessing, i.e., they would be giving the relevant feedback to themself. The trainer wouldn't be able to tell if what the trainee imagined really corresponded to what they were looking at, but the trainee would still be getting feedback. Moreover, if the trainee were a good artist, they could draw what they imagined and together with the trainer they could then compare the drawing to the picture in the book. This way, there would be direct feedback from the trainer on how well they were doing.

To give another example, suppose we wanted to see whether imaginative mindreading skills were improvable with training. A research team could recruit some undergraduates and hire them to work on their imaginative skills for an hour a day, three to five days a week. During this training, various emotional people would be brought in front of the undergraduates, who would be asked to look and listen and then to imagine what the people were feeling. When the undergraduates report their judgments, the trainers could provide immediate feedback as to whether and to what extent those judgments were accurate.[15]

I suspect that each of these three examples could be nitpicked – and I don't have any special expertise at experimental design – but the point here isn't really about whether these kinds of training exercises are particularly well-designed or especially effective. Rather, the point is that the possibility of imagination training *that provides feedback to the imaginer* is not an incoherent one. Just as we can provide feedback to ballroom dancers in training and rememberers in training, we can also provide feedback to imaginers in training.

27.4 Concluding remarks

As the discussion of this chapter has shown, imagination seems to fit the general model of skills-based activities developed in Section 27.1. It is under one's intentional control, can be done more or less well, and is improvable via practice/training. At this point, however, one final question arises. What are the philosophical benefits to thinking of imagination this way? What are the payoffs for philosophers in reminding ourselves that imagination is a skill?

I will here briefly mention three. First, as we started to see in Section 27.2 above, there are a lot of different senses of imagination in play in the current literature. It's my suspicion that thinking of imagination as a skill – or perhaps as a set of skills – has the potential to unify some of the discussion and also give us a principled way of carving up the terrain. Second, thinking of imagination as a skill helps us to make sense of some conflicting claims about imagination that we encounter in the philosophical literature. This literature is rife with disagreements about what can and cannot be imagined. While these disagreements are often taken as a sign that imagination is not to be trusted, as a reason to disparage imagination, reminding ourselves that imagination is a skill shows that such disagreements are not a bad sign but are exactly what should be expected. Given that imagination is a skill, people will vary in their imaginative capacities. Thus, when one person claims to be unable to imagine some state of affairs that another person claims to be able to imagine, rather than throwing up our arms in despair and viewing both claims with suspicion, we should instead explore whether one of the individuals might be a more gifted imaginer than the other. Third, and relatedly, thinking of imagination as a skill helps us to think more clearly about the limits of imagination. In particular, when we make claims about what can and cannot be imagined, and especially when we take those claims to have philosophical importance, we should be sure that the claims are based on what can and cannot be done by skilled imaginers. The fact that an unskilled runner cannot run a 100-meter course in under 10 seconds does not mean that it can't be done. Likewise, the fact that an unskilled imaginer cannot imagine some proposed state of affairs does not mean that it can't be done.

These three payoffs are specific to philosophical inquiry. But it's worth also noting that reminding ourselves that imagination is a skill has a further non-philosophical payoff. Claims are often made about the importance of imagination. Einstein, for example, famously said that imagination is more important than knowledge.[16] Recognizing that imagination is a skill can spur us to take action in inculcating it, both in ourselves and in our children. I close with a quotation from science fiction writer Ursula Le Guin that seems particularly apt in this context:

> The imagination is an essential tool of the mind, a fundamental way of thinking, an indispensable means of becoming and remaining human. We have to learn to use it, and how to use it, like any other tool. Children have imagination to start with, as they have body, intellect, the capacity for language: things essential to their humanity, things they need to learn how to use, how to use well. Such teaching, training, and practice should begin in infancy and go on throughout life. Young human beings need exercises in imagination as they need exercise in all the basic skills of life, bodily and mental: for growth, for health, for competence, for joy. This need continues as long as the mind is alive.
>
> *Le Guin 2016: 4*

Acknowledgments

Thanks to Ellen Fridland and Bence Nanay for helpful comments on a previous draft of this essay.

Notes

1 Thanks to Alon Chasid for pointing me to this example.
2 For a couple of passing references to imagination being a skill, see White (1990: 138) and Taylor (1981: 206).
3 While there are some other features of skill that Stanley and Krakauer mention, these additional features relate specifically to motor skills.
4 Stanley and Krakauer put this point in terms of "rational control," but in explicating what this means they say: "The manifestations of what we would colloquially describe as skills are *paradigm examples* of intentional action, and are hence under our rational control." It thus seems plausible that we can understand "rational control" as "intentional control." Doing so also enables us to ascribe skills to non-human animals whom we might be hesitant to characterize in terms of rationality.
5 For a nice discussion of the great variety of activities that are generally recognized as skills, see Fridland 2014: 79.
6 Stanley and Krakauer seem clearly to take each feature on the list to be necessary to skill, though they don't seem to intend these features to be jointly sufficient.
7 This case is lightly adapted from a case I used in Kind (2016a).
8 Compare Noë's discussion of digestion (Noë 2005: 279).
9 In what follows, I will usually just refer to "imagination" rather than "sensory and experiential imagination," but these are the types of imagination I will have in mind.

10 A third example comes from someone whose imaginative processes I've discussed at length in other work: Temple Grandin. See Kind (2016b) and Kind (2018). For her own descriptions of her imaginative processes, see Grandin (1995).

11 See Phillips (2014) for a useful overview of this literature.

12 Similar results have been achieved for other mental skills such as mental math. Researchers at Carnegie Mellon working with two ordinary undergraduates turned them into "lightning calculators" able to mentally solve multiplication problems involving two-digit by four-digit problems and two-digit by five-digit problems, e.g., 47×2568 or 59×79486. After about 300 hours of practice over four years, both undergraduates massively improved their performance and one of them became about as fast and as accurate as one of the known "expert" calculators. See Staszewski (1988).

13 For two discussions of these visualization techniques from the popular press, see Clarey (2014) and Maese (2016). For a scholarly overview, see Suinn (1994).

14 As originally utilized, image rotation experiments were meant to test whether the subjects' representations of the figures were pictorial in nature (Shepard and Metlzer 1971). Underlying the experiment was the thought that if a subject's response time corresponded to the amount the second figure would have to be rotated in order to confirm its similarity to the first figure (such that response time was longer when the figures needed more mental rotation and took shorter when the figures needed less mental rotation), that would suggest that subjects were working with pictorially encoded representations. Subsequent researchers have done work with image rotation figures that is relevant to the kind of imaginative training that I mention in the text above; see, e.g., Kail and Park (1990).

15 This example relates to the kind of empathy training often undergone by physicians discussed by Leslie Jamison (2014; see especially Ch. 1). It also relates to the kind of empathy exercises often used on college campuses in sexual assault ally training. For a discussion of empirical evidence that "supports the general hypothesis that individuals can be trained to harness their imaginative activities in order to increase their empathic abilities," see Frank (1978: 336).

16 This remark came in a 1929 interview with a reporter for the *Saturday Evening Post*. See www.saturdayeveningpost.com/2010/03/imagination-important-knowledge/

References

Clarey, C. (2014) "Olympians use imagery as mental training." (February 22, 2014) Available at www.nytimes.com/2014/02/23/sports/olympics/olympians-use-imagery-as-mental-training.html

Ericcson, K., Chase, W., and Faloon, S. (1980) "Acquisition of a memory skill," *Science*, 208(4448), pp. 1181–1182.

Frank, S.J. (1978) "Just imagine how I feel: How to improve empathy through training in imagination." In J. Singer and K. Pope, eds., *The Power of Human Imagination: New Methods in Psychotherapy*. New York: Springer US, pp. 309–346.

Fridland, E. (2014) "Skill learning and conceptual thought: Making our way through the wilderness." In Bana Bashour and Hans Muller, eds., *Contemporary Philosophical Naturalism and Its Implications*. New York: Routledge, pp. 77–100.

Grandin, T. (1995) *Thinking in Pictures*. New York: Random House.

Jamison, L. (2014) *The Empathy Exams*. Minneapolis, MN: Graywolf Press.

Kahn, J. (2006) "The extreme sport of origami," *Discover*, 27(7), pp. 60–63.

Kail, R. and Park, Y. (1990) "Impact of practice on speed of mental rotation," *Journal of Experimental Child Psychology*, 49(2), pp. 227–244.

Kind, A. (2018) "How imagination gives rise to knowledge." In F. Dorsch and F. Macpherson, eds., *Perceptual Memory and Perceptual Imagination*. Oxford: Oxford University Press, pp. 227–246.

—— (2016a) "Introduction: Exploring imagination." In A Kind, ed., *Routledge Handbook of Philosophy of Imagination*. Abingdon: Routledge, pp. 1–11.

—— 2016b "Imagining under constraints." In A. Kind and P. Kung, eds., *Knowledge Through Imagination*. Oxford: Oxford University Press, pp. 145–159.

—— (2001) "Putting the image back in imagination," *Philosophy and Phenomenological Research*, 62(1), pp. 85–109.

Kind, A. and Kung, P. (2016) "Introduction: The puzzle of imaginative use." In A. Kind and P. Kung, eds., *Knowledge Through Imagination*. Oxford: Oxford University Press, pp. 1–37.

Le Guin, U.K. (2016) "The operating instructions." In *Words Are My Matter*. Easthampton, MA: Small Beer Press, pp. 3–6.

Luria, A. (1968) *The Mind of a Mnemonist*. New York: Basic Books. Translated by Lynn Solotaroff.

Maese, R. (2016) "For Olympians, seeing (in their minds) is believing (it can happen)." *Washington Post* (July 28, 2016). Available at www.washingtonpost.com/sports/olympics/for-olympians-seeing-in-their-minds-is-believing-it-can-happen/2016/07/28/6966709c-532e-11e6-bbf5-957ad17b4385_story.html?utm_term=.aeb1b1195e5c

Noë, A. (2005) "Against intellectualism," *Analysis*, 65(4), pp. 278–290.

Pavese, C. (2016) "Skill in epistemology I: Skill and knowledge," *Philosophy Compass*, 11(11), pp. 642–649.

Phillips, I. (2014) "Lack of imagination: Individual differences in mental imagery and the significance of consciousness." In J. Kallestrup and M. Sprevak, eds., *New Waves in Philosophy of Mind*. London: Palgrave Macmillan, pp. 278–300.

Ryle, G. (1949) *The Concept of Mind*. Chicago, IL: University of Chicago Press.

Shepard, R. and Metzler, J. (1971) "Mental rotation of three-dimensional objects," *Science*, 171(3972), pp. 701–703.

Stanley, J. and Krakauer, J. (2013) "Motor skill depends on knowledge of facts," *Frontiers in Human Neuroscience*, 7, pp. 1–11.

Stanley, J. and Williamson, T. (2017) "Skill," *Noûs*, 51(4), pp. 713–726.

Staszewski, J.J. (1988) "Skilled memory and expert mental calculation." In M. Chi, R. Glaser, and M.J. Farr, eds., *The Nature of Expertise*. Hillsdale, NJ: Lawrence Erlbaum Associates, Inc., pp. 71–128.

Suinn, R. (1994) "Visualization in sports." In A. Sheikh and E. Korn, eds., *Imagery in Sports and Physical Performance*. Amityville, NY: Baywood Publishing Company, pp. 23–42.

Taylor, P. (1981) "Imagination and Information," *Philosophy and Phenomenological Research*, 42(2), pp. 205–223.

Tesla, N. (1921) "Making your imagination work for you," *American Magazine*. Available at https://teslauniverse.com/nikola-tesla/articles/making-your-imagination-work-you.

—— (1919) *My Inventions: The Autobiography of Nikola Tesla*, edited by Ben Jonhston (reprinted 2017 by Digireads.com).

White, A. (1990). *The Language of Imagination*. Oxford: B. Blackwell.

28

EMOTION RECOGNITION AS A SOCIAL SKILL

Gen Eickers and Jesse Prinz

28.1 Introduction

At first glance, emotion recognition seems to be a rather strange topic to characterize as a skill. A skill is usually referred to as something we learn and can improve with training. Emotions and emotion recognition, on the other hand, are often conceived as something that is innately within us and does not need to be learned or trained. Skills differ from mere instincts, in that they are sensitive to context, flexible, and potentially complex; emotion recognition, in contrast, is often presumed to involve strict mappings from features to categories. In addition, skills are characteristically practical, hence active, whereas recognition is paradigmatically passive. Here, we will take on this orthodoxy and argue that emotion recognition is a skill. A skill perspective on emotion recognition draws attention to underappreciated features of this cornerstone of social cognition. We will ultimately suggest, too, that emotions themselves may be skills.

In what follows, we will begin with a brief analysis of skills. We will then review prevailing theories of social cognition and argue that they are problematic in ways that imply failures to fully appreciate the extent to which emotion recognition is a skilled activity. After that, we will introduce our own preferred account, which appeals to the notions of scripts. The script account entails that emotion recognition is indeed a skill.

28.2 Skills

The term skill can be used in many ways, and the English term, which is quite broad in meaning, has no exact analogue in some languages (Pavese 2016a, 2016b). For the purposes of this discussion, we will characterize skills as having three features, already intimated above:

Improvability. Skills can vary in success, as a function of training together with individual differences.
Practicality. Skills are cases of know-how, which means their possessors can perform actions in virtue of possessing them.
Flexibility. Skills are context-sensitive, and are often complex, with parts that can be recombined to address variable features of context.

Pear (1928: 611), in a pioneering analysis, defines skill as "an integration of well-adjusted performances." Our notion of flexibility corresponds to Pear's analysis of integration; practicality echoes his concept of performance; and improvability captures his term "well-adjusted."

Improvability and practicality together imply that skills can be honed through practice: a form of training that involves doing. These alone might imply that skills are habits, but the third feature, flexibility, distinguishes skills from mere habits, which are usually conceived as relatively fixed responses to repeatable inputs (cf. Pear 1928). Flexibility and improvability distinguish skills from fixed abilities, such as the ability to curl your tongue, and practicality distinguishes skills from passive abilities, such as the ability to feel pain.

28.3 Standard accounts of emotion recognition

28.3.1 Evolved expression recognition

Much work on emotion recognition builds on the Darwinian view of emotional expression (Darwin 1872/1955). According to the standard reading of Darwin's view, each emotion elicits an emotional expression. That is, specific and visible physical changes in facial configuration, gestures, vocalization, and other physiological changes are caused by emotional states and can be used to detect an emotion. In the 20th century, Darwin's nativist approach to emotion recognition was taken up by Paul Ekman. Ekman and Friesen (1969, 1982; Ekman et al. 1988) developed an anatomical measure to detect and identify emotional expressions called the Facial Action Coding System (FACS). FACS relies on the minimal facial muscle actions needed to express a basic emotion (Awasthi and Mandal 2015). Each emotion corresponds to one or more patterns of facial actions. Facial expressions are standardized and quantified in FACS, so FACS can be used, and is frequently used, to test its assumptions. Ekman believes that FACS accurately represents the way that basic emotions are expressed, and also sheds light on how we ourselves recognize emotions. Much of his work has aimed to establish that certain expressions are universally recognized. This universality claim has become a widespread assumption in psychology.[1]

28.3.2 Accounts of social cognition

One can also extrapolate approaches to emotion recognition from prevailing accounts of social cognition. Social cognition accounts have come up with different explanations for the mechanism/s behind interpersonal understanding. "Interpersonal understanding" refers to a person's ability to understand persons, or other cognizant or sapient beings, as such. "Understanding" means finding something intelligible by classifying it, explaining it, and/or predicting how it will behave. Understanding of cognizant and sapient beings "as such" is meant to contrast with understanding inanimate things. When we encounter persons, we are capable of understanding their behavior in terms of underlying psychological states. Attribution of mental states is central to many social cognition accounts. That is, when one person interacts with another person (e.g., having a conversation about when to meet for dinner), both people, in order to understand the other's intentions, engage in attributing mental states to the other. This ability also includes emotional states. If we see a person weeping, we are able to interpret that as a sign of an emotional state.

28.3.2.1 Theory Theory

One of the leading accounts of social cognition is known as the Theory Theory. Theory Theorists say that, like theoretical explanation in science, mental-state attribution posits hidden causes and laws (e.g., Gopnik and Meltzoff 1997). Each of us uses a "folk psychology" on this view, which is a theory that, like scientific psychology, offers causal explanations with reference to hidden variables. For example, intentional actions are explained by appeal to beliefs and desires. These, in turn, are understood in terms of law-like causal roles: e.g., the desire that P will, ceteris paribus, cause us to try to make it the case that P (Fodor 1981). By analogy to science, such law-like principles are presumed to explain our success.

Theory Theorists do not typically offer theories of emotion recognition, but one can extrapolate that the approach is commited to something like causal inference: we infer from observations (such as approach behavior and expressions) to underlying mechanisms (such as desires and feelings), which are, in turn, understood in terms of their functional roles.

28.3.2.2 Simulation Theory

The other main approach for social cognition is Simulation Theory. At the most general level, Simulation Theory claims that we can understand and predict the actions of others by simulating them. That is, we use our own mechanisms for generating behavior to understand how others will act. This simulating process can proceed via low-level or high-level mechanisms (Gallese and Goldman 1998; Rizzolatti and Sinigaglia 2008). Low-level simulation helps us understand qualitative states. If we see someone in pain, we might imaginatively experience a state of pain, which then leads us to wince and prepare to withdraw and soothe the pain, leading us to form predictions about what the observed person in pain will do. High-level simulation is said to handle cases of mental states that may lack phenomenal qualities, such as beliefs. S. Niedenthal et al. (2017) claim that Simulation Theory is effective at describing and modeling how emotion recognition works. "Conceptual knowledge about emotion … can be represented by embodied simulation" (Niedenthal et al. 2017: 407). That is, if we see someone display anger, our bodies then conform to a comparable bodily state, which can facilitate prediction; e.g., we may predict that an angry person is inclined to aggress by introspecting our own vicarious anger.

Indeed, some authors even suggest that we cannot reliably recognize others' emotional expressions without routing through the brain systems that underlie our own emotions (Adolphs 2002a, 2002b). The idea here is that recognition is an empathetic process: we emulate the faces either overtly or by forming a motor plan, and then that overt or covert behavioral response excites the corresponding emotion. Sometimes this transition from observed expressions to inner feelings is said to be achieved by mirror neurons (Adolphs 2002a, 2002b). Mirror neurons are usually invoked to explain understanding of instrumental motor actions, such as grasping, but they have also been posited to explain emotion recognition (Gallese 2009). Thus, the simulation account comes with the added attraction of a possible neural mechanism.

28.3.2.3 Direct Perception

A more recent alternative is called Interaction Theory. Theory Theory and Simulation Theory deny that we have direct access to other minds. According to an Interaction Theory, which has been presented as the leading rival to these theories, we can directly perceive the mental states of others. Inference-based mechanisms and imagination are not necessary, according to this view, since our perception of other minds is direct; we simply pick up on all the information needed to make sense of social partners.

Gallagher and Hutto (2008), for example, claim that humans have a direct understanding of each other that is provided in seeing. Mental states, such as emotions, are directly perceivable because cognition is embodied and extended. This claim goes especially for emotions; they are perceivable since they are embodied (Gallagher and Varga 2013). While supporters of Direct Perception do not think we necessarily always perceive emotions directly, they do propose that there are sets of embodied elements that are specific to emotions. They conclude that emotion recognition works like pattern recognition (Gallagher and Varga 2013).

To summarize, imagine seeing an angry person. According to Theory Theory, we infer from observations (e.g., aggressive behavior) an inner state of anger; according to Simulation Theory, we spontaneously mimic the person, and then project the resulting inner experience, which is anger; according to Interaction Theory, anger is immediately perceived because it is literally written, or at least visible, on the person's face. The Darwinian view is most like this last alternative except that no assumption about directness is made; instead, we have an innate decoding mechanism akin to FACS.

28.4 Assessing leading accounts of emotion recognition

We now want to assess prevailing theories of emotion recognition and suggest that each of them faces serious objections. Along the way, we will suggest that these correspond to ways in which these theories fail to appreciate the role of skill in recognition. Proponents of each theory might devise responses to our objections, but we do think they motivate the search for other accounts. It will be the burden of Section 28.4 to sketch an alternative to the approaches that we are interrogating here.

28.4.1 Evolved expression recognition

As we have seen, the FACS developed in Paul Ekman's work on pancultural emotion recognition presupposes that there is a small set of emotions that can be recognized everywhere, and that universal recognition hangs, in turn, on a relatively fixed and univocal mapping between discrete emotions and movements of facial muscles. Here, we raise five reasons for doubt, synthesizing and expanding on objections in the literature.

First, some authors have argued that Ekman exaggerates the cross-cultural universality of his basic emotion expressions. In his influential cross-cultural research, Ekman tested recognition for six faces among the Fore, a group in Papua New Guinea, relatively isolated from the West. Using a forced choice method, Ekman claims that the Fore correctly associated each face with short vignettes indicating that they assign the same meaning to these faces as individuals in a Western comparison group. A closer look at the results suggests that this conclusion may be hasty. The vast majority of Fore do successfully identify a smile with a vignette that we interpret as involving happiness, but things are less clear for the other five emotions. For fear, anger, and disgust only about half the respondents make the predicted choice. This is better than chance, but hardly decisive evidence for a biologically fixed recognition program. For surprise and anger conditions, the Fore give responses that differ from Western respondents, replacing these emotions with fear and sadness, respectively. Thus, of the six tested expressions, the only one that gets impressive performance is happiness, which is the only positive emotion in the set. Of the five negatives, three show middling performance, and two go against Ekman's universalist hypothesis. Moreover, forced choice cannot settle whether a face was assigned the same meaning or whether it was just significantly better than other presented options (Russell 1994, 2003).

According to a second line of criticism, Ekman's FACS approach underappreciated the link between expression and behavior. A. Fridlund (1994) puts this starkly, saying that Ekman's expressions do not indicate emotions at all, but rather signal action plans. The so-called anger face indicates a plan to aggress on this view and smiling indicates readiness to affiliate. We think Fridlund pushes a bit too hard when he denies that such expressions can express emotions, but we share his conviction that expressions can be predictive of action. As such, they also invite or even demand actions from observers. Anger expressions invite various defense behaviors, and tears invite attending to an individual's suffering. Crucially, the invited behavior may be very sensitive to context.

A third line of objections challenges the theory of emotions underlying Ekman's account. Some researchers challenge the discrete emotion view, suggesting that our emotion terms actually label socially constructed assemblies of simpler psychological units (Barrett 2012). We believe in discrete emotions and have defended them elsewhere (Eickers et al. 2017), but we side with constructivists in saying that emotions may not be biologically fixed as Ekman supposes. Feleky (1916), for example, uses dozens of faces, not just six, and a large vocabulary of emotion terms. Her list includes such states as faith, enthusiasm, resolution, firmness, hope, interest, yearning, coyness, among many others. While it seems unlikely that there is a facial action uniquely corresponding to each of these, a good actor would have no difficulty embodying any of them, and, given context, an audience could decipher the meaning. In some cases, the expression may be the result of explicit cultural learning. Faith, for example, could be expressed in Christian cultures with hands clasped in prayer and glance toward the heavens. Cultures use gestures to express gratitude, approval, pride, offense, and many other things. Facial expressions may also reflect such cultural learning, and culture may even cultivate distinctive emotions.

A fourth worry concerns methodology: forced choice methodology has also been challenged with domestic samples (Russell 1994, 2003; Barrett et al. 2007; Barrett 2012). The very same face might have many different meanings. When an experimental design builds in a one-to-one mapping with pre-selected vignettes, it will inevitably provide support for Ekman's univocal meaning theory. But suppose an experiment included multiple vignettes that could go with a given face. To take an example from Barrett, a screaming face could indicate terror, rage, or the joy of victory. Tears can indicate despair, pride, nostalgia, relief, or joy, as when a beauty contestant wins a contest. A smile might indicate happiness, nervousness, embarrassment, or derision.

A final worry, already hinted at, is that the FACS approach is radically decontextualized. Ekman trains people to recognize faces using FACS in a way that abstracts from context. Learners are supposed to know what someone is feeling from the face alone. In real life this seems implausible. We usually have a lot of contextual information, and there is good reason to think (as already noted) that this contributes to recognition. Context can matter in a variety of ways. First, consider the individuals involved. A smile from a coach can mean approval; from a friend it can indicate affection or support; from a flirtation partner it can signal romantic interest. Situational context matters too. A smile after opening a door for someone will connote gratitude; a smile at a political protest can express solidarity. There are many social norms about when to smile, and these play a role in interpretation. The FACS approach may help us understand something about default meanings, but, by abstracting away from context, there is little reason to think that the interpretation dictated by FACS reveals the meaning of the expressions we encounter in real life.

This suggests that, for Ekman, there is an innate version of FACS in an encapsulated module, which differs from the FACS methods used in his workshops. Our ordinary capacity for recognition is biologically given. If culture shapes emotions, in contrast, recognition must depend heavily on learning, and is thus improvable. The Darwinian approach also treats recognition passively, with no link to action. Our third objection hints at the possibility that recognition carries immediate practical implications, and thus that a good theory of recognition must be practical. The fourth and fifth objections point out that expressions are ambiguous, and this requires more flexibility than Darwinians tend to allow. In sum, the Darwinian theory underestimates improvability, practicality, and flexibility, or, in a word, skill.

28.4.2 Theory Theory

For Theory Theorists, we might suppose that each emotion is understood as an inner state that has law-like effects. If we see a person yelling, for example, we might infer that they are angry, because of a law that tells us that anger is an inner state that tends to cause people to raise their voices. This sounds plausible enough, but there are at least two reasons to resist the Theory Theory of emotion recognition.

First, Theory Theory emphasizes understanding rather than interaction; it underestimates practicality. Philosophers often distinguish between theoretical and practical rationality. Theoretical reasoning is a kind of inference that one does from the position of a passive observer. Its aim is comprehension and explanation rather than action. Practical deliberation tells us how to act. We certainly recognize that emotion recognition can be largely passive, as when we watch a film or read a novel. But, more often, it arises in contexts where we are active or potentially active participants. Here recognition is bound up with reaction. Observed emotions compel us to respond, and knowing what they are partially involves knowing what they demand from us. Theory Theory could represent such knowledge in the form of action-guiding causal roles, but such a move would depart from the spirit of the approach, which emphasizes an analogy between social cognition and scientific explanation. It also departs from the idea that mental states are hidden entities with causal powers. Observed emotions do not cause us to act the way a pool cue causes a ball to roll. Our responses are compelled by overarching social norms. The link to action is normative, rather than descriptive—externally and symbolically mediated, rather than physically evoked.

Second, the emphasis on law-like principles makes Theory Theory ill-equipped to accommodate the kind of context sensitivity we have been discussing. One might think there are laws like this: If one is angry, one will yell, ceteris paribus. This loses intuitive appeal, however, when one starts to think about how one would fill in the ceteris paribus clause. There is an open-ended set of conditions in which yelling would not occur during an episode of anger, and no set of conditions under which yelling always arises. There is not a causal disposition to yell that operates reliably within some boundary conditions. Whether anger promotes yelling is constrained by personality, intended aims, attitudes toward current interaction partners, social roles, situational context, and culturally specific norms.

One might try to push for Theory Theory by pointing out that emotion recognition sometimes resembles the scientific method: there can be hypothesis formation and testing. Suppose a friend stops responding to your email, and you infer that they might be mad at you. You can test your hypothesis by asking or looking for other signs of anger, or by investigating a competing hypothesis: maybe they are just busy. This looks like theory testing, and we certainly do not want to rule out that this sometimes occurs. We would note two things in response, however. First, such hypothesis testing is probably infrequent in emotion recognition. Second, and more importantly, even this would not entail a Theory Theory account of emotions. Hypothesis testing can occur in domains that do not principally involve hidden variables and laws (as when a detective investigates a crime, or a historian explains a war). When wondering whether your friend is mad, you don't need to suppose that there is law-like generalization linking anger and email inactivity. Rather, the link is less directed, and might itself have many intervening pathways: are they avoiding you, allowing themselves time to cool down, giving you time to apologize, or trying to make you suffer? You may not have a hypothesis about this. Instead, you are relying on a multiply realized regularity between emotions and email behavior, with beliefs about the underlying motives. We think the theory analogy distracts from the real ends of emotion recognition. As social agents, we are not trying to arrive at good models of human behavior; we are trying to figure out what our interaction partners are feeling on each particular occasion, so we can decide what to do about it. The theory analogy removes social cognition from its practical orientation, aiming at fixed rules rather than flexible, action-oriented skills.

28.4.3 Simulation Theory

Let us turn now to Theory Theory's most prominent competitor: Simulation Theory. Unlike Theory Theory, which is only rarely emphasized in accounts of emotion recognition, Simulation Theory is often said to play a role.

This is not the place to fully assess mirror neuron accounts of Simulation Theory, but we do harbor some skepticism (for general critiques, cf. Heyes 2010; Hickok 2014; Brinker 2015). For present purposes, let it suffice to recall that the mapping between expressions and emotions is many to many, so no brain cell could be charged with responding to both an emotional expression and the corresponding emotion, since many emotions would correspond. The deficits in emotion recognition that have been recorded in patients with impaired emotions do not establish that there are individual cells doing such double duty. It may just be that flattening of a given emotion tends to make us neglect that emotion when ignoring others, just as a person who is impervious to insults may forget that others are less so.

These remarks on mirror neurons draw attention to the fact that simulating a facial expression is not sufficient for understanding it. Expressions are ambiguous. Equally obvious is the fact that simulations are not necessary. We can interpret expressions without engaging in emotional imagination. For example, we might come to recognize the fluffed-up feathers of birds as a mating signal without being overtaken by attraction for birds (similarly for swollen monkey butts and canine erections). Likewise, there is no reason to suppose that simulation is necessary for recognition of human emotions.

Conceding this, the Simulation Theorist might say that simulation is not necessary but that it often plays a role, nonetheless, for example, in vicarious emotions. But consider what happens when we see the joy of those we detest, like crowds cheering for a political candidate whose agenda we adamantly oppose. Here, the recognition of joy may be accompanied by seething hatred. Vicarious emotions do not entail that simulation is used to arrive at an attribution. It seems at least as likely that vicarious emotions are the result of attribution, not the other way around. Consider cases where we feel joy on hearing of a friend's good news. This would occur without seeing the friend's expression. Seeing someone writhe in pain might seem to be the exception here, since the vicarious response seems to be so fast and automatic that it is hard to imagine an intervening interpretive step. Simulation Theorists sometimes call this low-level simulation. But research suggests that vicarious pain is mitigated by such things as outgroup bias and social status (Brewer et al. 1993; Brewer and Silver 2000; Fiske 2004; Heyes 2011; Fischer and Manstead 2016) and knowledge that the person in pain deserves to be punished (Singer et al. 2008, though this mitigation effect was observed only in men). Thus, seeing pain does not always lead to vicarious pain. Social and situational knowledge play a role here. The appearance of automaticity and immediacy may be deceptive.

We have been suggesting that simulation is neither necessary nor sufficient for emotion attribution, and also that it is unlikely to be the primary means by which we recognize emotions. We have one final worry about Simulation Theory, which is that it tends to underestimate the rich intricacy of emotion comprehension. The emphasis on imitation might lead one to think that the most important consequence of an emotional state is the expression that it causes. Emotions do much more than make us smile or frown. Each emotion has a complex and varied range of causes and effects. Emotion recognition is not simply a matter of imaginatively recovering the feeling underlying a face. It may involve reconstructing background, understanding circumstances, and thinking through possible coping strategies and outcomes. Recognition involves bringing to bear knowledge of the roles that emotions play in human life.

Simulation Theory could, in principle, accommodate this. It could say that we interpret other people's emotions by engaging our own elaborate, socially governed emotion rules. But this move would place its explanatory burdens on the content of those roles, not simulation as such. What is to be gained by insisting that it is our own first-personal rules that guide emotion understanding rather than third-personal rules? We think these rules may be one and the same. A rule that makes sense of others' behavior may also be one that we rely on when deciding what to do. If so, there is a collapse between Simulation Theory and an alternative account that makes no mention of simulation. Worse still, the insistence that we use our own rules belies the fact that emotions operate differently in different individuals. Consider gender norms. In a patriarchy, men might be expected to act callously while women are expected to show feelings under certain circumstances. A man who has conformed to this role can nevertheless make sense of a norm-conforming woman. He does so by virtue of his mastery of these norms, not by imagining how he would act. *Ex hypothesi*, the rules that govern his behavior differ from the rules that govern hers. Such role-specific variability is a pervasive phenomenon, and, once this is brought to the fore, the simulation approach loses much of its initial appeal.

These objections can be summarized by pointing out that Simulation Theory is inadequately flexible—spontaneous simulations are more like habits than skills. Simulation Theory also places little emphasis on improvability and practicality: it emphasizes innate mechanisms (mirror neurons) and treats the main function of recognition as mental-state attribution rather than behavioral interaction.

28.4.4 Direct Perception

Direct Perception seems comparatively practical in orientation, since its proponents emphasize real-time interaction. We like this aspect of the approach but we do not think it is helpful to characterize emotion recognition as direct.

The directness claim implies that emotion attribution can be inferred from what is presented perceptually, without reliance on background knowledge or context. This makes emotion recognition look more like a habit than a skill: a fixed mapping from inputs to outputs. But background information often matters. Consider cultural differences in politeness norms: an American who fails to smile and say thank you may seem disgruntled, but a Russian who did the same, would strike a knowledgeable interaction partner as quite ordinary. Recognition requires flexibility. Recognition is also improvable, and this improvement often involves learning about cultural norms, not learning to pick up on subtle perceptual cues, as Direct Perception Theorists imply.

Another pressing problem with Direct Perception, which also threatens the other theories, is that it does not account for dehumanization. The theories seem to assume that, given certain inputs such as a facial expression, we will automatically attribute mental states (via Direct Perception on this account, or by FACS mechanisms, theoretical inference, or simulation). Given the same input we should assign the same emotional significance. With dehumanization, this does not happen. When viewing the expression of an outgroup member, for example, we assign less emotional meaning than the corresponding expression would receive for the in-group. We think dehumanization depends on extra-sensory processes. For example, when a white person underestimates pain in a person of color, there is no failure to see the pain expression; rather there is a failure to regard the person as fully sentient, or perhaps a racist belief that non-white people can tolerate harsh treatment. Such examples show that recognition is not just a perceptual skill, but a social skill—a skill involving social knowledge and resulting in more or less successful responses to social situations.

As we have seen, emotion recognition is highly flexible, improvable, and practical; it is important for social interactions. Prevailing theories face many objections, and most of these correspond to failures to fully appreciate these features. In the following, we want to propose a script-based account of emotion recognition, that places emphasis on improvability, practicality, and flexibility—an account that treats rejection as a skill.

28.5 A proposal: emotion recognition via scripts

We offer a sketch of our alternative here. We are content to show that it has advantages over rivals and deserves consideration. As will become clear, our preferred approach is also more overtly skill-like in key respects, and this, we shall argue, is one of its key strengths.

28.5.1 Scripts

There is already a considerable body of research out there explaining how emotions can be understood by appeal to scripts. We will describe this work before turning to emotion recognition.

Russell formulated the perhaps best-known script account of emotions (Russell 1994, 2003; see also Hochschild 1979; Averill 1980). Following Lakoff, he considers emotions to have different components and to be scripts in the sense of being a sequence of subevents (Lakoff 1987; Russell 1994, 2003). The subevents include: causes, beliefs, feelings, physiological changes, desires, overt actions, and vocal and facial expressions (Russell 1994, 2003). Those different subevents are sequentially related and together make up an emotion. By stating that an emotion works like a script (i.e., an emotion's "features are ordered … in much the same way that actions are ordered in a playwright's script" (Russell 1991: 442; see also Russell 1994, 2003)), Russell implies that an emotion is something like an action, and an emotion is something we can learn about. This goes against the standard orthodoxy according to which emotions are passive and innate.

Emotion scripts differ from playwright's scripts in that they are not always rigidly followed. Rather, we think they embody norms, in both the statistical and philosophical sense (Eickers 2019). They describe what we should come to expect, based on prior experience, but also what might be expected of us as appropriately conforming members of society. A love script that includes courtship, dating, and ultimately cohabitation tells us that this is how love operates in our society, while also promoting such a pattern of behavior. This behavior may include physical actions, such as handholding or staring into a lover's eyes, as well as more protracted actions, such as going on a date.

Evidence for learning of scripts can be found in the aforementioned fact that emotions differ cross-culturally. For example, there are culturally specific behaviors such as bowing, flicking-off, and clapping. In addition, cultures differ in whether they encourage people to act aggressively when angry or to quietly sulk or brood (see Goddard (1996) on Malaysia), while other cultures discourage brooding (see Briggs (1970) on the Ifaluk). This suggests that anger is not an automatic response with a fixed action tendency, but rather a role that we act out in culturally prescribed ways. That doesn't mean people take themselves to be merely pretending or performing when they respond emotionally. The sociologist Arlie Hochschild compared emotional episodes to "deep acting"—a kind of performance that we are so caught up with that we do not realize we are performing.

We take Russell's understanding of scripts as a starting place for our proposal. Following Russell, we understand scripts to be meaningful, context-dependent entities we acquire over time through practice and thus mastery.[2]

28.5.2 Scripted emotions

Influenced by Russell's account of emotions as scripts, various researchers have come up with proposals about how exactly emotions are to be conceived of as something one is actively engaged in rather than something that is happening to us in a passive manner. The script approach also draws attention to the fact that emotions often unfold in social settings.

Fridlund (1994) and Griffiths and Scarantino (2009), for example, argue that both culturally learned practices and also situational contexts are crucial for emotion. For example, a display of anger might be useful when trying to get a non-compliant social partner to act, but it might be harmful when trying to restore calm during a squabble with a loved one. The transactional model suggests that emotions are designed to function in social contexts; that is, they are socially situated goal-oriented responses. Griffiths and Scarantino (2009: 438) describe emotions as "signals designed to influence the behavior of other organisms, or as strategic moves in ongoing transaction between organisms."

Fischer, too, considers emotion to be scripted. She portrays a developmental perspective on emotion scripts and describes how children, by being constantly exposed to others and to media, and simply by being members of the social world—that is, taking part in social activities (e.g., communication)—acquire emotion scripts (Fischer 1991; Parkinson et al. 2005).

28.5.3 Scripting emotion recognition

Our proposal here is to extend Russell's approach and emotional transaction theory to emotion recognition. We will argue, based on the information and arguments provided in the previous sections, that emotion recognition works via scripts.[3] If knowing the meaning of emotion terms includes knowledge of scripts (Russell 1994, 2003), and if having emotions also involves following scripts, then it is plausible that emotion recognition works via these very scripts.[4] That is, we associate each emotion with a range of context-specific scenarios in which interacting individuals behave in specific ways, and when we see a situation unfold that resembles one of these scenarios, we use this knowledge to predict what will unfold, and to participate depending on what role we happen to occupy.

As a simple example, consider various anger scripts we might have: demanding to speak to a manager in a store, pouting after being insensitively treated by a lover, shouting in sync at a political demonstration, and scolding a child who misbehaves. These are extremely different behaviors that require considerable cultural knowledge, yet they are all forms of anger. To recognize them as such, we need to be able to interpret a range of expressions (a firm demand to speak to a manager, a curled lip, a rhythmic shout, parental finger-wag). The script theory of emotions invites a script theory of recognition. We know that the pouting lover is mad, and not, say, sad or merely moody, because we recognize that such displays have a standard communicative role in that context. The pout says, "I don't like how you've treated me, and I won't show affection until you make amends." Recovering this meaning requires interpretation, and scripts are well-suited to play a role in that.

On any account of emotions, there is a performative aspect to expression. Thus, a script-based approach to recognition may be attractive even to those who resist the script-based theory of emotions that we have been endorsing.

28.5.4 Script-based emotion recognition as a skill

Our proposal for a script-based approach entails that emotion recognition is a form of skillful engagement. Using scripts can be thought of as a skill. Just, the mechanism underlying emotion recognition is script following—speaking of skills describes a phenomenon, not a mechanism.

On the analysis given in Section 28.1, skills have three features that distinguish them from related notions such as habits and mere abilities: they are improvable, practical, and flexible. Each of these applies to the script-based theory of emotion recognition.

Let's begin with improvability. Though not explicitly emphasized in script theories, it is implicit in one of the central tenets of that approach: scripts and script-based recognition skills are not innate. There may be considerable innate contributions to our emotion scripts, but they get elaborated in ways that reflect cultural norms. This means that recognition of emotional scripts requires learning. This can be seen when we move from one culture to another, and find ourselves unsure of the local emotional cues. There will also be individual differences. Introverts may get less practice at emotion recognition, for example, and frequent travelers may gain skills in emotional translation. In relationships, we learn to recognize emotions of those we love, and good managers can feel the pulse of their teams.

Script theory also entails flexibility. Recall the example of anger scripts that differ in their expression depending on context: we need to adapt to contexts in order to be able to make sense of these displays. Here emotion scripts differ from scripts used on stage, which tend to be fixed. Emotion scripts can be recombined and adapted (Eickers 2019). For example, if you never misgendered someone, you might discover that doing so causes anger and is not remedied by making excuses; you learn, thereby, that misgendering is an occasion for apologizing.

Practicality is also a central commitment of the script approach. Unlike Theory Theory and Simulation Theory, which emphasize attribution, scripts are tools for behavioral interaction, and one cannot recognize that a script is being instantiated without thereby knowing how one might respond. Theory Theory implies that emotion recognition is a kind of know-how, like knowing the names of US presidents; simulation treats recognition as an instinctive habit, and Interaction Theory treats recognition as an emotional ability. Script theory, in contrast, treats emotions on the model of know-how.

28.5.5 Three objections

Before concluding, we want to consider three objections to the script theory focusing specifically on our claim that emotion recognition is a skill. First, with respect to improvability, one might think we have moved too far beyond Darwinian models. Granting that culture can have some impact on how emotions are expressed, there are decades of research suggesting that people can recognize decontextualized faces, and this suggests that some recognition is both innate and independent of scripts.

We reject this interpretation of such research. Success in decontextualized facial recognition is measured by experimenters' a priori stipulations about what those faces signify. In the real world, faces are always contextualized, and research shows that context matters, including vocalizations, postures, surrounding faces, situations, and settings (Wieser and Brosch 2012). Considered in isolation, faces are always ambiguous (Fernández-Dols and Crivelli 2013), and the features that help to fix interpretations speak to the role that the emotion is playing, as predicted by a script theory.

Second, one might worry that our theory fails to satisfy the practicality requirement. Scripts include knowledge of social interactions, but, for all we have said, that could be knowledge that rather than knowledge how. Perhaps script theory, like Theory Theory, is committed only to the view that emotion recognition deploys beliefs about how emotions impact behavior rather than physical dispositions to react.

We grant that there has been too little empirical work on the physical impact of emotion recognition on recognizers, but we venture a conjecture. Since emotion recognition ordinarily serves social interaction, rather than mere third-person attribution, there is good reason to think that recognition instigates or constitutively involves behavioral dispositions. Think about how your body reacts when confronted with someone very angry. You might cower in fear, or aggress in retaliation, or apologize or try to calm. It is hard to be indifferent. On our view, this is because the recognition of an emotion immediately brings to mind context-specific scenarios in which the emoter acts and others react. Emoting involves doing something and that places demands on others who are present and recognize the emotion.

Third, turning to flexibility, one might think that the script-based theory is too cognitive to qualify as a skill. It requires knowing facts about culture and can be applied in the context of deliberation (as when we ask ourselves, "I wonder if that email means they are mad at me?"). In contrast, skills have traditionally been understood to be low-level (Dreyfus 2004), and are often equated with motoric responses.

We offer two replies. First, in recent years, arguments against a low-level understanding of skills have come up, and researchers have developed definitions of skill that involve higher cognitions to different degrees, even in cases where there is a motor component (Fridland 2014, 2016; Christensen et al. 2016). E. Fridland (2014: 83) claims that "in order for a skill to be successfully instantiated, one must adjust, shift, and respond to the very particular features of the environment in which the skill is being performed." That is, according to Fridland, the motor system is directly responsive to higher-order cognitions, and specifically to personal-level goals. Our account of script-based emotion recognition is consistent with this aspect of Fridland's analysis.

In addition, we think the knowledge contained in scripts need not be entirely propositional in the way "higher-cognition" implies. Scripts incorporate behavioral dispositions, as pointed out in response to the proceeding objection. The flexibility they embody is not simply a matter of knowing what a contextualized emotion signifies, but knowing how to respond fluidly in real time. Consider the difference between someone who "over-thinks" the emotions expressed by others. Their response may seem stilted. Someone more skilled at emotion recognition, like a fluent language speaker, will respond without skipping a beat, and that suggests a kind of knowledge that has been integrated with behavior. Consider the host who notices a guest looking slightly alienated and immediately approaches with a warm, but not overwhelming smile. The host doesn't say, "let me smile thusly"—the smile just arises.

In sum, we think emotion recognition is essentially contextual, intelligent, and embodied. These features are underemphasized by other accounts, and integral to skills.

28.6 Conclusion

Our discussion began with an analysis of skills as improvable, practical, and flexible. We think these three features are also essential to an adequate theory of emotion recognition. Prevailing theories of emotion recognition do not always recognize this. For example, Darwinian theories underestimate improvability by emphasizing innateness, the Theory Theory underestimates practicality by focusing on theory-like knowledge, and Simulation Theory underestimates flexibility by assuming that we can recover any emotion by bodily imitation, rather than drawing on knowledge of culture and context. These and other problems motivated a search for an alternative theory. We proposed that emotion recognition involves scripts and that scripts are improvable, practical, and flexible. Scripts, in other words, are skills. We have only sketched this alternative here, but we hope we have offered enough to motivate further investigation, and, more generally, to approach emotion recognition as a skilled practice.

Acknowledgments

We are grateful to Ellen Fridland and Michael Brownstein for supremely helpful comments.

Notes

1 Universality claim: Tomkins 1962, 1963; Ekman 1972; Izard 1994, 2011; Matsumoto et al. 2008; Ekman and Cordaro 2011; Tracy and Randles 2011; Tracy 2014.
2 In Section 28.4.4 we compare Russell's account of scripts and our understanding of scripts to Dreyfus's approach to skill and expertise (Russell 1994, 2003; Dreyfus 2004).
3 This is not necessarily an extension of Russell's approach but more of an exemplification of what implicitly follows from some of Russell's statements, e.g.:

> In short, according to the script hypothesis, categories of emotion are defined by features. The features describe not hidden essences but knowable subevents … . To know the meaning of a term like happiness, fear, or jealousy is to know a script for that emotion. In other words, the script hypothesis is that the meaning of each such word, the concept it expresses, is a script.
>
> *Russell 2003*

4 We use "emotional expression" as an umbrella term that includes vocal and facial expressions (Russell 2003).

References

Adolphs, R. (2002a) "Recognizing Emotion from Facial Expressions: Psychological and Neurological Mechanisms," *Behavioral and Cognitive Neuroscience Reviews* 1: 21–62.
—— (2002b) "Processing of Emotional and Social Information by the Human Amygdala," in M. Gazzaniga (ed.) *The Cognitive Neurosciences*, Cambridge, MA: MIT Press.
Averill, J. R. (1980) "A Constructivist View of Emotion," in R. Plutchik and H. Kellerman (eds.) *Theories of Emotion*, Vol. 1, San Diego, CA: Academic Press, pp. 305–39.
Awasthi, A., and Mandal, M. K. (2015) "Facial Expressions of Emotions: Research Perspectives," in A. Awasthi and M. Mandal (eds.) *Understanding Facial Expressions in Communication: Cross-Cultural and Multidisciplinary Perspectives*, New Delhi. India: Springer, pp. 1–18.
Barrett, L. F. (2012) "Emotions Are Real," *Emotion* 12: 413–29.
Barrett, L. F., Lindquist, K. A., and Gendron, M. (2007) "Language as Context for the Perception of Emotion," *Trends in Cognitive Science* 11: 327–32.

Brewer, M. B., and Silver, M. D. (2000) "Group Distinctiveness, Social Identification, and Collective Mobilization," in S. Stryker, T. Owens, and R. White (eds.) *Self, Identity, and Social Movements*, Minneapolis, MN: University of Minnesota Press, pp. 153–71.

Brewer, M. B., Manzi, J. M., and Shaw, J. S. (1993) "In-Group Identification as a Function of Depersonalization, Distinctiveness, and Status," *Psychological Science* 4: 88–92.

Briggs, J. L. (1970) *Never in Anger: Portrait of an Eskimo Family*, Cambridge, MA: Harvard University Press.

Brinker, M. (2015) "Beyond Sensorimotor Segregation: On Mirror Neurons and Social Affordance Space Tracking," *Cognitive Systems Research* 34: 18–34.

Christensen, W., Sutton, J., and McIlwain, D. F. J. (2016) "Cognition in Skilled Action: Meshed Control and the Varieties of Skill Experience," *Mind & Language* 31: 37–66.

Darwin, C. (1872/1955) *The Expression of the Emotions in Man and Animals*, New York: The Philosophical Library.

Dreyfus, S. E. (2004) "The Five-Stage Model of Adult Skill Acquisition," *Bulletin of Science, Technology & Society* 24: 177–81.

Eickers, G. (2019) *Scripted Alignment: A Theory of Social Interaction*, Diss., Freie Universität Berlin.

Eickers, G., Loaiza, J., and Prinz, J. (2017) "Embodiment, Context-Sensitivity, and Discrete Emotions: A Response to Moors," *Psychological Inquiry* 28: 31–8.

Ekman, P. (1972) *Emotions in the Human Face*, New York: Pergamon Press.

Ekman, P., and Cordaro, D. (2011) "What Is Meant by Calling Emotions Basic," *Emotion Review* 3: 364–70.

Ekman, P., and Friesen, W. V. (1969) "The Repertoire of Nonverbal Behavior: Categories, Origins, Usage, and Coding," *Semiotica* 1: 49–98.

—— (1982) "Felt, False and Miserable Smiles," *Journal of Nonverbal Behavior* 6: 238–52.

Ekman, P., Friesen, W. V., and O'Sullivan, M. (1988) "Smiles When Lying," *Journal of Personality and Social Psychology* 54: 414–20.

Feleky, A. (1916) "The Influence of the Emotions on Respiration," *Journal of Experimental Psychology* 1: 218–41.

Fernández-Dols, J. M., and Crivelli, C. (2013) "Emotion and Expression: Naturalistic Studies," *Emotion Review* 5: 24–9.

Fischer, A. H. (1991) *Emotion Scripts: A Study of the Social and Cognitive Aspects of Emotion*, Leiden, Netherlands: DSWO-Press.

Fischer, A. H., and Manstead, A. S. R. (2016) "Social Functions of Emotion and Emotion Regulation," in L. Barrett, M. Lewis, and J. Haviland-Jones (eds.) *Handbook of Emotions*, New York: Guilford Press, pp. 456–69.

Fiske, A. P. (2004) "Four Modes of Constituting Relationships: Consubstantial Assimilation; Space, Magnitude, Time, and Force; Concrete Procedures; Abstract Symbolism," in N. Haslam (ed.) *Relational Models Theory: A Contemporary Overview*, Mahwah, NJ: Lawrence Erlbaum Associates, pp. 61–146.

Fodor, J. A. (1981) *Representations*, Cambridge, MA: MIT Press.

Fridland, E. (2014) "Skill Learning and Conceptual Thought: Making Our Way Through the Wilderness," in B. Bashour and H. Muller (eds.) *Philosophical Naturalism and Its Implications*, New York and London: Routledge, pp. 77–100.

—— (2016) "Skill and Motor Control: Intelligence All the Way Down," *Philosophical Studies* 174: 1539–60.

Fridlund, A. J. (1994) *Human Facial Expression: An Evolutionary View*, San Diego, CA: Academic Press.

Gallagher, S., and Hutto, D. (2008) "Understanding Others Through Primary Interaction and Narrative Practice," in J. Zlatev, T. Racine, C. Sinha, and E. Itkonen (eds.) *The Shared Mind: Perspectives on Intersubjectivity*, Amsterdam, Netherlands: John Benjamins, pp. 17–38.

Gallagher, S., and Varga, S. (2013) "Social Constraints on the Direct Perception of Emotions and Intentions," *Topoi* 33: 185–99.

Gallese, V. (2009) "Mirror Neurons, Embodied Simulation, and the Neural Basis of Social Identification," *Psychoanalytic Dialogues* 19: 519–36.

Gallese, V., and Goldman, A. (1998) "Mirror Neurons and the Simulation Theory of Mind-Reading," *Trends in Cognitive Sciences* 12: 493–501.

Goddard, C. (1996) "The 'Social Emotions' of Malay (Behasa Melayu)," *Ethos* 24: 426–64.

Gopnik, A., and Meltzoff, A. N. (1997) *Words, Thoughts, and Theories*, Cambridge, MA: MIT Press.

Griffiths, P. E., and Scarantino, A. (2009) "Emotions in the Wild: The Situated Perspective on Emotion," in P. Robbins and M. Aydede (eds.) *Handbook of Situated Cognition*, Cambridge, UK: Cambridge University Press, pp. 437–53.

Heyes, C. (2010) "Where Do Mirror Neurons Come From?" *Neuroscience and Biobehavioral Reviews* 34: 575–83.

—— (2011) "What's Social About Social Learning?" *Journal of Comparative Psychology* 126: 193–202.

Hickok, G. (2014) *The Myth of Mirror Neurons: The Real Neuroscience of Communication and Cognition*, New York: WW Norton & Company.

Hochschild, A. R. (1979) "Emotion Work, Feeling Rules, and Social Structure," *American Journal of Sociology* 85: 551–75.

Izard, C. E. (1994) "Innate and Universal Facial Expressions: Evidence from Developmental and Cross-Cultural Research," *Psychological Bulletin* 115: 288–99.

—— (2011) "Forms and Functions of Emotions: Matters of Emotion–Cognition Interactions," *Emotion Review* 3: 371–8.

Lakoff, G. (1987) *Women, Fire and Dangerous Things: What Categories Reveal About the Mind*, Chicago, IL: University of Chicago Press.

Matsumoto, D., Keltner, D., Shiota, M. N., Frank, M. G., and O'Sullivan, M. (2008) "What's In a Face? Facial Expressions as Signals of Discrete Emotions," in M. Lewis, J. M. Haviland, and L. Feldman Barrett (eds.) *Handbook of Emotions*, New York: Guilford Press, pp. 211–34.

Niedenthal, P., Rychlowska, M., and Wood, A. (2017) "Feelings and Contexts: Socioecological Influences on the Nonverbal Expression of Emotion," *Current Opinion in Psychology* 17: 170–5.

Parkinson, B., Fischer, A. H., and Manstead, A. S. R. (2005) *Emotion in Social Relations: Cultural, Group, and Interpersonal Processes*, New York: Psychology Press.

Pavese, C. (2016a) "Skill in Epistemology I: Skill and Knowledge," *Philosophy Compass* 11: 642–9.

—— (2016b) "Skill in Epistemology II: Skill and Know How," *Philosophy Compass* 11: 650–60.

Pear, T. H. (1928) "The Nature of Skill," *Nature* 122: 611–14.

Rizzolatti, G., and Sinigaglia, C. (2008) *Mirrors in the Brain: How We Share Our Actions and Emotions*, New York: Oxford University Press.

Russell, J. A. (1991) "Culture and the Categorization of Emotions," *Psychological Bulletin* 110(3): 426–50.

—— (1994) "Is There Universal Recognition of Emotion from Facial Expression? A Review of the Cross-Cultural Studies," *Psychological Bulletin* 115: 102–41.

—— (2003) "Core Affect and the Psychological Construction of Emotion," *Psychological Review* 110: 145–72.

Singer, T., Snozzi, R., Bird, G., Petrovic, P., Silani, G., Heinrichs, M., and Dolan, R. J. (2008) "Effects of Oxytocin and Prosocial Behavior on Brain Responses to Direct and Vicariously Experienced Pain," *Emotion* 8(6): 781–91.

Tomkins, S. S. (1962) *Affect, Imagery and Consciousness. Volume I: The Positive Affects*, New York: Springer.

—— (1963) *Affect Imagery Consciousness. Volume II: The Negative Affects*, New York: Springer.

Tracy, J. L. (2014) "An Evolutionary Approach to Understanding Distinct Emotions," *Emotion Review* 6(4): 308–12.

Tracy, J. L., and Randles, D. (2011) "Four Models of Basic Emotions: A Review of Ekman and Cordaro, Izard, Levenson, and Panksepp and Watt," *Emotion Review* 3(4): 397–405.

Wieser, M. J., and Brosch, T. (2012) "Faces in Context: A Review and Systematization of Contextual Influences on Affective Face Processing," *Frontiers in Psychology* 3: 471.

PART V

Skill, language, and social cognition

29

SKILL AND EXPERTISE IN JOINT ACTION

James Strachan, Günther Knoblich, and Natalie Sebanz

29.1 Introduction

Developing an individual skill is a daunting undertaking. Take learning a musical instrument: when a person first picks up a guitar, she must learn the basic motor actions that will produce prescribed chords, how each string is supposed to sound and be tuned, and her own motoric constraints of what kinds of chords she can produce and the speed with which she can transition. Only then can she progress to adapting these to suit her own needs. Now imagine the guitarist wants to learn guitar so that she can play as part of a band, and this individual skill must transition to a joint skill where, in addition to learning the guitar she must also contend with the performance of her bandmates. Now, as well as producing her own music she must also anticipate and adapt to production features that are outside of her control.

This chapter focuses on two questions related to skilled joint action. The first question is what are the mechanisms that allow people to perform skilled joint actions. The second question is how context affects skilled joint action, such as whether coordination occurs in the course of a cooperative or competitive interaction. In addressing these questions, we draw on studies from a wide range of skilled joint actions, including music, sports, and dance, as well as on more basic coordination tasks designed to investigate fundamental mechanisms of coordination. While acquiring specific joint actions – such as dancing tango or playing in a string quartet – may entail challenges that are unique to a specific domain, there are also general principles of skilled joint action performance. Such principles can not only be derived from studies on "experts" who have been trained to perform joint actions in particular domains; rather, any typical human being can to some extent be considered a joint action expert, given our life-long engagement in joint actions such as handshakes, object transfers, and conversations.

29.2 Mechanisms in skilled joint action

When performing a joint action, coordinating with other individuals is vital. In this section we introduce and describe empirical evidence of coordination processes and mechanisms that expert actors can rely on to facilitate the performance of skilled joint actions: strategic action modulations, joint action planning and monitoring, and action prediction.

29.2.1 Strategies of action modulation

Making oneself predictable. Several studies have shown that when people are instructed to synchronise their actions with a partner, their actions become less variable than when they act alone (Vesper et al. 2011, 2016). In particular, by increasing the speed of their actions, interaction partners reduce their temporal variability. Furthermore, they may choose trajectories and velocities that are easy to predict. In a study of joint improvisation, Hart et al. (2014) asked participants to synchronise their actions in a simplified version of the mirror game, an exercise from improvisational theatre that requires two people to perform the same actions at the same time without knowing what their partner will do next. They found that experienced improvisers systematically modulated the velocity profile of their movements in order to achieve synchrony with their partner, considerably deviating from their way of moving individually. These adjustments were interpreted as attempts to make themselves more predictable for their partner, thereby facilitating coordination. On the one hand, the strategy of making one's actions less variable and more predictable appears to be very basic, as it can be found in simple coordination tasks that do not require specific training and has even been reported in macaque monkeys (Visco-Comandini et al. 2015). On the other hand, for specific skilled joint actions, such as joint improvisation in the mirror game, considerable training may be necessary in order to learn how to make one's actions more predictable.

Ancillary movements. Head and instrument movements in musicians that are not directly linked to music production but are an integral part of musical performance are examples of ancillary movements (as opposed to instrumental movements that are necessary to produce a sound; Nusseck and Wanderley 2009). For example, ancillary gestures are related to musical expression in clarinet players, as they use more frequent and variable ancillary movements when asked to play expressively than when asked to play inexpressively (Wanderley 2001; Wanderley et al. 2005; Palmer et al. 2009). The question then is how and whether these gestures of musical expression occur differently in a context where music is produced as part of an ensemble; whether musicians maintain their own rhythm of gestures, whether they copy others' gestures, or whether they use ancillary gestures strategically to coordinate.

Coordination of ancillary movements in music production can serve to maximise predictability of different expert players in an ensemble, without necessarily sacrificing their expressivity. Glowinski et al. (2013) asked professional and student violinists to play five pieces of music on their own and as part of a quartet while they monitored players' head movements using motion capture. They found that, while the violinists produced task-irrelevant head movements in all playing conditions, these movements were significantly more regular when they were playing as part of their ensemble compared with when they were playing a solo. Given that increasing regularity and decreasing variability can facilitate coordination (Vesper et al. 2011, 2016), this is to be expected. According to Palmer et al. (2009), who found that lower variability of movement related to lower ratings of expressivity in music production, we might also expect that these coordinative ensemble productions would be judged as less expressive. However, when Glowinski et al. showed videos of the performances to both non-expert and expert violinists, more regular head movements were not rated as any less expressive. Rather, observers could tell if the production was a solo or ensemble performance based on the violinists' head movements – and this judgement accuracy was related to expertise: professional violinists found it easier than novices to tell whether head movements came from an ensemble performance.

Importantly, the collaborative function of ancillary movements can be used strategically to adapt to adverse conditions. If auditory feedback during joint music making is noisy or absent, pianists make efforts to adjust according to the available information (Goebl and Palmer 2009). They try to compensate for reductions in auditory feedback through increased synchrony of postural swaying and other physical movements that can serve as visual signals to timing (ibid.). This suggests that in adverse conditions players can establish a common understanding of timing using ancillary movements.

Controlling entrainment. In physical terms, entrainment is the process by which oscillating systems assume the same period in time. In psychological terms it means much the same: entrainment of behaviour refers to the process by which two or more individuals producing regular patterns of behaviour fall into the same rhythm. For example, two people walking side by side along a quiet street will typically fall into a rhythm of footsteps, either in-phase (both left feet forward at the same time) or anti-phase (one person's left foot forward at the same time as the other person's right foot). Entrainment is considered as an emergent, non-strategic phenomenon that is the result of strong automatic coupling between action and perception (Schmidt and Richardson 2008).

Entrainment has been proposed as a key component of everyday skills such as turn-taking in speech (Cummins 2009). There is also evidence that entrainment increases attention to an interaction, which can improve subsequent memory for features unrelated to the entrained behaviour (Macrae et al. 2008), and can increase participants' sense of social affiliation with the coupled entrainment partner (Hove and Risen 2009). In the context of skilled joint action, two questions arise: whether experts entrain differently from novices, and whether they differ in terms of their experience of the social and cognitive consequences of entrainment.

There is surprisingly little research that examines entrainment as an emergent property in experts. Interestingly, some instances of expert behaviour, such as running, require resistance to entrainment (Blikslager and de Poel 2017; but cf. Varlet and Richardson 2015). This is a particularly difficult task, as there is a natural tendency to fall into a rhythm with other people even when trying to maintain one's own unique rhythm. Participants entrain to another's rhythm if they are visually coupled despite having been told to maintain their own preferred rhythm and in light of different ecological constraints (Schmidt and O'Brien 1997; Richardson et al. 2007b) and they maintain this entrained rhythm even when visual information about the other is removed (Oullier et al. 2008). However, there are instances of joint skilled behaviour, such as dancing or ensemble music playing, where one must avoid entraining to a partner's (or partners') rhythms in order to produce one's own part. As such, expert dancers or musicians should be better able to resist entrainment than the novices tested in these studies.

To test this experimentally, Sofianidis et al. (2014) asked expert Greek dancers – who are skilled at dancing to music in haptically connected groups of dancers – and novice dancers to close their eyes and sway their bodies according to a metronome they heard over headphones. Participants swayed while they either touched fingers with a partner next to them who was doing the same task, or they stood independently. Crucially, the two partners were always guided by different metronome speeds, such that while one would be tasked with swaying fast the other would sway slowly. While novice dancers were likely to show interference from their partner's rhythm when they were touching each other, experts showed little interference from the partner and matched to the rhythm of the metronome. This shows that entrainment in expert joint action can be selectively inhibited. It suggests that one crucial aspect of expertise in joint action is the ability to strategically suppress otherwise automatically processed information from a partner or partners.

This can also be seen in contexts where synchronisation within a group is desired, but entrainment with other groups is not. Take the Congado, an Afro-Brazilian religious tradition where teams of musicians all play at the same time in the same place and all try to maintain a unique rhythm within their own group while not entraining to other groups around them. Resisting the natural tendency to synchronise with other groups is used to demonstrate the cohesive identity of one's own group, as well as one's own group's musical competence (Lucas et al. 2011).

More generally, strategically adapting to specific sources and resisting entrainment with others may constitute a hallmark of joint action expertise. To illustrate, consider team rowers who face a particular challenge when deciding how to use available environmental information. In a two-person row team, both rowers face the same way, which means that one rower has access to more visual information than the other as they can see their partner's movements. As such, one strategy the second rower might use would be to couple their actions to the rhythm and movement of the visually disadvantaged rower, taking into account their environmental constraints. However, a study of Olympic and World Championship rowers found that rather than focus on this feature, rowers who could see their partner instead coupled themselves to the invariant haptic signals from the boat, and the perception of water passing (Millar et al. 2013). That is, rather than couple themselves to the primary coordination target (their teammate) they instead coupled to the environmental features that they knew their target would use in order to improve coordination.

Finally, it should be noted that music novices are also able to adjust their coordination strategies to different contexts (Honisch et al. 2016). It remains to be seen how experts' ability to use these timing strategies directly compares with that of novices.

29.2.2 Action prediction

Joint actions rely not only on modulating one's own actions: it is important to be able to read and anticipate the actions of others. Expert action perception is therefore a crucial component of skilled joint action. Expert tennis players, for example, are faster to respond to their opponents' strokes than are novices, and there is evidence that this is related, at least in part, to more effective visual search strategies (Williams et al. 2002). This relationship appears to be causal: when recreational players are trained to use the same visual search strategy that experts use, their tennis performance improves more than if they are instructed with a placebo strategy.

There has been a growing body of research aiming at identifying the underlying structure of expert advantage in action perception. Expert dancers are able to identify dance moves in an upright configuration even when these sequences have been reduced to point-light displays (the videos only show a series of white dots that correspond to landmarks at various joints on the body, while all other perceptual information is removed; Calvo-Merino et al. 2010). When the same dance moves are shown in an inverted configuration, experts perform as poorly as novices. This indicates that experts use a configural processing strategy to process the kinematic information in these low-information displays. Similar results with badminton players have shown that experts can pick up kinematic cues from point-light displays even from only short segments of the action (Abernethy and Zawi 2007) and that experts perform similarly to point-light displays as they do for full videos, indicating that these configural kinematic features are sufficient to explain the expert advantage in this particular task (Abernethy et al. 2008).

Perceptual and motor expertise are fundamentally linked. Action observation often recruits relevant motor systems (Cross et al. 2009), and motor experience plays a key role in perceptual expertise. Elite basketball players are better at predicting the success of observed free-throws than people with comparable visual experience such as their coaches or sports journalists, and this appears to be related to specific motor activation during action observation (Aglioti et al. 2008). In novices, even short periods of blindfolded motor learning can enhance later perceptual judgements (Hecht et al. 2001; Casile and Giese 2006).

This perceptual expertise in experts is also highly specific to the nature of actors' action repertoires. For example, expert cricketers are better than novices at predicting the direction of a bowled ball and moving to meet it, and they show this advantage even before the ball has left the bowler's hand. However, a study found that this expert advantage was significantly more prominent when experts made physical movements to intercept the ball, and this was even greater when they held a cricket bat in their hands. Although the visual information was the same, the context of holding a cricket bat improved experts' accuracy in anticipating the direction of an incoming bowl even when the only visual information came from the bowler's actions up until the point of ball release (Mann et al. 2010). Other studies have found that in long-term experts many of these neural responses are stronger for a dancer's own school of dance compared with a different school (e.g., ballet vs. capoeira; Calvo-Merino et al. 2004). There is also some evidence that female experts are better than male experts at matching point-light upright dance sequences modelled by female dancers even when all models and observers come from the same school (Calvo-Merino et al. 2010). This could suggest that the specificity of this action simulation is greater even within established roles from the same school of dance.

The studies discussed above provide support for action simulation – that is, experts recruit both action perception and production mechanisms during action observation to simulate and anticipate the observed action, which allows for more efficient action understanding and prediction. In doing so, they rely on so-called internal forward models in the motor system that are used both for predicting the outcomes of one's own actions and the outcomes of others' actions (Wolpert et al. 2003). Accordingly, greater similarity between the system making the predictions and the system to be predicted improves prediction and ultimately coordination. In an experiment with skilled pianists, Keller et al. (2007) asked participants to perform one half (that is, one hand's part) of a piece along with a pre-recording of the other half that either the participant themselves or one of the other participants had played. They found that participants achieved better temporal coordination when playing duets with their own recordings than with others' recordings. Furthermore, participants who were better at identifying their own idiosyncrasies from the recordings (see also Repp and Knoblich 2004) showed a greater self-synchronisation advantage than those who could not recognise their own playing. A follow-up study by Loehr and Palmer (2011) found that this extended beyond playing duets with one's own recordings – the degree of a priori similarity between performers playing together affected their success of achieving temporal coordination. Such findings suggest that during duet or ensemble performances musicians internally simulate the actions of other musicians, and that similarity of personal idiosyncrasies can aid this simulation.

Skilled joint action performance may particularly benefit from predictions that are not only made by one interaction partner about the other, but by reciprocal, coupled predictions. This idea was put forward by Noy and colleagues based on findings from an experimental version of the mirror game (Noy et al. 2011). They found that expert performance was marked by stretches of time during which both interaction partners moved smoothly in synchrony without one of them leading and the other following. According to their model, engaging in this "co-confident" motion hinges on predictive internal models in the motor system that are coupled so that the output of one controller is the input for the other.

29.2.3 Joint action planning and monitoring

Planning. When planning a joint action, actors must consider the affordances and limitations of their co-actors, which allows for sophisticated coordination and distribution of tasks (Richardson et al. 2007a). Studies examining the mechanics of how people represent others' affordances and limitations in a joint action task are limited, but evidence with transcranial magnetic stimulation (TMS) has shown that the size of motor evoked potentials (MEPs; a measure of motor excitability) to objects depends on how accessible the objects are to the participant: MEPs are stronger to objects that the participant can act upon than to those that are out of reach (Cardellicchio et al. 2011). Interestingly, enhanced MEPs can also be elicited when the object is out of participant's reach if they are within reach of another agent (Cardellicchio et al. 2013), suggesting that participants spontaneously accommodate another's affordances during object processing.

As well as accommodating the joint action partner's affordances, one must also consider their action constraints. That is, it is not enough to consider whether a partner *can* act, but how costly their action would be relative to one's own, and how that might affect the joint outcome. Experimental evidence shows that people do take the difficulty of another person's task into account when they attempt to coordinate. Vesper et al. (2013) instructed participants to make coordinated forward jumps – each participant had a different distance to jump forward onto a target plate, and their task was to land at the same time. While they could not see or hear their partner, participants knew how far their partner had to jump, as well as how far they themselves had to jump. Participants distributed the coordination effort according to the task difficulty, such that those with the easier task (a shorter distance to jump) made more adjustments to coordinate with the partner who had the more demanding task. Further evidence suggests that this asymmetry in adjustment is not just a result of a general slowing down on the part of the person with an easier task – in an experiment where participants had to move objects between two sites with an aim to landing at the end point at the same time, unobstructed participants adjusted their movement profiles if their partner had to move around an obstruction (Schmitz et al. 2017). These adjustments were not just a result of slowing down; these participants moved as though they were also moving around an obstacle, indicating that they were not just representing coarse information but specifically representing the nature of the obstacle.

Electrophysiological evidence shows that participants plan not only their own actions, but also include a task partner's actions in their planning. Kourtis et al. (2013) studied this by providing participants with an instruction cue (a symbol representing the type of action they were about to perform) followed one second later by a "go" or imperative stimulus that indicated that they should start to perform the action. This gave a 1,000 ms window where participants had to plan the action they were about to perform, during which electroencephalography (EEG) was recorded on both participants. The cues either informed participants that they would perform an individual action – grasping an object, raising it off the table, then returning it to the starting position; a joint passing action – grasping the object and then passing it to the other person on the other side of the table; or a joint receiving action – taking the object as it was passed to them by their partner.

Kourtis et al. found that planning to perform the joint action reduced the magnitude of the right lateral P3b component, a component that reacts strongly to information related to processing of group-relevant information. The fact that this component was smaller in the joint action conditions indicates that participants evaluated the instruction cue in terms of relevance for the group (themselves and their partner) rather than just to themselves. The right lateral P3b component is thought to arise in the temporoparietal junction, an area of the brain associated with mentalising. This suggests that participants did not just represent what they had to do but also what their partner would have to do.

To investigate how similar the planning of one's own and another's actions is, a later EEG study compared unimanual actions (lifting a cup from a table), bimanual actions (lifting two cups and touching them together), and joint actions (two people lifting cups and touching them together, as people do when toasting) while EEG was recorded from one participant (Kourtis et al. 2014). The contingent negative variation (CNV; a slow potential that reflects time-based motor preparation) was not only larger during joint action planning than during individual action, but just as large when planning a joint action as when planning a bimanual action. This suggests that participants planned their own action together with the other's action, much in the same way as planning a coordinated action with their two hands.

Behavioural evidence also shows that, even as novices, participants represent their partners' actions in an effort to achieve a joint goal. Piano novices were asked to perform simple melodies, either individually or as a duet (Loehr and Vesper 2016). They then reproduced the melodies in a test block, either with or without accompaniment. If, during learning, participants approach a joint task with an individual mind-set – that is, a focus on producing their own melody regardless of what their partner does – then participants should perform best in the absence of any shared feedback as they can focus on their own melody without interference. However, if even novices represent the shared goal of the duet, then they should perform better when playing with an accompaniment and experiencing the full duet. Loehr and Vesper found that participants did indeed represent the joint goal, and that this was specific to when they played a duet with another person – the same results were not found for computer-generated accompaniments. This suggests that even from an early stage of proficiency, efficiently achieving joint goals relies on practicing and learning within a joint context, and that representing the other's task is a key feature of successful joint action.

However, to represent another's task in the same way as one's own is not always conducive to joint action. If two people are playing a duet, one player cannot allow their duet partner's melody to interfere with their own or the necessary complementarity of the two productions would be lost. Novembre et al. (2012) had musicians play the right-hand part of a piano piece that they had learned to play bimanually, either alone or listening to another person play the left-hand accompaniment. While they played, the experimenters applied TMS and measured MEPs in the left hand (the resting hand) to see if corticospinal excitability associated with action representations of the left-hand part differed as a result of whether the musician played alone (an individual context where they have to inhibit the known left-hand part in order to produce the right-hand part) or as part of a duet (where someone else is playing the left-hand part and so the left hand becomes associated with the other person). They found stronger MEPs in the joint condition, when the left-hand accompaniment was associated with the other, than in the individual condition where it was associated with the self. Importantly, the same results were found in a control condition where the participants could not hear the other player but still believed that they were playing the accompaniment. In a self-relevant condition, where the participant is the only player, the un-played accompaniment must be inhibited to avoid interfering with the right-hand melody. However, participants do not appear to exert the same inhibition in a joint task where the action has been assigned to the partner.

Many of the tasks used in laboratory joint action studies are very simple motor tasks designed to examine specific mechanisms. But these are not necessarily comparable to highly skilled – and often highly idiosyncratic – expert behaviours. Our own base motor expertise in, for example, clinking glasses in a toast (Kourtis et al. 2014) allows us to make accurate predictions about a partner's movements without ever having toasted with a particular partner before. However, experts must often form much more specialised and temporally fine-grained predictions about their co-actors' movements in order to achieve optimal performance, such as musicians playing in an orchestra or football players anticipating each other's running paths. As such, it is necessary not only to know what another is going to do, but also *how* they are going to do it and what sort of idiosyncrasies characterise their playing style. Greater familiarity with a duet partner's part but no experience with actually playing with that partner leads to more asynchronies and poorer coordination, and these asynchronies are driven in part by each individual's own playing style (Ragert et al. 2013). Experts in domains such as music, therefore, must develop fine-grained action predictions and plans that are tailored to the individuals and context with which they perform those joint actions.

Monitoring. As a joint action requires the input of more than one individual to achieve a joint goal, it is not sufficient to represent what another *could* do. It is also necessary to monitor what that person *does*, particularly with regard to any errors made, so that one can adjust one's own behaviour or prepare for any costs incurred. Loehr et al. (2013) used EEG to study error monitoring in pianists playing a series of chords in a duet. On some trials, either the participant's or the partner's keyboard was programmed to play the wrong note resulting in an error that either affected the overall harmony of the combined chords (the joint outcome) or only affected the individual harmony (individual outcome). While they showed that feedback-related nega-tivity (an ERP component that emerges early, around 200 ms following an error) reflected a similar response to all errors regardless of who produced them, a later positive potential known as the P300 showed evidence of specific action monitoring with a stronger response to a partner's errors that affected the joint outcome than to errors that affected only the individual outcome. As such, while earlier, low-level monitoring of errors appears to monitor all errors equally, later processes then show sensitivity not only to the source (self vs. other) but to the significance of the error (affecting only one person's outcome vs. affecting the joint outcome).

There is evidence that participants represent others' errors in a similar way to their own. In reaction time studies, there is a well-established phenomenon where participants slow down on trials immediately following an error they made. During joint tasks, where participants are asked to perform different tasks simultaneously, participants also show post-error slowing in response to observed errors (Schuch and Tipper 2007; de Bruijn et al. 2012). This adds to a series of studies that show similar results from neuroimaging, indicating that others' errors are also represented in a similar way to one's own at the neural level (Bates et al. 2005; Kang et al. 2010; de Bruijn and von Rhein 2012; Picton et al. 2012).

Allowing others' errors to impact one's own performance can be costly in skilled joint action, as such monitoring makes demands of limited cognitive resources. However, evidence that participants are prone to post-error slowing suggests that monitoring others' errors encourages people to slow down and approach tasks more cautiously. This means that others' errors may serve as cues to or reminders of task difficulty. In addition to that, in contexts where the joint outcome is prioritised over the individual goal, such as in music, dance, or high-risk joint actions such as surgery, it would make sense for experts to treat any error as their own in order to be better able to adapt to and compensate for it.

29.3 Action contexts: cooperation vs. competition

So far this chapter has discussed joint action largely from the perspective of it being an inher-ently cooperative endeavour. That is, individuals share a goal and coordinate their actions in time and space to achieve that goal together. While many accounts of joint action in philosophy (e.g.,

Bratman 1992) and communication (e.g., Clark 1996: 61) exclude competitive interactions from definitions of joint actions, we believe it can be useful to include them: competition involves some of the same coordination mechanisms described so far, such as strategic modulations of action, resisting entrainment, action prediction, monitoring, and co-representation (Ruys and Aarts 2010).

This is not to say that all of the processes involved in cooperation and competition are the same, however. For example, different action contexts lead to reliance on different aspects of perceptual information about others' actions. Streuber et al. (2011) invited participants to play either competitive (standard rules) or cooperative table tennis games (instructed to pass the ball back and forth as many times as possible) in a dark room with glowing markers attached to the players' bodies or paddles – creating a live impression of a point-light display. Being able to see the movements of one's own body improved participants' performance regardless of context. However, participants benefited in the cooperative condition if they could see the other's racket movements, whereas in the competitive condition they benefited if they could see the other's body movements. The authors interpret this as suggesting that action prediction (which relies on being able to see the opponent's body movements) is more important in competitive than cooperative actions. Given that predictability is a key feature of cooperative joint action, where efforts are taken to minimise any unexpected or unanticipated behaviours (Glover and Dixon 2017; Issartel et al. 2017), the inverse must be true for competition, in that a player must do their best to minimise predictability for an opponent, and the opponent is by extension driven to form predictions on the basis of subtle behavioural changes.

Knowing that an opponent is monitoring one's behaviour in order to predict future behaviour can be an advantage. An often-used competitive strategy is to disguise one's true intentions by deliberately providing misleading cues. Basketball players often feint when passing using gaze misdirection, and this kind of misleading gaze cue is difficult to inhibit, and so serves as a powerful deceptive cue. However, evidence also shows that experts are better able to resist these misleading gaze cues than are novice players, and that this is specific to participants' experience – basketball players are able to inhibit their response to misleading gaze cues following a previous basketball feint, but football players (who are skilled athletes but without the same domain-specific expertise) and non-athletes could not (Weigelt et al. 2016).

In addition to action prediction, other aspects of joint action differ between cooperation and competition. One example is error monitoring. While there is evidence that others' actions are treated in a similar way to one's own and that this can result in similar electrophysiological responses to errors (de Bruijn and von Rhein 2012) and behavioural adjustments (Schuch and Tipper 2007; de Bruijn et al. 2012), there is also evidence that treating others' errors as one's own is sensitive to the context of these errors. One's own error is typically a negative and potentially costly event, and in a cooperative context a partner's errors can be seen as also negative for the self. However, in a competitive context an opponent's errors can be a rewarding or positive event, as these create the opportunity for exploitation, and a growing body of research suggests that others' errors are represented differently at a neural level depending on whether they occur in a competitive or cooperative context (de Bruijn et al. 2009; Koban et al. 2010).

An outstanding question with regard to skilled joint action in competitive contexts is the role of teams. In the laboratory, many studies investigate competition and cooperation in isolation. This means that the role of the team, a crucial element of many competitive skilled actions, is often ignored. In sports such as football, rugby, or basketball, each player must strike up a balance within themselves in terms of communication and coordination. Given that skilled team players must cooperate with their own team (e.g., by making their actions more predictable) and compete with the opposing team (making themselves *less* predictable), how do they deal with these competing demands? Furthermore, there is the question of joint skill learning. While there is some limited research looking at how joint skills can be learned, there is little theoretical or empirical consideration of how competitive team players (e.g., football or rugby players) acquire this ability to balance cooperative and competitive motivations. This kind of cognitive juggling act that skilled players perform between the conflicting motivations of cooperation and competition offers a rich avenue for future research.

29.4 Conclusion

At first glance, skilled joint actions can appear to be largely by-products of skilled individual actions. In this view, skilled joint actions simply rely on developing an individual skill and then applying it to a joint context. However, true joint skill cannot be acquired individually. Good coordination with others is a skill in its own right, and one that is highly specific to particular action contexts. Skilled joint actors are not only good at producing task-relevant action features and adapting their behaviour to accommodate their interaction partners, but they can also use incidental or emergent behaviours strategically to communicate context and intention to other actors.

As well as showing expert advantage in action production, expertise also leads to benefits in action prediction and perception, and these are closely linked with motor expertise. That is, even with comparable visual experience, one cannot acquire the same expert advantage in action perception without motor experience.

With regard to action planning and error monitoring, there is little evidence for large qualitative differences between experts and novices. Indeed, novices are able to represent joint goals, plan joint actions, and monitor both their own and others' errors while also processing the source and significance of those errors. The key difference may not be in the mechanisms that experts use but in the resolution at which they apply them – creating much more temporally and spatially tuned predictions than novices who rely on an established interaction history.

The context of a particular action is a critical element of how skill emerges: cooperative and competitive actions make use of different action parameters and features. This applies not only to action production – where skilled actors must maximise predictability for cooperators while minimising predictability for competitors – but also action perception, where competitors' deceptive or misleading behaviours must be accurately identified and compensated for. The role of expertise in maintaining these conflicting motivations, and how this is acquired through learning and training, remains to be seen.

References

Abernethy, B., and Zawi, K. (2007) "Pickup of Essential Kinematics Underpins Expert Perception of Movement Patterns," *Journal of Motor Behavior* 39: 353–67, https://doi.org/10.3200/JMBR. 39.5.353-368.

Abernethy, B., Zawi, K., and Jackson, R. C. (2008) "Expertise and Attunement to Kinematic Constraints," *Perception* 37: 931–48, https://doi.org/10.1068/p5340.

Aglioti, S. M., Cesari, P., Romani, M., and Urgesi, C. (2008) "Action Anticipation and Motor Resonance in Elite Basketball Players," *Nature Neuroscience* 11: 1109–16, https://doi.org/10.1038/nn.2182.

Bates, A. T., Patel, T. P., and Liddle, P. F. (2005) "External Behavior Monitoring Mirrors Internal Behavior Monitoring," *Journal of Psychophysiology* 19: 281–8, https://doi.org/10.1027/0269-8803.19.4.281.

Blikslager, F., and de Poel, H. J. (2017) "Sync or Separate? No Compelling Evidence for Unintentional Interpersonal Coordination between Usain Bolt and Tyson Gay on the 100-Meter World Record Race," *Journal of Experimental Psychology: Human Perception and Performance* 43: 1466–71, https://doi. org/10.1037/xhp0000315.

Bratman, M. E. (1992) "Shared Cooperative Activity," *The Philosophical Review* 101: 327–41.

Calvo-Merino, B., Ehrenberg, S., Leung, D., and Haggard, P. (2010) "Experts See It All: Configural Effects in Action Observation," *Psychological Research PRPF* 74: 400–6, https://doi.org/10.1007/s00426-009-0262-y.

Calvo-Merino, B., Glaser, D. E., Grèzes, J., Passingham, R. E., and Haggard, P. (2004) "Action Observation and Acquired Motor Skills: An fMRI Study with Expert Dancers," *Cerebral Cortex* 15: 1243–9, https://doi.org/10.1093/cercor/bhi007.

Cardellicchio, P., Sinigaglia, C., and Costantini, M. (2011) "The Space of Affordances: A TMS Study," *Neuropsychologia* 49: 1369–72.

—— (2013) "Grasping Affordances with the Other's Hand: A TMS Study," *Social Cognitive and Affective Neuroscience* 8: 455–9, https://doi.org/10.1093/scan/nss017.

Casile, A., and Giese, M. A. (2006) "Nonvisual Motor Training Influences Biological Motion Perception," *Current Biology* 16(1): 69–74.

Clark, H. (1996) *Using Language*, Cambridge: Cambridge University Press, https://doi.org/10.1016/S0378-2166(97)83330-9.

Cross, E. S., Kraemer, D. J. M., Hamilton, A. F. D. C., Kelley, W. M., and Grafton, S. T. (2009) "Sensitivity of the Action Observation Network to Physical and Observational Learning," *Cerebral Cortex* 19: 315–26, https://doi.org/10.1093/cercor/bhn083.

Cummins, F. (2009) "Rhythm as Entrainment: The Case of Synchronous Speech," *Journal of Phonetics* 37: 16–28, https://doi.org/10.1016/J.WOCN.2008.08.003.

de Bruijn, E. R. A., de Lange, F. P., von Cramon, D. Y., and Ullsperger, M. (2009) "When Errors Are Rewarding," *Journal of Neuroscience* 29: 12183–6, https://doi.org/10.1523/JNEUROSCI.1751-09.2009.

de Bruijn, E. R. A., Mars, R. B., Bekkering, H., and Coles, M. G. H. (2012) "Your Mistake Is My Mistake … or Is It? Behavioural Adjustments Following Own and Observed Actions in Cooperative and Competitive Contexts," *The Quarterly Journal of Experimental Psychology* 65: 317–25, https://doi.org/10.1080/17470218.2010.545133.

de Bruijn, E. R. A., and von Rhein, D. T. (2012) "Is Your Error My Concern? An Event-Related Potential Study on Own and Observed Error Detection in Cooperation and Competition," *Frontiers in Neuroscience* 6: 8, https://doi.org/10.3389/fnins.2012.00008.

Glover, S., and Dixon, P. (2017) "The Role of Predictability in Cooperative and Competitive Joint Action," *Journal of Experimental Psychology: Human Perception and Performance* 43: 644–50, https://doi.org/10.1037/xhp0000362.

Glowinski, D., Mancini, M., Cowie, R., Camurri, A., Chiorri, C., and Doherty, C. (2013) "The Movements Made by Performers in a Skilled Quartet: A Distinctive Pattern, and the Function That It Serves," *Frontiers in Psychology* 4: 841, https://doi.org/10.3389/fpsyg.2013.00841.

Goebl, W., and Palmer, C. (2009) "Synchronisation of Timing and Motion Among Performing Musicians," *Music Perception* 26: 427–38, https://doi.org/10.1525/MP.2009.26.5.427.

Hart, Y., Noy, L., Feniger-Schaal, R., Mayo, A. E., and Alon, U. (2014) "Individuality and Togetherness in Joint Improvised Motion," *PLoS One* 9: e87213, https://doi.org/10.1371/journal.pone.0087213.

Hecht, H., Vogt, S., and Prinz, W. (2001) "Motor Learning Enhances Perceptual Judgment: A Case for Action-Perception Transfer," *Psychological Research* 65: 3–14, https://doi.org/10.1007/s004260000043.

Honisch, J. J., Elliott, M. T., Jacoby, N., and Wing, A. M. (2016) "Cue Properties Change Timing Strategies in Group Movement Synchronisation," *Scientific Reports* 6: 1–11, https://doi.org/10.1038/srep19439.

Hove, M. J., and Risen, J. L. (2009) "It's All in the Timing: Interpersonal Synchrony Increases Affiliation," *Social Cognition* 27: 949–60.

Issartel, J., Gueugnon, M., and Marin, L. (2017) "Understanding the Impact of Expertise in Joint and Solo-Improvisation," *Frontiers in Psychology* 8: 1078, https://doi.org/10.3389/fpsyg.2017.01078.

Kang, S. K., Hirsch, J. B., and Chasteen, A. L. (2010) "Your Mistakes Are Mine: Self-Other Overlap Predicts Neural Response to Observed Errors," *Journal of Experimental Social Psychology* 46: 229–32, https://doi.org/10.1016/J.JESP.2009.09.012.

Keller, P. E., Knoblich, G., and Repp, B. H. (2007) "Pianists Duet Better When They Play with Themselves: On the Possible Role of Action Simulation in Synchronization," *Consciousness and Cognition* 16: 102–11, https://doi.org/10.1016/j.concog.2005.12.004.

Koban, L., Pourtois, G., Vocat, R., and Vuilleumier, P. (2010) "When Your Errors Make Me Lose or Win: Event-Related Potentials to Observed Errors of Cooperators and Competitors," *Social Neuroscience* 5: 360–74, https://doi.org/10.1080/17470911003651547.

Kourtis, D., Knoblich, G., Woźniak, M., and Sebanz, N. (2014) "Attention Allocation and Task Representation During Joint Action Planning," *Journal of Cognitive Neuroscience* 26: 2275–86, https://doi.org/10.1162/jocn_a_00634.

Kourtis, D., Sebanz, N., and Knoblich, G. (2013) "Predictive Representation of Other People's Actions in Joint Action Planning: An EEG Study," *Social Neuroscience* 8: 31–42, https://doi.org/10.1080/17470919.2012.694823.

Loehr, J. D., Kourtis, D., Vesper, C., Sebanz, N., and Knoblich, G. (2013) "Monitoring Individual and Joint Action Outcomes in Duet Music Performance," *Journal of Cognitive Neuroscience* 25: 1049–61.

Loehr, J. D., and Palmer, C. (2011) "Temporal Coordination between Performing Musicians," *Quarterly Journal of Experimental Psychology* 64: 2153–67, https://doi.org/10.1080/17470218.2011.603427.

Loehr, J. D., and Vesper, C. (2016) "The Sound of You and Me: Novices Represent Shared Goals in Joint Action," *Quarterly Journal of Experimental Psychology* 69: 535–47, https://doi.org/10.1080/17470218.2015.1061029.

Lucas, G., Clayton, M., and Leante, L. (2011) "Inter-Group Entrainment in Afro-Brazilian Congado Ritual," *Empirical Musicology Review* 6: 75–102.

Macrae, C. N., Duffy, O. K., Miles, L. K., and Lawrence, J. (2008) "A Case of Hand Waving: Action Synchrony and Person Perception," *Cognition* 109: 152–6, https://doi.org/10.1016/j.cognition.2008.07.007.

Mann, D. L., Abernethy, B., and Farrow, D. (2010) "Action Specificity Increases Anticipatory Performance and the Expert Advantage in Natural Interceptive Tasks," *Acta Psychologica* 135: 17–23, https://doi.org/10.1016/j.actpsy.2010.04.006.

Millar, S. K., Oldham, A. R., and Renshaw, I. (2013) "Interpersonal, Intrapersonal, Extrapersonal? Qualitatively Investigating Coordinative Couplings Between Rowers in Olympic Sculling," *Nonlinear Dynamics, Psychology and Life Sciences* 17: 425–43.

Novembre, G., Ticini, L. F., Schutz-Bosbach, S., and Keller, P. E. (2012) "Distinguishing Self and Other in Joint Action. Evidence from a Musical Paradigm," *Cerebral Cortex* 22: 2894–903, https://doi.org/10.1093/cercor/bhr364.

Noy, L., Dekel, E., and Alon, U. (2011) "The Mirror Game as a Paradigm for Studying the Dynamics of Two People Improvising Motion Together," *Proceedings of the National Academy of Sciences* 108: 20947–52, https://doi.org/10.1073/pnas.1108155108.

Nusseck, M., and Wanderley, M. M. (2009) "Music and Motion: How Music-Related Ancillary Body Movements Contribute to the Experience of Music," *Music Perception: An Interdisciplinary Journal* 26: 335–53, https://doi.org/10.1525/mp.2009.26.4.335.

Oullier, O., de Guzman, G. C., Jantzen, K. J., Lagarde, J., and Scott Kelso, J. A. (2008) "Social Coordination Dynamics: Measuring Human Bonding," *Social Neuroscience* 3: 178–92, https://doi.org/10.1080/17470910701563392.

Palmer, C., Koopmans, E., Carter, C., Loehr, J. D., and Wanderley, M. (2009) "Synchronization of Motion and Timing in Clarinet Performance," *Proceedings of the International Symposium on Performance Science 2009*: 159–64.

Picton, L., Saunders, B., and Jentzsch, I. (2012) "'I Will Fix Only My Own Mistakes': An ERP Study Investigating Error Processing in a Joint Choice-RT Task," *Neuropsychologia* 50: 777–85.

Ragert, M., Schroeder, T., and Keller, P. E. (2013) "Knowing Too Little or Too Much: The Effects of Familiarity with a Co-Performer's Part on Interpersonal Coordination in Musical Ensembles," *Frontiers in Psychology* 4: 368, https://doi.org/10.3389/fpsyg.2013.00368.

Repp, B. H., and Knoblich, G. (2004) "Perceiving Action Identity: How Pianists Recognize Their Own Performances," *Psychological Science* 15: 604–9.

Richardson, M. J., Marsh, K. L., and Baron, R. M. (2007a) "Judging and Actualizing Intrapersonal and Interpersonal Affordances," *Journal of Experimental Psychology: Human Perception and Performance* 33: 845.

Richardson, M. J., Marsh, K. L., Isenhower, R. W., Goodman, J. R., and Schmidt, R. C. (2007b) "Rocking Together: Dynamics of Intentional and Unintentional Interpersonal Coordination," *Human Movement Science* 26: 867–91.

Ruys, K. I., and Aarts, H. (2010) "When Competition Merges People's Behavior: Interdependency Activates Shared Action Representations," *Journal of Experimental Social Psychology* 46: 1130–3, https://doi.org/10.1016/j.jesp.2010.05.016.

Schmidt, R. C., and O'Brien, B. (1997) "Evaluating the Dynamics of Unintended Interpersonal Coordination," *Ecological Psychology* 9: 189–206.

Schmidt, R. C., and Richardson, M. J. (2008) "Dynamics of Interpersonal Coordination," in A. Fuchs and V. K. Jirsa (eds.) *Coordination: Neural, Behavioral and Social Dynamics* (pp. 281–308), Berlin, Heidelberg: Springer, https://doi.org/10.1007/978-3-540-74479-5_14.

Schmitz, L., Vesper, C., Sebanz, N., and Knoblich, G. (2017) "Co-Representation of Others' Task Constraints in Joint Action," *Journal of Experimental Psychology: Human Perception and Performance* 43: 1480–93, https://doi.org/10.1037/xhp0000403.

Schuch, S., and Tipper, S. P. (2007) "On Observing Another Person's Actions: Influences of Observed Inhibition and Errors," *Perception & Psychophysics* 69: 828–37.

Sofianidis, G., Elliott, M. T., Wing, A. M., and Hatzitaki, V. (2014) "Can Dancers Suppress the Haptically Mediated Interpersonal Entrainment During Rhythmic Sway?" *ACTPSY* 150: 106–13, https://doi.org/10.1016/j.actpsy.2014.05.002.

Streuber, S., Knoblich, G., Sebanz, N., Bülthoff, H. H., and de la Rosa, S. (2011) "The Effect of Social Context on the Use of Visual Information," *Experimental Brain Research* 214: 273–84, https://doi.org/10.1007/s00221-011-2830-9.

Varlet, M., and Richardson, M. J. (2015) "What Would Be Usain Bolt's 100-Meter Sprint World Record Without Tyson Gay? Unintentional Interpersonal Synchronization Between the Two Sprinters," *Journal of Experimental Psychology: Human Perception and Performance* 41: 36–41, https://doi.org/10.1037/a0038640.

Vesper, C., Schmitz, L., Safra, L., Sebanz, N., and Knoblich, G. (2016) "The Role of Shared Visual Information for Joint Action Coordination," *Cognition* 153: 118–23, https://doi.org/10.1016/J.COGNITION.2016.05.002.

Vesper, C., van der Wel, R. P. R. D., Knoblich, G., and Sebanz, N. (2011) "Making Oneself Predictable: Reduced Temporal Variability Facilitates Joint Action Coordination," *Experimental Brain Research* 211: 517–30, https://doi.org/10.1007/s00221-011-2706-z.

—— (2013) "Are You Ready to Jump? Predictive Mechanisms in Interpersonal Coordination," *Journal of Experimental Psychology: Human Perception and Performance* 39: 48–61, https://doi.org/10.1037/a0028066.

Visco-Comandini, F., Ferrari-Toniolo, S., Satta, E., Papazachariadis, O., Gupta, R., Nalbant, L. E., and Battaglia-Mayer, A. (2015) "Do Non-Human Primates Cooperate? Evidences of Motor Coordination During a Joint Action Task in Macaque Monkeys," *Cortex* 70: 115–27, https://doi.org/10.1016/j.cortex.2015.02.006.

Wanderley, M. M. (2001) "Quantitative Analysis of Non-Obvious Performer Gestures," in I. Wachsmuth and T. Sowa (eds.) *Gesture and Sign Language in Human-Computer Interaction* (pp. 241–253), Berlin, Heidelberg: Springer.

Wanderley, M. M., Vines, B. W., Middleton, N., McKay, C., and Hatch, W. (2005) "The Musical Significance of Clarinetists' Ancillary Gestures: An Exploration of the Field," *Journal of New Music Research* 34: 97–113, https://doi.org/10.1080/09298210500124208.

Weigelt, M., Güldenpenning, I., Steggemann-Weinrich, Y., Alhaj Ahmad Alaboud, M., and Kunde, W. (2016) "Control over the Processing of the Opponent's Gaze Direction in Basketball Experts," *Psychonomic Bulletin & Review* 24: 828–34, https://doi.org/10.3758/s13423-016-1140-4.

Williams, A. M., Ward, P., Knowles, J. M., and Smeeton, N. J. (2002) "Anticipation Skill in a Real-World Task: Measurement, Training, and Transfer in Tennis," *Journal of Experimental Psychology: Applied* 8: 259–70, https://doi.org/10.1037/1076-898X.8.4.259.

Wolpert, D. M., Doya, K., and Kawato, M. (2003) "A Unifying Computational Framework for Motor Control and Social Interaction," *Philosophical Transactions of the Royal Society of London. Series B: Biological Sciences* 358: 593–602.

30

SELF- AND OTHER-AWARENESS IN JOINT EXPERT PERFORMANCE

Shaun Gallagher and Jesús Ilundáin-Agurruza

30.1 Introduction

On some phenomenological conceptions of expert performance, the expert operates completely on the pre-reflective (i.e., tacit, non-observational, non-objectifying) level of experience. Any sort of reflective consciousness or appeal to reflective knowledge is characterized as an interruption or decline in performance level. This view is most frequently associated with Hubert Dreyfus' explanation of expertise, which draws on phenomenological accounts of everyday bodily actions (Dreyfus 1997, 2002, 2005; Dreyfus and Dreyfus 1980). Merleau-Ponty also emphasizes the pre-reflective nature of action and the disruption that can occur by taking a reflective attitude. As he puts it, "my corporeal intending of the object of my surroundings is implicit and presupposes no thematization or 'representation' of my body or milieu" (1964: 89). Or again:

> I have no need of representing to myself external space and my own body in order to move the one within the other. It is enough that they exist for me and that they constitute a certain field of action held around me.
>
> *Merleau-Ponty 2012: 186*

For Dreyfus, both everyday coping and expert performance follow this same pre-reflective logic.

In contrast, there are accounts that suggest that expert performance in some contexts requires a reflective or mindful awareness of one's body. For Richard Shusterman (2008), for example, explicitly conscious somatic sensations or perceptions of one's body, including "distinct feelings, observations, visualizations, and other mental representations of [one's] body and its parts, surfaces, and interiors" can play an important role in performance. Such

> mindfully conscious somatic perceptions can help us to perform better. A slumping batter, by looking at his feet and hands could discover that his stance has become too wide or that he is choking up too far on the bat. A dancer can glance at her feet to see that they are not properly turned out.
>
> *Shusterman 2008: 53*

We explore these views by looking at empirical and phenomenological studies of expert performance. After reviewing some theoretical debates about the nature of individual self-awareness during expert performance, we examine some accounts of individual self-awareness in athletics and dance. We then turn to questions about the role of self-awareness and the awareness of others during joint actions, and in team and collaborative performances. We show that the contrasting positions represented by Dreyfus and Shusterman, respectively, are both off the mark, and we advocate an alternative pluralist model that helps refine the analysis of self- and other-awareness in expert performance.

30.2 The Dreyfus model

Dreyfus' analyses of action and perception, drawn from phenomenological writings (Heidegger 1962; Todes 2001; Merleau-Ponty 2012), provide an account of expertise that emphasizes, paradoxically, its mindless nature (Dreyfus and Dreyfus 1980; Dreyfus 2005). Experts engage in action such that they do not think about the specifics of practice. Expert attention is not directed to the motoric specifics of the action; if anything, it is rather intentionally directed outward and forward to the environment and action goals:

> A phenomenology of skill acquisition confirms that, as one acquires expertise, the acquired know-how is experienced as finer and finer discriminations of situations paired with the appropriate response to each. Maximal grip names the body's tendency to refine its responses so as to bring the current situation closer to an optimal gestalt. Thus, successful learning and action do not require propositional mental representations. They do not require semantically interpretable brain representations either.
>
> *Dreyfus 2002: 367*

Dreyfus generalizes this view, claiming that we are all experts in everyday embodied practices, such as walking, riding a bike, etc. Someone who is coping with his environment "does not need to be aware of himself even in some minimal way" (2007a: 374).

To summarize, for Dreyfus, experts engage in a highly proficient bodily coping, know what to do intuitively, without thinking, and without consulting a set of rules, as novices might do. This gives experts the ability to be mindlessly in the flow. Dreyfus appeals to the model of Aristotelian *phronesis*, especially regarding the emphasis on gaining expertise through practice without following a set of rules (2005). Many of these themes get followed up in Dreyfus' debate with John McDowell.

Dreyfus (2005) rejects McDowell's idea that perception is conceptual and defends his long-held views on non-conceptual embodied skills and everyday coping. He rejects the "myth of the mental," and maintains that perception and action typically occur without mental intervention. In response, McDowell (2007) argues that perception and embodied coping are conceptual, rational, and not as "mindless" as Dreyfus contends. The kind of rationality involved in action does not have to be situation independent. McDowell likewise appeals to the Aristotelian notion of *phronesis*. In contrast to Dreyfus (2005: 51) who takes *phronesis* to be "a kind of understanding that makes possible an immediate response to the full concrete situation," for McDowell *phronesis* involves an initiation into conceptual capacities: "the practical rationality of the *phronimos* is displayed in what he does even if he does not decide to do that as a result of reasoning" (2007: 341). This means there is a kind of reasoning built into action understood as the activity of deciding which affordances to respond to and how to go about responding to them. This "means-end rationality" involves a "stepping back" into a stance of deliberation (2007: 341–2). For McDowell, the fact that we can give reasons for our action, even if such action was not informed by prior deliberative reasons, suggests that our actions and embodied copings have an implicit rational structure amenable to conceptuality.

Dreyfus will have none of this. For him, the concept of rationality involves detached, reflective thoughtful processes related to propositional discourse, the space of reasons, and conceptual articulation. But such processes are not involved in everyday coping or expert performance. He agrees that we can "step back" and reflect, but this type of "free distanced orientation" interferes with performance and skillful coping (Dreyfus 2007b: 354). In one telling example, Dreyfus suggests that an expert skier in the flow of his performance loses his expertise if he starts to reflect on possible changes in the snow further downhill.[1]

30.3 The phenomenology of expert performance

In contrast to Dreyfus, who emphasizes the lack of reflection and thought in expert performance, we can find studies that suggest a more mindful phenomenology. John Sutton et al. (2011) claim that expertise is not without some sort of self-awareness. Their example is the cricket player, who, with less than half a second to execute hitting a hard fast pitch traveling at 140 km/h, draws not only on smoothly practiced batting, but also on game-relevant context and conditions, in order to hit a shot with extraordinary precision through a slim gap in the field. This performance is "fast enough to be a reflex, yet it is perfectly context-sensitive. This kind of context-sensitivity, we suggest, requires some forms of mindedness" (Sutton et al. 2011: 80). The expert cricket player is not on automatic pilot – she has trained up her body-schematic movement control, but what she needs to do in the context of a game is more than that. In contrast to the Dreyfus model, where finely tuned motor control processes (or an attuned body schema) is all the expert needs, Sutton et al. claim that skill within a context of a game involves something more – a mindful strategic sense of where the batter is going to put the ball:

> Skill is not a matter of bypassing explicit thought, to let habitual actions run entirely on their own, but of building and accessing flexible links between knowing and doing. The forms of thinking and remembering which can, in some circumstances, reach in to animate the subtle kinaesthetic mechanisms of skilled performance must themselves be redescribed as active and dynamic. Thought is not an inner realm behind practical skill, but an intrinsic and worldly aspect of our real-time engagement in complex physical and cultural activities. ... So expert performers precisely counteract automaticity, because it limits their ability to make specific adjustments on the fly. ... Just because skillful action is usually pre-reflective, it does not have to be mindless.
>
> *Sutton et al. 2011: 95*

Clearly the cognitive processes at stake are not heavy reflective processes, or a detailed awareness of one's body. Rather, they engage an awareness of the situation and a procedural or performative know-how that involves "[selective] target control for some features, such as goal, one or more parameters of execution, like timing, force, a variation in the sequence, and so on" (Christensen et al. 2013: 50). The cricket player can see the potential shot in the situation and "can 'feel' when her motor system has the right configuration" (Christensen et al. 2013: 59).

Christensen et al., thus suggest a "meshed" architecture model that integrates perceptual and cognitive elements with body-schematic control (Christensen et al. 2016).

Such models work best the more flexible they are, given the high specificity of sports skills: cricket is premised on attentional resources honed for high-speed action, whereas freediving 300 feet underwater relies on a capacity for maximal serenity under literal and figurative pressure. As Jørgen Eriksen (2010) posits, Dreyfus' analysis presents a monolithic view that is inapplicable to all sports. We need the right tool for the right job. Eriksen finds that risk sports are specially problematic because although they prevent deliberation – skiing down a 60° slope or "big wave surfing" 60-foot behemoths leaves no room for distraction or measured reflection – they do require full attention rather than mindlessness. Aligned with this, Gunnar Breivik (2013) arguing that elite sportspeople do not cope mindlessly, quotes ultra-marathoner Bernd Heinrich:

> I often noticed that muscle tenseness could be relaxed by conscious effort. I then focused attention on my calves, thighs, arms, trying to relax them even during training runs, so that the most essential running muscles would be exercised. For a mile or so I would monitor and hence try to control the kick of my arm swings, to make sure no energy was wasted in side-to-side motion.
>
> *Breivik 2007: 129*

The underlying subtext is that Dreyfus' view of everyday expertise embodies a low standard of performance when compared with elite performers (Ilundáin-Agurruza 2016). In fact, Dreyfus' model fails to capture elite performers' phenomenology. Everyday skillful coping enables us to mindlessly drive to the store. Marvelous as this is, it does not explain the *engagement* that top performance needs. Elite performers' highly refined kinetic repertoires enable them to discriminate among stimuli all but undetectable for others. Additionally, much like consummate pianists use the full range of keys, they move across the full register between conscious control and pre-reflective consciousness, between external and internal attentional foci, and between automatism and spontaneous, improvised responsiveness to pertinent conditions. Thus, in less demanding settings, experts may well be distracted or even mindless, but in do-or-die scenarios they are hyper-focused and highly aware. In short, expert performance as a fully situated and transactional process between performers and their environment involves a multilevel and dynamic attunement.

Barbara Montero (2012, 2016), in agreement with the foregoing, also rejects that expert performance somehow is effortless or thoughtless. Rather, although certain types of bodily awareness may interfere with well-developed skills, such awareness is typically not detrimental to the skills of expert athletes or performing artists. "In expert-level performance thinking is generally better than not thinking" (Montero 2015: 127). Empirical studies that purport to show that paying attention to certain bodily aspects of performance will interfere with performance, she argues, are not ecological. For example, one study asks a player to pay constant attention to his feet as he dribbles a soccer ball (e.g., Ford et al. 2005). This type of cognitive effort is not found in usual practice.

Montero – a former dancer – focuses on the kind of body awareness involved in dance. On one view, that awareness stays pre-reflective. Rather than taking the body as an intentional object, a pre-reflective performative awareness "provides a sense that one is moving or doing something, not in terms that are explicitly about body parts, but in terms closer to the goal of the action" (Gallagher 2005: 73). Dorothée Legrand (2007) characterizes this kind of heightened pre-reflective attention to the body as a performative focus. "A dancer is very concerned with his body and while dancing he is intensively attending to it. But he is not attending to it reflect-ively as an object. Rather, his awareness of his body as subject is heightened" (512). The expert dancer can put this subjective character of experience "at the front" of his experience without turning experience, action, or body into an explicit intentional object (Legrand 2007: 512; see Toner et al. 2016). Although Montero allows for the possibility that expert performers, in dance or musical performance, stay pre-reflective, occasionally even entering a mindless zone, she also thinks that optimal performance often coincides with thoughtful performance, perhaps involving even a step up from enhanced pre-reflective or performative awareness. Taking the lead from the cellist Ingal Segev, she writes:

> The idea that you should get lost in the music and simply let it lead you was mistaken, she thinks, as it proscribes thought. If being in the zone for a musical performance means performing at one's best, being in the zone according to Ingal means, it seems, extensive conscious thought about what to do and when to do it.
>
> *Montero 2015: 136*

Likewise, Montero points to qualitative studies in athletics where a more detailed type of con-scious monitoring improves performance. She cites Timothy Gallwey, a pro-tennis player:

> [W]hen you increase your stroke speed to normal and begin hitting, you may be par-ticularly aware of certain muscles. For instance, when I hit my backhands, I am aware that my shoulder muscle rather than my forearm is pulling my arm through.
>
> *Montero 2015: 135*

Olympic swimmer Jim Montgomery corroborates this:

> As soon as I jump in the water, I begin to concentrate on my stroke deficiencies. Am I carrying my head too high, dropping my right elbow midway through the pull, or not finishing through with my left arm? All these things can occur in my freestyle stroke when fatigue sets in.
>
> *Montgomery and Chambers 2009: 35*

This form of self-monitoring comes close to specific types of awareness identified by Shusterman (2008). As we mentioned, he argues that both explicit exteroceptive consciousness, and more implicit proprioceptive and kinaesthetic awareness can help to improve performance. Concerning the latter, he claims that "through systematic practice of somaesthetic awareness this proprioceptive consciousness can be significantly improved to provide a sharper and fuller picture of our body shape, volume, density, and alignment without using our external senses" (53–4). He identifies two types of explicit consciousness: conscious somatic perception and reflective somatic perception with explicit awareness. The first includes a visual or propriocep-tive sense of one's body parts, their relations with other body parts, posture and with objects in the environment. We can also be aware of breathing, or of tensions in the body. In the second type of explicit reflective consciousness,

> we are not only conscious of what we perceive as an explicit object of awareness but we are also mindfully conscious of this focused consciousness as we monitor our awareness of the object of our awareness through its representation in our consciousness.
>
> *Shusterman 2008: 55*

That is, we are self-consciously aware of our own perceptual monitoring.

Shusterman proposes that one reason these explicit kinds of self-awareness can improve performance is the inaccuracy involved in pre-reflective awareness. On the basis of pre-reflective awareness, or simply not having an awareness at all, "I may think I am keeping my head down when swinging a golf club, though an observer will easily see I do not. I may believe I am sitting straight when my back is rounded" (Shusterman 2008: 64). Without a trained explicit attention to one's posture, performance could easily decline.

Both Montero and Shusterman make it clear that the phenomenology of the expert performer is an expert phenomenology. That is, the type of awareness required for expert performance is a trained awareness. We will refer to this as the *trained awareness model*. Not just any old form of awareness will do. In this respect, they disagree with Dreyfus, not only in his downgrading of self-awareness but in his attempt to construe everyday coping as a type of expertise. Outside of a trained self-focus, everyday performance may not be optimal. To be clear, in this trained awareness model there are a range of possible foci posited in varying circumstances, as in the thick of a performance or competition, or in practicing a drill, from kinaesthetic and proprioceptive, pre-reflective awareness, to what appears to be a reflective attention to a body part, such as "my shoulder is pulling my arm through," or, "my left foot is lagging behind." We argue below, however, that it is actually more complicated – and interesting– than this, especially in cases of team or collaborative performances.

Before turning to examples of such performances, consider some complexities involved in Japanese swordsmanship, *kenjutsu*, 剣術, as practiced between the 1500s and the mid-1600s. This practice involves, specifically, a state of heightened performance called *mushin*, 無心.[2] Literally, and misleadingly, it translates as "no-mind," but is better rendered as a mindfully fluid attentive awareness unhindered by distracting thoughts. Zen priest Takuan Sōhō (1986), who wrote an extended letter to peerless samurai Yagyū Munenori on swordsmanship, is adamant that *mushin* is not a state of inattentiveness. Rather, it involves a hyper-awareness where swordsmen react *immediately* and with their *whole* being: "It is called [*mushin*] when the [heart-mind] has neither discrimination nor thought but wanders about the entire body and extends throughout the entire self" (Sōhō 1986: 33).[3] Thus, awareness partakes of both reflective and pre-reflective consciousness. It is also modulated in response to an opponent who is trying to be deceptive (deception is analyzed below with reference to soccer).

Mushin is closely connected to *muga*, 無我, no-self. For some, this may lead to viewing *mushin* as disposing of the self completely. But, it is not as simple as that. For clarity's sake, and at the risk of oversimplification, the idea is that Zen Buddhist soteriology, which informs samurai swordsmanship, aims at eliminating attachments, the delusion of the self, and overcoming the fear of death through embodied practice. The delusion here concerns the metaphysical claim that there is self as an enduring substance; phenomenologically there is still an experience of the self, but realizing such delusion leads to freedom from attachments and liberation from suffering. The idea is to minimize discrimination, which in this context involves a harmful concern for the self and fear for one's life. Otherwise there will be gaps; worry and anxiety will disturb our heart-mind (our embodied awareness). This is bound to hamper performance and get the swordsman killed.

30.4 Performing with others

The debates we have just rehearsed focus on individual expert performance and action. What happens when experts engage in joint action? Or when expert teams work toward some goal? Ultimately, we will contend that there are evident differences in terms of awareness among experts across different practices, e.g., musical quartet, soccer team, or army platoon. We first consider the received phenomenological view and vet it with an example from musical expertise.

Similar to claims about individual performance, in the phenomenological tradition we find accounts suggesting that reflection also interrupts team or cooperative performance, and that working together best remains pre-reflective. Alfred Schutz (1976), for example, proposes that working together requires a pre-reflective sense or understanding of the person with whom one is working. The ability to understand the other is based upon a pre-reflective "Thou-orientation" (1976: 24). Even if I am not interested in the other person's behavior, gestures, bodily movements, etc., per se, the thou-orientation just is an orientation to such embodied aspects of the other, since only in those aspects am I able to see the other as another person. If this orientation is mutual – if we are interacting in a reciprocal framework – the thou-orientation becomes a "we-relation," which Schutz characterizes as a face-to-face relation (1976: 25). My awareness that we are jointly attending to something, for example, may be based on my perception of "movements of your body and expressions of your face during these movements" (25), and in this fashion "I experience my fellow-man 'directly' in a We-relation" (26). But for Schutz this is still a pre-reflective experience, and when we start to reflect on the meaning of the other's action, the directness, the face-to-face is lost (27).

Let's test these intuitions against a detailed study of expert musical performance. Simon Høffding, in his study of the Danish String Quartet, conducted phenomenological interviews and focused on the precise experiences the musicians had while playing their best. It turns out that each member of the quartet had different experiences while playing, but all of them reported they could be thinking of or experiencing different things:

> [E]xpert musicians can undergo a wide range of different experiences while playing, from thinking about where to go for beers after the performance, to worrying whether one's facial expression looks interesting to the audience, to enjoying the fact that the playing seems to be unfolding smoothly, and finally to a deep absorption in which one experiences a profound transformation of consciousness.
>
> *Høffding 2015: 11*

This is surprising were we looking for some consistency with either the Dreyfus model or the contrasting trained awareness model. Høffding (2015) himself takes this result to undermine Dreyfus' claims, siding with some aspects of trained awareness. But one could think that if a performer can start thinking about the pub, or about his facial expression, and yet not have this interfere with his playing, that playing must be a process that happens precisely at the pre-reflective level that Dreyfus describes, and in such a way that it frees the performer to think about whatever comes to mind. At the same time, it seems that Dreyfus is wrong to think that any kind of reflective thinking necessarily interrupts performance. Further, in some practices and situations expert performance may need to go beyond the mindless coping or reflective thinking dichotomy, needing a more flexible model.

Høffding distinguishes four different states of awareness in expert performance:

1. *Absent-minded playing* (automatic performance) – something that would be consistent with the Dreyfus model.
2. *Playing under stress* (e.g., after interruption) and striving to get back – "just barely keeping up without missing the notes, yet coping nevertheless, managing to perform without mistakes" – a state that would be more consistent with trained awareness.

3. *Deep absorption or blackout*: Lack of self-awareness – again seemingly consistent with the Dreyfus model.
4. *Heightened awareness* of self and surroundings – again consistent with trained awareness.

As Høffding puts it, absorption and heightened awareness

> are not best understood in terms of a certain relation between reflective and pre-reflective consciousness because [they] can encompass moments of both and because the overall phenomenology of expert musicianship is far too rich to be reduced to this particular relation.
>
> *2015: 159–60*

More relevant to these states, Høffding's musicians experience modulations in the sense of agency: a diminished sense of agency in deep absorption; an increased sense of agency in heightened awareness. Here is a description of heightened awareness from Asbjørn, one of the musicians:

> You are both less conscious and a lot more conscious I think. Because I still think that if you're in the zone, then I know how I'm sitting on the chair, I know if my knees are locked, I know if I am flexing my thigh muscle, I know if my shoulders are lifted, I know if my eyes are strained, I know who is sitting on the first row, I know more or less what they are doing, but it is somewhat more, like disinterested, neutrally registering, I am not like inside, I am not kind of a part of the set-up, I am just looking at it, while I'm in the zone.
>
> *Høffding 2015: 116*

As the musicians describe it, in both states, absorption and heightened awareness, there is a certain *letting go* that involves *passivity*. Even with increased sense of control in heightened awareness, the performer doesn't intervene in the process but lets it happen.[4]

Høffding's analysis indicates four factors that account for the performance being carried along such that it involves this kind of passivity: body schema, affect, the music itself, and the other players. We will briefly discuss the first three, then focus on the question of the other players.

First, through sustained practice musicians can attune their bodily performance, which allows musicians to play "from the body schema" (Høffding 2015: 181) and thereby forget about many of the motoric details. This gives them freedom to focus on selective target control (see Bowman 2004). But attunement of the body schema is insufficient for the kind of expert performance found in either deep absorption or heightened awareness. Høffding suggests, second, that the affective factor may help to differentiate musical and athletic performances. This does not mean that athletic performance lacks in affect or emotion,[5] but that affect is different in musical performance in the way that it integrates the other factors. With respect to movement under body-schematic control, for example, we may want to distinguish a relatively affectively neutral *instrumental* movement from an affectively rich *expressive* movement. Musical expression can work like gesture and language and go beyond simple motor control. It is also possible that music allows exploring, developing, or regulating emotion differently. Still, if affective factors in some way drive expressive movement during music performance, this doesn't happen without body-schematic control. *Mutatis mutandis*, the body schema doesn't work independently of affect, delivering technically proficient movement to which we then add an expressive style.

Rather, affect can modulate body-schematic processes – slowing them down or speeding them up, for example, or leading to the adoption of postures that may influence the performance in an ongoing manner.

Third, affective and body-schematic processes are also integrated with the music itself. Regarding the musical instruments themselves, empirical studies show that we tend to incorporate tools and instruments into our body schema (e.g., Maravita and Iriki 2004). In that regard, body-schematic processes add to the playing of the music. It goes deeper than that, however, since the music itself reciprocally moves us; it engages the body schema through its links to rhythm, material resonance, muscle, movement, and action.

Does this fit with Schutz's notion that working or playing with others involves a pre-reflective attunement to the other's intentions? What precisely is the performing musicians' consciousness of others in the performance?

30.5 Other-awareness in synchronic performance

Let's first note that Dreyfus is silent on this issue. The social dimension is missing in his account of expertise:

> From Dreyfus's perspective, one develops the affective comportment and intuitive capacity of an expert solely by immersion into a practice; the skill-acquiring body is assumed to be able, in principle at least, to become the locus of intuition without influence by [social and cultural] forces external to the practice in which one is apprenticed.
>
> *Selinger and Crease 2002: 245; see also Young 1980; Collins 2004*

Engaging in apprenticeship, on the way to expertise, usually means learning from others, but Dreyfus' account of apprenticeship lacks any analysis of what that might mean. This also raises problems with his use of the concept of *phronesis*, which, according to Aristotle, one cannot attain without learning from the right people (see Gallagher 2007, 2016).

In contrast to Dreyfus, there is good evidence that intersubjectivity is an important factor in performance (Salice et al. 2019). One way to explicate this relation is through recent research that shows that while working (or playing) together in joint action we form "joint body schemas" (Soliman and Glenberg 2014), and that one's peripersonal space extends to include instruments *and* other people with whom we are playing. In Soliman and Glenberg's experiment, coordinated action produces modulations that show up in both neuronal and behavioral measures. One might argue that what changes are simply processes in each individual – individual body schemas expand, altering subpersonal processes that may generate an *individual* sense of joint agency – a feeling of being in sync with the other. Alternatively, one might argue that the two bodies form a larger action system, so that the joint body schema belongs only to this larger system (two parts constituting a larger whole). In either case this type of physically attuned embodied alignment may very well be limited to synchronous interactions such as dancing together, or playing music together.[6] These processes are clearly subpersonal, and if they generate some kind of feeling or experience, it would be a pre-reflective experience. One finds indications of this in accounts of the role of gestures and motor actions in joint musical performance (Glowinski et al. 2013; Gnecco et al. 2013), supporting the idea of an established entrainment or sensorimotor synchronization in performance (Repp and Su 2013).

What about more explicit awareness of the others with whom one is performing? In those cases that Høffding calls *playing under stress* (struggling to get back into the smooth flow of playing together), might one be more aware of precisely what the other performers are doing? Rune, one of Høffding's musicians, describes this state: "you start thinking about 'here we are not together', 'here it is not in tune', such that you begin to look for errors" (Høffding 2015: 132). In another instance of playing under stress, the musicians recognized that the audience had lost their attunement to the music (133). Yet, even in these cases the struggle seems to be more about getting oneself back into sync with the music rather than with the others; there is very little said (in Høffding's interviews) about an awareness of others in performance. Even less is said about this in the other states of awareness. There is not much *explicit* attention being paid to the others, even as one is playing into their performance.

This seemingly goes against the claims of several psychologists who develop the notion of joint musical attention. Høffding cites several studies. Seddon and Biasutti (2009), for instance, claim that "to reach empathetic attunement, musicians must decentre and see things from other musicians' musical points of view" (119–20) And Keller (2008: 205) suggests that "to produce a cohesive ensemble sound, the pianists must hold a common goal; a shared representation of the ideal sound." One could think this requires a kind of mindreading or simulationist sensitivity to the other player's mental states (see Keller et al. 2007: 102). Alternatively, the musicians may be predicting joint musical outcomes in a way that does not involve mindreading or separate predictions for the other players' actions. Rather, it may involve only the predicting of one's own actions with respect to jointly produced consequences (see Loehr et al. 2013). But, is explicit attending to or representation of either the other players' mental states or of one's own future actions necessary for performance? It seems not. One of Høffding's musicians, Asbjørn Nørgaard, indicates this in his description of events involving the other quartet members, Frederik Øland, Fredrik Sjölin, and Rune Tonsgaard Sørensen:

> [R]ecently, there was this concert, in which Frederik, because of his father [who had recently passed away] was very moved by a movement of Beethoven, where Rune hadn't noticed at all that he [Frederik Ø] had been crying and Rune decisively hadn't seen it.
> But you saw it?
> I saw it and Fredrik also saw it. And another time on the last England tour, where Rune had all kinds of problems with his Beethoven Quartet in which Frederik [Ø] played first violin and Rune second violin, and Rune had been sitting and placed his arm on the thigh whenever he could and Fredrik and I were immediately afterwards towards Rune "Are you ok?" and where Frederik [Ø] hadn't discovered anything what so ever, even if he had been looking at him.
>
> *Høffding 2015: 203–4*

Asbjørn's comments suggest that what musicians attend to varies in different circumstances. More generally, if, while playing, one musician is thinking of going to the pub later, and another is thinking of how his facial expressions look to the audience, and a third is being carried away in deep absorption, it's not clear that an explicit consciousness of the other players, or an explicit attending to one's actions is always needed to make the performance work. This suggests that at least in some cases, in line with Dreyfus' analysis, and assuming that the performance remains expert rather than sub-optimal, the real work is being done in a manner that involves skillful automaticity or, a minimally pre-reflective level. One of Høffding's descriptions makes clear the latter possibility:

In the fall of 2014, I gave a talk, in which Rune and Asbjørn participated, to illustrate the nature of the research project. They played a Mozart duo and I performed a mock interview inquiring into the differences between performing as a quartet and then this unusual configuration of just the two of them. [...] Asbjørn asked whether the audience had heard a distinct *rallentando* (slowing down) during the last movement. No one in the audience had noticed. Asbjørn had noticed that Rune had to turn pages and slowed down to give him time to do so. Rune, when asked, expressed that he was clearly aware that Asbjørn slowed down to give him time to turn the page. When asked how he knew to slow down, Asbjørn stated that it wasn't because he explicitly knew that Rune had to turn the page and then planned to slow down, but rather because he felt a slight disturbance in Rune's playing ... he simply sensed directly that something was off and slowed down to remedy the situation.

2015: 210–11

Again, there appears to be no explicit or reflective attending to the other musician, but something closer to a (possibly enhanced) pre-reflective awareness. Høffding concludes:

Perfectly coordinated musical interaction is possible without perception of others in a full-blown sense, and it seems to me that to even begin making sense of this, one must appeal to a fundamental bodily reciprocity or interaction that bypasses high-level cognition.

2015: 212

How then should we characterize attunement to partners in performance? The members of the quartet offer a variety of characterizations. They use terms such as "hive-mind," "zone-forces," being in sync, and trusting in the process. They speak of an intuitive know-how:

When you perform in the quartet, you know precisely when to play the tones, you know what the others are doing without looking at them. When everyone in the quartet is in this state, it is just like there is a bubble of sound over every ones' heads that you can just form as you wish.

Høffding 2015: 213–14

Here Høffding invokes Merleau-Ponty's notion of intercorporeity, a concept consistent with the notion of a joint body schema. But one is also led to the idea that the music ("the bubble of sound") itself situates the intercorporeity, and pulls the quartet into this kind of synchronic relation. In just such synchronic performances this pre-reflective intercorporeity seems central to explaining the kind of situated (in the music, or in the dance) other-awareness that is possible. This kind of account, however rich, is limited to those kinds of performances. It is not clear that one can say the same for all forms of expert performance. How would this play out on a different ground such as the soccer pitch?

30.6 Variations on expert experience

There are clear differences between a quartet that plays music together and teams that work together jointly. Examples of the latter may include cockpit crews, and firefighters, surgery, and athletic teams. But there are also significant differences among all of these teams, specifically in terms of team-member location, function, types of movement, etc. In trying to answer the general question involving social cognition or social perception in joint expert action or performance, other-awareness in synchronic joint performance such as musical performance represents one extreme where (sometimes heightened) pre-reflective, intercorporeal synchrony is close to the rule. In contrast, in varied situations, answers are going to differ in detail. In close quarters (e.g., cockpits, surgeries) the routine of procedures combined with visuals of those procedures and the other team members' actions likely constrain the requirements for how we are conscious of those others. In a range of more dispersed environments (e.g., firefighting, team athletics) as well as risky conditions, planned strategies, or the presence of opponents, likewise make for differences in how we are conscious of others. On a theoretical level where the question is precisely about the nature of self- and other-consciousness in joint expert actions and performances across these different conditions, the rule is that there is no rule; one has to go case-by-case. This is where theory collapses into (or is strongly guided by) practice, a situation that calls for *phronesis* in phenomenological investigations as much as in expert performance. The phenomenology of expert performance may indeed differ case-by-case given the inherent contextual uniqueness of each activity and high skill specialization involved. This is precisely what *phronesis* allows for. In some cases, performers may be required to reflectively focus on one or other factor of the situation; in other cases, the situation may allow for letting go. Experts know when to focus and when to let go. Just because of these variations in self- and other-awareness the phenomenological analysis will need to capture nuanced differences case-by-case.

Such variations can be found, for example, in team athletic performance. With respect to other-awareness, some sports experiences are aligned closer to Høffding's analysis than others. Closed-skill team sports where performance involves fixed sets of movements and stable environment better align with the musical case, particularly if these are closer to dance or music, such as rhythmic gymnastics or synchronized swimming. But in open-skill team sports that require adjusting dynamically to competitors there are significant differences. In contrast to music, there is no score, choreographed movements, or pre-set patterns (there may be tactics, but these are often thwarted, this being the opponents' goal). For example, in soccer there is an analogous reciprocity among players on the same team but, signally, the "synchrony" is predicated on the opponents' very attempt to disrupt the performance. Kenneth Aggerholm (2013: 211) suggests, "it would be more appropriate to describe it as a being-against-the-Other."

The player feints right and goes left as the defense tries to anticipate the move. The key action in this antagonistic context, to be deceptively creative, is the feint. Aggerholm et al. (2011) develop an analysis of soccer – which considers the Dreyfus model on the one side and on the other the trained awareness model of Montero and Shusterman – on the basis of the feint as the locus of the game's creativity. The answer is found

> somewhere in a continuum between the two accounts. Performance in high-level football obviously involves intentions and the players certainly have a tendency to perform in specific ways that make sense in relation to the common objective. But no matter how good you are, you always have to move into an open situation and relate and adapt to the social situation of the game as it unfolds.
>
> *Aggerholm et al. 2011: 351*

The feint presents a unique phenomenological situation: to be effective it demands a "sensitivity and openness to the dynamic configuration of the social situation" (ibid., 354); its foundation is the attempt to transcend, within the rules, the opponents' expectations to attain an advantage (ibid., 348). That is, here the common goal of the soccer players is to *strive together* (from L. *com* + *petitio*) in facilitating occasions for being attuned to and anticipating the others' intentions when these are deceptive. In fact, for players to be aware of opponents in their intent to deceive, they need to be aware of the others as the others perceive them in a kind of compound awareness. It might be thought that this competitive facet could disrupt expert performance by bringing deliberation into the fray. This *can* be the case when the opponent thwarts the feint, the case of a foul being clearest. But, when the player succeeds, as when Argentinian Diego Maradona scored his most memorable goal against six defenders in the 1986 World Cup to the dismay of the English, his performance was predicated precisely on the sort of situated, anticipatory, and responsive attunement where the unwilling opponent is integrated into the totality of the play. Someone might suggest that the trained awareness model – whether Montero's or Shusterman's – can also account for this kind of adaptation. Perhaps. Nonetheless, like Dreyfus, that model centers on individual performance. Montero's brief discussion of social coordination (2016: 114), still requires the sort of deliberate attention that would be ruled out in this case in lieu of a more transactional process that can modulate across a wider attentional register.

30.7 Conclusion

Studies of the phenomenology of expert performance can tell us about the various forms of self- and other-awareness at work in different situations. Consider the different characterizations from the above discussion (which could mix differently with varied practices and performers' skill level).

- Situated strategic reflection (the downhill skier)
- Selective target control (the cricket batter)
- Performative awareness (a dancer's goal-related, pre-reflective sense of body-as-subject, which may include the sense of a rightly configured body)
- A more explicit conscious monitoring of the body (a dancer or athlete)
- Deep absorption and heightened awareness (during musical performance)
- Heightened awareness with minimal self-awareness (as with the swordsmen)
- Socially attuned awareness of the possible deception of the other (the soccer players)

We can certainly expect further variations in different types of collective and team arrangements. In some of these arrangements, given relevant differences in spatial and temporal arrangements and purpose, it may very well be that the kind of pre-reflective, intercorporeal experiences typical of some collaborative musical performances are impossible. In such cases shared representations, plans, communicative, or narrative practices, and other more reflective forms of cognition may be involved in our experience of or with others. In some regards this pluralist model goes against both the Dreyfus model and the trained awareness model understood as exclusive accounts of expertise, but makes room for both of them as phenomenological accounts of some limited number of many variations in expert performance.

Acknowledgments

Both authors are part of and receive support from the project *Minds in Skilled Performance*, Australian Research Council. Australia (Grant number: DP170102987); SG's research has also been supported by the Humboldt Foundation's Anneliese Maier Research Award.

Notes

1 Dreyfus made this claim at a meeting in Oslo in 2004, in response to an Olympic trainer who was describing one of her best skier's experience.
2 With some modifications this readily extends to athletic contests and risk sports. In sports, the analogous state is called "flow." As states characteristic of heightened performance, both flow and *mushin* are functionally equivalent. There are, however, subtle but telling phenomenological and cultural differences (Krein and Ilundáin-Agurruza 2014; Ilundáin-Agurruza 2016).
3 To emphasize the attentive, dynamic, and fluid nature [*mushin*] replaces the translator's use of "No-Mind"; likewise, the bracketed "heart-mind" is a more accurate rendition of the original Japanese rather than the translator's use of "mind." "Heart-mind" translates the Japanese 心, which depending on the context may refer to *shin* or *kokoro*. Either rendition is tantamount to a holistic bodyminded integration of emotion, will and intellect psychosomatically blended and resulting in superior achievement.
4 In contrast, the sense of agency in the case of *kenjutsu* (discussed above), rather than leading to passivity in the "letting go" process, as in the musical performance, engages the performers in open, dynamic responsiveness to the situation. There is superior performance with awareness of self minimally kept to the pre-reflective level. We might speak of a fifth state of awareness, were we not inclined to taxonomical deflationism.
5 In athletics there are cases where affect is instrumentally suppressed or aroused, depending on the type of sport and the athlete's temperament. Sports like boxing or MMA fighting attract contestants who often pump themselves up before the fight. Other sports, such as target shooting, archery, or freediving, demand emotional temperance. Sports where expressiveness is operative, e.g., rhythmic gymnastics or synchronized swimming, are closer to dance or music in terms of affective richness.
6 It may also be the case, as one reviewer pointed out, that this effect is limited to haptic coupling (as in the experiment). This is an open, empirical question. It seems reasonable, however, to think that if haptic coupling can modulate body-schematic sensory-motor connections, auditory coupling in the case of playing music together may do the same.

References

Aggerholm, K. (2013) "Express Yourself: The Value of Theatricality in Soccer," *Journal of the Philosophy of Sport* 40: 205–24.
Aggerholm, K., Jespersen, E., and Ronglan, L.T. (2011) "Falling for the Feint: An Existential Investigation of a Creative Performance in High-Level Football," *Sport, Ethics and Philosophy* 5: 343–58.
Bowman, Q. (2004) "Cognition and the Body: Perspectives from Music Education," in L. Bresler (ed.) *Knowing Bodies, Moving Minds: Toward Embodied Teaching and Learning*, 29–50, Dordrecht: Kluwer Academic Press.
Breivik, G. (2007) "Skillful Coping in Everyday Life and in Sport: A Critical Examination of the Views of Heidegger and Dreyfus," *Journal of the Philosophy of Sport* 34: 116–34.
—— (2013) "Zombie-Like or Superconscious? A Phenomenological and Conceptual Analysis of Consciousness in Elite Sport," *Journal of the Philosophy of Sport* 40: 85–106.
Christensen, W., Sutton, J., and McIlwain, D. J. (2013) "Cognitive Control in Skilled Action," https://waynechristensen.wordpress.com/2013/08/15/cognitive-control-in-skilled-action/.
—— (2016) "Cognition in Skilled Action: Meshed Control and the Varieties of Skill Experience," *Mind & Language* 31: 37–66.
Collins, H. M. (2004) "Interactional Expertise as a Third Kind of Knowledge," *Phenomenology and the Cognitive Sciences* 3: 125–43.
Dreyfus, H. L. (1997) "Intuitive, Deliberative, and Calculative Models of Expert Performance," in C. Zsambok and G. Klein (eds.) *Naturalistic Decision Making*, 37–48, London: Psychology Press.
—— (2002) "Intelligence Without Representation: Merleau-Ponty's Critique of Mental Representation," *Phenomenology and the Cognitive Sciences* 1: 367–83.
—— (2005) "Overcoming the Myth of the Mental: How Philosophers Can Profit from the Phenomenology of Everyday Expertise," in *Proceedings and Addresses of the American Philosophical Association*, 47–65, Newark, DE: American Philosophical Association.
—— (2007a) "Response to McDowell," *Inquiry* 50: 371–7.
—— (2007b) "The Return of the Myth of the Mental," *Inquiry* 50: 352–65.

Dreyfus, S. E., and Dreyfus, H. L. (1980) "A Five-Stage Model of the Mental Activities Involved in Directed Skill Acquisition," (No. ORC-80-2), Berkeley Operations Research Center, California University.

Eriksen, J. W. (2010) "Mindless Coping in Competitive Sport: Some Implications and Consequences," *Sport, Ethics and Philosophy* 4: 66–86.

Ford, P., Hodges, N. J., and Williams, A. M. (2005) "Online Attentional-Focus Manipulations in a Soccer Dribbling Task: Implications for the Proceduralization of Motor Skills," *Journal of Motor Behavior* 37: 386–94.

Gallagher, S. (2005) *How the Body Shapes the Mind*, Oxford: Oxford University Press.

—— (2007) "Moral Agency, Self-Consciousness, and Practical Wisdom," *Journal of Consciousness Studies* 14: 199–223.

—— (2016) "The Practice of Thinking: Between Dreyfus and McDowell," in T. Breyer (ed.) *The Phenomenology of Thinking*, 134–46, London: Routledge.

Glowinski, D., Mancini, M., Cowie, R., Camurri, A., Chiorri, C., and Doherty, C. (2013) "The Movements Made by Performers in a Skilled Quartet: A Distinctive Pattern, and the Function That It Serves," *Frontiers in Psychology* 4: 841.

Gnecco, G., Badino, L., Camurri, A., D'Ausilio, A., Fadiga, L., Glowinski, D., et al. (2013) "Towards Automated Analysis of Joint Music Performance in the Orchestra," in *International Conference on Arts and Technology*, 120–7, Heidelberg: Springer.

Heidegger, M. (1962) *Being and Time*, trans. J. Macquarrie and E. Robinson, New York: Harper.

Høffding, S. (2015) *A Phenomenology of Expert Musicianship* (PhD thesis), Department of Philosophy, University of Copenhagen, Copenhagen.

Ilundáin-Agurruza, J. (2016) *Holism and the Cultivation of Excellence in Sports and Performative Endeavors: Skillful Striving*, London and New York: Routledge.

Keller, P. E. (2008) "Joint Action in Music Performance," in F. Morganti, A. Carassa, and G. Riva (eds.) *Enacting Intersubjectivity: A Cognitive and Social Perspective on the Study of Interactions*, 205–21, Amsterdam: IOS Press.

Keller, P. E., Knoblich, G., and Repp, B. H. (2007) "Pianists Duet Better When They Play with Themselves: On the Possible Role of Action Simulation in Synchronization," *Consciousness and Cognition* 16: 102–11.

Krein, K., and Ilundáin-Agurruza, J. (2014) "An East-West Comparative Analysis of Mushin and Flow," in G. Priest and D. Young (eds.) *Philosophy and the Martial Arts*, London and New York: Routledge.

Legrand, D. (2007) "Pre-Reflective Self-Consciousness: On Being Bodily in the World," *Janus Head* 9: 493–519.

Loehr, J. D., Kourtis, D., Vesper, C., Sebanz, N., and Knoblich, G. (2013) "Monitoring Individual and Joint Action Outcomes in Duet Music Performance," *Journal of Cognitive Neuroscience* 25: 1049–61.

Maravita, A., and Iriki, A. (2004) "Tools for the Body (Schema)," *Trends in Cognitive Sciences* 8: 79–86.

McDowell, J. (2007) "What Myth?" *Inquiry* 50: 338–51.

Merleau-Ponty, M. (1964) *Signs*, Evanston, IL: Northwestern University Press.

Merleau-Ponty, M. (2012) *Phenomenology of Perception*, trans. D. A. Landes, London: Routledge.

Montero, B. G. (2012) "Practice Makes Perfect: The Effect of Dance Training on the Aesthetic Judge," *Phenomenology and the Cognitive Sciences* 11: 59–68.

—— (2015) "Thinking in the Zone: The Expert Mind in Action," *The Southern Journal of Philosophy* 53: 126–40.

—— (2016) *Thought in Action: Expertise and the Conscious Mind*, Oxford: Oxford University Press.

Montgomery, J., and Chambers, M. (2009) *Mastering Swimming*, Champaign, IL: Human Kinetics.

Repp, B. H., and Su, Y. H. (2013) "Sensorimotor Synchronization: A Review of Recent Research (2006–2012)," *Psychonomic Bulletin & Review* 20: 403–52.

Salice, A., Høffding, S., and Gallagher, S. (2019) "Putting Plural Self-Awareness into Practice: The Phenomenology of Expert Musicianship," *Topoi* 38: 197–209.

Schutz, A. (1976) *Collected Papers* Vol II, Dordrecht: Springer.

Seddon, F. A., and Biasutti, M. (2009) "Modes of Communication between Members of a String Quartet," *Small Group Research* 40: 115–37.

Selinger, E. M., and Crease, R. P. (2002) "Dreyfus on Expertise: The Limits of Phenomenological Analysis," *Continental Philosophy Review* 35: 245–79.

Shusterman, R. (2008) *Body Consciousness: A Philosophy of Mindfulness and Somaesthetics*, Cambridge: Cambridge University Press.

Sōhō, T. (1986) *The Unfettered Mind: Writings of the Zen Master to the Sword Master*, Tokyo: Kodansha.

Soliman, T. M., and Glenberg, A. M. (2014) "The Embodiment of Culture," in L. Shapiro (ed.) *The Routledge Handbook of Embodied Cognition*, 207–19, London: Routledge.

Sutton, J., McIlwain, D., Christensen, W., and Geeves, A. (2011) "Applying Intelligence to the Reflexes: Embodied Skills and Habits between Dreyfus and Descartes," *Journal of the British Society for Phenomenology* 42: 78–103.

Todes, S. (2001) *Body and World*, Cambridge, MA: MIT Press.

Toner, J., Montero, B. G., and Moran, A. (2016) "Reflective and Prereflective Bodily Awareness in Skilled Action," *Psychology of Consciousness: Theory, Research, and Practice* 3: 303–15.

Young, I. M. (1980) "Throwing Like a Girl: A Phenomenology of Feminine Body Comportment Motility and Spatiality," *Human Studies* 3: 137–56.

31

THE EVOLUTION OF SKILLED IMITATIVE LEARNING

A social attention hypothesis

Antonella Tramacere and Richard Moore

Humans possess many skills that other animals do not. Among our distinctively and perhaps uniquely human skills are the uses of a range of sophisticated motor tools (such as tools that modify or extend the control of biological effectors, like hands or legs), sensorial tools (that enhance the capacities of sensory organs) and cognitive and communicative tools (including the natural number system and natural languages). Given the unique nature of our skillset, questions arise about its origins. Are these human-specific skills biologically inherited, or are they learned? And if they are learned, what explains our capacity for learning them?

Some uniquely human skills are thought to arise partly on the back of our possession of another more fundamental skill: a uniquely human form of social learning – imitation.[1]

Imitation is a form of action copying in which an agent is concerned to replicate the precise strategy of an observed demonstration (Fridland & Moore 2015; after Tomasello 2010). This concern allows imitative learners to reproduce faithfully the actions that they watch others perform, and to accumulate knowledge through observation of their peers.

In recent accounts that emphasise the role of social learning in the development of the human skillset, imitation has been thought to play a foundational role, because its mastery allows for the rapid acquisition of a large number of further skills (Richerson & Boyd 2008; Moore 2013a; Fridland 2018). Since imitation is available even to cognitively undeveloped individuals, including pre-verbal infants, it constitutes a simple mechanism through which further cognitive, manual and sensory tools can be developed. To illustrate with examples, the acquisition of spoken language seems to require (among other things) vocal imitation. The words and sentences of a natural language are usable only to the extent that they are copied with a high degree of accuracy, since poorly imitated utterances might be incomprehensible. Imitation, therefore, seems necessary for the development of natural languages in ontogeny and phylogeny (Fridland & Moore 2015; Moore 2013a; Tomasello 2010; Tramacere & Moore 2018).

Imitation has also been argued to be important for the production and mastery of manual tools, such as the spears and long bows needed for hunting large prey (Boyd et al. 2011; see also Moore 2016). Many tools could, in principle, be produced by individuals in isolation through trial and error. Indeed, recent findings support the view that hominini invented and re-invented tools many times during hominid evolution (Tennie et al. 2017; Braun et al. 2019). However, as the number and complexity of tools used by a given population increased, copying technological solutions from others would have become an adaptive strategy. Agents who were able to copy an expert demonstrator's tool-making techniques could have quickly produced a stock of high-calibre equipment, and by using the same skills to copy demonstrations of tool use could train themselves to use those tools. Meanwhile, agents who copied poorly would have been more likely to produce poor-quality tools, and to use them without skill. Alternatively, they might have been forced to spend time and effort reinventing tools for themselves. Thus, imitation is hypothesised to have been central to explaining our human ancestors' ability to adapt to and survive in a variety of climates since their migration out of Africa sometime between 50,000 and 120,000 years ago.[2]

Since imitation contributes to the accumulation of human knowledge and cultural products and is shared by other species only in limited respects, it seems well placed to contribute to an explanation of why some elements of human cognition are uniquely human. Comparative studies show that humans use imitative learning strategies to acquire cultural practices by copying others' actions (e.g., Henrich 2015; Tennie et al. 2009; Tomasello 2010). In contrast, neither monkeys nor apes seem to imitate, although apes sometimes use other forms of social learning such as emulation (see Whiten & Ham 1992; Moore 2013b for discussion). These typically result in less faithful forms of cultural learning. A chimpanzee, for example, might learn that a certain tool can be used to retrieve a piece of food, but typically won't pay close attention to the techniques with which others use it. Thus, chimpanzees will fail to learn behaviours that can be learned only with high fidelity copying. Tennie and collaborators (Tennie et al. 2009) demonstrated this by showing that chimpanzees were unable to produce a rope lasso to retrieve food even after watching others use one. Meanwhile four-year-old children learned the same skill with relative ease (ibid.). For this reason, chimpanzee communities seem unable to support processes of cultural evolution where imitation is required.

The scarcity of imitation in non-human species, and its ubiquity in human activities, has the potential to explain why other primate species fail to learn skills humans learn easily. Thus, imitative learning in humans seems to be important for understanding the origins of human cognition and culture, because it facilitates the learning of other valuable skills. It makes learning to imitate a crucial cognitive achievement in human history. For this reason, cognitive scientists have wondered whether imitation is itself an adaptation, or whether it has been learned through cultural processes.

In this chapter we address an ongoing debate about the origins of human imitation. Specifically, we discuss whether the observation and execution of fine-grained manual and vocal actions associated with imitative learning is the result of biological or cultural changes in the hominin lineage, with particular reference to the Mirror Neuron System hypothesis.

There are currently two central hypotheses about the origins of human imitation. According to one influential view, defended by Michael Arbib among others, the Mirror Neuron System (MNS) in humans is a candidate for being the neural substrate of action copying behaviour. According to Arbib, the MNS possessed by humans emerged in the hominin lineage under selection pressure for the skilled copying of manual behaviour, in the service of better tool use and gestural communication (Arbib 2005, 2012, 2017). The emergence of a complex manual imitation system supported by an evolved MNS distinguished the hominin lines from the great apes and enabled us to acquire new skills through imitative learning. During phylogeny this manual imitation system extended to the vocal domain when our ancestors, who communicated using gestures, switched to vocal communication in order to free their hands for other tasks. Thus, according to Arbib's view, we possess domain-specific adaptations for manual and vocal imitation: a bodily mapping schema for matching others' actions to one's own. It is because selection for this system occurred after humans split from our last common ancestor with great apes that we alone are imitators par excellence.

Against this view, a group of psychologists led by Celia Heyes argue that imitation is a product of cultural and not biological evolution; and that the MNS is composed of only domain-general cognitive processes that are shared with other species and trained in human ontogeny (e.g. Heyes 2018). According to this view, if humans are good imitators it is because we have learned to be so – possibly with the assistance of cultural practices developed to cultivate imitative success. Thus, what makes humans but not great apes good at imitative learning is not a matter of our biological inheritance but our having participated in the right sorts of cultural entrainment.

In this chapter, we suggest a third account of the origins of human imitation. It borrows elements from both the nativist and non-nativist hypotheses while offering a parsimonious explanation of the cognitive and neurobiological differences between humans and other species. Consistent with Arbib's view, we argue that hominini underwent biological changes that supported the development of fine imitative skills. However, contra Arbib, we will propose that these changes may not have been triggered by selective pressure for imitation per se; and they did not result in an MNS specialised for complex imitation in humans. In agreement with Heyes, we argue that high-fidelity imitative skills are learned and depend on changes in the social environment. Contra Heyes, though, we posit that humans have been adapted for social learning – by undergoing selection for better social attention combined with selection for enhanced motor control in the manual, facial and vocal domains. On our view, the emergence in humans of sophisticated and multimodal social learning strategies exploited a combination of biological and socio-environmental resources.

Our story has implications for, among other things, the characteristics of the cortical MNS (i.e., the temporo-fronto-parietal network of the human brain supporting observation and execution of skilled actions) and the mechanisms for social attention connected to it. It explains why humans alone are exceptional imitators and so why our acquired cultural skillset so exceeds that of other species.

31.1 Uniquely human skills: manual, vocal and orofacial imitation

Imitation is a form of action copying in which the agent is concerned to replicate the precise observed strategy of a demonstration. In light of this concern, an imitator pays attention to the way the copied agent acts and subsequently tries to recreate her actions as carefully as possible (Fridland & Moore 2015). Where an imitator can identify the goals of others and carefully copy the actions they are pursuing in order to achieve those goals – either by uttering words, or performing manual actions – an imitating individual can acquire new resources (e.g., a natural language or mastery of a new tool).

At the cognitive level, imitation involves a perceptual representation of an observed sequence of behaviours that are matched to a pattern of motor activation that can produce the same sequence of behaviours. Consequently, imitative learning requires that agents recognise intentional actions and can match their own voluntary bodily actions to those of an observed agent. This involves abilities for recognising others' goals, selecting appropriate goal-directed movements for performing a task, controlling motor output based on predictions about the actions needed to realise that task, and being guided by perceptual feedback in order to make adjustments to improve one's chances of success. Attention to others' actions and fine motor control of the biological effectors (e.g. hand, mouth and larynx) used to reproduce actions are therefore fundamental for imitative success.

While infants from one year of age are able to reproduce complex action sequences, both in the manual and the vocal domain (Jones & Herbert 2008), great apes do not. Chimpanzees are capable of what has been called simple imitation (Arbib 2002), or emulation (Tennie et al. 2009). This allows actions to be acquired through a focus on the end product of the observed activities. However, a number of experiments suggest that while chimpanzees are capable of recognising the goals with which others are acting through observations of their behaviour, they do not spontaneously perform high-fidelity action copying (Arbib 2005; Tennie et al. 2006, 2009, 2012; Tomasello 1990). Rather than copying others' manual and vocal behaviours, they recreate their own ways of achieving the goal they have watched others pursue. In the more restrictive characterisation of imitation useful for cultural evolution research (see Fridland & Moore 2015), this makes chimpanzees capable of emulation but worse at imitation.

31.2 The Mirror Neuron System as a neural substrate of imitative learning

Recent work in cognitive neuroscience suggests that imitative learning is implemented by the temporo-fronto-parietal (TFP) network, a network of cortical regions associated with the execution of a range of actions including hand gestures, tool actions and vocalisations. Specific parts of the TFP network activate during the observation of the same or similar actions performed by others. This network is therefore collectively defined as the Action Observation Network (AON) or the Mirror Neuron System (MNS).

In this section, we review evidence suggesting that the execution of goal-directed manual and vocal actions involves activations of the TFP network computing individual sensorimotor coordination. Moreover, the perception of these actions performed by others activates parts of the TFP network (the MNS) and facilitates their reproduction and learning (for reviews and meta-analysis see Caspers et al. 2010; Van Overwalle & Baetens 2009; Molenberghs et al. 2012).

A review of existing findings on the neural substrates of the MNS shows that, while the MNS associated with the observation and execution of goal-directed manual and vocal actions are all present in humans, an MNS for the matching of vocal perception and reproduction is not present in non-human primates (Tramacere et al. 2017, 2019). Further, the MNS associated with hand and tool perception and execution present interesting neurophysiological differences between humans and apes. Consequently, the comparative analysis of these networks supports the hypothesis that action copying in humans and apes is governed by different neural mechanisms. This may give important insights into an understanding of how humans evolved to become good imitators, and how imitation supported the historical emergence of a number of associated cultural tools, such as the use of language and technology.

In human and non-human primates, a subclass of sensorimotor neurons called mirror neurons (MNs) fires both when an individual performs an action and when she observes that same or similar action performed by another (Gallese et al. 1996). MNs are embedded in the MNS (Keysers & Perrett 2004; Rizzolatti & Craighero 2004) comprising specific sectors of the frontal (i.e., premotor and motor) and parietal cortices that contain MNs, plus the superior temporal sulcus (STS) that contains only sensorial neurons. In recent years, additional neurophysiological and neuroanatomical studies have led some scholars to propose an "extended MNS", which includes not only these regions of the brain but also the primary motor, the secondary somatosensory and the ventrolateral prefrontal cortex, together with specific limbic and subcortical structures (Bonini 2016; Bruni et al. 2018). Since we are here interested in the high-level multimodal representations associated with the intentional reproduction of perceived actions, we will consider only the cortical TFP regions of the MNS, which are activated during the perception and execution of goal-directed actions.

MNS can be classified in different sub-systems, using two unambiguous physiological criteria: the modalities of sensory input triggering the response, and the effectors involved in the motor output (Tramacere et al. 2017). Consequently, we treat the hand visuomotor and the audio-vocal MNS as independent mirror systems. In this way we can analyse independently how hand and vocal actions are represented in the brain, and identify the neurobiological correlates of different sensorimotor skills and their behavioural implementations across species. We refer to the hand visuomotor MNS (hereafter hand MNS) as the network of neuronal cells activated by the observation of others' hand gestures that are also involved in the control of one's own hand actions. We use the term audio-vocal MNS to refer to the network of neurons that discharge during both listening and vocalising.

The recruitment of the human hand MNS is associated with imitative tasks performed in a social context (Cross & Iacoboni 2014a; Iacoboni 2005; Kessler et al. 2006). For instance, the execution of manual actions after observation of the same action performed by another leads to an increased activation of the MNS compared to when the same manual action is performed in response to a symbolic cue, suggesting that the hand MNS works by mapping sensory information to motor knowledge (Iacoboni et al. 1999). Further, a number of Transcranial Magnetic Stimulation and kinematic experiments show that the observation of some manual actions prime (and thereby facilitate) the execution of similar actions. This shows that the observation and execution of specific movements relies on the same neural mechanisms (Cross & Iacoboni 2014b).

Using imaging studies, the activation of the chimpanzee and human hand MNS has been compared during observation of goal-directed and non-goal-directed grasping actions. Results show the human parietal and occipitotemporal regions of the MNS activated significantly more, especially during non-goal-directed actions (Hecht et al. 2012). This finding correlates with those showing that in chimpanzees there is a greater discrepancy between the ventral (frontal with superior temporal lobe) and the dorsal streams (frontal with parietal lobe), with the ventral components larger than and strengthened relative to the dorsal ones (Hecht et al. 2013). In humans this difference is not present. Further, in humans but not in chimpanzees an additional dorsal pathway passes through the parietal opercular white matter to the anterior supramarginal gyrus, with the latter univocally implicated in tool-use (Orban 2016; Peeters et al. 2009). Finally, the link between the mirror parietal region (enlarged in humans and associated with spatial coding) and the inferior temporal sulcus, where objects and tools are recognised, is more developed in humans than in chimpanzees (Hecht et al. 2013).

Functionally speaking, the ventral stream is considered the What route, devoted to identifying objects and events and to computing what has been defined as "vision for perception". The ventral stream may be used in processing the end-results of observed actions, because it works "to select the goal object from the visual array" (Goodale & Milner 2013: 100). On the contrary, the dorsal stream (known as the Where-How route) supports the kinds of visuomotor transformation in which visual input leads to manual actions such as reaching, grasping and manipulating objects (Goodale et al. 2004). The dorsal stream can be considered a "vision for action" pathway that processes the spatial mapping of movements and allows the extraction of a finer level of action kinematics (Goldenberg & Spatt 2009; Johnson-Frey et al. 2003).

The findings of the selectively greater activation in the ventro-parietal cortex during observation of goal-directed and especially non-goal-directed actions in humans compared to chimpanzees can be interpreted in the light of this evidence. A greater portion of the human parietal cortex is dedicated to finer level action processing. These areas are recruited during the observations of others' actions, potentially for inferring the proximate goals of these actions, and for translating observed actions for the performance of similar actions (Kilner et al. 2007).

In support of this hypothesis, studies in patients with specific impairments in the parietal cortex further show that the dorsal stream is implicated in processing the causal relation of objects that are commonly used in sequence (e.g., a hammer and nails), a phenomenon called paired-object affordance. Moreover, selective lesions in uniquely human-represented sectors of the parietal cortex indicate a dissociation between the neural mechanisms that support the simple grasping of an object and those that support using an object following specific action plans (Binkofski & Buxbaum 2013; Johnson-Frey 2004). This provides evidence that the human-specific expansion of sectors of the parietal cortex is implicated in understanding the general principles of tool use and causal interactions between objects.

The role of the frontoparietal pathway in visuomotor transformation has also been generalised to the auditory-vocal domain. Concerning the auditory domain, both human and non-human primates seem to possess a similar kind of auditory processing (Rauschecker & Scott 2009), while a dramatic difference between human and non-human primates lies in their respective abilities for vocal production. Classically, vocal communication in non-human primates has been attributed to mesial and subcortical structures and thought to be involuntary, due to mainly emotional and motivational control (Jurgens 2002). Consequently, non-human primates have been typically described as lacking the discrete and voluntary vocalisation that can be detected in humans and that can be ascribed to the somatosensory motor control found in the frontoparietal pathways of the human cortex.

However, several sources of evidence now speak in favour of a greater control of voluntary vocalisation in non-human primates. Recent experiments showed that the monkey homologue of Broca's area, as well as the premotor and/or primary motor cortices, are all involved in the initiation of volitional calls that have been uttered in response to visual or auditory stimuli (Coude et al. 2011; Hage & Nieder 2013). Further, a fraction of neurons in these areas exhibit responses to auditory stimulation with species-specific calls (Hage & Nieder 2015). Since the auditory responses do not temporally match the pattern of vocal output, these neurons cannot be considered audio-vocal MNs (by definition). However, the findings suggest that the frontal cortex in primates is involved in the multisensory control of oro-facial cues and may constitute a precursor of cortical control in the evolution of vocal learning (Hage & Nieder 2016). Interestingly, studies in songbirds show that vocal learning is grounded in a mechanism of matching between vocal output and auditory feedback (both in a social and a first-person perspective), which involves, at the sub-personal level, neurons that show a precise temporal matching between auditory and vocal stimuli (Prather et al. 2008).

We interpret this evidence as showing that the more the performance of a specific action requires a fine level of kinematics and complex causal control, the more it involves larger regions of the TFP network and temporally precise matching between sensory and motor stimuli (Tramacere et al. 2019). The stronger activation of the MNS in humans with respect to manual and vocal perception in a social context can, thus, be interpreted in terms of humans possessing more developed capacities for manual and vocal fine-grained and sequential (i.e. skilled) motor control. In sum, the neurobiological evidence described so far suggests that there are substantial neurological differences between human and non-human primates with respect to the areas of the brain that have been identified as playing a role in imitative learning. It is a further question whether these differences are a product of our evolutionary history or whether they are learned in ontogeny.

31.3 The evolution of the MNS

In recent years a debate has arisen concerning the origins of the MNS and its status as an important neurobiological candidate for explaining imitative learning. It is a matter of ongoing debate whether the neurobiological differences described above are the product of a process of natural section or whether they might themselves arise as a product of cultural learning. Two rival hypotheses, discussed in the sections below, have been proposed: (1) the associative hypothesis (Cook et al. 2014; Heyes 2014) and (2) the adaptive hypothesis (Arbib 2005; Rizzolatti & Arbib 1998; for a review see also Ferrari et al. 2013). Proponents of the associative hypothesis argue that the ability of humans to imitate (and thereby acquire advanced linguistic and techno-logical skills) is a product of cultural and not biological evolution. On the contrary, proponents of the adaptive hypothesis argue that human beings possess adaptations for imitation and that these enable their skilled learning of cultural practices and products.

31.3.1 Mirror neurons and imitation are not in our genes

According to the associative learning (ASL) hypothesis, MNs are forged through associative learning, which connects observing and executing the same actions. Associative learning offers a parsimonious explanation for how neurons acquire mirroring properties: contingent and repeated activation of the sensory and motor representation of an action cause sensorimotor associations. Sensorimotor associations at the behavioural level produce Hebbian learning at the subpersonal level: sensory and motor "neurons that fire together, wire together" (Hebb 2005). Sensorimotor neurons are, first, associated through the observed experience of our own behaviour. A subpart of these neurons also activates during the observation of others' behav-iour. Clusters of neurons thus acquire differential observation-execution matching properties through a domain-general process of associative learning.

As a by-product of individual learning, MNs may play a functional role in social learning but they need not have a specific adaptive function (Cook et al. 2014). According to the associative hypothesis, biological evolution has played a non-specific background role in the evolution of MNs and associated cognitive skills, including imitation. The general abilities for associative learning and connectivity between the sensory and motor cortices are genetic adaptations, while the characteristic matching properties of MNs are forged by sensorimotor learning.

In particular, the associative hypothesis states that (i) neither human nor non-human pri-mates have a specific genetic predisposition to develop MNs; these animals do not inherit a set of MNs, or even a domain-specific learning mechanism that promotes the develop-ment of MNs. (ii) Human and non-human primates have genetic predispositions to develop (a) connections between particular sensory and motor areas of the cortex, which evolved because it promotes precise visual control of action, and (b) a domain-general capacity for asso-ciative learning. (iii) When individuals with these predispositions receive correlated experience of observing and executing the same actions they develop MNs for those actions. (iv) MNs are primarily a collateral result of individual sensorimotor learning and social interactions and, although MNs may contribute to behaviour in a number of important ways once they have been developed, they are not an adaptation for any specific social learning function (Cook et al. 2014; Heyes 2014).

On this associative view, MNs and imitation are not products of biological evolution. They result from a process of the generalisation of individual sensorimotor learning. We learn to imitate through culture-specific forms of social interaction. These include culturally trained processes of socialised attention, and activities such as perceiving one's own and others' oro-facial and manual actions. Experiences of our own and others' bodies in everyday life are further trained by cultural practices such as looking at ourselves in mirrors – practices that are predicted to contribute substantially to the maturation of the MNS in ontogeny. The same neural and behavioural mechanisms mediate individual motor learning and social cognitive skills. Bodily movements are represented in the same way during individual visual feedback in the course of motor coordination and during observations of other's actions. In the case of imitation for example, the domain-general mechanisms of motor learning process social input – i.e. the observed actions of others – rather than executed individual bodily movements. Processing of this input is made possible by a set of bidirectional excitatory links or vertical associations, each of which connects sensory (usually visual) and motor representations of the same movement. MNS, and thus imitation, are not genetically programmed. What makes us good imitators lies in the social environment in which we are raised and in general processes of cultural evolution (Heyes 2011, 2016a)

31.3.2 Evolving imitation for a language ready brain

In contrast to the associative hypothesis, some scholars have formulated an adaptive hypothesis. They propose that macaque and human MNS are an evolutionarily conserved neural mechanism that has been selected during phylogeny for accomplishing high-level cognitive functions, such as action understanding, imitation, mind-reading and language (Arbib 2005; Gallese & Goldman 1998; Gentilucci & Corballis 2006; Rizzolatti & Craighero 2004). One function of this system is (paraphrasing Heyes 2018) to map the felt-but-not-seen movements of our own bodies to the seen-but-not-felt movements of others' bodies. (Heyes calls this process "solving the correspondence problem".) Once observers have mapped others' actions to their own movements they can use first personal abilities to infer the goals that others' actions were intended to realise. Thus, this mapping system generates knowledge of the goals underlying others' actions.

Michael Arbib has defended one variant of this adaptive proposal. We focus on his account, because he has clearly explained the cognitive functions (imitation and language) that are hypothesised to drive the evolution of the human MNS. Arbib's mirror system hypothesis claims that the MNS for grasping present in macaques and chimpanzees evolved into a key component of the mechanisms that rendered the brain of recent human ancestors ready for learning imitatively a proto-language consisting of manual gestures, and subsequently a syntactically structured vocal language (Arbib 2005). Specifically:

> [I]mitation is seen as evolving via a so-called simple [mirror] system such as that found in chimpanzees (which allows imitation of complex "object-oriented" sequences) to a so-called complex system found in humans (which allows rapid imitation even of complex sequences, under appropriate conditions) which supports pantomime. This is hypothesized to have provided the substrate for the development of ... protosign and protospeech then developing in an expanding spiral. ... [T]hese stages involve biological evolution of both brain and body.
>
> *Arbib 2005: 105*

Arbib specifies that possessing a macaque-like MNS for grasping does not guarantee the development of any imitative or linguistic abilities. The MNS associated with hand actions shared by the common ancestor of human and monkeys is simply the necessary first step for developing imitative skills in the manual and vocal domains. This prototypical hand MNS enabled only the voluntary control of hand actions and the understanding of manual gestures for communicative purposes. In contrast, the common ancestor of chimpanzees and humans shared a hand MNS sufficient for not only the voluntary control of hand actions but also for emulation – the form of action copying that apes are able to perform.

According to Arbib, only in the recent hominin lineage (i.e. hominini who were ancestors of humans but not chimpanzees and bonobos) did a further biological step enable the emergence of "true imitation" in the vocal domain, following selection pressure for the mastery of a gestural protolanguage. The development of this protolanguage was made possible only by imitation in the manual domain: prior to the emergence of sophisticated vocal communication, our ancestors communicated using imitatively learned gestures. It was only at a later stage of evolution that communication migrated into the vocal domain (see Tramacere & Moore (2018) for discussion).

This evolutionary step is hypothesised to have brought a series of biological changes. Starting from the connections between the premotor, parietal and temporal areas in macaques (which we shall call the "monkey MNS"), changes "lifted" the premotor homologue of the common ancestor of human and monkey to yield the human (premotor and frontal) Broca's area, and also "lifted" the other regions to yield (the parietal) Wernicke's area and other areas that support imitation and subsequently language development in the human brain (Arbib 2005: 106).

Setting aside Arbib's metaphorical and somewhat opaque talk of "lifting", the view that emerges here is that human imitation is a product of evolutionary changes that occurred during our accession to language. These changes equipped us with an inborn ability to map others' actions to our own, and thereby interpret the intentions underlying them. This in turn gave us new abilities for imitative learning.

31.3.3 *The evolution of the MNS: the social attention hypothesis*

Proponents of the adaptationist and associative accounts have responded to each others' arguments at length. Heyes (2018) has argued, for example, that imitative tongue-protrusion apart, there is no evidence that children are born with imitative learning abilities (see Heyes 2016b; Oostenbroek et al. 2016). Consequently she argues that there is "no good reason to believe that the capacity for imitation is genetically inherited" (Heyes 2018: 129). Heyes also points to evidence that imitative abilities improve following sensorimotor experience (see Catmur et al. (2009) and Cook et al. (2014) reviews) as evidence that imitation is learned.

Proponents of the adaptationist view argue that the proponents of the associative view have constructed a straw-man argument against the adaptive view, because they work with a concept of adaption that is unnecessarily rigid. They claim that even though the proponents of the associative view convincingly proved that the MNS is modulated by experience, this does not mean that our capacity to match sensory and motor representations is not an adaptation (Lingnau & Caramazza 2014).

We would add that Heyes' hypothesis that the human skill for social learning is itself learned fails to explain why our species is so uniquely good at social learning. On current formulation it says very little about the behavioural and neurological differences between humans and other primates – differences that seemingly support our differential abilities for skilled action copying. Yet it is consensus – as Heyes herself acknowledges (2018) – that apes are not capable of learning to imitate as skilfully as humans do. This may be because the differences between human and ape social learning are correlated with unlearned biological differences.[3]

For reasons of space we will not evaluate in full the arguments for and against the adaptationist and associative views here. However, we want to suggest that a third option is also consistent with existing data. It takes elements from both views and gives a plausible account not only of the complex human abilities for imitation, and the specific human neural circuitry that supports them, but also of the role of social learning in the development of imitation in human ontogeny.

The starting point of our hybrid account is that both the associative and adaptive accounts are to some extent plausible and heuristically fruitful. The associative hypothesis is a parsimonious and testable account of how any brain possessing connectivity between sensory and motor cortices and capable of associative learning could give rise to something like an MNS. Meanwhile the adaptive hypothesis provides a valuable working hypothesis for identifying and explaining the changes associated with species-specific differences in cognitive functions based on brain properties and non-equivalent social learning abilities.

At the same time both accounts are also somewhat limited. The associative hypothesis does not explain why chimpanzees are poor at social learning. One plausible explanation of this difference is that species that imitate well have undergone selection pressure for imitation-relevant abilities, if not imitation per se.

We suggest that a variety of cerebral and cognitive mechanisms – e.g., hierarchical coding and control of own movements, coarse-grained sensorimotor connectivity, selective attention for others' actions and specific input representation – are necessary for the development of an MNS that is consistently activated during the perception of others' actions, and for social cognition in general (Bonaiuto 2014). In other words, connections between sensory and motor regions plus associative learning are necessary but not sufficient for MNS involvement in imitative learning. Specifically, the MNS can be better understood as a neural system connecting expanded cortical areas evolved for facilitating sensorimotor development in an individual and social perspective. Such systems likely evolved in environments where the monitoring and continuous comparison of one's own and others' actions was fundamental for cognitive development.

Following Heyes, our account endorses the proposition that sensorimotor experience plays a constitutive role in the development of MNs through associative learning, but adds that without special-purpose social learning mechanisms (such as an adaptation that predisposes agents to be attentive to others, and to the actions that they perform) the development of imitative learning as we observe it in humans would not have arisen. According to this account, extant ancestors of macaques and humans developed flexible mechanisms of sensorimotor control, such as the MNS, by relying on specific connectivity between sensorial and motor areas of the brain. During phylogeny, developing MNS started to play a key role in social cognition as a result of increased social demands (e.g. action monitoring and copying). Consequently, selection pressures emerged that led to the development of flexible sensorimotor mechanisms sensitive to and modulated by social conditions, so that the properties and distribution of the MNS reflected not only sensorimotor experiences, but also the socio-cognitive evolution of species (Ferrari et al. 2013; Tramacere et al. 2015, 2017).

31.4 The evolution of skilled imitative learning

The central content of our proposal here is that humans are not biologically adapted for imitation per se. Rather, we have undergone selection to be more attentive to the actions of our peers.[4] Additionally we have undergone selection for fine-grained motor control and sequential learning of complex actions. Because humans are biologically prepared to attend to others' motor actions, and to physically perform these actions, we are particularly good at copying others' intentional behavioural sequences. As a result, imitation is learned, and learned on the back of evolved skills for attending to and performing fine-grained motor actions, thus making human social attention sensorimotor in nature. Our imitative skills are a by-product of natural selection for both skilled motor control (particularly in the manual and oro-facial domains) and social attention – specifically toward the motor actions performed by others (again, particularly oro-facial and manual actions).

While the study of attentional patterns of humans and great apes is in its infancy, some differences between our species have become apparent already (see Hirata & Myowa 2018). These are consistent with our hypothesis that there are evolved differences in the way that humans and great apes attend to actions.

No studies that we know of have yet looked at whether there are differences in the ways that humans and other ape species attend to actions. However, we predict that differences would be apparent. In particular, we hypothesise that humans would be better than non-human great apes at attending to the manual and vocal actions of others, and at recognising both goals and motor strategies with which actions are performed. In contrast, we would expect chimpanzee attention to be more oriented to the objects on which an agent acted. This would be reflected in differences in how chimpanzees and humans reproduce the actions they had observed – with the humans' manual actions being more carefully and accurately reproduced.

It follows from our view that imitation must be learned. (This would be true even if attentional differences are unlearned.) Given that imitation must be learned, it's likely that developed skills for imitation have been honed by human cultural practices like those described by Heyes, and that there would be changes in both imitation (and perhaps also changes to attention) in ontogeny. Nonetheless, we hypothesise that human (but not great ape) ancestors underwent selection for better social attention and motor control. If this is right, our cultural practices build on a biological preparedness to learn from others. Chimpanzees raised in a human environment might become better imitators than if they were raised in the wild, but they would still not be as adept at motor execution and observation as we are, simply because they are not capable of the same flexible control, and because their social attentional resources are comparatively poor.

This social attention hypothesis has yet to be tested directly. However, it is consistent with a number of lines of evidence from comparative studies of primate and human cognition. For example, great apes seem to be less attentive to one another, and to human caregivers, than are humans to their peers (Moore, personal observation). This difference likely stems from a number of sources. These include the greater need for humans to communicate in order to solve coordination problems and secure food (see Moore 2017; Moore et al. 2015) and the greater reliance of humans on social learning (Fridland & Moore 2015; Henrich 2015; Moore 2013a, 2013b). Our hybrid view is also attractively parsimonious, since small tweaks to social attention could have improved both our ancestors' communicative abilities (Moore 2017) and their social learning skills. It may be, for example, that a chimp-like tendency in our ancestors to look to the world for solutions to their problems was replaced by a human-like tendency to look to peers for solutions (Kano et al. 2018). We think this proposal is worthy of further investigation, in both empirical and conceptual domains.

Notes

1 Whether or not imitation is itself a skill will, of course, depend on what we take skills to be. But – as this chapter will argue – it seems to possess at least one key feature of many skills: it is learned and perfected through practice.
2 For discussion of the importance of social learning to hominin and human survival see Boyd, Richerson, and Henrich (2011), Sterelny (2012) and Moore (2016). For an argument that the importance of imitation for tool mastery has at least sometimes been overstated in phylogeny see Tennie et al. (2017). For recent discussion of ancestral migrations out of Africa, see Timmermann and Friedrich (2016).
3 Another possibility is that great apes have not been enculturated and trained in imitation in ways that would make comparisons with human imitators legitimate. This concern is reasonable but given the dubious ethics of raising chimpanzees in human environments it is not likely to be tested any time soon (see Leavens, Bard, & Hopkins 2019).
4 For an application of our social attention hypothesis to the interpretation of differences in human and chimpanzee understanding of referential communication see Kano et al. (2018).

References

Arbib, M. A. (2002) "The mirror system, imitation, and the evolution of language", in K. Dautenhahn & C. L. Nehaniv (eds.) *Imitation in Animals and Artifacts* (pp. 229–280). Cambridge, MA: MIT Press.
—— (2005) "From monkey-like action recognition to human language: an evolutionary framework for neurolinguistics", *Behavioral and Brain Sciences, 28*(2), 105–124; discussion 125–167.
—— (2012) "Tool use and constructions", *Behavioral and Brain Sciences, 35*(4), 218–219.
—— (2017) "Toward the language-ready brain: biological evolution and primate comparisons", *Psychonomic Bulletin & Review, 24*(1), 142–150.
Binkofski, F., & Buxbaum, L. J. (2013) "Two action systems in the human brain," *Brain and Language, 127*(2), 222–229.
Bonaiuto, J. (2014) "Associative learning is necessary but not sufficient for mirror neuron development", *Behavioral and Brain Sciences, 37*(2), 194–195.
Bonini, L. (2016) "The extended mirror neuron network: anatomy, origin, and functions", *Neuroscientist, 23*(1), 56–67.
Boyd, R., Richerson, P. J., & Henrich, J. (2011) "The cultural niche: why social learning is essential for human adaptation", *Proceedings of the National Academy of Sciences, 108*(Supplement 2), 10918–10925.
Braun, D. R., Aldeias, V., Archer, W., Arrowsmith, J. R., Baraki, N., Campisano, C. J., … Feary, D. A. (2019) "Earliest known Oldowan artifacts at >2.58 Ma from Ledi-Geraru, Ethiopia, highlight early technological diversity", *Proceedings of the National Academy of Sciences, 116*(24), 11712–11717.
Bruni, S., Gerbella, M., Bonini, L., Borra, E., Coude, G., Ferrari, P. F., … Rozzi, S. (2018) "Cortical and subcortical connections of parietal and premotor nodes of the monkey hand mirror neuron network", *Brain Structure & Function, 223*(4), 1713–1729.
Caspers, S., Zilles, K., Laird, A. R., & Eickhoff, S. B. (2010) "ALE meta-analysis of action observation and imitation in the human brain", *NeuroImage, 50*(3), 1148–1167.
Catmur, C., Walsh, V., & Heyes, C. (2009) "Associative sequence learning: the role of experience in the development of imitation and the mirror system", *Philosophical Transactions of the Royal Society of London B: Biological Sciences, 364*(1528), 2369–2380.
Cook, R., Bird, G., Catmur, C., Press, C., & Heyes, C. (2014) "Mirror neurons: from origin to function", *Behavioral and Brain Sciences, 37*(2), 177–192.
Coude, G., Ferrari, P. F., Roda, F., Maranesi, M., Borelli, E., Veroni, V., … Fogassi, L. (2011) "Neurons controlling voluntary vocalization in the macaque ventral premotor cortext", *PLoS One, 6*(11), e26822.
Cross, K. A., & Iacoboni, M. (2014a) "Neural systems for preparatory control of imitation", *Philosophical Transactions of the Royal Society of London. Series B, Biological Sciences, 369*(1644), 20130176.
—— (2014b) "To imitate or not: avoiding imitation involves preparatory inhibition of motor resonance", *Neuroimage, 91*, 228–236.
Ferrari, P. F., Tramacere, A., Simpson, E. A., & Iriki, A. (2013) "Mirror neurons through the lens of epigenetics", *Trends in Cognitive Sciences, 17*(9), 450–457.

Fridland, E. (2018) "Do as I say and as I do: imitation, pedagogy, and cumulative culture", *Mind & Language, 33*(4), 355–377.

Fridland, E., & Moore, R. (2015) "Imitation reconsidered", *Philosophical Psychology, 28*(6), 856–880.

Gallese, V., Fadiga, L., Fogassi, L., & Rizzolatti, G. (1996) "Action recognition in the premotor cortex", *Brain, 119 (Pt 2)*, 593–609.

Gallese, V., & Goldman, A. (1998) "Mirror neurons and the simulation theory of mind-reading", *Trends in Cognitive Sciences, 2*(12), 493–501.

Gentilucci, M., & Corballis, M. C. (2006) "From manual gesture to speech: a gradual transition", *Neuroscience & Biobehavioral Reviews, 30*(7), 949–960.

Goldenberg, G., & Spatt, J. (2009) "The neural basis of tool use", *Brain, 132*(Pt 6), 1645–1655.

Goodale, M., & Milner, D. (2013) *Sight Unseen: An Exploration of Conscious and Unconscious Vision*: Oxford: Oxford University Press.

Goodale, M., Westwood, D. A., & Milner, A. D. (2004) "Two distinct modes of control for object-directed action", *Progress in Brain Research, 144*, 131–144.

Hage, S. R., & Nieder, A. (2013) "Single neurons in monkey prefrontal cortex encode volitional initiation of vocalizations", *Nature Communications, 4*, 2409. doi:10.1038/ncomms3409

—— (2015) "Audio-vocal interaction in single neurons of the monkey ventrolateral prefrontal cortex", *Journal of Neuroscience, 35*(18), 7030–7040.

—— (2016) "Dual neural network model for the evolution of speech and language", *Trends in Neurosciences, 39*(12), 813–829.

Hebb, D. O. (2005) "The first stage of perception: growth of the assembly", in *The Organization of Behavior* (pp. 102–120). London: Psychology Press.

Hecht, E. E., Gutman, D. A., Preuss, T. M., Sanchez, M. M., Parr, L. A., & Rilling, J. K. (2012) "Process versus product in social learning: comparative diffusion tensor imaging of neural systems for action execution–observation matching in macaques, chimpanzees, and humans", *Cerebral Cortex, 23*(5), 1014–1024.

Hecht, E. E., Murphy, L. E., Gutman, D. A., Votaw, J. R., Schuster, D. M., Preuss, T. M., … Parr, L. A. (2013). "Differences in neural activation for object-directed grasping in chimpanzees and humans", *Journal of Neuroscience, 33*(35), 14117–14134.

Henrich, J. (2015) *The Secret of Our Success: How Culture Is Driving Human Evolution, Domesticating Our Species, and Making Us Smarter*. Princeton, NJ: Princeton University Press.

Heyes, C. (2011) "Automatic imitation", *Psychological Bulletin, 137*(3), 463–483.

—— (2014) "Tinbergen on mirror neurons", *Philosophical Transactions of the Royal Society of London. Series B, Biological Sciences, 369*(1644), 20130180.

—— (2016a) "Born pupils? Natural pedagogy and cultural pedagogy", *Perspectives on Psychological Science, 11*(2), 280–295.

—— (2016b) "Imitation: not in our genes", *Current Biology, 26*(10), R412–R414.

—— (2018) *Cognitive Gadgets: The Cultural Evolution of Thinking*. Cambridge, MA: Harvard University Press.

Hirata, S., & Myowa, M. (2018) "Understanding about others' action in chimpanzees and humans", In K. Shigemasu, S. Kuwano, T. Sato, & T. Matsuzawa (eds.) *Diversity in Harmony: Proceedings of the 31st International Congress of Psychology* (pp. 85–103). Hoboken, NJ: John Wiley & Sons.

Iacoboni, M. (2005) "Neural mechanisms of imitation", *Current Opinion in Neurobiology, 15*(6), 632–637.

Iacoboni, M., Woods, R. P., Brass, M., Bekkering, H., Mazziotta, J. C., & Rizzolatti, G. (1999) "Cortical mechanisms of human imitation", *Science, 286*(5449), 2526–2528.

Johnson-Frey, S. H. (2004) "The neural bases of complex tool use in humans", *Trends in Cognitive Sciences, 8*(2), 71–78.

Johnson-Frey, S. H., Maloof, F. R., Newman-Norlund, R., Farrer, C., Inati, S., & Grafton, S. T. (2003) "Actions or hand-object interactions? Human inferior frontal cortex and action observation", *Neuron, 39*(6), 1053–1058.

Jones, E. J. H., and Herbert, J. S. (2008) "The effect of learning experiences and context on infant imitation and generalization", *Infancy, 13*(6), 596–619.

Jurgens, U. (2002) "A study of the central control of vocalization using the squirrel monkey", *Medical Engineering & Physics, 24*(7–8), 473–477.

Kano, F., Moore, R., Krupenye, C., Hirata, S., Tomonaga, M., & Call, J. (2018) "Human ostensive signals do not enhance gaze following in chimpanzees, but do enhance object-oriented attention", *Animal Cognition, 21*(5), 715–728.

Kessler, K., Biermann-Ruben, K., Jonas, M., Siebner, H. R., Baumer, T., Munchau, A., & Schnitzler, A. (2006) "Investigating the human mirror neuron system by means of cortical synchronization during the imitation of biological movements", *Neuroimage, 33*(1), 227–238.

Keysers, C., & Perrett, D. I. (2004) "Demystifying social cognition: a Hebbian perspective", *Trends in Cognitive Sciences, 8*(11), 501–507.

Kilner, J. M., Friston, K. J., & Frith, C. D. (2007) "Predictive coding: an account of the mirror neuron system", *Cognitive Processing, 8*(3), 159–166.

Leavens, D. A., Bard, K. A., & Hopkins, W.D. (2019) "The mismeasure of ape social cognition", *Animal Cognition, 22*(4), 487–504.

Lingnau, A., & Caramazza, A. (2014) "The origin and function of mirror neurons: The missing link", *Behavioral and Brain Sciences, 37*(2), 209–210.

Molenberghs, P., Cunnington, R., & Mattingley, J. B. (2012) "Brain regions with mirror properties: a meta-analysis of 125 human fMRI Studies", *Neuroscience and Biobehavioral Reviews, 36*(1), 341–349. https://doi.org/10.1016/j.neubiorev.2011.07.004.

Moore, R. (2013a) "Imitation and conventional communication", *Biology & Philosophy, 28*(3), 481–500.

—— (2013b) "Social learning and teaching in chimpanzees", *Biology & Philosophy, 28*(6), 879–901.

—— (2016) "Pedagogy and social learning in human development", in J. Kiverstein (ed.) *Routledge Handbook of Philosophy of the Social Mind* (pp. 35–52). London: Routledge.

—— (2017) "Social cognition, stag hunts, and the evolution of language", *Biology & Philosophy, 32*(6), 797–818.

Moore, R., Call, J., & Tomasello, M. (2015) "Production and comprehension of gestures between orang-utans (Pongo pygmaeus) in a referential communication game", *PLoS One, 10*(6), e0129726.

Oostenbroek, J., Suddendorf, T., Nielsen, M., Redshaw, J., Kennedy-Costantini, S., Davis, J., … Slaughter, V. (2016) "Comprehensive longitudinal study challenges the existence of neonatal imitation in humans", *Current Biology, 26*(10), 1334–1338.

Orban, G. A. (2016) "Functional definitions of parietal areas in human and non-human primates", *Proceedings of the Royal Society B: Biological Sciences, 283*(1828).

Peeters, R., Simone, L., Nelissen, K., Fabbri-Destro, M., Vanduffel, W., Rizzolatti, G., & Orban, G.A. (2009) "The representation of tool use in humans and monkeys: common and uniquely human features", *Journal of Neuroscience, 29*(37), 11523–11539.

Prather, J. F., Peters, S., Nowicki, S., & Mooney, R. (2008) "Precise auditory-vocal mirroring in neurons for learned vocal communication", *Nature, 451*(7176), 305–310.

Rauschecker, J. P., & Scott, S. K. (2009) "Maps and streams in the auditory cortex: nonhuman primates illuminate human speech processing", *Nature Neuroscience, 12*(6), 718–724. doi:10.1038/nn.2331

Richerson, P. J., & Boyd, R. (2008) *Not by Genes Alone: How Culture Transformed Human Evolution.* Chicago, IL: University of Chicago Press.

Rizzolatti, G., & Arbib, M. A. (1998) "Language within our grasp", *Trends in Neurosciences, 21*(5), 188–194.

Rizzolatti, G., & Craighero, L. (2004) "The mirror-neuron system", *Annual Review of Neuroscience, 27,* 169–192.

Sterelny, K. (2012) *The Evolved Apprentice.* Cambridge, MA: MIT Press.

Tennie, C., Call, J., & Tomasello, M. (2006) "Push or pull: imitation vs. emulation in great apes and human children", *Ethology, 112*(12), 1159–1169.

—— (2009) "Ratcheting up the ratchet: on the evolution of cumulative culture", *Philosophical Transactions of the Royal Society of London. Series B, Biological Sciences, 364*(1528), 2405–2415.

—— (2012) "Untrained chimpanzees (Pan troglodytes schweinfurthii) fail to imitate novel actions", *PLoS One, 7*(8), e41548.

Tennie, C., Premo, L. S., Braun, D. R., & McPherron, S. P. (2017) "Early stone tools and cultural transmission: Resetting the null hypothesis", *Current Anthropology, 58*(5), 652–672.

Timmermann, A., & Friedrich, T (2016) "Late Pleistocene climate drivers of early human migration", *Nature, 538*(7623), 92.

Tomasello, M. (1990) "10 Cultural transmission in the tool use and communicatory signaling of chimpanzees?", in S. Parker & K. Gibson (eds.) *'Language' and Intelligence in Monkeys and Apes: Comparative Developmental Perspectives*, (pp. 274–311). Cambridge: Cambridge University Press.

—— (2010) *Origins of Human Communication.* Cambridge, MA: MIT Press.

Tramacere, A., Ferrari, P. F., & Iriki, A. (2015) "Epigenetic regulation of mirror neuron development, and related evolutionary hypotheses", in P. F. Ferrari & G. Rizzolatti (eds.) *New Frontiers in Mirror Neurons Research* (pp. 222–244). Oxford: Oxford University Press.

Tramacere, A., & Moore, R. (2018) "Reconsidering the role of manual imitation in language evolution", *Topoi, 37*(2), 319–328.

Tramacere, A., Pievani, T., & Ferrari, P. F. (2017) "Mirror neurons in the tree of life: mosaic evolution, plasticity and exaptation of sensorimotor matching responses", *Biological Reviews of the Cambridge Philosophical Society, 92*(3), 1819–1841.

Tramacere, A., Wada, K., Okanoya, K., Iriki, A., & Ferrari, P. F. (2019) "Auditory-motor matching in vocal recognition and imitative learning", *Neuroscience, 409*, 222–234.

Van Overwalle, F., & Baetens, K. (2009) "Understanding others' actions and goals by mirror and mentalizing systems: a meta-analysis", *NeuroImage, 48*(3), 564–584.

32

SEMANTIC COMPETENCE

Diego Marconi

The notion of *linguistic* competence was introduced by Noam Chomsky (1965: 3–4) to designate knowledge a speaker/hearer has of her own language, as distinct from her *performance*, i.e., her actual use of language. It is the task of linguistics to infer competence from performance, in spite of the many factors, besides competence, that contribute to the latter. A description of competence is called a *grammar*. What a grammar aims at describing – competence in a language – is an aspect of a speaker's mind, though not one of which speakers themselves are aware: mental processes a grammar deals with "are far beyond the level of actual or even potential consciousness" (Chomsky 1965: 8).

Chomsky insisted that linguistic competence was not to be conceived as a practical ability or a kind of know-how. Ability to use a language may decline or even be lost because of some injury without the underlying knowledge being affected, as is shown by the ability being recovered once the injury's effects recede (e.g., Chomsky 1985: 9). It appeared to follow that competence is a form of propositional knowledge; but, as many philosophers objected (see e.g., Stich 1971), how could it be, as it was both unavailable to consciousness and unjustified? Chomsky's response was that our indisputable ability to differentially assign the appropriate meanings to phonetic structures, to tell well-formed from not well-formed sequences of sounds, etc., showed that we were in some epistemic relation (for a while, he called it "cognizing") with rules and principles such that, if "miraculously" we became aware of them, we would not hesitate to call our relation to them "knowledge" (Chomsky 1980: 70).

Only more recently (1999–2000) he distanced himself from the notion of knowledge of language (or of grammar), arguing that

> one should not expect such concepts [including *knowledge of language*] to play a role in systematic inquiry into the nature, use, and acquisition of language and related matters any more than one expects such informal notions as "heat" or "element" or "life" to survive beyond rudimentary stages of the natural sciences.
>
> *Chomsky and Stemmer 1999: 396*

This move was part of a more general anti-intentionalist turn, rejecting intentional vocabulary in favor of internal states and computational mechanisms (Chomsky 2000: 23). Such a turn may well be connected with the evolution of "substantial" Chomskyan linguistics: from the principles and parameters phase to minimalism, the focus has been on high-level entities such as principles, parameters, and procedures like *Merge*, that are not plausible candidates for being objects of a speaker's knowledge in the intentional sense (Matthews 2006: 204–207).

Chomsky consistently believed that no single part or aspect of linguistic competence corresponded in content to the philosophers' semantics; particularly, the philosophers' "theory of reference" was no part of the scientific study of language. The notion of reference as a technical notion introduced by some philosophical theories, if at all coherent, seems to Chomsky to be irrelevant to the scientific study of natural language (Chomsky 2000: 40–42, 150–152), whereas as an ordinary notion it is not a conceptual tool of any science but an object of study for ethnoscience, the study of folk-scientific conceptions (Chomsky 2000: 172–173). However, he conceded that some phenomena philosophers would regard as semantic – e.g., pronominal anaphora, distinctions such as mass/count and telic/atelic, analyticity, and more – were indeed relevant to the science of language. Some of them were to be brought back to syntax: e.g., in some cases syntactic principles determined semantic properties (as with pronominal anaphora), while in others, semantic properties constrained syntax. For example, in Italian some verbs require the auxiliary *avere* (*to have*) when they form atelic verbal predicates, whereas they require *essere* (*to be*) when they form telic predicates:

Gianni ha/*è corso
[John ran]
Gianni *ha/è corso a casa
[John ran home]

Higginbotham 1997: 108

That Chomsky himself tended to regard properties such as *telic* as syntactic, whereas others, working within his program broadly understood, chose to see them as semantic doesn't make much difference: the point is that principled connections involving syntax should be considered as part of linguistic competence in the narrow sense. Other allegedly semantic facts and properties, such as hyponymy, analyticity, selectional restrictions, etc., were instead excluded by Chomsky from the core of grammar and ascribed to the conceptual-intentional module of the language faculty, hence part of linguistic competence in the broad sense. Still others, e.g., that "Hesperus" and "Phosphorus" are coreferential or that "water" refers to H_2O, were definitely outside the scope of linguistic theory.

Meanwhile, in the work of Donald Davidson and Richard Montague and his school, "philosophical" semantics of natural language had been developing (since the late 1960s) along the path that had been traced by Frege, Russell, Wittgenstein, Tarski, Carnap, Church, and Quine among others, hence on the pattern of semantics for artificial languages such as the languages of logic. The two main programs, Davidson's and Montague's, though differing in important respects, agreed in identifying the aim of semantics with providing "an account of how the meanings of sentences depend upon the meanings of words" (Davidson 1967: 304; cf. Thomason 1974: 52), i.e., with bringing out the compositional rules that compute the meanings of complex expressions from the meanings of their constituents. In Montague's more developed version, such semantic compositional rules "mirrored" syntactic rules throughout: to each syntactic rule of formation for a type of complex expressions (such as noun phrases, verb phrases, etc.), a semantic rule corresponded that computed the semantic value of expressions of that kind from the values of its immediate constituents, as singled out by syntactic analysis (= "rule-by-rule" compositionality). Montague's syntax was *ad hoc*: it was designed to facilitate compositional semantics and didn't claim psychological plausibility (i.e., it was not regarded as a component of linguistic competence). Montague famously believed that semantics was part of mathematics, not of psychology. Davidson paid some tribute to Chomsky's early work, hinting at a possible "rapprochement" between generative grammar and "a sound theory of meaning"(Davidson 1967[1984]: 30); in fact, he made no use of Chomskyan grammars, relying instead on syntactic analysis of logical languages as exemplified in Frege's and Tarski's work (and occasionally extending it).

Originally, neither Davidson's truth-theoretic semantics nor Montague's model theoretic semantics were intended to be models of human semantic competence. Compositional semantic rules were not meant to reflect or explicate actual semantic processing of language: they were intended to yield the right truth conditions for sentences of a natural language such as English, where "language" is understood as *public* language (not an idiolect) under its standard interpretation. Both theories were subject to empirical test: in Davidson's case, the theory had to fit our intuitive knowledge of the conditions under which a sentence is true (Davidson 1970[1984]: 61–64); in Montague's case, the theory had to fit our intuitions of semantic ambiguity and – prominently – our *inferential* intuitions: inferences that came out valid according to the theory would be recognized as such by a normal speaker. This raises the issue of so called "material" inferences (a normal speaker would infer "Milan is south of Berlin" from "Berlin is north of Milan", though not by way of logic): Montague's theory would validate such inferences as well, provided it is augmented with the appropriate meaning postulates (on which see below) (Thomason 1974: 51–55). But in spite of both theories being controlled by the speakers' performance and their assessment of it, neither was intended as a theory of human language processing.

In both cases, however, more recent versions took a "cognitive" turn. Davidsonian semantics was presented as "a component of the larger enterprise of cognitive linguistics", spelling out the content of the specifically semantic module of the language faculty (Larson & Segal 1995: 22–24); Montagovian semantics, in turn, was described as internal to the generative tradition and aiming at modelling a speaker's competence, more particularly, semantic competence (Chierchia & McConnell-Ginet 1990: 2–6). Such a turn, however, did not appear to involve special attention to psychological or neurophysiological plausibility, let alone grounding, of the semantic categories and processes that were conjectured.

Among objections to the dominant semantic programs, one was prominent: both truth-theoretic and model-theoretic theories specified *lexical* meanings to a very limited extent. But without a fuller account of the meaning of words, a semantic theory cannot claim to be describing *sentential* meaning either, i.e., what a speaker comes to know when she understands a sentence. The objection was first raised by Michael Dummett (1975) in connection with Davidsonian truth-theoretical semantics. Dummett argued that statements of truth conditions such as "'The moon is round' is true if and only if the moon is round" do not account for a competent speaker's knowledge of the meaning of "The moon is round"; moreover, adding that "the moon" refers to the moon, while "is round" refers to the property *round* does not significantly improve on the amount of information provided. A *full-blooded* theory of meaning for a language L would both explain what it is for a speaker to grasp the concepts expressible in L (e.g., the concepts *moon* and *round*) and associate each concept with an expression of L; or in other words, it would explicitly state what it is for a speaker to grasp the meanings of such expressions (Dummett 1975: 101). Some noticed that statements of truth conditions did provide *some* lexical semantic information, as they made a sentence's "logical skeleton" explicit, thereby informing about the logical type of every lexical item involved (e.g., "the moon" is a noun phrase, so it cannot mean *red* or *run*) (Higginbotham 1989). The same could be said in favor of model-theoretic semantics *à la* Montague, which explicitly specified the logical type of each lexical item. However, it had to be conceded that this was much less than a Dummettian full-blooded theory was supposed to explain.

Concerning Montague-style model theoretic semantic theories, the objection took a somewhat different form. Proponents of such theories believed that much of lexical meaning could be spelled out by integrating the theory with meaning postulates, i.e., statements like "For every x, if x is red then x is colored" or "For every x, x is a bachelor if and only if x is an unmarried male". However, Barbara Partee remarked that no amount of meaning postulates could "tie down the intensions to their extralinguistic content" (Partee 1981: 71), i.e., determine the lexical items' reference. Partee's difficulty (as well as Grandy's (1974), to which she referred) was that though meaning postulates are informative about semantic relations among lexical items, they (obviously) do not tie down *any* of them to a reference in the real world (or in any possible world). Hence, a system of meaning postulates, no matter how extensive, does not fully encompass a speaker's lexical competence, which supposedly includes knowledge of reference. In Partee's words, some language-to-world *grounding* was needed (1981).

It may be surprising that such objections were raised, as proponents of both truth-theoretic and model-theoretic semantic theories had been fully aware that they were about the dependence of sentential meanings on word meanings, i.e., that they were, essentially, theories of the semantic import of syntax. Indeed, some believed that this was (almost) all that semantics, properly understood, could be. "We should not expect a semantic theory to furnish an account of how any two expressions belonging to the same syntactic category differ in meaning" – e.g., explicitly to distinguish the meaning of "cat" from the meaning of "table" – for that is a dictionary's business, and "the making of a dictionary demands considerable knowledge of the world" (Thomason 1974: 48). This response, of course, presupposes a sharp distinction between semantic knowledge and world knowledge, which, besides being at odds with Quine's famous criticism of the analytic/synthetic distinction, may not fit our intuitions about semantic competence. Later, indeed, others would agree with Thomason about the limits of semantic theory as part of linguistics, while recognizing that, exactly because of such limits, what went under the name of "semantics" was not *quite* a theory of meaning: semantic theory "[has] nothing at all to say about our recognitional capacities" (on which our lexical semantic competence is partly based); hence, "we cannot expect that a linguistic semantics ... could deliver the full meaning of any particular utterance" (Higginbotham 1997: 105).

Concurring criticism of the limitations of formal semantics came from cognitive psychologists and computer scientists working in natural language processing (a sub-field of AI). For example, Philip Johnson-Laird pointed out (like Partee) that "unless a theory relates language to the world ... it is not a complete theory of meaning", and that meaning postulates were inadequate to the task (Johnson-Laird 1983: 230); in the same spirit, he insisted (like Grandy) on some procedural fleshing out of lexical intensions, which would explicitly exhibit "what has to be computed in order to specify [a word's extension]" (Johnson-Laird 1983: 172–173). Such *desiderata* had partly been fulfilled by Terry Winograd's system SHRDLU (Winograd 1968–70; see Winograd 1972), in which lexical items (both monadic predicates such as "red", "big", and "cube", and relational predicates such as "on" and "taller than") were associated with procedures that identified objects and verified sentences in a virtual world of geometrical solids. SHRDLU looked like a toy model of one side of what Diego Marconi (1997) would later call "(lexical) referential competence", i.e., the ability humans have of singling out objects and relations in the real world to which a word applies ("application") and of verbally categorizing real objects and relations ("naming"). However, in SHRDLU, objects and relations were not accessed through perception; they were identified by proper names and described by nested predicates (e.g., B5 is a PYRAMID hence a MANIPULABLE OBJECT hence a PHYSICAL OBJECT). Thus, SHRDLU only pretends to be relating natural language words and sentences to a drastically impoverished "world"; in fact, it maps a fragment of natural language onto an artificial language.

Nevertheless, research leading to systems like SHRDLU was witness to the widespread opinion that a complete theory of meaning ought to relate language to the world, which required explicating the meaning of individual words. Partee (1981) introduced a distinction between *structural* semantics, dealing with the syntax-guided processes that build the semantic content of a complex expression from its constituents' contents, and *lexical* semantics, the characterization of the semantic contribution of words (it should be noted that, in linguistics, the phrase "lexical semantics" has also been frequently used for the analysis of the internal structure of the meanings of lexical items). Partee argued that while Montague-style formal semantics could be regarded (in principle) as implementing the structural side, its tools (i.e., meaning postulates) were radically insufficient to account for lexical meaning. In this context, she raised the issue of how lexical meaning could be *grounded* in words-to-world relations. The issue of "symbol grounding" (Harnad 1990) was widely discussed in the 1980s, often in response to John Searle's skepticism about artificial implementation of linguistic competence, based on his famous "Chinese room" thought experiment (Searle 1980). Searle's point was about AI; however, it easily generalized to any model of human competence. The point was that understanding could not consist of purely intralinguistic operations; hence, competence could not be identified with the ability to carry out such operations, as in translation, paraphrase, inference, etc. (Marconi (1997) would later collectively describe such abilities as constituting *inferential* competence.)

Essentially, two ways out of the Searlian predicament were proposed, one internalist, the other externalist; the latter, in turn, bifurcated into a cognitive and a non-cognitive view. Internalists such as Johnson-Laird (1983) and Ray Jackendoff (1992) thought that grounding did not require any connections with the external world: words got their meanings by being connected with internal representations and processes. This view was later appropriated by supporters of the "simulationist" paradigm (see below). Cognitive externalists such as Harnad and, later, Marconi believed instead that competence with lexical items was (partly) based on perceptual and motor connections with the world out there; e.g., knowing the meaning of words such as "pear" or "bed" involved both the ability to perceptually recognize pears and beds and the ability to appropriately respond, e.g., to commands involving such things. Non-cognitive externalists, such as Hilary Putnam (1975), thought that for many words – typically, though not exclusively, for names of natural kinds – grounding was brought about by objective causal connections with objects and properties in the environment, whether or not such connections affected the speaker's cognitive system. For example, in Putnam's celebrated Twin Earth thought experiment, Oscar and his Twin use "water" for two very different substances (H_2O and XYZ), even though their brain states are supposed to be identical. Oscar uses "water" to refer to H_2O because the word was originally introduced to name a substance that turned out, much later, to *be* H_2O; since its introduction, however, the word referred to whatever had the same nature as *that* stuff (namely H_2O) even though individual speakers, or even the whole linguistic community might not know about H_2O and, *a fortiori*, be unable to tell whether something is H_2O. Partee herself, in raising the grounding problem, appears to suggest some sort of reconciliation of Putnamian and cognitive externalism (Partee 1981: 68).

Concerning how to accommodate semantic competence within their framework, externalists disagreed. Putnam thought that a speaker's individual competence with a word W consisted in "some particular ideas and skills" connected with W; he particularly emphasized the role of *stereotypes*, mini-theories associated with W that specified salient properties of typical members of W's extension (i.e., that water is a liquid, transparent, thirst-quenching, etc.). Though stereo-types, far from determining the extension of W, might even be false of many of its members, Putnam eventually regarded the stereotype as a component of meaning (Putnam 1975: 269), thus as having semantic import. Indeed, he pointed out that "once we give up the idea that individual competence has to be so strong as to actually determine extension, we can begin to study it in a fresh frame of mind" (Putnam 1975: 246). By contrast, Michael Devitt identified individual competence (e.g., with the word "tiger") with a speaker's appropriate placement in a network of causal chains associated with the word: "a network involving other people's abilities as well as groundings and reference borrowings" (Devitt 1983: 89). A speaker's com-petence with "tiger" does not require any propositional beliefs (such as "Tigers are striped", etc.); it suffices that her thoughts be "grounded in tigers" (Devitt 1983: 89). Devitt was willing to make some room for a speaker's ability to, e.g., recognize a tiger when she sees one; how-ever, the respective weights of individual abilities (and beliefs) and objective groundings were not specified.

Internalist "grounders" often tried to conceive of internal representations and procedures so as to make them compatible with results of empirical psychology. For example, Johnson-Laird (1983) designed a procedure for interpreting syllogistic premises and finding their logical consequences whose computational implementation exhibited roughly the same perform-ance limitations as human subjects facing the same tasks. However, Marconi (1995) made one of the first attempts at looking for neuroscientific confirmation of hypotheses about lexical semantic competence. He brought back semantic competence with individual words to two separate (though cooperating) abilities: *inferential* competence, the ability to relate words to other words in material inference, definition, and other intralinguistic performances; and *refer-ential* competence:

> the ability to tell cats from cows by calling the former "cats" and the latter "cows", to describe a man as *running* rather than *walking*, and to pick up the appropriate tool if requested to obey the order "Bring me the hammer, not the pliers!"
>
> *Marconi et al. 2013: 2056*

Neuropsychological studies appeared to show that the two abilities were dissociated: there were patients who were badly impaired in referential performances such as object naming whereas their inferential abilities were intact; conversely (though less often), other patients exhibited good referential competence with very limited inferential ability. Neuropsychology also showed that within referential competence, *application* – the ability to find an object (or a picture) corresponding to a given word – was dissociated from *naming*, the ability to verbally categorize an object or a picture. Later, the distinction was to some extent confirmed by more neuroscientific research, including neuroimaging (see Calzavarini (2017) for an extensive survey).

In the last two decades, research on semantic competence was deeply affected by further neuroscientific research, often based on neuroimaging techniques such as PET and fMRI. Such research showed that understanding of (certain categories of) words correlated with neural activations "corresponding" to the semantic content of the processed words. Thus, e.g., it was shown that listening to sentences that describe actions performed with the mouth, hand, or leg activates the visuomotor circuits which subserve execution and observation of such actions (Tettamanti et al. 2005); that reading words denoting specific actions of the tongue ("lick"), fingers ("pick"), and leg ("kick") differentially activates areas of the premotor cortex that are active when the corresponding movements are actually performed (Hauk et al. 2004); and that reading odor-related words ("jasmine", "garlic", "cinnamon") differentially activates the primary olfactory cortex (Gonzales et al. 2006). Moreover, it was shown that understanding color words (such as "red") activates areas in the fusiform gyrus that have been associated with color perception (Chao et al. 1999; Simmons et al. 2007; for a survey of results concerning visual activations in language processing, see Martin 2007). Such research originated a neurally based version of internalistic grounding of (lexical) semantic competence, according to which "understanding is imagination" and "imagining is a form of simulation"; moreover, "what you understand of a sentence in a context is the meaning of that sentence in that context" (Gallese & Lakoff 2005: 456). Semantic competence can then be seen as the ability to simulate or *re-enact* perceptual (including proprioceptive and introspective) and motor experiences of the states of affairs that language describes, by manipulating memory traces of such experiences or fragments of them.

Lawrence Barsalou's (1999) theory of perceptual symbol systems can be read, in part, as an anticipated theoretical framework for such findings. According to the theory, cognition (including language understanding), though not identical with perception, is based on perceptual experience – including proprioception and introspection – and memory of it. The central claim is that "sensory-motor systems represent not only perceived entities but also conceptualizations of them in their absence" (Barsalou 1999: 589). Perception generates mostly unconscious "neural representations in sensory-motor areas of the brain" (p. 582), which represent schematic components of perceptual experience. Such "perceptual symbols" are not holistic copies of experiences but selections of information isolated by attention (p. 583). Related perceptual symbols are integrated into a *simulator* that produces limitless simulations of a perceptual component such as *red* or *lift*. Simulators are located in long-term memory and play the roles traditionally attributed to concepts (p. 587): they generate inferences and can be combined recursively to implement productivity. A concept is not "a static amodal structure" as in traditional, computationally-oriented cognitive science, but "the ability to simulate a kind of thing perceptually" (p. 604).

As far as language processing is concerned, the theory doesn't simply claim that mental imaging based on perceptual memory plays a role in understanding (an empirically well supported thesis, see e.g., Paivio (1986)); rather, understanding *consists* in "the construction of a perceptual simulation to represent the meaning of an utterance or text" (Barsalou 1999: 605). Linguistic symbols (i.e., auditory or visual memories of words) get to be associated with simulators; perceptual recognition of a word activates the relevant simulator, which simulates a referent for the word; syntax provides instructions for building integrated perceptual simulations, which "constitute semantic interpretations" (Barsalou 1999: 592). Thus, understanding is a thoroughly internalistic process; semantic competence is the ability to build *lato sensu* perceptual simulations in working memory. Barsalou grants that contents of perceptual symbols constrain but do not "specify [their] intentionality" (1999: 597), i.e., do not uniquely fix the reference of words; more generally, "the criteria for a simulation providing a satisfactory fit to a perceived entity remain unresolved in this theory" (Barsalou 1999: 609).

This difficulty is related with a more general issue. In traditional philosophical semantics, knowledge of sentential meaning has been identified with knowledge of a sentence's truth conditions. However, in Barsalou's theory (as in every simulationist theory) implementation of a sentence's meaning tends to be more restrictive than its truth conditions. For example, the meaning of the sentence "The cup on Anna's desk contains pens and pencils" is a simulation in which, by automatic inference, the pens and pencils sit vertically in the cup (Barsalou 1999: 605); however, the sentence would be true even if the pens and pencils lay horizontally on the cup's bottom. But in a perceptual simulation, they can have one or the other orientation, not both. (This could be called "Berkeley's problem", as the philosopher George Berkeley

(1710) was the first to point out that any mental picture a thinker might associate with the word "triangle" was bound to be inadequate by possessing particular features that were not implied by the word's meaning.) Barsalou suggests that the difficulty could be overcome by considering that "neurons can code information qualitatively", e.g. they can code a tiger's stripes without coding their number (Barsalou 1999: 585); however, simulation as a spontaneous process does not appear to be *a priori* constrained by truth conditions.

Another difficulty concerns the role of simulators. In Barsalou's theory, "once a simulator becomes established in memory for a category, it helps identify members of the category on subsequent occasions, and it provides categorical inferences about them" (Barsalou 1999: 587), i.e., it is active in both referential and inferential performances in the sense of Marconi (1995, 1997). Such performances may be impaired if the relevant neural areas are damaged: e.g., if visual areas are damaged then processing of categories specified by visual features (e.g., *bird*) is disrupted. However, the theory does not account for the well-established case of referential performances being severely impaired while inferential competence is fully preserved, in the absence of any damage to the visual areas (e.g., Kemmerer et al. 2001; review in Calzavarini 2017). Simulators do either both things or neither, which appears to be at odds with the neuro-psychological findings.

Finally, the theory, like all perception-based theories of cognition, has trouble with abstract words and concepts. Barsalou tries to show that, e.g., the content of "truth" can be perceptually implemented by a sequence of perceptual symbols such that the simulation of a propositional content "fits" a perceptually available physical situation, but the attempt is unconvincing.

As should be clear, psychological theories of understanding (and competence) that, like Barsalou's, are based on notions such as reenactment and "embodiment" are just a recent development of a turn that reflections on semantic competence started taking in the late 1970s. Dummett's criticism of truth-theoretic semantics and Partee's acknowledgment of the limitations of Montague's model theoretic semantics have led to the realization that such theories could not fully account for human understanding of language: genuine understanding must involve more than command of the compositional mechanisms of language (i.e., of how the meaning of complex expressions depends on the meanings of their constituents), and more than knowledge of semantic relations among lexical items as expressed by meaning postulates. That, in turn, invited the conclusion that *if* (sentential) meaning is identified with truth conditions (as in the tradition of philosophical semantics from Wittgenstein's *Tractatus* to Montague and Davidson) *and* knowledge of truth conditions is what is displayed by the then extant semantics theories, *then* knowledge of meaning does not amount to semantic competence. At the time, many believed (and some still believe) that the missing ingredient could be provided by Saul Kripke's and Putnam's (then) "new" theory of reference: lexical items were "grounded" in the real world by baptisms, causal chains, or simply by the use of language. However, the causal theory's externalist bent made it unsuitable as a basis for a theory of semantic competence: the essential semantic ingredient, i.e. reference, might not be cognitively accessible to otherwise competent speakers, as with the word "water" on both Earth and Twin Earth before the advent of chemistry. Though Putnam's "particular ideas and skills" provided content for a regular speaker's semantic competence, they could not guarantee his or her knowledge of truth conditions.

Meanwhile, debates within (and about) Artificial Intelligence dramatized the role of perception and motor action in the exercise of semantic competence: no artificial device could reasonably be attributed full semantic competence unless it could relate language to the world out there by answering questions, obeying orders, and describing perceptually accessible real-world situations. This inspired Harnad's, Marconi's, and others' attempts to conceive of semantic competence as involving several perceptual and motor abilities. Later, the relevance of such abilities to language understanding was emphasized by a flow of neuroscientific results that appeared to prove involvement of motor and perceptual brain areas in comprehension, and more generally, in language processing. Such research generated a partly new paradigm, which made language understanding *consist in* such (modal) activations. Now, there is little doubt that in many cases language production and comprehension are correlated with brain activations which appear to reflect the semantic content of the processed lexical materials: this is confirmed by constantly replicated experimental results. The role of such brain activity in linguistic performances is, however, still an object of controversy. As we saw, the radical claim that language understanding in general just *consists* in such activations faces some difficulties: e.g., much recent research does not find significant modal activations correlated with understanding of abstract words. Moreover, Berkeley's problem may indicate that whatever understanding is achieved by way of re-enactment is partial at best. In any case, there is more we need to know for a full-fledged empirical theory of language understanding to get off the ground. For example, what is the place and role of syntactic parsing in understanding? Moreover, what is the role of brain representation *of language itself*, i.e., of the phonetic, articulatory, visual, and motor representations of words we must somehow possess if we are to explain our ability to perceive language, to speak, to read, and to write? Could such representations – which we know to interact with one another – play the role of pegs onto which several ingredients of both understanding and production are hooked? Answers to such questions must await further research. What seems clear is that no future theory of understanding and semantic competence will be allowed to disregard evidence from psychology and neuroscience.

References

Barsalou, L. (1999) "Perceptual Symbol Systems," *Behavioral and Brain Sciences* 22, 577–660.

Berkeley, G. (1710) *A Treatise Concerning the Principles of Human Knowledge*, Dublin.

Calzavarini, F. (2017) "Inferential and Referential Lexical Semantic Competence: A Critical Review of the Supporting Evidence," *Journal of Neurolinguistics* 44, 163–189.

Chao, L. L., Haxby, A., & Martin, J.V. (1999) "Attribute-Based Neural Substrates in Temporal Cortex for Perceiving and Knowing About Objects," *Nature Neuroscience*, 2(10), 913–919.

Chierchia, G., & McConnell-Ginet, S. (1990) *Meaning and Grammar*, MIT Press, Cambridge Mass.

Chomsky, N. (1965) *Aspects of the Theory of Syntax*, MIT Press, Cambridge Mass.

—— (1980) *Rules and Representations*, Columbia University Press, New York.

—— (1985) *Knowledge of Language*, Praeger, New York.

—— (2000) *New Horizons in the Study of Language and Mind*, Cambridge University Press, Cambridge.

Chomsky, N., & Stemmer, B. (1999) "An On-Line Interview with Noam Chomsky: On the Nature of Pragmatics and Related Issues," *Brain and Language* 68, 393–401.

Davidson, D. (1967) "Truth and Meaning," *Synthese* 17, 304–323; later in D. Davidson (1984) *Truth and Interpretation*, Clarendon Press, Oxford, 17–36.

—— (1970) "Semantics for Natural Languages," in B. Visentini (ed.), *I linguaggi nella società e nella tecnica*, Edizioni di Comunità, Milan 177–88; later in D. Davidson (1984) *Truth and Interpretation*, Clarendon Press, Oxford, 55–64.

Devitt, M. (1983) "Dummett's Anti-Realism," *Journal of Philosophy* 80, 73–99.

Dummett, M. (1975) "What Is a Theory of Meaning?," in S. Guttenplan (ed.), *Mind and Language*, Oxford University Press, Oxford, 97–138.

Gallese, V., & Lakoff, G. (2005) "The Brain's Concepts: The Role of the Sensory-Motor System in Conceptual Knowledge," *Cognitive Neuropsychology* 21, 455–479.

Gonzales, J., Barros-Loscertales, A., Pulvermüller, F., Meseguer, V., Sanjuán, A., Belloch, V., & Avila, C. (2006) "Reading Cinnamon Activates Olfactory Brain Regions," *Neuroimage* 32, 906–912.

Grandy, R. E. (1974) "Some Remarks about Logical Form," *Nous* 8, 157–164.

Harnad, S. (1990) "The Symbol Grounding Problem," *Physica* D 42, 335–346.

Hauk, O., Johnsrude, I., & Pulvermüller, F. (2004) "Somatotopic Representation of Action Words in Human Motor and Premotor Cortex," *Neuron* 41, 301–307.

Higginbotham, J. (1997) "Reflections on Semantics in Generative Grammar," *Lingua* 100, 101–109.

—— (1989) "Knowledge of Reference," in A. George (ed.), *Reflections on Chomsky,* Blackwell, London, 153–174.

Jackendoff, R. (1992) *Languages of the Mind*, MIT Press, Cambridge Mass.

Johnson-Laird, P. (1983) *Mental Models*, Cambridge University Press, Cambridge.

Kemmerer, D., Tranel, D., & Barrash, J. (2001) "Patterns of Dissociation in the Processing of Verb Meanings in Brain-Damaged Subjects," *Language and Cognitive Processes* 16, 1–34.

Larson, R., & Segal, G. (1995) *Knowledge of Meaning*, MIT Press, Cambridge Mass.

Marconi, D. (1995) "On the Structure of Lexical Competence," *Proceedings of the Aristotelian Society* 95, 131–150.

—— (1997) *Lexical Competence*, MIT Press, Cambridge Mass.

Marconi, D., Manenti, R., Catricalà, E., Della Rosa, P. A., Siri, S., & Cappa, S. F. (2013) "The Neural Substrates of Inferential and Referential Semantic Processing," *Cortex* 49, 2055–2066.

Martin, A. (2007) "The Representation of Object Concepts in the Brain," *Annual Review of Psychology* 58, 25–45.

Matthews, R. J. (2006) "Knowledge of Language and Linguistic Competence," in E. Sosa & E. Villanueva (eds.), *Philosophy of Language (Philosophical Issues, 16)*, Blackwell, Boston & Oxford, 200–220.

Paivio, A. (1986) *Mental Representations: A Dual Coding Approach*, Oxford University Press, Oxford.

Partee, B. (1981) "Montague Grammar, Mental Representations and Reality," in S. Kanger & S. Öhman (eds.), *Philosophy and Grammar*, Dordrecht, Reidel, 59–78.

Putnam, H. (1975) "The Meaning of 'Meaning'," in *Philosophical Papers II*, Cambridge University Press, London, 215–271.

Searle, J. (1980) "Minds, Brains and Programs," *Behavioural and Brain Sciences* 3, 417–457.

Simmons, W. K. et al. (2007) "A Common Neural Substrate for Perceiving and Knowing About Color," *Neuropsychologia*, 45(12), 2802–2810.

Stich, S. (1971) "What Every Speaker Knows," *Philosophical Review* 80: 476–496.

Tettamanti, M., Buccino, G., Saccuman, M. C., Gallese, V., Danna, M., Scifo, P. et.al. (2005) "Listening to Action-related Sentences Activates Fronto-parietal Motor Circuits," *Journal of Cognitive Neuroscience* 17, 273–281.

Thomason, R. H. (1974) *"Introduction" to Formal Philosophy: Selected Papers of Richard Montague*, Yale University Press, New Haven Conn. and London, 1–69.

Winograd, T. (1972) "Understanding Natural Language," *Cognitive Psychology* 3, 1–191.

33
PRAGMATIC COMPETENCE*

Filippo Domaneschi and Valentina Bambini

33.1 Pragmatics and cognition

33.1.1 The Gricean view

In the linguistic and philosophical tradition, pragmatics is typically considered as the study of the use of language in context. This conception is strictly related to the seminal work of the philosopher Paul Grice. In 'Meaning' Grice (1957) faces a crucial question: why does a sign mean something? Grice notes that the same linguistic expression 'to mean' can have two different uses. First, an expression like 'These spots *mean* measles' is an example of *natural meaning*, i.e., a sign has a natural meaning when it means something simply because things in the world are in a certain way. Conversely, the use of *mean* in a sentence like 'Three rings on the bell *mean* that the pub is closing' is an example of *non-natural meaning*: in this case, a sign means something only because a certain speaker has the intention to communicate something to an audience by using a particular sign.

Within the realm of the non-natural meaning, Grice distinguishes between the sentence meaning and the utterer's meaning. *Sentence meaning* is the conventional meaning of an expression, which is given in terms of the *timeless-language-meaning* of an *utterance-type*: it is the linguistic meaning of structured and complete expressions pertaining to some type of sentence independently of a particular circumstance of use. Sentence meaning (or linguistic meaning) does not depend on the idiolect of a single individual; rather, it is the timeless meaning of a type-expression q socially determined within a community of speakers that share a language. According to Grice, the linguistic meaning of an expression q is simply a *clue* used by speakers to convey the *utterer's meaning* (or speaker's meaning), i.e., what a speaker S intends to communicate by uttering q in a specific verbal interaction.

The general conclusion of the Gricean analysis of the notion of meaning in terms of speakers' intentions is that, most of the time, what a speaker means to communicate does not coincide with what she explicitly says. This idea results in the distinction between *what is said* and *what is communicated* that has become Grice's best-known contribution. His notion of utterer's meaning is considered as being divided between:

1. what a speaker S *explicitly says* by the use of an expression E;
2. what a speaker S *implicitly communicates* by the use of the expression E.

The Gricean analysis has led contemporary linguists and philosophers to a mainstream view of pragmatics as the study of the speaker's meaning and of the inferential processes of reconstruction of communicative intentions.

33.1.2 Pragmatics: performance vs. competence

Pragmatics has long represented an area of philosophical investigation based on intuitions and on the observation of linguistic behaviour. During the mid-1980s, scholars in pragmatics embraced a more cognitively oriented perspective, which led to psychologically plausible models of communication (e.g., Relevance Theory) and to a closer look at the idea of a 'pragmatic competence'.

Until then, Pragmatics had received little attention for two main reasons. First, in linguistics, the early version of the generative grammar framework posited a distinction between *competence* and *performance* (Chomsky 1957). In later works, Chomsky (1980: 225) introduced the notion of 'pragmatic competence' to recognize that language users possess a knowledge of how verbal language is related to the specific circumstance of use. The seminal distinction between competence and performance, however, initially led many to include pragmatic phenomena in the domain of performance, thus excluding pragmatics from linguistic investigations focused instead on the level of competence, pertaining mainly to syntax. Second, the modular Theory of Mind (Fodor 1983) initially rejected the idea that pragmatic processing was associated with a specific, independently analysable module as a classic Chomskyan-intended competence was expected to be. Since the use of language involves a number of factors (e.g., the calculation of implicatures, understanding of speech acts, the turn-taking system, etc.), pragmatics was not considered as ruled by a single module, rather as pertaining to the central cognitive systems.

In this theoretical environment, the approach known as Cognitive Pragmatics arose as a first attempt to legitimize pragmatic investigation within a modular-generative perspective. On the one hand, Asa Kasher (1994) – who first used the term 'Cognitive Pragmatics' – suggested a revision of the Fodorian notion of module in order to account for pragmatic processing within a modular framework. Kasher argued that the use of language is based on two different types of pragmatic competence: purely linguistic pragmatic competence, and non-linguistic pragmatic competence. *Purely linguistic pragmatic competence* is ruled by a set of modules (with properties different from Fodor's modules) that drive specific pragmatic phenomena, e.g., the basic types of speech acts (e.g., assertions, orders, questions), turn-taking, etc. *Non-linguistic pragmatic competence*, according to Kasher, is not modular but general, namely, linked to more general cognitive systems devoted to rule all the pragmatic phenomena and it is based also on non-verbal information, e.g., the understanding of indirect speech acts, metaphors, irony, the rules of politeness, etc.

On the other hand, scholars in Relevance Theory initially rejected the thesis of the existence of an autonomous module for pragmatic processing. According to Sperber and Wilson (1986/1995), linguistic interpretation is an inferential process ruled by a general cognitive principle of relevance, according to which 'human cognition tends to be geared to the maximisation of relevance' and on the basis of a *communicative principle of relevance* which establishes that 'every act of overt communication conveys a presumption of its own optimal relevance'. Since, in understanding verbal language, users select the most relevant meanings on the basis of a variety of both perceptual and linguistic inputs, relevance theorists argued that pragmatic interpretation is a process based on the central system of thought. Later, however, Sperber and Wilson (2002) revised their position on modularism. They now argue that there is a specific module devoted to pragmatic interpretation, which is characterized by its own principles and mechanisms, which is the product of the evolution of the human capacity for 'mind reading'. Specifically, the mind-reading ability or Theory of Mind (ToM) is traditionally considered as the ability to attribute mental states to oneself and to other human beings and to use such attribution of mental states to derive predictions and to formulate explanations about oneself and others' behaviour (Premack and Woodruff 1978). Importantly, although the thesis of the modularity of pragmatics was well accepted within the Relevance Theory framework, the idea that pragmatics is a 'competence', intended *à la* Chomsky as a body of implicit knowledge, was contended. Carston (1997), for instance, argues that pragmatics is rather a performer operating within the constraints of real-time, on-line language processing.

Another prominent model that was shaped throughout the 1990s is Bara's Cognitive Pragmatics (Bara 2010), which interpreted theoretical pragmatics in a mentalistic key and emphasized the role of intentionality and cooperation in both linguistic and extra-linguistic communication. Cognitive pragmatics has offered a detailed characterization of communicative acts, which goes beyond the direct–indirect dichotomy and considers the length of the inferential chain required to derive the speaker's communicative intention. On this basis, simple and complex acts can be distinguished, related to different cognitive loads.

In the current state of the art, the problem of determining whether pragmatic processing is driven either by a single module or by the central system is overtaken. Rather, the Gricean inspired idea that pragmatics essentially coincides with the ability to infer speakers' communicative intentions has contributed to shape a widely shared assumption: as far as pragmatics can be intended as a competence, this should be largely tied, if not overlapped, with general mind-reading abilities, i.e., with ToM.

33.1.3 *The experimental turn in pragmatics*

In the last two decades, the cognitively oriented view of pragmatics paved the way to a further turn in pragmatic research, namely an 'experimental turn'. The goal of *Experimental Pragmatics* is to investigate pragmatic phenomena via experimental methods (Noveck and Sperber 2004; Noveck 2018), and specifically to test the theoretical models proposed in the field, deriving psychologically sound hypotheses from them. Experimental Pragmatics is based mainly on the behavioural data and techniques from psycholinguistics and cognitive psychology. More recently, also clinically oriented research ('clinical pragmatics'; Cummings 2017) and neuro-oriented research ('neuropragmatics'; Bambini and Bara 2012) developed considerably. The main aim of clinical pragmatics is to describe the profile of pragmatic impairment in clinical population, whereas the main goal of neuropragmatics is to characterize the cerebral localization and neurochronometry of pragmatic processes using methodologies that include fMRI, MEG, and EEG. Admittedly, distinctions among these areas are often difficult to draw, and in this work we will consider evidence from all strands of empirical research in pragmatics and use Experimental Pragmatics as an umbrella term for all these approaches.

In Experimental Pragmatics, the use of complex paradigms, relying on both experimental settings and on neuropsychological tests, has become crucial for identifying whether specific cognitive functions correlate with the processing of specific pragmatic phenomena (e.g., implicatures, presuppositions, figurative language). This approach has massively investigated the role of ToM but more and more interest has been devoted also to other cognitive functions such as executive functions, working memory, inhibitory capacity, etc. As a result, many studies allowed to shed new light on the relation between pragmatic processing and ToM (Cummings 2009), as well the complex interaction with other cognitive functions.

In what follows, we will try to argue that a careful survey of the most recent literature in Experimental Pragmatics can offer solid evidence in support of this thesis: pragmatic competence is not limited to the ability of understanding speaker's intentions and, hence, pragmatic competence cannot be reduced to ToM ability. One element supporting this thesis is that pragmatic competence has specific, i.e., distinct from ToM, characterization in terms of developmental trajectories, patterns of decay, and neural substrates. Indeed, pragmatic processing is supported by ToM but also, sometimes more prominently, by a cluster of other cognitive functions, in ways that differ across types of population and of pragmatic tasks. Our position differs from that of those who interpret the complexity of the cognitive underpinnings of pragmatics as indicative of the epiphenomenal nature of pragmatics, where this is seen as the emergent result of the interaction between linguistic, cognitive, and sensorimotor processes (Perkins 2005).

33.2 Dimensions of variation in pragmatic competence

33.2.1 Presupposition (and some but not all about scalar implicatures)

According to Stalnaker (2002), presuppositions are the background information communicated as taken for granted. They are usually activated by linguistic expressions that are referred to as *presupposition triggers*. For example, the verb *to give up* triggers the presupposition of an antecedent state, while in the sentence 'I regret that it's raining', *regret* triggers the presupposition 'it's raining' (Levinson 1983). There are two possible outcomes of using a presupposing utterance: suppose that someone utters the sentence, 'Sarah has given up smoking'. If it is already a common presupposition that Sarah used to smoke, then the presupposition is said to be *satisfied*. Conversely, an unknown or controversial presupposition leads to *a failure*. In this case, to make sense of the utterance, failure can be repaired via *accommodation*, i.e., the process whereby the presupposition that Sarah used to smoke is accepted (Lewis 1979).

Although presupposition has long represented a central topic of interest for theoretical investigation, experimental research on this topic is rather recent. The primary reason for the lack of experimental research is that, different from accounts of metaphor, of irony or of conversational implicatures, theoretical models of presupposition were mainly developed within a formal semantic framework. What the cognitive underpinnings of presupposition processing are remains unclear. The issue of which cognitive functions are involved in understanding information taken for granted is, in fact, still mostly open.

Recent studies, however, tried to investigate the relation between presupposition processing and cognitive functioning. Indeed, the evidence collected up to now suggests that presupposition represents an interesting case study for disentangling the role of working memory in supporting pragmatic competence. Domaneschi et al. (2014), for example, focused on the cognitive load of different presupposition triggers. In their experiment, a group of healthy young adults were presented with a series of stories containing different presupposition triggers. Afterwards, participants were required to answer a series of questions directly targeting the content of the presuppositions introduced in the stories. The task was performed in two conditions, one of high and one of low cognitive load, depending on the number of geometrical figures that participants were required to remember during the task. Results showed that, when people are in a condition of high cognitive load, the accommodation of a presupposition is difficult with temporal triggers and, in particular, with change-of-state verbs such as *stop* and *start* and with iterative expressions such as *return* and *again*, which require a demanding process of mental representation of temporally displaced events. This result constitutes first evidence in support of the idea that the process of updating the discourse mental model with a presupposed information is modulated by the working memory ability. The higher cognitive cost associated with change-of-state verbs has found further experimental support in an Event Related Brain Potentials (ERP) study, where Domaneschi et al. (2018) showed that the accommodation of presuppositions activated by change-of-state verbs, as compared to that of definite descriptions, is more effortful in the later stage of processing, i.e., the one reflecting the updating of the discourse model with the presupposed information (associated with the so-called P600 component).

The idea that working memory is prominently involved in updating the discourse model with presupposed information was further investigated in Domaneschi and Di Paola (2019). In a word-by-word self-paced reading paradigm, presupposition processing was investigated by comparing a group of young adults with a group of healthy elderly participants, to ascertain the role of the aging factor. Results support two conclusions. First, older adults, as compared to younger adults, exhibit higher on-line processing costs for presuppositions with change-of-state verbs as compared to definite descriptions. Second, the ability to recover information introduced in the discourse as taken for granted is affected by the aging factor: elderly subjects took longer in recovering presupposed information from the discourse mental model than the younger control group. Interestingly, the authors observed a significant correlation between the participants' working memory capacity and the ability to recall information previously introduced as presupposed.

These results offer initial evidence in support of the idea that for pragmatic phenomena such as presuppositions that do not typically convey the main point of an utterance, i.e., the speaker's meaning, pragmatic processing relies primarily on non-mindreading mechanisms. Understanding a presupposing utterance seems to require the ability of retaining in the working memory a mental representation of the discourse mental model and of recovering from that model the presupposition introduced by a trigger, a cognitive skill that seems to be mastered more by working memory capacity than by ToM.

Converging findings were reported for another largely investigated pragmatic phenomenon, namely scalar implicature, e.g., the meaning 'not all' derived from the use of expressions on a scale such as 'some' and 'any'. Using a dual task paradigm requiring both sentence verification and memorization of dot patterns, De Neys and Schaeken (2007) showed that participants derived less scalar implicatures under memory load. This is indicative of the non-automatic nature of scalar implicatures and of the involvement of executive resources. By contrasts, studies showed that autistic-like traits (considered as a proxy of ToM skills) are not crucial in the comprehension of scalars (Heyman and Schaeken 2015; Antoniou et al. 2016).

33.2.2 Conversational mechanisms

The variety of cognitive functions that contribute to determine language users' pragmatic competence emerges clearly with two pragmatic phenomena that play a key role in the organization of a conversational exchange: the turn-taking mechanism and politeness.

Turn-taking is the set of rules and mechanisms that coordinate the activity of speaking and listening in a conversation such that at any time of the talk exchange there is only one speaker (Sacks et al. 1978). Turn-taking mechanisms are usually considered universal (Stivers et al. 2009) and are displayed by both sign and verbal language with little quantitative and qualitative variation between them (Holler et al. 2015). There is compelling evidence that turn-taking skills are largely affected by executive functions and by joint attention.

The literature on typical development shows that turn-taking is among the first pragmatic mechanisms acquired by children: neonates take part actively in verbal interactions with smiles and sounds and coordinate their rhythm with that of the adults, showing distress in case of perturbation in the turns alternation (Murray 1998; Trevarthen et al. 1999). Turn-taking skills are significantly related to infants' joint attention capacity, which typically emerges at six months. Such a capacity slowly increases in the early development, resulting in an initial difficulty in planning an adequate response to an antecedent turn: Casillas et al. (2016), for instance, showed that young children answer questions with longer delays than adults due to the effort associated with planning and elaborating an appropriate answer.

Research on atypical development suggests that children with Pragmatic Language Impairment exhibit difficulties in providing clues for turn-taking (Bishop et al. 1994) and are more likely to share less information with the interlocutors, indicating a lack of joint attention (Murphy et al. 2014). Similar difficulties were documented also in children with Autism Spectrum Disorder (ASD). Although children with High Functioning Autism do participate in conversation and try to follow the turns alternation, they were shown to be less likely to answer questions (Eales 1993) and more likely to ignore adults' invites to converse than language-matched groups of typically developing children (Eigsti et al. 2007).

In the area of atypical development, the most informative case study in this respect is represented by subjects displaying Attention Deficit Hyperactivity Disorder (ADHD). Executive dysfunction, which is the main explanatory model for the symptoms of ADHD (Willcutt et al. 2005), is usually identified as the main reason behind the pragmatic problems in ADHD. The difficulty of ADHD children in sustaining attention, for example, was associated with difficulties in turn-taking/waiting (Staikova et al. 2013; Green et al. 2014).

Converging evidence comes from studies on adult clinical populations. Executive dysfunction has been associated with deficits in turn-taking both in subjects with brain tumour (Wolfe et al. 2013), non-Alzheimer dementia (Rousseaux et al. 2010), and Parkinson's disease (McNamara and Durso 2003).

Another promising line of research on the cognitive underpinnings of pragmatic processing revolves around politeness mechanisms. The rules of politeness and, in particular, the notion of positive and negative face have been argued to be universal components of human culture (Brown and Levinson 1987). Yet, developmental research has provided blatant evidence in support of the idea that the specific politeness rules of a linguistic community are culturally dependent and are acquired rather late as the result of explicit instruction provided by the parents (or other adults) to the children (Foster 1990). More specifically, the ability of formulating indirect requests as an instrument of politeness, which is typically taught between the ages of two to four years (Aksu-Koç and Slobin 1985), increases progressively in typically developing children. Empirical evidence collected seems to support the idea that the ability to use politeness rules as a function of the acquisition of social skills goes hand in hand with the development of ToM abilities. Another example in this respect are white lies used for politeness purposes – i.e., lies produced in situations where insincerity is considered socially appropriate. White lies display, in fact, a developmental trajectory which is symmetric with that of mind-reading abilities: children are typically not able to use white lies competently before the age of four (Broomfield et al. 2002; Airenti and Angeleri 2011) and this competence increases gradually together with their ToM abilities until the age of 11 (Ma et al. 2011). If a prominent correlation between politeness roles and mind-reading skills seems to characterize early pragmatic development, the picture is less clear and more fragmented with clinical subjects at a late stage of lifespan. First, in some patients with dementia, politeness skills, as well as other social skills, are partially preserved (Davis and Maclagan 2010), second, the correlation between deficits in socio-pragmatic skills and defective mind-reading abilities is not so clear especially in patients with Alzheimer's Dementia (Guendouzi and Savage 2017). Moreover, research suggests that politeness skills indeed may be compromised in subjects with Parkinson's Disease (Holtgraves and McNamara 2010) but no direct correlation between such a deficit and difficulties in ToM has been observed yet and, more importantly, as explained before, pragmatic deficits in this population seem to be linked more with a general disruption in executive functioning than with a compromised ToM (Kudlicka et al. 2011).

33.2.3 Metaphor

According to Grice's proposal (Grice 1975), metaphor represents a case of blatant violation of the Quality Maxim, leading to a conversational implicature. In Relevance Theory, the emphasis is on conceptual operations that lead the hearer to derive the speaker's meaning in a metaphor. Upon hearing "Sally is an angel", the hearer will adapt the concept ANGEL by narrowing its denotation (e.g., dropping logical properties such as being a supernatural creature) and broadening it to include people that share encyclopaedic properties of angels, such as being kind and gentle (Wilson and Carston 2007). These models, however, did not make explicit predictions in terms of time-course and processing. These aspects were discussed in psycholinguistic research, which hosted a long-lasting debate between Grice-inspired indirect access accounts and direct access models of figurative meanings (Gibbs 1990). As often happens, data support an in-between position. All other things being equal, the processing of a metaphor leads to increased costs with respect to its literal equivalent (Noveck et al. 2001; Bambini et al. 2013). However, context plays a crucial role and may reduce the costs of metaphors, together with other properties such as familiarity and salience (Giora 2003). Further evidence on processing came from the use of the ERP technique, which can track neural activity underlying metaphor comprehension with millisecond precision. Based on ERP evidence, metaphor comprehension seems to go through an early phase of lexical effort, indexed in the so-called N400 component, which is sensitive to context-based expectations; later, metaphor understanding elicits the so-called P600 component, reflecting inferential operations that lead to the communicated meaning (Weiland et al. 2014; Bambini et al. 2016).

The processing costs described above make metaphor a challenge in acquisition. Although the type of task can make the difference (Pouscoulous 2014), there is evidence that children do not fully master metaphor until the age of ten years (Winner et al. 1976). Moreover, metaphor is a challenge in atypical development, especially in children with ASD (Kalandadze et al. 2019). A seminal paper testing children with ASD claimed that metaphor comprehension requires first-order ToM, since it involves the interpretation of the speaker's thought (Happé 1993). The modern view, however, has toned down the claim about the role of ToM and evidenced the role of other factors, especially language and vocabulary skills (Norbury 2005). Interestingly, the relationship between metaphor and ToM might depend on the type of metaphors, being stronger for metaphors expressing psychological characteristics (e.g., *Daddy is a volcano*) rather than for metaphors expressing physical characteristics (e.g., *Dancers are butterflies*; Lecce et al. 2019).

Metaphors represent a hard challenge also for several adult clinical populations (Thoma and Daum 2006). Among them, the most relevant condition associated with problems in metaphor comprehension is schizophrenia, where literal interpretation of metaphor has been known since the early description of the illness and is referred to as 'concretism' (Kircher et al. 2007; Mossaheb et al. 2014). The literature has largely explored the neurocognitive underpinning of metaphor impairment in schizophrenia, reporting the involvement of a large range of cognitive skills, including ToM but not limited to it, and extending also to executive functions, intelligence, and symptoms (Champagne-Lavau and Stip 2010; Mossaheb et al. 2014). Likewise, neuroimaging studies on healthy populations reported the involvement of several brain regions devoted to different cognitive functions, from ToM to executive processing linked to the suppression of irrelevant information (Bambini et al. 2011). Overall, it seems impossible to link metaphor comprehension to a single cognitive component. Rather, a more fruitful approach is to see metaphor as a pragmatic task having its own patterns of processing, development, and decay, and involving other cognitive skills depending on the individual and stimulus characteristics.

33.2.4 Irony

In the previous sections, we have highlighted a number of pragmatic tasks where ToM proved not to be sufficient for a correct pragmatic behaviour. We shall end with a task where, indeed, the role of ToM seems more pervasive, namely irony. In the Gricean framework, irony was linked – just like metaphor – to a violation of the Quality maxim. Yet this account does not fully consider the complexity of irony, which is eminently a meta-cognitive phenomenon, related to the expression of attitudes. This aspect is captured by the echoic theory of irony proposed by Relevance Theory, where ironic utterances are seen as echoing a thought and conveying a derogatory or mocking attitude toward it (Wilson 2006).

In this framework, the link between irony and ToM becomes radical. Several studies investigated the developmental steps leading to full-fledged ironic abilities (Filippova and Astington 2008; Glenwright and Pexman 2010) and highlighted a relationship with ToM development, especially second-order ToM (Nilsen et al. 2011). Consistently, neuroimaging studies showed a large degree of overlap between the brain regions recruited by irony processes and the neural correlates of classic ToM tasks such as false beliefs (Spotorno et al. 2012). In the same vein, irony and social-cognition impairments are connected in atypical populations such as those with ASD (Happé 1993) and schizophrenia (Langdon et al. 2002).

It would be simplistic, however, to assume that irony can be collapsed into ToM. Bosco and colleagues have developed a research line targeting sincere, ironic, and deceitful communication in development and in clinical conditions, and consistently reported cases where ToM alone is not sufficient to explain behaviour in non-literal communication (Bosco and Gabbatore 2017; Bosco et al. 2018). There is clearly more involved than ToM alone in determining the ability to understand ironic meanings. For instance, it has been argued that an important predictor of the ability of individuals with traumatic brain injury to understand irony is general inferential reasoning (Martin and McDonald 2005), and executive functions too have been shown to play a role (Bosco et al. 2017).

33.3 Conclusion

Throughout this chapter, we tried to highlight a considerable body of research in theoretical and empirical pragmatics that offers compelling evidence in favour of an internal characterization of pragmatics, thus in favour of the idea of pragmatic competence. In our view, this amount of evidence indicates that pragmatic behaviour is not haphazard: speakers are equipped with a specific capability of activating certain procedures in communication, and such capability – or competence – can be described in terms of *specific* neurophysiological correlates, developmental trajectory, and patterns of decay. Yet pragmatic competence – just like any other cognitive aspect – is to some extent intertwined with other cognitive domains. The Grice-inspired idea, further elaborated in Relevance Theory, that pragmatics (and pragmatic competence) is a sub-module of ToM certainly captures a crucial aspect of pragmatics, i.e., the intentional nature of meaning. However, when interpreted in terms of an overlap between pragmatics and ToM, this view does not fully account for the available data, where the involvement of ToM in pragmatic tasks is fragmentary and unsystematic across the literature. In line with recent proposals in the field (Bosco et al. 2018), we argue that pragmatics and ToM do not overlap. A more likely scenario is that pragmatic competence is a specific capability, which in turn might exploit an array of other cognitive abilities, differently engaged depending on the specific communicative situation and properties of the interaction (Andrés-Roqueta and Katsos 2017). There might also be differences linked to the specific task: for instance, tasks such as metaphor and scalars might be linked to vocabulary knowledge and only minimally to ToM, while other tasks, such as irony, might greatly capitalize on mind-reading skills. Similarly, presuppositions seem to depend more on speakers' executive functioning and, in particular, verbal working memory skills. Differences might also be due to the specific cognitive profile of each population, where impairment in – for instance – executive functions or language skills might hamper pragmatic processing (Martin and McDonald 2003). Finally, it is worth noticing that ToM per se encompasses different aspects and does not constitute a single ability. ToM can be distinguished, for instance, in first- and second-person ToM, cognitive and affective ToM, first-, second- and third-order ToM: all these aspects might be differently engaged in pragmatic processing. The complexity of this scenario should be taken as indicative of a lively time in Experimental Pragmatics, ready for taking the challenge – after two decades dominated by discussion on the competence-performance dichotomy and on the role of ToM – of shaping a new and more mature account of pragmatic competence.

Note

* Author contribution: Although the two authors planned and revised the chapter jointly, FD is responsible for sections 33.1, 33.2.1 and 33.2.2, while VB is responsible for sections 33.2.3, 33.2.4 and 33.3.

References

Airenti, G., and Angeleri, R. (2011) "Situation-Sensitive Use of Insincerity: Pathways to Communication in Young Children," *British Journal of Developmental Psychology* 29: 765–82.

Aksu-Koç, A. A., and Slobin, D. I. (1985) "The Acquisition of Turkish," in D. Slobin (ed.) *The Cross-Linguistic Study of Language Acquisition. Vol. 1: The Data*, 839–78, Hillsdale, NJ: Lawrence Erlbaum.

Andrés-Roqueta, C., and Katsos, N. (2017) "The Contribution of Grammar, Vocabulary and Theory of Mind in Pragmatic Language Competence in Children With Autistic Spectrum Disorders," *Frontiers in Psychology* 8: 996.

Antoniou, K., Cummins, C., and Katsos, N. (2016) "Why Only Some Adults Reject Under-Informative Utterances," *Journal of Pragmatics* 99: 78–95.

Bambini, V., and Bara, B. G. (2012) "Neuropragmatics," in J.-O. Östman and J. Verschueren (eds.) *Handbook of Pragmatics*, 1–21, Amsterdam: John Benjamins.

Bambini, V., Bertini, C., Schaeken, W., Stella, A., and Di Russo, F. (2016) "Disentangling Metaphor from Context: An ERP Study," *Frontiers in Psychology* 7: 559.

Bambini, V., Gentili, C., Ricciardi, E., Bertinetto, P. M., and Pietrini, P. (2011) "Decomposing Metaphor Processing at the Cognitive and Neural Level through Functional Magnetic Resonance Imaging," *Brain Research Bulletin* 86: 203–16.

Bambini, V., Ghio, M., Moro, A., and Schumacher, P. B. (2013) "Differentiating among Pragmatic Uses of Words through Timed Sensicality Judgments," *Frontiers in Psychology* 4: 938.

Bara, B. G. (2010) *Cognitive Pragmatics*, Cambridge: MIT Press.

Bishop, D.V. M., Hartley, J., and Weir, F. (1994) "Why and When Do Some Language-Impaired Children Seem Talkative? A Study of Initiation in Conversations of Children with Semantic-Pragmatic Disorder," *Journal of Autism and Developmental Disorders* 24: 177–97.

Bosco, F. M., and Gabbatore, I. (2017) "Sincere, Deceitful, and Ironic Communicative Acts and the Role of the Theory of Mind in Childhood," *Frontiers in Psychology* 8: 21.

Bosco, F. M., Parola, A., Sacco, K., Zettin, M., and Angeleri, R. (2017) "Communicative-Pragmatic Disorders in Traumatic Brain Injury: The Role of Theory of Mind and Executive Functions," *Brain and Language* 168: 73–83.

Bosco, F. M., Tirassa, M., and Gabbatore, I. (2018) "Why Pragmatics and Theory of Mind Do Not (Completely) Overlap," *Frontiers in Psychology* 9: 1–7.

Broomfield, K. A., Robinson, E. J., and Robinson, W. P. (2002) "Children's Understanding about White Lies," *British Journal of Developmental Psychology* 20: 47–65.

Brown, P., and Levinson, S. C. (1987) *Politeness: Some Universals in Language Usage*, Cambridge: Cambridge University Press.

Carston, R. (1997) "Relevance-Theoretic Pragmatics and Modularity," *UCL Working Papers in Linguistics* 9: 1–27.

Casillas, M., Bobb, S. C., and Clark, E. V. (2016) "Turn-Taking, Timing, and Planning in Early Language Acquisition," *Journal of Child Language* 43: 1310–37.

Champagne-Lavau, M., and Stip, E. (2010) "Pragmatic and Executive Dysfunction in Schizophrenia," *Journal of Neurolinguistics* 23: 285–96.

Chomsky, N. (1957) *Syntactic Structures*, The Hague: Mouton.

—— (1980) *Rules and Representations*, New York: Columbia University Press.

Cummings, L. (2009) *Clinical Pragmatics*, Cambridge: Cambridge University Press.

—— (ed.) (2017) *Research in Clinical Pragmatics*, Cham: Springer Verlag.

Davis, B., and Maclagan, M. (2010) "Pauses, Placeholders and Fillers in Alzheimer's Discourse: Glueing Relationships as Impairment Increases," in N. Amiridze, B. Davis, and M. Maclagan (eds.) *Fillers and Placeholders in Discourse and Grammar*, 189–215, Amsterdam: John Benjamins.

De Neys, W., and Schaeken, W. (2007) "When People Are More Logical Under Cognitive Load," *Experimental Psychology* 54: 128–33.

Domaneschi, F., Canal, P., Masia, V., Lombardi Vallauri, E., and Bambini, V. (2018) "N400 and P600 Modulation in Presupposition Accommodation: The Effect of Different Trigger Types," *Journal of Neurolinguistics* 45: 13–35.

Domaneschi, F., Carrea, E., Penco, C., and Greco, A. (2014) "The Cognitive Load of Presupposition Triggers Mandatory and Optional Repairs in Presupposition Failure," *Language, Cognition and Neuroscience* 29: 136–46.

Domaneschi, F., and Di Paola, S. (2018) "The Processing Costs of Presupposition Accommodation," *Journal of Psycholinguistic Research* 47: 483–503.

—— (2019) "The Aging Factor in Processing Presuppositions," *Journal of Pragmatics* 140: 70–87.

Eales, M. (1993) "Pragmatic Impairments in Adults with Childhood Diagnoses of Autism or Developmental Receptive Language Disorder," *Journal of Autism and Developmental Disorders* 23: 592–617.

Eigsti, I., Bennetto, L., and Dadlani, M. (2007) "Beyond Pragmatics: Morphosyntactic Development in Autism," *Journal of Autism and Developmental Disorders* 37: 1007–23.

Filippova, E., and Astington, J. W. (2008) "Further Development in Social Reasoning Revealed in Discourse Irony Understanding," *Child Development* 79: 126–38.

Fodor, J. A. (1983) *The Modularity of Mind: An Essay on Faculty Psychology*, Cambridge, MA: MIT Press.

Foster, S. H. (1990) *The Communicative Competence of Young Children*, London: Longman.

Gibbs, R. W. (1990) "Comprehending Figurative Referential Descriptions," *Journal of Experimental Psychology: Learning, Memory, and Cognition* 16: 56–66.

Giora, R. (2003) *On Our Mind: Salience, Context and Figurative Language*, New York: Cambridge University Press.

Glenwright, M., and Pexman, P. M. (2010) "Development of Children's Ability to Distinguish Sarcasm and Verbal Irony," *Journal of Child Language* 37: 429–51.

Green, B. C., Johnson, A., and Bretherton, L. (2014) "Pragmatic Language Difficulties in Children with Hyperactivity and Attention Problems: An Integrated Review," *International Journal of Language and Communication Disorders* 49: 15–29.

Grice, H. P. (1957) "Meaning," *The Philosophical Review* 66: 377–88.

—— (1975) "Logic and Conversation," in P. Cole and J. Morgan (eds.) *Syntax and Semantics, Vol. 3, Speech Acts*, 41–58, New York: Academic Press.

Guendouzi, J., and Savage, M. (2017) "Alzheimer's Dementia," in L. Cummings (ed.) *Research in Clinical Pragmatics*, 324–46, Cham: Springer Verlag.

Happé, F. G. E. (1993) "Communicative Competence and Theory of Mind in Autism: A Test of Relevance Theory," *Cognition* 48: 101–19.

Heyman, T., and Schaeken, W. (2015) "Some Differences in Some: Examining Variability in the Interpretation of Scalars Using Latent Class Analysis," *Psychologica Belgica* 55: 1–18.

Holler, J., Kendrick, K. H., Casilla, M., and Levinson, S. C. (2015) "Editorial: Turn-Taking in Human Communicative Interaction," *Frontiers in Psychology* 6: 1919.

Holtgraves, T., and McNamara, P. (2010) "Pragmatic Comprehension Deficit in Parkinson's Disease," *Journal of Clinical and Experimental Neuropsychology* 32: 388–97.

Kalandadze, T., Bambini, V., and Næss, K. A. (2019) "A Systematic Review and Meta-Analysis of Studies on Metaphor Comprehension in Individuals With Autism Spectrum Disorder: Do Task Properties Matter?" *Applied Psycholinguistics* 40: 1421–54.

Kasher, A. (1994) "Modular Speech Act Theory: Programme and Results," in S. Tsohatzidis (ed.) *Foundations of Speech Act Theory*, 312–22, London: Routledge.

Kircher, T. T. J., Leube, D. T., Erb, M., Grodd, W., and Rapp, A. M. (2007) "Neural Correlates of Metaphor Processing in Schizophrenia," *NeuroImage* 34: 281–9.

Kudlicka, A., Clare, L., and Hindle, J. (2011) "Executive Functions in Parkinson's Disease: Systematic Review and Meta-Analysis," *Movement Disorders* 26: 2305–15.

Langdon, R., Davies, M., and Coltheart, M. A. X. (2002) "Understanding Minds and Understanding Communicated Meanings in Schizophrenia," *Mind and Language* 17: 68–104.

Lecce, S., Ronchi, L., Del Sette, P., Bischetti, L., and Bambini, V. (2019) "Interpreting Physical and Mental Metaphors: Is Theory of Mind Associated With Pragmatics in Middle Childhood?" *Journal of Child Language* 46: 393–407.

Levinson, S. C. (1983) *Pragmatics*, Cambridge: Cambridge University Press.

Lewis, D. (1979) "Scorekeeping in a Language Game," *Journal of Philosophical Logics* 8: 339–59.

Ma, F., Xu, F., Heyman, G. D., and Lee, K. (2011) "Chinese Children's Evaluations of White Lies: Weighing the Consequences for Recipients," *Journal of Experimental Child Psychology* 108: 308–21.

Martin, I., and McDonald, S. (2003) "Weak Coherence, No Theory of Mind, or Executive Dysfunction? Solving the Puzzle of Pragmatic Language Disorders," *Brain and Language* 85: 451–66.

Martin, I., and McDonald, S. (2005) "Evaluating the Causes of Impaired Irony Comprehension Following Traumatic Brain Injury," *Aphasiology* 19: 712–30.

McNamara, P., and Durso, R. (2003) "Pragmatic Communication Skills in Parkinson's Disease," *Brain and Language* 84: 414–23.

Mossaheb, N., Aschauer, H. N., Stoettner, S., Schmoeger, M., Pils, N., Raab, M., and Willinger, U. (2014) "Comprehension of Metaphors in Patients With Schizophrenia-Spectrum Disorders," *Comprehensive Psychiatry* 55: 928–37.

Murphy, S. M., Faulkner, D. M., and Farley, L. R. (2014) "The Behaviour of Young Children With Social Communication Disorders During Dyadic Interaction With Peers," *Journal of Abnormal Child Psychology* 42: 277–89.

Murray, L. (1998) "Contributions of Experimental and Clinical Perturbations of Mother-Infant Communication to the Understanding of Infant Intersubjectivity," in S. Bråten (ed.) *Intersubjective Communication and Emotion in Early Ontogeny*, 127–43, Cambridge: Cambridge.

Nilsen, E. S., Glenwright, M., and Huyder, V. (2011) "Children and Adults Understand that Verbal Irony Interpretation Depends on Listener Knowledge," *Journal of Cognition and Development* 12: 374–409.

Norbury, C. F. (2005) "The Relationship Between Theory of Mind and Metaphor: Evidence from Children With Language Impairment and Autistic Spectrum Disorder," *British Journal of Developmental Psychology* 23: 383–99.

Noveck, I. (2018) *Experimental Pragmatics: The Making of a Cognitive Science*, Cambridge: Cambridge University Press.

Noveck, I., Bianco, M., and Castry, A. (2001) "The Costs and Benefits of Metaphor," *Metaphor and Symbol* 16: 109–21.

Noveck, I., and Sperber, D. (2004) *Experimental Pragmatics*, Basingstoke: Palgrave Macmillan.

Perkins, M. R. (2005) "Pragmatic Ability and Disability as Emergent Phenomena," *Clinical Linguistics and Phonetics* 19: 367–77.

Pouscoulous, N. (2014) "The Elevator's Buttocks: Metaphorical Abilities in Children," in D. Matthews (ed.) *Pragmatic Development in First Language Acquisition*, 239–60, Amsterdam, Philadelphia: Benjamins.

Premack, D., and Woodruff, G. (1978) "Does the Chimpanzee Have a Theory of Mind?" *Behavioural Brain Sciences* 1: 515–26.

Rousseaux, M., Seve, A., Vallet, M., Pasquier, F., and Mackowiak-Cordoliani, M. A. (2010) "An Analysis of Communication in Conversation in Patients with Dementia," *Neuropsychologia* 48: 3884–90.

Sacks, H., Schegloff, E. A., and Jefferson, G. (1978) "A Simplest Systematics for the Organization of Turn-Taking in Conversation," in J. Schenkein (ed.) *Studies in the Organization of Conversational Interaction*, 7–55, New York: Academic.

Sperber, D., and Wilson, D. (1986/1995) *Relevance: Communication and Cognition*, Oxford: Blackwell.

—— (2002) "Pragmatics, Modularity and Mindreading," *Mind & Language* 17: 3–23.

Spotorno, N., Koun, E., Prado, J., Van Der Henst, J.-B., and Noveck, I. (2012) "Neural Evidence that Utterance-Processing Entails Mentalizing: The Case of Irony," *NeuroImage* 63: 25–39.

Staikova, E., Gomes, H., Tartter, V., McCabe, A., and Halperin, J. M. (2013) "Pragmatic Deficits and Social Impairment in Children With ADHD," *Journal of Child Psychology and Psychiatry* 54: 1275–83.

Stalnaker, R., (2002) "Common Ground," *Linguistics and Philosophy* 25: 701–21.

Stivers, T., Enfield, N. J., Brown, P., Englert, C., Hayashi, M., Heinemann, T., et al. (2009) "Universals and Cultural Variation in Turn-Taking in Conversation," *Proceedings of the National Academy of Sciences* 106: 10587–92.

Thoma, P., and Daum, I. (2006) "Neurocognitive Mechanisms of Figurative Language Processing – Evidence from Clinical Dysfunctions," *Neuroscience & Biobehavioral Reviews* 30: 1182–205.

Trevarthen, C., Kokkinaki, T., and Fiamenghi Jr., G. A. (1999) "What Infants' Imitations Communicate: With Mothers, With Fathers and With Peers," in J. Nadel and G. Butterworth (eds.) *Imitation in Infancy*, 127–85, Cambridge: Cambridge University Press.

Weiland, H., Bambini, V., and Schumacher, P. (2014) "The Role of Literal Meaning in Figurative Language Comprehension: Evidence from Masked Priming ERP," *Frontiers in Human Neuroscience* 9: 11–12.

Willcutt, E. G., Doyle, A. E., Nigg, J. T., Faraone, S. V., and Pennington, B. F. (2005) "Validity of the Executive Function Theory of Attention-Deficit/Hyperactivity Disorder: A Meta-Analytic Review," *Biological Psychiatry* 57: 1336–46.

Wilson, D. (2006) "The Pragmatics of Verbal Irony: Echo or Pretence?" *Lingua* 116: 1722–43.

Wilson, D., and Carston, R. (2007) "A Unitary Approach to Lexical Pragmatics: Relevance, Inference and AD Hoc Concepts," in N. Burton-Roberts (ed.) *Pragmatics*, 230–59, Basingstoke: Palgrave Macmillan.

Winner, E., Rosenstiel, A. K., and Gardner, H. (1976) "The Development of Metaphoric Understanding," *Developmental Psychology* 12: 289–97.

Wolfe, K. R., Walsh, K. S., Reynolds, N. C., Mitchell, F., Reddy, A. T., Paltin, I., and Madan-Swain, A. (2013) "Executive Functions and Social Skills in Survivors of Pediatric Brain Tumor," *Child Neuropsychology* 19: 370–84.

PART VI

Skill and expertise in normative philosophy

34

MORAL EXPERTISE

Julia Driver

There can be experts in astronomy, in engineering, in mathematics, and in chemistry. Intuitively, no one really challenges this. If I want to know something about astronomy, say, the number of rings circling Saturn, I will ask an astronomer or consult a book written by an astronomer, because astronomers are experts in the relevant area. When the astronomer tells me, "Seven ring groups and thousands of smaller rings," I am justified in believing her. Given the belief is true, then I have acquired some knowledge that I did not have before. I have acquired the *true* belief that Saturn has seven ring groups in a *justified* manner, on the basis of *expert* testimony. Of course, experts are not infallible. But justification does not require infallibility, it simply requires reliability, and the astronomer is a reliable source of information about the planets.

To describe someone as a moral expert *on analogy with* an astronomy expert, or an engineering expert, seems to describe them as someone who has (much) more knowledge about morality than the average person. Further, the analogy seems to commit one to viewing them as good sources of moral advice and testimony.

But astronomy is descriptive. "Saturn has seven ring groups" is not a prescriptive or normative claim. It describes a feature of our solar system as it *is*, not how it *should* be. Expertise in *normative* domains can be thought of as a separate issue, and moral expertise is normative. People who seek out moral experts want to know how things *ought* to be and what they *ought* to do. The issue of moral expertise is significant because it helps us to understand if and how there is a difference between moral knowledge and understanding, and descriptive knowledge and understanding. It also figures into debates regarding whether or not one ought to rely *solely* on expert testimony when deciding how to act. If one believes, for example, that correct moral judgments involve legislating *for oneself* (rather than believing and doing what someone else tells you to do), then one may believe that there really are no moral experts in the sense of someone who has better access to the truths of morality than anyone else. Further, if it turns out there are no moral experts, or that even if there are, we are not justified in relying on their testimony, that will have profound practical implications.[1] On some theories of virtue, the fully virtuous person is the same as the moral expert, and therefore the issue is important for developing a certain understanding of the morally virtuous person.

To start, consider claims such as:

(1) When Aubrey stole the food from the grocery store to feed his starving children, he did something wrong.
(2) People in affluent countries have a moral duty to try to alleviate famine.

Again, these sorts of claims are distinct from "Saturn has seven ring groups" because they are normative, they make claims about what we *ought* or *ought not* do, what is morally *right* or morally *wrong*, *virtuous* or *vicious*, etc. Thus, the moral expert will be someone who knows and/or understands how we ought to act and be. To say that a moral expert knows that *p* is to say that the moral expert has a justified true belief that *p*. To say that the moral expert understands that *p* is to say that the moral expert can also provide the correct justification for *p*, though as we shall see, some philosophers require even more for understanding.

Many philosophers have been skeptical of moral expertise. Gilbert Ryle argued there were no moral experts because there was nothing moral to be expert *about*. If there is no moral knowledge, because, perhaps, moral judgments and corresponding "assertions" are emotive or expressive and do not actually assert anything, then when an expert claims, "It is (*pro tanto*) wrong to steal" she is not actually passing along any knowledge she has, but simply expressing her feelings of disapproval toward stealing, and expressions of attitudes such as "Yuk!" or "Yay!" have no truth conditions, they are neither true nor false.

However, this suggests a much too narrow understanding of moral expertise. Even if there is no moral knowledge, there can still be other ways of spelling out moral expertise that accords with our considered views. "Correspondence with reality plus reliable access to that" is just one standard that we can employ. For example, an Emotivist might hold that the moral expert is one whose emotions are properly calibrated – they meet their fittingness or aptness conditions and/or suit their practical aims (of encouraging or discouraging others from similar behavior).

Thus, it is a mistake to dismiss expertise on these grounds since one can have an account of expertise in a domain as long as there are standards of correctness for the judgments and expressions themselves. One can even be a nihilist about morality, and believe that all moral claims are not true, and be better at moral judgments or acting morally than others. On this view there is no real moral knowledge, but we could have instrumental reasons for acting as if morality is true, or pretending that it is true, and those reasons would provide non-evidential justification for the moral claims, and form the standard by which the moral claims are evaluated.

However, in this chapter I will assume that there is moral knowledge. As noted earlier, one reason expertise has emerged as a significant topic of discussion in ethics has to do with its connection to the issue of deference to testimony, and whether or not one can acquire moral knowledge *solely* via the testimony of an expert. To *defer* to testimony is to accept what the putative expert has told you even though you don't understand the reasons why the direction that they have given you is correct. That is, you do not understand their justification. This is quite different from taking advice from an expert, which you think about for yourself and in which you come to understand the underlying justification for the expert's claims. No one challenges the view that there are many non-problematic ways that experts can help one acquire moral knowledge. Consider (1). Suppose that Candace can't decide whether or not Aubrey did something that was, all things considered, wrong. On the one hand, he stole, and stealing is *pro tanto* wrong. On the other hand, he has a *pro tanto* duty to take care of his children as well. Candace discusses this with her friend Celestine, who she reasonably takes to be a moral expert – Celestine has a long record of making correct moral judgments. Celestine explains that, under the circumstances, the duty to take care of his children is more important than the violation of the norm against stealing, because it is necessary to alleviate the children's suffering, and the store owner is simply losing a small amount of property. Suffering is more significant, morally. After Celestine talks to her about it, Candace comes to see for herself that, indeed, this makes a great deal of sense and acquires for herself the understanding that alleviation of suffering is a very, very significant moral reason in relation to other moral reasons. In this kind of case, there is no problem at all with listening to an expert. The problematic cases are those which involve someone relying only on the testimony of the expert in forming one's belief. Thus, in the above case, suppose that Candace listened to Celestine, but still had no sense of which reason was weightier, and did not acquire an understanding of how to weigh suffering against other goods and evils. Nevertheless, she trusts Celestine and believes her when she says, "Aubrey did the right thing." Candace now has a belief, and it is a true belief, but does the testimony itself provide sufficient justification? If the answer is "no" then there is a dramatic difference between expert testimony in descriptive cases as opposed to moral ones.

However, recent discussion has granted that one can acquire knowledge solely on the basis of expert testimony, and the problem has shifted to the issue of whether or not people should rely solely on moral testimony, when they lack an understanding of the underlying justification. For example, Alison Hills grants that one *can* acquire moral knowledge on the basis of expert moral testimony, but holds that one *should* not (Hills 2009). This is because, in part, moral *understanding* cannot be acquired this way, and it is moral understanding that is important. Moral understanding is understanding of the fundamental features of moral justification – moral reasons, and how those reasons factor into moral justification in a systematic way. So, according to Hills and others, a person with moral knowledge acquired via testimony but no moral understanding might perform the right action solely on the basis of this knowledge, but she would not be performing the right action *for the right reasons*, since she lacks an understanding, or an appreciation, of those reasons, and so the action would not be morally worthy or virtuous. For an action to be virtuous the agent must be performing the action for the right reasons. For example, if Cathy gives to charity for the sole purpose of reducing her tax burden, then she has done something that has good effects, but she hasn't done it for the right reasons, in this case, reasons that arise out of caring for the well-being of other people. Thus, her action lacks moral worth, and it is not truly virtuous. The notion of a morally worthy action is generally attributed to Immanuel Kant, who uses the example of a shopkeeper to illustrate (Kant 1998: 11). The shopkeeper is honest to his customers in order to acquire and maintain his reputation for honesty, so that he can compete successfully. Here the shopkeeper, in giving correct change, for example, is acting rightly, but not for the right reasons. The right reason to act honestly is that it is commanded by the moral law. Only a shopkeeper who gives correct change for the right reasons also performs an action with moral worth. Morally worthy actions are better than merely right actions because they indicate the agent is motivated to act by the right reasons, that is, for the reasons that actually morally justify the action.[2] Thus, the person performing the morally worthy action regards morality as binding on its own, separate from their own individual interests.

So, consider another case, similar to the Candance and Celestine case, in which one friend, Melissa, relies on another friend, Jamie, to help in cases of moral uncertainty. As Candace does with Celestine, Melissa correctly judges Jamie, on the basis of past experience, to be very reliable on moral matters. In this case, however, Melissa is not only worried about correctly judging, she is deciding on what to do, and wants to act rightly. Melissa is unsure about whether she should lie, to spare the feelings of someone else, or tell the truth. Limiting pain and honesty both provide moral reasons, she is just not sure which dominates in this situation. When Jamie tells her, "Normally lying is wrong, but in this particular case it is right," she believes her and acts accordingly. Jamie is the moral expert in this situation. On the view sketched above, Melissa acted rightly in telling the lie in this particular situation, but her action also lacks moral worth because she did so for the wrong reason – she did so on the basis of her friend's testimony and without a full and *systematic* understanding of the moral reasons that provide justification for the action. Not only must one know what the relevant reasons are, one must also know how they weigh against each other in particular circumstances. One must know how they work, so to speak. The defect is that she did not come to the right conclusion in a way that involved her own appreciation of the reasons and how they are weighed against each other. The moral experts are the ones who possess this understanding. Hills further holds that there is something morally defective about deferring to testimony. She points to the instrumental concerns that such a person is not developing her own moral understanding, and thus is undermining her character, as well as the worry that there is something intrinsically defective about it since one seems to be outsourcing one's autonomous decision-making.[3]

Further, Alison Hills argues that moral understanding cannot be reduced to moral knowledge on her view, nor can moral knowledge be understood itself in terms of moral understanding. They are distinct. One can know a proposition is true, but fail to understand why it is true, as the testimony cases seem to reveal. More controversially she holds that one cannot account for understanding why p is the case in terms of knowing why p is the case. It is important for her to maintain the two are distinct in order to argue that the knowledge possessed by the person who defers to expertise cannot be recast as a form of understanding, otherwise one could argue that understanding itself can be transmitted solely via testimony regarding the fundamental justificatory moral reasons.[4]

Other writers, such as myself, have challenged such a demanding view of moral expertise (Driver 2013). One can be a moral expert without possessing full understanding on my view, because moral expertise is understood as contrastive. A person can be a moral expert relative to a specific moral domain while lacking a full understanding of underlying moral reasons (Driver 2013). That person would be an expert relative to others with an even greater lack of understanding. Further, there are different ways in which someone can be an expert which involve very little in the way of moral understanding. This view is discussed further later in the essay.

Other writers are skeptical of expertise in another sense: they point out that even if, in principle, there are these moral experts, there is no real way to determine who they are, and then, even if we can determine who they are, we may have no reason to trust them. Plato, in the *Charmides*, was concerned with this issue.[5] How can the naive, non-expert person, tell someone who is pretending to be a doctor from a real doctor? It would seem that since they lack the knowledge of what it takes to be a doctor, they won't be able to properly judge. One response to this problem is to hold that one can tell over time when one keeps track of the person's success rate.[6]

However, one version of this argument points to the existence of serious moral disagreement to make the skeptical case. Many writers have noted that there is often great disagreement among people who are equally well credentialed (Cross 2016). This can occur at the theoretical level or the practical level. Consider a practical case: Maria is trying to decide whether or not she should respect her mother's Do Not Resuscitate (DNR) order, and allow her to die, or not respect it since she feels that her mother still has a fairly good quality of life: her mother is happy, enjoys watching television, and does not seem to be in any pain. She consults experts on moral decisions in end-of-life treatment, and finds that there is much disagreement about what she should do: some argue that she must respect her mother's prior, rational, wishes but others tell her that since her mother is enjoying life she ought to reject the DNR order as it does not represent her mother's current desires. Her mother now enjoys just sitting and watching children's shows on TV all day, something her mother, at the time she made the DNR order, would not have wanted for herself at all. Indeed, she would have been horrified at the thought of such a fate in which her primary concerns and goals are gone. Both experts provide her with arguments that seem quite reasonable. She has no idea who to believe, who to judge the genuine expert. Since very many practical issues are like this – involving disagreement between thoughtful, well-credentialed people on what one ought to do – it is very difficult, if not impossible, for the non-expert to pick out the genuine expert. While much has been made of the credentialing problem, this does not mark a principled difference between the descriptive and the prescriptive. As in the descriptive cases, the non-expert uses the best available evidence, and, of course, can still make mistakes on whom to trust. In these sorts of cases, the disagreement might undermine moral knowledge, as well, and if the moral expert is one who possesses moral knowledge (perhaps in addition to having other properties), then there can't be moral experts in areas of disagreement between equally well-credentialed "experts." In these cases we can still reasonably hold that experts are those with more in the way of justified beliefs in a given domain. There can be two experts on the subject who disagree even if at least one of them must be wrong.

Here I assume that there are moral experts and moral knowledge, but argue that the issue of moral expertise has been hampered by lack of clarity about what it *is*. As I have argued elsewhere, there is no single primary sense of "moral expertise." It can take different forms. The analogy I trade on is well known in ethics – it is the analogy between morality and language. Someone, for example, might not know anything about grammar at all, and be very well able to identify infelicitous expressions such as "Best the be to all" or "Forest swamped alert and by." One can identify the infelicitous without being able to analyze it or explain it. One can make the right judgment but then not be able to explain it. That is still a form of expertise. Further, one may be able to identify correct and incorrect grammar, but have trouble oneself *speaking* or *writing* grammatically.

There are moral experts when it comes to making moral judgments, "a is the right action in this situation," when it comes to practice or performance, "She reliably acts rightly," and in terms of analysis, "Her action was right because it was the kind thing to do in these circumstances." In this essay I will focus on *judgment* and *practice* expertise. It is these two that are closest to what most people have in mind when writing about the issue. Some theorists view the genuine moral expert as someone who is expert at both making the correct judgments and acting as they ought to act (Cross-reference to Bashour, Chapter 37).

34.1 Moral judgment

This type of expertise is similar to what Alvin Goldman refers to as cognitive expertise: "experts in a given domain … have more beliefs (or high degrees of belief) in true propositions and/or fewer beliefs in false propositions within that domain than most people do" (Goldman 2001: 91). If one is a moral expert in judgment then one makes judgments about moral matters that are more reliable than others. This could mean that when the expert judges that "x is wrong" that judgment is more likely to be correct than the same judgment made by the non-expert. One might also hold that to be an expert judge one must understand the underlying justificatory reasons that render the judgment correct. However, I believe that these can be separated when it comes to moral expertise, just as they can be separated in cases of non-moral expertise. For example, a person may be expert at sorting, and thus expert at judging whether or not a chick is male or female, without also being able to justify the judgment, or to explain why there is a difference. For them it is simply a matter of correct perception. They are responding to reasons, but not at a conscious level that they are able to articulate. Thus, one can be more likely to be correct in one's judgments without being able to provide justification.

The expert judge, then, makes more reliably correct moral judgments. But the expertise is understood relative to a contrast class. I may have a friend who is expert on free speech issues relative to me, and yet not expert relative to someone else. Goldman, in his analysis of expertise, also holds that it is comparative. However, he believes that the expert must reach some level of absolute command of the subject.

> If the vast majority of people are full of false beliefs in a domain and Jones Jones exceeds them slightly by not succumbing to a few falsehoods that are widely shared, that still does not make him an "expert" (from a God's eye point of view). To qualify as a cognitive expert, one must possess a substantial body of truths in the cognitive domain.
>
> *Goldman 2001: 91*

I agree with Goldman's claim in that we can distinguish between a God's-eye view of expertise, and then an on-the-ground view of expertise. In the idealized sense of "expert" we do require some high threshold of knowledge and understanding. We use the term "expert" sometimes as a kind of honorific. It denotes significant accomplishment. And, again, to that extent, Goldman is correct. However, in other situations we use it to pick out the best person to consult on a given topic, even if not very much is known regarding that topic. Utterances such as, "She's the expert, she knows more than anyone else, though nobody knows very much," seem to make sense. I may live in a community in which no one knows very much about medicine, but one person knows a bit more than others. That is the person it would be reasonable for me to go to for advice, to consult. She might not be an expert from the God's-eye point of view, but relative to anyone else I can consult in that community, she is. One could argue that in the case of fairly simple issues, where the choices are between "yes" and "no" and one isn't also hoping at least for a glimmering of understanding, on the view I am suggesting here there would not be any real experts if the body of knowledge of the putative expert were too low, so that the expert got it wrong more than half the time. In that case, one would be better off just flipping a coin to decide. That would be true (barring a consideration of the instrumental goods associated with seeking out advice, etc.), but that also does not seem to be a typical case. If we don't accept the full contrastive picture of expertise, then we are left with the possibility that, really, there are no experts. And that might be fine. The contrastive account also has a problem in that if everyone in the group has the same knowledge as everyone else then there are no experts, even if all of them know an awful lot about the norms in question. That seems odd, because utterances such as, "You can ask anybody, we are all experts," also seems to make sense. Most likely the best account distinguishes between purely contrastive expertise, God's-eye expertise, and something in between, the real on-the-ground standard of expertise, which sets a threshold in some non-idealized way. The on-the-ground expert needs to get things right at least greater than 50% of the time, and must be more reliable than others.

Thus, the moral expert in this sense is the person who makes more reliable judgments about what is right or wrong, or virtuous and vicious, etc. But this isn't clear enough. It is tricky because moral judgments are frequently made on the basis of both descriptive and prescriptive, or normative, facts. What does the distinctly *moral* part of the judgment consist in? *If* we understand the moral expert as someone who reliably makes correct judgments about what ought to be done, what policy should be implemented, etc., then some experts are those who can, for example, foresee what will happen better than others, or who have better empirical understanding. Consider again the second claim we began with: "People in affluent countries have a moral duty to try to give to famine relief charities." Two individuals may agree on the moral reasons in play, but disagree about whether or not this claim is true because they disagree about empirical facts. One person may believe that it is true because we ought to alleviate human suffering and working to end famine does that because it alleviates hunger. The second may think it false, because we ought to alleviate human suffering, but she thinks that giving to famine relief fails to accomplish that goal (perhaps due to corruption, or worries that famine relief makes the problem worse in the future).[7] In this particular case the one who is correct on the empirical facts makes the correct judgment. If I am trying to decide what to do, and I defer to the one who favors giving aid for famine relief purposes, then I am doing so because I believe that expert has better command of the empirical facts. This expert is not better than the other judge in terms of the possession of moral knowledge, knowledge of the underlying moral justification relevant to the question of famine relief.

But this is *impure* deference to moral expertise.[8] That is, this expert does reliably make better moral judgments than others, but does so through a better command of empirical facts. Distinctively *moral* expertise is expertise on the moral facts, it is expertise regarding the underlying moral justifications, the reasons that render the act right or wrong. We might understand this as a knowledge of what counts as a moral reason, or which moral consideration dominates in a given situation, etc.

However, many writers have viewed moral expertise as involving *both* descriptive and normative knowledge. For example, G. E. Moore believed that the moral expert was able to understand the right action in terms of good or bad, *and* cause and effect. The expertise consisted in identifying the good and then using empirical methods to appropriately judge cause and effect (Eggleston 2005). The two judgments "x is good" and "a causes x" are the two judgments that underlie "a is the right action". So, at least on Moore's view, the moral expert is one who has both descriptive and normative knowledge, and that is what underlies knowledge of what action is the right action. However, one could argue that distinctively moral knowledge would simply be the knowledge of the good as well as knowledge of the correct attitude to take toward the good. This would involve judgments of the form "x is good" and "m is the correct approach to the good" so the action that achieves x m-ly is the right action. These two claims are distinctly normative.

The charge against Moore's view would be that the moral expert may not also be an expert on empirical matters. So, "a causes x" is not a bit of moral knowledge, and a judgment that "a is the right action because a causes x and x is good" is not purely moral. So, the *moral* expert is the one who is correct about the *normative reasons* for performing a given action, or correct about what the underlying justifiers are for the action. Thus, if someone holds that an action is justified simply on the basis of respect for autonomy, and another holds that it is justified solely on the basis of limiting the amount of suffering in the world, then one of them, at least, is not a moral expert even though both agree on the policy itself.

Again, this observation has led some to regard moral expertise as a matter of having moral knowledge but also having moral *understanding*, which is, in turn, distinct from moral knowledge. Though both of the people who offer correct testimony know what the right thing to do is, only one has moral understanding, and that one is the real expert. As I noted earlier, there are varying standards for what this understanding requires, but the most demanding accounts require a great deal in terms of what sort of grasp of the reasons moral understanding involves.

Alison Hills believes that understanding requires systematic knowledge of what these reasons are and how they work together, and an ability to articulate those reasons and explain to others how they justify either the judgment or action. If we identify the moral expert with the fully virtuous person, then expertise in action is also required. All three forms of expertise combine in the moral expert (Hills 2009, 2015). These are very high standards for moral expertise. To take up the linguistic analogy again: the corresponding linguistic expert would be one who speaks grammatically, can recognize violation of grammatical norms, speaks well, *and* who is a linguist.

The requirement that the moral expert, either in judgment or practice, needs to be able to articulate the reasons that justify the action, is very controversial and has received some attention in the literature on moral expertise. In addition to Alison Hills, Julia Annas has also placed the requirement that the virtuous agent be able to articulate the correct justification for an action and judgment (Annas 2011). Matt Stichter has challenged Annas on this requirement since in part it seems easily subject to counterexample (Stichter 2007). Annas grants that there are skills that people have that don't seem to require the possession of the ability to articulate and explain the reasons supporting the action, but considers that these are not genuine skills, or at least not skills of the sort that concerned Socrates in developing the skill analogy. Part of Stichter's criticism is that if one restricts the comparison to "intellectualist" skills, then one is building into the concept the intellectual features that one should have to argue for, they can't simply be assumed.

It seems that a less intellectualist form of understanding can be developed – for example, as responsiveness to reasons that do not require skill in analysis, as the chicken sorters case illustrates (Arpaly 2002b). There is wide variation in the literature on expertise regarding the nature of moral understanding, or what it is to be "aware of" or "responding to" the right reasons in judgment and action. One can, for example, make use of accounts of reasons responsiveness that are not overly intellectualized, that reject what Errol Lord has referred to as a *Conceptualization Condition* for reasons responsiveness that requires the reasons responsive agent to possess "mental states whose contents are conceptualized via some normatively relevant contents" and, more specifically, the concepts employed in the correct moral theory (whatever that happens to be) (Lord 2017, 347). This is the account he attributes to Nomy Arpaly and Timothy Schroeder. Lord correctly notes that this account is much too intellectually demanding. If this were the correct account view, few of us would ever be acting for the right reasons. His view is that reasons responsiveness that underlies moral creditworthiness is a kind of *know-how*. Morally good people know how to do the right thing, or the morally good thing, and when they act as an expression of the know how they deserve credit. They care about what is right and good, even if they are not able to deploy the concepts of the correct moral theory, or even partially deploy them. This view has the virtue of being less intellectually demanding, and more realistically covers our intuitions on specific cases, such as cases in which someone, though confused, is clearly acting out of a concern for other people when he sees them suffering. This person would be an expert in practice, and even an expert in judgment, but needn't be an expert in analysis.

We have already discussed the supposed disanalogy between descriptive and normative expertise. We might also try to understand moral expertise by exploring analogies between different forms of normative expertise. Recently in the literature on testimony, analogies have been drawn between the moral expert and the aesthetic expert. This is an attractive analogy, and has figured into historical discussions of moral norms, particularly with the early sentimentalists. David Hume, for example, often drew on analogies between the aesthetic and the moral. These norms are both based in our sentiments. Their content depends upon human nature. There is some form of objectivity with respect to these norms in the sense that there are universal standards that apply to all *human beings*. But, as in the case of aesthetic claims, moral claims are not true of necessity.

Hume explored the issue of aesthetic expertise in "Of the Standard of Taste" (Hume 1965), arguing that the criteria for aesthetic expertise are that the expert in aesthetic judgment is someone who has good sense, a delicate taste (can detect even small differences), and is free from prejudice. These qualities can carry over to the moral expert. The *limit* of the moral expert might be thought of as an "ideal observer." The qualities one thinks are relevant to the ideal observer are the ones the moral expert must have – impartiality, some understanding of the moral reasons at play, and otherwise possessing good sense, or good reasoning abilities. Hume also believed that aesthetic experts *practiced* making judgments, and made themselves familiar with a wide variety of cases so that they could make informed comparisons.

Some of these criteria are simply developmental and shouldn't be part of a definition of moral expertise. For example, Hume claimed that experts develop through practice. Many contemporary writers on expertise note this as well. Even if it were true, it is not a necessary condition of expertise that the expert has gone through this process. Rather, it picks out the process by which normal human beings *become* experts.

34.2 Moral practice

One can also be an expert when it comes to *acting* morally. That is, certain people possess skills, or know-how, when it comes to acting morally. Just as a violinist possesses the skill, or know-how, in playing music that isn't simply a matter of possessing propositional knowledge about violin playing. This is distinct from being an expert in judgment, or an expert in analysis. This moral expert in this sense more reliably *does* the right thing relative to others. Such an expert may not judge the action to be the right one, though, in many cases, judgment and practice expertise coincide.

Recall the developmental point that in order for someone to become an expert that person must practice. Thus, for someone to become an expert pianist that person must practice enough that certain finger movements are completely automatic. They act properly automatically, and that's a feature of expertise. But, again, this is simply a contingent developmental feature of how expertise is *developed* in normal human beings. It has nothing to do with the concept of what an expert *is*. Similarly, how one becomes a bachelor isn't a question relevant to understanding what a bachelor is.

At least some have thought that this practice involves the non-expert explicitly applying rules to behavior in order to develop the skill. Over time, the action becomes automatic. This does not seem right at all, especially if one finds the analogy with language compelling. This would make the development of moral skill more like the acquisition of a second language. But growing up in social settings gives people plenty of practice in acting morally in normal contexts, and the skill can be developed this way, just as first language use is developed. Others have thought that the developmental picture in psychology has been "one-dimensional" and that expertise is actually "three-dimensional." Harry Collins (2013) suggests that it isn't just individuals who are experts, groups can be experts as well. We might get some intuitive support for this by considering claims like, "Plumbers are the experts on pipes." I'm skeptical that this is much of a difference, however, since it seems that the group is reducible to the individuals, though I concede that there could be cases in which the group possesses expertise that each individual lacks – a kind of higher-order expertise. In any case, he also views the explicit application of rules to the development of expertise to be misguided. Of course, that can happen, but especially when we look at groups, he argues that knowledge can be transmitted as *tacit* knowledge. We watch, we absorb. Collins adds that the knowledge possessed by the expert must also be esoteric, in order to distinguish widespread or ubiquitous tacit knowledge from expertise. This is quite different from what I am proposing: on my view, one accepts that there is language-speaking expertise even in situations in which the skill is widespread within society. It is just that expertise is understood contrastively, so that even though all normal adults speak well, they are experts when contrasted with the normal three-year-old.

But Collins's developmental point is correct. One can just "pick up" certain forms of expertise. I would go further and hold that it seems plausible that some people are born with expertise in some domain (that is, they are not born experts strictly speaking, but they are born with a capacity that they take no active measures to develop, nor is the expertise something that they pick up from their environment). This is certainly conceptually possible, and the way or manner in which someone becomes an expert is not something that figures into what an expert *is*. How someone becomes a bachelor does not figure into what a bachelor is.

Again, there are many writers on this issue who, for example, connect moral expertise in action with possession of moral virtue. They also require that the genuine expert in action is expert in judgment as well. This requires that the moral expert possesses both abilities, to judge properly better than others in the relative contrast class, and to act rightly more reliably as well.

The classic case used in the literature of someone who acts rightly without understanding why what he did was right, and in fact, actually thinking that what he did was morally bad, is the case of Huckleberry Finn.[9] However, since we are discussing expertise rather than the rightness of actions, imagine a Huck-like character who very reliably acts rightly, responding to the right reasons, but who does not judge or reason correctly about the moral character of his own actions. This would be someone who was an expert moral actor, though not an expert in judgment or analysis. The highly intellectualized views of moral expertise in action would deny that this is a kind of moral expertise (see Bashour, Chapter 37 in this volume). Again, to make this case there is often an appeal to an articulation requirement: Huck is not able to give an account of why his actions are, all things considered, justified precisely because in some of those cases he thinks they are not, all things considered, justified. There is still basic moral understanding, and responsiveness to moral reasons, in the sense that he does understand that he has moral reason to help his friend escape from slavery. He is not clueless about morality, but he has accepted the conventions of his time as moral truths, when in fact they are not.

In this essay the debates surrounding moral expertise in the literature have been sketched and discussed, and an account of moral expertise has been argued for that holds that there are different ways in which someone can be a moral expert, and that some of these do not require that the moral expert possess a full, systematic, understanding of morality. Further, deference to these experts is, in principle, much like deference to experts on descriptive or empirical matters.

Notes

1 For this reason, the topic of moral expertise figures extensively into the medical ethics literature. For some examples of recent discussions see Leah McClimans and Anne Slowther, "Moral Expertise in the Clinic: Lessons Learned from Medicine and Science," *Journal of Medicine and Philosophy* (2016) 41: 401–413; Nicky Priaulx, Martin Weinel, and Anthony Wrigley, "Rethinking Moral Expertise," *Health Care Analysis* (2016) 24: 393–406; Ben Cross, "Moral Philosophy, Moral Expertise, and the Argument from Disagreement," *Bioethics* (2016) 30: 188–194.
2 For more on moral worth, see Nomy Arpaly, "Moral Worth," *Journal of Philosophy* (2002a) 99: 223–245 and Julia Markovits, "Acting for the Right Reasons," *Philosophical Review* (2010) 119: 201–242.

3 Some writers have defended deference to moral testimony. See, for example, David Enoch, "A Defense of Moral Deference," *Journal of Philosophy* (2014) 111: 229–258; Gopal Sreenivasan, "A Plea for Moral Deference," *Etica & Politica* (2015) 17: 41–59.

4 For criticism of Hills' view that moral understanding is distinct from moral knowledge see Amber Riaz, "Moral Understanding and Knowledge," *Philosophical Studies* (2015) 172: 113–128, and Paulina Sliwa, "Moral Understanding as Knowing Right from Wrong," *Ethics* (2017) 127: 521–552.

5 Plato, *Laches and Charmides*, translated by Rosamund Kent Sprague (Hackett Publishing Company, 1992), 22 ff.

6 C. A. J. Coady challenges this approach in *Testimony: A Philosophical Study* (Oxford University Press, 1992).

7 One could argue that this is the nature of the disagreement between Peter Singer and Garrett Hardin on whether or not those in affluent countries to give to famine relief. Compare Singer, "Famine, Affluence and Morality" to Hardin's "Lifeboat Ethics: The Case Against Helping the Poor."

8 See Sarah McGrath, "The Puzzle of Pure Moral Deference," 322 ff. for more on the distinction between pure and impure moral deference.

9 See Jonathan Bennett, "The Conscience of Huckleberry Finn,"; Julia Driver, "The Virtues and Human Nature" and *Uneasy Virtue*; Nomy Arpaly, *Unprincipled Virtue*.

References

Annas, J. (2011) *Intelligent Virtue*, Oxford: Oxford University Press.

Arpaly, N. (2002a) "Moral Worth," *Journal of Philosophy*, 99: 223–245.

—— (2002b) *Unprincipled Virtue*, Oxford: Oxford University Press.

Bennett, J. (1974) "The Conscience of Huckleberry Finn," *Philosophy* 49: 123–134.

Collins, H. (2013) "Three Dimensions of Expertise," *Phenomenology and the Cognitive Sciences* 12: 253–273.

Cross, B. (2016) "Moral Philosophy, Moral Expertise, and the Argument from Disagreement", *Bioethics*, 30: 188–194.

Demeree-Cotton, J. (2016) "Do Framing Effects Make Moral Intuitions Unreliable?" *Philosophical Psychology* 29: 1–22.

Driver, J. (1998) "The Virtues and Human Nature," in Roger Crisp and Michael Slote (eds.) *How Should One Live?* Oxford: Oxford University Press, 111–130.

—— (2001) *Uneasy Virtue*, Cambridge: Cambridge University Press.

—— (2006) "Autonomy and the Asymmetry Problem for Moral Expertise," *Philosophical Studies* 128: 619–644.

—— (2013) "Moral Expertise: Judgment, Practice, and Analysis," *Social Theory and Practice* 30: 280–296.

Eggleston, B. (2005) "The Ineffable and the Incalculable: G. E. Moore on Ethical Expertise," in L. M. Rasmussen (ed.) *Ethics Expertise: History, Contemporary Perspectives, and Applications*, Dordrecht: Springer, 89–102.

Enoch, D. (2014) "A Defense of Moral Deference," *Journal of Philosophy* 111: 229–258.

Goldman, A. (2001) "Experts: Which Ones Should You Trust?" *Philosophy and Phenomenological Research* 63: 85–110.

Hardin, G. (1974) "Lifeboat Ethics: The Case Against Saving the Poor," *Psychology Today* 8: 38–43.

Hills, A. (2009) "Moral Testimony and Moral Epistemology," *Ethics* 120: 94–127.

—— (2015) "The Intellectuals and the Virtues," *Ethics* 126: 7–36.

Hume, D. (1965) "Of the Standard of Taste," in John W. Lenz (ed.) *Of the Standard of Taste and Other Essays*, Indianapolis: Bobbs-Merrill.

Kant, I. (1998) *Groundwork of the Metaphysics of Morals*, translated and edited by Mary Gregor, Cambridge: Cambridge University Press.

Lord, E. (2017) "On the Intellectual Conditions for Responsibility: Acting for the Right Reasons, Conceptualization, and Credit," *Philosophy and Phenomenological Research* 95: 436–454.

Markovits, J. (2010) "Acting for the Right Reasons," *Philosophical Review* 119: 201–242.

McClimans, L., and Slowther, A. (2016) "Moral Expertise in the Clinic: Lessons Learned from Medicine and Science," *Journal of Medicine and Philosophy* 41: 401–413.

McGrath, S. (2009) "The Puzzle of Pure Moral Deference," *Philosophical Perspectives* 23: 321–344.

—— (2011) "Skepticism about Moral Expertise as a Puzzle for Moral Realism," *Journal of Philosophy* 108: 111–137.

Priaulx, N., Martin, W., and Wrigley, A. (2016) "Rethinking Moral Expertise," *Health Care Analysis*, 24: 393–406.

Riaz, A. (2015) "Moral Understanding and Knowledge," *Philosophical Studies* 172: 113–128.

Rini, R. (2015) "How Not to Test for Philosophical Expertise," *Synthese* 192: 431–452.

Schwitzgebel, E., and Cushman, F. (2012) "Expertise in Moral Reasoning? Order Effects on Moral Judgment in Professional Philosophers," *Mind and Language* 27: 135–153.

Singer, P. (1972) "Famine, Affluence, and Morality, *Philosophy and Public Affairs* 1: 229–243.

Sinnott-Armstrong, W. (2006) "Moral Intuitionism Meets Empirical Psychology," in Terry Horgan and Mark Timmons (eds.) *Metaethics After Moore*, Oxford: Oxford University Press. doi:10.1093/acprof:oso/9780199269914.003.0016.

—— (2011) "Emotion and Reliability in Moral Judgment," *Emotion Review* 3: 288–289.

Sliwa, P. (2017) "Moral Understanding as Knowledge of Right and Wrong," *Ethics* 127: 521–552.

Sreenivasan, G. (2015) "A Plea for Moral Deference," *Etica & Politica* 17: 41–59.

Stichter, M. (2007) "Ethical Expertise: The Skill Model of Virtue," *Ethical Theory and Moral Practice* 10: 183–194.

35

A THEORY OF POLITICAL EXPERTISE

Alexander A. Guerrero

Although a prominent question in ancient Greek political philosophy, the question of political expertise or political skill is one that has received little recent philosophical discussion—particularly outside of debates about exactly how to read and interpret Plato. This is unfortunate, as the idea of political expertise or skill relevant to politics continues to be prominent in popular discussions of political candidates, in empirical research relating to voter and political official competence, and, implicitly, in discussions of what have come to be called technocratic or epistocratic political systems.

In this chapter, I argue that although we can countenance many different notions of skill or expertise that are, in some sense, "political" or related to politics, we should distinguish between (1) *expert political analysts* and *exceptionally effective political actors*, and (2) *normative political experts* and *expert political actors*. It is the latter group who we should think of as possessing political expertise such that they might plausibly merit possessing political power, and it is this latter group that has been of philosophical interest historically.

In any agential domain, we can identify what counts as skill or expertise in that domain only after we have identified the *purpose(s)* or *function(s)* or *aim(s)* of action in that domain. This is necessary so that we can determine what constitutes success in that domain. I argue that in the political domain, the relevant purposes of political action are those relating to the *moral* function(s) of political institutions: the aims which, if achieved, would serve to morally justify and legitimate political action. On this view, possessing normative political expertise and being an expert political actor are a matter of knowing what ought to be done to achieve the legitimating purposes of political institutions, and acting skillfully so as to achieve those aims.

The view of political expertise that I defend in the chapter is, accordingly, contextualist and functionalist. Before saying what is required for political expertise, what an agent must be like to be a political expert, one must fix the institutional context and corresponding institutional roles, identify the legitimating purposes of action in that role, and then ask: what is required of an agent to be successful in acting to achieve those purposes?

35.1 The political expert as expert political analyst

There is a way in which the question "are there political experts?" has a very boring answer. Yes, of course there are political experts. One can turn on the TV or the radio, or open a newspaper, and encounter all sorts of people brought in to opine on various things because they are political experts. Consider, for example, the professor and political commentator David Rebovich, discussed here in the *New York Times*:

> As far as who Mr. Rebovich is, you need look no further than the political pages of any newspaper or magazine in the state during a campaign. Turn on the television and it can seem as if his face has replaced the test pattern. When candidates begin making their pitch to voters, Mr. Rebovich, a 53-year-old political science professor at Rider University and avowed political addict, is nearly everywhere, analyzing and interpreting the shape of New Jersey politics.[1]

Rebovich and others like him are experts on politics in that they have knowledge about the following kinds of things:

Political systems and political rules: the details of political systems and processes, including rules of particular legislatures, parliamentary procedures, constitutional structures, and so on.
Political history: the history of political systems and institutions, political actors, and particular political decisions.
Descriptive political science: the relationships between various political institutions, actions, structures, demographic factors, and political outcomes, and the ways in which these are correlated with or causally related to each other.
Political psychology and political communication: the way in which political agents (citizens, voters, representatives, other political actors) are inclined to behave, feel, respond, interpret, and form beliefs in response to various events, policies, rules, structures, and so on.

This knowledge might be more or less general, focused on, say, just 21st-century New Jersey, or all of the United States, or all modern industrial democracies. And it might be more or less integrated into more general theories of psychology, history, law, sociology, economics, and so on.

Of course, there are also purported political experts who are not actually experts, because they do not actually possess knowledge about the political topics on which they teach or opine. But there will at least be a significant category of people who have engaged in extended research and study of topics such as these, whether in an academic setting or not, and who can be considered political experts in a fairly natural sense. Let us refer to this kind of political expert as an *expert political analyst*.

There are different ways of conceptualizing this kind of expert whose expertise is based on propositional knowledge. In general terms, we can say that an expert analyst in domain D is someone who:

(EA1) possesses a high absolute level of propositional knowledge regarding topics in D;
(EA2) is more able and more likely to answer a question in domain D correctly than people in the general population, and both this ability and likelihood is because of the propositional knowledge they possess;

(EA3) is able to identify considerations that are relevant to answering a question in D, even when they answer a question incorrectly; and

(EA4) is able to deploy methods in the future that will help develop answers to, or understanding of, other questions within D.

These are not necessary and sufficient conditions for being an expert analyst; rather, the better a person does with respect to each of (EA1)–(EA4), the more of an expert analyst they are with respect to D. And the broader D is, the broader the expertise of the analyst in question. Note that this conception of expertise includes both an absolute and a population-relative dimension. We can countenance expert analysts that satisfy (EA1) but not (EA2): perhaps everyone in the population is excellent at answering questions in some domain. And there might be expert analysts who are experts because they can get 45% of the questions in some domain right, while no one else in the population can correctly answer any of the questions, even though they still get more than half the questions wrong.

Many kinds of expert analysts will be relevant to political decisionmaking, even though their domain of expertise is not politics. Modern policymaking is incredibly technical and complex. Making law and policy in an epistemically responsible way requires drawing on expertise on a wide range of topics, basically the whole span of areas over which we do or might make law and policy: agriculture and food safety, telecommunications, immigration, education, taxation, energy policy, and so on. These expert analysts are not political experts, but they will be relevant to the discussion later.

It is natural to feel that this sense of political expert—political expert as expert political analyst—is uncontroversial, but also uninteresting. Even leading expert political analysts in this sense end up with rather narrow domains of expertise. And those who end up counting uncontroversially as expert political analysts also seem to lack any pro tanto claim to political authority or to it being a good idea to give them political power. There is something that this kind of expert seems to be lacking. Here's a hypothesis about what that thing is: expertise about what ought to be done, politically; expertise about what we as a political community ought to be doing, and how we ought to go about doing it.

Of course, on the understanding of expert political analyst offered above, we might simply take D to be the domain of *what ought to be done, politically*. Call this kind of expert political analyst a *normative political expert*. A normative political expert—an expert political analyst about this domain—is much closer to being a political expert in the sense of being an *expert political actor*. And it might seem more plausible that, *if* there were normative political experts, then it might be a good idea to give them political power, or more power and influence. But it will also be more controversial whether there are normative political experts.

35.2 The political expert as normative political expert or expert political actor

The political domain is an agential domain: there are many things that one might *do* in the political domain. It is not a purely theoretical domain. That means that there are questions of what one *ought* to do, questions of what *ought to be done*, and questions about how to be *skillful* in doing whatever it is that ought to be done.

As noted above, we can call someone who does well at knowing what ought to be done in the political domain, in the (EA1)–(EA4) sense identified above, a *normative political expert*. Call someone who is particularly skilled in doing what ought to be done in the political domain an *expert political actor*. Obviously, an individual might be both a normative political expert and an expert political actor. We might even think that being an expert political actor requires or presupposes that one is also a normative political expert. But let us take up that question in a moment.

Are there normative political experts and expert political actors? What would such people look like? In any agential domain, we can only identify what counts as skill in that domain after we have identified the *purpose(s)* or *function(s)* or *aim(s)* of action in that domain, so that we can determine what constitutes success in that domain. This is a general claim about skill, but one that has perhaps been overlooked in discussions of political expertise. A suggestion: most disagreements about the possibility of normative political experts and expert political actors stem from disagreement about the function or point of politics or of action in the political domain.

Some agential domains are relatively monolithic in the purpose that agents pursue in those domains, focused on one end. Other agential domains are pluralistic, including several or even many dimensions of potential achievement or success. Consider the domain of artmaking. An agent might create art as a means of self-expression, to engage and affect a real or potential audience, to support herself financially, to process a difficult experience, to communicate an idea, to represent some aspect of reality, and so on. It may be a matter of controversy which of any of these purposes should be associated with being an expert or skilled artist. But these are all purposes for which agents engage in the creation of art.

In the case of political action, the questions of purpose and success are complicated by ways in which the political domain is itself complex and multifarious, making attempts at general claims about expertise or success in acting in "the political domain" like attempts at general claims about expertise or success in "game-playing," or "artmaking" or some other large and variegated domain of action. We might be able to say something at this level of generality, but it won't be anything very interesting. Accordingly, it is worth trying to be more specific regarding the different subdomains of the political, so that we might be able to offer more interesting suggestions regarding normative political expertise and expert political action.

There are at least three significant dimensions of variance that affect what we might say about "action in the political domain" and the various purposes and success conditions of that action. First, there are institutional differences: which political institutions and practices exist in particular places and times differ, making possible different kinds of actions within the domain of the political. Second, there are role differences: even given an institutional setting, agents may occupy very different roles within the broader political structures, giving rise to different potential actions and different conditions for successful action. Third, there are functional differences: political institutions and roles within those institutions exist to achieve different kinds of purposes, so that different background sociopolitical contexts call for different conditions of political success. Let me say more about each of these, beginning with the last.

35.2.1 Functionalism

Elsewhere, I have argued for what I call "institutional functionalism":

> Political and legal institutions are only instrumentally or functionally valuable—they are tools that can be used to address various practical problems of moral significance that arise when certain kinds of creatures live in relative proximity to each other (e.g., problems of scarcity, ignorance, disagreement, conflict, irrationality, prejudice, and so on).[2]

This functionalist view of political institutions leads to contextualist, non-universalist commitments about what the proper purposes of politics are and what political institutions should be in place in a particular community. Different problems may arise for different communities, and so different tools—different political and legal systems—may be required, depending on the particulars of the problems that arise and the particulars of the relevant community. To say anything about what success in the political domain might look like, and to thereby have an account of what kind of person might count as an expert in bringing it about, we first need to say more about the political problems relevant for a given society and the corresponding potential functions of political institutions in that society. Once we have in mind some list of this sort, we can see how it might recommend various kinds of political and legal institutions, which in turn will include specific roles for political actors and opportunities for political action, which in turn will generate specific results regarding whether there is normative political expertise or whether there are expert political actors, and what either of those things might look like.

35.2.2 Institutional and role-based context

As mentioned above, differences of political function were only one of the variables relevant to assessing normative political expertise and the possibility of expert political actors. Along with that, there is also variability introduced by the specific political institutions that exist and the different roles that individuals do or might occupy within those institutions. Consider, for example, the way in which expert political action might differ depending on which of the existing political institutional arrangements (and corresponding set of political roles) is in place:

Electoral representative constitutional democracy: a political system like that in the contemporary United States, in which there are citizens, elected representatives, an elected executive, an entrenched constitution, and a constitutional court, along with "secondary" political actors (who are in various ways hired/appointed and managed by the primary political actors): police officers, prosecutors, lawyers, judges, administrative agency bureaucrats, executive branch cabinet, military officers, and so on.

Direct democracy: a political system like the above, except without elected representatives or an elected executive, in which citizens play a direct role in deciding law and policy—perhaps choosing to authorize and employ a similar panoply of secondary political actors.

Lottocracy: a political system in which ordinary citizens are randomly selected to serve on one of thirty different single-issue (e.g. education, transportation, immigration, etc.) legislative bodies.[3] Those randomly selected to serve on one of these bodies hear from experts, activists, and stakeholders during a Learning Phase, engage in community consultation with the broader citizenry, spend time deliberating and discussing with each other, and eventually vote to enact law and policy. There would be a legal and constitutional structure similar to that in most modern electoral representative systems, absent an elected executive, but with legislatively controlled administrative agencies, a constitutional court, prosecutors, police officers, lawyers, judges, and so on.

Totalitarian authoritarianism: a political system in which there is only one political party, no substantive electoral competition, and in which the state is run through a combination of a president/dictator, executive cabinet, and leading Party officials and Party representatives none of whom were elected in substantively competitive elections. To maintain control and stability, this kind of system employs extensive networks of secret police; neighborhood/community spying organizations; state control of the economic sector; extensive repression of freedom of speech, religion, and association through official monitoring and censorship; and widespread use of political prison and detention.

As should be clear, there are different roles within each of these institutional systems, and different potential purposes. The central suggestion is that these differences—of function, institution, and role—affect the details of what counts as success in acting in these domains and what might be required to achieve it. Just as we would expect different abilities, skills, and competencies to be relevant for whether one is expert at the "games" of chess, cricket, crossword-puzzle solving, marathon-running, and competitive powerlifting, so, too, we should expect different abilities and skills to be relevant for whether one is expert at "politics" in these different institutional settings and roles, aiming at one or several of these different functional purposes of politics.

One might be a citizen in a direct democracy, an elected representative, a judge on a constitutional court, a bureaucrat in a technocratic administrative agency, a president, a citizen-member of a lottocratic legislature, a prosecutor in a totalitarian state, and so on. Given this wide variance in political institutions and political roles within those institutions, as well as the background functions or purposes of political institutions, it is unsurprising that there is no simple, uniform account of what is required to be a normative political expert or an expert political actor—just as we wouldn't expect there to be a simple, uniform account of what is required to be an expert game player for all of the aforementioned games. There might be some common factors, but the list of these would be far from a comprehensive account of what is required. And there might not even be any common factors.

To say more, we will need to do more to specify the institutional and role context, as well as the background functional purpose. Prior to that, however, there is one additional question that must be addressed: the question of how to understand the connection between political function or purpose and what might be morally or normatively significant about political expertise.

35.2.3 Normative functionalism

There are at least three different levels of functional assessment or assessment regarding the purposes of artifactual entities (including objects, but also institutions and social practices): actual purpose(s), intended purpose(s), and normatively significant purpose(s). In the political case, we can call these the *de facto*, *de jure*, and *normatively legitimating* functions or purposes.

The *de facto* or actual function is what the artifactual entity actually accomplishes (brings about, causes) in the world. The *de jure* or intended function is what the artifactual entity was created or invented to accomplish (bring about, cause). The *normatively legitimating* function is what morally justifies the creation and existence of the artifactual entity (if it requires or has such a justification).

These can all be the same, in cases in which the artifactual entity is functioning well and functioning as designed. But they can also come apart. For example, perhaps the *de facto* purpose of political system X is to ensure that the wealthy elite maintain their socioeconomic power and are maximally well-off, but the *de jure* purpose (as inscribed in the constitution of system X) is to promote the well-being of the majority of the citizens of X. And we can suppose further that the only *legitimating* purpose of system X would be to promote the equality and well-being of all members of the society.

Which of these is the purpose that is connected to being either a normative political expert or an expert political actor? Recall that, just as a matter of terminology, being a normative political expert was defined in terms of knowing what *ought* to be done in the political domain, and being an expert political actor was defined as being particularly skilled in doing what *ought* to be done in the political domain. Accordingly, then, the most natural thought is that the purposes or functions of the political system that matter are just those that matter from a normative vantage point: those that serve to make certain political actions and political institutions legitimate, morally permissible, morally justified, or even morally required.

There might be other potential or actual functions of political institutions—functions other than those that serve to legitimate the existence and actions of those institutions. For example, political institutions might be used to bring about the personal enrichment of those occupying certain offices. Or they might be used by members of a certain racial group to maintain power and domination over others. They might be used by leaders of corporations or industries to create favorable economic and legal conditions for the success of those corporations or industries. Let us suppose that none of these things are connected to the legitimating function of political institutions.

Regarding those people who are excellent at acting within these institutions so as to achieve these aims and other possible non-legitimating functions of political institutions, we don't want to say that they are either normative political experts or expert political actors, at least not in the sense of being particularly skilled at doing what ought to be done in the political domain. But there is a sense in which they have a kind of skill or expertise. Let us refer to these people as *expertly effective political actors*. They are effective at getting things done through the system, accomplishing what they want by use of the existing political institutions.

One reason that people may have been dubious that "political experts" should rule is that they have been thinking of political experts either as the mundane *expert political analysts* discussed in the first section, or as *expertly effective political actors*. We think of shady political operatives, career politicians who unscrupulously act to obtain power and influence, excellent behind-the-scene operators whose efforts are naturally described as *machinations* or *schemes*. These are people that you might want to have on your side, given the realities of politics, but they rarely exhibit anything morally attractive that we might describe as leadership or normative political expertise.

The key to finding a more compelling vision of political expertise is to set aside these "merely" expertly effective political actors and expert political analysts, and to focus more narrowly on those who excel at helping to achieve the *legitimating* purposes of political institutions through their skillful judgment and action. To focus in this way requires a view about what those legitimating purposes are, and a full defense in that regard would take us too far afield. Rather than going that route, I will use a simple model of a set of political institutions, roles, and accompanying legitimating purposes for the sake of example, although I hope they correspond to plausible judgments about what actually might be legitimating purposes of existing political institutions and roles within those institutions. The hope is to show how judgments about normative political expertise and expert political actors are connected to specific institutional and role contexts and to specific views about the legitimating purposes of those political institutions and roles. This will provide the template for what I think is the correct way of thinking about political expertise in a normatively attractive light.

35.3 A contextually specific story of normative political expertise and expert political actors

Above, I have suggested that to say anything about normative political expertise or expert political action, we must first fix various parameters:

(1) the potentially legitimating purpose(s) of political institutions in a particular social context;
(2) the institutions that are available to be used to achieve these purposes in this context; and
(3) the role that an individual occupies in this institutional context.

Only after these three parameters are fixed can we identify what is required of an agent to be successful in acting to achieve the legitimating purpose, given the agent's role within the broader institutional context. In other words, only after fixing these parameters can we say what will likely be required for either normative political expertise or expert political action.

In this section, I will present one way of filling in (1)–(3) to provide a bit more flesh on the bones of the view of political expertise I am defending.

35.3.1 *The context: modern electoral representative constitutional democracy*

To fix the relevant social context, let us consider a sociopolitical context something like the contemporary United States: a large, relatively wealthy, racially and ethnically diverse, ideologically fragmented political community. Like the contemporary United States, this is a political community with significant problems: racial injustice; significant socioeconomic inequality and poverty; high crime and incarceration rates relative to similarly wealthy countries; significant numbers of people who lack adequate health care; unequal access to quality public education; powerful multinational corporations that resist environmental and safety regulation and taxation; and others.

Let us imagine, then, that the potentially legitimating purposes of political and legal institutions in this context include the following:

Preventing domination and harm: checking the most powerful and well-resourced members of society so that they do not have dominion over the less powerful, undercut their autonomy, harm them, violate their rights, and so on.

Minority rights and justice: protecting the rights of those whose interests or identities make them relatively vulnerable minorities within the broader political community, including redressing historical injustice perpetrated along racial lines.

Working together under conditions of disagreement and distrust: helping individuals and communities work together to solve various coordination and collective action problems, even when there is disagreement about what ought to be done and some distrust of those on the other side.

Information management and use: harnessing expertise to make epistemically responsible policy and to respond productively to information asymmetries with respect to consumer products, health, safety, scientific and medical expertise, and so on.

Respecting and promoting equality: promoting conditions of social equality and equality of opportunity, stemming from considerations of respect for the moral equality of all.

Respecting and promoting autonomy: promoting conditions of individual and group autonomy, so that people can form their own personal conceptions of the good and valuable and make and enact life plans that align with those conceptions.

Promoting welfare: providing for the worst off and making sure that all morally significant creatures have what they need to survive and flourish.

Assume that these are the central legitimating purposes of political and legal institutions in this context, so that if the extant institutions work to achieve these purposes, then they are legitimate—morally justified in acting, even though they act backed by coercive force. (Let us leave aside the complicated issues of how each of these different purposes is to be prioritized, how they interact with each other, what constraints there might be in how they can be pursued, and so on.)

Let us stipulate, too, that the political system is basically like that of the federal government of the United States: a bicameral elected legislature, elected executive, unelected constitutional court with strong powers of judicial review, extensive system of federal courts, large administrative state overseen by both the legislative and executive branches, and widespread (even if imperfect) rights of citizens to vote and participate in electoral politics.

Within these institutions, there are all kinds of different political and legal roles that a person can occupy: representative, president, secretary of state, supreme court justice, judge, prosecutor, EPA staff bureaucrat, voter, and more. For each role, we can ask what would be required for a person to have normative political expertise or to be an expert political actor.

The answer to these questions will be different for different roles. One significant difference is that some of these roles contribute to the achievement of the legitimating purposes, to the extent that they do, through tightly constrained behavior on the part of those who occupy those roles—behavior that often is not explicitly aimed at achieving *any* of the legitimating purposes directly. So, acting expertly in these roles might be a matter of acting only on a narrow set of reasons. For this reason, let us call these political roles *narrow political roles*. Consider, for example, the role of federal prosecutor or OSHA claim administrator. Individuals occupying those roles do have significant choices to make, and the best individuals in those roles will have expert knowledge of the relevant laws, rules, and a broader sense of the overall purpose of the institutions of which they are a part. But they will mostly not have a lot of discretion, and when we think of potential political experts we are unlikely to think of people in these roles.

Contrast these narrow political roles with what we might call *expansive political roles*. These are roles such that those occupying them have extensive discretion regarding what they will do, and a correspondingly complicated normative world to consider when trying to decide what they ought to do—what reasons ought to be considered, how those reasons ought to be weighed and assessed, and so on. Those individuals occupying these roles might well directly consider how their actions will or will not advance the legitimating purposes of the broader political and legal institutions of which they are a part. The specifics may still differ, depending on the details of the role, but all of these roles are ones for which we can fruitfully consider what might be required for normative political expertise or expert political action. Some central examples of these roles: elected legislative representative, supreme court justice, president, and democratic voter.

35.3.2 *Political expertise and elected political representatives*

Let us focus on the role of elected political representative. This is perhaps the quintessential expansive political role, and it is plausible that elected political representatives should be thinking about how to act to achieve the legitimating purposes of the political system directly. They are charged with crafting legislation and policy to help address these problems and achieve these purposes. Accordingly, as I've argued elsewhere, elected "representatives face multiple competing norms regarding how they ought to behave: norms of fidelity (doing as they said they would), norms of deference (doing as their constituents would presently prefer), norms of guardianship (doing as would be best for their constituents), and moral norms of a more general sort,"[4] including moral norms regarding what would be best for the whole political community, what justice requires by way of helping the world's worst off, the future inhabitants of the political community, and future generations, and so on. And, in addition to all the different individuals whose interests might be relevant, there are different normative dimensions to those interests that might be relevant: equality, welfare, autonomy, and justice, for example. They must work to represent the majority as well as minority interests, to think of the present but also the future, to think of the people they represent but also the world, and, in every extant example of elected representatives, to do so in a generalist way—trying to discern what the right thing to do is regarding topics as diverse as agricultural production, education, healthcare, national defense, trade, transportation, and water regulation.

Given this normative complexity, it is no surprise that political expertise has often been equated with *moral* expertise. This is evident in the tradition discussing political expertise going back to Plato. As is well known, in the *Republic*, Plato defends the idea that those with political power should be a certain very particularly educated elite, rather than those who have prevailed in democratic elections. Their claim to rule depends, in large part, on their knowledge of the good and their virtuous moral character.[5] The Platonic tradition stemming from the *Republic* provides a useful way of understanding one view of what would make even an elected political representative an expert political actor. Here's Melissa Lane, discussing the view of political expertise set out in the *Republic*:

> By making the claim of the philosophers to rule depend on their knowledge of the good and of the other Platonic Forms (in conjunction with their moral character and tested practical experience), the dialogue vindicates the Socratic and Platonic thought that ruling well—what we might call "rule" proper—requires a rare form of expertise rather than lay judgment, rhetorical advice, or common knowledge. In the *Republic*, the knowledge required for rule is not specialized, but comprehensive: the knowledge of the good and the Forms is somehow to translate into an ability to make laws as well as the everyday decisions of rule.[6]

Given the nature of expansive political roles, it is no surprise that an account of expert political action in those roles will require something other than highly specialized knowledge. Moral knowledge or moral expertise is an attractive option. But it cannot be the full story. There are at least two problems with the simple equation between political expert and moral expert.

The first is that, given modern policy complexity, it is implausible that moral expertise is *sufficient* for political expertise. Even Plato stressed that practical experience and broad education would also be important. But there is a larger worry that the sheer evidential complexity of making laws and policies that will help to advance the legitimating purposes of political institutions will make *epistemic* qualities essential for an elected representative to be either a normative political expert or an expert political actor.

Which qualities? Well, consider the significant epistemic burden elected representatives face in order to have a correct or even plausible view about what ought to be done. It is not realistic to expect any one person to be (a) an expert political analyst (an expert about what there is to be known about political science, the subtle workings of political institutions, political psychology, political history); (b) an expert on all of the domains relevant to modern policymaking (broad academic-level domains such as economics, sociology, and history, as well as other relevant domains such as healthcare economics, insurance, financial instruments, environmental science, agricultural science, trade regulation, constitutional law, etc.); (c) an expert on all of the substantial policy proposals; (d) an expert on constituent beliefs and preferences regarding all of these; (e) an expert on the likely effects of these proposals if they were to be implemented

... and then, even having a mastery of the entire "descriptive" side of the equation, to also be a moral expert regarding the normative import of these descriptive facts.

Rather than being an expert on all these topics, spanning all these domains, it is more plausible that electoral representative expertise will involve representatives exhibiting certain epistemic virtues or engaging in certain epistemic practices, in addition to whatever else we might want in terms of moral expertise. In particular, for electoral representatives to know what ought to be done or to do what ought to be done, they will also need to excel at exhibiting appropriate epistemic humility and an awareness of where one's knowledge runs thin, appropriate deference to legitimate experts, broad interest and minimal competence in a wide range of topics, the ability to gather information about constituent beliefs and preferences (where this may require empathy, engagement, and abilities beyond mere polling in cases in which constituents might not have formed beliefs and preferences), the ability to identify trustworthy assistants and delegate epistemic tasks to those individuals, the ability to discern the reliability of diverse sources of information, and so on. Call these the *epistemic virtues of expert political representatives.*

On this view, significant impediments to being an expert political actor or a normative political expert as an elected representative would be arrogance, overconfidence, an unwillingness to rely on others, a propensity to surround oneself with like-minded "yes people" who say what the representative wants to hear, an ideological approach to filtering experts and evidence based on non-epistemic considerations and consonance with the representative's prior views, a dogmatic reluctance to revise one's prior views, a dislike and corresponding distrust of those different from oneself, and so on. These are epistemic failings and limitations, and they would undercut the claim of someone who was otherwise a moral expert to be a political expert.

It is true, of course, that any well-designed institutional setting for elected representatives will provide those representatives with staff and opportunities for research, investigation, discussion, deliberation, constituent consultation, and so on. The suggestion here is that these will only result in potentially expert political action or normative political expertise if representatives in these settings possess the aforementioned epistemic virtues. Moral virtue alone will be insufficient—at least if it is construed, as is typical, to be compatible with the absence of these epistemic virtues.

This suggestion regarding the distinctive political importance of a subtle, open, curious, and flexible epistemic approach receives some support in recent empirical work concerning the reliability of expert judgment. Philip Tetlock, in his influential book on the topic, states his conclusion regarding the evidence of reliability and expertise:

> If we want realistic odds on what will happen next, coupled to a willingness to admit mistakes, we are better off turning to experts who embody the intellectual traits of Isaiah Berlin's prototypical fox—those who "know many little things," draw from an eclectic array of traditions, and accept ambiguity and contradiction as inevitable features of life—than we are turning to Berlin's hedgehogs—those who "know one big thing," toil devotedly within one tradition, and reach for formulaic solutions to ill-defined problems.[7]

Although his focus is on what makes for reliable expert judgment, not political expertise, this provides some reason to think that the epistemic component of being a political expert will also be better served by open-minded foxes rather than single-minded ideological hedgehogs.

A second reason to think that moral expertise alone may be insufficient for political expertise is that elected political representatives usually act against background conditions of deep disagreement about morality. It is implausible that what makes for an expert political representative is just being better than most at knowing the truth about morality. A significant part of being an expert political representative is knowing how one ought to proceed given deep and substantive disagreement about morality. On at least some occasions, that might mean doing what one knows is not the morally best thing. On other occasions, it might mean using one's judgment to effectively override a significant proportion of the political community. If we have an expansive conception of moral expertise such that it includes knowledge of when one ought to defer, compromise, or override in the face of moral disagreement, then this would perhaps not be a concern. But on a narrower conception of moral expertise, these important aspects would be left out.[8]

Normative political expertise and expert political action retain a thoroughly *political* element—where the political is tightly connected to conditions of extended and expected disagreement about what ought to be done. Sometimes the path to the morally best possible outcome is complicated and treacherous. Sometimes the shortest route to the good outcome is unlikely to achieve that outcome in a stable and lasting way. Sometimes it is difficult or impossible to know which paths forward are feasible. In some cases, having a sophisticated grasp of the moral considerations might be enough to discern what one ought to do. But in other cases, all manner of non-moral, empirical considerations will be relevant—how extensive is the disagreement, what are its sources, which means are actually available, what is currently feasible, what will happen if X or Y is put in place, and so on. If this is correct, then political expertise will require more than just moral expertise, even expertise regarding knowledge of conditional claims such as "if X is the case empirically, then we morally ought to do A." It will also involve being expert at knowing or investigating when these various empirical antecedents hold—no easy task in the case of complex political circumstances—as suggested in the previous discussion of the epistemic virtue required for political expertise. And it will involve difficult decisions regarding compromise, conflict resolution, mediation, and the need to override dissenting opinion. Call this the skill of expert *disagreement navigation*.[9]

The above considerations suggest that moral expertise is not *sufficient* for elected representatives to be normative political experts or expert political actors—but is moral expertise *necessary*? If we are skeptical about the possibility of moral experts, this might generate another reason for skepticism about political expertise. An initial question is what is meant by *moral expertise* (see Driver, Chapter 34 in this volume). A full discussion would take us too far afield, but it is worth drawing a distinction between at least two senses of moral expert: the expert moral analyst (an expert in the *knowledge that* sense) and the expert moral actor (an expert in the *knowledge how* sense, who is particularly skillful as a moral actor).

The former sense of expert will be familiar from our earlier discussions. On this view, a moral expert is just an expert analyst with respect to morality (using the terminology from the beginning of the chapter), meaning that the person possesses a high absolute and population-relative level of propositional knowledge regarding morality, is able to identify relevant considerations, and develop methods to help answer and understand future moral questions.

The other sense of moral expert—the sense that focuses on being an expert moral actor—connects moral knowledge with acting and living well. This is a familiar idea from the Ancient Greek philosophical tradition. As Julia Annas describes the view: "[m]oral knowledge is knowledge which is, among other things, about how to act; it is also knowledge that is put into practice" and "[w]hen moral knowledge is thought of as a skill ... its object is global—namely, your life as a whole."[10] Moral expertise in this sense is constituted by acting and living particularly well (see Bashour, Chapter 37 in this volume).

For an elected representative to be a normative political expert or an expert political actor, must that representative be an expert moral analyst or be living particularly well in moral terms? Are either of these a requirement of being an expert political representative? Recall that success in acting in this institutional context is defined as success in helping to bring about the legitimating purposes of the extant legal and political institutions. We can ask: does doing this require moral expertise in either of these senses?

It doesn't seem to require that one be living *unusually* well—in a way that is better than most people. It is plausible that to be an effective elected representative one must not engage in certain kinds of morally bad behavior, since some such behavior will undermine one's credibility and real or perceived legitimacy as a representative. And one is perhaps more likely to be an expert political actor as an elected representative if one is living in a way that reinforces those ideals that are necessary to achieve the legitimating aims of political institutions: preventing harm, supporting social equality, protecting minority rights and interests, fostering peaceful and productive interactions, creating stable communities of trust and cooperation even in the face of disagreement, promoting individual autonomy and welfare, and so on. Just as there are ways in which institutions can help accomplish these aims, so, too, there are ways in which we as individuals can contribute to them. Harmony between one's personal actions and one's efforts qua political representative is likely to be helpful in achieving these institutional efforts. This is one place where ideas of personal *leadership* might be usefully invoked. But must one also be an excellent friend, a loyal sibling and child, a person who enjoys the higher pleasures rather than zoning out in one's free time playing video games or watching silly movies? These seem to be of only peripheral relevance to being an expert political actor, since they do not very closely connect to these core purposes of political institutions. Call those moral virtues related to the broader legitimating purposes of political institutions the virtues related to *ethical leadership*.

Does one have to be an expert moral analyst in order to be a normative political expert or an expert political actor? It does seem that ability in this regard will be significant, precisely because of the difficulty involved in acting to achieve the legitimating aims of political institutions. There is, as noted earlier, significant non-moral complexity and expertise that is relevant to making good political decisions. But even when much of the empirical evidence is in, hard questions remain. Thinking how all the relevant moral considerations interact is a difficult and serious project. This doesn't mean that a person needs to be a moral philosopher—a trained expert moral analyst in that sense. Rather, it means that to be a normative political expert or an expert political actor, one must be attuned to a wide range of moral considerations, to be—as with other, non-moral domains—epistemically open and alive to inquiry, and to be willing to think seriously about the real moral complexity that exists when considering the many distinct legitimating purposes of political institutions in the modern political context. One must possess a high degree of moral sensitivity in order to act well consistently given this complexity, which suggests that one will need to be at least relatively expert as a moral analyst more generally.

35.4 Conclusion

To sum up: to be a normative political expert and an expert political actor as an elected political representative—given the expansive nature of that role and the moral complexity of the legitimating purposes of modern political institutions—one will need to (a) exhibit a wide range of epistemic virtues concerning open-minded, thoughtful inquiry and practices of appropriate epistemic deference and trust; (b) excel at the skills required for disagreement navigation and conflict resolution; (c) act in ways that exhibit the moral virtues of ethical leadership in terms of how one engages with others; and (d) be relatively expert as a moral analyst, sensitive to a wide range of moral considerations, and relatively good at thinking through complex moral issues. The suggestion is that the better one is at (a)–(d), the better one will be at acting so as to achieve the legitimating purposes of the political institutions described in Section 35.3.1.

Crucially, this is *not* a general account of what is required for political expertise; it is not even a general account of what is required to be an expert political representative, as there might be other institutional settings in which some or all of (a)–(d) are not relevant, or for which other components would be. The account is supposed to highlight the embedded and contextual nature of political expertise, focusing only on what would be required of certain individuals in certain roles in certain institutional contexts in order for them to act so as to help achieve the legitimating purposes of those institutions.

Due to the functionalist, contextualist nature of the account, it is also a view about political expertise that is fundamentally "hostage" to empirical considerations. The account I have sketched is something of a prediction or guess at what will be required for elected political representatives to act expertly in the kinds of sociopolitical contexts described at the beginning of Section 35.2.2, where that just means: to act so as to collectively bring about the legitimating purposes of the institutions of which they are a part. It is possible that the features (a)–(d) that I have put forward are not actually necessary or sufficient to do this. It is also possible that whether they are or not may depend on, for example, what the other political representatives are like, whether they also possess those qualities, and so forth. Ideally, these suggestions would come to be tested through modeling or empirical study—although there are hard questions about how to operationalize these features, how to measure success, and much else. The philosopher's role here is to propose a theory, but that shouldn't be the end of the project. This normative functionalist, contextualist view of political expertise sets out a template for offering accounts of what makes for political expertise in other contexts and for other political roles, but it doesn't answer those questions directly, suggesting a place for future research and argument.

It also helps us see the way in which our extant political institutions implicitly or explicitly require people with certain skills in order for those institutions to achieve their legitimating purposes. This, in turn, might lead us to be skeptical either that there are any such people (perhaps the expertise demanded isn't possessed by anyone), or that the mechanisms in place for putting people into roles within the institutions are not doing a good job of putting people with those skills in the appropriate roles. We might ask, for example, whether elections as structured in the United States actually do a good job selecting people who possess the skills required to be expert political actors in those roles—the previously discussed epistemic virtues, skill in navigating disagreement, virtues of ethical leaders, and moral sensitivity and sophisticated moral sensibility. If they do not, then we have a problem on our hands, and it might suggest either institutional reform or reform in what we are asking of people in the various roles.

Notes

1 Sullivan, J. (2002). "In Person; The Answer Man," *The New York Times*, available at: www.nytimes.com/2002/08/25/nyregion/in-person-the-answer-man.html
2 Guerrero, A. (2017) "Political Functionalism and the Importance of Social Facts," in K. Vallier and M. Weber (eds.) *Political Utopias*, Oxford: Oxford University Press.
3 For further discussion, see Guerrero, A. (2014) "Against Elections: The Lottocratic Alternative," *Philosophy and Public Affairs*, Vol. 42, pp. 135–178).
4 Guerrero, A. (2010) "The Paradox of Voting and the Ethics of Political Representation," *Philosophy and Public Affairs*, Vol. 38, p. 281.

5 As one of the leading experts on the topic puts it, "In the *Republic,* the philosophers are to rule not in virtue of any peculiarly political knowledge they possess, but rather in virtue of their synoptic and pervasive understanding of the Good" (Lane, M.S. 1998) *Method and Politics in Plato's 'Statesman',* Cambridge: Cambridge University Press, p. 3.

6 Lane, M.S. (2017) "Ancient Political Philosophy," *The Stanford Encyclopedia of Philosophy,* E. Zalta (ed.), available at https://plato.stanford.edu/archives/sum2017/entries/ancient-political/.

7 Tetlock, P. (2017) *Expert Political Judgment,* Princeton, NJ: Princeton University Press, p. 2.

8 One would expect that even those who reject public reason political liberalism as the correct framework for political philosophy would acknowledge that in at least some cases of actual moral disagreement, political leaders might be *morally* required to pursue compromise or other non-morally optimal options. For a prominent critic of public reason views, see Enoch, D. (2015) "Against Public Reason," *Oxford Studies in Political Philosophy,* Vol. 1 (David Sobel, Peter Vallentyne and Steven Wall, eds.). That compromise in the face of disagreement is sometimes required in this way is itself a substantive commitment of political morality.

9 This second limitation of the simple equation between political and moral expertise—the need for a certain kind of refined political sensitivity and navigation in the face of disagreement—suggests that while Plato of the *Republic* might be in trouble, Plato of the *Statesman* might be on the right track for providing an attractive conception of what is required for being an expert political representative. The *Statesman* offers a conception of political expertise on which the political expert has "the unique role of commanding when each expert should perform his [*sic*] work and so coordinating the work of different experts" resulting in a view on which "[p]olitical expertise is neither meta-knowledge nor another species of knowledge, but rather knowledge of the relation between other forms of knowledge and the temporal demands of the moment of action, or the *kairos*" (Lane 1998, pp. 3–4). A second dimension of political expertise is explicitly concerned with responding to the *political* situation:

> The political expert is also to carry out the task of weaving together two conflicting factions in the city. Each of these factions is conceived as characteristically disposed to err on one side or the other of the mean, in making evaluative judgments.
>
> *Lane 1998: 10*

As Lane summarizes the view:

> The statesman is wholly defined by the possession of that knowledge of when it is best to exercise the other arts and its exercise in binding the different groups of citizens together, a knowledge which depends on a broader philosophical grasp but which is peculiarly political.
>
> *Lane 2017*

10 Annas, J. (2001) "Moral Knowledge as Practical Knowledge," *Social Philosophy and Policy* 18(2), pp. 244, 253.

References

Annas, J. (2001) "Moral Knowledge as Practical Knowledge," *Social Philosophy and Policy* 18(2), 236–256.

Enoch, D. (2015) "Against Public Reason," *Oxford Studies in Political Philosophy* 1(20), 112–142.

Guerrero, A. (2010) "The Paradox of Voting and the Ethics of Political Representation," *Philosophy and Public Affairs* 38(3), 272–306.

—— (2014) "Against Elections: The Lottocratic Alternative," *Philosophy and Public Affairs* 42(2), 135–178.

—— (2017) "Political Functionalism and the Importance of Social Facts," in K. Vallier and M. Weber (eds.) *Political Utopias,* 127–150, Oxford: Oxford University Press.

Lane, M. S. (1998) *Method and Politics in Plato's "Statesman,"* Cambridge: Cambridge University Press.

—— (2017) "Ancient Political Philosophy," in E. Zalta (ed.) *The Stanford Encyclopedia of Philosophy,* available at: https://plato.stanford.edu/archives/sum2017/entries/ancient-political/.

Sullivan, J. (2002) "In Person; The Answer Man," *The New York Times,* available at: www.nytimes.com/2002/08/25/nyregion/in-person-the-answer-man.html

Tetlock, P. (2017) *Expert Political Judgment,* Princeton, NJ: Princeton University Press.

36

SKILLS OF JUSTICE

Paul Bloomfield

On reflection, being that there are only four cardinal virtues, it is practically scandalous that justice has received so little attention from contemporary virtue theorists, both moral and epistemological. While justice has a pre-eminent presence in socio-political philosophy, where it is thought of as the most important virtue of institutions, the literature on justice as a personal moral virtue barely exists. Until recently, epistemologists have likely thought of justice as being wholly out of their wheelhouse. Miranda Fricker's *Epistemic Injustice* (2007) has thankfully changed that, and many socially minded epistemologists are now interested in the effects of epistemic injustice on society, particularly upon those who have been oppressed. Still, even here, the focus has been on epistemic injustice and its social effects rather than on a direct study of epistemic justice considered as a personal intellectual virtue, alongside, for example, open-mindedness and intellectual courage. How do just people think?

Taking justice as a character trait, in personal and not social or institutional terms, the line between morality and epistemology becomes interestingly blurred and frequently even dissolves. There are supposed to be basic differences between the two to keep them separate, in particular in their relation to voluntarism: morality is all about the choices we voluntarily make and the actions for which we can be held responsible ("ought implies can"), while beliefs are supposed to be, in an important way, involuntary. In virtue theoretic terms, this has played out as a difference between voluntary or agential judgment, on the one hand, and perceptual belief, on the other. In technical terms, this is the difference between responsibilists and reliabilists.[1]

If justice requires us to blur the lines between morality and epistemology, as will be argued below, it seems like this would cause conceptual confusions at the outset. There is a solution to the problem, however, to be found in thinking of justice epistemologically as a skill: locating epistemic justification in the nature of skill allows us a way to render moot the distinction between judgment and belief, between cognition within our epistemic discretion and cognition which is epistemically involuntary, however important it may remain in terms of understanding various forms of cognition and how the mind works. We will return to this set of issues at the end of the chapter.

The general way to see epistemology and morality being unified is fairly simple when we think of quintessential justice: in much the same way that we think the paradigm of courage is found in a virtuous soldier on the battlefield, the paradigm of justice can be found in a virtuous judge, sitting on a judicial bench, delivering judgments of innocence or guilt. The judge is doing something intrinsically moral, namely rendering verdicts concerning who to hold morally responsible for what: the innocent are set free, the guilty are punished, the victims get restitution. The function of a judge is to come to a fair and accurate assessment of the situation, a just assessment, yielding a just verdict. But producing an assessment of a moral situation is an epistemic affair. So, when a judge finds a defendant innocent or guilty, this is simultaneously a moral and an epistemic act, and understanding justice as a character trait forces us to elide the traditional distinction between the two discourses, however equally normative they may otherwise be.

It is worth pointing out that it is not only judges who are involved in making this sort of judgment, we all do it regularly, whenever we assess some set of facts for the sake of forming an opinion, whenever we make a judgment. The same holds for the assessment of testimony, or deciding who to trust and who not to trust and, importantly, the same holds when we make assessments of ourselves and our standing and accomplishments in our relations to others. What we want to understand is what happens when a judge gets it right, when justice is done, and what it takes for us to be fair to others and to ourselves. When we succeed in this, the success itself is equally moral and epistemic, the very same judgment "gets it right" in both ways: it cannot be a moral success without its also being an epistemic success and vice versa.[2] Justice requires both moral fairness and epistemic accuracy. Still, we can analytically prise these apart, as justice can play a role in contexts that are not moral, social, or political. When scientists assess their data and make judgments based on it, their conclusions must be fair and accurate and so, at a formal level, must engage the same cognitive traits as the judge. To keep these apart, we can call "Justice" with a capital "J", the justice that applies to moral, social, and political contexts, and "justice" with a lower case "j" will refer to the broader contexts in which the forms of justice are purely epistemic.[3] As we will see, justice turns out to play a unique role in all cognition insofar as the application of concepts to experience requires us to treat like cases alike, just as judges are supposed to do in the courtroom.

Even limiting our attention to Justice, the situation is more complicated than it seems, since we cannot simply attend to a distinction between getting Justice right and getting it wrong, and thereby assume that when it goes wrong, there is a failure of Justice. We can learn something substantive and direct about courage from cowardice in a way that we cannot learn about Justice from injustice. This can be seen through a brief interchange between Rosalind Hursthouse and Christine Swanton (Hursthouse 1980–81: 64; Swanton 2003: 21). Imagine an army quartermaster in charge of supplies who sells the soldiers' chocolate on the black market for the sake of enriching herself. Clearly, this quartermaster has done an injustice to the troops. Compare her, however, to another quartermaster who is horribly and akratically gluttonous, and who binges on the chocolate for the sake of sating his need. This quartermaster also does an injustice to the troops, and from the point of view of the troops, there is no difference between the two forms of injustice. And yet, the cause of the first quartermaster's injustice is the fact that she is an unjust person, she lacks the virtue of justice, while the second quartermaster's injustice is caused by his incontinence, he lacks the virtue of temperance. Given these cases, it is not hard to imagine injustices being caused by gullibility, cowardice, recklessness, foolishness, obsequiousness, and many other moral and intellectual vices. So, it will be hard to get a direct insight into the virtue of Justice per se, again considered as a personal character trait, by attending to particular cases of injustice.[4]

If not through injustice, how then should we approach the virtue of Justice? In fact, despite the small amount of work that has been done on the topic, there are other more socially oriented approaches that have been or are being pursued and all may contribute to a full account of the matter.[5] Bernard Williams' view of Justice as a virtue is a bit of a misfire, as he places it as secondary to an independent socio-political theory of Justice, which takes it out of any kind of standard virtue theory where the normative guidance comes from the virtues themselves.[6] A more mainstream yet innovative approach has been developed by the legal scholar Lawrence Solum, which he calls "virtue jurisprudence", or the study of judicial judges and which intellectual traits they ought to instantiate.[7] This, however, takes a narrow view of Justice as being bound by legality and our concerns are wider. In social and political philosophy, there are both more conservative and more liberal approaches to thinking of Justice in personal terms. David Schmidtz and John Thrasher consider Justice primarily in terms of "people getting their due" and understand this in terms of negative duties of non-interference (Schmidtz and Thrasher 2014: 59–74). For them, beneficence is the virtue which determines how and when to positively help others; "mere" Justice determines jurisdictions within which those agents who are in charge may act on their own discretion. Jay Drydyk's (2012) "capability approach" is more liberal in that it takes Justice to involve not merely closing inequalities but raising the capabilities of humans. He looks broadly at how individuals may characteristically act in ways that further the ends of social Justice by, for example, taking care of the worst off as a first priority and promoting entitlements that protect everyone from social exclusion.

These socio-political accounts are extremely helpful for understanding the range of phenomena they intend to capture, and it has long been thought that Justice is essentially a social phenomenon. While Fricker (2007) does treat Justice as a proper intellectual virtue, she only discusses this insofar as epistemic Justice is seen as the "anti-prejudicial virtue": it prevents "identity prejudice", or prejudice against a person as a result of that person's social type, since it "neutralizes prejudice … in judgments of credibility" (p. 92), and this keeps it well in the social world. Michael Slote (2007) discusses the virtue of Justice from the perspective of the ethics of care and empathy, arguing that Justice is caring about the social good, which again is helpful as far as it goes, but does not move us much closer to an understanding of Justice's epistemology.[8]

In virtue theory, it is common to distinguish the self-regarding virtues of courage and temperance from other-regarding virtues where Justice is the prime example. Nevertheless, there is something undoubtedly true when Philippa Foot says, "if justice is not a good to the just man, moralists who recommend it are perpetrating a fraud" (1978: 125–6). So, if we disagree with those like Callicles and Hume's Sensible Knave, and assume that Justice really is an excellence of character, then it must be a benefit to its possessor and therefore cannot be only interpersonal but is also in part intra-personal. The lesson here is that how we judge and treat others does not swing free of how we judge and treat ourselves. Justice is manifested in social circumstances in groups of either two or more, but it is also monadic or reflexive: just as we can be fair or unfair to others, we can be fair and unfair to ourselves, and indeed there are reasons to think we cannot succeed in being fair to ourselves if we are unfair to others, and vice versa. So, Justice is a self-regarding virtue as well as an other-regarding virtue.[9]

If we assume that Justice is limited to socio-political contexts, we will fail to cast it as broadly as a true virtue theory requires, and as it was understood by the ancient Greeks. By attending to Justice in its most general sense we can begin to comprehend a basic epistemology for it which allows us to see (all) justice as a skill (and not just Justice as a skill). It was the ancient Greeks who first determined that Justice was one of the four cardinal virtues. Their word, "*dikaiosyne*", which we translate as "Justice", is the virtue that mediates all social or interpersonal relations.[10] Thus, we expand our conception of *Justice* beyond the judicial or socio-political realm of interacting fellow citizens to include a sense of Justice or fairness that can be found in good friendships and even in familial relationships.[11] The cardinal virtues, Justice included, all begin with the self's relation to the self, and extend out to others from there: from family, to friends, to "fellow members of the tribe", to all of humanity.[12] Virtue begins in our character, in our psychology and our will, and as such, it is the basis for both our autonomy and our sociality.

Skills come more clearly into the picture because among the ancient Greeks there was a general consensus, including Socrates, Plato, the Epicureans, and the Stoics, that all the virtues are skills. And even Aristotle, who denied that the virtues are skills, acknowledged that the virtues are very similar to skills, since they are learned or acquired in the same way that skills are. Famously, he writes, "[W]e become builders by building and lyre players by playing the lyre. So too we become just by doing just actions, temperate by temperate actions, and courageous by courageous actions" (Aristotle 2000: 1103a29–1103b3).[13] That is, even if the virtues are not skills, they have the same (or a very similar) epistemology as skills. Aristotle and his followers were alone among the ancients in rejecting the thesis that the virtues are a proper subset of skills, however, and the thesis that they are skills has been picked up and developed by a few contemporary philosophers, most notably, Julia Annas and Matt Stichter.[14] One way of developing this thought is to note that becoming an expert in any skill, including the virtues, requires some amount of practical rationality (*phronesis*), the sort of experiences just indicated by the quote from Aristotle, as well as a mastery of the *logos* of the skill, or its intellectual structure or logic.[15]

So, Justice, understood broadly as *dikaiosyne*, will also fit this pattern. Expertise in being Just will require practical rationality, or the general ability to solve practical problems, as well as requiring experience in life with both fairness and unfairness. For our purposes here, however, we will best approach Justice as a skill by first understanding its moral psychology, so that we can see how the Just agent acts in comparison to those who fail in this trait, and thus how Justice figures into moral, social, judicial, and political philosophy. From there, we can move onto looking at Justice's purely epistemic aspects, as seen in justice (note the lower case "j"), and by giving the beginnings of an analysis of its *logos*. And what we find, upon looking into this *logos*, is that epistemic justice can be seen even more broadly than in the combination of inter- and intra-personal relations: in the most general terms, the virtue of justice is present in any context in which we find someone exercising "good judgment".

We can begin to see how Justice fits into a person's moral psychology by asking whether or not justice fits into Aristotle's doctrine of the mean, as answering this question takes us to the heart of Justice. Williams (1980) argues that Justice does not fit the model of a mean between extremes, because one cannot be "too just". This, however, is uncharacteristically off the mark for Williams, as this is not how the doctrine of the mean works: one does not become reckless by being "too courageous" nor does one become a "stick-in-the-mud" and incapable of having fun by being "too temperate". Rather, as Aristotle says, "[J]ustice is a mean between committing injustice and suffering it, since the one is having more than one's share, while the other is having less" (Aristotle 2000: 1133b30).[16] The ancient Greeks took the canonical vice of Justice to be *pleonexia*, which is often translated as "greediness", but involves all those circumstances in which one arrogantly takes more than one's due.[17] They saw the opposite of this trait, characteristically taking *less* than one's due, as being so contrary to how they understood human nature that it did not have a name. This, however, seems like too narrow of view of humanity, as we now know of how abject humility, servility, and adaptive preferences can lead people to willing accept less than they deserve.

Such a view of Justice allows us to see it as a mean between arrogance and servility, as it requires seeing oneself for who one truly is, not more, not less; it requires having an accurate measure of oneself, and thereby what one is due and what one is not due. These are Justice's self-regarding aspects. Expanding from the first-person point of view, Justice requires knowing oneself and others well enough to discern what everyone deserves, from circumstance to circumstance.

Socrates' intellectualism about virtue aside, knowledge is not by itself sufficient for right action, and when it comes to Justice what is required is that people actually respect themselves and each other as they deserve. And thus, it is having knowledge of oneself and others and respecting everyone properly that leads to Just outcomes. The respect involved is of two kinds, recognition respect and appraisal respect, now familiar in the literature (Telfer 1968; Darwall 1977). Recognition respect involves the recognition of a person as a person, and not as a thing or an "it", so as to establish a base-line level of treatment that all people unfailingly deserve, while appraisal respect is based on appraisals of the differing characters and accomplishments of individuals. The former respects what we all have in common while the latter respects what makes us each unique. Respecting properly is necessary for acting Justly. Notice that both forms of respect rest on accurate judgments of the people being assessed: the recognition in "recognition respect" is an epistemic achievement, while the appraisals in "appraisal respect" require evaluation and judgment. Justice, at its base, is the virtue of people who respect themselves as fundamentally neither better nor worse than other people, and as such lies at a mean between those who arrogantly think they are better than others, or deserve more for simply being who they are, and those who are servile, or who have a surfeit of humility, and therefore see themselves as being "less than", or not as worthy of being treated with the respect that others deserve. What characterizes Justice, as it figures in moral, social, judicial, and political philosophy is that it requires one to take proper account of oneself and of others in deciding what to do: one must avoid improper partiality to oneself and one must recognize other people as people and treat them with the respect and consideration they deserve.

So far, this begins to articulate the position of *Justice* as a character trait in the landscape of moral psychology. But as noted above, the intellectual virtue of justice (small "j"), has a cognitive role to play in many cases where respecting other people is not germane. We can begin our investigation of this general intellectual virtue by noting that the most fundamental principle of the *logos* of justice has been described in many ways but is captured succinctly by the idea of "treating like cases alike".[18] In political philosophy, this is expressed through the "rule of law". In jurisprudence, this is expressed by the concept of *stare decisis*, or the rule of precedent, while in general metaphysics it is captured by a fairly weak form of supervenience, whereby the good judgment of a case supervenes upon the facts of the matter: differing judgments ought to be grounded in a difference in cases.[19] These are all parts of Justice, but in fact "treating like cases alike" has a far wider range of application than moral, social, judicial, or political contexts, and an even deeper cognitive import. This was touched on in an early work of John Rawls, though unfortunately, it seems that he never embellished the idea. Nevertheless, he wrote:

> One can view this principle [what would come to be his "first principle of justice"] as containing the principle that similar cases be judged similarly, or if distinctions are made in the handling of cases, there must be some relevant difference between them (a principle which follows from the concept of a judgment of any kind).[20]
>
> *Rawls 1957: 654*

It is the final parenthetical phrase here that should capture our interest. Why does "treating like cases alike" follow from the concept of *judgment*? A Kantian answer to this will be suggested below, but as Kant also realized, the thought actually goes cognitively deeper than what happens as a person forms a judgment.[21] All judgment involves a fairly sophisticated kind of cognition, and treating like cases alike is more basic than that: one can see how the employment of concepts in cognition necessitates treating like cases alike. In order for me to possess the concept of a *dog*, I have to be able to judge dogs as being dogs; were I, on one occasion where the lighting is good, and I have adequate time, etc., to categorize a pig as a dog, this would count against my possession of the concept of a *dog*. Concepts are useless unless they are employed consistently across cases, and this consistency is what is captured by the idea of "treating like cases alike". So, while Rawls' point is that all judgment formation requires that like cases be treated alike, the more general point is that all concept application, all identificatory and re-identificatory judgments of the form "x is *f*" ought to manifest the essence of justice.

Concepts are like rules in that they govern how the items of sensibility are to be cognitively categorized. In this sense, "concept application" is another name for categorization. And this is the sense in which all cognition and epistemology are normative: from the cognitive and epistemic points of view, things can go well (judging a dog to be a dog) or things can go badly (judging a pig to be a dog). And here we are able to see the role of "treating like cases alike" as necessary but insufficient for making *valid judgments*, where *validity* comes in because of the truth-preserving inference involved in identifying some x to be *F*. So, from the centrality of *justice* to the process of concept application, we move to its centrality to the process of judging and what used to be called the "faculty" of judgment in general. The concept of *judgment* has famously played a large role in the history of philosophy, particularly in early modern philosophy, and there are various conceptions of it. For our purposes, Kant's view of the matter is particularly helpful. If we take a basic Kantian claim of his First Critique, that the faculty of understanding "deals with concepts" (Kant 1998: A130/B169), then in the section of that work entitled, "On the logical use of the understanding in general", he writes: "We can, however, trace all actions of the understanding back to judgments, so that the understanding in general can be represented as a faculty for judging" (1998: A69/B94). And he elaborates later in the section entitled, "On the transcendental power of judgment in general": "If the understanding in general is explained as the faculty of rules, then the power of judgment is the faculty of subsuming under rules, i.e., of determining whether something stands under a given rule (*casus datae legis*) or not" (A132/B171).

So, the nominal "power of judgment" or acts of "judging", taking the verb to be basic, is manifest in the application of a rule to a case. Primarily, judging is something that one does.[22] This is an importantly normative matter: it can be done well or poorly. Whatever one thinks "objectivity" amounts to, it will be objectively better to have good judgment than bad. If one judges well, then one first chooses the correct rule to apply to the case and then correctly applies it, treating like cases alike.[23] The essence of judgment is the essence of justice. In its broadest cognitive understanding, the personal virtue of justice simply is having good judgment, and so, from the point of view of pure virtue epistemology, there is arguably no intellectual virtue more central or important than that of justice.

And how is this related to skill and its acquisition? We can continue to take our cue from Kant. He takes a pessimistic view of the pedagogy involved in teaching the skill of good judgment, but it is nevertheless properly seen as a developed use of talent:

> [T]his is also what is specific to so-called mother-wit, the lack of which cannot be made good by any school; for although such a school can provide a limited understanding with plenty of rules borrowed from the insight of others and as it were grafted onto it, nevertheless the faculty for making use of them correctly must belong to the student himself, and in absence of such a natural gift no rule that one might prescribe to him for this aim is safe of misuses. A physician therefore, a judge, or a statesman, can have many fine pathological, juridical, or political rules in his head, of which he can even be a thorough teacher, and yet can easily stumble in the application, either because he

is lacking in natural power of judgment (though not in understanding), and to be sure understands in abstracto but not distinguish whether a case in concreto belongs under it, or also because he has not received adequate training for this judgment through examples and actual business. This is also the sole and great utility of examples: that they sharpen the power of judgment.

1998: A133–4/B172–3

The lack of this natural gift is called by Kant "stupidity" and "such a failing is not to be helped" (1998: A133/B172). This might well infuse virtue epistemology, in general, with elitism, which may nevertheless be more excusable than it is in virtue ethics: not everyone may be capable of perspicacity regardless of how good their will might be. There are fools and geniuses and in most cases no amount of work or effort will change a genuine fool into a genius. Now, some psychologists do think that we can, by dint of effort, "grow" our intelligence (Dweck 2016). The thought is that, at some non-metaphorical level, the brain works like a muscle insofar as it can be trained or developed to function better. Perhaps this is true, and if so, then there would be some degree of responsibility we would have to assume for our intelligence. Nevertheless, those sadly lacking in intellectual capacity will not become geniuses no matter how hard they work. So, while it is epistemically elitist to say that some have a better sense of judgment than others, it is justly egalitarian to note that this gift or talent only makes a difference for appraisal respect, and when it comes to recognition respect, no form of arrogant elitism is justifiable.[24] Regardless of intellectual standing, everyone's opinion should be treated with respect, even if, in the end, it is rejected. We all have whatever abilities we have and, still consistent with egalitarianism, each of us ought to do as much as we can with what we have.

As for applications of what Kant says to the skill of justice, many are obvious.[25] The importance of experience and the use of examples in learning, or how it "sharpens" the judgment, has already been touched upon in the discussion of Aristotle's general epistemology of virtues and skills (we become builders by building, etc.). If we understand discourses, such as medicine, the law, and statesmanship, (roughly) as sets of rules to follow, then the ability to have intellectual understanding of a discourse and yet be unable to apply it practically to cases is a familiar phenomenon, however unfortunate it may be. Slightly different is the way in which the raw talent for making good judgments in general is one thing, while the application of this talent to different and particular areas of discourse is another. Thus, there seems to be a formal difference between the role that justice plays in good judgment, understood in complete generality, and the role it plays in moral contexts wherein substantive questions of Justice arise. We expect, for example, scientists to make fair and accurate judgments about their data and not, for example, to draw conclusions that go beyond what the data supports. This is to apply justice to the rules of good scientific practice. In this way, we can see justice in non-moral contexts, a form of epistemic justice which transcends even the broadly understood *dikaiosyne* of the ancient Greeks. Of course, good judgment is also necessary in moral contexts as well: this would be to address once again Justice and not merely justice, and the substantial principles of Justice comprising its *logos*.

The entire *logos* of the intellectual virtue of justice is unsurprisingly going to be broader and more complicated than can be adduced in a single essay. If we wish to understand good judgment more fully in the broad sense, we will have to attend to how it relates to consistency in general, to the skills of basic reasoning and what philosophers teach to undergraduates under the guise of "critical thinking", with the canons of logic in the background. Further canons are also at play: in purely jurisprudential thought, there are a variety of principles and informal canons for interpreting the law, and we should expect to find similar canons in justice writ large (Scalia 1997). We presume innocence, while guilt must be proved; there is the "rule of lenity", for example, which says that when a rule, or a statute, or treaty is ambiguous, the ambiguity is to be resolved in favor of the defendant, etc. (Note that there is a distinction between the skills involved in designing a legal system and those involved in implementing it.) The relation of justice to the other virtues is also a large and difficult matter. We should expect some virtues to be plainly subordinate to justice, such as honesty, loyalty, and mercy.[26] As noted above, *phronesis* or practical rationality is necessary for the moral virtues, and so it is necessary for Justice; it might well be the case that *sophia* or theoretical wisdom is needed for justice. But a moment's reflection will reveal that distinguishing Justice and justice from either practical wisdom or theoretical wisdom would be one of the most sublime intellectual tasks imaginable: what is wisdom if not excellence in judgment?[27] So, while we have already made a start, we are far from a full understanding of the *logos* of either Justice or justice. Still, there is one other crucially important aspect of the intellectual virtue of justice that should be brought to the fore.

We can begin here again with an early slogan from Rawls, when he claims that "essentially, justice is the elimination of arbitrary distinctions" (1957: 653). It seems clear that if I, as a professor, give better grades to those students who have brown eyes rather than some other color, then I am allowing an arbitrary distinction to improperly affect my judgment. And, obviously, all sorts of prejudice and bigotry are the result of letting arbitrary distinctions affect one's deliberations. Here, we may reference back to Fricker's view of justice as the "anti-prejudicial" virtue, but we should take "prejudice" in the widest sense possible, that of prejudging any kind of case (colloquially, "judging a book by its cover"), and not just involving cases of what she calls "identity prejudice" aimed at people. But clearly, the difficulty in "eliminating arbitrary distinctions" is in how to apply it: which distinctions count as arbitrary? There is obviously no simply answer. Notice that in order to understand what an "arbitrary distinction" is between cases, we must first have a grasp of what it is for one thing to be like another, we need an account of *similarity*, and understanding similarity is an on-going question in metaphysics.[28] Beyond understanding similarity, there is the issue of what *relevance* or *salience* is, as these are the relevant contraries of *arbitrariness*.[29]

Despite not having a complete account of the "salient/arbitrary" distinction, one way of saying something helpful here comes by way of a discussion of impartiality and partiality. There is proper and improper impartiality, where improper impartiality can be seen as a kind of "strict moralism", or being "moralistic" in the pejorative sense, and proper and improper partiality, where forms of improper partiality are forms of "bias" or "prejudice" understood generally. We can be improperly impartial when mercy or indulgence is apt and we can be improperly partial toward ourselves and loved ones. Figuring out when to be impartial and when to be partial can lead to the most difficult problems in morality, though arguably it is the virtue of Justice that properly determines the answer. Our most famous archetype of Justice is as being blindfolded, and impartiality is of course correct for judges sitting on the bench, officers of the law, or umpires, referees, and similar authorities who are required to deliver fair judgments regardless of whether it is strangers or loved ones who fall under their authority. Any form of prejudice, bias, or partiality in these cases is most clearly improper.

It was long thought that Justice, or even morality as a whole, always demands strict impartiality, until the 1970s when Michael Stocker and Bernard Williams wrote about the ways in which strict moral impartiality leads to forms of self-alienation or "moral schizophrenia" in Stocker's terms: a break between the values that we accept as right and proper and the so-called "demands" of impartial morality (Stocker 1976; Williams 1973, 1981, 1985).[30] To take an example of Charles Fried which Williams made famous in this context:

[S]urely it would be absurd to insist that if a man could, at no risk or cost to himself, save one of two persons in equal peril, and one of those in peril was, say, his wife, he just treat both equally [impartially], perhaps by flipping a coin. One answer is that where the potential rescuer occupies no office such as that of captain of a ship, public health official or the like, the occurrence of the accident may itself stand as a sufficient randomizing event to meet the dictates of fairness, so he may prefer his friend, or loved one. Where the rescuer does occupy an official position, the argument that he must overlook personal ties is not unacceptable.

Fried 1970: 227

The implications for our discussion of justice seem obvious. Absent some official capacity that places special duties upon people, it seems fair and Just to allow personal connections to affect one's deliberations in a way that would count as biased or partial from a perfectly impartial point of view in which all people are treated equally.

The difficulty with this approach is in determining what counts as an "official capacity". Consider, for example, the role of *being a parent*, which in a variety of ways, many of them legal or social, counts as an "official capacity". There are certainly some situations in which being the parent of a child justifies all sorts of partiality toward the child in comparison to how a parent treats the children of other adults: without any injustice at all, I buy Christmas gifts for my children but not the next-door-neighbors' children; I rightly only go to parent/teacher meetings for my children and no one else's. If, however, I do my neighbors a favor by offering to watch over their children one evening, and a fire breaks out in my house, it is surely wrong of me to steadfastly think only partially and purposefully save my own children first and the neighbor's children only if there is time. The responsibility I have taken on involves an imperative to treat my neighbor's children as if they were my own. Or, taking a different example, if I have many children, it is unfair and unjust of me to regularly and arbitrarily favor one child over the others.

The present issue is not, of course, to settle upon principles by which we can always determine when a distinction is arbitrary. As has been noted, doing so would require a better grasp of *similarity*, *salience*, and *arbitrariness* than we currently have, not to mention *partiality* and *impartiality*. Perhaps more to the point is that, as has been much discussed, virtue theory is not rule governed in a way that allows for recursive procedures to determine the correct answers to moral problems (Hursthouse 1999; Annas 2011). The *logoi* of the virtues are not codifiable. So, even if these theoretical terms were clearly defined, they would not yield substantial principles or rules that we could unthinkingly follow; at best, we could get "rules of thumb" or *pro tanto* rules. Exercising good judgment requires keeping an eye out for those cases that are genuine exceptions to the rule. Some salient distinctions will only be discerned by the wisest of judges.

This can be modeled in the jurisprudential context. Legally, the methodology behind treating like cases alike is to appeal to a combination of law and precedent in the history of the court with a legal and moral theory that is supposed to make sense of these laws and precedents and to tell us, in future cases, when the precedent applies.[31] As Ronald Dworkin puts it, individual precedents have "gravitational force" on a decision, depending on how salient they are to the case under consideration. Jurisprudential genius is found in the ability to apply precedents with strong gravitational force to cases in which there are no superficial similarities whatsoever. Similar methods are at least sometimes acceptable in situations demanding justice in the purely epistemic sense: e.g., the scientific method requires treating like cases alike and looks for law-like similarities between seemingly diverse phenomena which could reveal deep truths about nature. But often in moral situations, we come up on novel situations without precedent: moral situations can be so complex that they become (at least for all intents and purposes) unique, and there is certainly no guarantee of a precedent to which one might appeal. At moments such as these, it will only be those who are truly just and wise who will have the insight to know the right thing to do.

Albeit briefly and in conclusion, the epistemology of such "insight" is the final topic to be addressed, as it brings us back again to skills. "Insight" is, perhaps, a better term than "intuition", but both words bring in the large recent literature on "dual processing", fast vs. slow thinking, emotional reactions vs. rational reflection, etc. From the point of view of general epistemology, a parallel debate exists between internalists and externalists, and in virtue epistemology in particular, between perceptual belief vs. agential judgment and reliabilists and responsibilists. The suggestion is not that these debates all map the same distinctions, nor cover the same range of issues. Rather, it is that they are all concerned with how much and what kind of access we have to our desiderative procedures, and how access bears on the justification of the cognitive output. With regard to epistemic justice per se, we might ask which view of the process of making just judgments is best, though we should not expect there to be one right answer for all judgments about justice (or Justice). If we have to judge whether or not to trust a stranger quickly, this is obviously going to be a case of fast thinking: we have to go by gut feel. There is now evidence suggesting that we learn how to make judgments such as these in non-conscious ways, using "encoding algorithms" to learn relations between facial expressions and behavioral traits (Lewicki et al. 1992). On the other hand, there are more difficult judgments involving Justice which are likely to be best made through cool and conscious reflection, such as whether or not a defendant is guilty of a crime. These are judgments that are supposed to hold up to public scrutiny, and so the justification for the judgment should be explicitly rendered. These various judgments of people we do not know personally, assessing their trustworthiness or their guilt, need not stay distinct: my gut feelings can inform my considered judgment, though they ought not to have such influence without considering other non-conscious processes such as implicit bias or self-deception (Holroyd 2012). There is even some evidence for the idea that slow *non-conscious* processing produces the best results for some kinds of judgments about justice: in judgments requiring comparisons of complex options, evidence indicates that it can be helpful to be distracted from thinking about the problem for a significant number of minutes or even "sleeping on it" (Ham et al. 2009).[32]

Notice that this last bit of data suggests that for some deliberations, fast thinking is not sufficient, but neither is slow thinking if this is identified with reflection: some cognitive processing happens best at a slow, calm pace, but when, for periods of time, the deliberation is unconscious, it happens automatically. As introspective and consciously thoughtful as experts may be, there is a great deal of expertise to which even the most consummate of experts do not have access. Their skills are not explained fully by either reliabilists or responsibilists, externalists or internalists, considered in isolation.

While these problems about access have been flummoxing epistemologists for quite some time, thinking of justice as a skill provides a neat solution.[33] Consider the differences between learning a language as a child at mother's knee and doing so as a college student in a classroom. Since being able to speak and understand a language is a skill, what we see here is that there are two distinct ways to acquire a single skill, both of which may lead to its mastery. But the differences in access to the knowledge involved is obviously great: people do not need explicit knowledge of the rules of grammar for the languages we learn as children, while for adults learning a second language, the rules of grammar have to be learned by rote and understood explicitly. There is no reason, however, to say that one way of knowing a language is better or more justified than the other: the only thing that matters is how fluently one communicates in the language, exactly how one does it is irrelevant. The conclusion to draw from this is that if we ground our concept of *justification* in skills, then questions about access fall away. Skillful behavior will be justified, independently of whether or not one can cite the grounds of one's justification. This is not to suggest that there are not interesting, important, and empirical questions about how much access we have to our various mental processes, how well experts can understand their own expertise, but that these questions no longer bear on the analysis of *justification* per se. This is not, of course, to claim that there will be no cases in which a person's judgment requires an articulated justification for it to hold sway among others, especially in cases of disagreement. But giving justifications is different than being justified, and the former is most important only if we want others to agree with us or we want them to do things our way. If that is not an issue, then neither is the ability to articulate reasons, other than to aid in auto-didactic learning. The requirement of "articulating one's reasons" primarily plays a social and not a purely epistemic role. So, if we adopt virtue epistemology as our method for developing an account of justification, and accept the thesis that the virtues are skills, then we have a unified and unifying theory of epistemic justification which ought to command more investigation and exploration. It would be epistemically unjust to do otherwise.[34]

Notes

1 This is one of the few differences that divide these camps. For responsibilism, see, e.g., Linda Zagzebski, *Virtues of the Mind* (Cambridge: Cambridge University Press) 1996; Jason Baehr, *The Inquiring Mind* (Oxford: Oxford University Press) (2011). For reliabilism, see e.g., Ernest Sosa, *A Virtue Epistemology* (Oxford: Oxford University Press) 2007; John Greco, *Achieving Knowledge* (Cambridge: Cambridge University Press) 2010. For discussion of the differences between these two types of theory, see Heather Battaly, "Virtue Epistemology", *Philosophy Compass* 21 July 2008, doi.org/10.1111/j.1747-9991.2008.00146.x.

2 Is this in fact a unity and there is no difference between morality and epistemology here or is the relation more like that of renates to cordates? I do not know.

3 There might be some reason to think that the purely epistemic form of justice should be thought of as something like "fair-mindedness". This is how Jason Baehr (2011) uses the term, "Fair-mindedness is a matter of judging or using reason in a consistent or even-handed manner" (p. 24), though he says little else substantive about it. Linda Zagzebski (1996) seems, however, to see fair-mindedness as a moral virtue, "Intellectual prejudice, for example, is an intellectual vice, and the virtue that is its contrary is fair-mindedness, but clearly we think of prejudice as a moral failing and fair-mindedness as a morally good quality" (p. 148). In the end, she takes no stand on whether a moral and an intellectual virtue can be a single character trait. In the end, cases like that of the judicial judge lead one to conclude that it is the judge's intellectual virtue of justice that is being applied to moral context, and this leads me to use one word "justice" for both the intellectual and moral virtues, distinguishing them only by the case of the "J".

4 Arguably, Fricker (2007) misses this point. On page 4, she identifies "identity prejudice" as the "central" cause of epistemic injustice, where "identity prejudice" is prejudice against a person as a result of that person's social type. Then, on page 92, as she introduces the "anti-prejudicial virtue", the particular purpose of which is that it "neutralizes prejudice in … judgments of credibility". In identifying this virtue, she writes, "Let us call it (what else?) the virtue of *testimonial justice*". But if I downgrade your testimony because I am fearful of people like you and those of your social group, then my prejudice and the injustice I do to you is caused by cowardice and not injustice. For more on this see my "Epistemic Temperance", *American Philosophical Quarterly* vol. 56, no. 2: 109–124 (2019).

5 There is one paper on Aquinas' view of justice, similar in spirit to the present essay, by Stewart Clem, "The Epistemic Relevance of the Virtue of Justice", *Philosophia* vol. 41: 301–311 (2013). Clem's paper is, however, more focused on applications, such as the role of justice in assessing testimony, than it is to an investigation of the general logos of justice itself. Another paper on how Aquinas' voluntaristic view of justice focuses on its relation to the will is Jean Porter, "Dispositions of the Will", *Philosophia* vol. 41: 289–300 (2012).

6 Bernard Williams, "Justice as a Virtue," in *Essays on Aristotle's Ethics*, A. O. Rorty (ed.) (Berkeley: University of California Press) 1980.

7 Ronald Dworkin's character of the judge he calls Hercules, in *Taking Rights Seriously* (1977), could easily be seen as the start of this project, while virtue jurisprudence per se has been led by Lawrence Solum and Colin Ferrally. See Solum's "Virtue Jurisprudence: A Virtue Centered Theory of Judging", *Metaphilosophy* vol. 34, no. 1/2: 178–213 (2003) and Colin Farrelly and Lawrence Solum (eds.) *Virtue Jurisprudence* (New York: Palgrave MacMillian) 2008.

8 Slote, *The Ethics of Care and Empathy* (Abingdon: Routledge) 2007, chapter 6.

9 This argument is expanded upon in my "Justice as a Self-Regarding Virtue", *Philosophy and Phenomenological Research* vol. LXXXII, no. 1: 46–64 (2011).

10 Gregory Vlastos writes, "I shall use 'justice' and 'just' merely as counters for dikaiosyne and dikaios, whose sense is so much broader, covering all social conduct that is morally right" (see his "The Argument In The Republic that 'Justice Pays'", *Journal of Philosophy*, vol. LXV, no. 21: 665–674 (1968). Julia Annas pursues the implications of acknowledging the proper scope of *dikaiosyne* in *Platonic Ethics: Old and New* (Ithaca: Cornell University Press) 1999.

11 For a conception of justice within marriage, see Jean Hampton, "Feminist Contractarianism", in *A Mind of One's Own*, edited by Louise Antony and Charlotte Witt (Boulder, CO: Westview Press) 1993a, and for a discussion of how we can be unfair to ourselves, see Hampton's masterful, "Selflessness and Loss of Self," *Social Philosophy and Policy* vol. 10, no. 1: 135–165 (1993b).

12 For the extending circle metaphor, see the quote from Hierocles in *The Hellenistic Philosophers* vol. 1, edited by Anthony Long and David N. Sedley (Cambridge: Cambridge University Press) 1987, p. 349.

13 *Nicomachean Ethics*, translated by Roger Crisp (Cambridge: Cambridge University Press) 2000. Aristotle's arguments against the virtues actually being skills are not strong and depend upon thinking of skills as crafts, such as carpentry. For example, he claims that the virtues are focused on the performance of actions while skills are concerned with the production of objects, even though this ignores those skills, such as playing a musical instrument like the lyre, which is all about performance and has no concrete product. For an extended critique of Aristotle's arguments on this score, see my *Moral Reality* (New York: Oxford University Press) 2001, pp. 92–102.

14 See Annas "Virtue as a Skill," *International Journal of Philosophical Studies* vol. 3, no. 2, 1995: 227–243, and *Intelligent Virtue* (New York: Oxford University Press) 2011; Matthew Stichter, "Ethical Expertise," in *Ethical Theory and Moral Practice* vol. 10, 2007a: 183–194, and "The Skill Model of Virtue" in *Philosophy in the Contemporary World* 14: 39–49 (2007b); "Virtue as Skill", in *Oxford Handbook of Virtue*, edited by Nancy Snow (New York: Oxford University Press) 2018. See, too, my "Virtue Epistemology and the Epistemology of Virtue," *Philosophy and Phenomenological Research* 60 (1), 2000: 23–43, "Some Intellectual Aspects of the Moral Virtues", in *Oxford Studies in Normative Ethics* vol. 3, edited by Mark Timmons (Oxford: Oxford University Press) 2014a, and *Moral Reality* (2001: ch. 2).

15 For an argument concluding that practical rationality is necessary but not sufficient for the virtues, see my "Some Intellectual Aspects of the Cardinal Virtues" in *Oxford Studies in Normative Theory* vol. 3, edited by Mark Timmons (Oxford: Oxford University Press) 2014a. I develop this tripartite account of a skill in my *Moral Reality* (2001), chapter 2. For more on the epistemic role of *logoi* in virtue, see Jessica Moss, "Right Reason in Plato and Aristotle: On the Meaning of Logos", *Phronesis* vol. 59, no. 3: 181–230 (2014).

16 *Nicomachean Ethics*, translated by Roger Crisp (Cambridge: Cambridge University Press) 2000.

17 For more on pleonexia, see David Sachs, "Notes on Unfairly Gaining More: Pleonexia", in *Virtues and Reasons: Philippa Foot and Moral Theory*, edited by R. Hursthouse, G. Lawrence, and W. Quinn (Oxford: Oxford University Press) 1998. See also my "Justice as a Self-Regarding Virtue" (2011).

18 A wonderful example of this kind of thinking can be found in an unpublished note of Abraham Lincoln's from 1854, in which he wrote,

> If A. can prove, however conclusively, that he may, of right, enslave B. — why may not B. snatch the same argument, and prove equally, that he may enslave A?–You say A. is white, and B. is black. It is color, then; the lighter, having the right to enslave the darker? Take care. By this rule, you are to be slave to the first man you meet, with a fairer skin than your own. You do not mean color exactly?–You mean the whites are intellectually the superiors of the blacks, and, therefore have the right to enslave them? Take care again. By this rule, you are to be slave to the first man you meet, with an intellect superior to your own. But, say you, it is a question of interest; and, if you can make it your interest, you have the right to enslave another. Very well. And if he can make it his interest, he has the right to enslave you.
>
> *Basler 1953: 222–223*

19 For the jurisprudential discussion, see, e.g., H. L. A. Hart, *The Concept of Law* (Oxford: Clarendon) 1961, ch. VIII; for the supervenience of judgments on facts of the case, see R. M. Hare, "Universal Prescriptivism", in *A Companion to Ethics*, edited by Peter Singer (Oxford: Blackwell) 1991, p. 456.

20 "Symposium: Justice as Fairness", *Journal of Philosophy* vol. LIV, no. 22: 653–662 (1957). Rawls was not the first to make this observation. For example, Isaiah Berlin, "Equality", *Proceedings of the Aristotelian Society* vol. 56: 301–326 (1955–6); Richard Wasserstrom mentions the point in reference to rationality in "Rights, Human Rights and Racial Discrimination", *Journal of Philosophy* vol. 61: 628–641 (see pp. 634–635); J. B. Schneewind quotes Clarke on the issue, noting without reference in a footnote that Cumberland also comments on it, see *Proceedings and Addresses of the American Philosophical Association*, vol. 70, no. 2: 25–41 (1996).

21 Kant writes,

> Thinking is cognition through concepts. Concepts, however, as predicates of possible judgments, are related to some representation of a still undetermined object. The concept of a body thus signifies something, e.g., metal, which can be cognized through that concept. It is therefore a concept only because other representations are contained under it by means of which it can be related to objects. It is therefore the predicate for a possible judgment, e.g., "Every metal is a body".
>
> *Kant 1998: A69/B94*

22 The reasons to take the verb "to judge" to be basic are twofold: first since this allows for the normativity of "judging well" and "judging badly", and second because the virtues themselves must be character traits of agents and not mere outputs: one might exhibit "good judgment" in a case by getting the right response as a "one-off" or by accident. Judging well, however, does not happen by accident. For more on this see Roger Crisp, "A Third Method of Ethics?", *Philosophy and Phenomenological Research* vol. 90, no. 2: 257–273 (2015).

23 I'm grateful to Matthew Stichter for pointing out this distinction here. One may note that this makes things difficult for legal pragmatism or some forms of legal realism: it seems backwardly inapposite to first render a verdict of innocence or guilty and only after that search for a rule to cover the case.

24 Obviously, issues of moral luck abound. For discussions of elitism in virtue theory see Julia Driver, *Uneasy Virtue* (Cambridge: Cambridge University Press) 2001, and my *Virtues of Happiness* (2014), pp. 230–231.

25 Kant's theory of moral reflection or conscience is explicitly built on the idea of a judge in a courtroom. Exploring this would take us too far afield, but the juridical aspects of Kant's Critiques are central to his project. See Allen Wood, "Kant on Conscience", in *Kantovski Sbornik* (Kaliningrad) 2009; Marijana Vujošević, "The Judge in the Mirror: Kant on Conscience", *Kantian Review* vol. 19, no. 3: 449–474 (2014).

26 For more on this see David S. Oderberg, "On the Cardinality of the Cardinal Virtues", *International Journal of Philosophical Studies* vol. 7, no. 3: 305–322 (1999); see also my "Virtues as Excellences", MS.

27 Thanks to Heather Battaly for discussion on the difficulty of this point. There are, of course, other ways to conceptualize wisdom. For example, Matthew Stichter argues that wisdom is inherently moral and does not extend to other non-moral contexts. As a brief response, one might ask what we should think, on this view, of the actions of wise people when they are not in moral situations? Why not say they are wise throughout their lives, if the patterns of thought and experience garnered through morality have application outside moral contexts? Surely, we want to say that Einstein had *theoria*. If a farmer uses wisdom to raise children, might there not be an application of these skills of care and "tending to" which are applicable to his crops? I see no loss of meaning in "practical wisdom" or "practical rationality" if it is extended to non-moral contexts. The issue in the end may be semantic. See Stichter, "Practical Skills and Practical Wisdom in Virtue", *Australasian Journal of Philosophy* vol. 94, no. 3: 435–448 (2016).

28 David Lewis takes similarity as a primitive notion in his *On the Plurality of Worlds* (1986). A classic treatment of similarity can be found in David Armstrong, *A Theory of Universals* (Cambridge: Cambridge University Press) 1980. A sample of more recent work on the issue is Ben Blumson, "Two Conceptions of Similarity", *Philosophical Quarterly* vol. 68, no. 270: 21–37 (2018).

29 This problem is most famously familiar to Kantian ethics, given their reliance on universalizability based on relevant descriptions. See, for instance, chapters 2 and 3 of Onora O'Neill, *Acting on Principle* 2nd edition (Cambridge: Cambridge University Press) 2014; chapter 2 of Mark Timmons, *System and Significance* (New York: Oxford University Press) 2017. For an article on how epistemic salience figures

into virtue generally, Richard Yetter Chappell and Helen Yetter-Chappell, "Virtue and Salience", *Australasian Journal of Philosophy* vol. 94, no. 3: 449–463 (2016). For a theory of virtue epistemology, similar to a skill analysis as discussed here, which rests on a notion of "explanatory salience", John Greco, "Knowledge and Success from Ability", *Philosophical Studies* vol. 142: 17–26 (2009). In general philosophy, the issue centers itself on *salience*, yet typically it employs salience rather than gives an analysis of it. But see, J. Mehta, et al., "The Nature of Salience: An Experimental Investigation of Pure Coordination Games", *American Economic Review* vol. 84: 658–673 (1994), and a response to this by Gerald Postema, "Salience Reasoning", *Topoi* vol. 27: 41–55 (2008).

30 Stocker, "The Schizophrenia of Modern Ethical Theories", *Journal of Philosophy* vol. 73: 453–466 (1976); Williams, "A Critique of Utilitarianism", in *Utilitarianism: For and Against*, co-written with J. C. C. Smart (Cambridge: Cambridge University Press) 1973, pp. 77–150; *Moral Luck* (Cambridge: Cambridge University Press) 1981, chap. 1; and *Ethics and the Limits of Philosophy* (Cambridge, MA: Harvard University Press) 1985, chap. 10.

31 I do not mean to imply that the role of precedents and how they are used in the law is uncontentious. The view glossed in the text is from Ronald Dworkin, *Taking Rights Seriously* (Cambridge, MA: Harvard University Press) 1977. See his discussion of the ideal judge, whom he names "Hercules", in chapter 4.

32 Some data suggests that we learn, in part, some tasks while we sleep. For example, psychologists Daoyun Ji and Matthew Wilson write of rats learning mazes:

> One reason for calling such a learned information structure a representation is that it exhibits information-value-sensitive processing that is substantially independent of current experience or context. During episodes of REM sleep after a day of training in a maze, a rat's acquired spatial representations of the maze can be observed to be repeatedly re-activated.
>
> *Ji and Wilson 2007: 100–101*

See also, A. S. Gupta, M. A. A. van der Meer, D. S. Touretzky, and A. D. Redish, "Hippocampal Replay Is Not a Simple Function of Experience," *Neuron* 65: 695–705 (2010).

33 An earlier development of this following argument can be found in my "Virtue Epistemology and the Epistemology of Virtue", *Philosophy and Phenomenological Research* vol. LX, no. 1: 23–43 (2000).

34 Matthew Stichter gave me comments on a draft of this chapter for which I am grateful. Also, I'd like to thank the following people for their helpful comments and discussion: Teresa Allen, Heather Battaly, Jeffery Brian Downard, Georgi Gardiner, Nathan Kellen, Yuhan Liang, Bill Lycan, Michael Lynch, Lionel Shapiro, and Ufuk Topkara.

References

Annas, J. (1995) "Virtue as a Skill", *International Journal of Philosophical Studies* vol. 3, no. 2: 227–243.
—— (1999) *Platonic Ethics: Old and New*, Ithaca, NY: Cornell University Press.
—— (2011) *Intelligent Virtue*, New York: Oxford University Press.
Aristotle (2000) *Nicomachean Ethics*, translated by Roger Crisp, Cambridge: Cambridge University Press.
Armstrong, D. (1980) *A Theory of Universals*, Cambridge: Cambridge University Press.
Baehr, J. (2011) *The Inquiring Mind*, Oxford: Oxford University Press.
Basler, R. (ed.) (1953) *Collected Works of Abraham Lincoln* vol. 2, New Brunswick, NJ: Rutgers University Press.
Battaly, H. (2008) "Virtue Epistemology", *Philosophy Compass*, July 21, doi.org/10.111/j.1747-9991. 2008.00146.x.
Berlin, I. (1955–56) "Equality", *Proceedings of the Aristotelian Society* vol. 56: 301–326.
Bloomfield, P. (2000) "Virtue Epistemology and the Epistemology of Virtue", *Philosophy and Phenomenological Research* vol. 60, no. 1: 23–43.
—— (2001) *Moral Reality*, New York: Oxford University Press.
—— (2011) "Justice as a Self-Regarding Virtue", *Philosophy and Phenomenological Research* vol. LXXXIII, no. 1: 46–64.
—— (2014a) "Some Intellectual Aspects of the Moral Virtues", in Mark Timmons (ed.) *Oxford Studies in Normative Ethics* vol. 3, 287–313, Oxford: Oxford University Press.
—— (2014b) *Virtues of Happiness*, Oxford: Oxford University Press.
—— (2019) "Epistemic Temperance", *American Philosophical Quarterly* vol. 56, no. 2: 109–124.
Blumson, B. (2018) "Two Conceptions of Similarity", *Philosophical Quarterly* vol. 68, no. 270: 21–37.

Chappell, R. Y., and Yetter-Chappell, H. (2016) "Virtue and Salience", *Australasian Journal of Philosophy* vol. 94, no. 3: 449–463.

Clem, S. (2013) "The Epistemic Relevance of the Virtue of Justice", *Philosophia* vol. 41: 301–311.

Crisp, R. (2015) "A Third Method of Ethics?", *Philosophy and Phenomenological Research* vol. 90, no. 2: 257–273.

Darwall, S. (1977) "Two Kinds of Respect", *Ethics* vol. 88, no. 1: 36–49.

Driver, J. (2001) *Uneasy Virtue*, Cambridge: Cambridge University Press.

Drydyk, J. (2012) "A Capability Approach to Justice as a Virtue", *Ethical Theory and Moral Practice* vol. 15: 23–38.

Dweck, C. (2016) *Mindset*, New York: Ballantine Books.

Dworkin, R. (1977) *Taking Rights Seriously*, Cambridge, MA: Harvard University Press.

Ferrally, C., and Solum, L. (eds.) (2008) *Virtue Jurisprudence*, New York: Palgrave Macmillan.

Foot, P. (1978) "Moral Beliefs", reprinted in *Virtues and Vices*, 110–131, Berkeley: University of California Press.

Fricker, M. (2007) *Epistemic Injustice: Power and the Ethics of Knowing*, Oxford: Oxford University Press.

Fried, C. (1970) *An Anatomy of Values*, Cambridge, MA: Harvard University Press.

Greco, J. (2009) "Knowledge and Success from Ability", *Philosophical Studies* vol. 142: 17–26.

—— (2010) *Achieving Knowledge*, Cambridge: Cambridge University Press.

Gupta, A. S., van der Meer, M. A. A., Touretzky, D. S., and Redish, A. D. (2010) "Hippocampal Replay Is Not a Simple Function of Experience", *Neuron* vol. 65: 695–705.

Ham, J., van den Bos, K., and Van Door, E. (2009) "Lady Justice Thinks Unconsciously", *Social Cognition* vol. 27, no. 4: 509–521.

Hampton, J. (1993a) "Feminist Contractarianism", in Louise Antony and Charlotte Witt (eds.) *A Mind of One's Own*, Boulder, CO: Westview Press.

—— (1993b) "Selflessness and Loss of Self", *Social Philosophy and Policy* vol. 10, no. 1: 135–165.

Hare, R. M. (1991) "Universal Prescriptivism", in Peter Singer (ed.) *A Companion to Ethics*, Oxford: Blackwell.

Hart, H. L. A. (1961) *The Concept of Law*, Oxford: Clarendon.

Holroyd, J. (2012) "Responsibility for Implicit Bias", *Journal of Social Philosophy* vol. 42, no. 3: 274–306.

Hursthouse, R. (1980–81) "A False Doctrine of the Mean", in *Proceedings of the Aristotelian Society* vol. 81: 57–72.

—— (1999) *On Virtue Ethics*, Oxford: Oxford University Press.

Ji, D., and Wilson, M. A. (2007) "Coordinated Memory Replay in the Visual Cortex and Hippocampus during Sleep", *Nature Neuroscience* vol. 10: 100–107.

Kant, I. (1998) *A Critique of Pure Reason*, trans. and ed. Paul Guyer and Allen Wood, Cambridge: Cambridge University Press.

Lewicki, P., Hill, T., and Czyzewska, M. (1992) "Nonconscious Acquisition of Information", *American Psychologist* vol. 47, no. 6: 796–801.

Lewis, D. (1986) *On the Plurality of the Worlds*, Oxford: Blackwell Publishing Ltd.

Long, A., and Sedley, D. N. (eds.) (1987) *The Hellenistic Philosophers* vol. 1, Cambridge: Cambridge University Press.

Oderberg, D. (1999) "On the Cardinality of the Cardinal Virtues", *International Journal of Philosophical Studies* vol. 7, no. 3: 305–322.

O'Neill, O. (2014) *Acting on Principle*, 2nd ed., Cambridge: Cambridge University Press.

Porter, J. (2012) "Dispositions of the Will", *Philosophia* vol. 41: 289–300.

Postema, G. (2008) "Salience Reasoning", *Topoi* vol. 27: 41–55.

Rawls, J. (1957) "Symposium: Justice as Fairness", *Journal of Philosophy* vol. LIV, no. 22: 653–662.

Sachs, D. (1998) "Notes on Unfairly Gaining More: Pleonexia", in R. Hursthouse, G. Lawrence, and W. Quinn (eds.) *Virtues and Reasons: Philippa Foot and Moral Theory*, Oxford: Oxford University Press.

Scalia, A. (1997) *A Matter of Interpretation*, Princeton, NJ: Princeton University Press.

Schmidtz, D., and Thrasher, J. (2014) "The Virtues of Justice", in Kevin Timpe and Craig Boyd (eds.) *Virtues and Vices*, 59–74, Oxford: Oxford University Press.

Slote, M. (2007) *The Ethics of Care and Empathy*, Abingdon: Routledge.

Solum, L. (2003) "Virtue Jurisprudence: A Virtue Centered Theory of Judging", *Metaphilosophy* vol. 34, no. 1/2: 178–213.

Sosa, E. (2007) *Virtue Epistemology*, Oxford: Oxford University Press.

Stichter, M. (2007a) "Ethical Expertise", in *Ethical Theory and Moral Practice* vol. 10: 183–194.

—— (2007b) "The Skill Model of Virtue", *Philosophy in the Contemporary World* vol. 14: 39–49.

—— (2016) "Practice Skills and Practical Wisdom in Virtue", *Australasian Journal of Philosophy* vol. 94, no. 3: 435–448.

—— (2018) "Virtue as Skill", in Nancy Snow (ed.) *Oxford Handbook of Virtue*, 57–82, New York: Oxford University Press.

Stocker, M. (1976) "The Schizophrenia of Modern Ethical Theories", *Journal of Philosophy*, vol. 73: 453–466.

Swanton, C. (2003) *Virtue Ethics: A Pluralistic View*, New York: Oxford University Press.

Telfer, E. (1968) "Self-Respect", *Philosophical Quarterly* vol. 18: 114–121.

Timmons, M. (2017) *System and Significance*, New York: Oxford University Press.

Vlastos, G. (1968) "The Argument in The Republic that 'Justice Pays'", *Journal of Philosophy*, vol. LXV, no. 21: 665–674.

Vujošević, M. (2014) "The Judge in the Mirror: Kant on Conscience", *Kantian Review* vol. 19, no. 3: 449–474.

Wasserstrom, R. (1964) "Rights, Human Rights and Racial Discrimination", *Journal of Philosophy* vol. 61: 628–641.

Williams, B. (1973) "A Critique of Utilitarianism", in B. Williams and J.C.C. Smart *Utilitarianism: For and Against*, 77–150, Cambridge: Cambridge University Press.

—— (1980) "Justice as a Virtue", in A. O. Rorty (ed.) *Essays on Aristotle's Ethics*, 189–199, Berkeley: University of California Press.

—— (1981) *Moral Luck*, Cambridge: Cambridge University Press.

—— (1985) *Ethics and the Limits of Philosophy*, Cambridge, MA: Harvard University Press.

Wood, A. (2009) "Kant on Conscience", in *Kantovski Sbornik* (Kaliningrad).

Zagzebski, L. (1996) *Virtues of the Mind*, Cambridge: Cambridge University Press.

37

WHY MORAL PHILOSOPHERS ARE NOT THE MOST VIRTUOUS PEOPLE

Bana Bashour

It's that time of the year again when philosophers get together at the Eastern Division Meeting of the American Philosophical Association (APA). George and Moe, two friendly departmental colleagues, walk into the annual smoker discussing moral philosophy. As always, George is finding it difficult to articulate his version of moral skepticism and Moe is running circles around him. As soon as they are in the room, as happens every year, Moe scans the room for a famous philosopher and darts over to introduce himself, but not before telling George: "Who knows what kind of doors this chance encounter will open up for me?" Moe walks over, chats with the famous philosopher, and impresses her with his clever interpretation and defense of Kant's second formulation of the categorical imperative and how well he can apply it to contemporary social and political issues. George, as is his habit, looks for nervous graduates of his department he knows to be on the job market. He finds a few of them and goes around to comfort them, give them advice and wish them the best. The graduate students, as always, are very grateful for this drop of kindness in a very harsh and competitive environment.

This is not an alien or unfamiliar scenario. Moe may be an excellent moral philosopher and George a mediocre one at best, but most of us would agree that George's actions are more virtuous than Moe's (in this scenario that is). In this chapter, I wish to argue that behaving virtuously requires having a set of skills that are separate from what is required for making moral judgments. In order to motivate the need to discuss virtuous behavior in terms of skills, I will rely on recent discussions of skill in the philosophical literature. Section 37.1 will focus on arguments partly motivated by some fleshed-out examples, such as that of Moe and George above, which serve to show that having an appropriate judgment is neither necessary nor sufficient for behaving virtuously. This suggests that we need to think of a new way of behaving virtuously that is distinct from making moral judgments, so I will put forth the alternative of thinking of virtuous behavior in terms of skills. In Section 37.2, I examine some contemporary accounts of skill as well as how they can be related to virtue. I will illustrate my preferred account with the case of musical performance and show how it can also be applied to virtuous action. Just as the best music critic need not be the best musician, the best moral philosopher (or anyone who is good at making moral judgments) may not be the most virtuous agent.

Before beginning the first section, I would like to emphasize the significance of discussing morality in terms of skills. Aristotle famously wrote:

> Virtues, however, we acquire by first exercising them. The same is true with skills, since what we need to learn before doing, we learn by doing; for example, we become builders by building, and lyre-players by playing the lyre. So too we become just by doing just actions, temperate by temperate actions, and courageous by courageous actions.
>
> *Artistotle 2005 1103b: 23*

Unlike other moral philosophers, specifically ones who believe moral behavior involves acting in line with a specific judgment informed by a principle or set of principles, virtue ethicists argue that the question we ought to be concerned with in morality is not what principle or set of principles we ought to follow, but what kind of a person we ought to be. In order to do that, we need to understand how to become the kind of person who behaves virtuously in a reliable manner, and that requires gaining a set of skills that can be improved by practice as Aristotle notes above.[1]

37.1 Moral judgment and virtuous behavior

In this section I will give some arguments for why being a good moral judge is neither necessary nor sufficient for being a virtuous agent. The vignette at the beginning of this chapter waves in the direction of that argument. I will stipulate that the reason that our moral judgments and virtuous behaviors can come apart is that we need to think of virtuous behavior in terms of skills.

Before turning to these examples, it is important to understand the role they are playing in the argument. Since I would like to argue that being a good moral judge is neither necessary nor sufficient for being a virtuous moral agent I need to present two distinct kinds of examples: the first involving an agent who has made a good moral judgment but did not behave virtuously and the second involving an agent who behaves as a virtuous moral agent but is unable to make a good moral judgment.

37.1.1 Good moral judges, non-virtuous agents

The case of George and Moe brings out these two kinds of examples. Moe is a talented Kantian scholar who argues for the immorality of treating another person as a mere means to one's ends, yet at the APA and various other social situations, he violates this formulation and tries to get the most out of whomever he meets. Moe may be a brilliant moral philosopher and may be able to point out the features of an action that make it immoral, perhaps even recognizing that his actions violate the Kantian principle, but he is more concerned with his self-interest than he is with doing the right thing.[2] He may represent the virtuous behavior under the guise of the good (Smith 1994), perhaps even convincing others to follow it, but he does not feel the need to follow it himself.[3] Perhaps the heart of such examples is captured by the mantra: "do as I say not as I do" which is repeated by parents and educators everywhere. They are explicitly stating that they are better at judging moral or other appropriate behavior than acting in line with such judgments. At this point, these kinds of cases should show that people can be good moral judges without behaving like virtuous agents.

37.1.2 *Bad moral judges, virtuous agents*

Now we can turn to the second set of examples, namely those of George above and the more popular example of Huckleberry Finn (Arpaly & Schroeder 1999). Starting with George, although he may not be a very good moral philosopher, and although he may have difficulty making moral judgments, he can still behave virtuously. He argues for an account of moral skepticism and insists that no behavior can be deemed more virtuous than another but still behaves in a kind and considerate fashion. He may be tuned to people's feelings, his attention captured by another's discomfort or pain and that attracts him to help. In other words, it may be the very same features of the action that make it virtuous that capture George's attention and motivate him, though he does not recognize them as so doing, i.e. he does not represent it to himself under the guise of the good (Smith 1994; Railton 2014). He may, for instance, simply like the graduate students and enjoy helping them any chance he gets, and he does not see that as morally relevant but as a personal quirk of his: he thinks he is just a big softie and that's his personality. He is motivated by what makes it virtuous but fails to recognize it *as* virtuous. This is very similar to the familiar example of Huckleberry Finn who refuses to turn in the slave Jim. Arpaly and Schroeder call this a case of "inverse akrasia" since Huck believes that, all things considered, the virtuous action is to turn Jim in but he fails to do so (Arpaly & Schroeder 1999). However, in reality, not turning him in is the right thing to do. Huck may not be good at making, arguing for or explaining his moral judgments, but he is able to be motivated by the same features that make an action a virtuous one. It is the fact that Jim seems to be no different from Huck and deserves respect and treatment as such, that motivated Huck, but he did not recognize these as features that make the behavior virtuous. Arpaly and Schroeder argue that because he was motivated by the right set of features, and although he fails to recognize his action as a virtuous one, he should still be said to have acted virtuously in this situation.[4]

In their later work, Arpaly and Schroeder present Spare Conativism as a theory of virtuous behavior that takes such cases into account (Arpaly & Schroeder 2013) The central thesis of Spare Conativism is that: "To be virtuous is to have significant good will and lack ill will. To be vicious is to have significant ill will or significant moral indifference" (Arpaly & Schroeder 2013: 203).

Good will is defined in terms of intrinsic desires for the right or good correctly conceptualized (Arpaly & Schroeder 2013: 162). This means that one is considered to be virtuous if one desires the very same feature that makes an action praiseworthy and represents it to oneself in the relevant way. So if what makes an action praiseworthy is the fact, for instance, that it generates the greatest amount of happiness, then what makes someone virtuous is the fact that she desires the greatest amount of happiness even if she does not recognize the fact that this has anything to do with virtue. This desire is not instrumental for other purposes, but one that the agent has for its own sake. For example, in the case of Huck Finn, he clearly has an intrinsic desire for the welfare of Jim and conceives of it as such. He does not have it so that people will look upon him favorably as the hero who saved Jim. He is simply concerned with the well-being of his friend and salvaging his friend's freedom is all he aims at. While that is what makes his action virtuous, he need not conceive of it under the guise of the good for him to count as having acted virtuously. So what determines the quality of one's will and thereby one's virtue, is the content of one's intrinsic desires and how this content is conceived.

I agree with Arpaly and Schroeder's account in that it drives a wedge between our theoretical understanding of morality and the relevant practical features that allow people to behave virtuously. I do not see Arpaly and Schroeder's account as conflicting with the thesis I wish to argue for in this chapter. However, I do wish to argue for a different way of explaining this wedge by emphasizing the skillful nature of virtuous behavior and its sensitivities to features of the environment that allow a person to behave virtuously.

So why is it that making moral judgments can be separated from performing virtuous action? I would like to propose that virtuous behavior requires a set of skills while making moral judgments does not, or if it does, it requires a different set. The rest of the chapter will be an attempt to motivate this proposal by appealing to contemporary theories of skill acquisition in general as well as ones relevant to virtue.

37.2 Virtuous behavior as skilled action

In order to motivate the account that virtue and virtuous behavior can be thought of in terms of skills, it is necessary to delve into the literature on the matter. I will first look at some prominent accounts of skill and skill acquisition most notably by Hubert and Stuart Dreyfus as well as the intellectualist account of Jason Stanley. I will then turn to what can be called the intellectualist and anti-intellectualist accounts of skill and virtue, namely those of Julia Annas and Matt Stichter.[5] I will argue that all these accounts are problematic. I finally turn to the account of skill that seems promising, that of Ellen Fridland. I will illustrate her account with the example of musical skills rather than the traditional example of sports because it is closer to moral skills. Finally, I will apply her account to virtue.

37.2.1 Different accounts of skill

There have been surprisingly few detailed accounts of skill in contemporary analytic philosophy. Perhaps the two most prominent ones are the anti-intellectualist account of Hubert and Stuart Dreyfus (Dreyfus & Dreyfus 1986; 2004; Dreyfus 2007) and the intellectualist account of Jason Stanley (Stanley 2011; Stanley & Krakauer 2013; Stanley & Williamson 2017). Space does not allow me to discuss these accounts in detail, but a brief summary may be helpful.

Dreyfus and Dreyfus (1986, 2004) argue that there are five stages for skill development. It is only in the earlier stages that the novice needs to rely on rules. As the learner gains expertise, she relies more on her holistic intuition that is formed through her experiences over time. This enables her to pick out relevant features of a situation and behave appropriately. By the time someone becomes an expert, she need not be able to verbally articulate her skills or tell you how she is doing what she is doing. She will rely heavily on the phenomenology of expertise in order to make her case, and argue that an expert does not consult rules or follow directions, she just does. In fact, Dreyfus and Dreyfus (1986) argue that a significant difference between computing machines and humans is that the former can only function in response to explicit rules, whereas the latter give them up when they gain expertise. This, according to them, rules out the possibility of Artificial Intelligence taking over some tasks requiring skill (e.g. being a teacher or a manager). It is, therefore, clear why their account can be considered an anti-intellectualist one. However, this account leaves a lot to be desired. For instance, many have argued that instead of this being an account that explains the nature of skill, this account leaves us wondering if there is anything else to be learned about skill. In other words, just stating that the skilled expert performs her task intuitively is uninformative. One may still ask what this intuitive ability consists in, how it is formed, how it is improved and what features of the environment it picks out.[6] One can also raise a whole slew of questions regarding the relation between the sub-personal non-cognitive mechanisms involved in the expert's intuitive skilled performance and the plans and goals of that expert (e.g. planning a specific performance at a specific time). If these mechanisms have no content as Dreyfus (2007) argues, then it may be impossible to explain how linguistically represented plans and goals can have an effect on a skilled performance (Fridland 2014a). These problems make this account of skill deeply unsatisfactory.

The intellectualist account of skill presented by Jason Stanley and Timothy Williamson (2017) suggests that to have a skill is to have a disposition to know or to acquire knowledge states including knowledge-how. In previous works, Stanley (2011) had argued that know-how is just like any knowledge-wh (know what, where, when, whom …) and so can be expressed as propositional knowledge. Knowledge-how is not strictly declarative but has a practical component, so the agent may not be able to verbally articulate this knowledge despite possessing it. This allows one to see how knowledge can generate behavior. On that view, knowing how to play the guitar involves the agent's standing in a knowledge relation to some way w to play the guitar that is contextually relevant to the context she is in and she represents this way w in a practical mode. However, though his account of skill is strongly connected to knowledge, he does not believe that this knowledge needs to be explicitly formulated by the skillful agent. Note that this knowledge is what constitutes having a skill, but performing a skillful action also requires unintelligent, non-cognitive, sub-personal motor routines, like the specific nuanced differences in the movements of fingers of an amateur guitarist and those of a professional (Stanley & Krakauer 2013). But a major problem arises for Stanley's account, namely that he makes such a sharp distinction between the knowledge a skilled agent has and the unintelligent, mechanical, sub-personal motor acuity, and though these are meant to work in tandem in the cases of skillful action, it is unclear how this can work. In other words, how can knowledge that is contentful and cognitive allow for non-contentful non-cognitive motor acuity to give rise to the intended performance of skill? (Fridland 2014a).

We can now turn to accounts of skill as it is related to virtue. Julia Annas argues on the side of the intellectualist view, albeit a different one from Stanley's, and Matt Stichter follows Dreyfus and Dreyfus's model of the anti-intellectualists.

37.2.2 Virtue and skill

Julia Annas (1995, 2008, 2011) argues in support of an intellectualist view of skill (and of virtue as skill) that she inherits from Plato. Note that Annas is not interested in spelling out an account of skills in general, but only interested in skills as they are relevant to virtues. According to this view, there are three elements that are necessary for a skill. The first is that the skill is teachable, in other words the one who has it can, to some degree, teach it to others. Second, there are some unifying principles underlying the whole field that the skillful person is able to grasp and that allow for flexibility when applying the skill in unfamiliar situations. Finally, the skilled person is able to give an account of this skill. It is impossible, on this view, for someone to have a skill and yet be unable to explain how it is that they rely on this skill. On this account, a virtue is a skill, and that involves an intellectual structure that the virtuous person is able to grasp, and that makes it a matter of explicit knowledge that the agent possesses. One can see that this account is quite different from that of Stanley discussed above, but they are both dubbed "intellectualist" because of their reliance on the necessity of knowledge for skill. For Annas it needs to be explicit though not so for Stanley.

On the other hand, Matt Stichter (2007, 2011, 2013, 2016) argues against Annas's overly intellectual account and in support of an Aristotelian anti-intellectualist or empiricist position. He argues that if one were to take an account of virtue as skill seriously, then one ought to rely on a strong and fleshed-out account of skill and not simply discuss skills only as they are related to virtues as Annas does. He believes that Dreyfus and Dreyfus provide us with the most prom-ising account of skills and so relies on it to flesh out how he sees virtues as skills. On his account one can have a skill without being able to explain what one is doing when performing skillful actions. Stichter agrees with Dreyfus and Dreyfus that skills are perfected through experience and therefore need not have intellectual representations or explicit knowledge. Even if an agent were to apply rules at the beginning stages of acquiring a skill, she ceases to do so when she becomes an expert since her experience would have provided her with the necessary intuitions to skillfully perform her tasks. On this view, one can become a skillful expert who consistently makes the right call without being able to say anything about one's skill. Stichter agrees with Annas that virtue should be thought of as a skill, but with this understanding of skill rather than the intellectualist one presented by her.

One implication of the claim I defended in the first section of this chapter is that one can behave virtuously without recognizing oneself to be doing so, and without being able to explain how one is doing so. Julia Annas (2011) argues that this cannot be true. In fact, she argues in support of a distinction between having a knack for something, which means picking it up without telling you how and why, and being skilled at it. This distinction lies at the heart of the disagreement between intellectualist and anti-intellectualist accounts of virtue as a skill. Annas adds that one difference between a knack and a skill is that a skill is consistent because the skilled person can give an account of what principles or rules she is following, and can hence apply them in a variety of different cases. But one who has a knack for something may not be able to do so, and therefore is not as reliable.

There are several ways of responding to her claim. First, the first part of this chapter argues for the dissociation of virtuous behavior and making moral judgments. Annas's view does not account for this dissociation as she believes that for skillful performance of a virtuous act to be distinguished from a knack, the agent must appeal to moral judgments that explain the virtue of the behavior. Earlier in the chapter, I argued in support of this dissociation by showing that one can do one without the other, so an agent can behave virtuously without being able to explain her behavior. Annas seems to take the opposite for granted and that is unwarranted and clearly problematic.

Another critique of Annas's distinction between a knack and a skill, and one that is specific to virtue as a skill. She relies on a *false dilemma* between skills requiring either explicit know-ledge or no knowledge at all. An agent can have knowledge related to a skill without being able to verbalize what it is that she is doing and why. Even Jason Stanley, the other intellec-tualist about skills discussed above, gives an account of skill that makes a distinction between knowing something and knowing something explicitly. For Stanley, the knowledge-how that is required for skillful performance is propositional but is represented in a practical mode. Another ingenious model of implicit competence and one that is relevant to virtue is fleshed out by Peter Railton in which he argues that our intuitions and affective reactions generally may be based on experience and knowledge we may not know that we possess.[7] In fact, he also gives a detailed account about how this implicit moral knowledge, or moral intuitions are learned in developing children (Railton 2017). In addition, if what I have argued for above is true, namely that one can behave virtuously without being able to explain or justify her behavior, someone who is skilled at performing virtuous actions also need not have any way of explaining or justifying his actions. Aside from insisting on the account that skilled virtuous behavior requires giving an account, which I have argued above is not supported either by accounts of skills or any account of virtue, there is no reason to think that John, an extremely thoughtful and kind man consistently helping others and always sensitive to their plights, does not have a skill because he is unable to give you an account of how and why he is so acting.

In this case, saying of John that he simply has a knack for doing the right thing but is not virtuous seems odd. After all, what is virtue if not having the right set of attitudes that allow one to behave reliably in a morally praiseworthy way?

Given the problems raised for Annas's account as well as those raised earlier for Dreyfus and Dreyfus (and therefore for Matt Stichter), one is left with no satisfactory account of virtue as a skill. In the next section, I will look into one possible avenue for such a view, though there remains much work to be done on that front.

37.2.3 Promising avenue

Ellen Fridland (2014a, 2014b, 2017) argues that none of the contemporary accounts mentioned above can explain the central role control plays in skill, and so she begins to formulate such an account (see Fridland, Chapter 19 in this volume). It is early days yet for this research project, but it seems quite promising. I will now turn to spelling out Fridland's account, but instead of illustrating the various levels of control with examples from sports psychology, I will do so with examples from music learning and the psychology of music.

37.2.4 Why music?

People often think of skills in terms of competitive sports, and most of the philosophers mentioned in this chapter do so as well. Although learning about sports psychology may be helpful in explaining the nature of skill in general, a more appropriate analogy if we are interested in virtue and skill is that of music. I believe that is the case for several reasons that highlight similar features between the virtuous behavior and musical performance, and these help us understand virtue as a skill: First, music, like virtue, necessarily involves an affective as well as cognitive component.[8] Affective feedback may directly alter a musical performance, as both the cognitive and affective elements are essential to it. This makes it more similar to virtues. Second, just like virtue or pro-sociality, most of us have a natural propensity for music that we simply fine tune over time. Infants respond to music quite early on in life, as they do for pro-social behavior (Railton 2017). Third, music, like virtue, is accessible to everyone. Though some may consider themselves tonally deaf, anyone can learn music with enough practice (Lehman et al. 2007). Finally, music, like virtue, is a universal phenomenon despite there being some nuanced differences across cultures. String instruments take different forms (guitar, violin, oud, sitar, etc.) as does vocalization, but the overarching system is to some degree overlapping (e.g. music is ritualistic, is sometimes meant to evoke emotions, different instruments are meant to simulate the different vocal ranges, etc.) This seems to suggest that these similar features between skillful performance of music and skillful performance of virtuous action may shed light on the latter.

37.2.5 Fridland's three levels of control

Now we can turn to Fridland's three levels of control required for skill: strategic control, selective, top-down attention and motor control. Note that these are meant to be found in all cases of skilled embodied action.

An essential feature of any skilled performance is the employment of strategic control. Fridland writes: "Strategic control ought to be identified with the goals, plans, and strategies that the agent uses in order to guide various instantiations of motor skill" (Fridland 2014a: 2744). This means that the agent must consciously select how the skill should be instantiated to serve the specific purpose of the performance. I will use the example of choral singing throughout as this is a hobby I practice and so am quite familiar with it. In order to perform a piece, a singer needs to understand the message being relayed and therefore the style, mood, and method she ought to use when performing it. You cannot, for instance, sing the Lacrimosa movement of Mozart's *Requiem* from the throat or in a cheerful manner. Similarly, Handel's Hallelujah movement from *The Messiah* sung in a slow gloomy tempo will completely defeat its purpose. One thing to keep in mind is that strategic control is not the same as conscious theoretical knowledge. First off, this kind of control may be exerted intuitively without having the ability to give any explicit justification, which is different from cases of explicit theoretical knowledge. Second, it is a practical kind of decision based exclusively on practical considerations which may become automated with practice, and that also marks a difference with theoretical knowledge. So one can clearly distinguish between strategic control and theoretical knowledge, and although it may be the case that some cases of the former involve the latter (e.g. learning some music theory may help one make a strategic decision to play a piece one way rather than another), it is not necessarily the case.

The next level of control is that of attention. She writes: "[Selective, top-down, automatic attention] is responsible for selecting the relevant features in an environmental array that a skilled agent should gather information about and respond to, given her goals, plans, and strategies" (Fridland 2014a: 2746).

There are many different things happening whenever someone is performing a skilled action, and one of the differences between the novice and expert is that the former does not know what to pay attention to, whereas this comes quite naturally to the expert. Some features of a situation are essential for the skilled behavior to be successful, and an expert selectively pays attention to those features (Fridland 2017). To go back to choral singing, a novice often concentrates on her score, trying to ensure that she gets all the notes right, whereas an expert pays attention to many significant features of a performance to sing masterfully as part of a collective, for instance not only does she need to be aware of the notes but she also needs to pay attention to the conductor as well as the entrances of all other singers and instruments. You need to train yourself to be attentive to the right elements of the performance and sometimes adjust it so you are in sync with others who may slow down or speed up. Selective attention is crucial in the development of any skill, be it a musical one, an athletic one, or as I will argue next, the skill of virtue.

Finally, on motor control, Fridland writes: "Motor control is constituted by the automatized motor routines that are learned through practice and training" (Fridland 2014a: 2748). This is the kind of control most people usually associate with skill, as it involves the nuanced changes in one's motor routines that people seek to make when continuing to practice. In the case of musical instruments, such as playing the guitar or piano, these are the fine and fast movements of the fingers as they seamlessly slide from note to chord. As for choral singing, it involves changes in stomach muscles, changes in breathing techniques, finding and perfecting one's mouth resonance and other such examples. In the case of virtue, an agent may mimic a victim's physical cues in an attempt to express empathy, or she may speak in a tone that is comforting for someone in a state of panic, which comes naturally and without forethought from the training she has had as a clinical psychologist. Many skilled jazz improvisers perform their acts intuitively by suddenly moving their fingers in a way that somehow meshes with the rest of the instrument to make a familiar pattern generate a whole new rhythm. This is another example of how nuanced motor routines may effect a performance but not in the traditional way we think of.[9]

If one were to take the analogy between virtues and musical skills seriously, one may see another parallel, namely that despite the presence of all three levels of control in the case of a musical performance, none of this is happening in a similar way in cases of evaluating a musical performance. Starting with strategic control, while a critic may note the strategic decision that the performer made, her skill does not require that she make the right choice herself, only that she is able to evaluate the performer's decision. As for having selective attention, the requirement for a critic is to be able to see how the different elements of a performance mesh together without being an active participant trying to fit in, thereby requiring a different kind of attention. Finally, in the case of musical performance, motor skill is key, and the mouth resonance or quick movements of the fingers are fundamental for a good performance, but they are wholly absent in the case of musical evaluation. You may be a fantastic music critic without having mastered any instrument. Just as in the case of virtue mentioned above, in which one can drive a wedge between moral judgment and virtuous behavior, so too can one see it in the case of music critics and musical performers. The best music critics are not the best musicians, and the best musicians are not the best critics. Similarly, the best moral judges may not be the most virtuous agents and the most virtuous agents may not be great moral judges. Evaluation and performance are separate in both cases.

If we want to see how this new account of skills fares when applied to virtue, we need to see if these three levels of control are found in cases of virtuous behavior. This is what we will turn to next.

37.2.6 Virtue and skill

In Section 37.1, I argued in support of driving a wedge between moral judgments and virtuous behavior. In order to explain this divergence, I have hypothesized that while virtuous behavior involves skilled performance, making moral judgments involves a different process. In this final section I wish to illustrate how virtuous behavior can be seen as skilled performance by two morally relevant though somewhat commonplace examples.

In the first, a friend of yours is suicidal and she is confiding exclusively in you, putting you in a unique position to help. You need to approach the situation very carefully and in a way not to lose that friend's trust. However, circumstances vary and it is not the case that there is a one-size-fits-all solution. Imagine, for instance, being in the United States where a professional can be of help. One can say that in this case the strategic decision should be to encourage your friend to seek the help of professionals. Unfortunately, if you are in a place where the professionals are not as reliable or even non-existent, you may need to think twice about that and try to find an alternate method. In any case, a strategic decision needs to be made about how to deal with it. You need to also deploy selective top-down attention as you should be aware of some warning signs or cries for help. Finally, motor control is necessary for continuing to put your distressed friend at ease. You need to be in tune with her and ensure that no subtle movement you make or remark you utter will be perceived as threatening.

Second, you are at a dinner, and one of the guests makes a rape joke. This guest is unaware that one of his audience was a rape victim, but you are aware of that fact. Again, here you are in a unique position to either let it pass or do something to alleviate your friend's distress, and thus a strategic decision needs to be made. You need to non-verbally gauge how the friend prefers this to be handled, but also how the other audience members, including the joker, will react. If, for instance, they are deeply insensitive to rape victims or will react by looking down on your friend for her sexual activities (imagine being in an extremely conservative society that lays blame on rape victims), then it may be a good idea to let it go. However, all these nuanced differences need to be weighed carefully before making the strategic decision, and once again, the selective top-down attention is crucial for recognizing all the different features of the situation. Finally, motor control, though it seems uninteresting in this case, is utilized even in the non-verbal communication you have with your friend, assuring her that you are there to be supportive. That involves nuanced bodily movements to relay this detailed information.

Those are some illustrations of how different levels of control may be at play in virtuous behavior, but I would go even further in claiming that they are likely to be present in most cases of virtuous behavior.

37.3 Conclusion

In this chapter I have argued for conceiving of virtue in terms of skill. In the first part I did so by driving a wedge between the ability to make moral judgments and the ability to behave virtuously. In the second part I explored some accounts of skills in the contemporary literature and finally relied on one that seems to have a promising future. So to answer the question posed by the title of this chapter, why moral philosophers are not the most virtuous people, I can say that it is because virtue requires a set of skills different from those found in making moral judgments.[10] So just like watching sports does not make you a good athlete or listening to music does not make you a good performer, learning moral philosophy does not make you behave virtuously. But I want to end on a positive note for moral philosophy and speculate that if you do it right, in tandem with practicing virtue, then just like in sports and music, it may help.

Notes

1 For example, Annas (1995, 2008, 2011), Stichter (2007, 2011, 2013, 2016)
2 Note that this is a case in which an agent comes to his judgment through reason, but the same can apply if he had come to his judgment through affect, for instance one's affinity toward someone because of historical familiarity may allow one to be more lenient in one's judgment of that person and that is not based on reason but affect.
3 Some may say that these are similar to examples of weakness of will, in which someone judges that, all things considered, she should perform some action X, but still fails to do so. However, the reason my examples are more commonplace is that I do not want to focus on one case in which there is a divergence between a judgment and an action, because I want to emphasize a pattern. One slip-up does not suggest anything about the presence or absence of some skill, but a pattern does.
4 See Arpaly and Schroeder (1999, 2013) and Arpaly (2002) for good examples of such cases.
5 Although Matt Stichter has developed a more recent account, I will only discuss his earlier work in this chapter. I plan on discussing his later work in detail elsewhere.
6 For a more detailed rejection of Dreyfus and Dreyfus's account of skill, see Fridland (2014a) or Stanley and Williamson (2017).
7 Railton (2014) gives some neuro-scientific justifications for his claims and illustrates them with a detailed example of a litigator.
8 For example, Railton (2014), Haidt (2001).
9 Buskell (2015) argues that Fridland's account is incomplete since her focus on motor control is too focused on athletic skills and does not make room for semantic skills (such as comedians, story-tellers, writers). In an amendment to her account he suggests that instead of the three levels of control one can see control as an instantiation of two features: normative sensitivity and opportunistic robustness. I will not address his account here, but I believe it to fit as well with the account of virtue as skill as Fridland's, if not more so.
10 Some, following Haidt (2001), may argue that learning moral philosophy will not even improve making moral judgments as those are based on affect rather than reason. That may be the case, but my claim about learning moral philosophy stands either way.

References

Annas, J. (1995) "Virtue as a Skill", *International Journal of Philosophical Studies* 3(2): 227–243.

—— (2008) "The Phenomenology of Virtue", *Phenomenology and the Cognitive Sciences* 7(1): 21–34.

—— (2011). *Intelligent Virtue*. Oxford: Oxford University Press.

Aristotle (2005) *Aristotle: Nicomachean Ethics*, edited by R. Crisp. Cambridge: Cambridge University Press.

Arpaly, N. (2002) *Unprincipled Virtue: An Inquiry into Moral Agency*. New York: Oxford University Press.

—— (2014) "Duty, Desire and the Good Person: Towards a Non-Aristotelian Account of Virtue", *Philosophical Perspectives* 28(1): 59–74.

Arpaly, N. and Schroeder, T. (1999) "Praise, Blame and the Whole Self", *Philosophical Studies* 93(2): 161–188.

—— (2013) *In Praise of Desire*. New York: Oxford University Press.

Bandura, A. (2002) "Selective Moral Disengagement in the Exercise of Moral Education", *Journal of Moral Education* 31(2): 101–119.

Bashour, B. (2013) "Can I Be a Good Animal?", in B. Bashour and H. Muller (eds.) *Contemporary Philosophical Naturalism and its Implications*. New York: Routledge, pp. 182–193.

Buskell, A. (2015) "How to Be Skillful: Opportunistic Robustness and Normative Sensitivity", *Synthese* 192(5): 1445–1466.

Dickey, M. (1992) "A Review of Research on Modeling in Music Teaching and Learning", *Bulletin of the Council for Research in Music Education* 113: 27–40.

Dreyfus, H. L. (2007) "The Return of the Myth of the Mental", *Inquiry: An Interdisciplinary Journal of Philosophy* 50(4): 352–365.

Dreyfus H. and Dreyfus, S. (1986) *Mind Over Machine: The Power of Human Intuition and Expertise in the Era of the Computer*. Oxford: Basil Blackwell.

—— (2004) "The Ethical Implications of the Five-Stage-Skill-Acquisition Model", *Bulletin of Science, Technology and Society* 24(3): 251–264.

Fridland, E. (2014a) "They've Lost Control: Reflections on Skill", *Synthese* 191(12): 2729–2750.

—— (2014b) "Skill Learning and Conceptual Thought: Making our Way through the Wilderness", in B. Bashour and H. Muller (eds.) *Contemporary Philosophical Naturalism and Its Implications*. New York: Routledge, pp. 77–100.

—— (2017) "Motor Skill and Moral Virtue", *Royal Institute of Philosophy Supplement* 80: 139–170.

Haidt, J. (2001) "The Emotional Dog and its Rational Tail: a Social Intuitionist Approach to Moral Judgment", *Psychological Review* 108(4): 814–834.

Lehmann, A., Sloboda, J. and Woody, R. (2007) *Psychology for Musicians: Understanding and Acquiring the Skills*. Oxford: Oxford University Press.

Railton, P. (2014) "The Affective Dog and its Rational Tale", *Ethics* 124(4): 813–859.

—— (2017) "Moral learning: Why learning? Why moral? And why now?", *Cognition* 167: 172–190. http://dx.doi.org/10.1016/j.cognition.2016.08.015

Smith, M. (1994) *The Moral Problem*. New York: Blackwell.

Stanley, J. (2011) *Know How*. Oxford: Oxford University Press.

Stanley, J. and Krakauer, J. W. (2013) "Motor Skill Depends on Knowledge of Facts", *Frontiers in Human Neuroscience* 7: 503.

Stanley, J. and Williamson, T. (2017) "Skill", *Noûs* 51(4): 713–726.

Stichter, M. (2007) "Ethical Expertise: The Skill Model of Virtue", *Ethical Theory and Moral Practice* 10(2): 183–194.

—— (2011) "Virtues, Skills, and Right Action", *Ethical Theory and Moral Practice* 14(1): 73–86.

—— (2013) "Virtues as Skills in Virtue Epistemology", *Journal of Philosophical Research* 38: 333–348.

—— (2016) "Practical Skills and Practical Wisdom in Virtue", *Australasian Journal of Philosophy* 94(3): 435–448.

38

VIRTUE AS SKILL

Self-regulation and social psychology

Matt Stichter

38.1 Introduction[1]

Skills have become increasingly important to virtue theory, given the recent trend of concep-tualizing virtue as a skill in both virtue ethics and virtue.[2] Given that I and others have laid out these accounts elsewhere (including in some of the other contributions in this volume), I will not cover that ground again here. However, in this chapter I will be adding to these accounts by grounding an account of skill within the larger framework of the psychological research on self-regulation.[3] Self-regulation theories cover both the considerations involved with setting goals and striving to accomplish those goals.[4] Since skill acquisition is essentially a sophisticated form of self-regulation, this approach will shed further light on the nature of skill and thereby virtue.

The main issue I hope to shed light on in this chapter is what moral skill training might look like, given what we know about self-regulation and skill acquisition. Skills are improved by deliberate practice, where in such practice you are attempting to improve by correcting past mistakes and overcoming your current limitations. So, in acquiring moral virtues as skills, we have reason to focus on some of the common moral mistakes we make, along with other fre-quent obstacles to acting well.[5]

Here this project converges with the situationist critique on virtue, as social psychology experiments highlight some of our current weaknesses when it comes to acting morally.[6] Experiments have shown that whether people act morally well or poorly is often strongly influenced by irrelevant (and sometimes trivial) factors of a situation. Whether people stop to help someone in need, for example, can be affected by whether there are passive bystanders nearby (Latané and Darley 1970). Furthermore, our moral judgments can be influenced by stereotypes, or how moral dilemmas are framed (Tversky and Kahneman 1981). Then there are the more (in)famous experiments, such as the Milgram obedience experiment, where it seems far too easy to elicit cruel behavior out of average people (Milgram 1974).

Fortunately, there are resources in the self-regulation and skills literature to devise strategies to combat these situational influences. In the rest of this chapter, I will begin by outlining some general features of the psychological research on self-regulation and skill.[7] I will then discuss the results of some social psychology experiments (such as framing effects and the bystander effect), and what kinds of training can be used to overcome those obstacles to better moral behavior.

In the process I will show how a skill model of virtue can respond to the situationist critique, as we can view the results of the experiments as presenting us with opportunities to further develop virtue.

38.2 Self-regulation: goal setting and goal striving

Self-regulation theories in psychology begin with commitment to a goal, which implies adopting certain standards of behavior by which one judges oneself.[8] This also has an affective dimension, as Albert Bandura relates, because "self-regulatory control is achieved by creating incentives for one's own actions and by anticipative affective reactions to one's own behavior depending on how it measures up to personal standards" (Bandura 1999: 176).[9] In terms of self-reactions, achieving a goal is usually a source of self-satisfaction, while failing to do so can lead to self-censure. Furthermore, the strength of the self-reaction, in terms of the motivation it provides for self-regulation, depends in part on how the goal is valued.[10] Goals that are highly valued can provide more self-satisfaction from achievement, and likewise more self-censure from failing to achieve them, than goals that are only minimally valued. A highly valued goal will make you feel really bad for violating it or really good for conforming to it. So, motivation to strive for the goal arises from self-evaluative reactions (anticipated feelings of self-satisfaction or self-censure), the strength of which depends in part on the degree of value placed on the goal.

The value that a goal has (its desirability), however, is not the only factor to affect motivation. The above assumes a situation where the person believes that the desired outcome can be achieved, or the undesirable outcome can be avoided, by acting. If instead someone believes that they are not capable of achieving the desired outcome, she will have little motivation to self-regulate. As Bandura notes:

> Among the self-referent thoughts that influence human motivation, affect and action, none is more central or pervasive than people's judgments of personal efficacy … Unless people believe that they can produce desired results by their actions, they have little incentive to act or to persevere in the face of difficulties.
>
> *Bandura 1999: 180–181*

'Perceived self-efficacy' then refers to people's beliefs about what they are capable of achieving, and self-efficacy beliefs can strengthen or undermine one's motivation to engage in self-regulation.[11] Thus, goal setting is both a matter of perceived desirability and feasibility.

Setting a goal frequently leads to adopting a set of goals that are organized hierarchically, as a complex or abstract (or superordinate) goal will give rise to more context-specific subsidiary (or subordinate) goals (Carver and Scheier 2003: 189). It could be that the goal itself is complex and thus requires many intermediary steps to accomplish, or that the goal itself is abstract enough that it requires a more concrete specification to act on. For example, wanting to do well in an academic class will require achieving several minor subgoals along the way, such as registering for the class, picking up the textbooks, etc. The relationship between the differing levels of the goals need not be merely a product of means–end reasoning, though, as sometimes the lower order goals provide the constitutive elements of a higher order goal.[12] Achieving an abstract goal such as being kind, for example, often requires a more practical specification in circumstances, like how being kind to a friend might require that you now tell that person a hard truth.[13]

Once you have committed yourself to realizing a goal, it is time to start figuring out how you are going to realize it, and this marks a transition from goal setting to goal striving. This distinction is important, as deciding whether to commit to a goal in the first place, or later whether to maintain commitment to that goal, requires a different kind of mindset from the activities associated with striving to achieve a goal (which involves planning and acting) (Achtziger and Gollwitzer 2007; Heckhausen 2007). In short, in phases of goal setting you are undecided about your goal commitments, whereas phases of goal striving assume a decided goal commitment that you are now trying to realize.[14] Bandura notes this connection in self-regulation, stating that "people motivate themselves and guide their actions anticipatorily through the exercise of forethought. They anticipate likely outcomes of prospective actions, they set goals for themselves, and they plan courses of action designed to realize valued futures" (Bandura 1989: 19). Committing yourself to a goal is part of this process of forethought. It motivates the next phase of forethought in planning what steps to take to achieve that goal, where you are likely trying to figure out what needs to be done, how you are going to do it, when and where you will take action, etc.[15]

With self-regulation it matters how the goals are spelled out, as more specific and proximate goals (as compared to vague or distant goals) allow for better planning before acting, and better feedback after acting. Similarly, not all plans of action for implementing those goals are equally effective. We can make plans of action in the moment, responding to our current situation and trying to determine what act would best further our goals. But that approach suffers from two main drawbacks. First, it is often cognitively demanding to figure out how to achieve a goal (especially in the given context), and you may have to decide quickly on what course of action to take in the moment. Second, with this reactive approach you are forced to respond to the current situation, and you may find out that the situation you have gotten yourself into is not conducive to achieving your goals (such as trying to quit drinking alcohol but then agreeing to meet up with friends at a bar).

A more effective route to achieving your goals is through the use of implementation intentions, which differ from the kinds of intentions we have when we decide to commit ourselves to goals (i.e. goal setting). Trötschel and Gollwitzer explain the difference as follows:

> In contrast to goal intentions, implementation intentions specify a plan on the when, where, and how of acting on one's goal intentions. Implementation intentions are subordinate to goal intentions and have the format of "If situation x arises, then I will perform goal-directed behavior y!", thus linking an anticipated opportunity to a select goal-directed response. By forming implementation intentions, people plan out in advance (i.e., pre-select) which situations and behaviors they intend to use to achieve their goals (goal intentions).
>
> *Trötschel and Gollwitzer 2007: 581*

Basically, an implementation intention has an 'if-then' structure – if this situation arises, then I will respond in this particular way (in order to achieve the goal I have committed myself to). Perhaps this sounds rather obvious as a strategy to realize one's goals, but people frequently do not form detailed implementation intentions at all, and rely instead on having just a very specific goal intention (e.g. I am going to snack less than I do now). Furthermore, there is evidence that forming a mere goal intention has a low correlation with actually acting on that intention (Webb and Sheeran 2006). Numerous studies have shown, however, that forming implementation intentions that detail when, where, and how a behavior will be performed significantly increase goal attainment (Trötschel and Gollwitzer 2007). To take an example connected to a virtue like temperance, to achieve the goal of snacking less often, you might form the intention 'if I find myself filling up my plate at a buffet line in a restaurant, I will choose fruit instead of cake for dessert'. Forming such intentions requires you to anticipate the kinds of situations that might provide opportunities to advance your goal, or those that might threaten to undermine your goal, and decide on a course of action to take in response. So, for example, exercising temperance for someone trying to quit alcohol might involve trying to find places other than at a bar to get together with friends.

There are a few generic advantages to having implementation intentions of this kind. First, the kind of planning it involves requires you to do some thinking in advance as to what kind of situations you want to seek out, or avoid, in order to be in the best position to achieve your goal. This is certainly acknowledging the power of situational influences. Second, forming an implementation intention does not require conscious awareness of the situational cue in order to prompt the goal-directed behavior you decided on earlier.[16] As Weiber et al. note, "[b]ecause forming an implementation intention entails the selection of a critical future situation, the mental representation of this situation becomes highly activated and hence more accessible" (Wieber, Gollwitzer, and Sheeran 2014: 32). This is especially helpful when a goal is not easy to implement because one has habitual responses that steer one away from the goal (for example, being in the habit of ordering dessert when you have recently formed a new goal of losing weight). In essence, forming the implementation intention will prompt the intended goal-directed response, thus pre-empting the prior habituated response (Gollwitzer 1999). This represents an interesting interplay between deliberative and automatic processes, as you are using a deliberate self-regulatory strategy (i.e. implementation intentions) in advance, which works by later prompting "goal-directed behavior efficiently and in the absence of conscious intention" (Fujita, Trope, Cunningham, and Liberman 2014: 56). Interestingly, this kind of automaticity develops even without repetition, in contrast to how automaticity is usually the result of repeated performance.[17]

38.3 Skill acquisition, deliberate practice, and automaticity

Skill acquisition is basically a sophisticated form of self-regulation, and skills enable us to achieve a desired goal in a domain of high complexity.[18] It is important to note that a skill involves some flexibility in how one goes about achieving that outcome (to cope with changes in one's environment – which is part of what makes the domain complex), as well as a broad view of the outcome (such as in learning how to speak a language, rather than a single phrase). In committing yourself to acquiring a skill, you begin internalizing standards about what counts as a good performance, which will guide your efforts to learn the skill. Skill acquisition involves a progression from tackling simple tasks to more challenging tasks, no matter what level of skill you are aiming at, and as one advances in skill development which tasks count as 'simple' or 'challenging' will change. Learning how to be a competent and safe driver on the road can be one's superordinate goal, and reaching that goal requires successfully achieving many subgoals along the way (e.g. learning how to start the car, how to change gears, how to back out of a driveway, how to parallel park, etc.). Each of those subgoals requires planning how to achieve them (e.g. 'if I reach 20 mph, then I switch to third gear'), and there is a progression of difficulty in the subgoals that requires successful completion of the previous subgoal.

This progressive mastering of subgoals requires 'practice, practice, practice'. However, neither mere experience, nor rote repetition, is sufficient for improvement. People reach a certain level of acceptable performance, after which further experience does not lead to any improvement in performance. Additional experience may make performing at that level of skillfulness easier, but that is not the same as actually improving one's performance.

What more is needed? Research indicates that a particular kind of experience is necessary for improvement, as it turns out that the quality of the practice matters just as much as the quantity. Improving your level of skill requires not the mere repetition of things you already know how to do, but continually striving to do things that you currently cannot do. This kind of experience is referred to as 'deliberate practice'. Deliberate practice requires having specific goals in mind for improvement, rather than the vaguer goal of 'getting better', as is true with self-regulation in general. There need to be specific aspects of your performance that you go about planning how to improve, which then structures the kind of deliberate practice you engage in (Horn and Masunaga 2006: 601). As you engage in deliberate practice you seek out feedback about your performance, in the hopes of identifying and correcting errors. You keep monitoring your progress as you practice. If you do not seem to be progressing, you may need to redesign your practice sessions. If instead you keep up a steady progression, then at some point you achieve your current goal. At that point it is time to set out to strive to accomplish the next more difficult goal (i.e. you advance to planning how to achieve the next higher-ordered subgoal on the vertical hierarchy). This is how you improve upon your current level of performance.[19]

Not only does practice allow you to improve your level of skill, it can also function as a form of planning for actual performances if the practice session attempts to simulate actual conditions under which someone will perform. For example, pilots can use simulators to engage in deliberate practice with regard to emergencies, and Ericsson reports on findings that show that "if prior to the emergency event the expert pilots had practiced the same emergency situation in the simulator, they were reliably more successful in dealing with the actual event" (Ericsson 2006: 693). However, since skill acquisition is needed to deal with complex domains of action, where one has to be able to respond dynamically to the current situation, plans formed in the planning phase will either be vague in detail or will specify a default approach to take – both of which one has to be prepared to modify while acting.[20] So, for example, a firefighter might go into a fire with a certain plan of how to keep it under control, but if the wind unexpectedly shifts, it will likely require a change in plans. Thus, to remain in control, one must be able to develop some flexible hierarchical structures to guide action in a dynamic context.[21]

In order to make progress in learning a skill, the currently effortful tasks need to become relatively effortless, in order to free up your attention to handle more complicated tasks. As Daniel Kahneman explains, you have

> a limited budget of attention that you can allocate to activities, and if you try to go beyond your budget, you will fail. It is the mark of effortful activities that they interfere with each other, which is why it is difficult or impossible to conduct several at once.
>
> *Kahneman 2011: 23*

With practice, tasks can be accomplished more effectively and more efficiently. This allows a person to devote less attention to the tasks at hand without any reduction in performance, and to shift that attention to other matters. This phenomenon is referred to as automaticity, and it is what allows one, through practice, to make progress on tackling ever more difficult tasks (Feltovich, Prietula, and Ericsson 2006: 53).

Novices learning a skill will have to pay a lot of attention to what they are doing, and attention is a scarce resource. Due to limitations in our short-term or working memory, we can only focus our attention on a limited number of activities at one time. For example, you are not going to be able to pay full attention to changing lanes in heavy traffic if you still have to pay a lot of attention to changing gears. You need that changing of gears to happen with little attention or effort, so that you can focus your effort on a more demanding task. As performance becomes more automatic in its implementation, cognitive resources are freed up, either for engaging in multi-tasking, like carrying on a conversation (deliberate) while driving (automatic).[22] But importantly for skill acquisition, one's attention is now freed up for more control over the performance, such as being able to pay closer attention to traffic patterns or road conditions while driving.[23]

Automaticity reflects the fact that the processes by which one engages in self-regulation can be broadly characterized by dual-processes theories of cognition. The first is cognition that is automatic, intuitive, fast, and effortless; while the second is cognition that is deliberate, analytic, slow, and effortful. Daniel Kahneman distinguishes the two processes as System 1 (automatic) and System 2 (deliberate).[24] However, while much of the dual-process literature makes it sound as if you are guided by either one process or the other, a more nuanced view sees the two systems as working together, as will be shown with skill acquisition.[25]

Deliberate practice clearly involves a transition from deliberate to automatic processing, as Ericsson notes that "[c]onsistent with the mental demands of problem solving and other types of complex learning, deliberate practice requires concentration that can be maintained only for limited periods of time" (Ericsson 2006: 699), and furthermore,

> the requirement for *concentration* sets deliberate practice apart from both mindless, routine performance and playful engagement, as the latter two types of activities would, if anything, merely strengthen the current mediating cognitive mechanisms, rather than modify them to allow increases in the level of performance.
>
> *Ericsson 2006: 692*

Chess players, for example, when engaging in deliberate practice will spend time studying opening moves and playing through past games played by grandmasters (to see if the move they made turns out to be the same move made by the expert player). This kind of study takes focused concentration, as you are trying to figure out the mistakes you are prone to make, and how to correct them.

This is why, as I mentioned earlier, the findings of the social psychology experiments are helpful to improving our existing levels of moral skillfulness, as they reveal the mistakes we are prone to making, and thus can serve as the target of deliberate practice (when conceiving of virtues as skills). That is, if virtues are skills, skills are improved through deliberate practice, and deliberate practice requires focusing on specific mistakes to correct; then the situationist experiments provide us with feedback on the mistakes we are prone to make. They are helpful in providing us some structure for deliberate practice, so that we can improve our moral skillfulness (i.e. virtues). So, the next step is then figuring out what kind of strategies we can implement to correct for these mistakes.

38.4 Framing effects, stereotypes, and the bystander effect

One seemingly irrelevant factor that has a significant impact on our moral decision making is the way a moral issue is framed. For example, Tversky and Kahneman (1981) tested subject's responses to a public health crisis, specifically a disease that threatened to kill 600 people. They presented the subjects with two treatment options, where both treatment options had the same predicted outcome in terms of how many people would survive, but one was framed in terms of a 100% chance of saving 200 lives and the other in terms of a 33% chance of saving 600 lives (and 66% chance of saving none). Subjects overwhelmingly preferred the first treatment, even though the treatments had the same predicted outcome. However, the really surprising result was that if the same two treatment options were framed instead in terms of chances that people will die (i.e. 400 lives lost), they overwhelmingly preferred the second treatment. It seems as though we react differently to issues when framed in terms of gain (positive) or loss (negative), such that we want to secure a definite gain but we try to avoid a definite loss.

The literature on implementation intentions, as a way to self-regulate, offers a way to resist some framing effects. Trötschel and Gollwitzer studied the effects of using implementation intentions on achieving prosocial goals (such as fairness and cooperation) in negotiations, specifically in respect to loss framing. The framing effect in this context is that the outcomes of negotiations depend on whether they are framed in terms of gains or losses. People appear to be more motivated to avoid a loss than to seek a gain, and so if the outcomes are framed in terms of losses then people are less likely to make concessions in negotiations, such that "loss frames lead to comparatively unfair outcomes and hinder the finding of integrative solutions" (Trötschel and Gollwitzer 2007: 580). In other words, while framing in terms of gains leads to fairer outcomes, those who adopt a loss frame typically come out ahead of the other person. This, of course, just provides incentives to go in with a loss frame to start.

However, they found that this effect could be mitigated if people supplied their goals (e.g. be fair) with implementation intentions specifying how they would be fair. In the experiment, "participants were randomly assigned to play the role of one or the other representative of two neighboring countries (blue nation vs. orange nation) disputing over an island, said to be close to the main land of both countries" and one group had neither goal nor implementation intentions, a second group had the goal to be fair but not implementation intention, and the third group had both the goal and were supplied with the implementation intention "if I receive a proposal on how to share the island, then I will make a fair counterproposal!" (Trötschel and Gollwitzer 2007: 583). The first group experienced the typical framing effect, the second group partially mitigated the effects of the framing, and the third group managed to fully mitigate the loss frame effects. Importantly, the results of these experiments have implications beyond just the context of negotiations, for

> negotiations are cognitively very demanding tasks in which a large amount of information has to be processed on-line and the course of events is hard to predict. Thus, negotiations can be understood as the prototype of a complex situation in which the pursuit of desired goals can easily become derailed.
>
> *Trötschel and Gollwitzer 2007: 582*

Given how easily the pursuit of moral goals can become derailed, as the social psychology literature highlights, the effects of implementation intentions will likely be of use in resisting some situational influences.

Implementation intentions are not the only way to resist the effects of some situational influences. Deliberate practice programs and skilled training can be used, for example, to resist stereotypes and problematic situational influences. Plant et al. (2005) studied how to counteract automatic racial bias in a situation that mirrored police encounters with potential criminals. The subjects were shown a picture of a face of someone with either black or white skin, and an object that was either a gun or something with a similar shape to the gun – a camera, cellphone, or wallet. Subjects had to make an instant reaction as to either shoot or not shoot the suspect, based on these two factors. Initial reactions by subjects showed a racial bias – they were more likely to mistake a gun for something harmless when the picture was of a white person, and more likely to mistake something harmless for a gun when the picture was of a black person. Sadly, this is what we see in the many recent real-life examples of police shooting black males who were actually unarmed.

Plant et al. were able to eliminate the bias in this task after participants went through a program designed to make race a non-diagnostic factor in determining criminal behavior. Their approach emphasized training the subjects that race was not relevant to determining the presence of a weapon, via practice with a program where statistically the faces were equally likely to be black or white, and each face was equally likely to be paired with a gun or a harmless object. After extensive practice with the program, the initial bias of the subjects was eliminated on the task when tested both immediately after the practice, and 24 hours later. A similar result was obtained in experiments performed by Kawakami et al. (2000). They had participants practice saying 'No' when presented with stereotypic representations of social categories (e.g. elderly are afraid), and 'Yes' when presented with counter-stereotypic representations. After training, participants demonstrated significantly reduced levels of stereotype activation, both immediately after the training, and 24 hours later as well.

Two aspects of Plant et al.'s results are worth pointing out. First, it might be supposed that the automatic bias was counteracted by a conscious and deliberate response. However, they found that "training directly influenced the degree of automatic racial bias as opposed to resulting in some degree of controlled, conscious compensation for the bias" (Plant, Peruche, and Butz 2005: 153). So the deliberate practice is leading to changes in later automatic responses. Second, this result could have occurred either because the program changed the positive or negative associations someone had with those racial categories, or because people were not thinking in terms of racial categories at all. They found that it was the latter, since "race was non-diagnostic and paying attention to race only impaired performance on the shoot/don't shoot task, extensive exposure to the program encouraged the inhibition of the participants' racial categories" (Plant, Peruche, and Butz 2005: 152). So this gives hope to overcoming some of our automatic biases with deliberate practice.

Another situational influence to impact helping behavior is the presence of an unresponsive bystander, but deliberate practice can also mitigate this influence. Latané and Darley (1970) did a series of experiments that showed that when people are alone and witness an emergency (like someone having a seizure), they show high rates of responding to the emergency. But all it takes is the presence of one unresponsive bystander in the situation, and helping rates decrease dramatically. There are, however, some examples of being able to mitigate the bystander effect with deliberate practice. Cramer et al. (1988) found that registered nurses were not subject to the bystander effect when it came to an emergency situation in which they were skilled in responding. The experiment involved a group of registered nurses who were part of a nursing program, and a group of students who were part of a general education program. Half of each group were working alone in a room when they heard a person fall off a ladder in an adjoining room, and the other half were working with a partner in the room when the same event occurred. When each subject was initially led to their room they passed by a person working on a ladder, but the sound of that person falling off the ladder was produced by a prerecorded tape.

Cramer et al. found that when alone, both groups of students responded to the emergency with the same frequency (about 75%). When with a bystander, the general education students rate of helping dropped by half, thus showing the bystander effect. However, the registered nurses helped just as often when with a bystander as when alone. Cramer et al. attributed the difference to the greater competency of the nurses:

> As expected, high-competent subjects reported that when the emergency occurred they felt more confident about their ability to help the workman, and more sure about what steps to take to help than their low-competent counterparts. Even among the subjects who helped, high-competent subjects compared to low-competent ones reported feeling more confident about their abilities, and about what steps to take to help. Thus, minimization of the bystander effect appears to have been mediated, in part, by the nurses' skill at emergency responding.
>
> *Cramer, McMaster, Bartell, and Dragna 1988: 1142*

So, some practice with helping in an emergency situation has an influence on self-efficacy beliefs and minimizing the bystander effect.[26] It seems we underestimate just how uncertain people are about how to respond to emergency situations without some skilled training.

Further support for the importance of self-efficacy beliefs and the bystander effect can be found in studies on bullying. Bullying is a pervasive problem in schools, and such behavior frequently occurs with bystanders who do not intervene to help. Thornberg and Jungert (2013) studied the bystander effect in bullying situations, and found that a significant factor that was positively associated with those who intervened to help was self-efficacy beliefs. That is, those adolescents who had strong beliefs about their ability to successfully intervene were more motivated to actually help. Those who lacked such beliefs did not see intervention as a feasible goal, even if they knew it was the right thing to do, and so did not strive to intervene. I suspect attempts at moral training stop too often at having mere goal intentions or appropriate attitudes and miss the kind of training that would be needed to actually realize such intentions. It would be a great benefit for adolescents to get this kind of training in school, to curb the pervasive harm of bullying, and likely there are other kinds of moral training we should be receiving long before we reach adulthood.

Some work has been done on putting moral courage training programs into effect, to mitigate against the bystander effect. Brandstätter and Jonas (2012) have been involved with training programs aimed at increasing people's abilities to intervene in situations of intolerance, discrimination, and violence within their community. The problem is that while people typically express attitudes that they and others should intervene to stop displays of intolerance and discrimination, it rarely translates into actual behavior. Brandstätter and Jonas describe the work being done by a couple of moral courage training programs taking place in Germany and Switzerland (Brandstätter 2007). The programs "aim to strengthen an individual's assertiveness and self-efficacy, on the one hand, while preparing the ground for establishing behavioral routines, on the other hand, as core competencies for bystander intervention" (Brandstätter and Jonas 2012: 273).

The programs use the work of Latané and Darley to help identify the different psychological mechanisms that can impede intervention, in order to formulate a training program to help counter those mechanisms. The training has three main components. The first is to increase the knowledge base of the participants, including both potential problems brought out in the work of Latané and Darley on bystander intervention, as well as general strategies for self-regulation as discussed by Gollwitzer (1999). Of special note is that:

> participants learn about what to do and what to refrain from doing in diverse situations of neighborhood violence (e.g., put the victim at the center of your intervention; never touch the perpetrator; never intervene directly in a fist fight; make an emergency call). Notably, participants are informed about the emergency services in their community, which is an important issue in combating neighborhood violence,

since bystanders often remain passive simply because they lack the knowledge of how to activate the emergency system.

Brandstätter and Jonas 2012: 277

What is important about this is that it reinforces the point above that lack of knowledge, and connected to that low self-efficacy beliefs, about how to handle emergency situations is a significant part of the problem. I imagine that some of the tips they give about what to do or not do in a situation of violence are likely to be new to you, the reader, as well. After all, without proper training, how could you be expected to know these things?

The second component is the use of role-playing and mental simulations to simulate situations of harassment and violence, so people can try out different ways to respond to such situations. Of interest here is that "participants practice useful de-escalating behavioral strategies in different role-playing situations (e.g., inviting the insulted victim to leave the situation; speaking up in a non-aggressive way; seeking collaborators; confusing the perpetrator by doing something unexpected)" (Brandstätter and Jonas 2012: 277). Again, I think it helpful to highlight the kind of tactics that may never occur to someone outside of training, and even if they do it is probably difficult to find ways to practice them on your own. Role-playing the tactics gives a chance to practice them and get feedback on what might be the most effective response, and how best to carry it out. The third component is for the participants to form some specific goal and implementation intentions that are relevant to their personal situations, in the manner documented by Gollwitzer (1999).

This is a great example of deliberate practice aimed at overcoming a specific moral weakness. There is also some evidence of their effectiveness, though of course it is harder to gauge as we cannot simply place the participants in dangerous situations to see what happens. But participants in the training had much stronger self-efficacy beliefs about their abilities to intervene even months after the program. Memory tests also showed that they had a high retention of the information provided in the training, which Brandstätter and Jonas note "is important in that the greater mental presence of the concept of moral courage is an important prerequisite for strengthening the corresponding behavior" (2012: 278). The training has helped make the concept of moral courage more accessible, thus it should make the participants more likely to see situations through this perspective.

After seeing such a program laid out, it seems unwarranted to expect untrained people to reliably act well in such situations. In which case, it is no surprise that people are generally not intervening when they should, as they do not have the skills and corresponding self-efficacy beliefs they would need to reliably respond well. In support of this, in their studies of bystander effects and moral courage, Osswald et al. reported that "in moral courage situations people feel less competent to intervene compared to other prosocial incidents" (Osswald, Frey, and Streicher 2011: 400). Moral training really does need to go beyond having mere goal intentions or appropriate attitudes. Osswald et al. have offered training courses based on Brandstätter's work, to impart more practical knowledge of how to successfully intervene. They found that "participants feel more responsible to show moral courage and they indicate to have more specific self-efficacy concerning how to intervene well – always compared to a control group and not only directly after the training but also 6 weeks later" (Osswald, Frey, and Streicher 2011: 402). This is a promising result, but they also note that more research would need to be done to determine the longer-term effects of the training.

Overall, the moral courage training programs offer hope for mitigating the bystander influence, and a path toward increasing our skillfulness in courage. Granted, it is still at a speculative stage, as we cannot directly test the effects of such programs by intentionally putting people in dangerous situations and seeing how they respond. But there are some other reasons to be hopeful. First, the training program is using methods that have proved efficacious elsewhere (i.e. implementation intentions – Gollwitzer (1999); deliberate practice for emergencies – Ericsson (2006)). Second, out of the outcomes that could be documented from the programs, there is an increase in practical knowledge and self-efficacy beliefs. Since we know that greater self-efficacy beliefs are positively associated with greater intervention (Cramer et al. 1988; Thornberg and Jungert 2013), then that provides additional reasons to think that the training will actually pay off in some situations. Finally, a larger lesson to draw is that this is a helpful illustration of how social psychology experiments can make us aware of obstacles to moral behavior (e.g. the bystander effect), as well as providing us some information useful to strategizing how to overcome such obstacles (e.g. affected by self-efficacy beliefs), such that we can design deliberate practice routines aimed at improving our moral skillfulness.

38.5 Situationism and the rarity of virtue

There are ways to mitigate the effects of situational influences through self-regulatory strategies, deliberate practice, and skilled training. I take these examples to point to a reason why we might expect virtue to be rare, at least currently. Insofar as people think of moral education in terms of merely internalizing moral standards, the research on implementation intentions shows that much more work needs to be done to effectively implement those standards. It requires you to consider the potential obstacles in your way, and to develop plans ahead of time for how to respond. Specific kinds of deliberate practice may then be required to effectively implement one's goals. To the extent that people do not tend to think of moral development in terms of the self-regulation strategies and deliberate practice that goes into skill acquisition, people presumably have not been doing the kinds of activities that they would need to engage in to significantly develop virtue. That is, because it has not been well-known what steps are required to overcome the more troublesome obstacles to appropriate moral behavior, people have not usually been taking those steps. So, is it really any surprise if we frequently test low for moral competency?

If full virtue is not widespread, then the situationist critique loses much of its power, given that in these experiments some smaller percentage of people manage to still act well, and so the experiments do not necessarily undermine the possibility of acquiring high degrees of virtue. However, there may be a cost to going this route. Mark Alfano argues that the idea that virtue possession is fairly widespread is deeply ingrained in our traditional conceptions of virtue. As he points out, "[i]f virtues are what humans need, but the vast majority of people don't have them, one would have thought that our species would have died out long ago" (Alfano 2015: 134). I think the skill model of virtue can accommodate this thought, if we distinguish between different levels of skill acquisition. I think without some basic competency with respect to many of the virtues, it would be hard for humans as a social species to survive. So we might have some minimal levels of virtue, but that's also consistent with us having a lot of room for improvement. To use a skill analogy, people need to display some basic competencies with driving a car in order to get a driver's license, to ensure that those on the road are not a constant hazard to themselves and others. You do not need to exhibit expertise, though, to get a license, as it certainly does not take 10,000 hours of training to get a handle on the basics of driving.

But that basic competency is compatible with finding people driving poorly in a variety of situations (such as in the snow, or while texting). It is also the case that those who have put in a lot more training in driving will have a higher level of skill than the minimum we

497

require to get a license. With skill acquisition, improvement in skill can be a matter of being more reliable in familiar situations (e.g. driving with greater safety), extending your current level of performance in a more difficult situation (e.g. driving as safely in wintry conditions as dry conditions), or tackling a more complex task (e.g. driving while also navigating to a new location). So we can view virtue possession as a matter of degree in the same way – there are some basic levels that you need to attain so that you are not a constant danger to yourself and others, while also recognizing that there are higher levels of performance above our minimum expectations of people. While we might need basic moral competency to survive, higher levels of moral skill development can enable us to live well, and this is consistent with virtue theorists who conceive of virtues as constitutive of living well (and not merely surviving).[27]

In this respect, I think the skill approach gives a different twist to the situationist critique. Instead of viewing situational influences as barriers to moral development and acquiring virtue, the skill model of virtue can view the overcoming of these influences as opportunities for further developing virtue. That is, improvements in skill come about through awareness of our errors and limitations, along with deliberate practice and strategies targeted at correcting those errors and expanding our abilities. Without that process, one remains at a fixed level of skill development. In that sense, the situationist literature is helpful in bringing out shortcomings we were not fully aware we had, so that we can begin the process of strategizing how to overcome those shortcomings, and increase our level of moral skillfulness. While we should expect that we have acquired lower degrees of virtue than we might have initially suspected, it also means that the situation can be remedied (at least to some extent) once people learn what steps they need to take to further their moral development. A better account of moral development should thus lead to improvements in moral education and development, and there is much work to be done in identifying our most important weaknesses and devising training to improve our current levels of moral and intellectual skills.

Notes

1 My thanks to Ellen Fridland and Walter Sinnott-Armstrong for very helpful advice in revising this chapter.
2 See for example: Annas, 2011; Sosa 2007; Stichter, 2017.
3 This essay draws from chapters in my book: *The Skillfulness of Virtue: Improving our Moral and Epistemic Lives*, Cambridge University Press (2018), reprinted with permission of Cambridge University Press © Cambridge University Press.
4 Self-regulation is thus much broader in scope than what is more narrowly thought of as 'self-control', which is merely one aspect of self-regulation.
5 Given limited space, I will confine my discussion to implications for moral skills, though there are also implications for epistemic skills.
6 I will not go into detail on the situationist critique itself, as there is already a voluminous literature on it. However, I will discuss some of the findings of the experiments themselves later in this chapter. For the situationist critique, see Doris (2002), Alfano (2013), and Miller (2013).
7 Space permits only a brief overview of some aspects of the empirical literature on self-regulation and skill here, so I will highlight those aspects most relevant for responding to the findings of the social psychology experiments. Also, since there is research in psychology showing how to resist some situational influences with self-regulation strategies, I provide a framework for self-regulation from the perspective of psychology, rather than, say, from a philosophical perspective on action (though there is sure to be a lot of overlap between the two).
8 Some goals need not necessarily be adopted with a conscious goal commitment, such as goals related to satisfying basic needs like hunger.
9 This does not mean, however, that such anticipation is necessarily conscious to the agent.

10 How much a goal is valued may depend in part on whether the goal is intrinsically or instrumentally valued, or how closely a goal is tied to one's identity, but these need not always go together. My thanks to Walter Sinnott-Armstrong for pushing this point.

11 Connected to self-efficacy are people's beliefs regarding whether the abilities needed to reach the goal are ones that are relatively fixed, or malleable through improvement, as setbacks tend to undermine motivation to improve in the former. Of note is that skills (and thus virtue) when viewed in terms of deliberate practice as I describe in detail later, represent a malleable view of abilities (see Dweck and Leggett, 1988).

12 In fact, this is how many virtue theorists view the relationship between virtues and living well. Virtues are not merely means to the end of living well, but rather the virtues are constitutive of what it means to live well.

13 Also, given that we set for ourselves many different types of superordinate goals, there inevitably arise situations in which our different goal commitments conflict (e.g. I want to study, and I want to party). How we resolve these dilemmas is another aspect of self-regulation, but one I don't have space to cover here.

14 See Achtziger and Gollwitzer, 2007. Though, as Heckhausen (2007: 168) points out, while it is common and usually efficient to move sequentially through these phases, "individual agents can be expected to perform these switches from goal choice to goal engagement and from goal engagement to disengagement and evaluation imperfectly."

15 I will go into further detail on strategies for improved planning (i.e. implementation intentions) later on in the chapter. I don't have space to address issues that come up when acting, such as the need for self-control (i.e. virtues of willpower) to prevent acting in a way that undermines one's goal commitments.

16 For evidence that implementation intentions are still effective even under dual-task interference tasks, see Brandstätter, Lengfelder, and Gollwitzer (2001).

17 As Fujita et al. (2014, p. 55) point out:

> What is remarkable about implementation intentions, however, is unlike habits and acquired skills, they do not appear to require repeated practice to automate. Indeed, simply repeating an implementation intention several times ("If I see the number 5 on the computer screen, then I will type in my response particularly fast!") is sufficient in prompting cognitively efficient goal-directed behavior when the context specified by the plan is later encountered.

18 That is, not all acquired abilities are necessarily skills. Some tasks are so simple, such as tying one's shoelaces or opening doors, that once you have done it a few times there is nothing else to learn. The need to acquire sophisticated competencies such as skills arises when dealing with complex issues, since the skills enable one to handle the complexity by progressively developing one's abilities (via deliberate practice). So I agree with Ellen Fridland (2014a) when she claims that skills "are characterized by the fact that they are refined or developed as a result of effortful attention and control to the skill itself."

19 This helps to explain why Ellen Fridland (2014b: 2740) takes "attention-governed, practice-related improvement as a criterion of skill".

20 This likely has overlaps with philosophical accounts of intention and planning, like those put forth by Michael Bratman. Space, however, does not permit me to going into detail on the connections. My thanks to Ellen Fridland for drawing my attention to this.

21 Note that changing plans in such a situation is not a matter of changing goal commitments – which, for example, remains stopping the fire – but rather to the 'when, where, and how' details of goal striving.

22 Furthermore, you are unlikely to be able to recount all the driving conditions you experienced afterwards, since you were not paying explicit attention to them. Dual-process also explains how we can be paying conscious attention to one matter while simultaneously engaged in another activity.

23 By this, though, I don't mean to deny Ellen Fridland's (2017) argument that attention can be deployed automatically as well.

24 Kahneman, 2011. For concerns regarding dual-process theory, see Keren and Schul (2009). For a defense of dual-process theories, see Evans and Stanovich (2013).

25 See Christensen et al. (2016).

26 Furthermore, as detailed in the following paragraphs, one does not need as much training as a nurse to mitigate the bystander effect. While some situations may call for specialized training, other forms of helping, like giving basic first aid or being able to deescalate a situation, will apply across a variety of

situations. It is even helpful just for people to know better how to effectively contact someone who can help in situations, rather than doing nothing at all (as happens with the bystander effect).

27 Virtue in this regard is necessary, but not sufficient, for living well. Economic, political, and other social factors matter significantly in this regard.

References

Achtziger, A., and Gollwitzer, P. M. (2007) "Motivation and Volition in the Course of Action", in J. Heckhausen and H. Heckhausen, eds., *Motivation and Action*. New York: Cambridge University Press, pp. 202–226.

Alfano, M. (2015) "Ramsifying Virtue Theory", in M. Alfano, ed., *Current Controversies in Virtue Theory*. New York: Routledge, pp. 124–135.

—— (2013) "Identifying and Defending the Hard Core of Virtue Ethics", *Journal of Philosophical Research* 38, pp. 233–260.

Annas, J. (2011) *Intelligent Virtue*. Oxford: Oxford University Press.

Bandura, A. (1999) "Social Cognitive Theory of Personality", in L. A. Pervin and O. P. John, eds., *Handbook of Personality: Theory and Research*. New York: The Guilford Press, pp. 154–196.

—— (1989) "Self-Regulation of Motivation and Action through Internal Standards and Goal Systems", in L. Pervin, ed., *Goal Concepts in Personality and Social Psychology*. London: Lawrence Erlbaum Associates, pp. 19–85.

Brandstätter, V. (2007) "Kleine Schritte statt Heldentaten. Ein Training zur Förderung von Zivilcourage gegen Fremdenfeindlichkeit" [Small steps instead of heroic deeds: A training to increase moral courage against xenophobia], in K. J. Jonas, M. Boos, and V. Brandstätter, eds., *Zivilcourage trainieren! Theorie und Praxis* [Training moral courage: Theory and practice], Göttingen: Hogrefe, pp. 263–322.

Brandstätter, V. and Jonas, K. J. (2012) "Moral Courage Training Programs as a Means of Overcoming Societal Crises", in K. J. Jonas and T. A. Morton, eds., *Restoring Civil Societies: The Psychology of Intervention and Engagement Following Crisis*. West Sussex: John Wiley & Sons, pp. 265–283.

Brandstätter, V., Lengfelder, A., and Gollwitzer, P. M. (2001) "Implementation Intentions and Efficient Action Initiation", *Journal of Personality and Social Psychology*, 81, pp. 946–960.

Carver, C. S. and Scheier, M. F. (2003) "Self-Regulatory Perspectives on Personality", In T. Millon and M. J. Lerner, eds., *Handbook of Psychology: Volume 5 Personality and Social Psychology*. Hoboken, NJ: John Wiley & Sons, Inc., pp. 185–208.

Christensen, W., Sutton, J., and McIllwan, D. (2016) "Cognition in Skilled Action: Meshed Control and the Varieties of Skill Experience", *Mind & Language*, 31(1), pp. 37–66.

Cramer, R. E., McMaster, M. R., Bartell, P. A., and Dragna, M. (1988) "Subject Competence and Minimization of the Bystander Effect", *Journal of Applied Social Psychology*, 18(13), pp. 1133–1148.

Doris, J. (2002) *Lack of Character*. Cambridge: Cambridge University Press.

Dweck, C. S. and Leggett, E. L. (1988) "A Social-Cognitive Approach to Motivation and Personality", *Psychological Review*, 95(2), pp. 256–273.

Ericsson, K. A. (2006) "The Influence of Experience and Deliberate Practice on the Development of Superior Expert Performance", in K. A. Ericsson, ed., *The Cambridge Handbook of Expertise and Expert Performance*. Cambridge: Cambridge University Press, pp. 683–704.

Evans, J. and Stanovich, K. (2013) "Dual-Process Theories of Higher Cognition: Advancing the Debate", *Perspectives on Psychological Science*, 8(3), pp. 223–241.

Feltovich, Paul J., Prietula, Michael J. and Ericsson, K. Anders (2006) "Studies of Expertise from Psychological Perspectives", in K. Anders Ericsson, ed., *The Cambridge Handbook of Expertise and Expert Performance*. Cambridge: Cambridge University Press, pp. 41–68.

Fridland, E. (2017) "Automatically Minded", *Synthese* 194(11), pp. 4337–4363.

—— (2014a) "Skill Learning and Conceptual Thought: Making a Way through the Wilderness", in B. Bashour and H. Muller, eds., *Philosophical Naturalism and its Implications*. New York: Routledge, pp. 13–77.

—— (2014b) "They've Lost Control: Reflections on Skill", *Synthese*, 191, pp. 2729–2750.

Fujita, K., Trope, Y., Cunningham, W. A., and Liberman, N. (2014) "What Is Control? A Conceptual Analysis", in J. W. Sherman, B. Gawronski, and Y. Trope, eds., *Dual-Process Theories of the Social Mind*. New York: The Guilford Press, pp. 50–65.

Gollwitzer, P. M. (1999) "Implementation Intentions: Strong Effects of Simple Plans," *American Psychologist*, 54(7), pp. 493–503.

Heckhausen, J. (2007) "The Motivation-Volition Divide and Its Resolution in Action-Phase Models of Developmental Regulation", *Research in Human Development*, 4(3–4), pp. 163–180.

Horn, J. and Masunaga, H. (2006) "A Merging Theory of Expertise and Intelligence", in K. A. Ericsson, ed., *The Cambridge Handbook of Expertise and Expert Performance*. Cambridge: Cambridge University Press, pp. 587–612.

Kahneman, D. (2011) *Thinking, Fast and Slow*. New York: Farrar, Straus and Giroux.

Kawakami, K., Dovidio, J. F., Moll, J., Hermsen, S., and Russin, A. (2000) "Just Say No (To Stereotyping): Effects of Training in the Negation of Stereotype Associations on Stereotype Activation", *Journal of Personality and Social Psychology*, 78, pp. 871–888.

Keren, G. and Schul, Y. (2009) "Two Is Not Always Better Than One: A Critical Evaluation of Two-System Theories", *Perspectives On Psychological Science*, 4, pp. 533–550.

Latané, B. and Darley, J. M. (1970) *The Unresponsive Bystander: Why Doesn't He Help?* New York: Appleton-Century-Crofts.

Milgram, S. (1974) *Obedience to Authority*. New York: Harper and Row.

Miller, C. (2013) *Moral Character: An Empirical Theory*. Oxford: Oxford University Press.

Osswald, S., Frey, D., and Streicher, B. (2011) "Moral Courage", in E. Kals and J. Maes, eds., *Justice and Conflicts*. Heidelberg: Springer, pp. 391–405.

Plant, E. A., Peruche, B. M., and Butz, D. A. (2005) "Eliminating Automatic Racial Bias: Making Race Non-Diagnostic for Responses to Criminal Suspects", *Journal of Experimental Social Psychology*, 41, pp. 141–156.

Sosa, E. (2007) *A Virtue Epistemology: Apt Belief and Reflective Knowledge, Volume 1*. Oxford: Oxford University Press.

Stichter, M. (2018) *The Skillfulness of Virtue: Improving our Moral and Epistemic Lives*. Cambridge: Cambridge University Press.

Stichter, M. (2017) "Virtue as Skill", in N. Snow, ed., *Oxford Handbook of Virtue*. New York: Oxford University Press, pp. 57–84.

Thornberg, R. and Jungert, T. (2013) "Bystander Behavior in Bullying Situations: Basic Moral Sensitivity, Moral Disengagement, and Defender Self-Efficacy", *Journal of Adolescence*, 36(3), pp 475–483.

Trötschel, R. and Gollwitzer, P. M. (2007) "Implementation Intentions and the Willful Pursuit of Prosocial Goals in Negotiations", *Journal of Experimental Social Psychology*, 43, pp. 579–598.

Tversky, A. and Kahneman, D. (1981) "The Framing of Decisions and the Psychology of Choice", *Science*, 211(30), pp. 453–457.

Webb, T. L. and Sheeran, P. (2006) "Does Changing Behavioral Intentions Engender Behavior Change? A Meta-Analysis of the Experimental Evidence", *Psychological Bulletin*, 132(2), pp. 249–268.

Wieber, F., Gollwitzer, P. M., and Sheeran, P. (2014) "Strategic regulation of mimicry effects by implementation intentions", *Journal of Experimental Social Psychology*, 53, pp. 31–39.

39

DE-BIASING, SKILL, AND INTERGROUP VIRTUE

Michael Brownstein

Inherent in the idea of democratic society is the possibility of changing one another's beliefs, attitudes, and behavior, albeit in limited and modest ways. It is difficult to imagine maintaining faith in democracy as a political system without believing that we can sometimes move one another without resorting to force. And yet, in practice, the challenge of changing others' minds is maddeningly familiar. This is particularly so when it comes to diminishing biases and prejudices.

I begin here with the observation that some people are better at this than others. And so I ask: what kind of skill does it take to be good at changing people's biases and prejudices? What are the strategies, abilities, or traits associated with being a successful "de-biasing agent?"[1]

Before trying to answer this question, I offer a few caveats and clarifications.

(1) I focus here on the skills individuals might seek, practice, and master. I have in mind situations of interpersonal interaction, perhaps between family members, friends, neighbors, and citizens. In focusing in this way, I do not mean to implicitly criticize other deeply worthwhile anti-discrimination and anti-prejudice activities, such as organizing protests, crafting legislation, establishing case law, amending corporate human resources policies, and militating for changes in public policy. I will return briefly in the conclusion to discuss how the ideas I present here relate to the ongoing debate between proponents of "individual" versus "structural" approaches to social change.

(2) Nor do I mean to imply that the *self*-regulation of prejudice and stereotyping is unimportant. I have biases and prejudices. It is my responsibility to try to diminish them. Indeed, as I discuss below, reducing prejudice is more a matter of modeling desirable behavior than it is a matter of persuading people to believe what you want them to. If this is right, then skilled de-biasing depends in part upon one's ability to regulate one's own prejudices. I have addressed the self-regulation of prejudice elsewhere;[2] here I address what people should consider doing if they want to combat injustice by trying to change the biases their fellow citizens hold. Concomitant to this, it is important to remember that many people want to be fair minded and to act in relatively egalitarian ways. In this sense, it is worth considering how to help each other challenge our biases.

(3) "Bias" is sometimes used in a pejorative sense, sometimes not. In the non-pejorative sense, a bias is a disposition to perceive or cognize things in a particular way, given some trait or feature of one's identity. Classical musicians might be biased in favor of the classical music radio station in this sense; orthopedic surgeons might be biased against letting their kid play on the jungle gym. In the pejorative sense, biases are inherently unfair, or they obscure the truth in some way. Racists are biased in the pejorative sense. What makes racist beliefs biased is not just that they are skewed by the racist's own idiosyncratic view of things. Racist beliefs are biased because they are unfair, untrue, or unjustified. They are *flawed*, whether factually or morally (or both). This pejorative sense of "bias" is the one I use in this chapter.[3] Below I will note some important differences in the psychology underlying the relevant kinds of factual and moral errors.

(4) As I understand them, prejudices are negative attitudes (i.e., evaluative feelings and thoughts, otherwise known as likings and dislikings) about people in virtue of their social group membership; stereotypes are generalizations about the traits of groups; and discrimination is unfair treatment on the basis of social group membership, often driven by prejudice and stereotyping.[4] Despite their distinct meanings, prejudice, stereotyping, and discrimination are fellow-travelers. Elsewhere, I have defended a view that there is a blurry boundary, at best, between these concepts.[5] This issue won't matter much here, although I will revisit it briefly in Section 39.1.

(5) Regarding "skill," I intend to stay neutral with respect to theories contending that skill is a form of knowledge-how (Ryle 1949); a particular way of responding to "affordances" (Dreyfus 2002a, 2002b); or a disposition to know certain propositions (Stanley & Williamson 2017). That is, I am here less interested in the nature of skill than I am in the specific skills a successful de-biaser might display. What abilities must such a person possess? What knowledge must she have? What strategies should she use? I operate with the assumption that de-biasing *is* a skill, however. Like dancing, debating, and drawing well, de-biasing is something one can learn and improve over time with practice. Acquiring the skill involves a combination of adopting the right goals, learning the right information, and simply practicing the relevant actions repeatedly. Doing so enables one to become fluent, that is, able to respond to different kinds of situations in appropriate ways on the fly. Most people, I suspect, can call to mind exemplars of de-biasing, people whom they believe were unusually skilled at it. What is it that these exemplars do?

39.1 Resisting argumentation

First, skilled de-biasers tend to resist the temptation to try to argue people out of their opinions. One reason for this is to avoid being condescending or perceived as holier-than-thou. People tend not to like being told that they are prejudiced.[6]

"Opinions" is a purposely vague term. As I'll discuss below, argumentation can be successful for changing people's factual beliefs, but usually much less so for changing people's attitudes, intentions, and behavior. It suffices to be wary of it as a route for combating prejudice, stereotyping, and discrimination. Of course, not everyone feels the temptation to argue people out of their opinions equally. But feeling it is common, perhaps particularly among intellectuals whose professional currency is ostensibly argumentation.

The fact is, however, that arguments are often ineffective tools. Long-standing laboratory research on belief perseverance, confirmation bias, and motivated reasoning (e.g., Ross et al. 1975; Lord et al. 1979; Kunda 1990; Nickerson 1998; Kahan et al. 2017; Mandelbaum 2019) shows, at least minimally, how steep the hill to climb is. These streams of research have, unsurprisingly, been applied in contexts involving intergroup attitudes (e.g., Kunda & Sinclair 1999; Ulhmann & Cohen 2005). Activists and canvassers engaged in shifting individuals' opinions about specific public policies have absorbed these lessons and tend now to shy away from trying to win arguments.[7] And good reasons are given for the ineffectiveness of argumentation in research on the evolutionary psychology of reasoning, the most compelling accounts of which (e.g., Mercier & Sperber 2011, 2017) suggest that reasoning in human beings evolved to facilitate cooperation, group cohesion, and the sustainment of social identity rather than to evaluate the strength of arguments, make good causal inferences, and so on.

Of course, there are important caveats here. Consider research on political beliefs and the so-called "backfire effect." A series of highly-cited papers suggests that correcting people's misperceptions about, for example, weapons of mass destruction in Iraq (Nyhan & Reifler 2010), belief in Obamacare "death panels" (Nyhan et al. 2013), and potential health impacts of climate change (Hart & Nisbet 2012) ironically leads people to double-down on their false beliefs about these topics. Telling people their beliefs are false leads them to hold on to their mistaken beliefs more strongly, in other words. Or so the story went. But it turns out that things are more complex than this. More careful and high-powered studies have failed to find evidence that correcting false beliefs leads people to believe the opposite of the truth (Cameron et al. 2013; Wood & Porter 2016). These follow-up studies have led some to suggest that the backfire effect ought to be thrown in the dustbin of history of much-hyped but ultimately illusory psychological phenomena.[8]

The warranted caveat here is that arguments and facts *can* correct false beliefs, and so in the domain of prejudice and stereotyping, there may be a time and a place for the skilled de-biaser to inform her racist uncle that violent crime is not on the rise in the United States or that China and India (not Mexico) are the sources of the largest number of people currently migrating to the United States.[9]

But more than this is unwarranted, and for two central reasons. First, while the evidence for backfire effects on factual beliefs is weak, there is mixed evidence at best in the above studies that participants have meaningful uptake of true beliefs. In other words, while participants don't double-down on their false beliefs in the way the original studies suggested, moving in the opposite direction of truth as a result of being given the facts, participants also don't move consistently in the direction of the truth once they have the facts.[10] The dynamics of this process—the "continued-influence effect" (Lewandowsky et al. 2012)—are not entirely understood. Repetition of factual corrections, presenting information in worldview-affirming ways, and other tactics appear to diminish it (Lewandowsky et al. 2012; see also Anderson 1982). Skilled de-biasers will need to learn these, as well as to adumbrate the strategy of "going factual" to contextual and personality variables.

Second, and perhaps more importantly, researchers *do* find evidence of backfire effects when it comes to intentions and attitudes, as compared to factual beliefs. For example, Nyhan and Reifler (2015) find that correcting the false belief that the flu vaccine gives you the flu reduces people's belief in this myth but also *reduces* people's intent to get vaccinated. And Nyhan and colleagues (2017) find that correcting false claims made by Donald Trump reduces belief in those claims among Trump supporters, but it does *not* affect their attitudes toward Trump.[11] This is crucial when it comes to combating prejudice, stereotyping, and discrimination. While these are separate constructs, in practice they are nearly inseparable.[12] As a result, changing "opinions" about social groups will nearly inevitably involve changing the kinds of attitudes that *do* appear susceptible to backfire effects. As Gordon Allport presciently said, "information seldom sticks unless mixed with attitudinal glue" (Allport 1954: 485).

The idea that the backfire effect is complex—that it works in some contexts but not others, for people with certain traits but not others—applies to persuasion in general (and, really, to just about any psychological phenomenon[13]). The experimental literature on persuasion is vast and successes are, of course, well-documented. But while persuasion sometimes works, it is often unclear *why* it works. Proposed explanations involve the credibility, stature, and even attractiveness of the message-giver, the emotional state and meta-cognitive awareness of the message-receiver, the sheer number and length of arguments in a message and how many times the message is repeated, the concomitant presentation of particular images (e.g., brain scans), and so on (for review see Petty & Briñol 2008). It is crucial to understand why persuasion works, when it does, because (a) in many cases these ostensible moderators cut both ways (e.g., in some studies happy people appear more receptive to persuasive arguments and in other studies they appear more resistant to persuasive arguments) and (b) it is possible that what makes persuasion sometimes effective has nothing to do with the strength of one's arguments. This is clear when attractive interlocutors are more persuasive than others.

All of this said, it is undeniable that providing people with knowledge about prejudice, stereotyping, and discrimination is crucial for creating social change. Effective attitude change techniques do just this. For example, Patricia Devine's "habit-breaking" approach to prejudice-reduction focuses on providing people with knowledge about the mechanisms of bias, along with motivation to avoid its effects and strategies for effectively avoiding it. Devine and colleagues' (2012, 2017) research is noteworthy for creating durable change in participants' attitudes and behavior, for example, leading to increased hiring of women in STEMM fields. But providing a person with knowledge is not tantamount to persuading them to change their mind. Devine's approach packages knowledge with motivation and tools in an effort to frame bias as a bad habit, not a false ideology. Other approaches provide knowledge by telling someone, "here is how prejudice has affected me," without prescribing what message-receivers are supposed to conclude from this. (See Section 39.4 for more on this tactic.)

As I granted above, some contexts may be more conducive than others to changing beliefs, attitudes, and behavior via argumentation. Debate societies and peer-reviewed journals, for example, are ostensibly appropriate venues for persuasion. While it's unclear how often people change their minds in these contexts, and there are worries about who has access to these venues, persuasion is certainly at home here. There are also other, less formal situations in which persuasion and argument may be appropriate. Some friendships and marriages are built on it! But success in these contexts is likely to be built upon mutual trust and a shared set of experiences, which are precisely what is often lacking in intergroup exchanges. These background conditions are more the exception than the norm. One thing that helps to promote them is what psychologists call "intergroup contact."

39.2 Intergroup contact

Here's a truism: doing things cooperatively with other people tends to lead people to like each other. But that this is a truism doesn't diminish its significance. Promoting cooperative intergroup interaction is at the core of the "contact hypothesis," which is perhaps the most influential and longest-standing research program on prejudice-reduction in existence. Allport's (1954) central proposition was that intergroup contact promotes intergroup liking. (Put in less sterile terms: doing things with people unlike yourself leads you to like them.) High-powered, longitudinal studies have demonstrated the salutary effects of intergroup contact. Colette Van Laar and colleagues (2005), for instance, studied the effects of both randomly assigned and voluntary intergroup roommate assignment at UCLA over four years and found that for nearly[14] all groups they studied (White, Asian American, Latino, and African American), living with a member of another group decreased prejudice and, perhaps even more significantly, this effect generalized to feelings about members of other outgroups. Similar positive effects as a result of intergroup roommate assignment have been found on implicit racial attitudes (Shook & Fazio 2008).[15]

So, at first glance, an obvious answer to the question of how to become a skilled de-biaser might be to embrace the contact hypothesis. But I will not dwell extensively on this approach. My reason is that it does not fit naturally within the scope of the question I am asking. Intergroup contact is essential for changing one's own prejudices. Moreover, it is an important goal for legislation and litigation (e.g., *Brown v. Board of Education of Topeka*). But it is unclear how an individual could "deploy" intergroup contact as a tactic in the relevant sense. One could try to persuade people to enter situations in which they will interact with outgroup members. But in many cases this puts the cart before the horse, because prejudice is often what prevents people from wanting to engage with others outside their own social group.[16] Intergroup contact can be conceived of as an end, in this sense, that the skilled de-biaser helps people to embrace, rather than as a means to that end.

39.3 Personal connections

Here's another seeming truism: changing people's minds about things they care about requires making a personal connection with them. For example, Jeremy Bird, the national field director for President Obama's 2012 re-election campaign, reported, "we trained our volunteers to connect with voters at the door on a personal and values level, not to talk at them with scripted talking points."[17] A recent highly publicized study on reducing transphobia substantiates this idea. David Broockman and Joshua Kalla (2016) showed that short conversations (approximately ten minutes) with voters in Miami, Florida, in which canvassers asked voters to recall a time in which they had been judged negatively for being different and then to relate that feeling to the experiences of transgender people, significantly increased positive feelings toward transgender people. The effect was large; it was greater than the average increase in positive feelings toward gay men and lesbians among Americans between 1998 and 2012. The effect was also common to both registered Republicans and Democrats, as well as to voters whose feelings toward transgender people started off above and below the average. Most strikingly, the effect of these short conversations did not diminish after three months.[18]

Broockman and Kalla's canvassers didn't try to convince voters of anything. They simply identified themselves as working with an LGBT organization; informed voters that they might have to vote whether to repeal a law protecting transgender people; asked voters if they had an opinion about the law and to explain their opinion if so; showed them a short video that defined the term "transgender," described simple arguments for and against the law, and identified that they were transgender, if they were[19]; asked the voters to recall an experience as described above and to relate that experience to the experiences of transgender people[20]; and then asked the voters whether the conversation had in any way changed their minds.

It isn't certain what *was* responsible for Broockman and Kalla's canvassers' success. The researchers themselves understood the intervention as a way of encouraging effortful active processing and analogic perspective-taking (i.e., encouraging voters to actively reason about what it would be like to experience the world as a transgender person). This builds upon previous successes in lab-based research using these techniques (e.g., Galinsky & Moskowitz 2000). But as the authors note, the focus on external validity means we cannot be certain that perspective-taking is responsible for any effects or that active processing is responsible for their duration; being primarily concerned with external validity and seeking to limit suspicion, we did not probe intervening processes or restrict the scope of the conversations as a laboratory study would.

Broockman & Kalla 2016: 222

It certainly seems clear that canvassers made *some* kind of personal connection to voters, compared with controls. Indeed, voters in the control group were simply informed that they may have to vote on a law requiring supermarkets to charge for plastic bags, asked what they thought about this, and then thanked. So, in addition to differences in the content of the discussion across conditions, not only did voters in the control condition not experience the active processing and analogical perspective-taking intervention, but they did not experience any kind of meaningful connection with the canvasser. This leaves open a number of possibilities. Broockman and Kalla's canvassers may have had success in the experimental condition because they encouraged active processing, because they managed to get voters to take the perspective of transgender people, or because they simply made a personal connection with them, notwithstanding the active processing and perspective-taking (or only because they did all three of these things together). Hopefully future research will replicate Broockman and Kalla's results as well as consider these possibilities as isolated independent variables. Until then, de-biasers would do well to try all three, much in the mold of Broockman and Kalla's canvassers.

39.4 Social referents and the perception of norms

I have a speculative suggestion about why Broockman and Kalla's canvassers were successful. They were effective de-biasers, I suggest, because they changed people's perceptions of norms. They did this, moreover, because they became what Betsey Levy Paluck calls a "social referent" (Paluck & Shepherd 2012; Tankard & Paluck 2016). Social referents are people with particular influence over other people's perceptions of norms. If correct, the upshot of this idea is that instead of trying to change people's beliefs or attitudes directly, successful de-biasers change people's perceptions of what *other* people believe and feel.

The idea that de-biasing agents become social referents draws upon a large and growing body of research on the psychology of norms. The basic claim of this body of research is that people's perceptions of norms are crucial determinants of their social attitudes and behavior. There is robust debate about how exactly to understand this claim, of course (e.g., Bicchierri 2005, 2016; Brennan et al. 2013; Henrich 2015; Kelly & Davis 2018). Much of this debate is orthogonal to the discussion here, although below I will note a few commitments I make to contested positions. Much of the debate homes in on a particular sense of the terms norms and normativity, a sense that is different from the way in which these terms are typically deployed in other disciplines. In the most general sense, norms refer to what is required, allowed, or forbidden (Kelly & Davis 2018). When philosophers refer to norms and normativity, they usually consider the nature of claims about what is required, allowed, or forbidden. Are those claims coherent, justified, universal, etc.? Moral philosophers, for example, try to ground normativity in this sense on various kinds of theoretical foundations (e.g., the promotion of the greatest good for the greatest number, according to utilitarians). In contrast, when economists, sociologists, and anthropologists talk about norms and normativity, they usually refer to what's normal or prevalent in a polity. Mixed-gender schooling is the norm in some cultures but not in others, for example. Norms in this sense are just regularities regarding what's required, allowed, or forbidden; economists and other social scientists aren't usually interested in whether these regularities are well-justified, for example. Psychologists (in particular, evolutionary psychologists) usually understand norms and normativity in a third sense, one that sits somewhat squarely between the philosopher's and the economist's senses. Psychologists tend to study people's *perceptions* of what's required, allowed, or forbidden; how and why these perceptions are formed, in terms of the architecture and evolution of the mind; and how perceptions of norms affect people's attitudes, beliefs, and behavior in distinctive ways (i.e., different from other influences on their attitudes, beliefs, and behavior). Of course, in reality, there is a lot of disciplinary overlap. I make these generalizations in order to clarify that it is in the third sense—the psychologist's sense—that I suggest that successful de-biasing agents become social referents for people's perceptions of norms.

There are many reasons to think that prejudice, stereotyping, and discrimination are illuminated by norm psychology.[21] An overarching reason is that norm psychology helps to explain how social groups maintain cohesion and, by definition, group cohesion requires a distinction between ingroup members and outgroup members. This is, in some sense, the very distinction underlying prejudice, stereotyping, and intergroup discrimination. But there are more specific reasons too. I'll identify three.

First, people's attitudes and behavior are influenced by their perception of what other people think it's appropriate or inappropriate to do, and this effect applies to the context of social attitudes and behavior. A well-known example compared the effects of different ways of framing an anti-theft message to visitors at Arizona's Petrified Forest National Park. Some visitors saw a sign that informed them that "[m]any past visitors have removed the petrified wood from the park," others saw a sign reading "the vast majority of past visitors have left the petrified wood in the park," and others only saw a message pleading with them to refrain from removing wood from the park (Cialdini et al. 2006). Those who were informed that the norm is to steal wood ("[m]any past visitors have removed the petrified wood from the park,") stole *more* wood than people who received the other messages. The same principle is found in research on stereotyping. For example, Michelle Duguid and Melissa Thomas-Hunt (2015) found that telling people that "*the vast majority of people* have stereotypical preconceptions" leads them to express more stereotypes and to act in more stereotype-consistent ways, compared with people who are told that "*very few people* have stereotypical preconceptions" (Duguid & Thomas-Hunt 2015: 347).[22]

Second, social practices influenced by norms typically involve rewards and punishments. This is a core tenet of the literature on the evolution of cooperation and has been explored extensively in game theoretic conditions, which often show that people are readily willing to incur costs for enforcing norms against norm-violators (see Henrich 2015 for review). Expectations of punishment also help to explain motivated reasoning in public policy contexts (see note #6) and public behavior, such as voting. Gerber and colleagues (2008) show that telling people that their participation in an election will be publicized is far more effective for increasing turnout than reminding people of their civic duty to vote or telling them that their participation will be monitored.[23] In research on social attitudes and discrimination, one of the very founding concerns behind the "implicit revolution" was that people are motivated to conceal their biases and prejudices when they perceive those attitudes to be socially proscribed. The idea that rewards and punishment underlie the expression of bias is particularly central to neuroscientific approaches to prejudice and stereotyping (e.g., Amodio 2014).

Third, as Daniel Kelly and Taylor Davis (2018) argue, norms have intrinsic motivational force. That is, to acquire a norm typically entails feeling motivated to obey it. One feels compelled to tip around 20% in a restaurant once one knows that most people think that you ought to tip about 20% at a restaurant. This doesn't mean that one *will* tip 20%, just that in the typical case one will feel some motivation to do so. One could say that norm perception has a tripartite structure. Acquiring a norm involves a belief about others' beliefs or attitudes, a feeling that one ought to do what others do, and a behavioral inclination to act in a way consistent with the norm. Now, compare this to Jack Dovidio and colleagues' characterization of the traditional conception of prejudice:

> prejudice is typically conceptualized as an attitude that, like other attitudes, has a cognitive component (e.g., beliefs about a target group), an affective component (e.g., dislike), and a conative component (e.g., a behavioral predisposition to behave negatively toward the target group).
>
> *Dovidio et al. 2010: 5*[24]

If I am right that the expression of prejudice and stereotyping involves the psychology of norms, then there should be effective norms-based approaches to de-biasing. Paluck and colleagues (2016) offer a dramatic example. They sought to reduce student conflicts in 56 public middle schools (with a total of 24,191 students) by training small "seed groups" of students to model anti-conflict strategies. This modeling was explicitly intended to publicize new norms in the school—wearing wristbands signifying conflict-mitigation behavior, creating hashtag slogans, making posters linking seed group students' images to anti-conflict slogans, etc.—not to persuade students about correct and incorrect behavior. Compared with control schools, disciplinary reports of student conflicts were reduced by 30% over one year. Even more strikingly, at schools in which at least 20% of the seed group was composed of students whom Paluck and colleagues identified as social referents, there was a *60% reduction* in disciplinary reports. Social referents were defined as students whose behavior was likely to be observed by many other students. These students were identified with questionnaires aimed at mapping social networks, in particular by determining how many social connections each student at the schools had.

My contention is that Broockman and Kalla's canvassers may have also been successful because they acted as social referents for the voters they met. One way this might have happened was by simply embodying the norm of acceptance of transgender people, thus shifting the voters' perceptions of what other people think is normal and acceptable. Recall that the canvassers established a personal connection with the voters; this is important, given that people more readily uptake normative information from individuals with whom they identify (Festinger 1954; Wilder 1990). Moreover, there is evidence that people sometimes have more egalitarian ideals than they are willing to express publicly, when such ideals are perceived as socially unacceptable (e.g., Lessig (1995) argues that many American southerners privately opposed hiring discrimination against African-Americans prior to the civil rights movement, but only expressed support for anti-discrimination laws after legal changes in the 1960s changed their perceptions of what was socially (un)acceptable). Perhaps the canvassers demonstrated changing social norms, a demonstration that licensed the voters to express their egalitarian ideals.

Of course, my contention about the role of norm psychology in Broockman and Kalla's research might be wrong. The contention could be tested in several ways in future research. For example, participants might be asked what they think people like them think about the relevant laws. They might be asked whether they support penalties for people who do not share the view they hold. And their feelings about the laws themselves might be assessed; how motivated are they to vote? These three items follow from the features of norm psychology I emphasized above.

There are a number of open questions about the idea that skill in de-biasing involves becoming a social referent. Broockman and Kalla found no difference in the effectiveness of transgender canvassers and cisgender canvassers. But a norms-based approach suggests other possibly important traits to consider. For example, virtually all theories of norm psychology identify heuristics people use to choose from whom to learn important information. These "learning biases" (here "bias" is used in the non-pejorative sense) include prestige, success, and skill (i.e., people have biases toward learning from prestigious people, etc.). Does this suggest that de-biasers perceived as prestigious would be more effective than de-biasers who are perceived as ordinary? (The ghost of Stanley Milgram's white-coated Yale-affiliated "scientist" lurks here, particularly given that subjects in a variant of Milgram's original experiment were far less likely to shock the "learners" when the confederate instructing them to administer shocks identified himself as a lowly graduate student (Milgram 1975/2009).) Besides specific traits to consider, contextual variables are likely to influence a de-biaser's success in acting as a social referent. Tankard and Paluck (2016) argue, for example, that norms interventions are likely to be most useful in contexts where others' beliefs and behavior aren't publicly observable (e.g., whether others are likely to regularly check their tire pressure) and contexts where rewards and punishments are particularly strong (e.g., racial attitudes). Tankard and Paluck also address strategies de-biasers could study and utilize for successfully framing norms (e.g., describing changes in social attitudes, such as support for gay marriage, as gaining momentum, as in "more and more people are supporting gay marriage" (Tankard & Paluck 2016: 198).

39.5 Which norms?

Still, there is an open question about *which* norms de-biasing agents ought to represent. One reason for this is that there is surprisingly little empirical research focused on intergroup *virtues* rather than intergroup *vices*. Indeed, in *The Nature of Prejudice*, Allport wrote, "it is the pathology of bigotry and not the wholesome state of tolerance that, as a rule, interests social scientists" (Allport 1954: 425–426). Research in intergroup psychology has mostly followed this rule, focusing almost exclusively on vices such as hatred, fear, disgust, or indifference toward members of social groups. As a result, comparatively little is known about which norms de-biasing agents have and spread. The skills and techniques I've described thus far presume that intergroup virtue can be understood in terms of the absence of vices rather than the presence of virtues, such as compassion, open-mindedness, and respectfulness. Similarly, while philosophers have extensively considered intergroup prejudice, such as whether it is marked by ill will (Garcia 1999) or disrespect (Glasgow 2009), less attention has been paid to correlative virtues.

One exception is Lawrence Blum's (2007) theory of racial virtue, which prioritizes feelings of comfort in intergroup interactions, recognition and respect of marginalized groups, and the capacity to see others as individuals. This makes intergroup virtue a complex construct consisting in several epistemic and practical virtues. Exemplars of intergroup virtue must have knowledge of common stereotypes and prejudices, and accept that they themselves are likely to hold biases. Related to this epistemic virtue is the ability to recognize when social categories such as race or gender are relevant (e.g., when someone is being discriminated against;

Madva 2016). This is a virtue of attention, of knowing when to pay attention to social categories and when not to. Exemplars of intergroup virtue must be motivated to act respectfully and display a degree of imperviousness to acquiring negative feelings about others in virtue of their social group membership. Practically, virtuous agents must know how to navigate complex intergroup interactions, exhibiting what has been called "interpersonal fluency" (Railton 2009, 2014; Anderson 2010; Brownstein & Madva 2012; Madva 2012). Moreover, being exemplary requires displaying each of these virtues over time and toward members of many different social groups.

If Blum is on the right track, the next question is how these virtues feed into the skills de-biasing agents possess. In what ways do the displays of these virtues affect others, if they do? In what contexts and conditions do they have salutary effects, and in what contexts and conditions do they perhaps backfire?

39.6 Conclusion

I have argued that skilled de-biasers resist the temptation to argue people out of their prejudices; treat intergroup contact as a goal; make personal connections with people using tools such as perspective-taking; utilize the psychology of norms to change people's representations of what other people feel and believe; and, in some way that needs more definition, stand as exemplars of intergroup virtue and not just the absence of intergroup vice.

Does this all fall prey to the critique of "individual" approaches to prejudice-reduction?[25] Are putative skilled de-biasers wasting their time trying to change individual minds, one-by-one? Should they not instead focus on laws, demography, and social practices? I won't rehash the contours of the debate between individual and structural-institutional approaches to prejudice-reduction, but I will conclude by making two points about what I think the approach I've described here adds to that debate.

First, skill in de-biasing can have large societal effects, in part because of how the kinds of interventions I've described scale up. Recall Paluck and colleagues' (2016) conflict-reduction intervention in middle schools. This touched the lives of approximately 12,000 students in 28 schools.[26] It is not hard to imagine how it could grow far larger as well. Even Broockman and Kalla's canvassers, who talked with voters one-on-one, spent only approximately ten minutes with each voter. That is certainly not an onerous investment, given the apparent payoff.

Second, the kinds of norms-based approaches I have described make an implicit concession to (some of) the structural-institutional critics. The concession is that changing social meanings, in Sally Haslanger's (2015) sense—the social concepts, public narratives, and collective expectations with which we make meaning out of social situations—is indeed essential for creating social change. Crucially, changing people's perceptions of norms is *at the heart* of this effort to change social meanings. Skilled de-biasers effectuate social change in part by representing new norms. They do not try to persuade people to embrace more inclusive social concepts, narratives, and expectations. Instead, they embody them.

Notes

1 To my knowledge, the original use of the term "de-biasing agents" is found in Kang and Banaji (2006).
2 See Brownstein (2016, 2017).
3 See Beeghly (2015) for related discussion of descriptive versus evaluative senses of the term "stereotype."

4 On defining prejudice, see McConahay and Hough (1976), Nosek and Banaji (2009), and Dixon et al. (2012). Note that in defining prejudice in terms of attitudes, I employ the psychologist's sense of "attitudes," not the philosopher's (i.e., propositional attitudes, per se). On defining stereotypes, see Allport (1954), Ashmore and Del Boca (1981), and Stangor (2009).

5 See Madva and Brownstein (2016).

6 See, for example, Czopp et al. (2006).

7 See, for example, those employing "deep canvassing:" <https://knockeverydoor.org/how-it-works/index.html#deep-canvassing> and <www.ctctogether.org/>.

8 See Daniel Engber on *Slate*, for example: <https://slate.com/health-and-science/2018/01/weve-been-told-were-living-in-a-post-truth-age-dont-believe-it.html>.

9 For related critical discussion of Zack's (2003) proposal regarding combatting racism by disseminating scientific information about the biology of race, see Kelly et al. (2010).

10 Engber (*op. cit.*) writes:

> Yet even if boomerangs turn out to be unusual, [Brendan Nyhan] says, there's little cause for optimism. Facts are, at best, "sometimes mildly effective" at displacing grabby lies, and corrections clearly aren't working "if the standard is getting rid of misperceptions in the world." Ullrich Ecker, the debunking expert who failed to reproduce Schwarz and Skurnik's finding on the boomerang effect for facts and myths, agrees with Nyhan. "If there's a strong motivation to hold on to a misconception, then often the corrections are ineffective. Whether or not they backfire, that's up for debate," he says. "But look, if it's ineffective, that's pretty much the same story as if there's a small backfire effect."

11 See also Swire et al. (2017).

12 See Madva and Brownstein (2016).

13 For example, see Brownstein et al. (2020) for application of this point to research on implicit bias.

14 The exception was for participants who lived with Asian American students. Their attitudes toward *other* outgroups became more negative.

15 But note that Towles-Schwen and Fazio (2006) found that randomly paired interracial freshmen roommates engaged in less joint activity and their relationships were more likely to dissolve compared with randomly paired white freshmen roommates.

16 See Kelly et al. (2010) for discussion of this point. See also Pettigrew and Tropp (2006), Pettigrew (2018), and Paluck et al. (2018) for discussion of the many contextual factors that contribute to the success—or lack of success—of intergroup contact as a tool for prejudice reduction.

17 www.nytimes.com/2016/04/10/magazine/how-do-you-change-voters-minds-have-a-conversation.html?_r=0. For discussion of the Obama campaign's use of behavioral science in its field operations, see www.nytimes.com/2012/11/13/health/dream-team-of-behavioral-scientists-advised-obama-campaign.html.

18 Lest you confuse Broockman and Kalla's study for the discredited and retracted LaCour and Green (2014), please note that Broockman and Kalla were widely credited for catching and publicizing LaCour and Green's fraud (which was mostly LaCour's fraud). Admirably, Broockman and Kalla then ran an actual study, which was similar in a number of ways to what LaCour and Green claimed to have done. It is also worth noting that Broockman and Kalla's study is an exemplar in psychometric terms. It combines the use of random placebo control, a well-concealed outcome measure, longitudinal outcome measurement, and ecological validity in the field.

19 There was no effect of canvasser gender identity.

20 In some cases, canvassers would tell their own stories of feeling judged for being different.

21 See Mesoudi (2009) for discussion.

22 See also Blanchard et al. (1994) and Monteith et al. (1996) for similar findings.

23 An alternative explanation of this finding is that people are motivated by expected rewards for being known as a voter, rather than by expected punishment for being known as a non-voter.

24 See Madva and Brownstein (2016) for related discussion.

25 For review, see Madva (2016, 2017, 2020) and Ayala-López and Erin Beeghly (2020).

26 The full study included over 24,000 students in 56 schools, but half of these served as controls and received no intervention.

References

Akerlof, G. A., & Kranton, R. E. (2000) "Economics and identity," *Quarterly Journal of Economics, 115*, 715–753.

Allport, G. (1954) *The Nature of Prejudice*. Cambridge, MA: Addison-Wesley.

Amodio, D. M. (2014) "The neuroscience of prejudice and stereotyping," *Nature Reviews Neuroscience, 15*(10), 670–682.

Anderson, C. A. (1982) "Inoculation and counterexplanation: De-biasing techniques in the perseverance of social theories," *Social Cognition, 1*(2), 126–139.

Anderson, E. (2010) *The Imperative of Integration*. Princeton, NJ: Princeton University Press.

Ashmore, R. D., & Del Boca, F. K. (1981) "Conceptual approaches to stereotypes and stereotyping," *Cognitive Processes in Stereotyping and Intergroup Behavior, 1*, 35.

Ayala-López, S., & Madva, A. (2020) "Explaining Injustice: Structural Analysis, Bias, and Individuals," in Erin Beeghly & Alex Madva (Eds.), *An Introduction to Implicit Bias: Knowledge, Justice, and the Social Mind*. New York: Routledge, pp. 211–232.

Beeghly, E. (2015) "What is a stereotype? What is stereotyping?" *Hypatia, 30*(4), 675–691.

Bicchieri, C. (2005) *The Grammar of Society: The Nature and Dynamics of Social Norms*. Cambridge: Cambridge University Press.

—— (2016) *Norms in the Wild: How to Diagnose, Measure, and Change Social Norms*. Oxford: Oxford University Press.

Blanchard, F. A., Crandall, C. S., Brigham, J. C., & Vaughn, L. A. (1994) "Condemning and condoning racism: A social context approach to interracial settings," *Journal of Applied Psychology, 79*, 993–997. doi:10.1037/0021-9010.79.6.993

Blum, L. (2007) "Racial Virtues," in Rebecca L. Walker & P. J. Ivanhoe (Eds.), *Working Virtue: Virtue Ethics and Contemporary Moral Problems*. Oxford: Oxford University Press, pp. 225–250.

Brennan, G., Eriksson, L., Goodin, R., & Southwood, N. (2013) *Explaining Norms*. Oxford: Oxford University Press.

Broockman, D., & Kalla, J. (2016) "Durably reducing transphobia: A field experiment on door-to-door canvassing," *Science, 352*(6282), 220–224.

Brownstein, M. (2016) "Context and the Ethics of Implicit Bias," in M. Brownstein & J. Saul (Eds.), *Implicit Bias and Philosophy: Volume 2, Moral Responsibility, Structural Injustice, and Ethics*. Oxford: Oxford University Press, pp. 215–234.

—— (2017) "Implicit Attitudes, Social Learning, and Moral Credibility," in J. Kiverstein (Ed.), *The Routledge Handbook on Philosophy of the Social Mind*. New York: Routledge, pp. 298–319.

Brownstein, M., & Madva, A. (2012) "Ethical automaticity," *Philosophy of the Social Sciences, 42*(1), 67–97.

Brownstein, M., Madva, A., & Gawronski, B. (2020) "Understanding Implicit Bias: Putting the Criticism into Perspective," *Pacific Philosophical Quarterly*. https://doi.org/10.1111/papq.12302.

Cameron, K. A., Roloff, M. E., Friesema, E. M., Brown, T., Jovanovic, B. D., Hauber, S., & Baker, D. W. (2013) "Patient knowledge and recall of health information following exposure to 'facts and myths' message format variations," *Patient Education and Counseling, 92*(3), 381–387.

Cialdini, R. B., Demaine, L. J., Sagarin, B. J., Barrett, D. W., Rhoads, K., & Winter, P. L. (2006) "Managing social norms for persuasive impact," *Social Influence, 1*(1), 3–15.

Czopp, A. M., Monteith, M. J., & Mark, A. Y. (2006) "Standing up for a change: Reducing bias through interpersonal confrontation," *Journal of Personality and Social Psychology, 90*(5), 784–803.

Devine, P., Forscher, P., Austin, A., & Cox, W. (2012) "Long- term reduction in implicit race bias: A prejudice habit-breaking intervention," *Journal of Experimental Social Psychology, 48*(6), 1267–1278.

Devine, P. G., Forscher, P. S., Cox, W. T., Kaatz, A., Sheridan, J., & Carnes, M. (2017) "A gender bias habit-breaking intervention led to increased hiring of female faculty in STEMM departments," *Journal of Experimental Social Psychology, 73*, 211–215.

Dixon, J., Levine, M., Reicher, S., & Durrheim, K. (2012) "Beyond prejudice: Are negative evaluations the problem and is getting us to like one another more the solution?" *Behavioral and Brain Sciences, 35*(6), 411–425.

Dovidio, J. F., Hewstone, M., Glick, P., & Esses, V. M. (2010) "Prejudice, Stereotyping and Discrimination: Theoretical and Empirical Overview," in J. F. Dovidio, M., Hewstone, P. Glick, & V. Esses (Eds.), *The Sage Handbook of Prejudice, Stereotyping and Discrimination*. London: Sage, pp. 3–28.

Dreyfus, H. (2002a) "Intelligence without representation: The relevance of phenomenology to scientific explanation," *Phenomenology and the Cognitive Sciences*, *1*(4), 367–383.

—— (2002b) "Refocusing the question: Can there be skillful coping without propositional representations or brain representations?" *Phenomenology and the Cognitive Sciences*, *1*, 413–425.

Duguid, M. M., & Thomas-Hunt, M. C. (2015) "Condoning stereotyping? How awareness of stereotyping prevalence impacts expression of stereotypes," *Journal of Applied Psychology*, *100*(2), 343–359.

Engber, D. (2018) LOL Something Matters. *Slate*. < https://slate.com/health-and-science/2018/01/weve-been-told-were-living-in-a-post-truth-age-dont-believe-it.html>.

Festinger, L. (1954) A theory of social comparison processes. *Human Relations*, *7*, 117–140.

Galinsky, A. D., & Moskowitz, G. B. (2000) "Perspective-taking: Decreasing stereotype expression, stereotype accessibility, and in-group favoritism," *Journal of Personality and Social Psychology*, *78*(4), 708–724.

Garcia, J. (1999) "Philosophical analysis and the moral concept of racism," *Philosophy and Social Criticism*, *25*, 1–32.

Gerber, A. S., Green, D. P., & Larimer, C. W. (2008) "Social pressure and voter turnout: Evidence from a large-scale field experiment," *American Political Science Review*, *102*(1), 33–48.

Glasgow, J. (2009) "Racism as disrespect," *Ethics*, *120*(1), 64–93.

Hart, P. S., & Nisbet, E. C. (2012) "Boomerang effects in science communication: How motivated reasoning and identity cues amplify opinion polarization about climate mitigation policies," *Communication Research*, *39*(6), 701–723.

Haslanger, S. (2015) "Social structure, narrative, and explanation," *Canadian Journal of Philosophy*, *45*(1), 1–15. https://doi.org/10.1080/00455091.2015.1019176

Henrich, J. (2015) *The Secret of Our Success: How Culture Is Driving Human Evolution, Domesticating Our Species, and Making Us Smarter*. Princeton, NJ: Princeton University Press.

Kahan, D. M., Landrum, A. R., Carpenter, K., Helft, L., & Jamieson, K. H. (2017) "Science curiosity and political information processing," *Supplement: Advances in Political Psychology*, *38*(S1), 179–199.

Kang, J., & Banaji, M. R. (2006) "Fair measures: A behavioral realist revision of affirmative action," *California Law Review*, *94*, 1063–1118.

Kelly, D., & Davis, T. (2018) "Social norms and human normative psychology," *Social Policy and Philosophy*, *35*(1), 54–76.

Kelly, D., Faucher, L., & Machery, E. (2010) "Getting rid of racism: assessing three proposals in light of psychological evidence," *Journal of Social Philosophy*, *41*(3): 293–322.

Kunda, Z. (1990) "The case for motivated reasoning," *Psychological Bulletin*, *108*(3), 480–498.

Kunda, Z., & Sinclair, L. (1999) "Motivated reasoning with stereotypes: Activation, application, and inhibition," *Psychological Inquiry*, *10*(1), 12–22.

LaCour, M., & Green, D. (2014) *Science*, *346*, 1366–1369.

Lessig, L. (1995) "The regulation of social meaning," *University of Chicago Law Review*, *62*(3), 943–1045.

Lewandowsky, S., Ecker, U. K., Seifert, C. M., Schwarz, N., & Cook, J. (2012) "Misinformation and its correction: Continued influence and successful de-biasing," *Psychological Science in the Public Interest*, *13*(3), 106–131.

Lord, C. G., Ross, L., & Lepper, M. R. (1979) "Biased assimilation and attitude polarization: The effects of prior theories on subsequently considered evidence," *Journal of Personality and Social Psychology*, *37*(11), 2098–2109.

Madva, A. (2012) *The hidden mechanisms of prejudice: Implicit bias and interpersonal fluency*. Doctoral dissertation, Columbia University.

—— (2016) "A plea for Anti-Anti-Individualism: How oversimple psychology misleads social policy," *Ergo, an Open Access Journal of Philosophy*, *3*.

—— (2017) "Biased against de-biasing: On the role of (institutionally sponsored) self-transformation in the struggle against prejudice," *Ergo, an Open Access Journal of Philosophy*, *4*.

—— (2020) "Individual and Structural Interventions." In Erin Beeghly & Alex Madva (Eds.), *An Introduction to Implicit Bias: Knowledge, Justice, and the Social Mind*. New York: Routledge, pp. 233–270.

Madva, A., & Brownstein, M. (2016) "Stereotypes, prejudice, and the taxonomy of the implicit social mind," *Noûs*. DOI: 10.1111/nous.12182.

Mandelbaum, E. (2019) "Troubles with Bayesianism: An introduction to the psychological immune system," *Mind and Language*, *34*(2), 141–157.

McConahay, J. B., & Hough Jr, J. C. (1976) Symbolic racism. *Journal of Social Issues, 32*(2), 23–45.

Mercier, H., & Sperber, D. (2011) "Why do humans reason? Arguments for an argumentative theory," *Behavioral and Brain Sciences, 34*(2), 57–74.

—— (2017) *The Enigma of Reason*. Cambridge, MA: Harvard University Press.

Mesoudi, A. (2009) "How cultural evolutionary theory can inform social psychology and vice versa," *Psychological Review, 116*(4), 929–952.

Milgram, S. (1975/2009) *Obedience to Authority: An Experimental View*. New York: Perennial Classics.

Monteith, M. J., Deneen, N. E., & Tooman, G. D. (1996) "The effect of social norm activation on the expression of opinions concerning gay men and Blacks," *Basic and Applied Social Psychology, 18*(3), 267–288.

Nickerson, R. S. (1998) "Confirmation bias: A ubiquitous phenomenon in many guises," *Review of General Psychology, 2*(2), 175.

Nosek, B. A., & Banaji, M. R. (2009) "Implicit attitude," In P. Wilken, T. Bayne, & A. Cleeremans (Eds.), *Oxford Companion to Consciousness*, 84–85. Oxford: Oxford University Press.

Nyhan, B., Porter, E., Reifler, J., & Wood, T. (2017) "Taking fact-checks literally but not seriously? The effects of journalistic fact-checking on factual beliefs and candidate favorability," *Political Behavior*, https://doi.org/10.1007/s11109-019-09528-x.

Nyhan, B., & Reifler, J. (2010) "When corrections fail: The persistence of political misperceptions," *Political Behavior, 32*(2), 303–330.

—— (2015) "Does correcting myths about the flu vaccine work? An experimental evaluation of the effects of corrective information," *Vaccine, 33*(3), 459–464.

Nyhan, B., Reifler, J., & Ubel, P. A. (2013) "The hazards of correcting myths about health care reform," *Medical Care, 51*(2), 127–132.

Paluck, E. L., Green, S. A., & Green, D. P. (2018) "The contact hypothesis re-evaluated," *Behavioural Public Policy*, 1–30.

Paluck, E. L., & Shepherd, H. (2012) "The salience of social referents: A field experiment on collective norms and harassment behavior in a school social network," *Journal of Personality and Social Psychology, 103*(6), 899–915.

Paluck, E. L., Shepherd, H., & Aronow, P. M. (2016) "Changing climates of conflict: A social network experiment in 56 schools," *Proceedings of the National Academy of Sciences, 113*(3), 566–571.

Petty, R. E., & Brinol, P. (2008) "Persuasion: From single to multiple to metacognitive processes," *Perspectives on Psychological Science, 3*(2), 137–147.

Pettigrew, T. F. (2018) "The emergence of contextual social psychology," *Personality and Social Psychology Bulletin, 44*(7), 963–971.

Pettigrew, T., & Tropp, L. (2006) "A meta- analytic test of intergroup contact theory," *Journal of Personality and Social Psychology, 90*, 751–783.

Railton, P. (2009) "Practical competence and fluent agency," in D. Sobel & S. Wall (Eds.), *Reasons for Action*, 81–115. Cambridge: Cambridge University Press.

—— (2014) "The affective dog and its rational tale: Intuition and attunement," *Ethics 124*(4), 813–859.

Ross, L., Lepper, M. R., & Hubbard, M. (1975) "Perseverance in self-perception and social perception: Biased attributional processes in the debriefing paradigm," *Journal of Personality and Social Psychology, 32*(5), 880–892. doi: 10.1037/0022-3514.32.5.880

Ryle, G. (1949) *The Concept of Mind*. London: Hutchinson.

Shook, N., & Fazio, R. (2008) "Interracial roommate relationships an experimental field test of the contact hypothesis," *Psychological Science, 19*(7), 717–723.

Stangor, C. (2009) "The Study of Stereotyping, Prejudice, and Discrimination within Social Psychology," in T. D. Nelson (Ed.), *Handbook of Prejudice, Stereotyping, and Discrimination*. New York: Psychology Press.

Stanley, J., & Williamson, T. (2017) "Skill," *Noûs, 51*(4), 713–726.

Swire, B., Berinsky, A. J., Lewandowsky, S., & Ecker, U. K. H. (2017) "Processing political misinformation: Comprehending the Trump phenomenon," *Royal Society Open Science, 4*, 160802.

Tankard, M. E., & Paluck, E. L. (2016) "Norm perception as a vehicle for social change," *Social Issues and Policy Review, 10*(1), 181–211.

Towles-Schwen, T., & Fazio, R. H. (2006) "Automatically activated racial attitudes as predictors of the success of interracial roommate relationships," *Journal of Experimental Social Psychology, 42*(5), 698–705.

Uhlmann, E. L., & Cohen, G. L. (2005) "Constructed criteria: Redefining merit to justify discrimination," *Psychological Science, 16*(6), 474–480.

Van Laar, C., Levin, S., Sinclair, S., & Sidanius, J. (2005) "The effect of university roommate contact on ethnic attitudes and behavior," *Journal of Experimental Social Psychology*, *41*(4), 329–345.

Wilder, D.A. (1990) "Some determinants of persuasive power of ingroups and out-groups: Organization of information and attribution of independence," *Journal of Personality and Social Psychology*, *59*, 1202–1213.

Wood, T., & Porter, E. (2016) "The elusive backfire effect: Mass attitudes' steadfast factual adherence," *Political Behavior*, 1–29.

Zack, N. (2003) "Race and Racial Discrimination," in H. Lafollete (Ed.), *The Oxford Handbook of Practical Ethics*, 245–271. Oxford: Oxford University Press.

INDEX

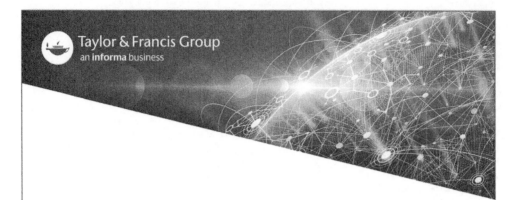